THE LATER POETIC MANUSCRIPTS
OF

Gerard Manley Hopkins

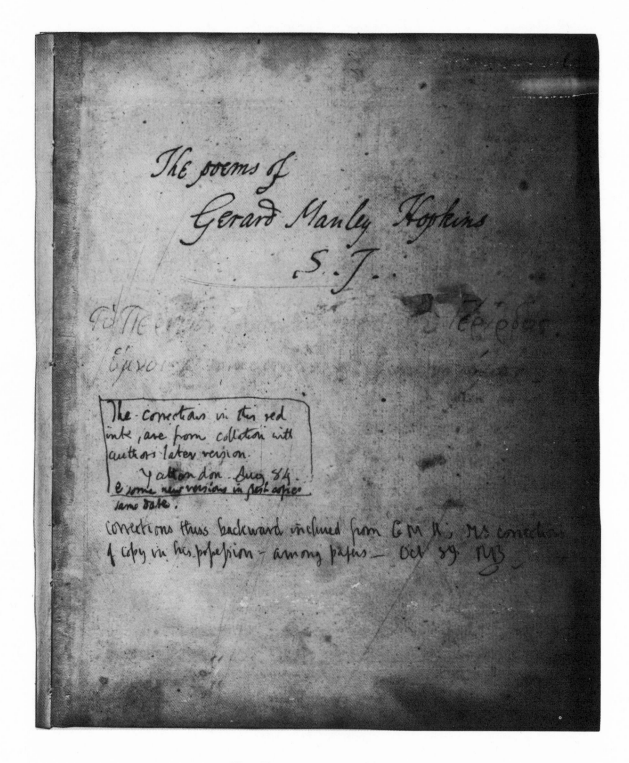

THE TITLE-PAGE OF MS. A.

Manuscript A is the fine old album of hand-made paper in which Robert Bridges preserved autographs of Hopkins's poems. The two lines of Greek, in pencil now mostly erased or smudged, concerned the "hymnoi" (odes, poems) "of Gerard." In the red rectangle Bridges has noted in red: "The corrections in this red ink, are from collation with author's later version [MS. B]. Yattendon. Aug 84." He adds in black ink: "And some new versions in fresh copies same date." "Corrections thus backward inclined from G.M.H.'s MS. corrections of copy in his possession—among papers—Oct. 89. RB" (i.e., versions found after his death—see, e.g., note below Plate 320, and Plates 420, 422, 453, 486). More details are given in the Introduction under "MS. A."

THE LATER POETIC
MANUSCRIPTS
OF

Gerard Manley Hopkins

IN FACSIMILE
Edited with Annotations
Transcriptions of Obscure Words
and an Explanatory Introduction

BY

NORMAN H. MacKENZIE

Garland Publishing, Inc.
NEW YORK & LONDON   1991

Introduction and textual commentary copyright © 1991 Norman H. MacKenzie.
All rights reserved

Library of Congress Cataloging-in-Publication Data

Hopkins, Gerard Manley, 1844–1889.
    The later poetic manuscripts of Gerard Manley Hopkins in facsimile / edited with annotations,
    transcriptions of obscure words and an explanatory introduction by Norman H. MacKenzie.
    p.   cm.
    Includes index.
    ISBN 0-8240-7444-0
    1. Hopkins, Gerard Manley, 1844–1889—Manuscripts—Facsimiles. 2. Manuscripts, English—
    Facsimiles. I. MacKenzie, Norman H. II. Title.
PR4803.H44A6 1991
821'.8—dc20   91-3809

The volumes in this series are printed on acid-free, 250-year-life paper.
Printed in the United States of America

Contents

ABBREVIATIONS AND SCALE

Abbreviations for MSS

A   An album of Hopkins's poems kept by Robert Bridges to preserve his autographs or transcripts. It is paginated, with odd numbers on the left in reversal of the convention. (Bridges Loan Collection, Bodleian Lib., Oxford.)

B   An album of transcriptions of Hopkins's poems made by Bridges, and corrected by the poet himself in 1884. Hopkins inscribed other poems or versions in autograph. (Bodleian MS. Eng. Poet. d.149)

D   MSS sent to Canon R.W. Dixon.

H.i.   A modern album into which the Bodleian guarded all the loose Hopkins MSS. bought from the Hopkins family in 1953--along with MSS. B and H.ii. (Bodleian Lib., MS. Eng. Poet. c.48)

H.ii.   An album created by Bridges in 1889 from poetic MSS. found after Hopkins's death. (Bodleian Lib., MS. Eng. Poet. d.150)

Initials of Persons (including Editors)

GMH	Gerard Manley Hopkins (1844-1889)
RB	Robert Bridges (1844-1930)
RWD	Richard Watson Dixon (1833-1900)
WHG	William H. Gardner (1902-1969)
HH	Humphry House (1908-1955)
NHM	Norman H. MacKenzie (1915-)
CLP	Catherine L. Phillips

Abbreviations for Published Hopkins Volumes

(all published by Oxford University Press)

P.   *Poems*
        1st edn. ed. RB, London: 1918
        2nd edn. ed. RB and Charles Williams, London: 1930
        3rd edn. ed. WHG, Lon.: 1948
        4th edn. ed. WHG and NHM, London: [1967] rev, 1970

OET   Poetical Works (Oxford English Texts), ed. NHM, Oxford: 1990

OA.   Oxford Authors (Poetry and Prose), ed. CLP, Oxford: 1986

N.   *Note-books and Papers,* ed. HH, Lon.: 1937

J.   *Journals and Papers,* ed. HH, completed by Graham Storey, Lon.: 1959

S.   *Sermons and Devotional Writings,* ed. Christopher Devlin, SJ, Lon.: 1959

L.i.   *Letters to Robert Bridges,* ed. C.C. Abbott, Lon.: [1935] rev. 1955

L.ii.   *Correspondence of GMH and R.W. Dixon,* ed. C.C. Abbott, Lon.: [1935] rev. 1955

L.iii.   *Further Letters,* ed. C.C. Abbott, [1938]. All refs. are to rev. and enlarged 2nd ed., Lon.: 1956

Sel.L.   *Selected Letters,* ed. Catherine Phillips, Lon.: 1990

Scale

├────────────┤ 50 mm of the original MS.

Acknowledgements

For long-sustained encouragement, as well as generous permission to reproduce the Hopkins material in this, the second of two volumes of facsimiles (much of it previously unpublished), I express my gratitude to the British Province of the Society of Jesus. This warm cooperation was extended to me first by Fr. Ronald Moffat and the permission was confirmed by Fr. Edward Ennis as Secretary of Trustees for Roman Catholic Purposes Registered (in whom the Hopkins copyright is now vested).

The rich collection of Hopkins manuscripts in Campion Hall, Oxford, that furnished a large proportion of the plates in *Facsimiles Vol. I*, has also been drawn upon in this successor, thanks to the courtesy of the Master and Librarian. The Rector of Stonyhurst College, Fr. Michael O'Halloran, obliged me with photocopies of Hopkins material from the editorial files of the *Stonyhurst Magazine* (still flourishing impressively after 110 years). Plates 398–407b have been reproduced from the *Month* of January 1882. Six years earlier that journal's first Jesuit editor, Fr. Henry Coleridge, Hopkins's oldest friend in the Society, had made the difficult but judicious decision not to print "The Wreck of the Deutschland" in the *Month*. The publication in 1876 of a lengthy ode, almost impervious to contemporaries, would (I am utterly convinced) have subjected its somewhat eccentric author to life-long chaffing by his colleagues, blighting his second poetic spring (see *Thought*, December 1990, 507–08). Hopkins posted the autograph of the "Deutschland," of which he had made no copy, to a succession of almost uniformly uncomprehending fellow Jesuits until, it seems, one of them lost it. Only the title of this masterpiece might now be known if his life-long supporter and literary trustee, Robert Bridges, had not taken the precaution of laboriously transcribing the 280-line poem into MS. A. But for his care and continual poetic stimulus, including the creation of MS. B (reproduced in the *Facsimiles* entire), only a fraction of the manuscripts in this volume might have been available for our study today.

The owners of the Hopkins manuscripts have offered me every assistance as well as their blessing on this edition. I am specially indebted to Robert Bridges's son, the late Edward, first Lord Bridges, and to his grandson Thomas, the present baron, both of whom among many kindnesses made special arrangements so that I could over prolonged periods compare the manuscripts they owned with other versions in Oxford. The staff of the Bodleian Library have treated me with great courtesy over the years: their Hopkins treasures include MSS. B, H.i, and H.ii, besides collections of letters from and about the poet. I have been much indebted to the late Robert Shackleton, former Librarian, to Douglas Vaisey the present Librarian, David Rogers who gave me special aid on many occasions, and Colin Harris. Edward Hall, for many years Director of the Oxford University Research Laboratory for Archaeology and the History of Art, provided expert help in differentiating Hopkins's inks from those used by Robert Bridges.

Other owners who provided me with photographs are the late Christabel, Lady Pooley, a direct descendant of Grace Hopkins, for whom the poet transcribed several sonnets; she sent me copies of them, and invited me to her home to examine the originals. Thanks to the Presidents and Librarians of Holy Cross College, Worcester, Massachusetts, and of Princeton University (Robert H. Taylor Collection), two little-known versions of celebrated poems are here reproduced—an early form of "Penmaen Pool" (Plates 272, 274, 276) and of "The Catholic Church Andromeda," a long-missing MS that surfaced very recently (Plate 372). I am also indebted to the Department of Manuscripts of the British Library, the Jesuit Archivist in Dublin, the Father Superior of St. Beuno's College in North Wales, and Fr. Michael Regan, Superior of Mount St. Mary's College, Spinkhill, Sheffield (who went to great lengths to help me). Though I failed in my efforts to locate the official MS of the sonnet "In Honour of St Alphonsus Rodriguez" sent to Majorca, I am deeply grateful to three Spanish friends who assisted me in my enquiries and correspondence, Dr. Pilar Abad Garcia, Dr. Felix Letemendia (who contributed notably to *Facsimiles Vol. I*), and Fr. Jaime Oraa, SJ, of Campion Hall, Oxford. Leo Handley-Derry found me the copy of "Ad Mariam" made by the poet's mother, Kate: although it was too late for the first volume, it is reproduced at the end of this one. Copies of her other transcriptions, now missing, had fortunately been preserved many years ago by Fr. A. Bischoff, SJ, to whom I once more record my deep gratitude.

For their contributions to the checking of doubtful readings in the Latin and Greek poems I again thank Colin Hardie, late of Magdalen College, Oxford, and Ross Kilpatrick, head of Classics in Queen's University; and for corresponding guidance with the Welsh, Marie Surridge, head of our Department of French. Fuller acknowledgement will be found in my Oxford English Texts edition of *The Poetical Works of Gerard Manley Hopkins* (cited here as *OET*). The origin of these *Facsimiles* volumes in that edition and their eventual separation from it were outlined in *Facsimiles I*, pp. 1–2, and in *OET*, pp. lxv–lxvii.

In the Introductions to both those volumes I have expressed my considerable debt to Catherine Phillips for undertaking at my request the exacting study of the evolution of Hopkins's handwriting, so as to enable me to arrange in chronological sequence in the *OET* and the *Facsimiles* not only the poems but the various autographs for each separate piece. Her own chronological edition of the poems, with liberal examples of Hopkins's prose (Oxford Authors, 1986), was the fruit of her independent work on the manuscripts. Her *Selected Letters* (Oxford, 1990) has with undue modesty silently corrected many of the transcriptions in Claude Abbott's standard three-volume edition, upon which we have all come to rely.

My many return visits to Oxford to study the manuscripts have been generously financed by the Canada Council and its successor, the Social Sciences and Humanities Research Council; or, during 1979–1981, the Killam Trust. The Dean of Graduate Studies and the Dean of Arts and Science at Queen's have also provided support. Among colleagues who have lent me practical encouragement I must name John Stedmond and the late George Whalley.

Successive Masters of Campion Hall, Oxford, offered me congenial hospitality while I was examining the poems; for this kindness I have been indebted to Jesuit Fathers Deryck Hanshell, E.J. Yarnold, the late Benjamin Winterborn, Paul Edwards, and Peter Hackett. Among helpful librarians and archivists I particularly remember Philip Endean, and the late Basil Fitzgibbon. I thank Penelope Bulloch of Balliol College and Christine Butler of Corpus Christi College, Oxford, for permission to use manuscripts in their care.

Two Oxford editors whom I must mention with gratitude are John Bell, a friend of many years' standing, and Frances Whistler, who saw the *OET* through its final transformation into a tangible volume. Thomas Collins, an outstanding Victorian scholar, now Provost and Vice-President of the University of Western Ontario, offered me the chance of contributing to the Garland series of nineteenth century poetic manuscripts. This happy invitation completely transformed the scope of the enterprise, largely owing to the wise advice of Ralph Carlson, formerly Vice-President of Garland Publishing, and my editor Elspeth Hart. I also take this opportunity of thanking Patricia Lalonde for the undeterred skill and patience with which she has converted the tangled MSS of my whole three-volume presentation of Hopkins poetic works, studded with myriad details, into immaculate typescripts, much of the *Facsimiles* in camera-ready copy.

I owe far more than can easily be put into words to my wife and our children for their unfailing support during the Hopkins editing that has preoccupied me for so many years. Rita helped me directly in the initial stages as far as her own professional pursuits in music and art permitted, and has given me valuable advice all through. Our daughter was of considerable assistance and encouragement, particularly when my professional duties with graduate students and administration drained time and energy from my very demanding editorial work.

NORMAN H. MACKENZIE
Queen's University at Kingston, Ontario
JANUARY 1991

Introduction

This volume, *Facsimiles II*, which embraces all Hopkins's mature verse from the "Wreck of the Deutschland" to his final sonnets in Ireland, completes an undertaking embarked upon many years ago—the editing and visual presentation of all his available autograph drafts or faircopies, as well as any valuable transcriptions of his poetry. Like its predecessor (*Facsimiles I*), *The Early Poetic Manuscripts and Note-books of Gerard Manley Hopkins in Facsimile* (New York: Garland Publishing, 1989), it forms part of a trilogy, the central volume being the Oxford English Texts edition of *The Poetical Works of Gerard Manley Hopkins* (Oxford: Clarendon Press, 1990). There have been since 1918 so many different Hopkins editions, all referred to as his *Poems*, that to avoid further confusion I chose the title *Poetical Works* and have used as an abbreviation the unequivocal acronym *OET*, since this Hopkins edition is the only one in that well-known Clarendon Press series, designed for scholarly use and provided with a textual apparatus or variant readings.

Plate and Poem Numbers

The three volumes have been integrated in various ways, with a minimum of overlap to avoid adding unnecessarily to bulk and cost. In the *OET* the poems are arranged in a basically chronological order and the headnote to each poem cites the plate numbers in the *Facsimiles* volume assigned to the reproductions of its MSS. In the *Facsimiles* volumes, the same sequence is followed for the poems, while the *OET* numbers appear in the running titles as well as the margins of the plates. The numeration of the plates is continuous: as *Facsimiles I* contained Plates 1 to 215 with four intercalaries (80a, 81a, 159a and b), *Facsimiles II* begins with Plate 220. Although much of the present volume was drafted in 1984–85, the experience of working with my Garland editor on *Facsimiles I* has led to the extensive revision of virtually all the layouts for plates and the consequent rewriting of almost all the notes I had prepared. Initially I tried to crowd as many different versions of a poem as possible onto a two-page double-spread to allow direct comparisons between them, but Garland urged that the reproductions should be on a much more generous scale, advice that I found compelling.

I delayed the insertion of plate numbers in the *OET* until early 1988, when that work emerged from a lengthy copy-editing stage in Oxford, but it was more than two years before I could return to a thorough revision of this volume: I was engrossed in seeing two complicated volumes through the press, while preparing some thirteen new Hopkins centenary lectures for delivery in Oxford, New York, Philadelphia, Washington, D.C.,

Rhode Island, and Boston. For the great majority of the mature poems my allocation of numbers proved to be just right, but for others when I reimmersed myself in the mature MSS I felt the need to print enlargements of the busiest sections where Hopkins squeezed successive revisions into ever-narrowing spaces (e.g., Plates 270, 335, 366, 465). In other instances it seemed advantageous to provide an extra plate in which corresponding lines from several different versions were printed one after the other—see, e.g., Plate 309a, the first five lines of the "The Windhover" in MSS. A¹, A², and B, with my commentary on the effect of the changes.

One newly discovered Hopkins autograph had, happily, to be fitted in: it came to my notice only in January 1989, in the Robert H. Taylor Collection recently acquired by Princeton University—"The Catholic Church Andromeda," signed in full "Gerard Manley Hopkins" without "SJ" (see Plate 372). For the *OET*, already in proof, only the generous sympathy of my current Oxford editor, Frances Whistler, enabled me to incorporate this exciting find. In *Facsimiles II*, however, I could make a place for it, as for other extra plates, by the simple expedient of adding an *a*, or *a* and *b*, to the last number(s) I had allotted to a particular poem. On the few occasions where my allocation of numbers had erred on the roomy side, I have either omitted the numbers with an explanatory note (e.g., 454–55), or made more appropriate use of the surplus: thus Plate 329, a few pages late, reproduces a contemporary engraving of the ill-starred H.M.S. *Eurydice*, along with details of the ship and of naval practice in shortening sail that tend toward the exoneration of Captain Marcus Hare.

In the case of the few poems published during Hopkins's lifetime I have reproduced the printed text (see such plates as 264, 396, 424, 524–25). One such publication defeated my search, just as it has eluded all Hopkins specialists since the only known copy disappeared from the British Library in the 1950s. Plate 374b describes this vestpocket miniature and appeals to readers to be on the look-out for it. I am specially curious to know in what form "Morning, Midday, and Evening Sacrifice" was published in Dixon's tiny book. On the other hand I have had much satisfaction, since the *OET* came out, in locating the printed text of the Nursery Rhymes in Latin. These were relegated to an appendix in the *OET* because the only text I had was transmitted orally: Plates 524–25 summarize the new evidence, which seems to support their attribution to Hopkins.

The Chief Albums of MSS: A and B

The Bodleian Library owns three of the principal volumes of Hopkins's poetry, purchased from the family in 1953, and Lord Bridges has very kindly placed MS. A, the volume of autographs in his possession, on loan in the Bodleian, though it can be consulted only with written permission from him. The Bodleian has on permanent exhibition MS. B (MS. Eng. Poet. d.149). The faircopies of early poems and drafts of others, to all of which Robert Bridges referred as "H," are in two volumes that, to avoid confusion, I have classified as "H.i" (MS. Eng. Poet. c.48) and "H.ii" (MS. Eng. Poet. d.150).

Albums A and B. For complex reasons associated with the complete dedication of his energies to the Church, after he became a Jesuit Hopkins seems to have kept no note-book corresponding to the two early Note-books reproduced in *Facsimiles I,* in which to enter drafts or faircopies of his compositions. The nearest approach was a rough scribbler, the Dublin Note-book, that received drafts of "Spelt from Sibyl's Leaves" and "St. Winefred's Well" in Ireland, along with lists of prescribed texts, examination grades, lecture material, and meditation notes (see Plates 426–27, 474–75). Instead, even before he entered the Novitiate, he began to use Robert Bridges as his literary trustee. The hard years of training from 1868 to 1875 were barren of spontaneous compositions, but after his poetic rebirth in December 1875 poems began to germinate once more. Bridges about 1878 demonstrated his faith in Hopkins's future as a copious poet by setting aside for his autographs a thick album of hand-made paper, MS. A. This volume now has over 300 pages, though a number were added from time to time and some were cut out.

In full realisation of the unique value of this collection as the only repository of his friend's poems, though Bridges showed album A to visitors likely to appreciate these strange experimental pieces, and even held out the opportunity of reading them to encourage Coventry Patmore to spend some time in his home, he appears never to have let album A out of his possession either by hazarding it in the mail or lending it to a friend. Instead, in 1883 he copied in an artistic italic hand most of the autographs into a second smaller book, album B, with the intention of lending it around to those most likely to recognise the originality and genius of Hopkins's verse.

Realising the uncertainties of interpreting the Jesuit's ambiguous stops or, with some "faircopies," of plucking the final version from a thicket of corrections, Bridges instead of sending MS. B to Coventry Patmore direct, posted it to the author for him to check and revise. Without these large-hearted actions—the time-consuming copying-out of album B, and the request to the poet himself to review the text—it is very doubtful if Hopkins could have revised the productions of his eight previous years: he had achieved an Ignatian detachment from his own work by failing to make or safeguard final copies of his poems. Nor is it likely that, if left to himself, he would have summoned energy enough to introduce those subtle touches by which, as these plates dramatically reveal, a merely adequate line or phrase in the MS. A version is suddenly lifted into the realm of inspiration in MS. B. With only slight changes—a superfluous article or syllable struck through or a word repeated or replaced—Hopkins reinforced the effects that have outlasted the popular successes of so many of his contemporaries. At times these alterations overlooked his own theoretical prosodic patterns (as in the first few lines of the "Deutschland," Plates 230 and 231, or in "Brothers," *OET* No. 143): Bridges seems to have been more aware of these rhythmic deviations than Hopkins was himself. But because Sprung Rhythm helped to liberate Twentieth Century English verse from the domination of the iambic two-step, we must not be too censorious of these metrical self-contradictions. Nor must his modern editors complain too loudly that Hopkins's eyes, alert to the finer detail of buds in ash trees or the flutes and combs in a hill-side brook, were unfocused proof-readers, leaving us frequently in doubt as to whether he passed, or simply passed over, minor departures in MS. B from the autograph that Bridges had copied out of MS. A.

Hopkins failed to change the Bridges transcription where it is self-evidently wrong, as where the priest's prayers are in B called "Froward" instead of "Forward" (i.e., "presumptuous"—Plate 369, line 48), or when clotted double-articulation is introduced by the intrusive middle *d* in "Double*d*-natured" in the "Wreck" (Plate 263, st. 34, *l*.2). The priest seems to have spent much less time and care in checking album B than Bridges devoted to inscribing it. His editors, unfortunately, have to reach hard decisions on minutiae that his poetic genius soared above. My annotations may seem to direct undue attention to the accidentals in which Bridges's transcriptions slipped away from the autographs and where Hopkins did not restore the integrity of his text. But such observations are essential in any study of a poem's intermediate stages, and more so in the evaluation of a final printed version. My only recourse has been to return to the autograph in A wherever it seems probable that Hopkins was neither responsible for the change in B nor even fully aware of it. After a quarter-century as a Hopkins editor I question the possibility of a definitive text, and wonder how often "MS. B after its revision by Hopkins" can be relied upon as the final authority for the poems of 1876 to 1883. This *Facsimiles* volume offers much of the evidence I have been able to muster in my long acquaintance with the originals. The untidiness of nearly every Hopkins faircopy is largely due to his mind-wandering inability to transcribe his own text, with line-spaces or indentations where he needed them—and his impulsive, disfiguring cancellations when he realised his mistake. Like a drowsy medieval monk, he dozed into dittography, repeating words from neighbouring lines or even from the last phrase. One pleasing exception is the birthday gift of two sonnets that he copied out for his mother in 1877 (Plates 285, 288).

Those of us whose activities as authors or editors began before word-processors were developed know the errors, like the inevitable dents and scratches in furniture-removal, that mar the transfer of material from one draft to another. The minor matters over which Bridges tripped in copying MS. B should have been smoothed out if Hopkins had been alert. The history of the main manuscript collections, A, B, H.i, and H.ii has been related in the *OET* (pp. xxviii to xxxix), but the process through which Bridges achieved an admirable first edition of the poems in 1918 deserves summary here.

Collection of the Autographs. With the exception of one or two "humorous" poems, Bridges does not seem to have lost a single autograph entrusted to him. The two long poems that Hopkins insisted upon taking charge of himself, so that he could lend them around to friends—his two rejected shipwreck pieces, Nos. 101 and 125—would have gone down without trace if Bridges had not copied them both out, twenty pages of verse, into MS. A. Plate 313a illustrates the author's own irresponsibility over the MS of the "Wreck of the Deutschland." The ode had taken months to compose, and reconstructing it from memory could have evoked only scattered fragments. Yet when Hopkins set out for a holiday in his parent's home in Hampstead in July 1877, he packed the unique MS in the heavy bag that had to travel in the guard's van. On the train's arrival in London the bag could not be found. It did not turn up till thirteen anxious days later. At that stage neither Bridges nor any of his own family appear to have seen the ode. A prudent man would forthwith have devoted whatever time was necessary to copying it out. Still wiser would have been to transcribe for lending the least dragonish section, the incomparable narrative stanzas that open Part the Second, being careful to stop short of the comparison in stanza 20 of Martin Luther to a wild boar tramping down the lilies. But the author took precautions neither against loss nor shock. The very next day after the MS's reprieve from extinction Gerard trusted it to Providence and the London Post, addressed to Robert Bridges for him to read and return.

Bridges's efforts to create an attractive album of Hopkins's poems, which he could not only preserve but show to congenial visitors, would have been eased if the poet himself had extended him more thoughtful consideration. The pages of album A vary slightly, but average 7.8" x 6.25". Bridges asked Hopkins to use paper of a size that would make mounting convenient (L.i.109, Sept. 1880), sitting comfortably on the page as "Spring and Fall" does (Plate 392). But Hopkins tended to leave the faircopying of a new poem to be rushed through before some deadline, usually after finishing a letter to Bridges, when he would seize any clean sheet at hand. Some of these he may have frugally carried round with him from one centre to another. Many sheets were of such poor quality that his quill spluttered over the page, so that ink-blots obscured deletions and soaked right through the paper.

A conspicuous illustration of the dilemmas that Hopkins occasioned his literary trustee is Plate 306, the earliest surviving version of "The Windhover" (A^1). Typically, it seems to have started as a faircopy. The sheet, though too tall for the album, proved to be not long enough for the sonnet owing to the false starts and second thoughts that graphically indicate new surges of inspiration. The undetected slip in the metrical note, "rhym" for "rhythm," imparts to admirers today a sense of its creator's excitement as this endlessly fascinating poem took shape; but contemporaries to whom he was simply an aspiring, markedly eccentric poet would have responded differently. The first line, numbered 1a in the margin, was impulsively deleted for some reason unknown, yet rewritten immediately below in virtually duplicate form and with no change in indenting. It was probably Bridges who cut the title off from above the metrical note and pasted it over the ugly deleted line (cf. his tidying up in Plate 468). As the intended faircopy evolved into a partial recasting, space was cumulatively lost until the bottom of the page was reached with three lines still to add. A practical man would have written the final tercet on a separate sheet to be pasted on the facing page of the album, but Hopkins, exasperatingly economical, turned the page over and sideways, to fit his three lines *at right angles down the back!* It became impossible to mount normally on an album page. The paper is so inferior that blotches from the verso disfigure the ends of lines 1 to 11, and the sheet had to be tipped or guarded into the album. Visitors to Bridges encountered this superb masterpiece with six of the lines heavily scored through: the poet did not bestir himself to spend fifteen further minutes creating a clean copy.

In contrast the next version of "The Windhover" (A^2, Plate 308) fitted neatly on the album page, with only one blot, in line 4, where the poet caught himself reverting to the earlier reading "hung" instead of the revised "rung." It was a little unfortunate, however, that the title had to be cut off for lack of space: Hopkins would certainly not have headed a poem only with the laconic "(Another version)."

Subsequent autographs reaching Bridges were sometimes so large as to require ingenious dismemberment into six pieces (e.g., "Brothers," Plate 389). Though certainly not the fault of Bridges as guardian, the aesthetic result is on occasion rather unattractive, as when the title had to be gummed down at right angles to a sonnet (see "Ribblesdale," Plate 417). With "The May Magnificat" (Plate 327a), the *y, g,* and *f* in the title, like the three blind mice, merely had their tails cut off when the metrical note written across them had to be excised and mounted sideways up the left margin: this is one of many cases where I have reconstituted the autograph into some resemblance to its original form.

Elsewhere I draw attention to the tops or descenders of letters that enable us to confirm that two poems were inscribed on a single sheet (Plates 453, 504).

Frequently Bridges mounted a title on one page and the text on the facing one. The gap is normally closed up in these plates to enable the lines to be reproduced on a larger scale. Bridges often used the intervening space for extracts from Hopkins's letters where the author either revised lines that had failed to satisfy, or offered, with a blend of amusement and defiance, an exegesis of some impenetrable passage Bridges had complained about (a sample is given on Plate 303a). Bridges's demand that Hopkins should explain himself served three desirable purposes: it reminded a man who quaintly claimed the extreme of popular style (L.iii.355) that he could be as obscure as the Delphic oracle; it stimulated him into a poetic mood through the realisation that at least one person was sufficiently engaged with his output to cross-examine him on it; and it saved early editors and critics from much precarious speculation. Because Hopkins's letters have since been published in full and his explications reprinted in editors' notes, these extracts are not republished in the *Facsimiles*, but they show that Bridges was systematically preparing himself to produce an annotated Hopkins edition.

Layers in MSS. A and B

These two albums are like geological sites, and my notes to the plates attempt to examine their successive layers of writing, starting, as stratigraphic studies do, with the oldest. Like rock-cuttings along a highway, however, not every MS exhibits all the strata, but I number them here for clarity. With the autographs of MS. A attention is first directed to the original text (let us call it "A.i"), and any deletions or revisions ("A.ii") that Hopkins made before sending the piece to Bridges. Let me remark that though the author may have been shown album A during his rare visits to Bridges's home, I cannot definitely point to any alteration that Hopkins himself entered in an autograph in A after it had reached Bridges. When Hopkins decided upon a revision, he normally sent the new wording in a letter, a reproduction of which I have sought always to include. On receiving this Bridges might copy into A the revision, with the date of the letter containing it (Plates 303a, 392). Sometimes, however, he had reason to feel that the change was no improvement (as with No. 139, Plate 375; cf. L.i. 97–98), just as Hopkins himself expressed strong criticisms of particular phrases in Bridges or Coventry Patmore. Unfortunately Bridges destroyed nearly all his letters to Hopkins, which had been returned to him from Ireland in 1889, so that the grounds of his objections are seldom preserved. W.B. Yeats later recorded his immense respect for Bridges's capacity to suggest ways in which another man's poems might be bettered.

The next stratum in the text of a poem written in those fertile years between 1876 and 1883 is in album B. Bridges was fully aware of the possible imperfections in the copies of the autographs that he had neatly transcribed in album B (let us call these "B.i"). Some slips he himself detected and put right ("B.ii"), but he also wished the author to have a chance of revising his texts. Hopkins had kept so few faircopies that, left to himself, he could scarcely have attempted to amend old poems, so before Bridges posted album B to Coventry Patmore, he arranged for Hopkins to "point" the poems (i.e., punctuate them) and "make a few corrections," by which Hopkins usually meant "improve the phrasing"

(L.i.189, 24 Oct. 1883; cf. L.i.42). These authorial amendments ("B.iii") I have made strenuous efforts to distinguish from the entries by Bridges already in the album. When the book first reached Stonyhurst it was a good deal neater than the collection of so-called faircopies in album A. Either out of respect for Bridges's ornate italic, or through lack of insight into the enigmas he was creating for Bridges and all future editors, Hopkins sometimes imitated Bridges's italic and his ampersands (Plate 301). He often doctored accidentals in B with such restraint that in spite of the extensive comparisons between the letter-shapes of Hopkins and Bridges that Catherine Phillips and I have carried out, it is frequently impossible to be sure which of the two was responsible for some stop or other feature in which the B transcription differs from the A autograph.

When Bridges seems to me to have improved the punctuation and Hopkins did not revert to the original, we would still like to know whether Hopkins was aware of the change and endorsed it by leaving it intact, or whether his attention simply flickered over that spot, intent on less trivial matters and more concerned with the ear than the eye. My espousal of the Infrared Image Converter (to be discussed presently) was an attempt to reach a scientific judgment on which marks in a B MS come from Hopkins's pen.

Album B might have been checked and amended with less desultory attention if Hopkins had been less worried, but he was confronting another uprooting, accompanied by wider responsibilities—promotion from the familiar securities of Stonyhurst to exile as Fellow in Classics in University College, Dublin. His self-fulfilling misgivings may account for his inefficiencies as an editor. Patmore, though a fellow Catholic and the author of an important study of "English Metrical Critics" (1857), repudiated as unnecessary all the prosodic marks Hopkins had added to B: unlike Johann Sebastian Bach, Hopkins was not content to omit directions as to how he wanted his work performed.

Patmore's curmudgeonly pronouncement that Hopkins's poems would never meet success (L.iii.352–53) contributed heavily to the priest's desolations in Ireland. What I have never seen emphasized is Patmore's failure to shake Bridges's own affection for them or his confidence that they would eventually emerge in print. When Patmore visited Bridges in July 1884, carrying album B back with him rather than trusting it to the mails, Bridges set out to open his eyes to the poetic beauties Patmore had missed (L.iii.356). So far from agreeing that Hopkins was scarcely worth publishing, the very next month Bridges carefully copied into album A all the revisions to his own transcriptions in B that he noticed Hopkins had carried out: we may call these A.iii. With the practical intelligence so deficient in the author himself, Bridges used red ink so that if MS. B ever followed the autographs of the two shipwreck poems into oblivion, he and any subsequent editor would be able to distinguish at a glance the original autographs in A from the revisions copied into them from B. Moreover, on the title page of album A (reproduced in the Frontispiece) Bridges recorded in the same red ink the date on which he had entered these revisions. When, shortly afterwards, Hopkins begged to be given album B as an encouragement and stimulus, Bridges was able to consign it to him with instant goodwill and a free conscience.

Five years later, on Hopkins's premature death, Bridges acted vigorously to rescue, perhaps even from the furnace, album B and any loose surviving drafts of the Jesuit's verse. Obituary notices in Dublin made no mention of his gifts as a poet, so that no special solicitude for his verse was to be expected. All the salvaged poetry sent back from Dublin to his family was loaned to Robert Bridges for him to sort into order (the origin of the H

MSS), but before returning these to Mrs. Manley Hopkins, Bridges copied any new items into MS. A, the central repository—another precaution against loss. (These transcripts have no authority, and as the originals have survived they are not reproduced in this volume.) He went through MS. B again, looking for further corrections and new versions (B.iv): some of these Hopkins had probably made before sending the album to Patmore, but so unobtrusively that Bridges had simply not noticed them. To enter these in the A autographs Bridges in 1889 employed a thin pen with black ink and backward sloping writing (A.iv), once again noting the procedure and the date on the title page. Examples will be found on Plates 304, 310, 312, 344, 420, 422, 453, and 486.

Finally, when Bridges was preparing for Oxford University Press the first edition of the *Poems*, he collated all the MSS in albums A and B, along with the drafts rescued from Dublin, which he had also sorted and arranged: these last are now in what the *OET* describes (xxix ff.) as MSS. H.i and H.ii. There is no need to repeat their history in this volume. The editorial notes Bridges pencilled in the margins of A we may think of as "A.v" and those he made in B as "B.v." In Plate 379, e.g., he notes that the date for "At the Wedding March" in that A version differs from the dating on which H and B agree. Proofs of the text reached him as early as May 1918, so that some of the collations in pencil may belong to 1917 or possibly even earlier: my "RB's pencil (1918)" or "(c. 1918)" can obviously not be precise.

What must never be underestimated, however, are the efforts Bridges made over the fifty years of his trusteeship to preserve the autographs, to record revisions, and before their publication to catch any errors for which he or the poet himself had been responsible. The text of the main body of mature poetry (apart from the "Deutschland") has been only slightly improved since the Bridges first edition (though the *OET* has attempted, there as elsewhere, to indicate to readers Hopkins's prosodic intentions). The least satisfactory section in album A is "The Wreck of the Deutschland," where Hopkins must bear the blame for the sole autograph having gone astray without his having made a copy. Of this perpetually challenging ode we would now have no more snippets than for many a lost Greek play but for the laborious transcriptions Bridges entered in album A (about December 1878?) and again from A into album B (August to October 1883). The annotations in the "Deutschland" section of *Facsimiles II* frequently allude to my hesitations as to what to print, and explain the numerous changes of text that I have felt compelled to introduce there.

"The Growth of the 'Windhover'"

It is not surprising, in view of the ten strata for which we should be on the lookout in poems having an autograph in A and a transcript in B with Hopkins's revisions, that there have been comparatively few published attempts to follow the development of any mature poem from start to finish. This is a pity, because it may prove a more profitable exercise than the measuring of his verse against some current theory of criticism which, despite contemporary enthusiasm, may turn out to be volatile or mirageous.

One celebrated pioneer study of three Hopkins MSS appeared in *PMLA* in October 1967, "The growth of 'The Windhover'" (82. No. 5. 465–68). I have in various places expressed appreciation of its general usefulness, but never explained how many mistakes the writer made in guessing the steps by which MSS. A² and B evolved. I do so now only to emphasize the need for explanatory notes to accompany photographic plates: in this *Facsimiles* volume the "Windhover" is represented by Plates 306, and 308 to 309a. My own earliest sets of copyflo prints have their margins crowded with pencilled observations made, during a succession of visits to Oxford, as I examined the MSS, all four albums side by side, with the best instruments I could find. The "Windhover" critic in the *PMLA* was severely disabled from the outset by his complete dependence upon photostats of a single poem. He could not differentiate ink from pencil, and was completely unaware of the precautionary colour code—red ink and black ink—used by Bridges to prevent some of the confusions that his article betrays. He assumes, incorrectly, that the first A version was the "slightly amended copy of the Falcon sonnet" Hopkins promised Bridges in L.i.56. He had apparently no misgivings about the risks scholars run when they try to identify who added what to a MS without having first familiarized themselves with the variations of handwriting of those who contributed to it. The writer of "The Growth of 'The Windhover'" knew Bridges only in his stylised italic transcriptions. He recognised neither of Bridges's two layers of contributions to A². The red ink entries in A that Bridges made in 1884 from Hopkins's revisions in B were thought to be the work of Hopkins himself, the differences in hand and the discrepancies in accidentals being attributed to Hopkins's comparative carelessness in copying them into A. Bridges's black ink of 1889 with its date "May 1877" was misread as "Maj," and again attributed to Hopkins. Bridges's ordinary rapid hand is often found illegible on a first encounter, as it was here.

The MS. B version of "The Windhover" was also incorrectly analysed, though an unknown third party, neither the poet nor his first editor, was credited with two features. In fact it was Hopkins who added the first—sixteen purple pencil stress marks so that posterity might have less difficulty in deciding where among his multisyllabled phrases the main emphases should fall. Having failed to recognise the stresses as the poet's own, the critic consequently took no account of these in establishing his "definitive" edition. And it was Bridges whose pencil around 1918 added the second feature—marginal collations, some of which caused the critic trouble: "After *l*.6 the same person has written ' = A'." From even the best semi-gloss or copyflo plates it may be difficult to tell what my annotations to Plate 309 report—that in the MS. B copy the hyphen in "bow-bend," omitted by Bridges and not restored by Hopkins, had been caught by Bridges in his careful collations for the 1918 First Edition, and inserted by him then *in pencil.* He frequently used an equals sign as a hyphen in the interests of clarity. Bridges's marginal comment after line 6 in B," = A," should therefore be spelt out: "the hyphen pencilled between 'bow' and 'bend' is taken from A."

The *PMLA* article is nevertheless the work of a man with a delicate feeling for Hopkins. It provided valuable information about three stages in the development of "The Windhover" that should have corrected or forestalled some influential misinterpretations of this exquisite poem.

Hopkins as Editor

The over-reactive conscience revealed by Hopkins's Anglican notes of self-examination (published for the first time in *Facsimiles I* and analysed in the Introduction to that volume with the aid of Dr. Felix Letemendia) prevented Hopkins from devoting to poetry or music anything more systematic than "spare" time. Of that relaxing tonic, through his notorious practical inefficiencies, he contrived for jaded body and mind much smaller infusions than did busier Jesuit colleagues. The same verdict must be pronounced on his "editorial" activities, whether in producing a faircopy for album A or in checking transcriptions in album B: the conundrums that tease an editor today are not due to Bridges but to the poet himself. On Plate 301 in lines 2 and 3 he imitated Bridges's italic (cf. Plate 317). He repeatedly told his two main correspondents that he had no thought of publishing—though one critic still persistently denies his sincerity (see, e.g., L.i. 65–66, 197; L.ii. 2, 8, 15, 27–31, 46–47, 51, 88–89, 93, 100, 132, 138, 140, 150), and the undulations of concentration shown by his uneven proofing of B might be attributed to an Ignatian detachment, even beyond the somewhat impoverishing way in which Victorian English Jesuits interpreted the *Spiritual Exercises* of their founder. Hopkins exhibited a mixture of courage and timidity in the face of both tradition and officialdom, and Fr. Philip Endean, SJ, produces persuasive arguments for his personal conviction that Hopkins would have been a better Jesuit if he had asked his superiors' permission for some of his verse to be printed by his friends (*HQ* 7.4, Winter 1981, 167–70). I speculate that a "cradle" Catholic, as distinct from a convert, might perhaps not have been as overawed by his rectors and parish priests as little Hopkins was. In our pleasure from the perpetual freshness of his poetry even today, however, we have to mute our grumbles over his characteristic lack of forethought for the most faithful transmission of it.

The Infrared Image Converter

While wrestling in the 1970s with the problem of determining what elements of the texts in B (in many important cases the latest authority) were added, overlooked, or accepted by Hopkins, I remembered a book published by the Director of the Home Office Forensic Science Laboratory in Cardiff, Dr. Wilson R. Harrison, *Suspect Documents: Their Scientific Examination* (London: 1958, 2nd impress. enlarged, 1966), which had interested me years before when I was dealing with seventeenth century historical and pseudo-historical sources. Among devices for detecting forgeries is an instrument that floods a MS with infrared light capable of penetrating ink overlays. Provided the ink below has not run, the instrument will reveal the shape of the original stop or letter below even dense black deletion lines (see notes on Plate 249). Moreover, the light reflected from the writing can be scrutinized in turn through a succession of alternative filters, each of which may be so constructed as either to transmit light in a very limited band centred on a particular wavelength (a "narrow-pass" filter), or to block all light waves up to a specified wavelength or colour (an "edge" filter). If two inks with different chemical ingredients have been used in a MS—as is often the case when a forger has changed part of a document—no matter how cleverly he has matched the ink in colour to deceive the naked eye, the Infrared Image Converter should be able to detect the intrusive ink. Since visual separation of Hopkins's revisions from the transcriptions of Bridges was often problematical, I suggested to the Bodleian Library that MS.B should be taken to the Document Examination Laboratory of Scotland Yard for a demonstration of their apparatus. I then made the special arrangements with the Laboratory's Director, Dr. Seeley. Dr. David Rogers, the senior research librarian who accompanied me, was so impressed that he enlisted Dr. Edward Hall of Oxford's Research Laboratory for Archaeology and the History of Art to construct a modified version of the instrument for the use of readers in the Bodleian.

I have described the apparatus and its process in *The Bodleian Library Record* (ix.4, June 1976, 234–40), "Forensic Document Techniques Applied to Literary Manuscripts," and I updated the account in the *OET* Introduction (xxxix–xliii). In 1972 the Bodleian Library became the first great humanistic library in the world to possess an instrument with these capabilities. The image in the eye-piece was of a few letters at a time faintly illumined in green, but unfortunately the Bodleian had no spare room where the instrument could be used under low lighting. Brilliant overhead tubes in the various reading rooms where it was temporarily housed not only hampered careful scrutiny but caused the deterioration of the delicate caesium-on-silver oxide cathode that converts the infrared photons into electrons. Moreover the apparatus often yielded inconclusive results because there was too little difference between some of the Jesuit inks and that used by Bridges in his transcriptions (e.g., Plate 301). With a minute field of view and poor working conditions only selected cruces on any one page could be examined. As the apparatus steadily lost its reliability the independent new readings I recorded on each of many return visits to the Bodleian began to show disturbing discrepancies.

Oxford's science libraries are housed in separate buildings with their own expert staff, but the Department of Western Manuscripts, which copes with a formidable range of documents from many centuries and in numerous languages, had no librarians with scientific training who could understand the Infrared Image Converter, nor could they afford a technician to maintain it. As visiting humanists with a Liberal Arts background asked for a demonstration of the instrument's ability to solve their own problems, the machine (nearly always waiting for me to readjust whenever I returned to use it) became burdensome to an increasingly understaffed department. Catherine Phillips and I were the main beneficiaries of Bodley's enterprising venture: we could both operate the apparatus without assistance. In November 1988 I fancied that I had found a permanent solution, when the Librarian, David Vasey, and Edward Hall both agreed with me in principle that the Infrared Image Converter should in future be housed and maintained a short distance away in the Laboratory for Archaeology and Art. This I reported in the *OET* (p. xliii). It is with regret that I have now to sound its requiem: when Dr. Hall examined the instrument he had made and paid for he found it damaged beyond repair, and replacing it would now be too expensive.

Meanwhile the British Library in London told me of their own interest. In view of the Bodleian's pioneer difficulties it seemed desirable that they should aim at an instrument specially adapted for literary work, with an infinitely graded filter, and that it should be under a qualified technician. Dr. Hall was himself a Trustee of the British Museum. The instrument installed in the Department of Manuscripts in the British Library is a Video Spectral Comparator, which can be linked with a photomultiplier to throw an enlarged image on a screen. Some of the results I report in this volume were obtained with its aid and with the assistance of the excellent technician, Tony Parker, who keeps himself abreast of developments by attending conferences; at these he frequently finds that he is the only person not on the staff of forensic department laboratories.

Arrangement of the Plates

The easiest way to have presented the Hopkins facsimiles would have been the one that has been adopted with other more voluminous poets—to reproduce each existing volume of MSS as a unit without any effort to bring together different versions of the same poem, except in a final index. My organising of the *Facsimiles* as companion volumes to the *OET* edition of the poems, however, ensured a chronological series of plates, illustrating the poet's career from Highgate school prizewinner to maladjusted priestly professor in self-accentuated exile, whose sublimated poems of distress were hidden even from his colleagues. Within each poem the *OET* lists the MSS in chronological sequence also, but if readers were to be able to compare autographs with transcripts, and, in reverse, the revisions Hopkins made in B with the entries Bridges made in A to record them, the plates had often to be arranged in a more complicated way.

With the "Wreck of the Deutschland," instead of printing all the A pages followed by all those in B, I have each A version in turn confronting its B counterpart across successive openings. Since in the albums there are only two stanzas to a page in A and three to a page in B, every B page had to be reconstituted in two-stanza units to keep the texts parallel. With "The Bugler's First Communion" (No. 137) scheme after scheme was devised and abandoned; certain pages were eventually given two plates each, four plates to an opening.

Intrusive Plates

Some surprise may be caused by my practice on various occasions of allowing a single plate, allotted to a piece with only one page of MSS, to squeeze itself into a sequence of three or five plates needed for a neighbouring poem. This madness, however, is born out of method. Take "Spring" (No. 117) as one example, where its three plates, 298 (even-numbered, so on the left) faces an intruder ("Hope holds to Christ . . .," 299), while over the page Plate 300 (the Pooley version of "Spring") has 301 (the B version of "Spring") to balance the next opening. But a right-hand plate cannot be compared with *any subsequent* plate without flicking pages back and forth, nor can a left-hand plate be held in the same visual field as any preceding one. I have so positioned the "Spring" MSS, however, that Plate 298 (the A version) can be read against 301 (the B transcript made from it) simply by holding the intervening sheet at right angles to the other two. We can likewise check backwards, to determine how accurately Hopkins's revisions in B were transferred in red ink to A by the same procedure. And as Pooley and B occupy the same opening, they too can be compared. The worst arrangement would have been to give 298, 299, and 300 to "Spring"; plates on the recto and verso of a sheet (like 299 and 300), are the most exasperating to compare.

"Binsey Poplars" (*OET* No. 130) has been awarded five plates: 334 to 337, and then 339. The missing plate, 338, reproduces, very appropriately, the printed notice concerning needlework and language classes on the back of which Hopkins frugally jotted the H² version of "Binsey Poplars" (on Plate 337), and it also carries the fragmentary No. 132, "Repeat that, repeat." But the chronological sequence of the plates is in this case also disrupted for good cause. The ravelled first draft (H¹, Plate 334, on the left) has opposite it an enlargement of the most agitated section, with a transcription (335). The second draft, H², should, in strict chronology, come next, but 336, a left-hand page, is necessarily blind to its predecessors; placing it there would have prevented us from comparing H[1] with H[2] without tedious page-shuffling—and I have borne in mind that major British libraries are apt to frown on photocopying. Instead Plate 336 is given to the third MS, namely A, which can then be examined across the hinge alongside its immediate predecessor in the growth of the poem, H[2] (Plate 337), and, by holding up that plate at right angles, also checked with its transcription in B, occupying the right-hand page of the next opening (Plate 339). The notes clearly indicate the sequence of the MSS ("earliest MS," MS. 2, MS. 3, MS. 4), so no confusion ought to result.

The Effect of Revisions: The Evolution of Poems

My annotations have been mainly directed towards the elucidations that will be found in the last section of this Introduction, but every now and then I return to my preferred role as a professor and literary critic. Setting one below the other the opening lines of "The Windhover" in three versions on Plate 309a I discuss the significance of the changes. So too on Plate 324 in "The Loss of the Eurydice." In the organisation of the MSS of the longer poems I have gone to a great deal of trouble to assist those who share my interest in the stages through which these fascinating pieces unfolded themselves.

"On the Portrait of Two Beautiful Young People" (No. 168) required careful disposition. The drafts are spread over eleven pages and occupy eight plates (478–85). On a large sheet I first listed down the margin the numbers 1 to 36 for the lines in its nine main stanzas, and in vertical columns across the page, corresponding with the MS folios, I recorded where each variant version of a line could be found.

Some lines reached their finished, almost invariable, shape at the very outset, such as the arresting first line, "O I admire and sorrow! The heart's eye grieves," or the fourth, "And beauty's fondest veriest vein is tears"—"fondest" was changed to "dearest" only because "fond" was more urgently needed as a rhyme word in line 13. But in between such inspired lines come others that had to be hammered, discarded, held again in the flame and reshaped. One was line 3, which he twisted through almost a dozen mutations and combinations, with juice / moisture running or riding through violets / bluebells / vine-leaves / brake-leaves; yet in the end, like Omar Khayyám, the poet came out, if not quite "by the same door as in he went," then very close to it.

Certain stanzas were wrestled out to his satisfaction in a concentrated bout: stanza 8 occupies most of Plate 479 and reaches finality on 480, but to interpret the enigmatic concision of "Your feast of; that most in you earnest eye" (*l.* 29f) we are compelled to consult the embryonic phrasings that preceded it in Plate 479: "Your lovely youth [*rev.* Your feast of youth] and that most earnest air" (29a), "Youth's festival in you" (29b), "The feast of you" (29d). Stanza 7 is another area of mystery in which variants assist our insight: "Man lives that list, that leaning in the will / No wisdom can forecast by gauge or guess" (25). Here earlier versions may be either plainer or more esoteric: "We live that leaning, least list in man's will/No wisdom would dare deal with, guage [sic] or guess" (25e, 26f). I spent a great deal of effort on various experimental arrangements of the MSS, but eventually returned to the one that seems closest to the probable evolution of this haunting portrait: H.ii. 93 recto, 94 recto, 93 verso, 94 verso, 97 recto, 96 recto, 96 verso; MS. A. To have arranged the MSS simply in the order of the foliation would have been far less helpful.

Line Numbers and Letters

My own pleasure in following the evolution of a poem through what can sometimes become a bewildering paper-chase has led me to encourage this pursuit among readers by adding letters to line numbers in some of the drafts. Letters are necessarily approximate where the precise succession is in doubt, or where that could be established only by the investment of even more time than I have already lavished. The numbers themselves, always based on the final version, may need to be clustered (e.g., "5, 6, 7") where a single line in an early sketch of a poem such as "Epithalamion" (Plates 495, 496) was expanded into two or more lines in the finished piece. As for the letters, 1a, 1b, 1c, etc., these are primarily attached to the numbers to enable the more exact identification of a specific portion of a MS. Even when a line appears to be the identical twin of one above it (though no two handwritten lines would on close inspection ever be found to be precise duplicates), I have given the second a different identification tab. I must freely admit to some inconsistencies in deciding when to assign several letters to a line with deletions and interlineations: the work has been spread over many years, with arduous final editing of two other volumes to distract me. But in spite of any imperfections, the marginal clues will make the growth of many poems far simpler, provided readers do not place too much confidence in the letters in the belief that they represent my settled opinion on the order in which the versions were modified. This is true of only some of them (see Plate 447, e.g.). With other poems a more searching examination would probably have modified my interim conclusions. To those who have hitherto known only the published final copies the imagery of Hopkins's footnoted alternatives in such poems as "The Starlight Night" (Plates 288a, 291) and "Spelt from Sibyl's Leaves" (Plate 474, 475) should bring new dimensions.

The Other Albums of Manuscripts: H.i and H.ii

For the pursuit of a poem from its earliest springs to its final flow the two volumes of drafts, H.i and H.ii, provide the most absorbing starting point. Sometimes they are also the end, as with "Epithalamion," which the poet abandoned on the brink of an allegorical precipice. Here we find nine excited pages in pencil and ink (Plates 494 to 502). The third set of drafts was committed to a spare examination answer-book, the cover of which heads Plate 500. The instructions to candidates struck Bridges as amusingly applicable to the professor's own procedures: he had certainly filled up all "the . . . blanks" and no one could fault him for failing to show the "rough work," though the "final results" that Bridges managed to extract are a greater tribute to the intrepid editor than to the author's penmanship. The pencilled signposts that Bridges left in the margins have proved of great assistance to aftercomers venturing into this wild scene. I have rearranged the plates in a sequence closer to the evolution of this strange marriage ode, and my numbering and lettering of the lines in the margins help to track the successive stages. Many lines have such numerous deletions and replacements as to provide multiple variants. I have set some of these out for the most heavily scored passages: though any reconstruction of such fleeting shapes is liable to elicit challenge, many experienced scholars fail to link up the deleted or revised words into any sort of syntactic sense. A Freudian slip uncovers a wounded reaction to those who rudely disturbed Hopkins's bower of bliss: on Plate 501, line 39b, we find "heavenfallen freshmen" (for "freshness")—his unruly students of classics, who flouted their lecturer unmercifully, must have seemed to him descendants of the rebellious angels.

ANNOTATIONS

"Anybody can read Hopkins's writing"

This phrase was the stock retort of one of my Oxford editors (while the *Facsimiles* plates were still part of the *OET*), any time I ventured to interpret a MS in any detail. But he wisely evaded my repeated offers of a monetary prize to any Oxford undergraduate of his choice who could transcribe a draft of one of the poems with complete accuracy. I doubt whether anyone living today has scrutinised the Hopkins autographs over a longer period than I have, yet I still approach them with circumspection, and before publishing any reading from a photocopy I try to check it against the prints of the MSS I have annotated in the margins with the originals in front of me. Scholars who can read a familiar faircopy with ease—thanks to the printed text—frequently stumble into error when they encounter an unpublished variant. On the other hand Catherine Phillips devoted endless hours to the detailed recording of the numerous shifting guises in which Hopkins and Bridges formed individual letters at different stages of their lives, a study from which I greatly benefited and to which I added. In *Facsimiles I*, p. 272, I reported on an attempt I made to produce a complete typographical transcription of a poem in ferment: this threatened to occupy far more space than the MSS themselves. In these annotations I have therefore offered help only in places where it would be easy to go astray, because of confusing signs, or strange dots over the letter *i*, or interlaced lines or heavily deleted words that are hard to decipher. Even experienced scholars can trip. Take "wince," Plate 447, line 6: this V was interpreted by a mature scholar, in a book submitted to a prestigious university press, as an indication that Hopkins wanted the reader's voice to descend and rise again on this single syllable. My note on the plate reveals it as simply the chance coming together of a swift "dot" over the *i* (drawn like a grave here and in many other places) and an acute stress mark, one of five in this line. In such annotations as these I try to pass on to the reader the results of repeated returns to the MSS themselves, examined in the best light Bodley could provide, and with the aid of the best instruments at my disposal.

Deletions

a) A deleted word or stop is always quoted *before* its replacement, following the chronological order, no matter if the poet has used common devices, such as a caret in front of the deletion, to lead the reader's eye to the new word first: e.g., in Plate 476, line 9, with "bleak light;⟋" in the MS clearly "light" was originally followed by a dash, and the semicolon before it was squeezed in later. The change is noted in logical sequence: "light⟋;"

b) When an uncompleted word has been deleted, I have often hazarded a guess at what it was going to be, judging from other variants, or the poet's tendency towards dittography, or his persistent auditory imagination that often suggested a homophone (Plates 300, *l*.4 "rin[g]" for "wring"; 288, *l*.9, "By / Buy"; 291, *l*.10, "Oar / orchard"; 365, "hour / our"). Some surmises are followed by a query. I have always set out with the unattainable aim of making sense of every mark on a page. My efforts may inspire some-one else to pursue a more thorough investigation.

c) With rare exceptions I have avoided the popular device of drawing a horizontal rule through a deleted passage, because this may obscure hyphens, dashes and the upper components of colons or semicolons, while also reducing the difference between such letters as *e* and *c.* Instead I have either struck the word or letters through on the slant, using a red pen to differentiate the strokes from the laser printer, or enclosed it in square brackets with "del.", or placed it in a list headed *"Deletions include:"*.

Punctuation

In the Introduction to the *OET* I commented upon difficulties that stem from some con-fusing stops used by Hopkins and Bridges. With Hopkins's hand, the blurring of distinc-tions between commas and periods applies more to the minute autographs in the two early note-books, C.i and C.ii, and to such notorious texts as *OET* No. 80 ("Summa"), or "Inundatio Oxoniana" (Plates 170, 171). In Plate 201 the abbreviation "A.M.D.G." seems to have three periods and a comma. Hopkins's "three-quarter colon" about which I jested in the *OET* is seen in such plates as 94, 96, 119, 122, 133, 138, 140, 203. They appear more numerous than they actually are because of the attention they provoke.

In the mature poems collected in this volume Hopkins's autographs usually exhibit admirably distinct punctuation. Trouble arises because the latest text for poems composed between 1876 and 1883 is a Bridges transcription corrected by Hopkins. Bridges showed minor interest in accidentals when copying his friend's verse, and, being aware of this, when he sent album B for Hopkins to check and revise he particularly asked him to "point it" (i.e., to punctuate it, L.i.189). This task Hopkins certainly did attempt, as my annota-tions indicate, but—with contemporary readers rather than future editors in mind—he incorporated his changes in the text so neatly that when Bridges examined album B in 1884 and again in 1889 he often failed to notice them. Only Bridges's meticulous collation with the autographs in 1918 brought many of them to light, and even then he sometimes mistook a deliberate change made by Hopkins for his own inadvertent departure from the autograph (e.g., Plate 345, note on line 10).

Hopkins characteristically gave his commas a curved tail, almost hooked, like the tails of Bridges's italic *g*s, and when these are found in a B transcript it is tempting to assume the author's intervention. Bridges's lack of concern for punctuation marks in B contrasts strangely with his ornately inscribed letters; commas he often flicked down between beau-tifully formed words without any care for their shape or size. They ranged from rapid straight strokes (as small as a millimetre period or as long as 4 mm.), to curves (some even made counter-clockwise, as his apostrophes can be) (Plates 260, st. 32:5, 255, st. 26:1). Confusion as to responsibility arises when he employs a hooked comma very similar to the Hopkins model he was copying. One of many occurs in A in his transcription of the "Wreck" st. 26:5 after "higher" (Plate 254). When we compare the B version (Plate 255)

> Blue-beating and hoary-glow height; and night, still higher,

it is hard not to conclude that both the commas are by Hopkins. Infrared, however, which confirms that the semicolon after "height" was originally a Bridges comma, reveals no stops under the commas in the second half of the line.

Because Hopkins often did not either change or clarify the punctuation where Bridges's stops are ambiguous, we should hesitate to interpret his inaction elsewhere as tacit approval. Robert Bridges's son, the first Lord Bridges, remarked to me that he could frequently not differentiate his father's commas from full-stops, particularly as RB might begin a new sentence with a lower case letter (see Plates 287 a, *l*4; 244, st. 16:7; cf. L.i.154: the reverse problem occurs in Plate 254, st. 26:6, 7). Many similar periods for commas Hopkins simply passed over when they occurred in B (see Plates 263b, st. 35:3; 287a, *l*8; 293, *l*14; 317, *l*1; 333, *ll*.10, 13; 381, *l*8; 383, *ll*.11,13 where two commas are almost invisible; 411, *l* 26; 413, *ll*. 35, 36). Such examples, plainly due to his lack of attention, challenge the reliability of founding the text of poems written between 1876 and 1883 upon "MS.B as corrected by GMH," our rule of thumb in the fourth edition of 1967.

I had hoped that infrared examination would eliminate confusion, but the B versions of "The Wreck of the Deutschland" and such poems as "Spring" (No. 117) were made and corrected in inks that the instrument I was using—and even the superior British Library Video Spectral Comparator—could not separate convincingly enough in cases of doubt for me to risk a definite attribution to GMH or RB. My normal editorial practice in the *OET* was then to fall back upon the original punctuation in A. For the "Deutschland," however, the A MS is itself a transcription, though likely to be in some measure more trustworthy because it was made from the now missing autograph, instead of being a copy of a copy as MS. B is for 34 of its 35 stanzas. My numerous changes to the text of the "Deutschland" are based upon A. Hopkins's editorial attention to B zigzagged over the lines like a dragonfly, working wonders where he alighted but missing much that he might have dealt with on more careful return flights; yet these expenditures of hours his conscience must have discouraged as an unprofitable use of time.

I have encountered no evidence that Hopkins revised the transcription of the "Wreck of the Deutschland" that Bridges, with wonderful fidelity to its layout, copied into album A. Yet MS. A is in theory likely to be closer to the lost autograph than the copy of a copy in B except in those places in B where we can be sure Hopkins intervened. Three imperfect processes confuse the "Deutschland" text:

1. Bridges's deciphering of what was no doubt often a much corrected autograph, and his transfer of this into A. His sometimes indistinguishable colons and semicolons may be seen, e.g., in Plates 230, 234, 242, 250, 252, 260, 262.

2. Bridges's transfer of his original transcription in A into MS. B. The text he provided Hopkins to edit was misleading in that the accidentals did not always match in A and B: e.g., he copied as a semicolon what I would read as a colon in A, and the other way round (e.g., sts. 21:5, 31:2).

3. Hopkins corrected B with no autograph to guide him, scarcely touching the flaws in one stanza and then tidying up the next in detail.

But the magnificent poetry shines out through all these shortcomings, deserving a more perfect text than we seem able to supply. Bridges had to admit that the loss of the autograph left him with a "stop uncertain" in various places (see Plate 254).

Finally, punctuation doubly earns its classification as an "accidental" in reproductions where a speck on the microfilm or on the MS page makes a comma masquerade as a semicolon on the plate (see, e.g., Plates 322, *l* 52; 373, *l* 17a, "cooling;" 381, *l* 6, "divined;").

Prosodic Marks

When I began editing Hopkins in 1964 scholars were often at a loss to decide who inserted the stress and other prosodic marks in MSS. A and B. As I became familiar with the MSS the answers seemed self-evident. In the A versions, the Hopkins autographs, the stresses are certainly by Hopkins himself except for rare cases where Bridges copied from the edited B version a few stresses important for the sense or rhythm—and then he used either red ink (1884) or black with a thin pen (1889) (see Plate 332). The A version of the "Wreck of the Deutschland" is, of course, an exception because it is a copy made from the autograph later lost; but as Hopkins had laid such emphasis upon the need for his blue chalk stresses, I have no reason to believe that any stresses in the lines marked (c. 100) were invented by Bridges himself rather than being transferred from the doomed original. Where Bridges reproduces a pattern of stresses from Hopkins, he is noticeably less particular than Hopkins in placing them: except when the tails of letters from the line above interfered, Hopkins aimed the stress at the (first) vowel in the accented syllable. Bridges allowed his stresses to land equally happily on vowels or consonants, or even on a mute *e* (e.g., in "elsé" Plate 254, st. 25: see Plates 332, note, last paragraph, and 382, *ll*.1 and 9).

When Bridges created the transcriptions in album B, as his note on the title page makes clear (Plate 220), he omitted nearly all the prosodic marks. Hopkins reacted equivocally (L.i.189): "You were right to leave out the marks: they were not consistent for one thing and are always offensive. Still there must be some. Either I must invent a notation applied throughout as in music [with every syllable, like a musical note, assigned a weight or length] or else I must only mark where the reader is likely to mistake, and for the present this is what I shall do." With the few exceptions to which I point in the notes (e.g., Plate 231), the prosodic marks in B were supplied by Hopkins: in a number of cases stresses or outrides were added to interlined revisions made in his undoubted handwriting (see, e.g., Plates 309, *ll*.4, 8, outrides; 313, *ll*.3, 13).

Dots below vowels. An apparently eccentric method of indicating stress is to be found in plates 271, 380, 489, 492, and 515—the use of a black dot below the first vowel of a stressed syllable. The earliest occurrence is in "The Woodlark" (No. 104), July 1876. The practice used to make more sense in Greek prosody, the source of his usage (which I cannot remember seeing identified). In what is now a badly dated discussion of versification in Greek, my old *Greek Grammar* by William Goodwin ([1879], 1902 edition, p. 348) uses dots below vowels to show the difference between the word-accents marked by graves and acutes, and the independent ictus. Unfortunately Hopkins succumbed to his usual temptation to add complicating refinements: in September 1880, writing to Bridges (L.i.109), he differentiated black balls (for "the real or heard stress") from white balls, "the dumb or conventional one." He forgot that with a worn or overloaded quill white balls tend to choke with ink. And when these symbols are sprinkled across poems in Sprung Rhythm (where conventional rhythms ought surely not to survive) the distinction may seem misguided (see Plates 489, 492).

Hyphenations, Compounds, and Penlifts

One controversial area is the delicate judgment as to whether two words separated by an unusually small space were meant by Hopkins or Bridges as a compound: I often comment "one word intended" or "probably intended." Particularly in theses, the acceptability of which may hinge upon a show of independence, these remarks may invite challenge, since absolute certainty may be impossible (see *OET*, introduction, xlvii). The matter is sometimes intertwined with the distribution of stresses in a line, where emphasis upon the second element in a hyphenation (as in "black-bírd") runs counter to linguistic analysis. The dilemma becomes acute in the "Deutschland," since we possess an autograph for only one out of 35 stanzas.

The decision on one word or two cannot be settled simply by refined scale measurements of the relative spaces between adjoining words: we have to scrutinize the poet's frequent penlifts within unquestionable single words in neighbouring plates, as well as the reverse, where he joins noun and verb without meaning them to be so printed. I have discussed this in Plates 504–505, though the problem faces us constantly. Bridges in his transcriptions from the autographs frequently omitted a hyphen (probably because that particular hyphenation was not then accepted: and any printer would have done the same), yet in these cases he often wrote the two elements in the hyphenation so close together that the author in checking his text could easily have joined them or bridged them with a hyphen. But the poet's sight, sharp if directed towards God's creation, was blunted by diffidence towards his own artifacts. When Hopkins in reviewing B did not change the Bridges copy in such places, we have no means of determining whether he accepted the hyphenless words as compound units, or was content to see them separated, or, as is equally possible, he gave them no consideration at all. Except with his longest poem, the "Deutschland," the editor can luckily have recourse to the autograph where reaching a conclusion may be less arduous, but in this matter as in so many others Hopkins was inconsistent (see, e.g., Plate 423).

Paper

While most of the poems in MS. B were inscribed, either by Bridges or Hopkins himself, on the pages of the album, most others were written on separate sheets of paper. With these I have been careful to remark upon any tears and creases that mimic letters and prosodic signs: thus on Plate 479, line 31a, a tear before "Worst" creates the illusion of a great colon. Details of the colour of the paper may help to tie two neighbouring poems together: sheets vary from pure white to paper yellowed and foxed by age, with occasional pages of blue and grey. Sometimes there is an invisible embossed address, as with Miss Cassidy's notepaper at Monasterevan (Plate 492, cf. 517). Strips of paper pasted over discarded versions are specially mentioned, with particulars of the original text thus obscured (Plates 237, 306, 409). I have also reported pages that were once part of a large sheet, e.g., Plate 437, where such information is of special value because of the vexed uncertainties of chronology among the poems written in Ireland.

Contents of the Chief Albums of MSS

Nearly thirty years ago, when I began to study the Hopkins MSS in Oxford, my first action was to make for each of the four albums a Table of Contents. These records have been of incessant use to me. At the end of this work I set them out in greater detail, adding the *OET* numbers of the poems and the Plate numbers in the two *Facsimiles* volumes. With MS. A, over 300 pages long, a description of Bridges's careful editorial entries inscribed between the mounted autographs would have occupied too much space: only the principal items are therefore inventoried. Bridges began a penciled list of contents (Plate 527), but this is almost illegible without my annotations. In MS. B I have distinguished between the four sections of poetic MSS and discussed who is most likely to have pasted in the final autographs. Brief annotations on the MSS in H.i help the evaluation of the autographs and the transcripts: many of the latter represent versions otherwise unknown.

The only album fully indexed by Bridges himself was H.ii (Plates 532–33); my notes provide the modern folio numbers to replace the ringed numbers Bridges wrote at the tops of the MSS. Plate 531 reproduces two notes by Bridges on the history of the volume, the first in 1889 when he created the album and the second in November 1918 after he had edited the First Edition of the *Poems*. When in 1917 he took the old scrapbook H out of a safe in Oxford, where it had been kept since the Hopkins family had sent it back to him from Haslemere, he found that the cover and some pages had become mouldy, though the MSS themselves had not suffered. He therefore transferred the poems to a new volume, preserving the old index and noting new pieces added to it. Graham Storey, faced with the task of preparing for the press Humphry House's Preface to the *Journals and Papers* (Oxford University Press, 1959) after the latter's untimely death, misunderstood House's account of MS. H, now printed in J. pp. xi–xii. House had written "there are no further references . . . until 1918. . . . In two letters to Kate Hopkins that autumn Bridges lists these papers. . . . On 14 October he [RB] wrote to her" describing the discovery of the mould. Storey, trying to clarify, added "1889" after "October." The letters, correctly dated "1918," were published in Donald Stanford's *Selected Letters of Robert Bridges*, vol. ii (Newark, University of Delaware Press, 1984, 742–45). Though Stanford missed the second page of the letter of 28 November 1918, he made it clear that the letters were to Miss Kate Hopkins, GMH's sister, not to his mother, Mrs. Kate Hopkins (see *OET* xxx).

Deterioration of the MSS

Hopkins's growing popularity, reflected by the numerous selected editions of his verse and celebrations all round the globe in 1989 of the centenary of his death, has imposed much wear and even fading on his autographs, both in the Bodleian Library and Campion Hall, Oxford. One of the driving motives in my completion of this two-volume edition of facsimilies has been the desire to make the benefits of manuscript study available to all serious students of Hopkins without exposing the original documents to unnecessary multiple use. Though there is no substitute for the autographs themselves as the final authority, that is all the more reason to save them from being handled more often than can be avoided. The Hopkins world owes an incalculable debt to those who have preserved and conserved his MSS, and to no one more than his life-long friend and literary trustee, Robert Bridges.

THE LATER POETIC
MANUSCRIPTS
OF

Gerard Manley Hopkins

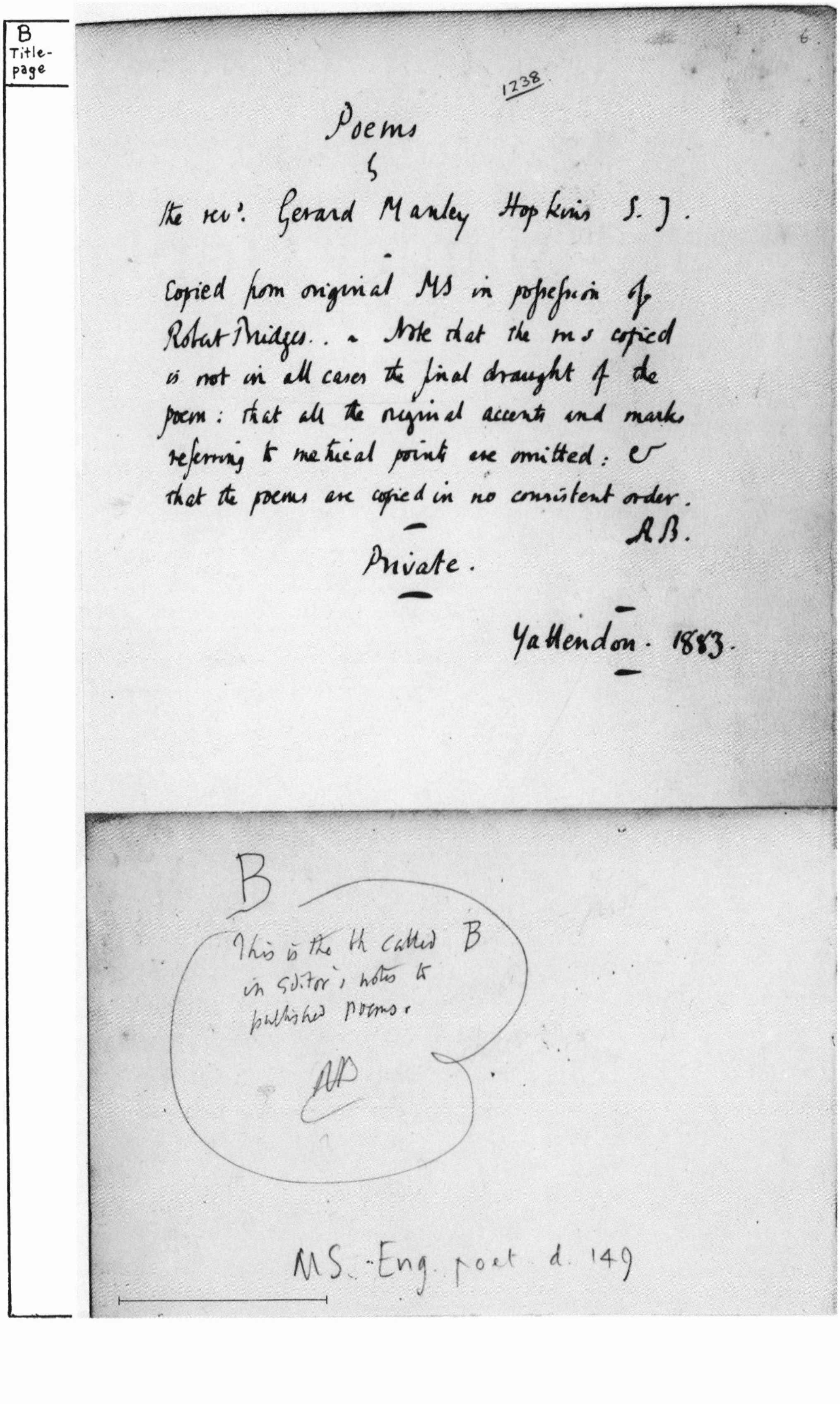

Poems
by
the rev?. Gerard Manley Hopkins S. J.

Copied from original MS in possession of Robert Bridges. . . Note that the m s copied is not in all cases the final draught of the poem: that all the original accents and marks referring to metrical points are omitted: & that the poems are copied in no consistent order.

R B

Private.

Yattendon. 1883.

B

This is the th called B in Editor's notes to published poems.

MS. Eng. poet. d. 149

Plate 220   Title-page of MS. B (f.6r)

This was the second album which Bridges devoted to the poetry of Hopkins. Showing more concern for the preservation of his verse than Hopkins did himself, Bridges never trusted his collection of Hopkins autographs in MS. A to the mail or loaned it to friends--though he often showed it to visitors who were likely to respond to this strange verse. In order to circulate the poetry and encourage the diffident priest, in 1883 Bridges copied many of his best poems into a second smaller album, MS. B, and sent it to Hopkins for correction and revision. He marked it "Private" to forestall unauthorised publication, a possibility which Hopkins was afraid would incur the displeasure of his superiors--see L.ii.30, 93, 150 and L.i.65-6.

RB's note in the lower part of the plate faces f.1r. The Bodleian Library shelf mark was added in 1953 when they acquired the album from the family.

PLATE 221. Metrical Preface to Hopkins's Mature Verse • 23

B
1r

1

5

10

15

20

25

30

The poems in this book are written some in Running Rhythm, the common rhythm in English use, some in
Sprung Rhythm, and some in a mixture of the two.
And those in the common rhythm are some counterpointed, some not.

Common English rhythm, called Running Rhythm
above, is measured by feet of either two or three
syllables and (putting aside the imperfect feet at the beginning and end of lines and also some unusual measures in which feet seem to be paired together and
double or composite feet to arise) never more nor less.

Every foot has one principal stress or accent, and
this or the syllable on which it falls on may be called
the Stress of the foot and the other part, the one or
two unaccented syllables, the slack. Feet (and
the rhythms made out of them) in which the stress
comes first are called Falling Feet and Falling
Rhythms, feet and rhythm in which the slack comes
first are called Rising Feet and Rhythms, and if
the stress is between the two slacks there will be
Rocking Feet and Rhythms. These distinctions are
real and true to nature; but for purposes of scanning it is a great convenience to follow the example
of music and take the stress always first, as the
accent or the chief accent always comes first in a musical bar. If this is done there will be in common
English verse only two possible feet— the so-called
accentual trochee and Dactyl, and correspondingly-
ly only two possible uniform rhythms, the so-called
trochaic and Dactylic. But they may be mixed

Plate 221   Metrical Preface to Hopkins's Mature Poems - MS. 1

B.1r.   These autograph notes on Running and Sprung Rhythm seem to have been written to accompany MS. B when GMH sent it on to Coventry Patmore, March 1884. They apply to the poems in album B ff.6 to 35r: if "Spelt from Sibyl's Leaves" (f.36r) had then existed it would surely have affected lines 115 and 161. When RB received album B back from Patmore in July, realising the unique value of the Preface he transferred it to album A (in which he preserved the autographs of GMH's poems): an uncompleted scribbled table of Contents for album A (see below, end of this volume) records "A preface to his poems MS." as beginning on p.8: the next item is listed as on p.16, and "The Deutschland preface" is listed further down as on p.24. This Preface to B was later professionally guarded into album B, occupying the rectos of ff.1 to 5, with an afterthought on f.3 verso.

and then what the Greeks called a Logaoedic Rhythm 2
arises. These are the facts and according to there ①
the scanning of ordinary regularly-written English verse
is very simple indeed and to bring in other principles
~~is here unnecessary~~
But because verse written, strictly, in these ~~rhythm~~ and by
these principles ~~strictly~~ will become same and tame the
poets have brought in licenses and departures from rule
to give variety; and especially when the natural
rhythm is rising, as in the ~~common~~ common ten-syllable
or five-foot ~~line~~ verse, rhymed or blank. These irregularities
are ~~principally~~ chiefly Reversed Feet and Reversed or
Counterpoint Rhythm, which two things are two steps or
degrees of licence in the same kind. By a reversed
foot I mean the putting ~~close top~~ the stress where, to
judge by the rest of the measure, the slack should be
and the slack where the stress, and this is done freely
at the beginning of a line and, in the course of a line, after
a pause; only scarcely ever in the second foot or place
and never in the last, unless when the poet designs
some extraordinary effect; for these places are characteristic and sensitive and cannot well be touched. But
the reversal of the first foot and of some middle foot after a strong pause is a thing so natural that our poets
have generally done it, from Chaucer down, without
remark and it commonly passes unnoticed, and cannot be said to amount to a formal change of rhythm, but rather is that irregularity which all natural growth and
motion shews. If however the reversal is repeated in
two feet running, especially so as to include the sensitive
second foot, it must ~~really~~ be due either to great
want of ear or else is a calculated effect, the super-
inducing or mounting of a new rhythm upon the old;

PLATE 223. Metrical Preface to Hopkins's Mature Verse • 25

B.3r

and since the new or mounted rhythm is actually
65 heard and at the same time the mind naturally
supplies the natural or standard foregoing rhythm,
for we do not forget that the rhythm is that by
rights we should be hearing, two rhythms are
in some manner running at once and we have
70 something answerable to counterpoint in music,
which is two or more strains of tune going on
together, and this is Counterpoint Rhythm. Of this
kind of verse Milton is the great master and
the choruses of _Samson Agonistes_ are written
75 throughout in it — but with the disadvantage that
he does not let the reader clearly know what the
ground-rhythm is and meant to be and so they
have struck most readers as merely irregular.
And in fact if you counterpoint throughout, since
80 only one of the counter rhythms is actually heard, the
other is really destroyed and cannot come to
exist and what is written is one rhythm only and
probably Sprung Rhythm, of which I now speak.

Sprung Rhythm, as used in this book, is
85 measured by feet of from one to four syllables, re-
gularly, and for particular effects any number
of weak or slack syllables may be used. It has
one stress, which falls on the only syllable, or, if there is only one, or,
there are more, then scanning as above, on the first, and so gives
90 rise to four sorts of feet, a monosyllable and
the so-called accentual trochee, Dactyl, and the
First Paeon. And there will be four corresponding natural rhythms; but nominally the feet are
mixed and any one may follow any other. And hence
95 Sprung Rhythm differs from Running Rhythm

Plate 223   Metrical Preface to B (cont.) - MS. 3
  B.3r. Deletion in 72-73: "This..has"   90 rh[ythm?]   Revision in 88-89 "if there is only one, or, if there are more, then"

B.
3 v.

105 Remark also that it is natural in Sprung Rhythm for the lines to
be *rove over*, that is for the scanning of each line immediately
to take up that of the one before, so that if the first has one or
more syllables at the end the other must have so many the fewer
at the beginning; and in fact the scanning runs on without
110 ~~x unless in the Echos,~~ ~~second line~~ break from the beginning, say,
of a stanza to the end and all the stanza is one long strain,
though written in lines asunder. ————

See
115 × Unless in the *Echos*, second line

PLATE 225. Metrical Preface to Hopkins's Mature Verse   •   27

in having or being only one nominal rhythm, a mixed 4
or "logaoedic" one, instead of three, but on the other hand
in having twice the flexibility of foot, so that ~~two~~ any
two stresses may either follow one another running or be
divided by one, two, or three slack syllables. But strict
sprung Rhythm cannot be counterpointed. In Sprung
Rhythm, as in logaoedic rhythm generally, the feet are
assumed to be equally long or strong and their seeming
inequality is made up by pause or stressing.

Two licences are natural to sprung Rhythm. The
one is rests, as in music; but of this an example is
scarcely to be found in this book.× The other is hangers or
outrides, that is one, two, or three slack syllables added
to a foot and not counting in the nominal scanning.
~~They are so called because~~ they seem to hang below the line or ride forward or
backward from it in another dimension than the line
itself, according to a principle needless to explain here.
These outriding half feet or hangers are marked by
a loop underneath them, and plenty of them will be
found.

The other marks are easily understood, ~~to wit~~ namely accents, where the reader might be in doubt which syllable
should have the stress; slurs, that is loops over syllables,
to tie them together into the time of one; little loops
at the end of a line to show that the rhyme goes on to
to the first letter of the next line; what ~~in~~ in music are
called pauses ⌢, to shew that the syllable should be
dwelt on; and twirls ∽, to mark reversed or
counterpointed rhythm.

Note on the nature and history of Sprung Rhythm —
Sprung Rhythm is the most natural of things. For (1)
it is the rhythm of common speech and of written prose,
when rhythm is perceived in them. (2) It is the rhythm of all

B.
4ᵛ.

100

104

113

115

120

125

130

135

Plates 224-5   Metrical Preface to B (cont.) - MSS. 4 and 5

B.4r,3v. At first the footnote to 115, indicated by an "x" ("Unless in the Echos, second line") was the only entry on
f.3v; it was deleted from 110 and rewritten below 112 when GMH added a para on rove over lines. In 110 "say," is
interpolated. Other deletions include: 106 t[o]   108 f[ewer?]   117 scanning   124 to wit   129 ar[e]

B 5r	

but the most monotonously monotonously regular music
so that in the words of choruses and refrains and
in songs written closely to music it arises. (3)
140 It is found in nursery rhymes, weather saws proverbs,
and so on; because, however these may have been
once made in running rhythm, the terminations
having dropped off by the change of language
the stresses come together and so the rhythm is
145 sprung. (4) It arises in common verse when reversed or counterpointed, for the actual rhythm
is then same reason. in spite of all this and

But nevertheless, though Greek and Latin
lyric verse, which is well known, and the old
150 English verse seen in <u>Pierce Ploughman</u> are in
sprung rhythm, it has in fact ceased to be used
since the Elizabethan age, Greene being the last
writer who can be said to have recognised it. For
perhaps there was not down to our days,
in English
155 in which spring rhythm is em-
ployed—not for single effects or in fixed places—
but as the governing principle of the scansion.
Say this because the contrary has been asserted;
if it is otherwise the poem should be cited.

160 Some of the sonnets in this book are in five-
-foot, some in six-foot or Alexandrine lines.
Nos. 1 and 25 are Curtal-sonnets that is
they are constructed in proportions resembling those
of the sonnet proper, namely 6 + 4 instead of 8 + 6,
165 with however a half line tailpiece (so that the equa-
tion is rather $\frac{12}{2} + \frac{9}{2} = \frac{21}{2} = 10\frac{1}{2}$).

Plate 226   Metrical Preface to B (cont.) - MS. 6
B.5r.   <u>Changes include</u>:   143 dé[cay?]   154 is not   162 - sonnets [s <u>mended to</u> S].
In 162 poems Nos. 1 and 25 become Nos. 121 and 140 in this volume.

REPORT OF AN INQUIRY

INTO THE CIRCUMSTANCES ATTENDING THE

LOSS OF THE STEAM SHIP "DEUTSCHLAND"

ON

THE KENTISH KNOCK SAND,

On the 6th day of December 1875.

Presented to both Houses of Parliament by Command of Her Majesty.

LONDON:
PRINTED BY GEORGE EDWARD EYRE AND WILLIAM SPOTTISWOODE,
PRINTERS TO THE QUEEN'S MOST EXCELLENT MAJESTY.
FOR HER MAJESTY'S STATIONERY OFFICE.

1876.

[C.—1403.]   *Price 10½d.*

REPORT.

Plate 227   No. 101: "The Wreck of the Deutschland"

Title-page and Contents of the official Inquiry into what caused the wreck of the Deutschland, conducted by the Board of Trade, and published 8 February 1876. As St. Beuno's College subscribed to The Times, Hopkins could read the detailed reports of the evidence and cross-examination before the Board: The Times published these, session by session, from 21 Dec. 1875 to 1 Jan. 1876. The British Library has a copy of the final report: Parliamentary Publications, 1876, vol. lxvii (Accounts and Papers, vol. 26: Pilotage, Wrecks and Casualties), pp.153-90.

A
P.24

Note — Be pleased, reader, since the rhythm in wh: 24
the following poem is written is new, strongly to mark the
beats of the measure, according to the number belonging to
each of the eight lines of the stanza, as the indentation
guides the eye, namely two & three and four and three &
five & five & four & six; not disguising the rhythm &
rhyme, as some readers do, who treat poetry as if it were prose
fantastically written to rule (which they mistakenly think the
perfection of reading) but laying on the beats too much stress,
rather than too little; nor caring whether one, two, three, or
more syllables go to a beat, that is to say, whether two or more
beats follow running — as there are three running in the
third line of the first stanza — or with syllables between, as
commonly; nor whether the line begin with a beat or not;
but letting the scansion run on from one line onto the next,
without break to the end of the stanza: since the dividing
of the lines is more to fix the places of the necessary rhymes
than for any pause in the measure. Only let this be obser-
=ved in the reading, that, where more than one syllable
goes to a beat, then if the beating syllable is of its na=
ture strong, the stress laid on it must be stronger the grea=
ter the number of syllables belonging to it, the voice tread=
=ing & dwelling: but if on the contrary it is by nature
light, then the greater the number of syllables belonging to
it the less is the stress to be laid on it, the voice passing=
flyingly over all the syllables of the foot & in some man=
ner distributing among them all the stress of the one beat.

Plate 228   No. 101: "The Wreck of the Deutschland" Note on the Rhythm of the "Wreck of the Deutschland" - MS. 1
A.p.24. Transcription by RB of an autograph now missing. It was copied on thinner paper, which was guarded into
album A. The paper bears the watermark of T & J Hollingworth, Turkey Mills, Maidstone, Kent.

A.
p.25

25

30

35

which syllables however are strong & which light is
better told by the Ear than by any instruction that cd
be in short space given: but for an example, in the
stanza which is fifth from the end of the poem & in
the 6th line the first two beats are very strong & the
more the voice dwells on them the more it fetches out the
strength of the syllables they rest upon, the next two
beats are very light & escaping, & the last, as well
as those which follow on the next line, are of a mean
strength, such as suits narrative. And so throughout
let the stress be made to fetch out both the strength of
the syllables & the meaning & feeling of the words.

The Wreck of the Deutschland

December 6. 7. 1875.

to the happy memory of five Franciscan nuns,
exiles by the Falck Laws, drowned between
midnight & morning of December 7.

The wreck of the Deutschland.   26

Part the first.

        Thou
God mastering me :
God! Giver of breath and bread ;
World's strand, sway of the sea ;
Lord of living and dead ;
Thou hast bound bones & veins in me, fastened me flesh,
And after at times almost unmade   what   with dread,
Thy doing : & dost Thou touch me afresh ?
Over again I feel Thy finger & find Thee.

                        2
    I did say yes
O At lightning & lashed rod ;
Thou heardst me, truer than tongue, confess
    Thy terror, O Christ, O God ;
Thou knowest the walls, altar & hour & night :
The swoon of a heart that the swoop & the hurl of Thee trod
Hard down with a horror of height :
And the midriff astrain with leaning of, laced with fire of stress.

                                    The

OET No. 101: "The Wreck of the Deutschland": GMH did not entrust RB with the autograph of this great ode, nor did he exert himself to make a copy. The original eventually disappeared. Fortunately, RB copied the poem out twice, once from the autograph (into album A), and in 1883 from A into album B, which he then sent to the author for checking and revision. When MS. B was returned to him, in Aug. 1884, RB recorded in A, using red ink to distinguish them, all the changes by GMH which he noticed. He ignored revised stresses and often overlooked accidentals. In Oct. 1889, after GMH's death, he added, in black backward-sloping letters, other corrections or additions made by the author (see, e.g., st.8:3; 13:7; 21:2; date and place at the end of the poem). Another copy of the "Wreck", made by Fr. Francis Bacon, SJ,was extant in 1918; RB asked Fr. Geof. Bliss to collate its readings when he was editing the first edition of the Poems. See OET p.316 for its later disappearance, and for its variant readings see notes below to sts. 4:7; 14:8; 16:7; 18:1; 21:2 and 8; 26:6; 34:8.

MS. A: The "Wreck" occupies A pp.26-43, two sts. per page, with st.35 by itself. On pp.26-28 the text is enclosed in red pencil borders. Most of the stress marks (no doubt copied from the autograph) are in blue pencil, but RB did not follow GMH in trying to place stresses only on vowels (see 2: ℓ.7, "down"). There is no evidence that any of the changes made in A were by anyone except RB.

MS. B: Ff.15r–20v. After the first two sts. each page has three, but to match MS. A the B versions have in this Facsimiles vol. been regrouped, 2 sts. per plate. In correcting MS. B, GMH appears to have strengthened or clarified many punctuation marks, especially in sts. 28-35.

PLATE 231. OET 101. "The Wreck of the Deutschland" • 33

Plate 230 (opposite) No. 101: "The Wreck of the Deutschland" A.p.26

St.1: Red ink corrections based on B: 1. "Thou" with caret, but "God" is del. in pencil. 2. "God!" and interlined "G" with del. (to show that "Giver" becomes ℓ.c.; the tail of that "G" is also crossed through in red). But RB preferred the orig. version of 1 and 2 (which fitted GMH's metrical pattern more closely). When RB publ. st. 1 by itself in The Spirit of Man (1916) he used the original text: hence his pencilled "stet" after ℓ.1, and pencilled del. of "Thou" (1) and "God!" (2). When editing 1st edn. of Poems in 1918 for a time he considered reverting to the orig. there also--see his note on B.f.15r. In A st.1:6 "at times" and "me" are del. in red ink; "it", "what" and final comma are added in red.

St.2: red ink changes--1. del. of "O" 2. "O" and stroke below "A" of "At" (to indicate ℓ.c.) are added. 6 "swoop" changed to "sweep"

Plate 231 (above) No. 101: "The Wreck of the Deutschland" B.15r.

Title: GMH interpolated the date; the tail of his "7" meets RB's flourish, forming a sort of "Z". RB's pencil note of Jan. 22 1918, "this [mended from or to "thou"] omitted from collation for the time", was made when he was preparing the 1st. edn. of the Poems. It probably refers only to the opening two lines as revised by GMH in the margin, or at most the opening st., where RB preferred the original version.

St.1: GMH's revisions in 1,2 are in the margin, in 6 interlined, with commas added after "unmade" and "dread". The (revised) stresses in 6 are GMH's (in purple pencil), but RB, who usually did not reproduce in B the stresses in A, had regarded the one on "thee" in 8 as too important to omit: he had marked it heavily in ink when transcribing B.

St.2: GMH revised 1,2,6, and, perhaps later, added a circumflex on "hour" (5). In 3 a word was erased below "tongue".

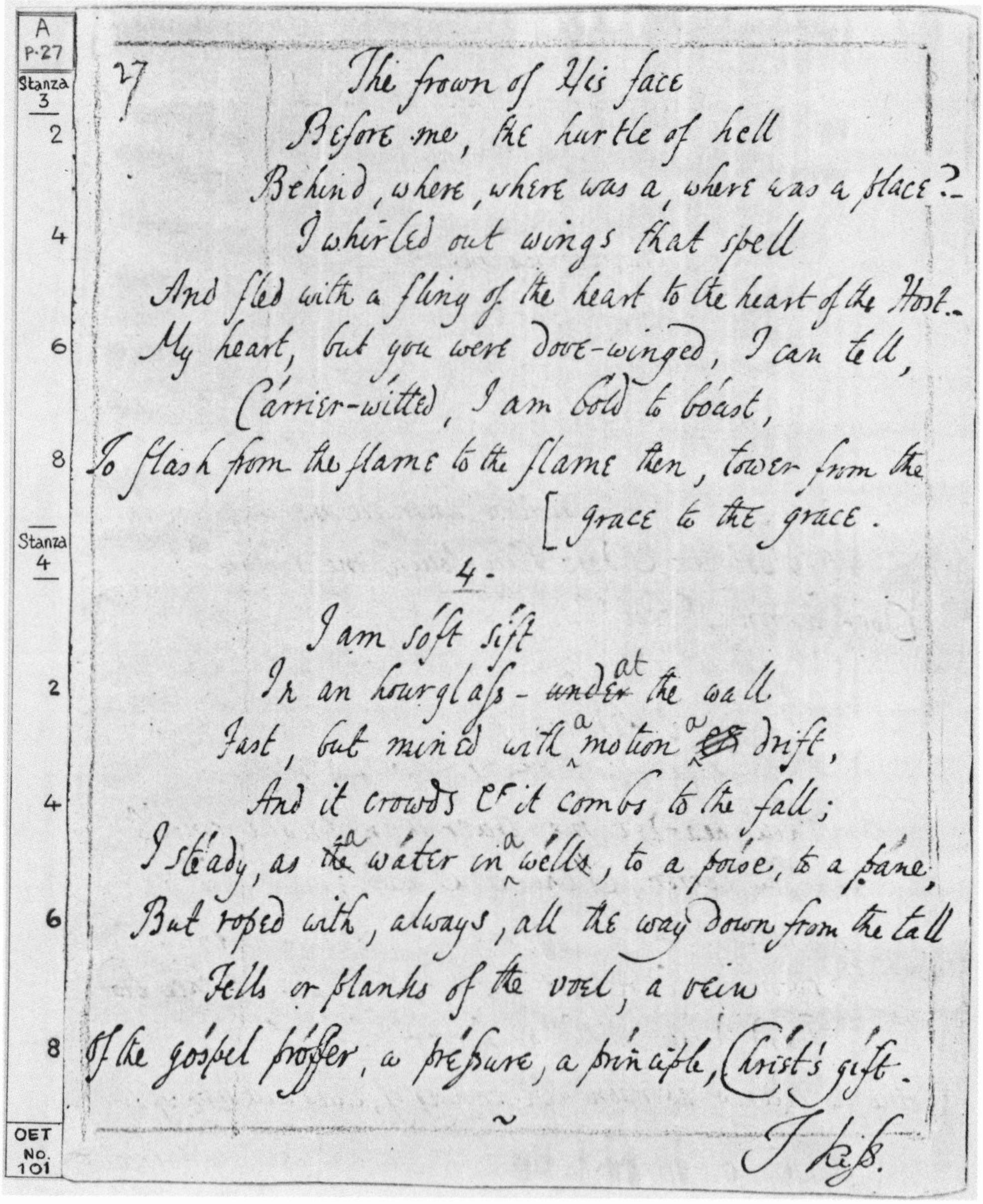

A
P·27

Stanza
3

2

27   The frown of His face
         Before me, the hurtle of hell
Behind, where, where was a, where was a, place?

4   I whirled out wings that spell
And fled with a fling of the heart to the heart of the Host.

6   My heart, but you were dove-winged, I can tell,
      Carrier-witted, I am bold to boast,

8 To flash from the flame to the flame then, tower from the
                [grace to the grace.

Stanza
4

            4.

       I am soft sift

2   In an hourglass - under^{at} the wall
Fast, but mined with^{a} motion^{a} drift,

4   And it crowds & it combs to the fall;
I steady, as the water in^{a} wells, to a poise, to a pane,

6 But roped with, always, all the way down from the tall
      Fells or flanks of the voel, a vein

8 Of the gospel proffer, a pressure, a principle, Christ's gift.
           ~
                       J.h.s.

OET
No.
101

Plate 232   No. 101: "The Wreck of the Deutschland" cont. A.p.27.
    St.3: Dashes at the ends of 3, 5 were obscured in the central crease: RB did not reproduce them in B, and editors before the OET have therefore also omitted them.
    St.4: Red ink changes in 2,3,5 copy revisions in B.

PLATE 233. OET 101. "The Wreck of the Deutschland" • 35

B.
15 v
St. 3
2

4

6

8

Stanza
4

2

4

6

8

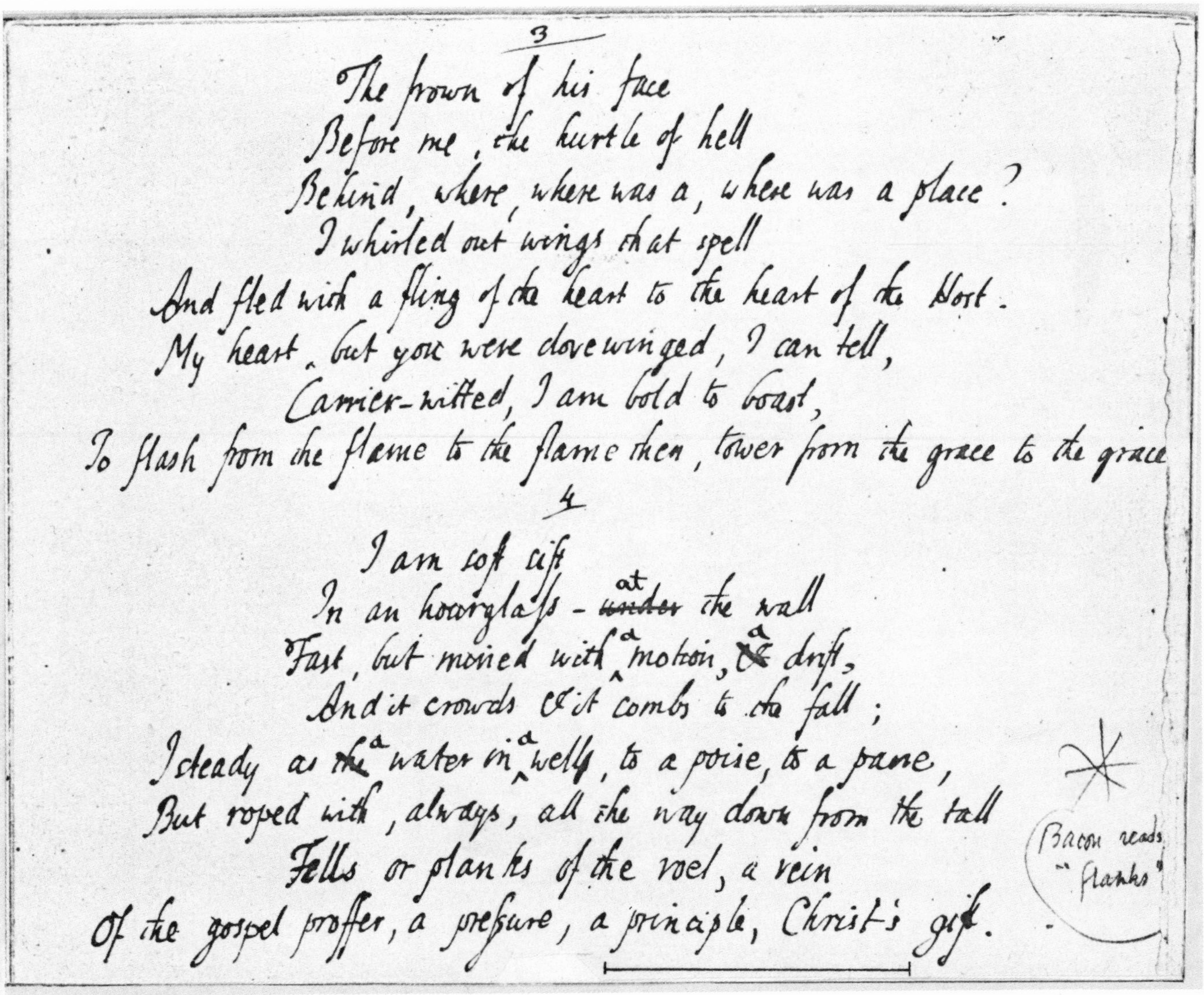

3

The frown of his face
Before me, the hurtle of hell
Behind, where, where was a, where was a place?
I whirled out wings that spell
And fled with a fling of the heart to the heart of the Host.
My heart, but you were dovewinged, I can tell,
Carrier-witted, I am bold to boast,
To flash from the flame to the flame then, tower from the grace to the grace

4

I am soft sift
In an hourglass — at under the wall
Fast, but mined with a motion, a drift,
And it crowds & it combs to the fall;
I steady as the a water in a wells, to a poise, to a pane,
But roped with, always, all the way down from the tall
Fells or planks of the voel, a vein
Of the gospel proffer, a pressure, a principle, Christ's gift.

Bacon reads
"flanks"

Plate 233   No. 101: "The Wreck of the Deutschland" cont.   B.15v.
    St.3:   8--the period after "grace" is obscured by the binding.
    St.4:   GMH revised 2, 3 (including comma after "motion"--one of the many changes in B not noticed by RB in 1884),
and 5, incl. del. of "s" in "wells": he did not reinstate the comma after "steady", found in A. RB's pencil (1918) notes in
the margin opposite "planks" (7): "Bacon reads 'flanks'" (see OET commentary).

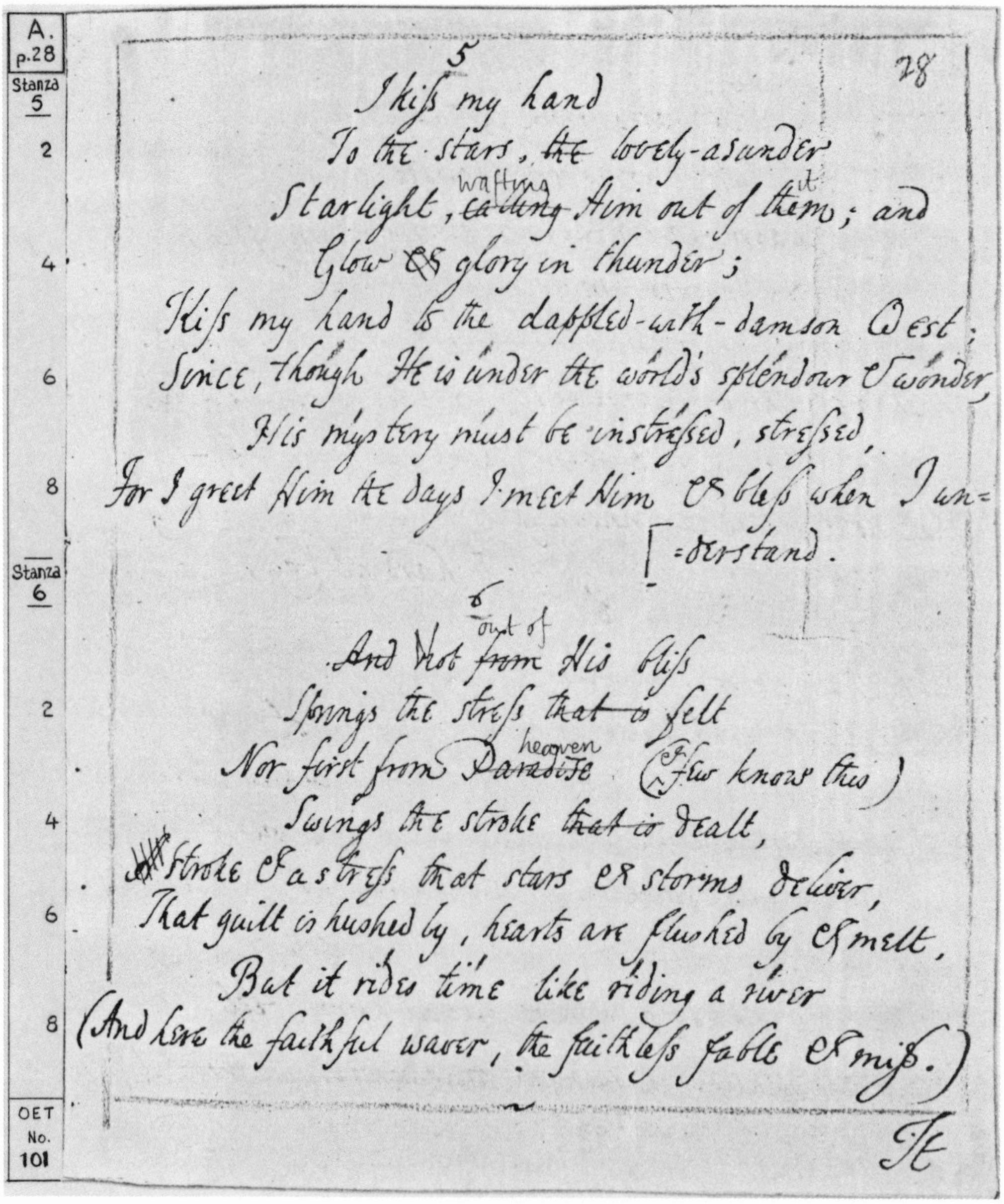

A.
p.28

Stanza 5

28

5

I kiss my hand
To the stars, the lovely-asunder
         wafting
Starlight, casting Him out of them; and
Glow & glory in thunder;
Kiss my hand to the dappled-with-damson West;
Since, though He is under the world's splendour & wonder,
His mystery must be instressed, stressed,
For I greet Him the days I meet Him & bless when I un-
         ⌈=derstand.

Stanza 6

         6
         out of
And not from His bliss
Springs the stress that is felt,
         heaven
Nor first from Paradise. (Few know this.)
Swings the stroke that is dealt,
Stroke & a stress that stars & storms deliver,
That guilt is hushed by, hearts are flushed by & melt,
But it rides time like riding a river
(And here the faithful waver, the faithless fable & miss.)

         ℋℋ

OET
No.
101

Plate 234   No. 101: "The Wreck of the Deutschland" cont.   A.p.28.
    St.5: Red corrections in 2,3 and 4 are based on GMH's revisions in B, but miss the comma now needed after "Glow"
(4). Note that in 7 "instréssed" shifts the emphasis to the second syllable, the verbal form.
    St.6: The first five lines record in red GMH's masterly revisions in B.

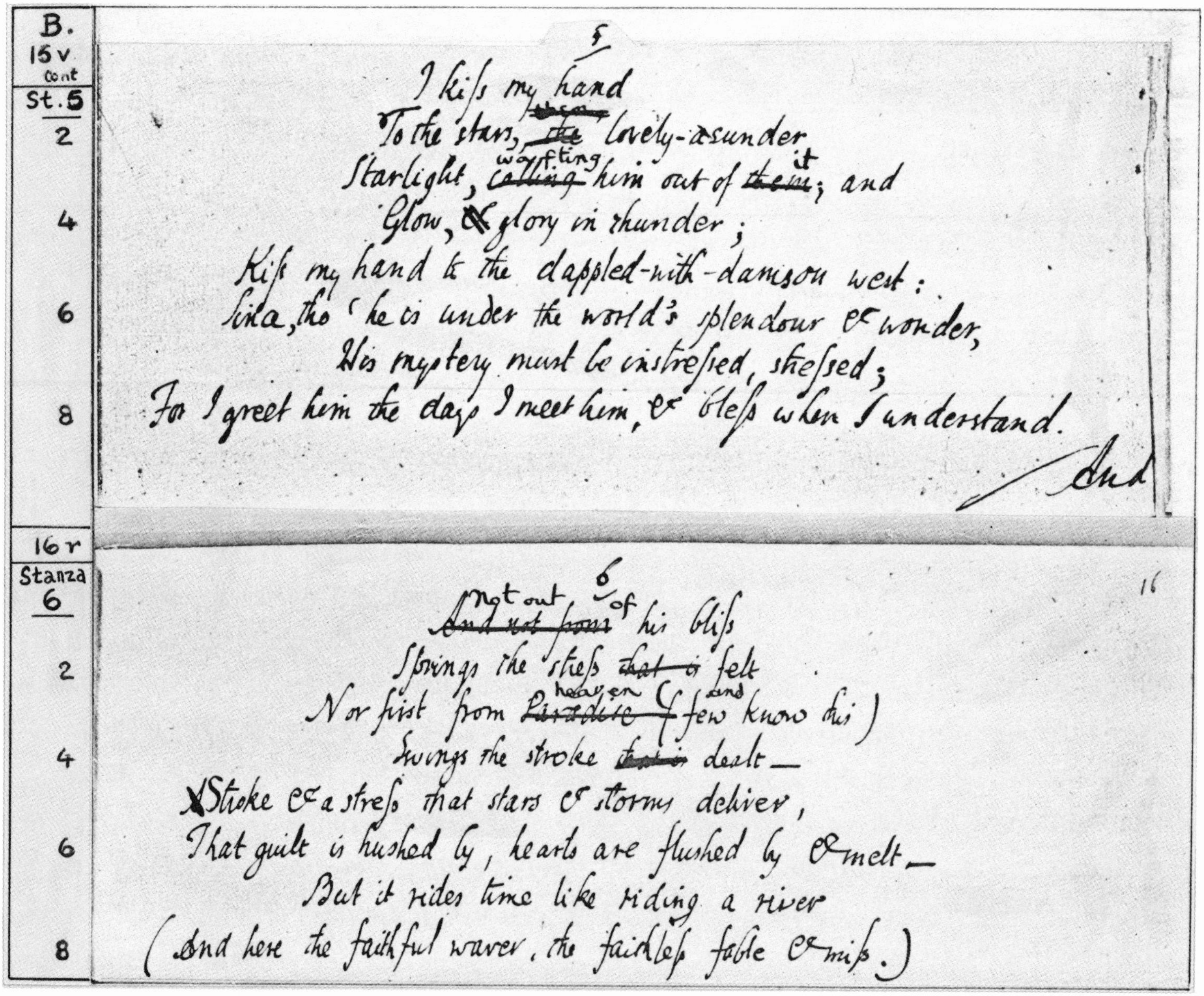

PLATE 235. OET 101. "The Wreck of the Deutschland"   •   37

B. **15 v** **cont**	5
St. 5	I kiss my hand
2	To the stars, ~~the~~ lovely-asunder
	Starlight, ~~calling~~ *waffting* him out of ~~them~~ *it*; and
4	Glow, & glory in thunder;
6	Kiss my hand to the dappled-with-damson west:
	Since, tho' he is under the world's splendour & wonder,
8	His mystery must be instressed, stressed;
	For I greet him the days I meet him, & bless when I understand.
	And

16 r **Stanza** **6**	6 *Not out, of* ~~And not from~~ his bliss
2	Springs the 'stress ~~that is~~ felt
	Nor first from ~~Paradise~~ *heaven* (& *and* few know this)
4	Swings the stroke ~~that is~~ dealt —
6	X Stroke & a stress that stars & storms deliver,
	That guilt is hushed by, hearts are flushed by & melt —
	But it rides time like riding a river
8	(And here the faithful waver, the faithless fable & miss.)

16

Plate 235   No. 101: "The Wreck of the Deutschland" cont.   B.15v. cont., 16r.
    St.5:   2 GMH interlined "then" above "the", but del. it also: he replaced RB's comma after "stars", which he had also del..   3 GMH revised two words and reinforced comma and semicolon. In 4 "Glow &" became "Glow,". In 7 the final punct. is GMH's. He strengthened stops elsewhere in the stanza. Note in 6 RB's "tho" with an apostrophe curving the wrong way, as his commas also sometimes do: "though" is written out in full in some 25 autographs of GMH's mature poems, justifying a change in the text here.
    St.6:   GMH revisions in 1-5 include the final dash in 4, marking an explanation the end of which he showed with another dash after "melt" (6). To conform to modern practice the final period in st.6 is usually placed outside the second parenthesis, to show that it ends the whole 8-line sentence, not simply the aside.

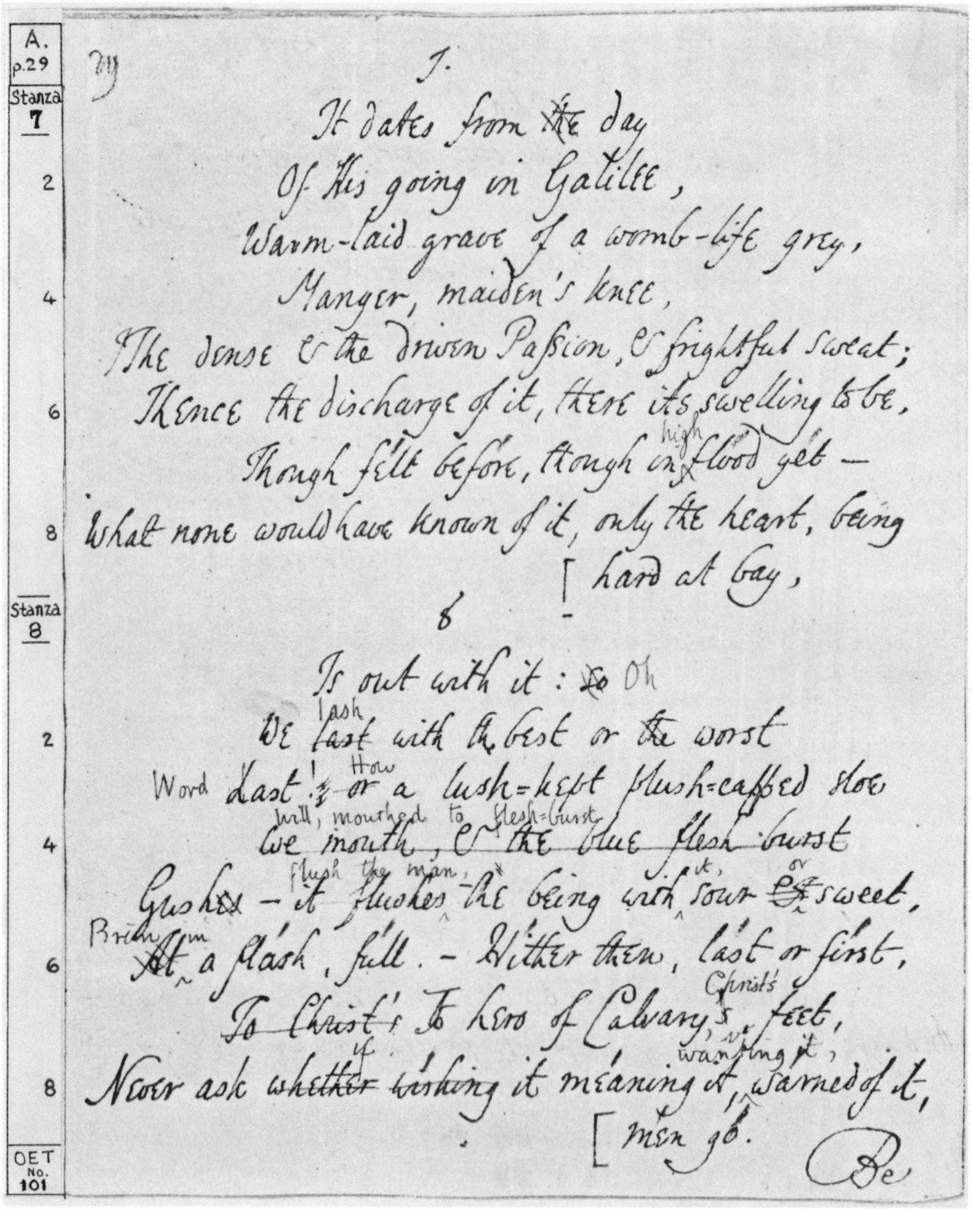

A.
p.29
Stanza
7

2

4

6

8

Stanza
8

2

4

6

8

OET
NO.
101

7.

It dates from the day
Of His going in Galilee,
Warm-laid grave of a womb-life grey,
Manger, maiden's knee,
The dense & the driven Passion, & frightful sweat;
Thence the discharge of it, there its swelling to be,
Though felt before, though in flood yet —
What none would have known of it, only the heart, being
[hard at bay,

8

Is out with it: Oh,
We lash with the best or the worst
Word last! — or a lush-kept plush-capped sloe
We mouth, & the blue flesh burst
Gushes — it flushes the being with sour or sweet,
At a flash, full. — Hither then, last or first,
To Christ's To hero of Calvary's feet,
Never ask whether wishing it meaning it, warned of it,
[men go.

Plate 236   No. 101: "The Wreck of the Deutschland" cont.   A.p.29.

St.7:   Note in 2 "his" mended in orig. ink to "His", and that in 5 RB began the line too far to the left and rewrote "T". RB's red ink in 1, 7 copies GMH's most obvious changes: in 4 GMH's deletion of the ampersand in B restores the reading of A. Note the invalidation in 7 of the prime stress on "flood" through the addition of "high".

St.8:   In 2 "We last" must have been RB's misreading of the lost autograph. All the corrections are in red ink, except the change in 3 of a semicolon to exclamation after "Last", which is in the black ink of 1889 (RB missed it in 1884). The orig. stresses in the first half of 6 are rendered doubtful by GMH's addition of "Brim": the line was allocated only five stresses in his metrical scheme, but now appears to have six. In 7 RB's red ink correction, "Calvary, Christ's feet", avoids GMH's eccentric comma before the apostrophe in "Christ's".

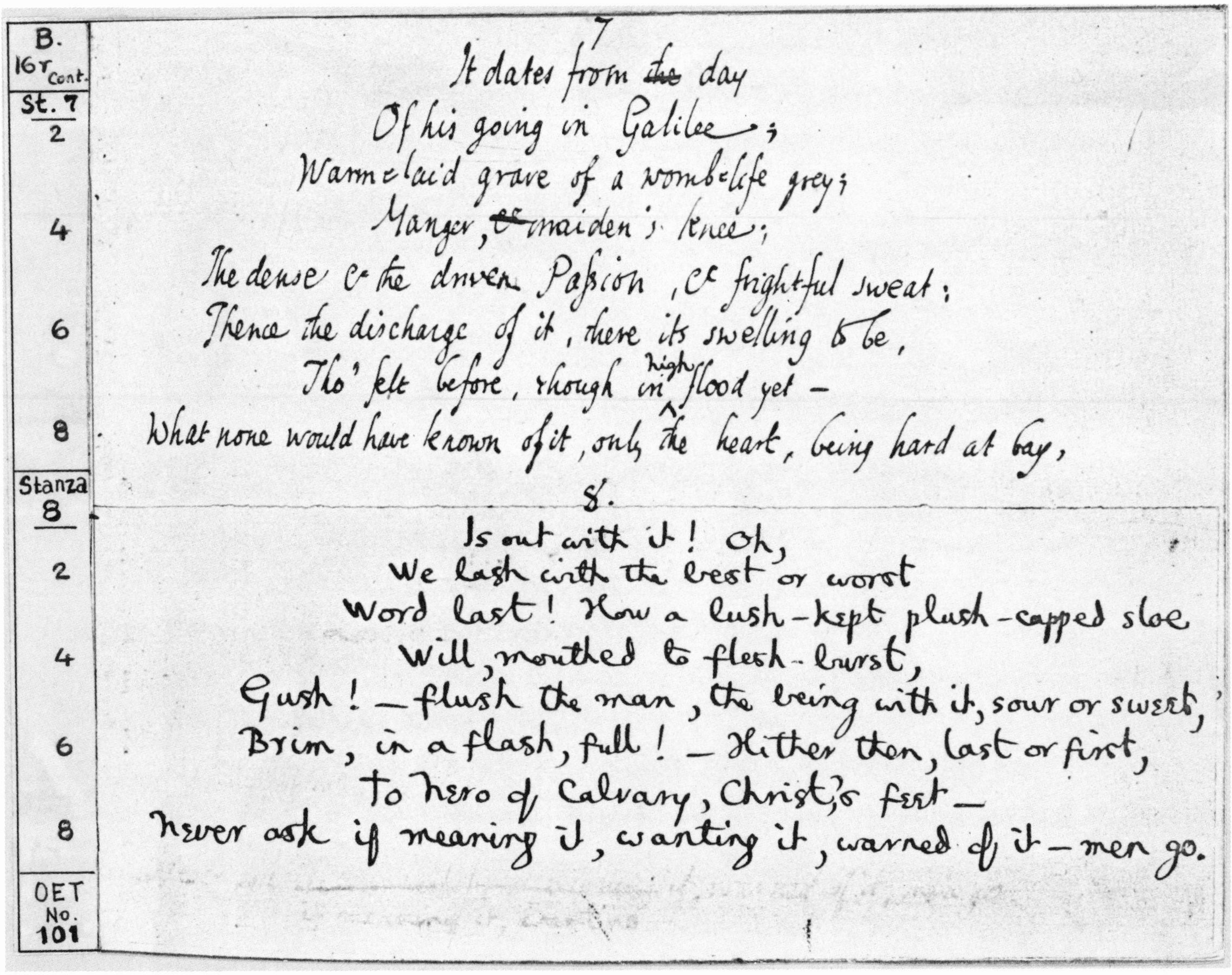

B.
16r cont.

St. 7

It dates from ~~the~~ day
Of his going in Galilee;
Warm=laid grave of a womb=life grey;
Manger, ~~&~~ maiden's knee;
The dense & the driven Passion, & frightful sweat:
Thence the discharge of it, there its swelling to be,
Tho' felt before, though in high *flood yet —*
What none would have known of it, only the heart, being hard at bay,

Stanza 8

Is out with it! Oh,
We lash with the best or worst
Word last! How a lush=kept plush=capped sloe
Will, mouthed to flesh=burst,
Gush! — flush the man, the being with it, sour or sweet,
Brim, in a flash, full! — Hither then, last or first,
To hero of Calvary, Christ's feet —
Never ask if meaning it, wanting it, warned of it — men go.

OET No. 101

Plate 237   No. 101: "The Wreck of the Deutschland" cont. B.16r. cont.

St.7: In 4 RB mistranscribed "Manger," as "Manger &" (ampersand). GMH corrected this, revised 1 by del. "the" before "day", changed the final commas to semicolons in 2,3,4, and added "high" in 7. He did not, as he frequently does elsewhere, clarify the ambiguous stop after "sweat" (5), where a colon marks this dividing point in sense in the st. better than a semicolon.

St.8: RB's transcription of A (covered by the paper bearing GMH's re-written version) omitted the hyphen in "plush-capped" (3) and added commas after "Christ's" (7) and "wishing it" (8). At first GMH made a few interim corrections in the transcription on the album page, but eventually he pasted over it his own revised version. His alignment of 2 with 4 and 3 with 7 is less precise than RB's, and I conjecture from his errors in indenting other poems that in the lost autograph of this very intricate pattern he scored through many lines because of false positioning and other slips, thus adding to the bewilderment of the ode's first readers.

Because st.8 is the only one in the B MS of the "Wreck" written wholly in GMH's hand, the opening 15v and 16r has faded through being a prime favourite during early exhibitions in the Bodleian.

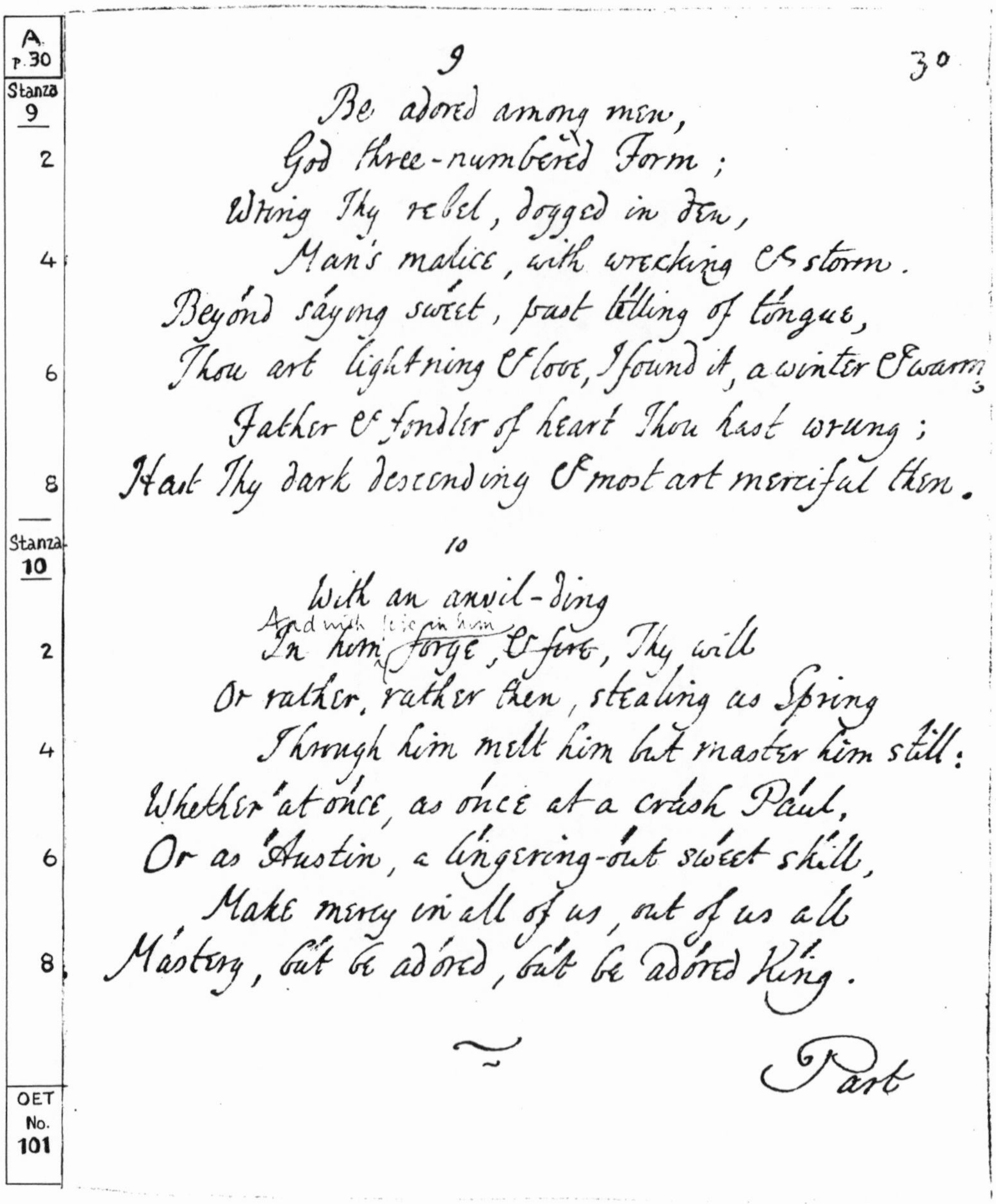
A. p.30
Stanza 9

9 30

Be adored among men,
God three-numberèd Form;
Wring Thy rebel, dogged in den,
Man's malice, with wrecking & storm.
Beyónd sáying sweet, past telling of tongue,
Thou art lightning & love, I found it, a winter & warm;
Father & fondler of heart Thou hast wrung:
Hast Thy dark descending & most art merciful then.

Stanza 10

10

With an anvil-ding
And with fire in him
In him forge, & fire, Thy will
Or rather, rather then, stealing as Spring
Through him melt him but master him still:
Whether 'at once, as once at a crash Paul,
Or as 'Austin, a lingering-out sweet skill,
Make mercy in all of us, out of us all
Mástery, but be adóred, but be 'adóred King.

~

Part

OET No. 101

Plate 238 No. 101: "The Wreck of the Deutschland" cont. A.p.30.

St.9: No corrections in red ink. In 4 "wrecking" shows traces of an erased "k" after "e": this is not a stress mark.

St.10: 2 corrections in red. Note in 5 the differences between RB's placing of the stresses over "at once" and GMH's in Plate 239 (over the vowels).

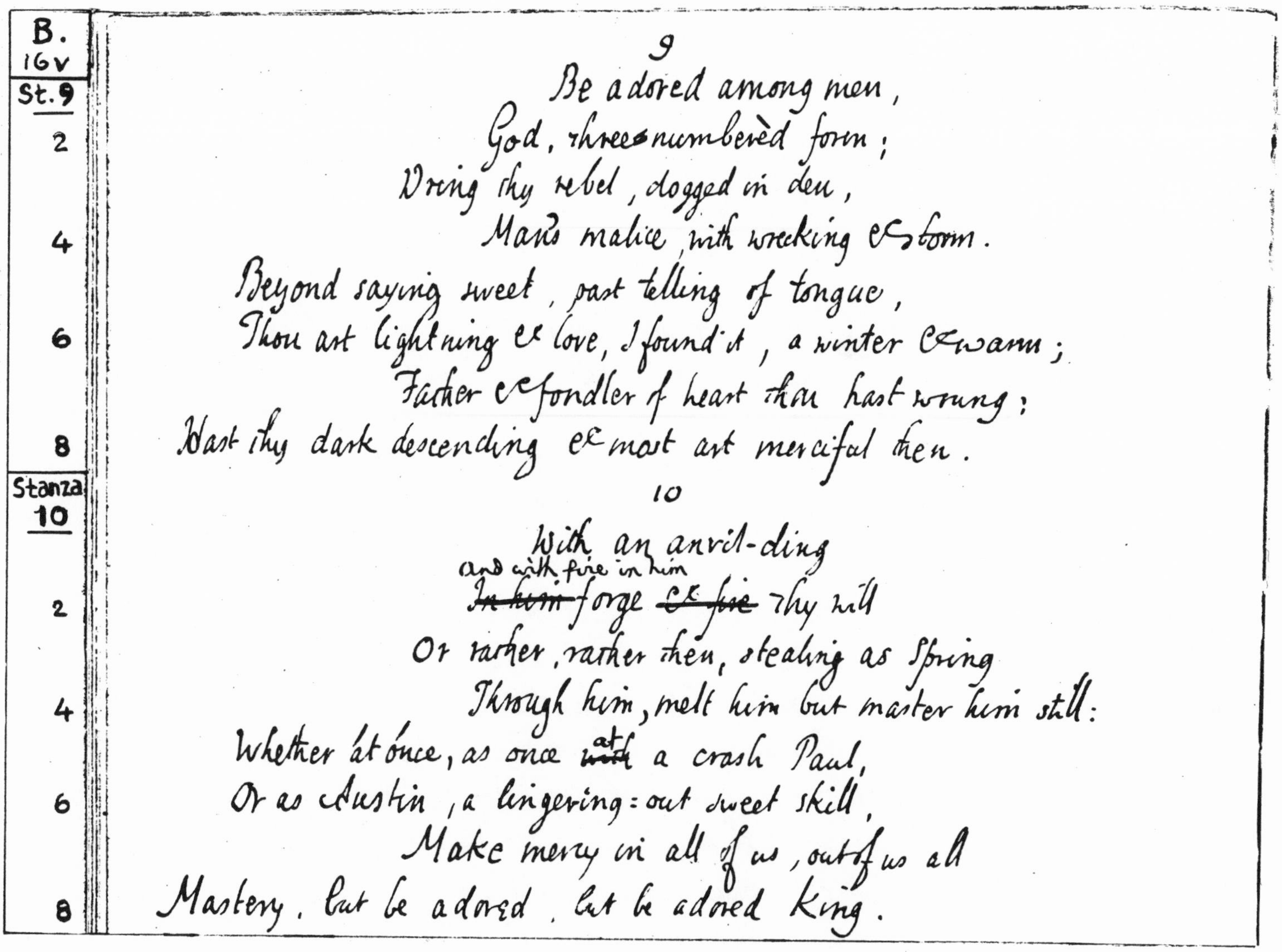

PLATE 239. OET 101. "The Wreck of the Deutschland"   •   41

B.
16v
St.9

9

Be adored among men,
God, three-numbered form;
Wring thy rebel, dogged in den,
Mark's malice, with wrecking & storm.
Beyond saying sweet, past telling of tongue,
Thou art lightning & love, I found it, a winter & warm;
Father & fondler of heart thou hast wrung:
Hast thy dark descending & most art merciful then.

Stanza
10

10

With an anvil-ding
and with fire in him
~~In him forge & fire~~ thy will
Or rather, rather then, stealing as Spring
Through him, melt him but master him still:
Whether at once, as once ~~with~~ at a crash Paul,
Or as Austin, a lingering=out sweet skill,
Make mercy in all of us, out of us all
Mastery, but be adored, but be adored King.

Plate 239   No. 101: "The Wreck of the Deutschland" cont.   B.16v.

St.9:   4 has a faint ink comma after "malice", and 7 ends with a stop where the upper mark is larger than the bottom--though Noppen reads this as a semicolon. Editors adopt A's semicolon after "wrung". The ampersands in 4 and 6 run into the next words: contr. those in A, where their tails are distinct.

St.10:   GMH's corrections in 2 and 5. In 5 the stresses are, as usual in B, in purple pencil: "with" for "at" was RB's slip, corrected by GMH (the ink did not run--contr. st.12:7). In sts.9:2 and 10:6 note RB's double hyphen (like an equals sign) to differentiate a hyphen from a dash. In 8 the two commas are minute.

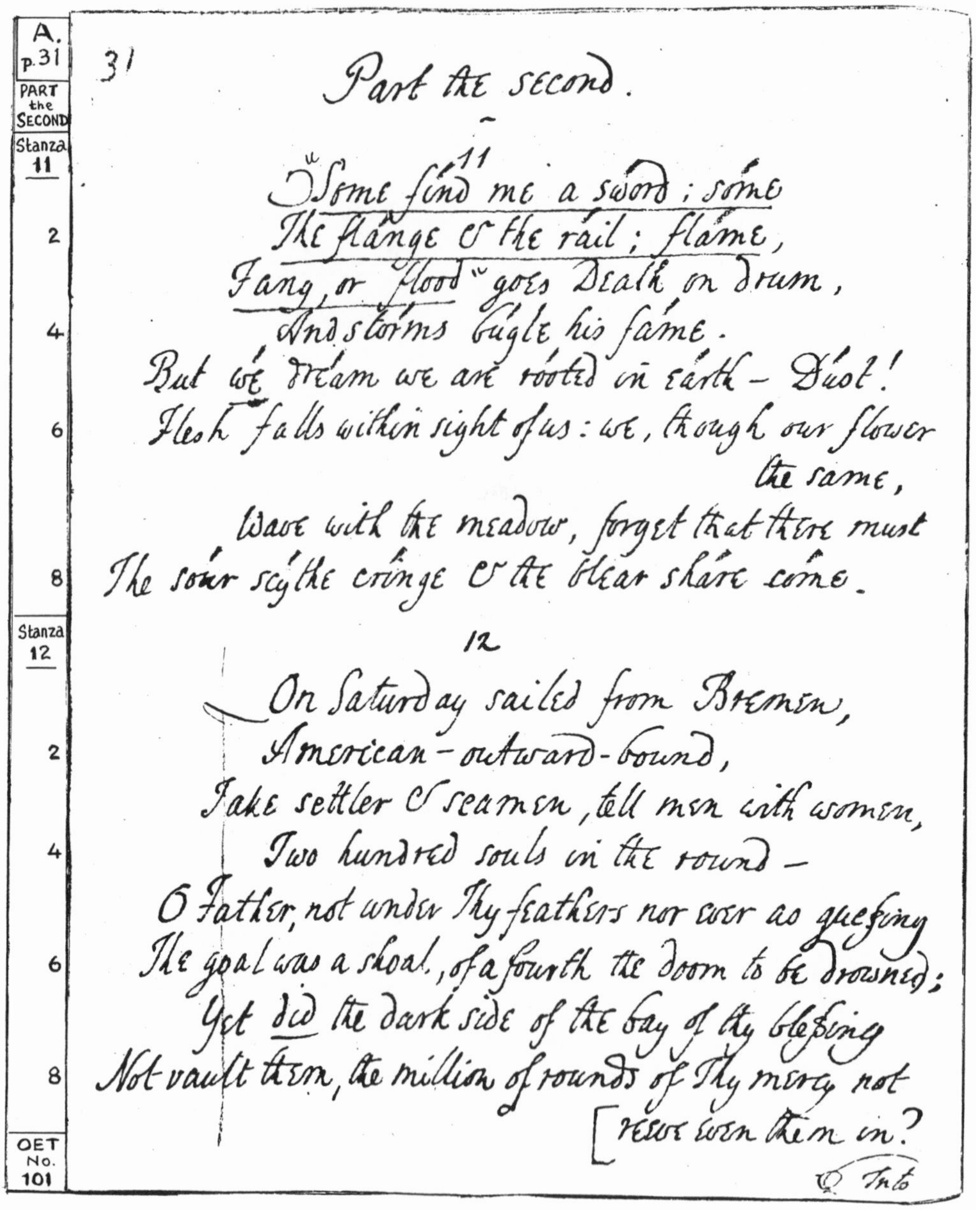

A.
p.31

PART
the
SECOND

Stanza
11

2

4

6

8

Stanza
12

2

4

6

8

OET
No.
101

31

Part the second.

11

Some find me a sword; some
The flange & the rail; flame,
Fang, or flood "goes Death on drum,
And storms bugle his fame.
But we dream we are rooted in earth — Dust!
Flesh falls within sight of us: we, though our flower
the same,
Wave with the meadow, forget that there must
The sour scythe cringe & the blear share come.

12

On Saturday sailed from Bremen,
American — outward — bound,
Take settler & seamen, tell men with women,
Two hundred souls in the round —
O Father, not under Thy feathers nor ever as guessing
The goal was a shoal, of a fourth the doom to be drowned;
Yet *did* the dark side of the bay of thy blessing
Not vault them, the million of rounds of Thy mercy not
[reeve even them in?

Q. Into

Plate 240   No. 101: "The Wreck of the Deutschland" cont. A.p.31.

Part the Second, St.11: GMH changed his metrical scheme in Part the Second by lengthening to three stresses the opening line of each stanza, to equal the second line. The ornament before "Some", appropriate for the beginning of a new section, also corrects the indentation. The italics in 1 to 3 and for "we" in 5 probably reflect the missing autograph: RB objected to GMH's use of italics in verse (see L.i.120, Jan. 1881) and GMH, somewhat reluctantly, agreed to give up the practice. In copying St.11 into B, RB in 1883 omitted the italics. GMH added quotes in B, which RB then copied in red ink in A. Both RB and GMH continued to use italics after 1881 (see, e.g., No. 178, ℓ.8): OET follows A (and presumably the lost autograph) in italicising "we" in 5.

St.12: The flourish before 1 marks the opening of the narrative section (cf. Arnold, 'Scholar Gipsy', ℓ.232, where a dash precedes the final epic simile). Note the vertical pencil line, used by RB to guide him with the difficult indentation, but normally erased. There are no red-ink corrections in A for sts.12,13,14,15 and 16: GMH was satisfied with these splendid narrative stanzas.

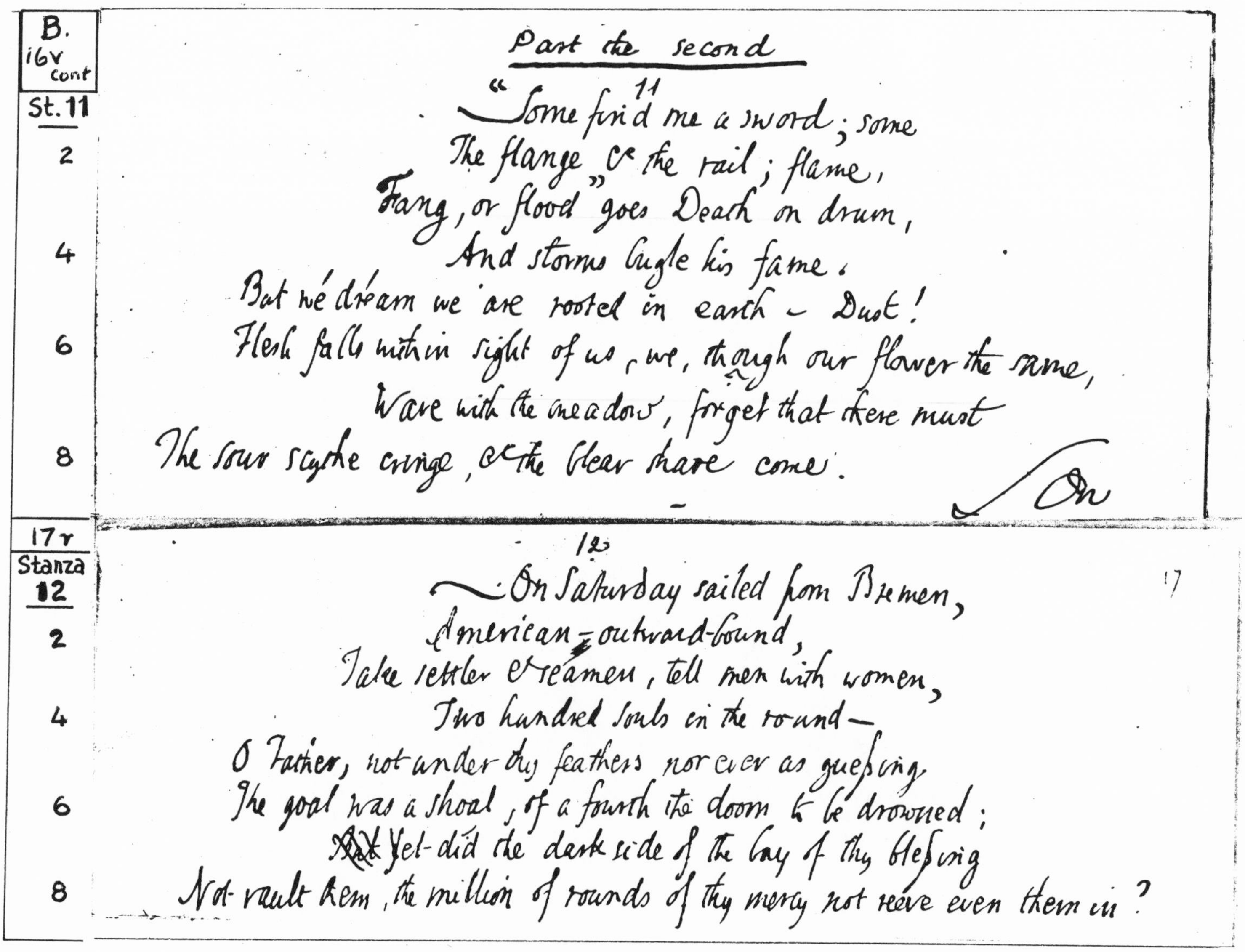

PLATE 241. OET 101. "The Wreck of the Deutschland" • 43

B.
16v
cont

St. 11

Part the second

11

"Some find me a sword; some

2　The flange & the rail; flame,

Fang, or flood" goes Death on drum,

4　　And storms bugle his fame.

But we´ dream we ´are rooted in earth ~ Dust!

6　Flesh falls within sight of us, we, though our flower the same,

　　Wave with the meadow, forget that there must

8　The sour scythe cringe, & the blear share come.

On

17 r
Stanza
12

12

~ On Saturday sailed from Bremen,

2　　American-outward-bound,

Take settler & seamen, tell men with women,

4　　Two hundred souls in the round —

O Father, not under thy feathers nor ever as guessing,

6　The goal was a shoal, of a fourth the doom to be drowned;

But Yet did the dark side of the bay of thy blessing

8　Not vault them, the million of rounds of thy mercy not reeve even them in?

17

Plate 241　No. 101: "The Wreck of the Deutschland" cont. B.16v. cont., 17r.

　Part the Second, St.11: The quotes in 1 and 3, and the stresses on "we dream" in 5, are by GMH. He also probably added the long tail to "Some" which corrects the indenting: this shows his characteristic pen-tracks and was made when the word was dry. He strengthened some stops (e.g., after "sword" in 1). In 6 note RB's first comma, curving the wrong way, in place of A's colon (cf. sts. 16:6, 20:8, etc.). The mark under "though" (6) is prob. accidental.

　St.12: In 2 (del. of comma) and 7 ("But" del. and "yet" changed to u.c. while the ink was wet) the corrections are by R.B. In 7 "did" (ital. in A) has a stress. Note the minute comma in 8 before "the million", which GMH left, though he strengthened the final stops in 1,2,3.

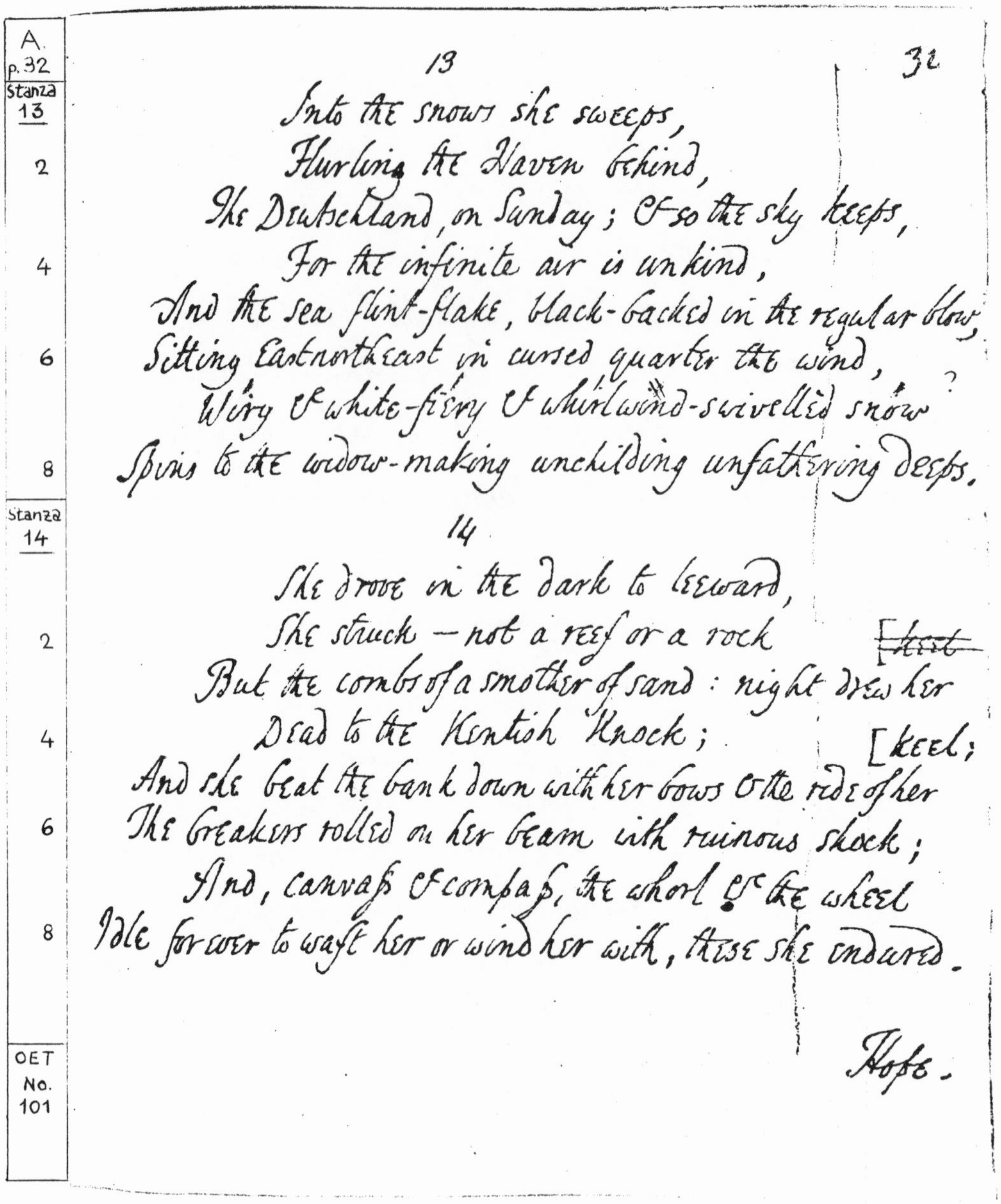

A.
p.32
Stanza
13

2

4

6

8

13

32

Into the snows she sweeps,
Hurling the Haven behind,
The Deutschland, on Sunday; or so the sky keeps,
For the infinite air is unkind,
And the sea flint-flake, black-backed in the regular blow,
Sitting Eastnortheast in cursed quarter the wind,
Wiry & white-fiery & whirlwind-swivellèd snow
Spins to the widow-making unchilding unfathering deeps.

Stanza
14

2

4

6

8

14

She drove in the dark to leeward,
She struck — not a reef or a rock   ~~first~~
But the combs of a smother of sand : night drew her
Dead to the Kentish Knock;   [keel;
And she beat the bank down with her bows & the ride of her
The breakers rolled on her beam with ruinous shock;
And, canvass & compass, the whorl & the wheel
Idle for ever to waft her or wind her with, these she endured.

Hope.

OET
No.
101

Plate 242   No. 101: "The Wreck of the Deutschland" cont. A.p.32.

St.13: In 7 where there is a "?" in the margin, RB used the black ink of 1889 to del. the blue pencil stress on "wind" (prob. his slip) and placed it over "whirl". In 1884 he had overlooked this stress in B.

St.14: In 3 the lost autograph may have had a slur after "drew her" to indicate that the run-on rhyme included the "D" of "Dead". In 7 there is a blot under the second ampersand, which can be seen through the sheet in st.16:6 above "tell".

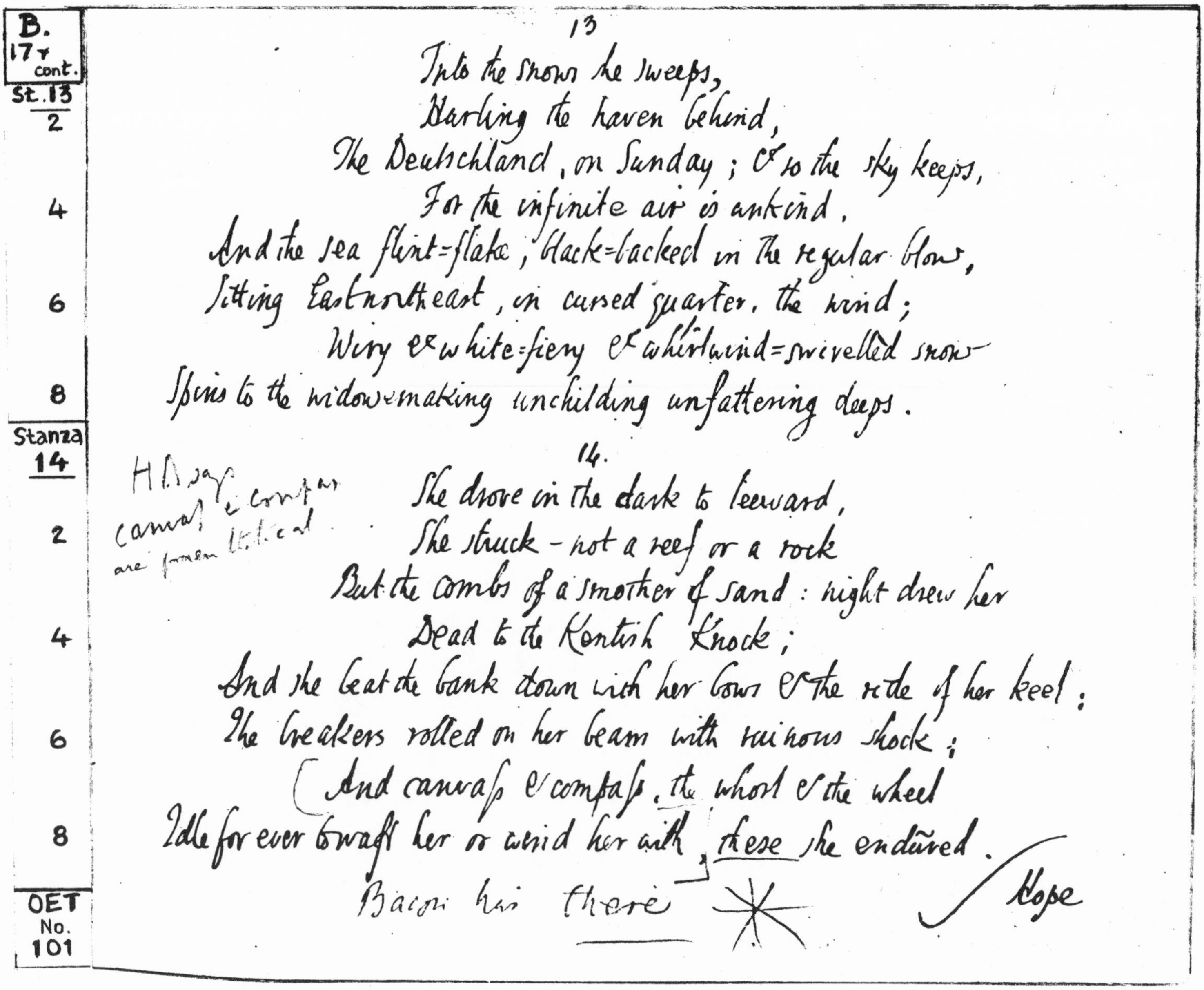

PLATE 243. OET 101. "The Wreck of the Deutschland" • 45

B.
17 r
cont.

St.13

2

4

6

8

Stanza
14

2

4

6

8

OET
No.
101

13

Into the snow he sweeps,
Starling the haven behind,
The Deutschland, on Sunday ; & so the sky keeps,
For the infinite air is unkind,
And the sea flint=flake, black=backed in the regular blow,
Sitting Eastnortheast, in cursed quarter, the wind;
Wiry & white=fiery & whirlwind=swivelled snow
Spins to the widow=making unchilding unfathering deeps.

14.

HB say canvas & compass are parenthetical

She drove in the dark to leeward,
She struck – not a reef or a rock
But the combs of a smother of sand : night drew her
Dead to the Kentish Knock ;
And she beat the bank down with her bows & the ride of her keel :
The breakers rolled on her beam with ruinous shock ;
(And canvass & compass, the whorl & the wheel
Idle for ever to waft her or wind her with, these she endured.

Bacon has there ✳ ✓ Hope

Plate 243   No. 101: "The Wreck of the Deutschland" cont.   B.17r.

St.13: GMH did not restore A's u.c. in "Haven" (2, i.e., Bremerhaven), which must have been in the lost autograph. He accepted the helpful commas in 6 enclosing "in cursed quarter". He either inserted or accepted the semicolon after "wind" (6), where A had a comma. In 8 the hyphen after "widow" is made of two curves (cf. st.7:3), resembling an "e". Some early reader or editor (not RB) wrote at the end of 8 "Why unfathering?"--an example of the problems the poem has created: the question was later erased.

St.14: Two pencil notes are by RB, 1918: a) "HB[Henry Bradley] says canvas & compass are parenthetical", but RB's pencilled square brackets in 7,8 show the parenthesis running to "with"; b) below the st.,starred to "these" underlined in l.8, he notes "Bacon has there". Note the dubious semicolons ending 5 and 6.

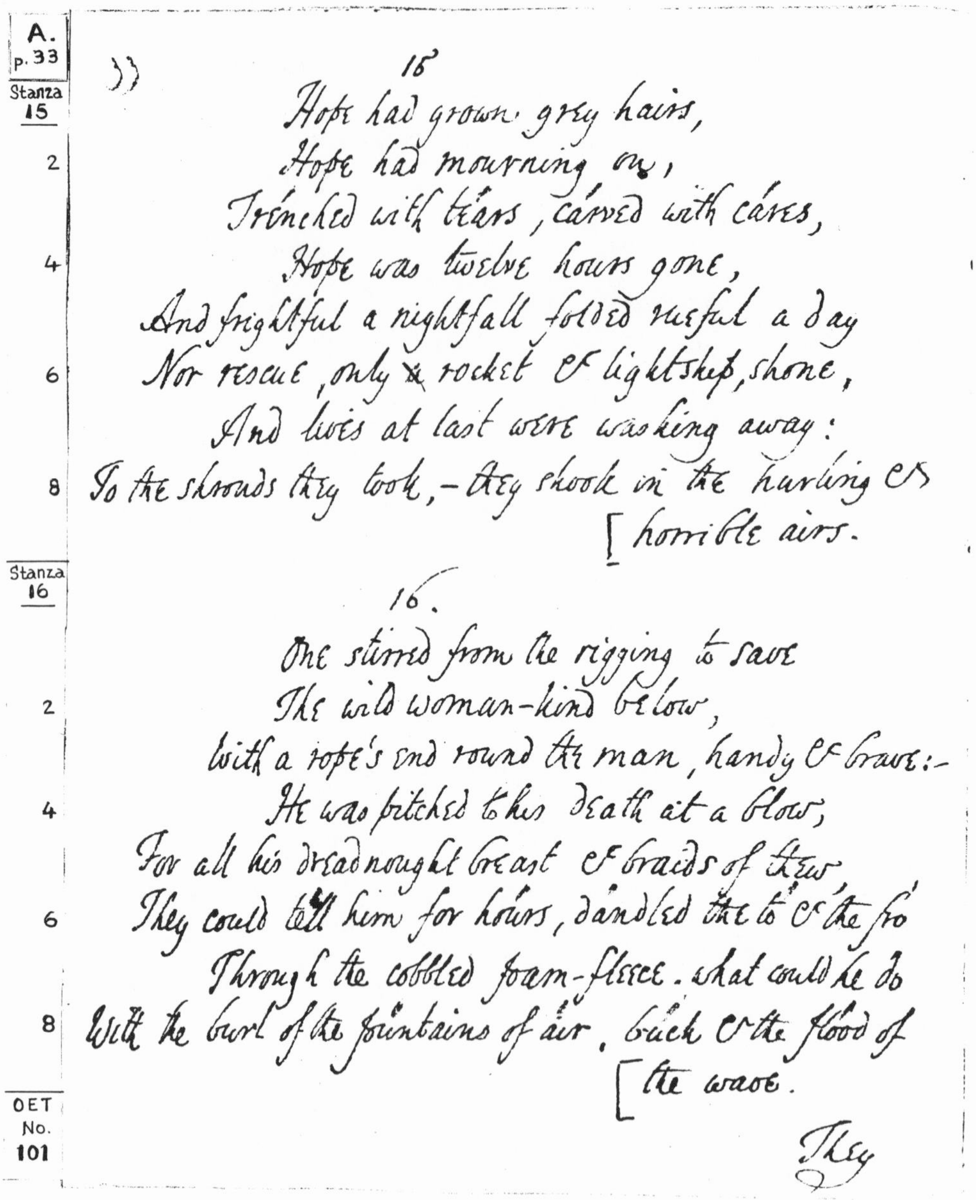

A.
p. 33
Stanza
15

))   15

Hope had grown grey hairs,
Hope had mourning on,
Trenched with tears, carved with cares,
Hope was twelve hours gone,
And frightful a nightfall folded rueful a day
Nor rescue, only a rocket of lightship, shone,
And lives at last were washing away:
To the shrouds they took, — they shook in the hurling and
[horrible airs.

Stanza
16

16.

One stirred from the rigging to save
The wild woman-kind below,
With a rope's end round the man, handy and brave:—
He was pitched to his death at a blow,
For all his dreadnought breast and braids of thew,
They could tell him for hours, dandled the to and the fro
Through the cobbled foam-fleece. what could he do
With the burl of the fountains of air, buck and the flood of
[the wave.

They

OET
No.
101

Plate 244   No. 101: "The Wreck of the Deutschland" cont. A.p.33.
    St.15: In 6 the del. of "a", while the ink was wet, is by RB. In 2 the blot below "on" comes from the "g" of "Hurling" in st.13:2.
    St.16: In 7, after the period RB copied "what" with a ℓ.c., where the autograph prob. had one of GMH's u.c. Ws which seem indistinguishable from ℓ.c.: his MS. letters to RB sometimes appear to spell names with ℓ.c., e.g., "waterhouse", "wooldridge", "whitby". Bacon assumed that the stop after "fleece" must be a comma (see RB's 1918 note in B). In 6 A's reading, "the to and the fro", prob. copied from the autograph, represents the even-handed pendulum swing of the body more closely than the normalized reading into which RB slipped in B--"the to and fro"--unbalanced and less evocative. The OET restores the second "the".

PLATE 245. OET 101. "The Wreck of the Deutschland" • 47

15.

Hope had grown grey hairs,
Hope had mourning on,
Trenched with tears, carved with cares,
Hope was twelve hours gone;
And frightful a nightfall folded rueful a day
Nor rescue, only rocket & lightship, shone,
And lives at last were washing away:
To the shrouds they took, — they shook in the hurling & horrible airs.

16

One stirred from the rigging to save
The wild woman-kind below,
With a rope's end round the man, handy & brave —
He was pitched to his death at a blow,
For all his dreadnought breast & braids of thew:
They could tell him for hours, dandled the to & fro
Through the cobbled foam-fleece. What could he do
With the burl of the fountains of air, buck & the flood of the wave?

[marginal annotations: "full stop RB" and ringed note "? what stop Bacon has)"]

Plate 245   No. 101: "The Wreck of the Deutschland" cont.   B.17v.

    St.15: In 4 the final semicolon after "gone", instead of the comma in A, is an improvement, which GMH either made or accepted. In 6 "light ship" could be intended as two words, as it sometimes was in contemporary official reports: A's compound is closer to GMH's usage.

    St.16: 3 orig. ended as "brave:" but GMH del. the top period and converted the lower one into a dash. In 5 GMH del. the final comma after "then" and substituted a colon, and either added or approved the query after "wave" (8). RB's marginal query "? what stop/Bacon has ," is connected by a faint pencil line to the ringed period in 7. His decision, entered above the query, is "full stop/RB". A marginal note below the stanza, with a pencil line across the page (visible in Plate 247), refers to RB's checking of the 1st. edn. in 1918: "Corrected proof to here".

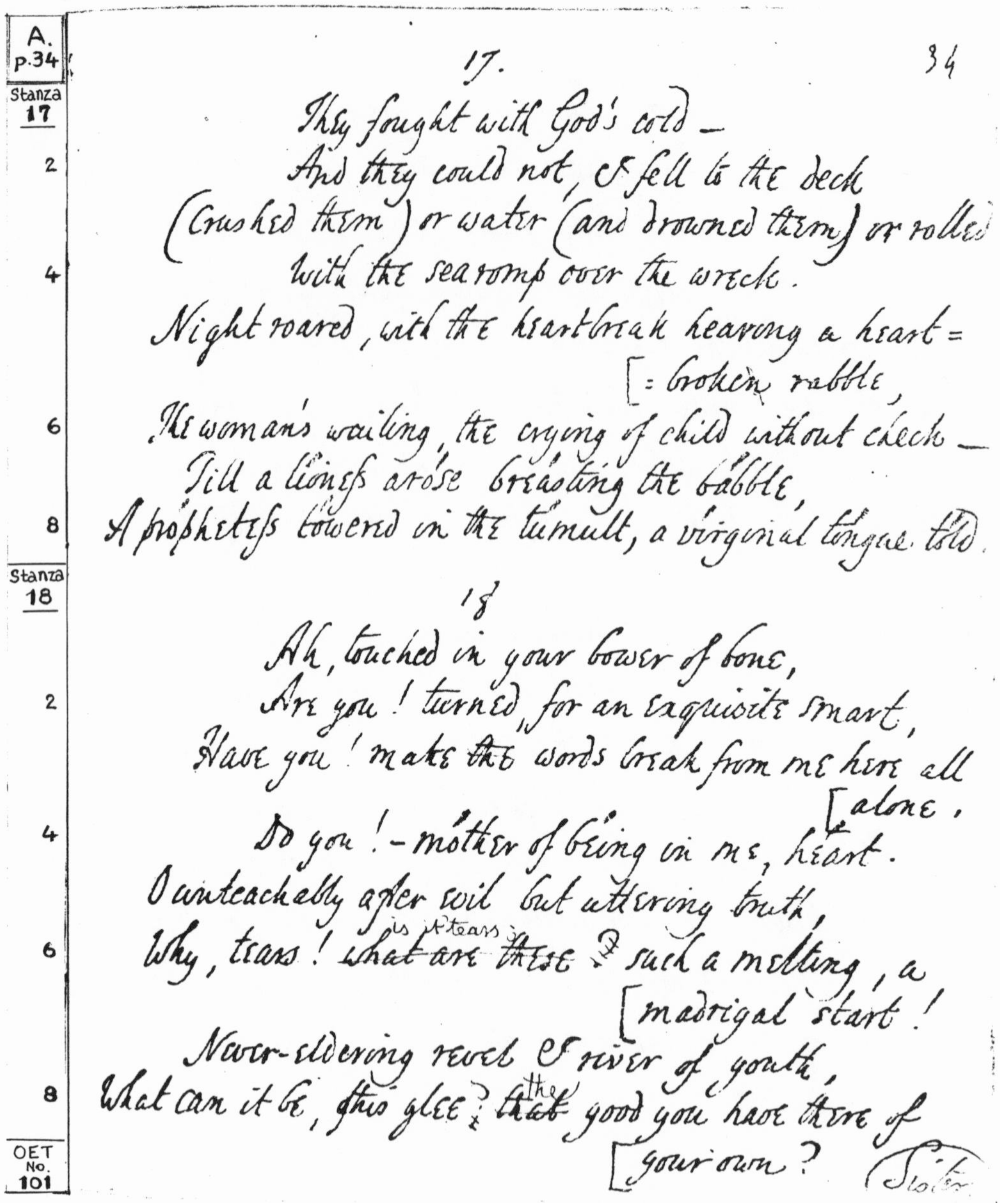

A.
p.34

17.　　　　　　　　　　　　　　　　34

Stanza
17

They fought with God's cold —
And they could not, & fell to the deck
(Crushed them) or water (and drowned them) or rolled
　　　　With the searomp over the wreck.
Night roared, with the heartbreak heaving a heart=
　　　　　　　　　　　　[= broken rabble,
The woman's wailing, the crying of child without check —
　　　Till a lioness arose breasting the babble,
A prophetess towered in the tumult, a virginal tongue told.

Stanza
18

18

Ah, touched in your bower of bone,
　Are you! turned, for an exquisite smart,
Have you! make the words break from me here all
　　　　　　　　　　　　[alone.
　　Do you! — mother of being in me, heart.
O unteachably after evil but uttering truth,
Why, tears! what are these ? such a melting, a
　　　　　　　　　[madrigal start!
　　Never-eldering revel & river of youth,
What can it be, this glee? that good you have there of
　　　　　　　　[your own ?

OET
No.
101

Plate 246　　No. 101: "The Wreck of the Deutschland" cont. A.p.34.
　　St.17:　As A was copied directly from the missing autograph, and RB tended to loosen word-structures in his transcriptions into B, there is good reason to believe that GMH orig. wrote "searomp" (4), "heartbreak", "heartbroken" (5, hyphenated only because of the line turn-over)--cf. st.25:6; 34:8): the OET here adopts compounds where B has hyphenations. In 5 the "n" in "heartbroken" is del. in red (from B).
　　St.18:　Corrections in red ink in 3,6,8 (after "glee" a query replaces a comma, not a semicolon; and "the" replaces "that"). In 8 RB began "glee" before "this". As suits a meditative stanza, there is heavier stopping in A in 1 and 2 than in B: A is the better model.

PLATE 247. OET 101. "The Wreck of the Deutschland" • 49

B.
17 v
cont.

St. 17

(Corrected proof)

17.

They fought with God's cold —
2 And they could not or fell to the deck
(Crushed them) or water (and drowned them) or rolled
4 With the sea-romp over the wreck .
Night roared , with the heart-break hearing a heart-broke(n) rabble,
6 The woman's wailing , the crying of child without check —
Till a lioness arose breasting the babble,
8 A prophetess towered in the tumult , a virginal tongue told.

18 r

Stanza
18

18

Bacon has
tower
18

Ah , touched in your (bower) of bone
2 Are you ! turned for an exquisite smart ,
Have you ! make the words break from me here all alone ,
4 Do you ! — mother of being in me , heart .
O unteachably after evil, but uttering truth ,
6 Why, tears ! ~~what are these~~ is, d? tears ? / such a melting, a madrigal start !
Never-eldering revel & river of youth ,
8 What can it be , this glee? that good you have there of your own ?

Plate 247   No. 101: "The Wreck of the Deutschland" cont.   B.17v. (cont.), 18r.

St.17:   See note on Plate 246 for RB's substitution of hyphenations for compounds. The del. of "n" in "heart-broken" (5) was by GMH (under infrared light, the "n" is clear below heavy obliteration: it did not run and the inks are different). But in 7 the "r" of "brabble" was wet when stroked through--obviously by RB.

St.18:   RB notes that in 1 "Bacon has 'tower'" for "bower". In 3 GMH del. "the" but RB corrected his own slip ("for", dittography from the line above, for "from") while the ink was wet. The exclamation after "heart" (4) is erased (RB's slip, corrected by him.) In 5 GMH added a comma after "evil", and revised 6 and 8 (B orig. read "glee, that").

A.
p.35
 	
Stanza
19
 	
2
 	
4
 	
6
 	
8
 	
Stanza
20
 	
2
 	
4
 	
6
 	
8
 	
OET
No.
101
	35
	
	19.
	
	Sister, a sister calling
	A master, her master & mine! —
	And the inboard seas run swirling & hawling.
	The rash smart sloggering brine
	Blinds her: but she that weather sees one thing, one,
	Has one fetch in her: she rears herself to divine
	Ears, & the call of the tall nun
	To the men in the tops & the tackle rode over the storm's
	       [brawling.
	
	20
	
	She was first of a five & came
	Of a coifèd sisterhood.
	(O Deutschland, double a desperate name!
	O world wide of its good!
	But Gertrude, lily, & Luther, <s>were</s> two of a town*,
	Christ's lily, & beast of the waste wood.
	From life's dawn it is drawn down,
	Abel is Cain's brother, <s>the</s> And breasts they have sacked <s>are</s> the
	       [same.
	       (Loathèd
	
	*Eisleben in Saxony, where S. Gertrude was
	born in 1263. Luther 220 years later ~

  St.19: In the second half all the stresses but the final one are marked.

  St.20: RB's red ink in 5 copies GMH's revision in B from "were" to "are"; but in 8 he did not del. the comma (curved the wrong way) after "brother": he also gave "and" a capital. The parenthesis begun with 3 is not closed in A, perhaps because GMH forgot to mark its end in his autograph.

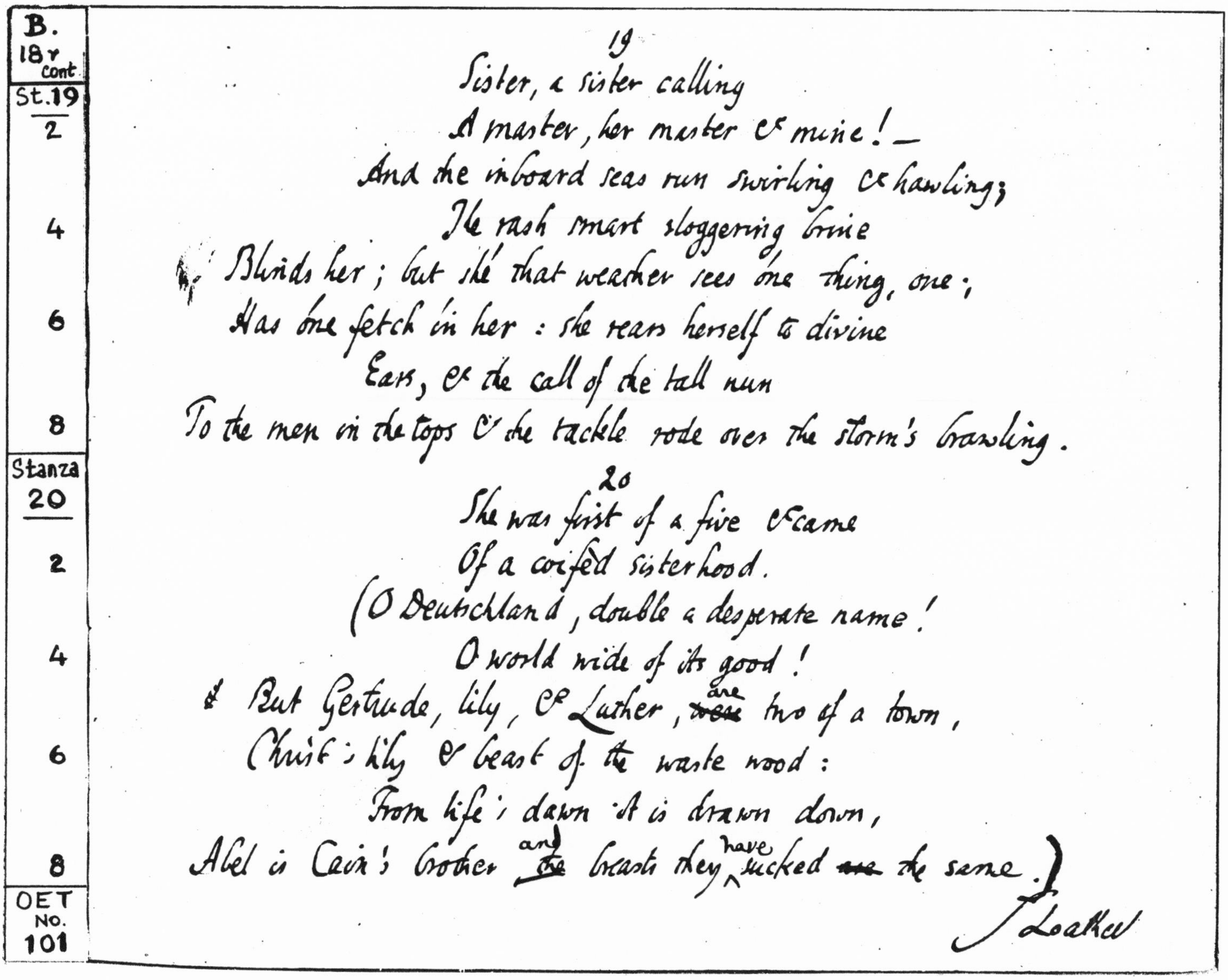

PLATE 249. OET 101. "The Wreck of the Deutschland" • 51

19

Sister, a sister calling
A master, her master & mine! —
And the inboard seas run swirling & hawling;
The rash smart sloggering brine
Blinds her; but she that weather sees one thing, one;
Has one fetch in her : she rears herself to divine
Ears, & the call of the tall nun
To the men in the tops & the tackle rode over the storm's trawling.

20

She was first of a five & came
Of a coifèd sisterhood.
(O Deutschland, double a desperate name!
O world wide of its good!
& But Gertrude, lily, & Luther, are two of a town,
Christ's lily & beast of the waste wood :
From life's dawn it is drawn down,
Abel is Cain's brother and the breasts they have sucked the same.)

Loaked

Plate 249   No. 101: "The Wreck of the Deutschland" cont. B.18r.cont.

St.19: GMH's clear semicolons end 3 and 5 where A has a "guess-stop" (3) and a comma (5). Under infrared, after "hawling" in B, RB's brown comma can be seen through GMH's black semicolon. In both sts.19 and 20 RB began his transcription of 5 too far to the left and had to erase or del. the false start.

St.20: GMH revised 5 and 8. RB had dotted in a closing parenthesis (missing from A and perhaps from the autograph) at the end of the stanza. These dots can be clearly seen with infrared filters through the intense black overlay of GMH's parenthesis confirming them.

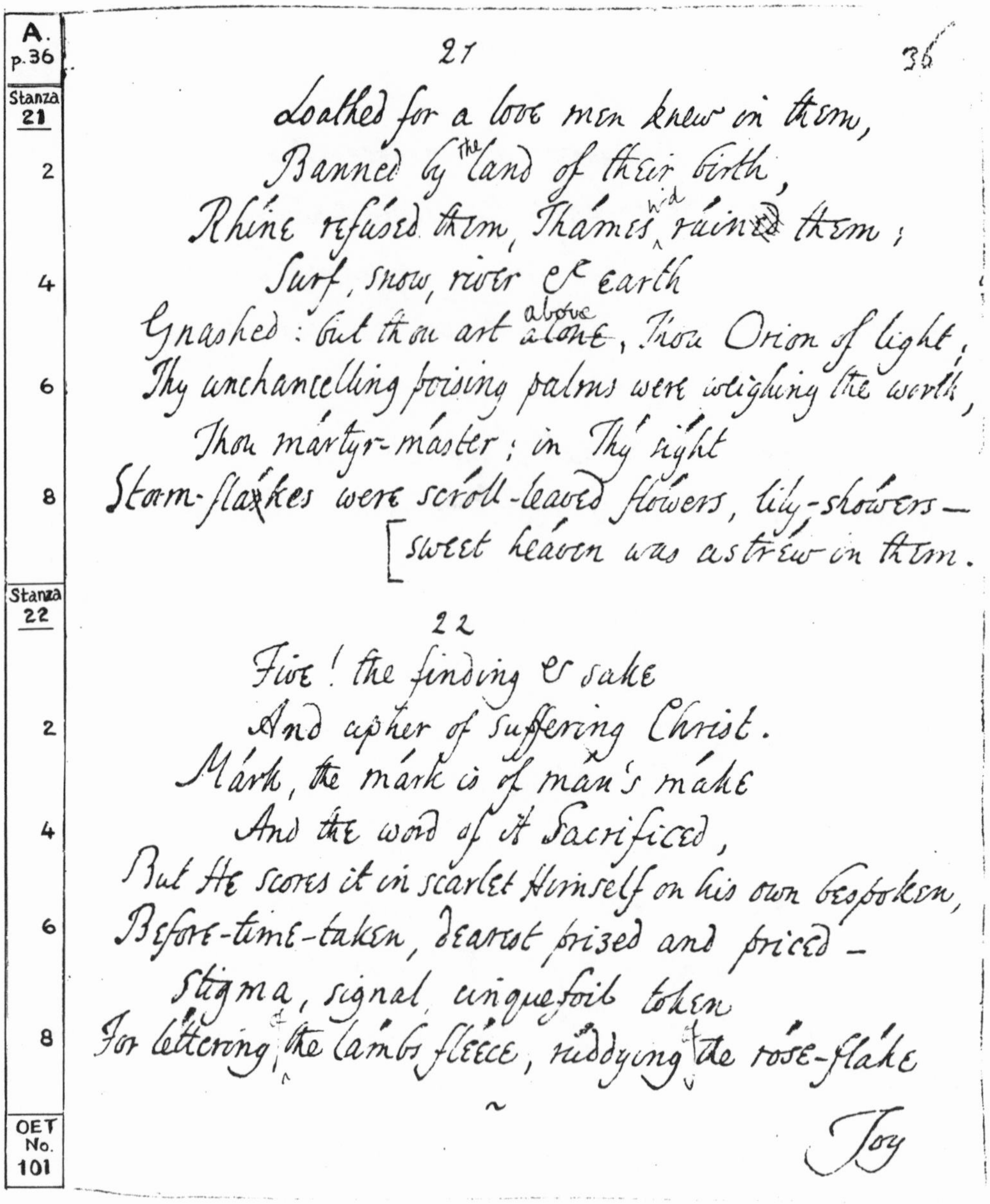

A.
p. 36

Stanza
21

21   36

Loathed for a love men knew in them,
Banned by the land of their birth,
Rhine refused them, Thames would ruin them;
Surf, snow, river & earth
Gnashed: but thou art above alone, Thou Orion of light;
Thy unchancelling poising palms were weighing the worth,
Thou martyr-master; in Thy sight
Storm-flakes were scroll-leaved flowers, lily-showers —
         [sweet heaven was astrew in them.

Stanza
22

22

Five! the finding & sake
And cipher of suffering Christ.
Mark, the mark is of man's make
And the word of it Sacrificed,
But He scores it in scarlet Himself on his own bespoken,
Before-time-taken, dearest prized and priced —
Stigma, signal, cinquefoil token
For lettering the lamb's fleece, ruddying the rose-flake

Joy

OET
No.
101

Plate 250   No. 101: "The Wreck of the Deutschland" cont. A.p.36.

St.21: In 2 "the" was added in the backward sloping black ink of 1889, but the two MSS. copied from the lost autograph (A and Bacon's) both omit it: so does the OET, assuming "the" to have been RB's slip in transcribing B. In 5 "alone" was a misreading of "above" in the autograph; the line ends with a "puzzle-stop" (cf. end of 3 and middle of 7). In 8 "flakes" was corrected when wet (by RB)--the ink ran; "astrew" appears to be one word.

St.22: In 4 "sacrificed" is mended to u.c.. In 8 each interpolated "of" is in red. The omission of the apostrophe in "lamb's" was not noticed.

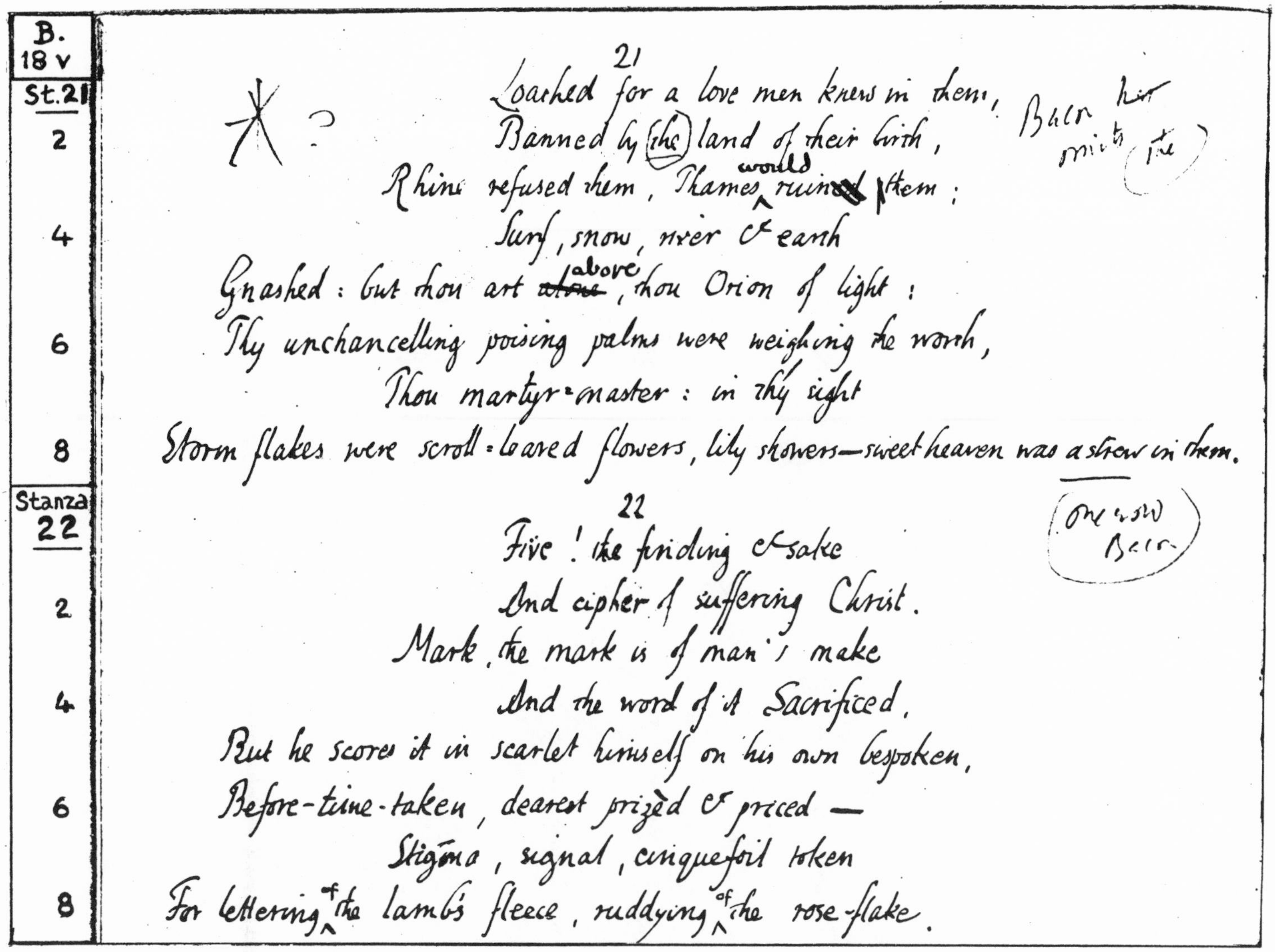

PLATE 251. OET 101. "The Wreck of the Deutschland" • 53

B. 18 v
St. 21

21

Loathed for a love men knew in them,
Banned by (the) land of their birth,
Rhine refused them. Thames would ruined them:
Surf, snow, river & earth
Gnashed: but thou art above, thou Orion of light:
Thy unchancelling poising palms were weighing the worth,
Thou martyr-master: in thy sight
Storm flakes were scroll-leaved flowers, lily showers—sweet heaven was a strew in them.

Bacon omits (the)

Stanza 22

22

Five! the finding & sake
And cipher of suffering Christ.
Mark, the mark is of man's make
And the word of it Sacrificed.
But he scores it in scarlet himself on his own bespoken,
Before-time-taken, dearest prizèd & priced —
Stigma, signal, cinquefoil token
For lettering of the lamb's fleece, ruddying of the rose-flake.

(one word Bacon)

Plate 251   No. 101: "The Wreck of the Deutschland" cont. B.18v.
    St.21:   In editing the 1st. edn. in 1918 RB ringed in pencil "the" before "land" (2), underlined it in red ink, with a query in red ink in the margin. He noted "Bacon [has del.] omits 'the'". GMH revised 3 (a mistaken colon is heavily deleted after "ruined") and 5. RB (1918) underlined "a strew" (8) and noted "one word Bacon" (as A appears to make it). In 8 "Storm flakes" and "lily showers" were left without the hyphens in A; linguists point out that hyphenations are normally stressed on their first elements. Since GMH stressed their second elements, as recorded in A, the OET also omits the hyphens.
    St. 22:   A blot was erased beneath "cipher" (2) and another crossed through above "stigma" (7). The grave on "prizèd" (6) is by GMH (cf. st.23:6), who interpolated "of" twice in 8. Note the minute commas in 3,4,5 and 8.

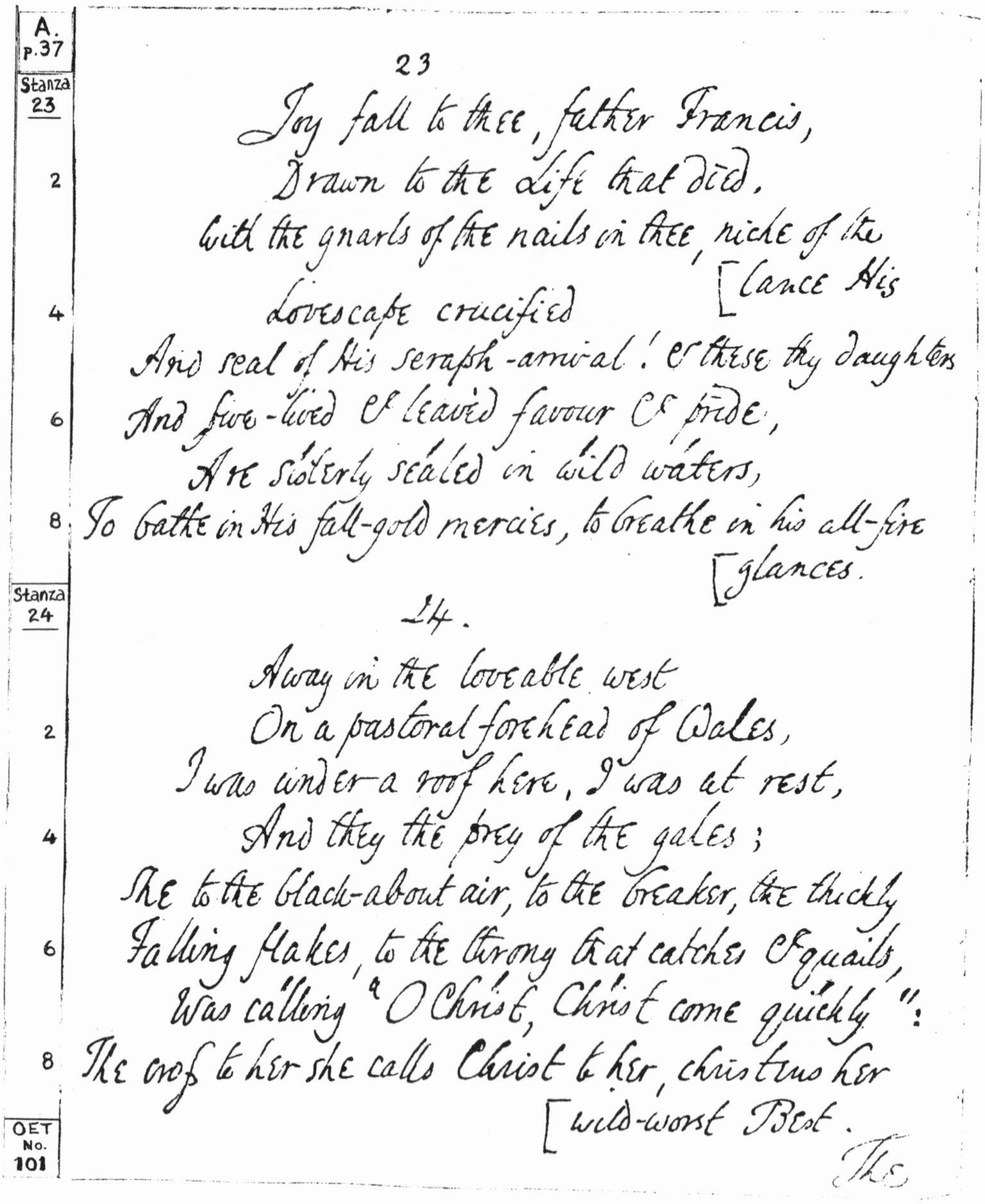

A. p.37

Stanza 23

23

Joy fall to thee, father Francis,
Drawn to the Life that died.
With the gnarls of the nails in thee, niche of the
[lance His
Lovescape crucified
And seal of His seraph-arrival! & these thy daughters
And five-lived & leaved favour & pride,
Are sisterly sealed in wild waters,
To bathe in His fall-gold mercies, to breathe in his all-fire
[glances.

Stanza 24

24.

Away in the loveable west
On a pastoral forehead of Wales,
I was under a roof here, I was at rest,
And they the prey of the gales;
She to the black-about air, to the breaker, the thickly
Falling flakes, to the throng that catches & quails,
Was calling "O Christ, Christ come quickly":
The cross to her she calls Christ to her, christens her
[wild-worst Best.
The

OET No. 101

Plate 252 No. 101: "The Wreck of the Deutschland" cont. A.p.37.

St.23: The final stop in 2 (though in the middle of a sentence), looks like a period, but RB copied it into B as a comma (in brown ink visible with infrared beneath GMH's semicolon).

St.24: No changes.

PLATE 253. OET 101. "The Wreck of the Deutschland" • 55

B.
18v
cont

St.23

23

Joy fall to thee, father Francis,
Drawn to the Life that died;
With the gnarls of the nails in thee, niche of the lance, his
Lovescape crucified
And seal of his seraph-arrival! or these thy daughters
And five-lived & leaved favour & pride,
Are sisterly sealed in wild waters,
To bathe on his fall=gold mercies, to breathe in his allfire glances.

Away

19r
Stanza 24

24

Away in the loveable west,
On a pastoral forehead of Wales,
I was under a roof here, I was at rest,
And they the prey of the gales;
She to the black=about air, to the breaker, the thickly
Falling flakes, to the throng that catches & quails
Was calling "O Christ, Christ, come quickly:"
The cross to her she calls Christ to her, christens her wildworst Best.

<u>Plate 253</u>   <u>No. 101: "The Wreck of the Deutschland"</u> cont.   <u>B.18v. cont., 19r.</u>
   <u>St.23:</u>   GMH revised several accidentals--he changed "died," to "died;" (2); he added a comma after "lance" (3);
restored his exclamation after "arrival" (5) where RB had only a comma; and placed a grave over the "ed" of "lived"
(6--contrast RB's unobtrusive grave in "leavèd"): RB's 1918 pencil notes the two accents in the margin. RB's 1st. edn.
restored the hyphen in "all-fire" (8).
   <u>St.24:</u>   GMH added commas not in A at the end of 1 and in 7 after the second "Christ" (note how small the "c" is,
no larger than in "come" or "christens", though it must be intended as u.c.). GMH did not restore the comma after
"quails" (6) where I feel it is needed. In 8 "wild worst" may have been accepted by GMH either as one word or two, so
A's hyphenation (restored by RB in the 1st. edn.) seems the safest text.

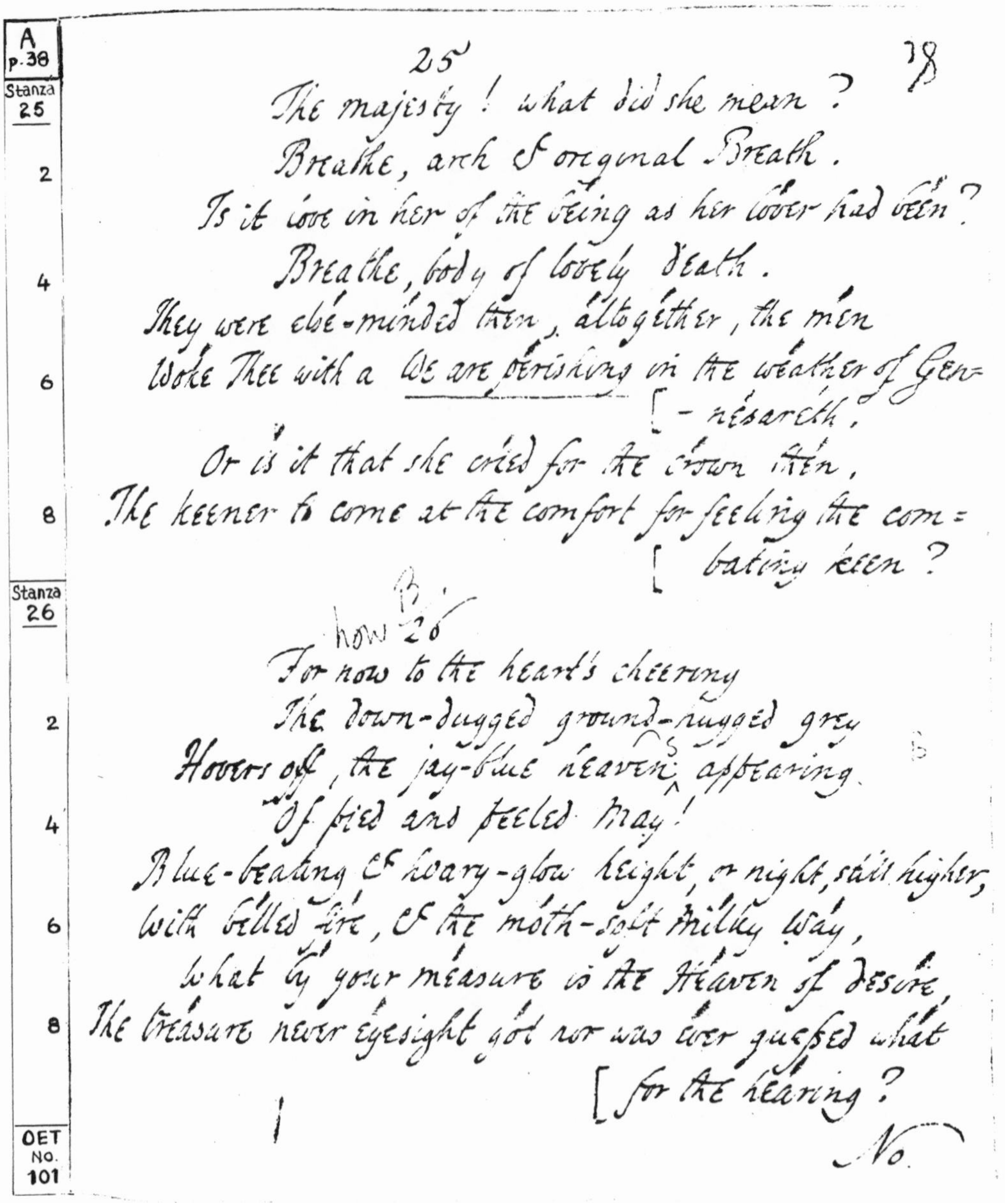

A
p.38

Stanza
25

25

The majesty! what did she mean?
Breathe, arch & original Breath.
Is it love in her of the Being as her lover had been?
Breathe, body of lovely Death.
They were else-minded then, altogether, the men
Woke Thee with a *We are perishing in the weather of Gen-*
                                    [*-nesareth.*
Or is it that she cried for the crown then,
The keener to come at the comfort for feeling the com=
                                    [forting keen?

Stanza
26

how 26
For now to the heart's cheering
The down-dugged ground-hugged grey
Hovers off, the jay-blue heavens appearing
Of pied and peeled May!
Blue-beating & hoary-glow height; or night, still higher,
With belled fire, & the moth-soft Milky Way,
What by your measure is the Heaven of desire,
The treasure never eyesight got nor was ever guessed what
                                    [for the hearing?
                                    No.

Plate 254   No. 101: "The Wreck of the Deutschland" cont. A.p.38.

St.25: In 5 RB's stress on "else" is casually placed on the mute "e".

St.26: RB's editorial pencil (1918) corrects, from GMH's corrections in B, "now" (1, a misreading of the autograph) to "how", and in 3 adds the "s" to "heaven". In 6 "milky way" was mended to u.c. while the ink was still wet. The comma following it in both A and B is described as "stop uncertain" in RB's note in the 1st. ed.--an indication that he felt the comma must be wrong. He adds that Bacon has a comma. The sense seems to demand a period.

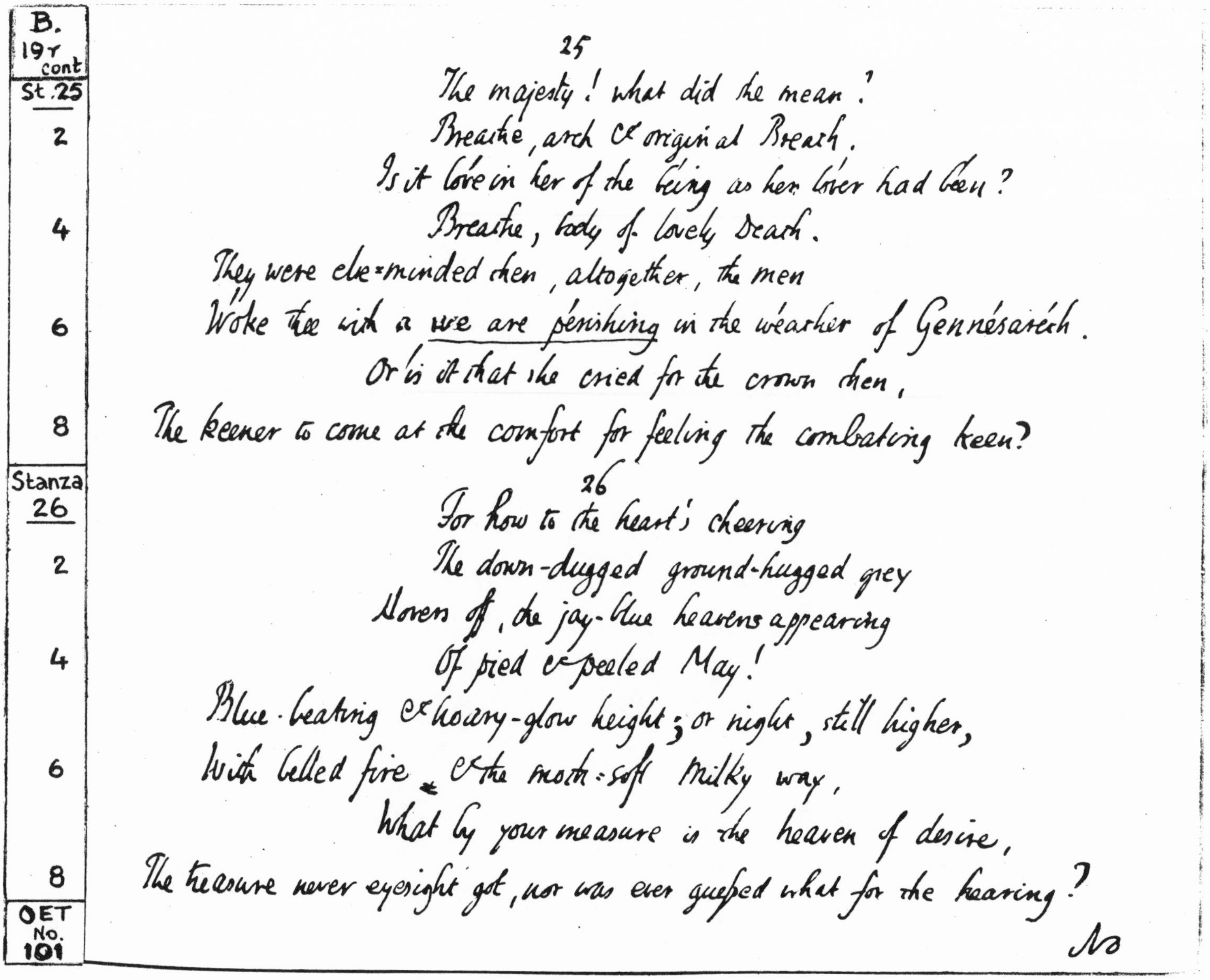

PLATE 255. OET 101. "The Wreck of the Deutschland"   •   57

B.
19r
cont

St.25

2

4

6

8

25

The majesty! what did she mean?

Breathe, arch & original Breath.

Is it love in her of the being as her lover had been?

Breathe, body of lovely Death.

They were else-minded then, altogether, the men

Woke thee with a *we are perishing* in the weather of Gennésareth.

Or is it that she cried for the crown then,

The keener to come at the comfort for feeling the combating keen?

Stanza
26

2

4

6

8

26

For how to the heart's cheering

The down-dugged ground-hugged grey

Hovers off, the jay-blue heavens appearing

Of pied & peeled May!

Blue-beating & hoary-glow height; or night, still higher,

With belled fire & the moth-soft Milky way,

What by your measure is the heaven of desire,

The treasure never eyesight got, nor was ever guessed what for the hearing?

OET
No.
101

No

Plate 255   No. 101: "The Wreck of the Deutschland" cont. B.19r. cont.

St.25:   In copying from A, RB gave "Death" (4) a capital (appropriate to distinguish the crucified Christ from the drowned nun).   In 6 he at first wrote "Woke thee with We", next erased the "We" to insert the missing "a", and then forgot the u.c. "W" when he rewrote the cry of the disciples.

St.26:   In 1 GMH changed "now" to "how", but so neatly that RB did not notice it till 1918, nor in 3 did RB see the "s" which GMH had squeezed in after "heaven": both changes were then made to A in pencil. Observe in 5 the minute dot for a hyphen in "Blue-beating": cf. GMH in his Early Note-book, C.i, e.g. in Facsimiles, i, Plate 75, C.i.215. After "height" (5) RB's brown comma can be detected below GMH's very black semicolon. It was prob. GMH who del. RB's comma after "fire" (6); he accentuated the query at the end of the stanza.

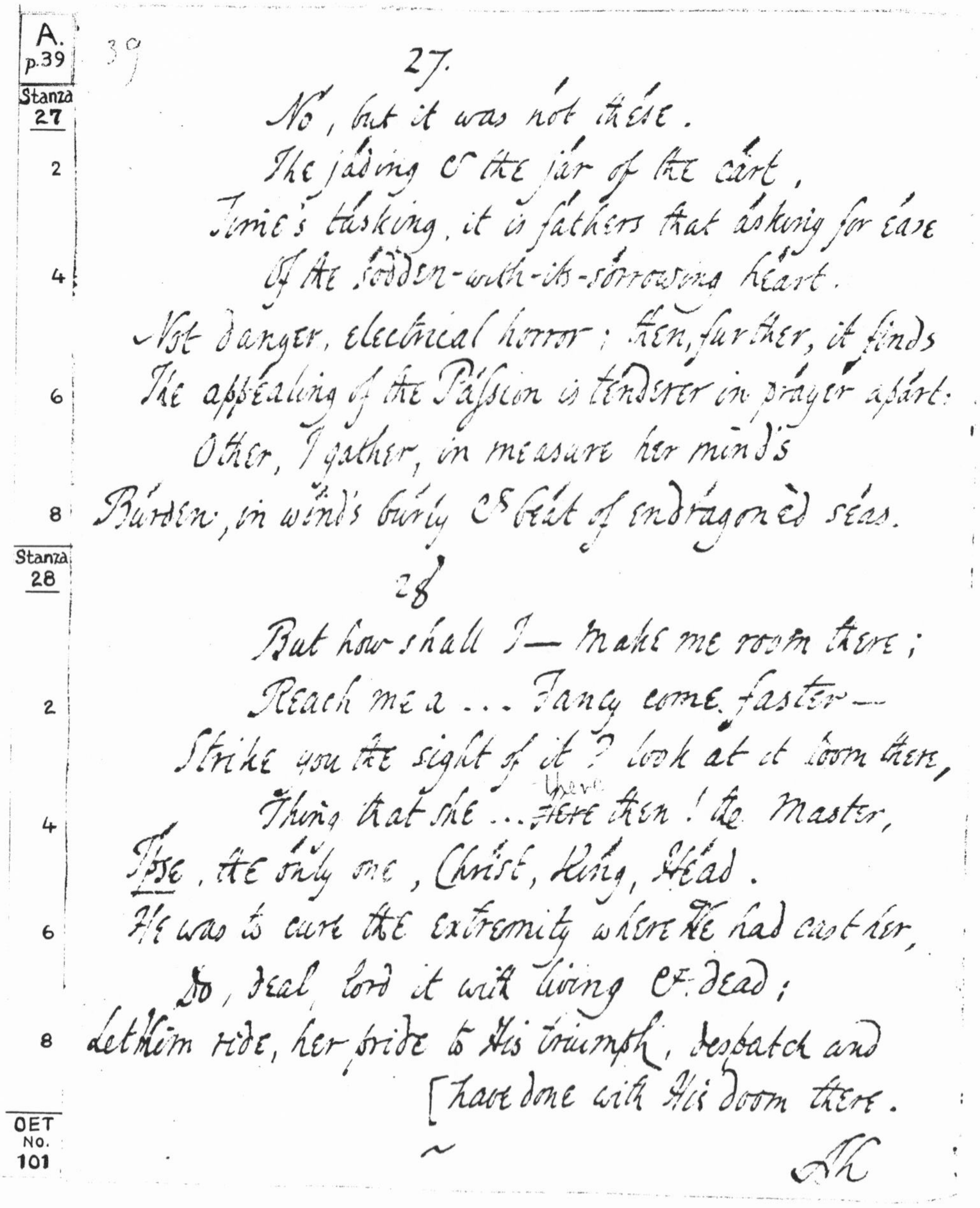

A.
p.39 39

Stanza
27

27.

Nŏ, but it was nŏt thĕse.
The jading & the jar of the cart,
Time's tasking, it is fathers that asking for ease
Of the sodden-with-its-sorrowing heart.

Not danger, electrical horror; then, further, it finds
The appealing of the Passion is tenderer in prayer apart.
Other, I gather, in measure her mind's
Burden, in wind's burly & beat of endragonèd seas.

Stanza
28

28

But how shall I— make me room there;
Reach me a ... Fancy come faster—
Strike you the sight of it? look at it loom there,
Thing that she ... There then! the Master,

Ipse, the only one, Christ, King, Head.
He was to cure the extremity where He had cast her,
Do, deal, lord it with living & dead;
Let Him ride, her pride to His triumph, despatch and

[have done with His doom there.

OET
No.
101

~

℞

Plate 256   No. 101: "The Wreck of the Deutschland" cont. A.p.39.

St.27:   In 2 the second "the" in "The jading and the jar of the cart", copied from the autograph, gives us an unrhythmic jolt evocative of a painfully unsprung tumbrel: as a more difficult reading than B's it may be the original one (GMH was a very unobservant proof-reader). In 5 the point between "electrical" and "horror" is best explained as a hyphen (cf. B, st.26:5). The commas after "then" and "further" (5) slow the rhythm appropriately.

St.28:   In 4 RB copies in red ink as "there" GMH's "There" (rev. of "Here") in B. Punctuation marks vary wildly in size and shape. In 8 "him" was mended to "Him"; "to His triumph" must surely be a slip, as though Christ were receding, not approaching.

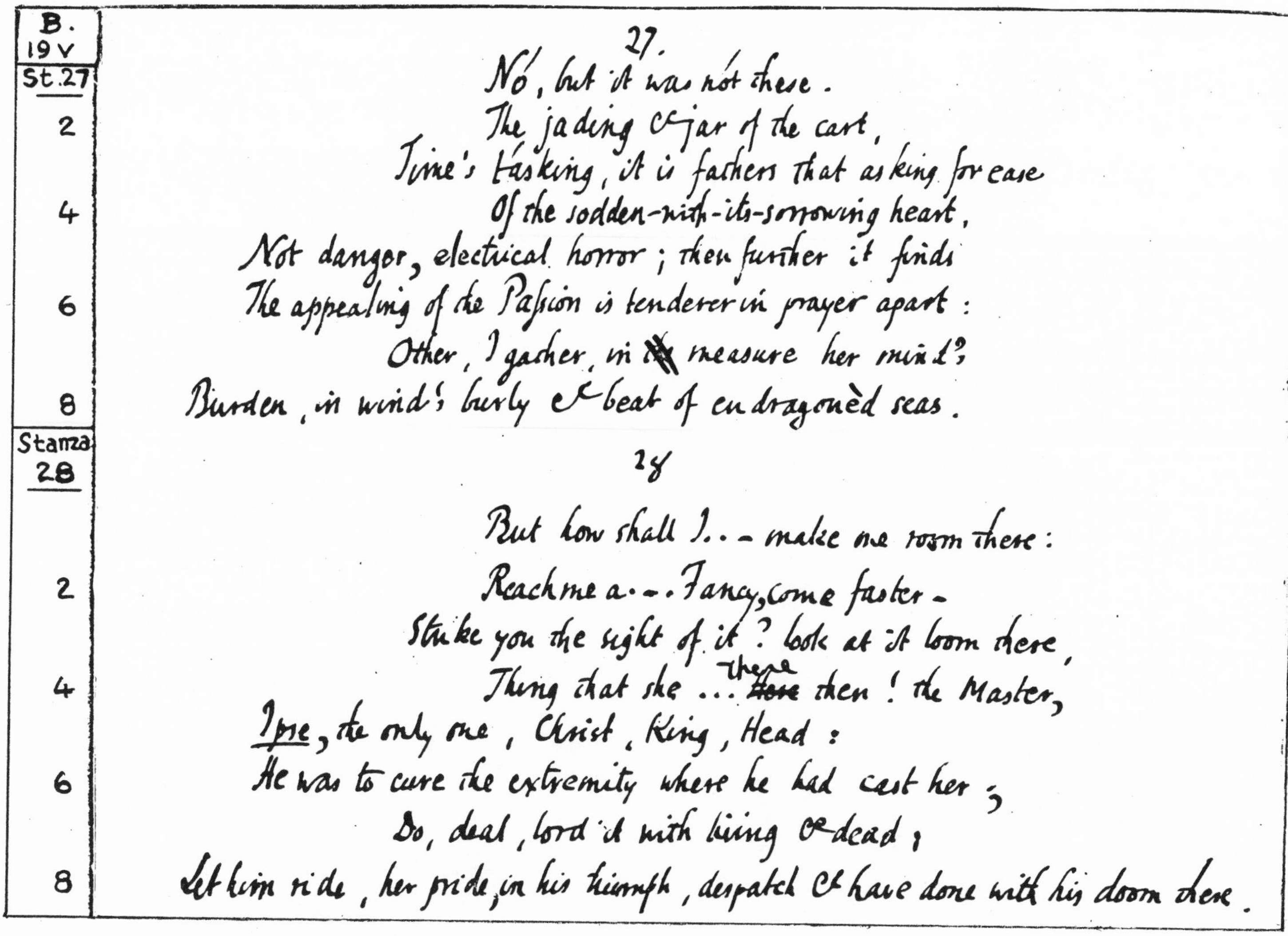

PLATE 257. OET 101. "The Wreck of the Deutschland" • 59

**B.
19 v
St.27**

27.

No', but it was not these.
The jading & jar of the cart,
Time's tasking, it is fathers that asking for ease
Of the sodden-with-its-sorrowing heart,
Not danger, electrical horror ; then further it finds
The appealing of the Passion is tenderer in prayer apart :
Other, I gather, in measure her mind's
Burden, in wind's burly & beat of endragonèd seas.

28

But how shall I.. — make me room there :
Reach me a.·.·. Fancy, come faster —
Strike you the sight of it ? look at it loom there,
Thing that she ... then ! the Master,
Ipse, the only one, Christ, King, Head :
He was to cure the extremity where he had cast her ;
Do, deal, lord it with living & dead ;
Let him ride, her pride, in his triumph, despatch & have done with his doom there .

**Stanza
28**

2

4

6

8

Plate 257   No. 101: "The Wreck of the Deutschland" cont. B.19v.

St.27: RB's slip in 7, "the" before "measure", was del. by GMH. In 5, beneath GMH's black comma after "danger", RB's small brown one may be detected.

St.28: RB recorded in A only GMH's rev. of "Here" (4) to "There". Not till 1918 did RB observe GMH's commas squeezed in after "Fancy" (2) and "pride" (8) and incorporate them in the 1st. edn.. The final stop in 7 seems a blurred semicolon, the same stop as A intends. GMH strengthened or changed a number of other punctuation marks: thus underneath his comma after "Master" (4) there is a short dash by RB, rather like the one ending 2; and he converted the final stop in ℓ.6 to a characteristically shaped semicolon.

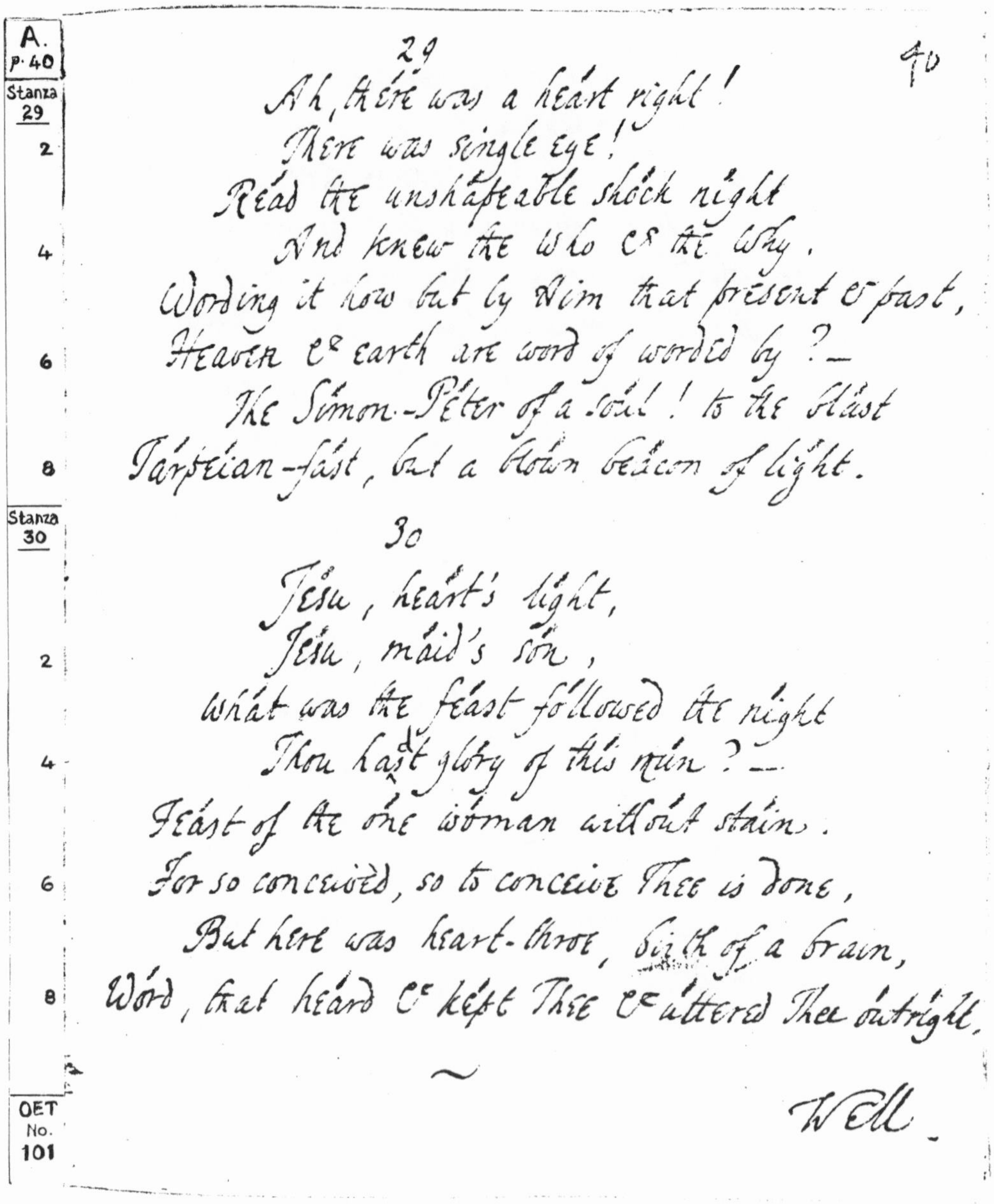

29

40

29

Ah, there was a heart right!
There was single eye!
Read the unshapeable shock night
And knew the who and the why.
Wording it how but by him that present and past,
Heaven and earth are word of, worded by?—
The Simon-Peter of a soul! to the blast
Tarpeian-fast, but a blown beacon of light.

30

Jesu, heart's light,
Jesu, maid's son,
What was the feast followed the night
Thou hadst glory of this nun?—
Feast of the one woman without stain.
For so conceived, so to conceive thee is done,
But here was heart-throe, birth of a brain,
Word, that heard and kept thee and uttered thee outright.

~

Well.

Plate 258 No. 101: "The Wreck of the Deutschland" cont. A.p.40.
St.29: No red ink corrections. As 4 flows into 5 in syntax, the ambiguous stop at its end, after "Why", should not be taken as a period: in B, GMH changed the stop there to a clear semicolon.
St.30: "hast" (4) is corrected to "hadst" in red ink (from B).

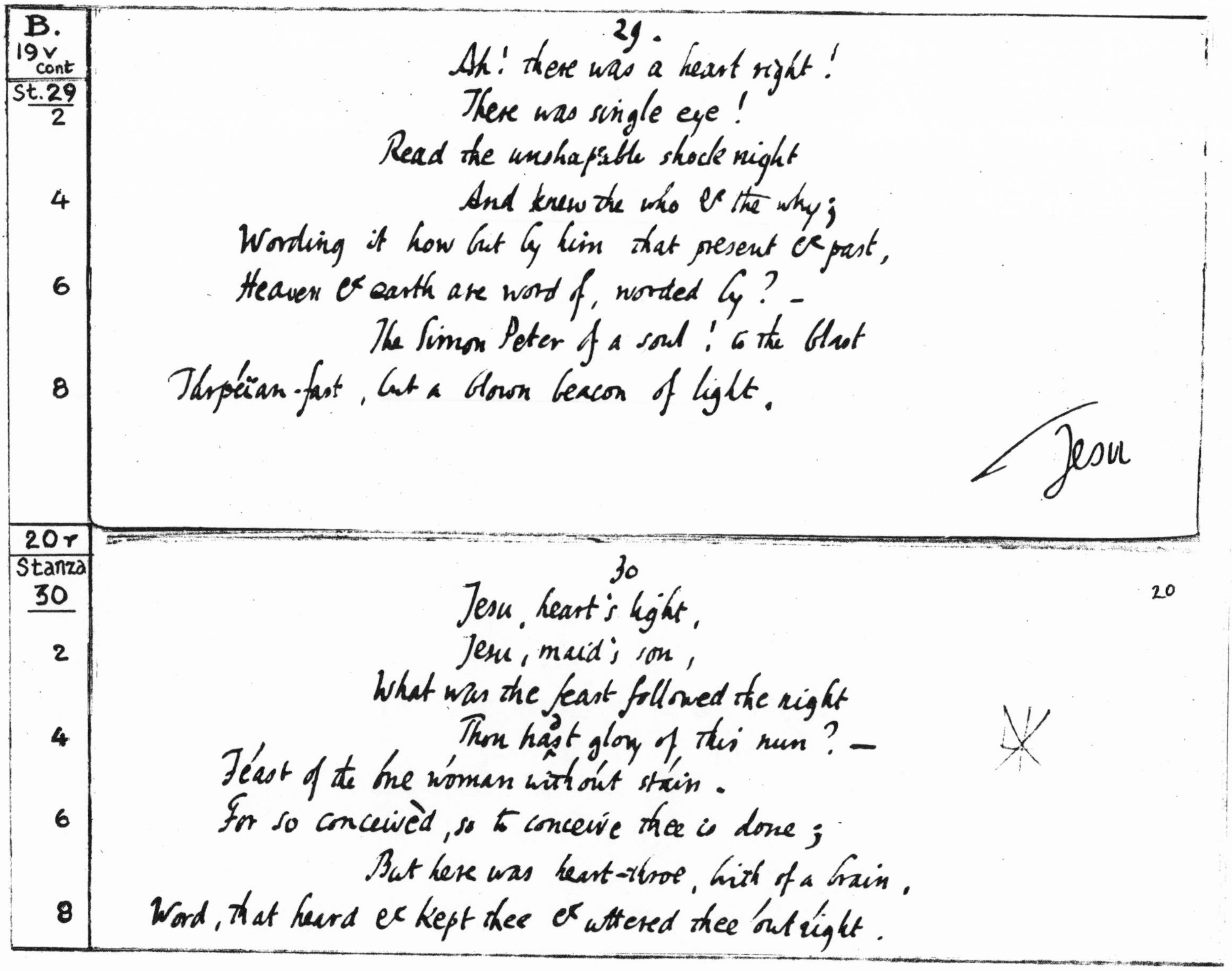

PLATE 259. OET 101. "The Wreck of the Deutschland" • 61

B.
19 v
cont

St. 29

2

4

6

8

29.

Ah! there was a heart right!
There was single eye!
Read the unshapable shock night
And knew the who & the why;
Wording it how but by him that present & past,
Heaven & earth are word of, worded by? —
The Simon Peter of a soul! to the blast
Tarpeïan-fast, but a blown beacon of light.

Jesu

20 r
Stanza
30

2

4

6

8

30

Jesu, heart's light,
Jesu, maid's son,
What was the feast followed the night
Thou hadst glory of this nun? —
Feast of the one woman without stain.
For so conceivèd, so to conceive thee is done;
But here was heart-throe, birth of a brain,
Word, that heard & kept thee & uttered thee outright.

20

Plate 259   No. 101: "The Wreck of the Deutschland" cont. B.19v. cont., 20r.

St.29:   In 3 RB used the alternative spelling, "unshapable", but he squeezed in the "e" later. RB also supplied the comma (not in A) needed in 6 after "word of", but the diaeresis on "Tarpeian" (not in A) was prob. supplied by GMH.

St.30:   GMH added the "d" in "hadst" (4)--note RB's pencil asterisk of 1918 to make sure that this important correction was not overlooked. GMH also lengthened RB's curt dash at the end of 4, and his grave accent on "conceivèd" (6). GMH's semicolon is easily recognizable at the end of that line.

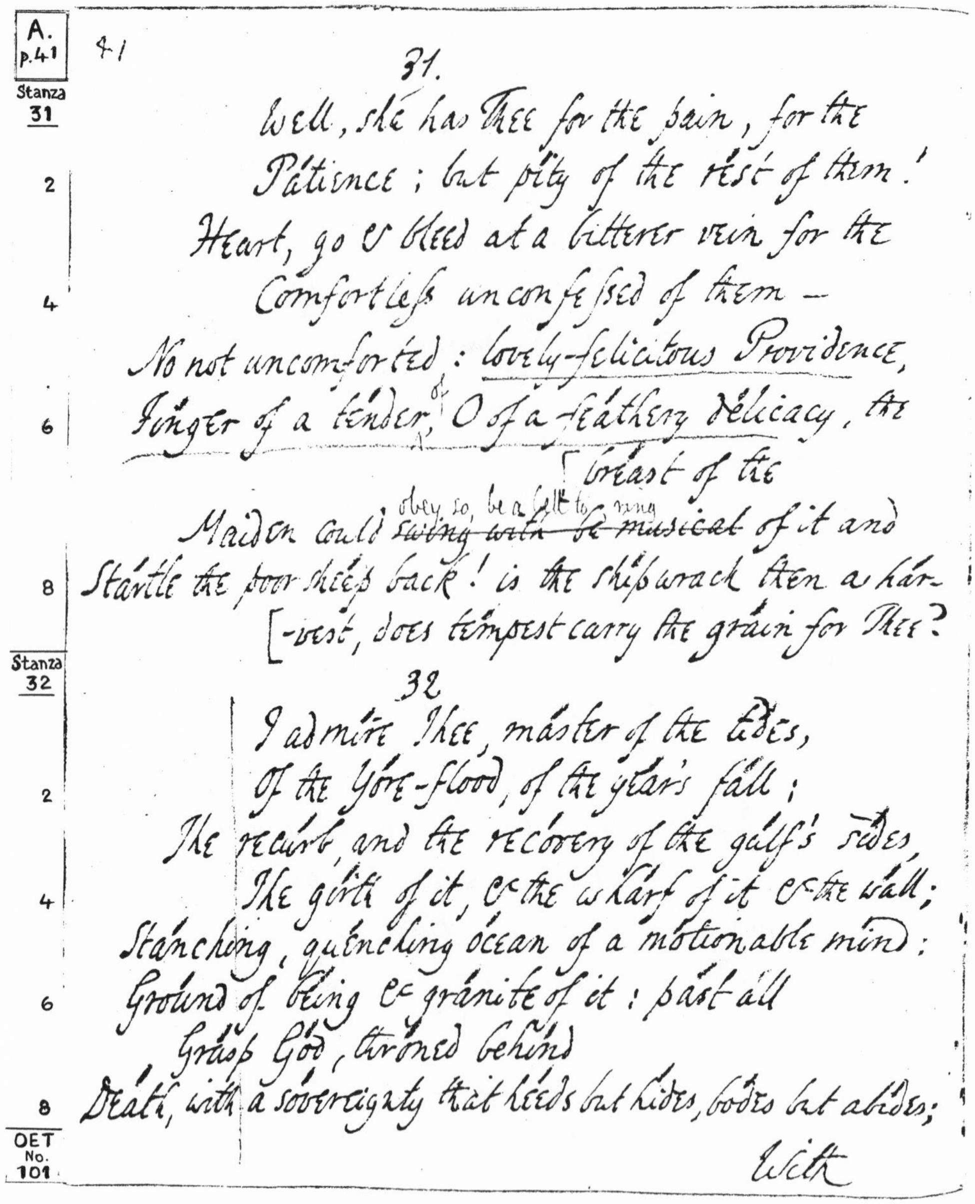

A.
p.41

Stanza
31

41

31.

Well, she has THEE for the pain, for the
Patience; but pity of the rest of them!
Heart, go & bleed at a bitterer vein for the
Comfortless unconfessed of them —
No not uncomforted: lovely-felicitous Providence,
Finger of a tender, O of a feathery delicacy, the
breast of the
Maiden could swing with be musical of it and
obey so, be a bell to ring
Startle the poor sheep back! is the shipwrack then a har-
[-vest, does tempest carry the grain for Thee?

Stanza
32

32

I admire Thee, master of the tides,
Of the Yore-flood, of the year's fall;
The recurb, and the recovery of the gulf's sides,
The girth of it, & the wharf of it & the wall;
Stanching, quenching ocean of a motionable mind;
Ground of being & granite of it: past all
Grasp God, throned behind
Death, with a sovereignty that heeds but hides, bodes but abides;

With

OET
No.
101

Plate 260   No. 101: "The Wreck of the Deutschland" cont. A.p.41.

St.31: RB's red ink copies GMH's revisions in 6 and 7, and (rather faintly) his stresses on "she" and "Thee" in 1. In 5 and 6 the light pencil underlining may relate to GMH's puzzling reference, in his Preface on the rhythm of this ode (Plate 229, line 31ff.) to "very strong" beats, and others "very light and escaping", in the "stanza which is fifth from the end of the poem"--no one has yet convincingly identified the passage. Cf. J.382.

St.32: Note (as in st.12) the vertical pencil guideline RB used to help with the complex indentation.

PLATE 261. OET 101. "The Wreck of the Deutschland"   •   *63*

B.
20 r
cont.

St. 31
2

4

6

8

Stanza
32

2

4

6

8

OET
NO.
101

31

Well, she has thee for the pain, for the
Patience (:) but pity of the rest of them!   *A ;*
Heart, go bleed at a bitterer vein for the
Comfortless unconfessed of them —
No not uncomforted : lovely-felicitous Providence
Finger of a tender,^of O of a feathery délicacy, the breast of the
Maiden could ~~swing with a musical~~ obey so, be a will to ring of it, and
Startle the poor sheep back ! is the shipwrack then a harvest, does tempest carry the
                                                                grain for thee?

32

I admire thee, master of the tides,
Of the Yore-flood, of the year's fall ;
The recurb & the recovery of the gulf's sides,
The girth of it & the wharf of it & the wall ;
Staunching, quenching ocean of a motionable mind ;
Ground of the being, & granite of it : past all
Grasp God, throned behind
Death with a sovereignty that heeds but hides, bodes but abides ;

Smith

Plate 261   No. 101: "The Wreck of the Deutschland" cont. B.20r. cont.

St.31:   GMH added "of" to 6, and extensively altered 7, stressing "óf it, and /S" to help the rove-over rhyme with "Providence". He failed to strengthen the comma after "Providence" (5), which is so faint as to appear erased, but which is clear in A, separating two phrases in apposition. RB's pencil (1918) ringed the colon after "Patience" (2) and added in the margin "A ;" (he corrected his slip in the 1st. edn.).

St.32:   GMH's strong stops end 2,3,4,5 and 8, but he paid less attention to internal punctuation. In A the extraordinary run of seven almost unrelieved stresses ("past...Death"), followed by a comma (now in the OET), is contrasted with clusters of two, three and four adjacent slacks in the rapid passages before and after it. In B however, RB intruded "the" before "being" (but del. it lightly when wet, as GMH did heavily later), and added a disruptive comma ("being,") which the OET rejects. GMH rewrote the ℓs in "all" (end of 6) where RB's two final letters were squeezed together.

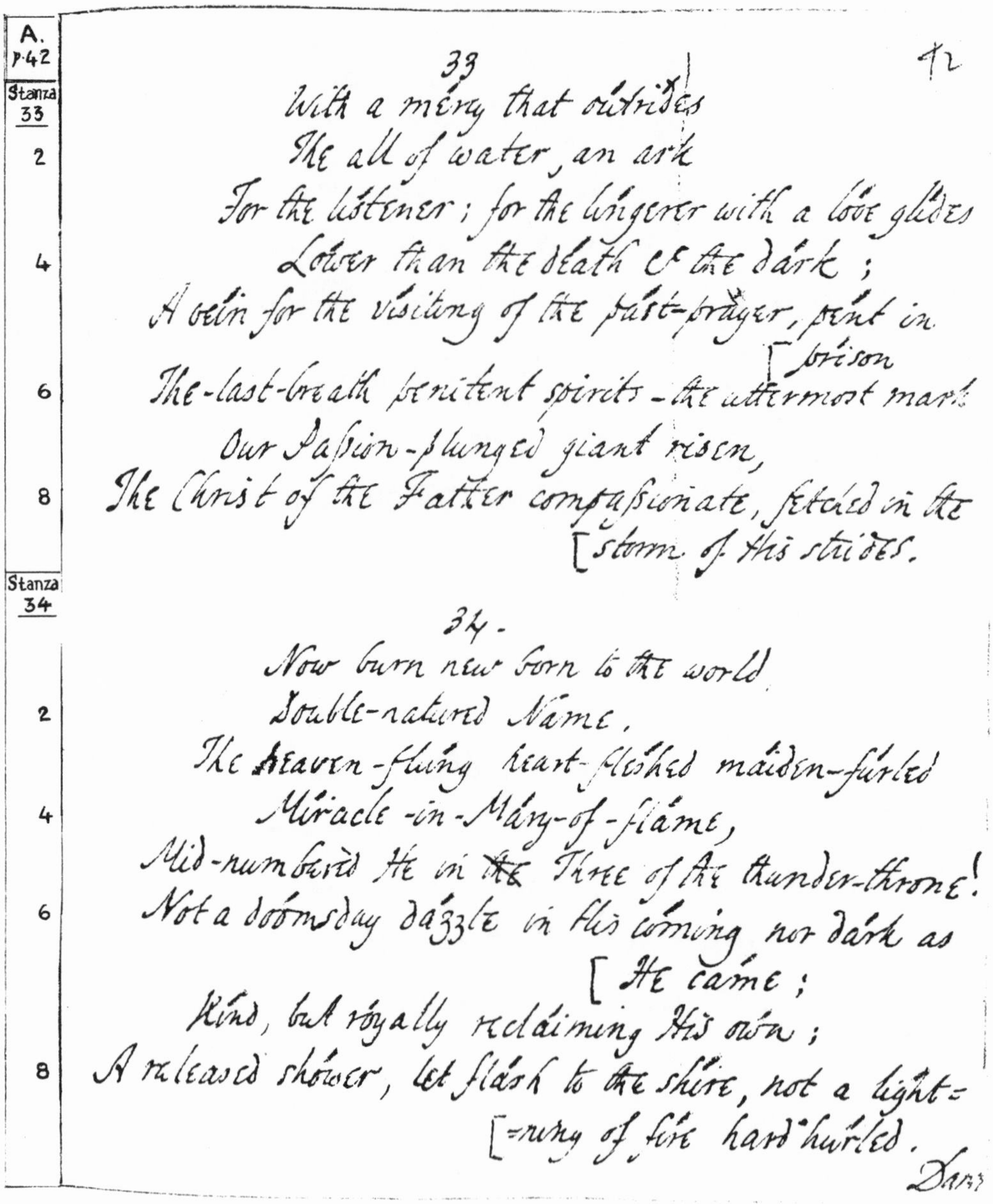

A.
p.42

Stanza 33

72

33

With a mercy that outrides

2 The all of water, an ark

For the listener; for the lingerer with a love glides

4 Lower than the death of the dark;

A vein for the visiting of the past-prayer, pent in

[prison

6 The-last-breath penitent spirits - the uttermost mark

Our Passion-plunged giant risen,

8 The Christ of the Father compassionate, fetched in the

[storm of his strides.

Stanza 34

34 -

Now burn new born to the world,

2 Double-natured Name,

The heaven-flung heart-fleshed maiden-furled

4 Miracle-in-Mary-of-flame,

Mid-numbered He in the Three of the thunder-throne!

6 Not a doomsday dazzle in His coming nor dark as

[He came;

Kind, but royally reclaiming His own;

8 A released shower, let flash to the shire, not a light=

[=ning of fire hard hurled.

Dan

Plate 262   No. 101: "The Wreck of the Deutschland" cont. A.pp.42.

St.33:   That more slips should occur through fatigue towards the marathon close of the poem is understandable: editing therefore becomes more difficult. RB added "the" twice in B st.32:6 and in A st.34:5; he seems to have done the same here, in A st.33:4 (before "death"). He has no note on Bacon's reading, and GMH, who rejected the other slips, did not insert "the" in B where it was omitted. In 5 RB's blue pencil stress on "prayer" is del. in the same pencil (the hyphen throws more stress on "past": the double alliteration of "prayer" and "prison" is no sure clue as to where GMH wanted emphasis). Note the vertical pencil guideline running through "outrides" to "storm".

St.34:   In 5 "the" is del. in red ink (1884). The comma at the end of 1 is faint, as though erased, but in B it is emphatically confirmed by GMH. Many linguists object to the second elements of hyphenations being given the prime stress: in 3 I would prefer "The héaven-flùng héart-flèshed máiden-fùrled"; this would be technically one stress short of GMH's pattern or two stresses too many, if secondary stresses are accepted, but GMH manipulated stresses freely (see, e.g., st.33:1, "óutrìdes"). In 8 the apparent hyphen high up between "hard" and "hurled", copied as such in B, is only a flaw in the paper, visible also on the verso (p.43, bot. left): the OET removes it because it shifts GMH's stress to the first element.

PLATE 263. OET 101. "The Wreck of the Deutschland" • 65

B.
20 v

St.33

33

—— With a mercy that outrides
—— The all of water, an ark

2

For the listener ; for the lingerer with a love glides
——— Lower than death & the dark ;

4

A vein for the visiting of the past-prayer, pent in prison,
The-last-breath penitent spirits — the uttermost mark

6

—— Our passion-plungèd giant risen,
The Christ of the Father compassionate, fetched in the storm of his strides.

8

Stanza 34

34

— Now burn, new born to the world,
— Doubled-naturèd name,

2

The heaven-flung, heart-fleshed, maiden-furled
————— Miracle-in-Mary-of-flame,

4

Mid-numbered he in three of the thunder-throne !
Not a dooms-day dazzle in his coming nor dark as he came ;

6

Kind, but royally reclaiming his own ;

8

A released shower, let flash to the shore, not a lightning of fire hard-hurled.

✗ B has shore

Plate 263   No. 101: "The Wreck of the Deutschland" cont. B.20v.

St.33:   Note the horizontal and vertical pencil guidelines which helped to make RB's transcripts neat. In 3 and 4 GMH's clear semicolons replace RB's ambiguous stops. After "prison" (5) RB had no stop in A or B; GMH added the comma, and the grave on "plungèd" (7).

St.34:   In 2 GMH overlooked RB's slip "Doubled", though he added the grave to "naturèd". He paid close attention to stops--"burn," (1, not in A or B orig.); "world," (1, over a minute comma); he accepted the commas in 3 (not in A); added clear semicolons after "came" (6) and "own" (7) (both over RB's ambiguous "three-quarter" colons). He del. "the" in 5. In the last line the slur over "A released" is in faded brown ink, prob. added by GMH at a later stage. RB himself mended "shore" to "shire". His 1918 pencil note abbreviates "Bacon" to "B"--in his 1st. edn., where Bacon is cited as G, RB writes "G has shore; but shire is doubtless right; it is the special favoured landscape visited by the shower"--an imaginative comment.

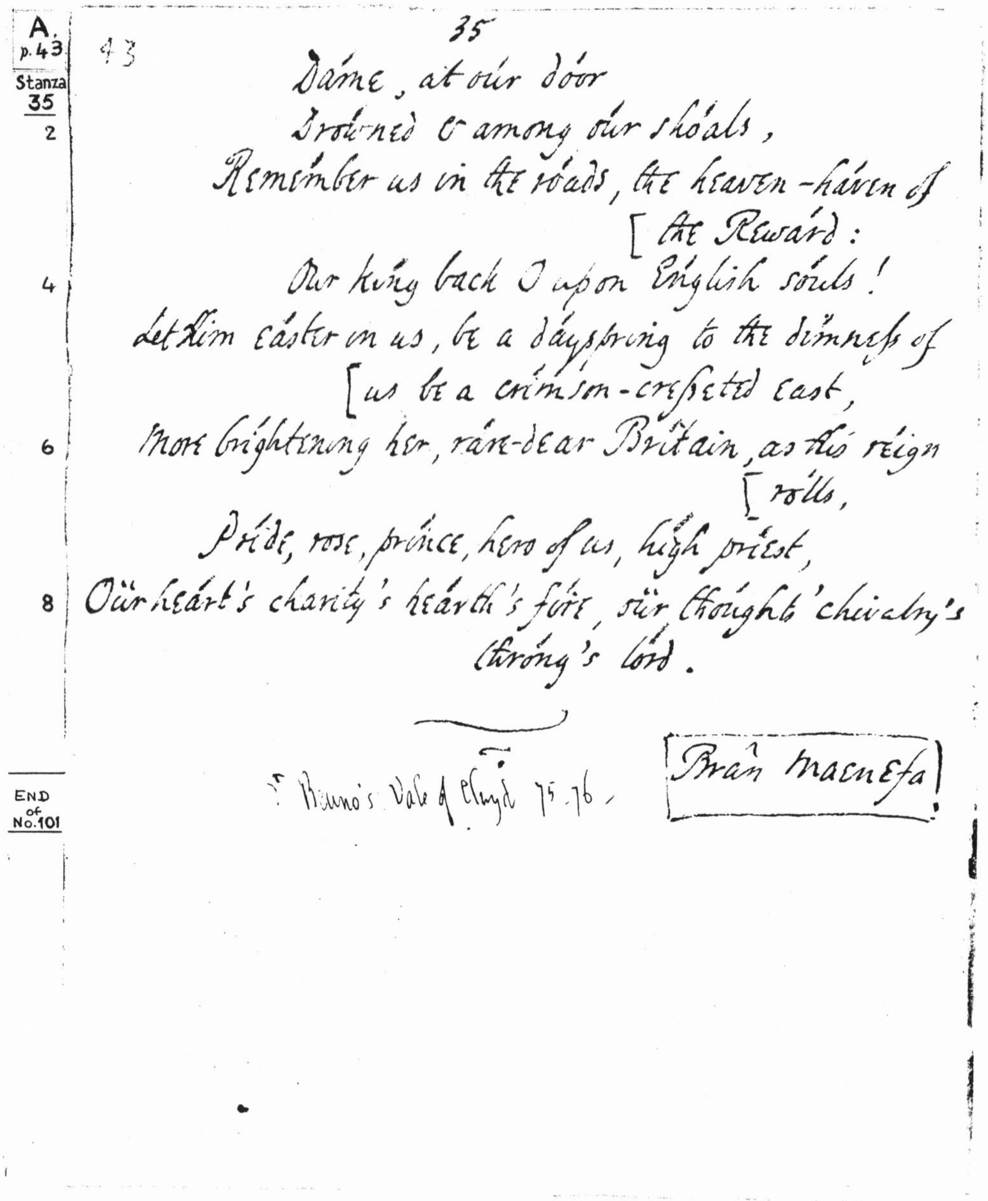

A.
p.43

43

35

Stanza
35

2

Dame, at our door
Drowned & among our shoals,
Remember us in the roads, the heaven-haven of
[the Reward :

4

Our king back O upon English souls !
Let him easter in us, be a dayspring to the dimness of
[us be a crimson-cresseted east,

6

More brightening her, rare-dear Britain, as his reign
[rolls,

8

Pride, rose, prince, hero of us, high priest,
Our heart's charity's hearth's fire, our thought's chivalry's
throng's lord .

S. Beuno's Vale of Clwyd 75.76.

[Brân Maenefa]

END
of
No.101

<u>Plate 263a</u>   <u>No. 101: "The Wreck of the Deutschland"</u> concl. <u>A.p.43.</u>

   <u>St.35</u>:   Stops are omitted in A which GMH accepted or added in B--after "Drowned" (2), before and after "O" (4), and after the second "us" (5). In 5 "him" is mended to "Him". The diaeresis on "Our" (8), not repeated in B, was in GMH's later usage replaced by a circumflex (see L.i.43). Note the discrepancies in capitalisation between A and B: A has u.c. for "Reward" (3) and "English" (4) where B has ℓ.c., while in 8 A has ℓ.c. for "lord', B has u.c. (where the <u>OET</u> follows it on this climactic term). In 4 both A and B have ℓ.c. for "king", though the stress mark in B makes this look like "K" in a black and white photograph (contr. u.c. K in st.14:4; 28:5; 34:7). RB did not copy into A GMH's rev. in 4. The place and date are added in the black backward-sloping ink of 1889. The bardic signature, "Brân Maenefa" was not repeated in B.

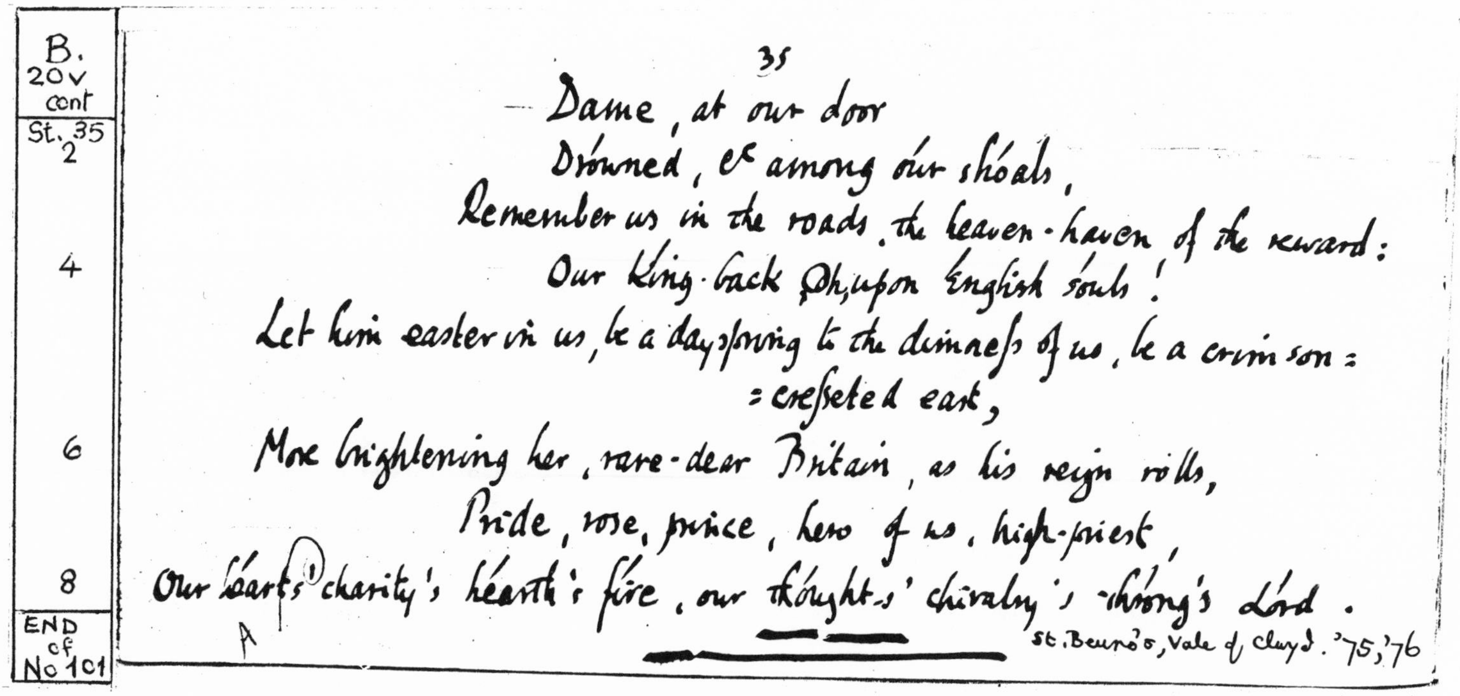

B.
20v
cont

St. 35
2

4

6

8

END
of
No 101

35

— Dame, at our door
Drowned, & among our shoals,
Remember us in the roads. the heaven-haven of the reward:
Our King back Oh, upon English souls!
Let him easter in us, be a dayspring to the dimness of us, be a crimson=
=cresseted east,
More brightening her, rare-dear Britain, as his reign rolls,
Pride, rose, prince, hero of us, high-priest,
Our hearts' charity's hearth's fire, our thoughts' chivalry's throng's Lord.

St. Beuno's, Vale of Clwyd. '75, '76

Plate 263b   No. 101: "The Wreck of the Deutschland" concl. B.20v. cont.

St.35:   In 4 GMH mended RB's "back, o upon" into "back, Oh, upon" (cf. "The Windhover", No.120, line 9), and strengthened the comma after "east" (5). RB's editorial pencil (1918) amends "hearts'" (8, apostrophe after "s", not challenged by GMH) to the A reading, "heart's". GMH's addition of the place and date here and in many other poems in album B was made after RB had given him back the volume for his own use.

H.i
27r

a. m. d. g.

27/

The Silver Jubilee

To ~~These~~ [Three] First Bishop of.
Shrewsbury

1.

Though no high-hung bells or din
of braggart bugles cry it in,
　　what is sound? Nature's round
4 Makes the Silver Jubilee.

2.

Five-and-twenty years have run
Since sacred fountains to the sun
　　Sprang, that but now were shut,
8 Showering silver jubilee.

3.

Feasts, when we shall fall asleep,
Shrewsbury may see others keep;
　　none but you this her true,
12 This her Silver Jubilee.

4.

Not today we need lament
Your wealth of life is some way Spent:
　　Toil has shed round your head
16 Silver, but for jubilee.

28r

5.

28

Then for her whose velvet vales
Should have pealed with welcome, Wales,
　　Let the chime of a rhyme
20 Utter silver jubilee.

L. D. S.

OET
No.
102a

here is a glimmer in the sky

THE SILVER JUBILEE.

Though no high-hung bells or din
Of braggart bugles cry it in—
　　What is sound?　Nature's round
　　　Makes the Silver Jubilee.

Five and twenty years have run
Since sacred fountains to the sun
　　Sprang, that but now were shut,
　　　Showering Silver Jubilee.

Feasts when we shall fall asleep,
Shrewsbury may see others keep;
　　None but you this her true,
　　　This her Silver Jubilee.

Not to-day we need lament
Your wealth of life is some way spent:
　　Toil has shed round your head
　　　Silver, but for Jubilee.

Then for her whose velvet vales
Should have pealed with welcome—Wales,
　　Let the chime of a rhyme
　　　Utter Silver Jubilee.

G. M. H.

Plate 264　　OET No. 102(a) - The Silver Jubilee　MS. H
H.i.27r (sts. 1 to 4), 28r (st.5). Autograph used for transcription into the presentation album.　In the subtitle (del. in pencil to show it must not be copied into the album) GMH at first confused Dr. Thomas Brown (Bishop over South Wales) with Dr. James Brown (Bishop of Shrewsbury, including N. Wales): GMH corrected his own slip. St.5 was smudged onto 27v. At the end, another hand added the first line of the poem to follow it in the album: "[T]here is a glimmer in the sky"--omitting the first letter, which was to be illuminated.

(Top right).　Published Version of 1876, printed on p.19 of *A Sermon/Preached at St. Beuno's College, July 30, 1876,/on the occasion of/The Silver Jubilee/of the/Lord Bishop of Shrewsbury/By John Morris,/Priest of the Society of Jesus.* London: Burns and Oates, 1876.

(Bottom right).　Letter from GMH to RB (MS. Letters, i.168), Feb. 15, 1879, correcting three errors in the MS. A version of st.4 (Plate 265a), but retaining a fourth ("lot" for "wealth").

St. Giles's, Oxford 1687 Feb. 15 2/79.

(Dearest Bridges, — I should have added in my last that the Silver Jubilee had been published. It was printed at the end of a sermon, bearing the same title and due to the same occasion; of Fr. John Morris's of our society. I have found it since I wrote and the copy I sent you from memory is not quite right: the third stanza should stand fourth and run —

　　Not today we need lament [spent:
　　Your lot of life is some way
　　　Toil has shed round your head
　　Silver, but for Jubilee.

the thought is more pointed. Please correct it if you put it into your album.

PLATE 265. OET 102(a). *The Silver Jubilee* • 69

Though no high-hung bells, or din
Of braggart bugles cry it in,
     What is sound? Nature's round
Makes the Silver Jubilee.

Five-and-twenty years have run
Since sacred fountains to the sun
     Sprang, that but now were shut
Showering   Silver Jubilee.

Feasts when we shall fall asleep,
Shrewsbury may see others keep:
     None but you this her true,
This her Silver Jubilee.

Not today we need lament
Your wealth of life is some way spent:
     Toil has shed round your head
Silver, but for Jubilee.

Then for her whose velvet vales
Should have pealed with welcome, Wales,
     Let the chime of a rhyme
Utter Silver Jubilee.

Plate 265   OET No. 102(a) - The Silver Jubilee . 2
    Illuminated page [69] in the beautiful album presented to the Bishop by St. Beuno's
College to mark his Silver Jubilee. The copy, in an unknown hand, was made from MS. H.
For a detailed description, see Alfred Thomas, SJ, "G.M. Hopkins and the Silver Jubilee
Album", in The Library, Fifth Series, xx, no.2, June 1965, 148-52. The album is kept in
St. Beuno's, North Wales.

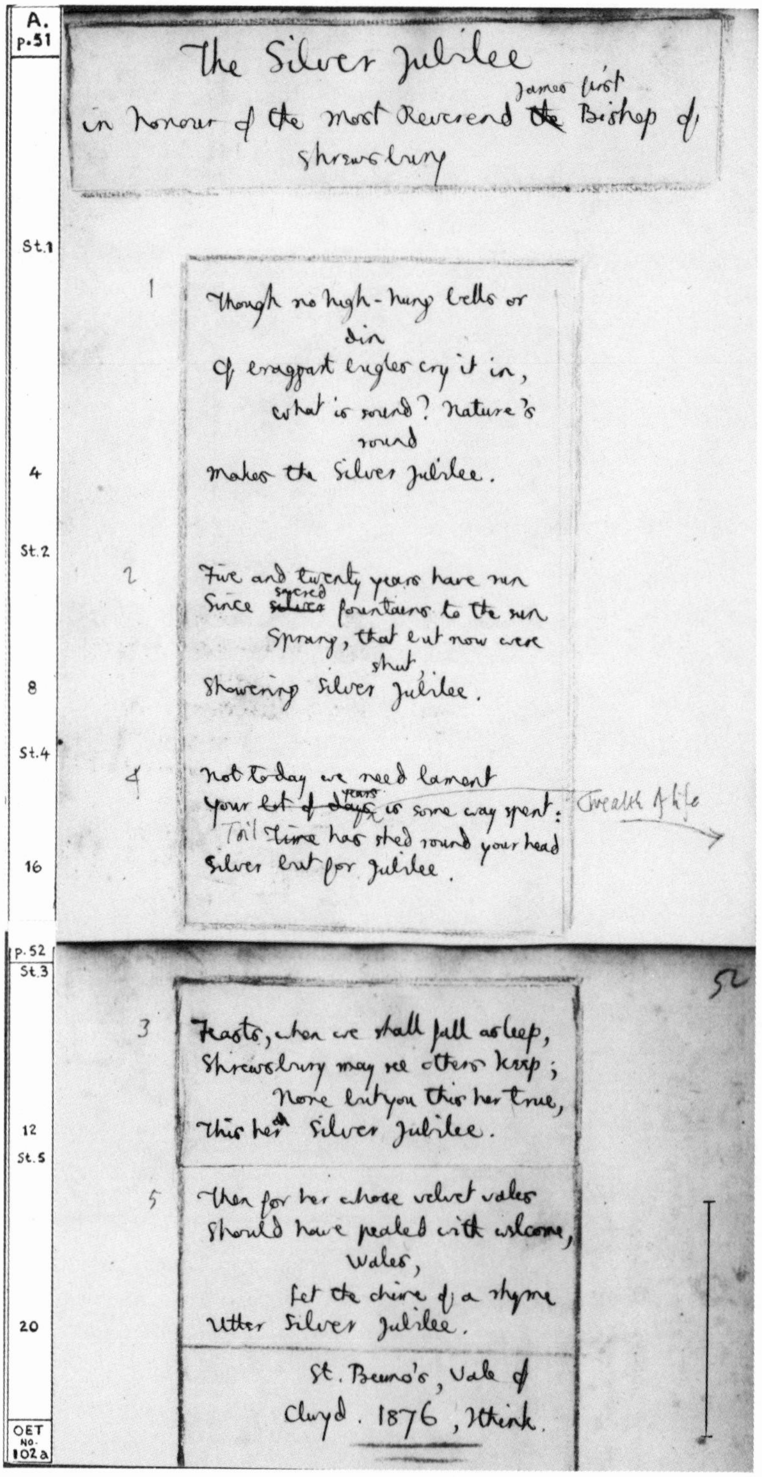

Plate 265a   OET No. 102(a) - The Silver Jubilee   MS. A

A.pp.51 (sts.1,2,4) and 52 (3,5). Autograph, cut and pasted into album A. GMH revised the subtitle, in ℓ.6 changed "silver" (a slip?) to "sacred", in 14 "days" to "years", and in 12 began to change "her" [? to "our", or possibly to "his"]. He wrote it from memory and probably reverted in st.4 to an earlier draft.

RB's red ink numbers the sts. (GMH had transposed sts.3 and 4, L.i.65), and corrects 14,15 from GMH's revised text in B. Below the poem (not included in plate) RB's pencil copies from GMH's letters of 29 Jan. and 15 Feb. 1879--note pencil arrow at 15.

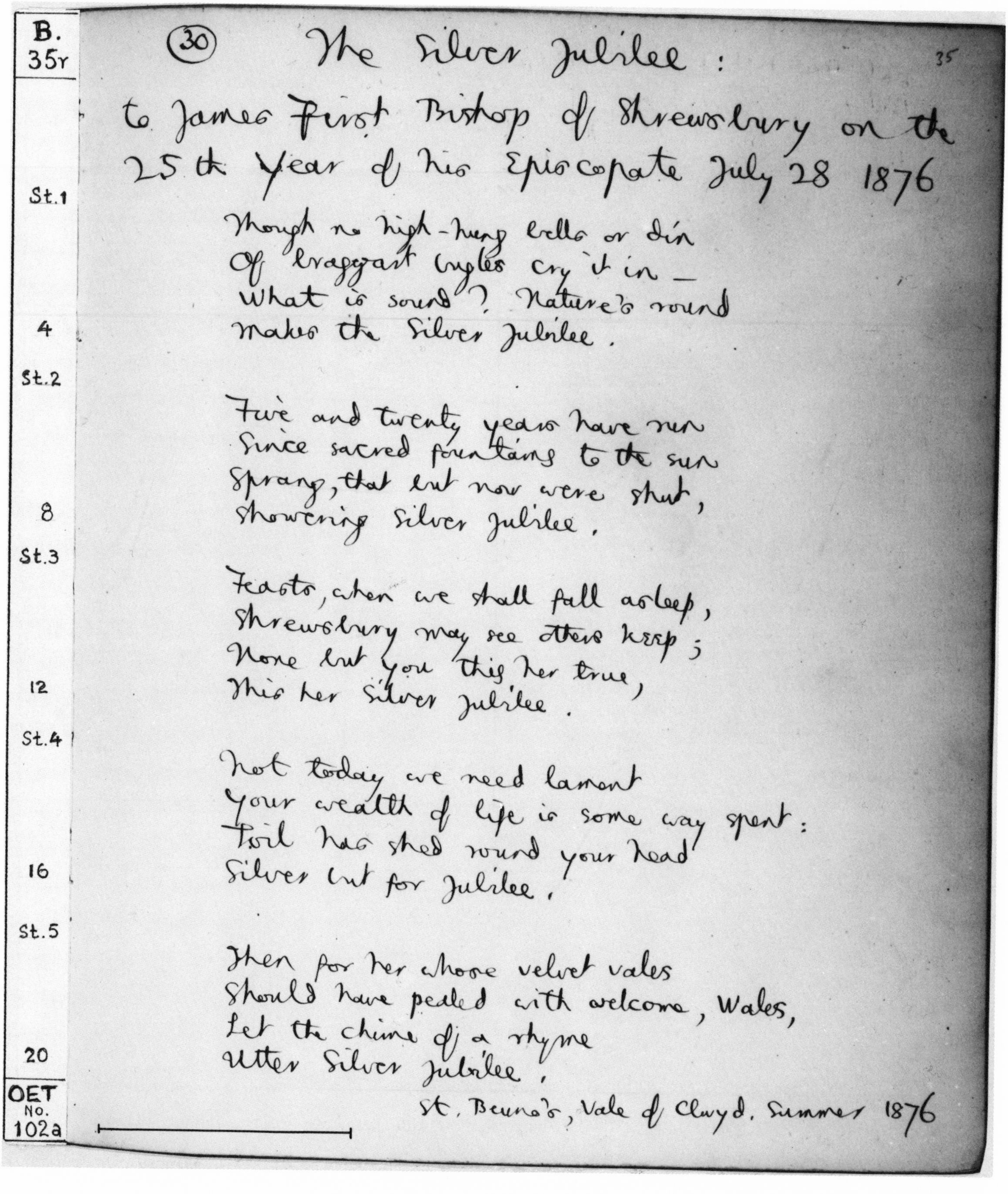

B. 35r

(30) The Silver Jubilee: 35

to James First Bishop of Shrewsbury on the 25th Year of his Episcopate July 28 1876

St.1
Though no high-hung bells or din
Of braggart bugles cry it in —
What is sound? Nature's round
Makes the Silver Jubilee.

St.2
Five and twenty years have run
Since sacred fountains to the sun
Sprang, that but now were shut,
Showering Silver Jubilee.

St.3
Feasts, when we shall fall asleep,
Shrewsbury may see others keep;
None but you this her true,
This her Silver Jubilee.

St.4
Not today we need lament
Your wealth of life is some way spent:
Toil has shed round your head
Silver but for Jubilee.

St.5
Then for her whose velvet vales
Should have pealed with welcome, Wales,
Let the chime of a rhyme
Utter Silver Jubilee.

St. Beuno's, Vale of Clwyd, Summer 1876

OET No. 102a

Plate 265b OET No. 102(a) - The Silver Jubilee MS. B

B.35r: Autograph, inscribed in album B, 1884, before it was sent to Patmore. In the title "first" and "year" have been mended to begin with capitals.

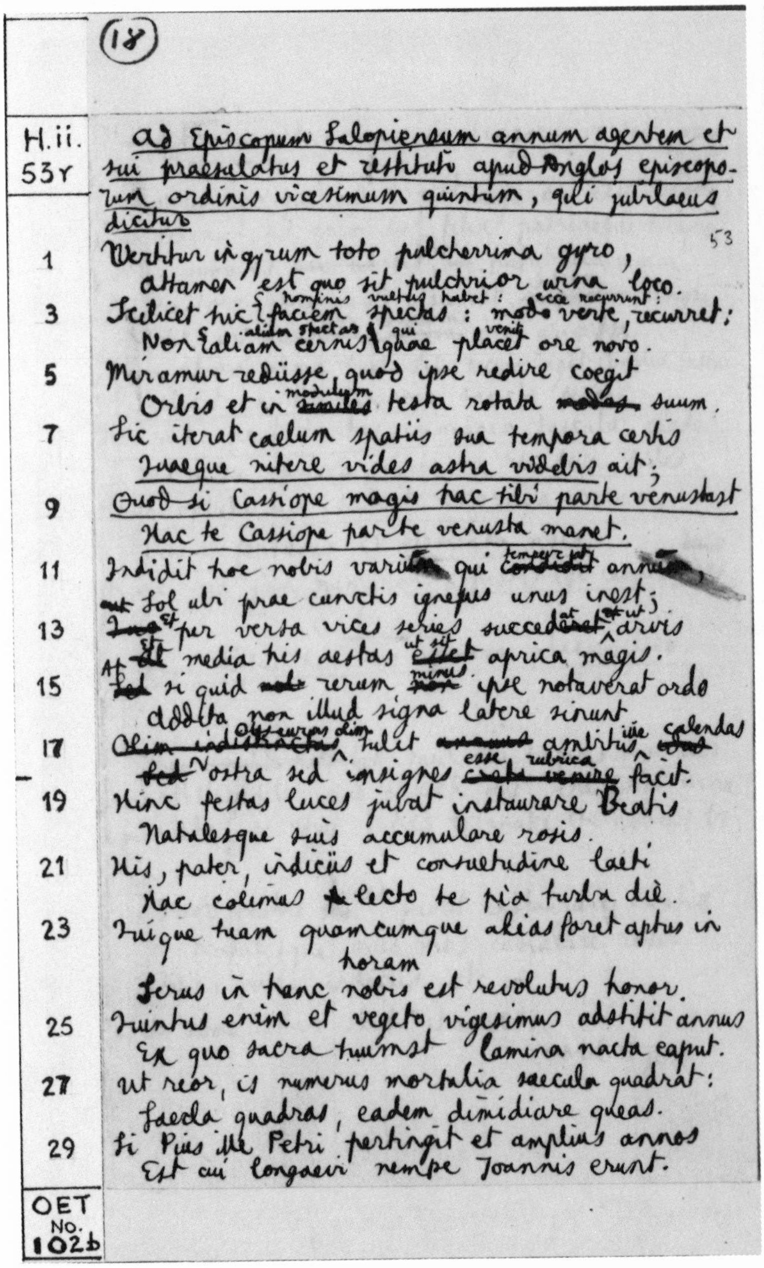

H.ii. 53r (18)

H.ii. 54r (18)

Left column (H.ii. 53r), lines 1–30:

Ad Episcopum Salopiensem annum agentem et
sui praesulatus et restituti apud ~~Anglos~~ episcopo-
rum ordinis vicesimum quintum, qui jubilaeus
dicitur

1 Vertitur in gyrum toto pulcherrima gyro,
   Attamen est quo sit pulchrior urna loco.
3 Scilicet hic faciem spectas : modo verte, recurret:
   Non taliam cernis quae placet ore novo.
5 Miramur rediisse, quod ipse redire coegit
   Orbis et in ~~similes~~ testa rotata ~~modas~~ suum.
7 Sic iterat caelum spatiis sua tempora certis
   Suaeque nitere vides astra videris ait;
9 ~~Quod si~~ Cassiope magis hac tibi parte venustast
   Hac te Cassiope parte venusta manet.
11 Indidit hoc nobis vario qui ~~condidit~~ tempore id annu
   ~~ut~~ Sol ubi prae cunctis igneus unus inest;
13 ~~Quo~~ et per versa vices series succedat drivis
   At et media his aestas ~~esset~~ aprica magis.
15 ~~Sed~~ si quid ~~not~~ rerum ~~non~~ ipse notaverat ordo
   Addita non illud signa latere sinunt.
17 ~~Olim indistinctas~~ tulit ~~annuus~~ ambitus calendas
   ~~Sed~~ Nostra sed insignes ~~creta venire~~ facit.
19 Hinc festas luces juvat instaurare Beatis
   Natalesque suis accumulare rosis.
21 His, pater, indiciis et consuetudine laeti
   Hac colimas lecto te pia turba die.
23 Suique tuam quamcumque alias foret aptus in
            horam
   Serus in hanc nobis est revolutus honor.
25 Quintus enim et vegeto vigesimus adstitit annus
   Ex quo sacra tuumst lamina nacta caput.
27 Ut reor, is numerus mortalia saecula quadrat:
   Saecla quadras, eadem dimidiare queas.
29 Si Pius ille Petri pertingit et amplius annos
   Est cui longaevi nempe Joannis erunt.

OET No. 102b

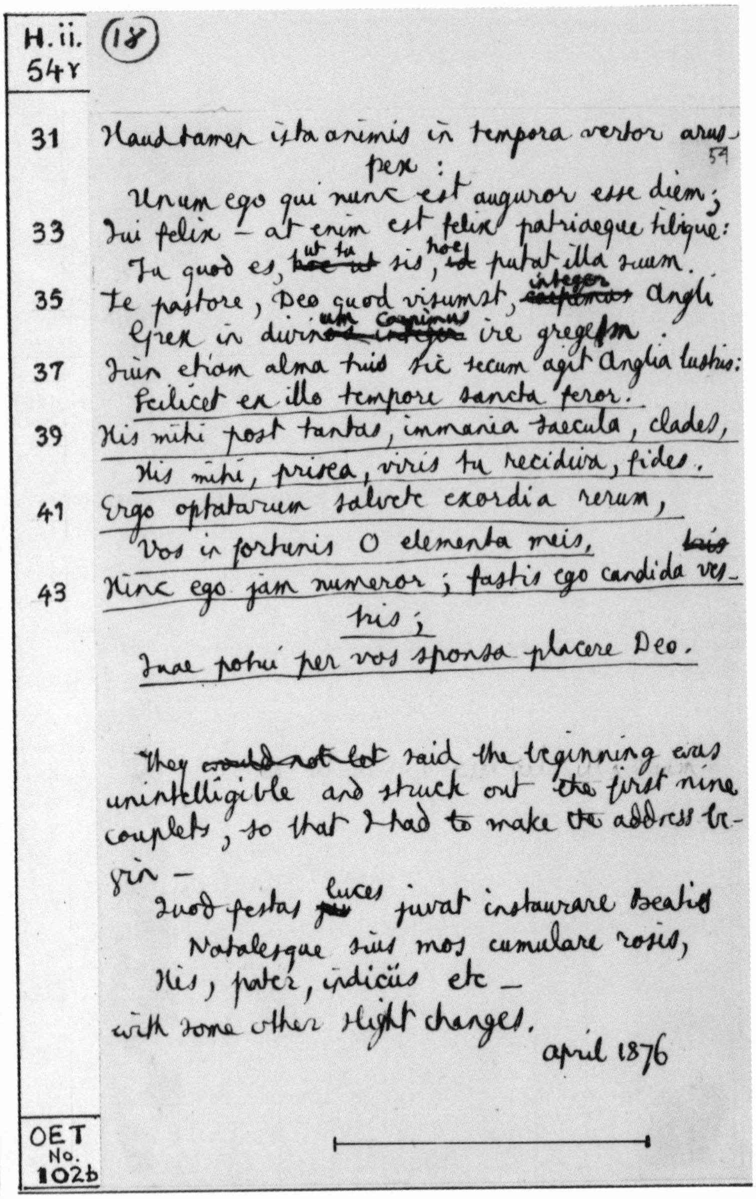

Right column (H.ii. 54r), lines 31–44:

31 Haud tamen ista animis in tempora vertor aruspex:
33 Unum ego qui nunc est auguror esse diem;
   Sui felix — at enim est felix patriaeque tibique:
35 Tu quod es, ut tu sis, hoc putat illa suum.
   Te pastore, Deo quod visumst, ~~caepimus~~ Angli
37 Grex in divino ~~integer~~ ire gregem.
   Suin etiam alma tuis sic secum agit Anglia lustris:
39 Scilicet ex illo tempore sancta feror.
   His mihi post tantas, immania saecula, clades,
41 His mihi, prisca, viris tu recidiva, fides.
   Ergo optatarum salvete exordia rerum,
43 Vos in fortunis O elementa meis,
   Hinc ego jam numeror ; fastis ego candida ver-
            his ;
   Suae potui per vos sponsa placere Deo.

They ~~could not let~~ said the beginning was
unintelligible and struck out ~~the~~ first nine
couplets; so that I had to make the address begin —

   Quod festas luces juvat instaurare Beatis
      Natalesque suis mos cumulare rosis,
   His, pater, indiciis etc —
with some other slight changes.
                              april 1876

OET No. 102b

Plate 266   OET No. 102(b) - Ad Episcopum Salopiensem

H.ii.53r (1-30), 54r (31-44). Autograph draft, with alternatives in 3,4, and footnote
explaining that the first nine couplets were rejected for the Silver Jubilee Album. Among the
"other slight changes" required was the correction in the title to "Salopiensem" from "...um".

Deletions include: 6 similes...modas. [? med. Lat. form used by St. Bernard for
"modos"]   11 vario...condidit anno   13 Quo/Ut...succederet et   14 At...esset   15
Sed...nob...non   17 Olim indistinctas...annuus...idus   18 Sed...creta venire   34 hoc ut...id
     35 caepimus   36 divinos integer...greges

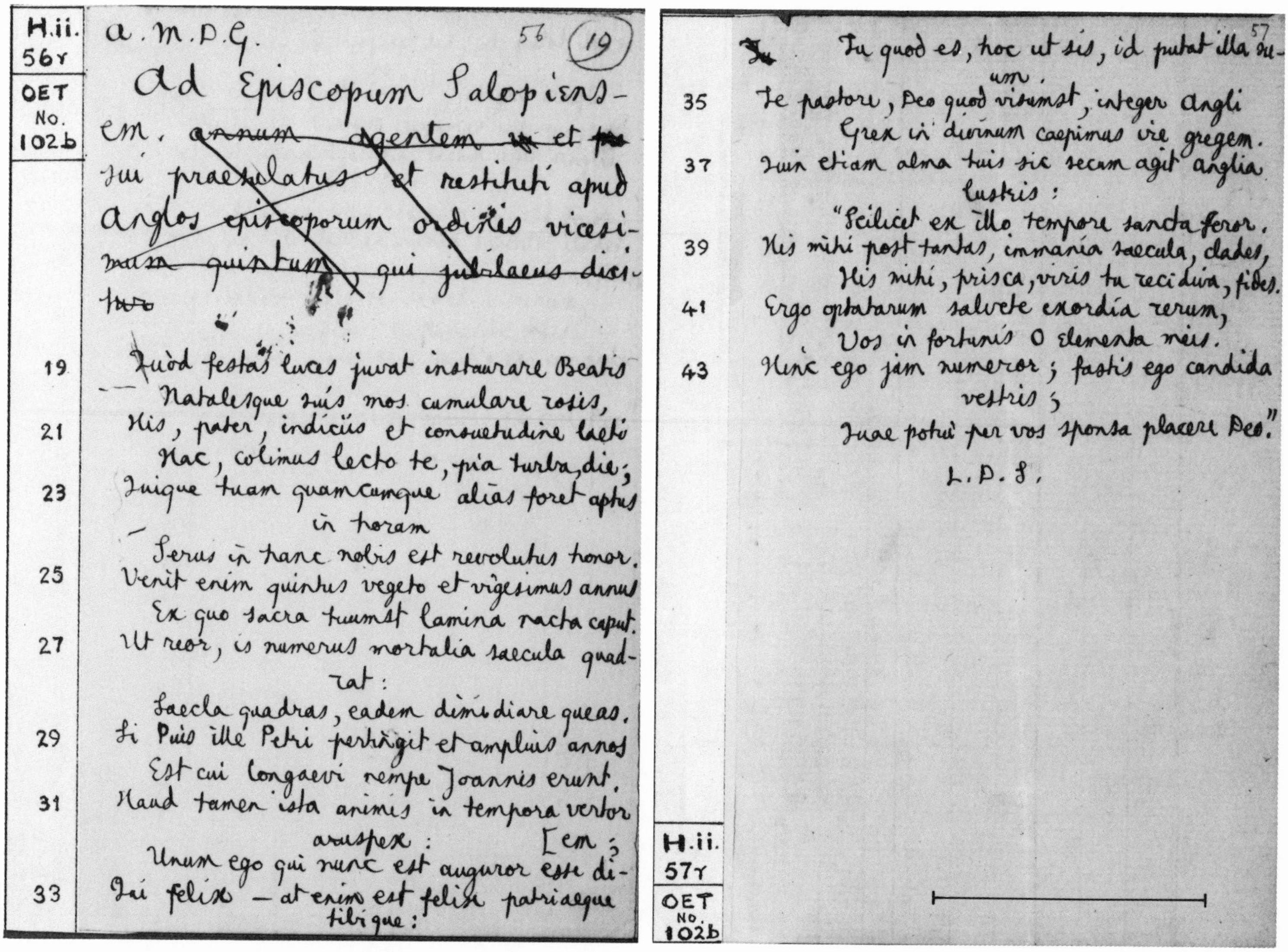

PLATE 267. OET 102(b). Ad Episcopum Salopiensem • 73

H.ii. 56r — OET No. 102b

a. m. p. g.   56 (19)

Ad Episcopum Salopiens-
em. ~~annum agentem et~~
~~sui praelatus~~ et restituti apud
Anglos ~~episcoporum~~ ordines vicesi-
~~mum~~ ~~quintum~~ qui ~~jubilaeus dici-~~
~~tur~~

19 Quòd festas luces juvat instaurare Beatis
    Natalesque suis mos cumulare rosis,
21 His, pater, indiciis et consuetudine laeti
    Hac, colimus lecto te, pia turba, die;
23 Tuique tuam quamcumque aliàs foret aptus
      in horam
25 Serus in hanc nobis est revolutus honor.
  Venit enim quintus vegeto et vigesimus annus
    Ex quo sacra tuum'st lamina tacta caput.
27 Ut reor, is numerus mortalia saecula quad-
      rat:
  Saecla quadras, eadem dimidiare queas.
29 Si Pius ille Petri pertingit et amplius annos
    Est cui longaevi nempe Joannis erunt.
31 Haud tamen ista animis in tempora vertor
      araspex: [em;
    Unum ego qui nunc est auguror esse di-
33 Qui felix — at enim est felix patriaeque
      tibique:

H.ii. 57r — OET No. 102b

    Tu quod es, hoc ut sis, id putat illa su-
       um.
35 Te pastore, Deo quod visum'st, integer Angli
    Grex in divinum caepimus ire gregem.
37 Quin etiam alma tuis sic secum agit Anglia
      lustris:
    "Scilicet ex illo tempore sancta feror.
39 His mihi post tantas, immania saecula, clades,
    His mihi, prisca, viris tu recidiva, fides.
41 Ergo optatarum salvete exordia rerum,
    Vos in fortunis O elementa meis.
43 Hinc ego jam numeror; fastis ego candida
      vestris;
    Tuae potui per vos sponsa placere Deo."

      L. P. S.

Plate 267   OET No. 102(b) - Ad Episcopum Salopiensem

H.ii.56r (19-33), 57r (37-44). Autograph, revised, faircopy, for transcription into the album being presented to the Bishop. The subtitle, not needed in the Silver Jubilee Album, was crossed through, along with the "Q" of the opening line, which was to be illuminated in the album. A pencil brace in the margin indicates to the transcriber that 23-24 form a couplet. The indentation was forgotten and corrected in 34.

Cywydd

H.ii. 67v

i Y annerch i'r tra pharchedig Dr.
ii Thomas Brown, esgob yr Am-
iii wythig, wedi cyrhaedd o hono
iv si bummed flwyddyn ar hugain,
v yr hon a elwir y jubil; a
vi chwyno y mae'r bardd fod dai-
vii ar a dŵr yn rhagor yn tysti-
viii olaethu yn mwy fwy hen gr efydd Gwynedd
ix nag y bydd dyn, a dywed hefy d
x fod yn mai gobeithia fod hyny gael i hyny ei
xi gyfnewid o craith yr esgob.

1 Y mae'n llewyn yma 'n llon
2 Â ffrydau llawer ffynon,
3 Gweddill gwyn gadwyd i ni
4 Gan Feuno a Gwenfrewi.
5 Glaw neu wlith, ni chai wlâd braidd
6 Tan rôd sydd fal hon iraidd.
7 Gân ddwfr a ddwg, nis dwg dyn,
8 Dyst ffyddlon am eu dyffryn;
9 Hên ddaiar ddenys di i gwedd
10 Ran drag'wyddawl o rinwedd;
11 Ni ddiffyg ond naws ddyniol,

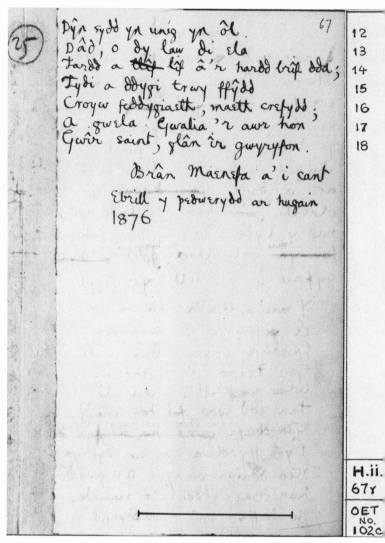

12 Dyn sydd yn unig yn ôl.
13 Dâd, o dy law di ela
14 Tardd a llif â'r tardd brif ddâ;
15 Tydi a ddygi trwy ffydd
16 Croyw feddygiaeth, maeth crefydd;
17 A gwela Gwalia 'r awr hon
18 Gwir saint, glân i'r gwyryfon.

Brân Maenefa a'i cant
Ebrill y pedwerydd ar hugain
1876

Plate 268   OET No. 102(c) - Cywydd

H.ii.67v (1-11), 67r (12-18). Autograph, faircopy with corrections. Recto numbered 25 in pencil (RB?)

Deletions: line i.   Ï...y   iii.   am gyrhaedd(i?)   vii.   yn rhagor   viii. mwy...am   ix,x. ei fod yn...o hyny   7. gwan yw, nidg[l]an ddyn   14. ḷ llîf

In line x "cael" had to be mended to "gael" because of the mutation caused by the insertion of "i" before the "c".

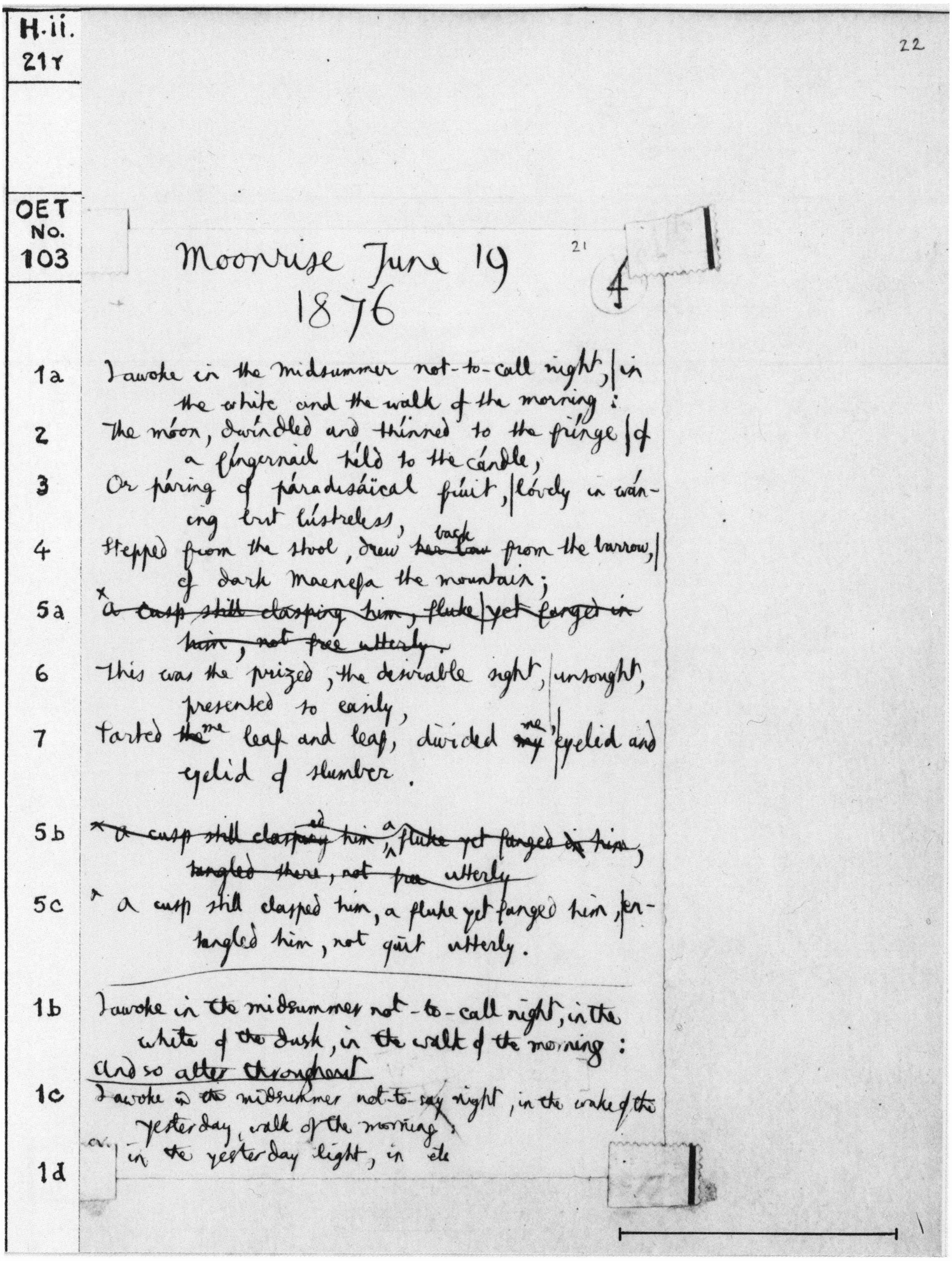

H.ii. 21r

OET No. 103

22

21

4

Moonrise June 19 1876

1a   I awoke in the midsummer not-to-call night, | in the white and the walk of the morning :

2   The moon, dwindled and thinned to the fringe | of a fingernail held to the candle,

3   Or paring of paradisáical fruit, | lovely in waning but listreless,

4   Stepped from the stool, drew ~~her~~ back ~~bow~~ from the barrow, | of dark Maenefa the mountain ;

5a   × ~~a Casp still clasping him, fluke | yet forget in him, not free utterly~~

6   This was the prized, the desirable sight, | unsought, presented so easily,

7   Parted ~~the~~ leaf and leaf, divided ~~my~~ eyelid and eyelid of slumber .

5b   × ~~a cusp still clasping him, a fluke yet fanged in him, tangled there, not free utterly~~

5c   ^ a cusp still clasped him, a fluke yet fanged him, entangled him, not quit utterly.

1b   I awoke in the midsummer not-to-call night, in the white of the dusk, in the walk of the morning : ~~And so alter throughout~~

1c   I awoke in the midsummer not to ~~say~~ night, in the wake of the yesterday, walk of the morning ,

1d   or in the yesterday light, in etc

<u>Plate 269</u>   <u>OET No. 103 - Moonrise June 19 1876</u>

    <u>H.ii.21r.</u> Autograph draft, with alternative metrical pattern begun at foot. GMH used ink for his stresses in 2,3 and caesuras (in 5a wrongly placed, corrected in 5c; omitted in 6, added in pencil, probably by RB). In 1c RB's pencil crosses out "say", as he preferred "call" (1b). Before 1d the "or" is almost concealed by the stamp paper fastening the MS to the page.

H.ii. 49ᵛ	

July 5 ~~just~~ 1876　　　The Woodlark

~~The~~ Teevo ~~&~~ cheevo, cheevio chee :

~~Teedy deedy leedy dee :~~

O*ʳ where , what can that be ?

Weedio-weedio : there again !　　　so dainty, ~~a darling a song,t~~

Such a tiny sweet strain ;　　　~~such a such a soft strain !~~

~~not to be found, all round~~,　　　why there ! a touch ~~in~~ strain !

~~In bough or bush or green ground~~,　　　and all round ~~of~~ not to be found

~~neither left neither right !~~　　　For brier, bough, furrow,

Nowhere in the sunlight ;　　　~~not anywhere in the sunlight~~.　　　or green ground

~~well, after all ! but listen~~.　~~O but hark~~—　~~Ah but hark !~~

am the little woodlark . My　　　Before or behind or far or at

~~Delight is to sing and fly~~　　　either left　hand　either right

"~~I am the little wood woodlark~~　　　anywhere in the sunlight.

~~To dainty, a darling a~~ ~~of~~ song-strain　　　well , after all ! Ah but hark—

"I am the little woodlark.

Today the sky ~~was~~ two and two

~~with strokes of white and strains of all blue~~

with white strokes,　and shains ~~of~~ the blue

Round a ring , around a ring

And while I sail (must listen) I sing

The skylark is my cousin and he

Is known to men more than me

OET NO. 104	

Right margin line numbers: 4d, 4c, 4b, 5b, }6b, 9b, 10c, 10b, }7, 8b, 9c, 10d, 11c

Left margin line numbers: 1b, 1a, 2, 3, 4a, 5a, 6a, 8a, 9a, 10a, 11a, 12a, 11b, 4e, 16, 17a, 17b, 14, 15, 12b, 13

first
July 5 ∧ -- 1876 The Woodlark

1b	~~Che~~ Teevo cheevo cheevio chee:	
1a	<u>Leedy-deeady-leedy-dee</u>:	
2	~~W~~O where, what can thát be?	so dainty, a, darling a song st　4d
3	<u>Weedio-weedio</u> : there again!	Such a, such a soft　4c ~~tin~~[y] strain.
4a ˣ	~~W~~Such a tiny sweet strain;	Why there's a touch　4b
5a	Not to be found, all round,	And all round, not to be found　5b
6a	In b[u]ough or bush or green ground,	For brier, bough, furrow,
8a	Neither left neither right,	or gréen ground　} 6b
9a	Nowhere in the súnlight,	Not ∧Anywhere in the súnlight.　9b Ah Yes　10c
10a	Well, after all! But listen. "I	O but hark,--Ah but hark!　10b
11a	Am the little woodlark. My	Before or behind or far or at
12a	Delight is to sing and fly	hand　} 7
11b	"I am the little ~~wod~~ wóodlark.	Either left either right　8b
		Anywhere in the súnlight.　9c
4e	tiny a trickle of	Well, after all! Ah but hark--　10d
ˣ	So ~~dainty, a, darling a,~~ sóng-strain	"I am the little wóodlark.　11c

is
16　Today the sky ~~was~~ two and two
17a　With strokes of white and strains of [bol] blue
　　　　　　　　　　and　　　　the
17b　With white strokes ∧ strains of ∧blue

14　Round a ring, around a ring
15　And while I sail (must listen) I sing

12b　The skylark is my cousin and he
13　Is known to men more than me

<u>Plate 270</u>　　<u>OET No. 104 - The Woodlark</u>　<u>MS. 1</u>

　　<u>H.ii.49 verso</u> -- Autograph draft, lines 1 to 17. The following transcript reproduces only the main features of the MS. In the top line the year is added in pencil. <u>Deletion lines</u> have been added only in special cases. <u>Mended letters</u> include:　2 W → O　4a W → Such [not a stress]　6a bu → bough　comma mended to caret in 17b.

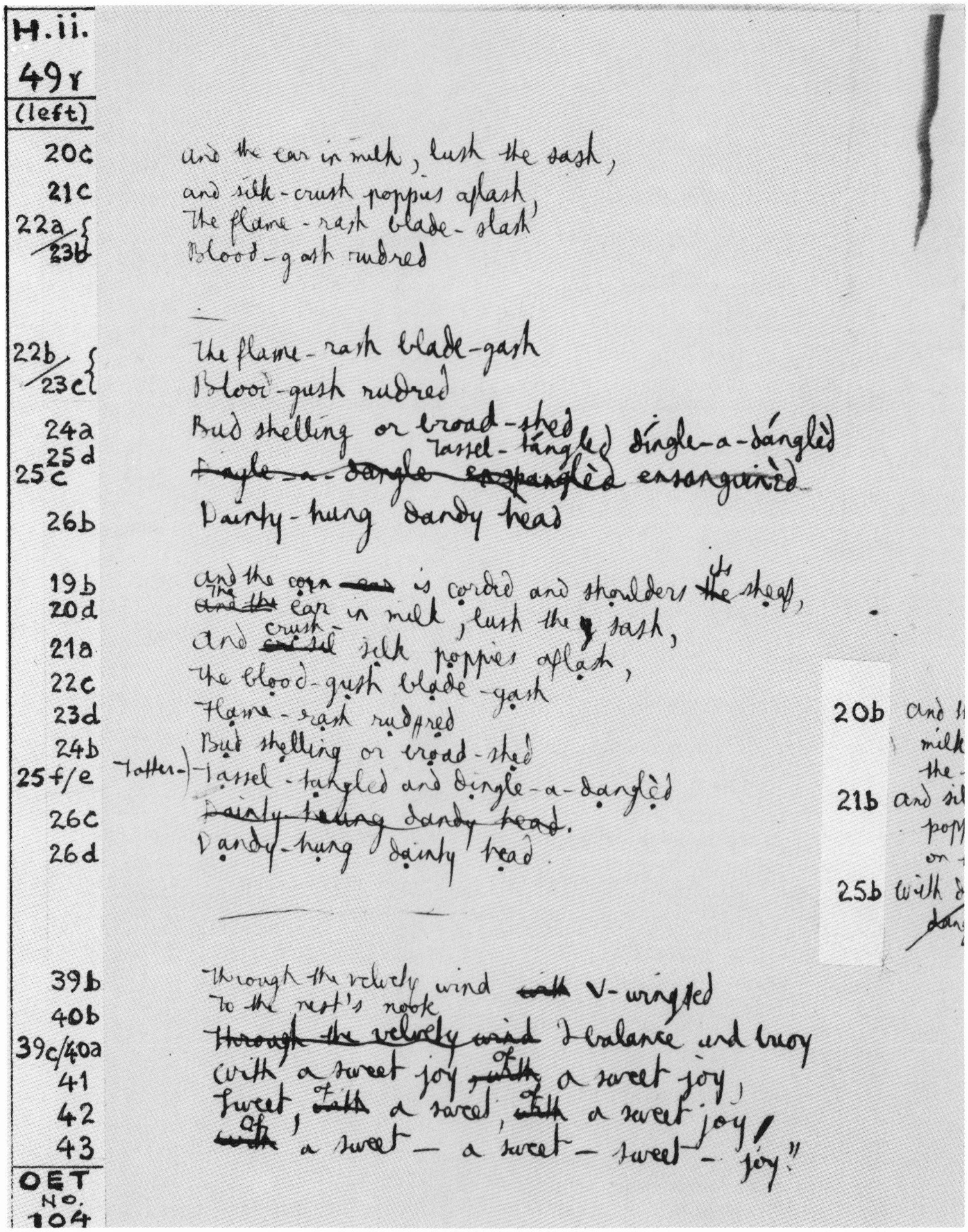

H.ii.
49ʳ
(left)

20c   And the ear in milk, lush the sash,
21c   and silk-crush poppies aplash,
22a   The flame-rash blade-slash
23b   Blood-gash rudred

22b   The flame-rash blade-gash
23c   Blood-gush rudred
24a   Bud shelling or broad-shed
25d   Tassel-tangled dingle-a-dangled
25c   Tagle-a-dangle enspangled ensanguined
26b   Dainty-hung dandy head

19b   And the corn-ear is cordid and shoulders the sheaf,
20d   And the ear in milk; lush the y sash,
21a   And crush-silk poppies aplash,
22c   the blood-gush blade-gash
23d   Flame-rash rud/red
24b   Bud shelling or broad-shed
25f/e   Tatter-)Tassel-tangled and dingle-a-dangled
26c   Dainty-taung dandy head.
26d   Dandy-hung dainty head.

39b   Through the velvety wind with V-winged
40b   To the nest's nook
39c/40a   Through the velvety wind I balance and buoy
41   with a sweet joy with a sweet joy,
42   sweet, with a sweet, with a sweet joy!
43   with a sweet — a sweet — sweet — joy!"

20b   And t
    milk
    the-
21b   and si
    pop
    on
25b   with
    dan

OET
NO.
104

Plate 271   OET No. 104 - The Woodlark cont.

H.ii.49r (left half of double sheet). Deletions include: 25c   Dingle-a-dangle enspanglèd ensanguinèd [last word del. in pencil]   19b   ear   the   20d   And the   g[ash? cf.22b]   21a   cri[mson?] sil[k]   23d   [hyphen in] rud/red   26c   Dainty--h[¢?]ung dandy head.   39b   with...wings   39c Through the velvety wind   41   , with   42 with...with [and final comma]   43   With.

Note on the right edge of this half sheet the beginnings of lines 20b, 21b and 25b, shown in full in the right half, Plate 271a. On the use of a dot below the vowel of a stressed syllable to show the rhythm see Introduction.

	H.ii.
49	49r
	(right)

when the cry within

Says Go on then I go on
till the longing is less and the good gone | 33
34
35

but down drop, if it says Stop,
to the all-a-leaf of the treetop
and after that off the bough | 36
37
38

I am

I am so very, o so very glad
That I do think there is not to be had | 31
32

20b	And the ear in	the blue ~~no~~ wheat-acre is underneath	18
	milk lush	And the braided ears breaks out of the sheaf,	19a
	the sash,	fall the ears trim the sash,	20a
		and crush-silk poppies are on the flash,	21a
21b	and silk-crush	and dingle dangle, the rudred	25a/23a
	poppies are	Dandy-hung dainty head	26a
	on the flash,		
25b	with dingle dan		
	dangle etc		

and down   the furrow dry
~~the~~ Sun spurge and ~~the~~ oxeye
{ and ~~but~~ lace-out lightly
{ Foam-tuft fumitory
{ And lace-~~leaf~~ ~~lovely~~ leaved lovely
{ Foam-tuft fumitory | 27
28
29a
30a
29b
30b

	OET
	NO.
	104

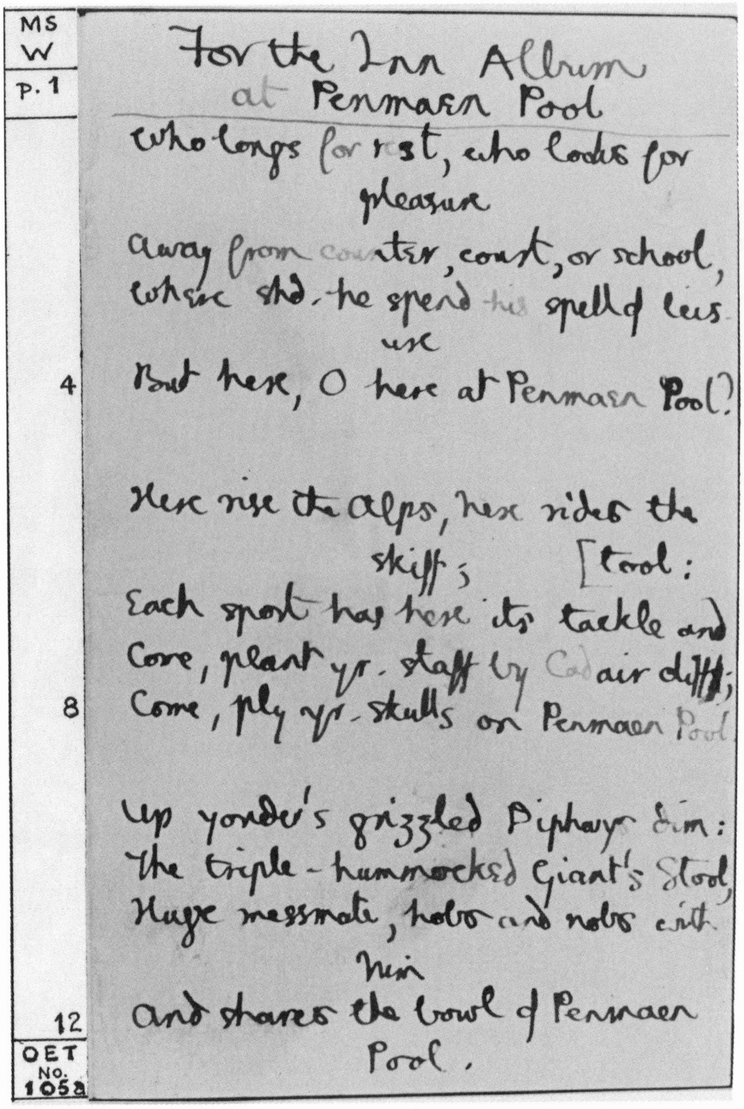

MS. W
P.1

For the Inn Album
at Penmaen Pool
Who longs for rest, who looks for
pleasure
Away from counter, court, or school,
where shd. he spend his spell of leisure
4 But here, O here at Penmaen Pool?

Here rise the Alps, here rides the
skiff;   [tool:
Each sport has here its tackle and
Come, plant yr. staff by Cadair cliff;
8 Come, ply yr. skulls on Penmaen Pool

Up yonder's grizzled Diphwys dim:
The triple-hummocked Giant's Stool,
Huge messmate, hobs and nobs with
him
12 And shares the bowl of Penmaen
Pool.

OET
No.
105a

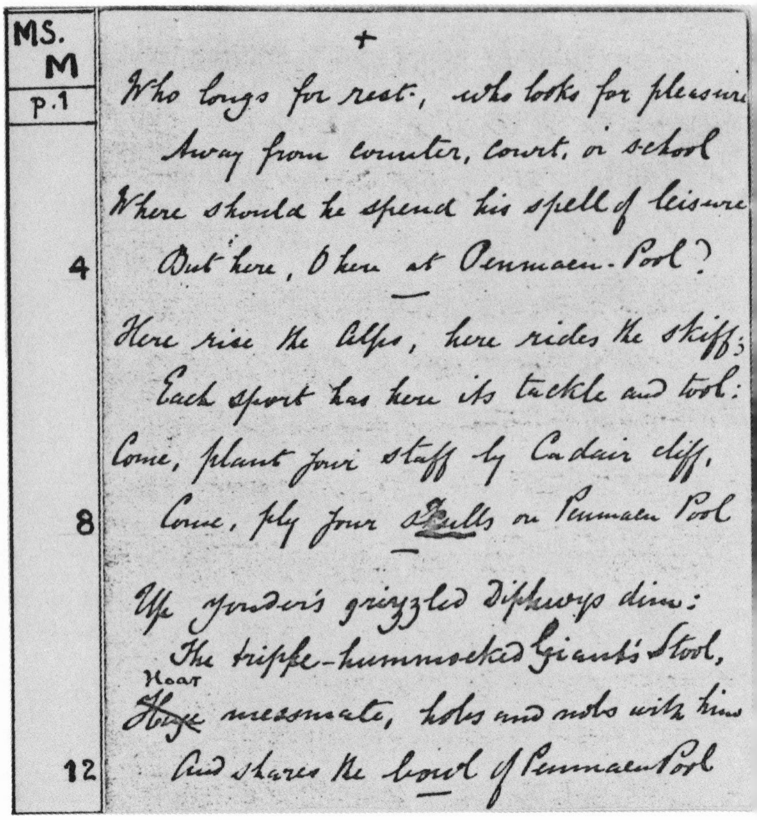

MS.
M
P.1

+

Who longs for rest, who looks for pleasure
Away from counter, court, or school
Where should he spend his spell of leisure
4 But here, O here at Penmaen-Pool?

Here rise the Alps, here rides the skiff;
Each sport has here its tackle and tool:
Come, plant your staff by Cadair cliff,
8 Come, ply your skulls on Penmaen Pool

Up yonder's grizzled Diphwys dim:
The triple-hummocked Giant's Stool.
Hoar
Huge messmate, hobs and nobs with him
12 And shares the bowl of Penmaen Pool

Plates 272,274,276 (left columns)   OET No. 105(a) - Penmaen Pool   (early version)

    MS. W pp.1-4--Autograph faircopy of an early version, sent to his family, with a "false rhyme" of which his father complained ("renewal/Pool", 34/36). Note how he allowed his pen to run almost dry every half-dozen words. In 6 "its" does not end with an illogical s-apostrophe; the extra stroke is part of the "s", more plainly seen in 1,12,14,26, etc.. Slips corrected include: 7 cliffs   14 tranquil   20 brighter   34 You'll's Date Aig. Other deletions: 17 The 31 over   32 High 33 And.   This autograph is now in the College of the Holy Cross, Worcester, Massachusetts.

Plates 272,274,276 (right columns)   OET No. 105(a) - Penmaen Pool   (early version)

    MS. M--Transcript of MS. W in an unknown hand, corrected by GMH: he changed "Huge" to "Hoar" (11) and "peace" to "ease" (37). He added a unique version of 33-36 as an alternative at the end, to eliminate the "false rhyme" to which his father objected. For the cross at the top of the MS cf. the Pooley version of "Spring" (OET No. 117).   MS. M is now in CH.

PLATE 273. OET 105(a). *Penmaen Pool* • 81

A.
P.101

Who longs for rest, who looks for pleasure
Away from counter, court or school
Where should he spend his spell of leisure
But here, O here at Penmän Pool?

4

Here rise the Alps, here rides the skiff:
Each sport has here its tackle & tool:
Come plant your staff by Cadair cliff:
Come ply your skulls on Penmaen Pool.

8

Up yonder's grizzled Dyphwys dim:
The triple-hummocked Giants-Stool,
Hoar messmate, hobs & nobs with him
And halves the bowl of Penmaen Pool.

12

3.   Spend where should such his lease of leisure
5.   To dare the Alp, to drive the skiff
6.   None here need want for tackle or tool:
9   What's yonder? Grizzled Dyphwys dim:
12   To halve. etc.

OET
No.
105a

Plates 273,275,277   OET No. 105(a) - Penmaen Pool   (early version)

A.pp.101-104.   Transcript in ink by RB of a version for which there is no autograph, with footnote variants, some from another missing version. In 4 a wavy ink line connects "here" with "Here" (5); note also "Penmän". After 21-23 in the footnote RB's pencil adds "this correct-/ion of above". The second "darksome" (32) is outlined in pencil with a footnote "danksome Keating" [i.e., Fr. Joseph Keating, quoting Fr. Bacon's transcript, MS. N]. This copy is a fine example of RB's penmanship.

MS.W cont. P.2

And this bright landscape under
survey   [rule
at tranquil times by nature's
To all repeated topsyturvy
In frank, in fairy Penmaen Pool.

16

And Charles's Wain, the wondrous
seven,   [white wool,
And sheep-flock clouds like soft
For all they shine so, high in heaven
Shew brighter shaken in Penmaen
Pool.

20

Here crips the Mawddach, whether
throtlled   [full
By tides that thrill her channel
Or mazy sandbanks, crisped and
wattled,   [Pool.
Waylay her steps from Penmaen

24

OET No. 105a

MS.M P.1 cont.

And this bright landscape under survey
At tranquil times by nature's rule
Is all repeated topsyturvy
In frank, in fairy Penmaen Pool

16

And Charlie's wain, the wondrous seven,
And sheep-flock clouds like soft, white
wool,
For all they shine so, high in heaven,
Shew brighter shaken in Penmaen Pool

20

Here trips the Mawddach, whether throttled,
By tides that thrill her channel full
Or mazy sandbanks, crisped & wattled,
Waylay her steps from Penmaen Pool

24

A.
p.102

102

And this bright landscape under survey
  At tranquil turns by nature's rule
Is all repeated topsyturvy —
  In frank, in fairy Penmaen Pool.

16

And Charles' Wain, the wondrous seven,
  And sheep-flock clouds like worlds of wool
For all they shine so high in heaven,
  Show brighter shaken in Penmaen Pool.

20

Here trips the Mawddach whether throttled
  When tides have thrilled her channel full,
Or crisping sandbanks water-wattled
  Waylay her, down from Penmaen Pool.

24

13 . And all the . etc .
15 Rides repeated topsy-turvy.
21. What stream trips her ? The Mawddack throttled
       At teeming flood that thrills her full
     By mazy sands all water-wattled   } this
                                          corrects

13
15
21
22
23

OET
No.
105a

MS.W cont.
p.3

But what's to see in stormy weath- [cool?
er,
When rains fall grey and gales blow
Why, water-roundels looped together
28 That lace the face of Penmaen Pool.

And even in weariest wintry hours
Of New Year's month or surly Yule
Tuft *after* tuft of snow-crest towers
32 *Tall* over darksome Penmaen
Pool.

while
if you're kept perforce at home.
You'll call (and that with fond
renewal) [foam
For ale that mantles like the
36 That purls an oar in Penmaen Pool.

Then come who care for peace or
pleasure
Away from counter, court, or school
and spend some measure of yr. treasure

p.4
40 To taste the treats of Penmaen
Pool.
Aug. 1876.

OET
No.
105a

But what's to see in stormy weather
When rains fall grey, and gales blow cool?
Why, water-roundels looped together
28 That lace the face of Penmaen Pool

And even in weariest wintry hours
Of New Year's month, or surly Yule
Tuft after Tuft of snow-crest towers
32 Tall over darksome Penmaen Pool

× While if you are kept perforce at home
You'll call, and that with fond renewal
For ale that mantles like the foam
That purls an oar in Penmaen Pool
36

Then come who care for peace or pleasure [case]
Away from counter, court, or school
And spend some measure of your treasure
40 To taste the treats of Penmaen Pool

Aug /76

× But if you're bound perforce at home 33
There's peace and pastime here and—who'll
But praise it?—ale like goldy foam
That purls an oar in Penmaen Pool 36

PLATE 277. OET 105(a). *Penmaen Pool* • 85

A.
p.103

But what's to see in stormy weather
     When grey showers gather & gusts are cool?
Why, raindrop-roundels heaped together
     That lace the face of Penmaen Pool.

28

Then even in weariest wintry hour
     Of New Year's month or surly Yule
Snow-charges, tuft above tuft tower
     From darksome, darksome Penmaen Pool.

32

And ever, if hardest bound at home
     You've parlour-pastime here, and—who'll
But praise it?—ale like goldy foam
     That frocks an oar in Penmaen Pool.

36

31

31. Furred snows, charged tuft above tuft, tower
      Pick { over
              up from darksome Penmaen Pool.

32

                    Darksome. Keats

p.104

---

p.104

Then come who pine for ease or pleasure
     Away from counter, court, or school,
Spend here your measure of time & treasure
     And taste the treats of Penmaen Pool.

40

                    —

                              August 1876

OET
No.
105a

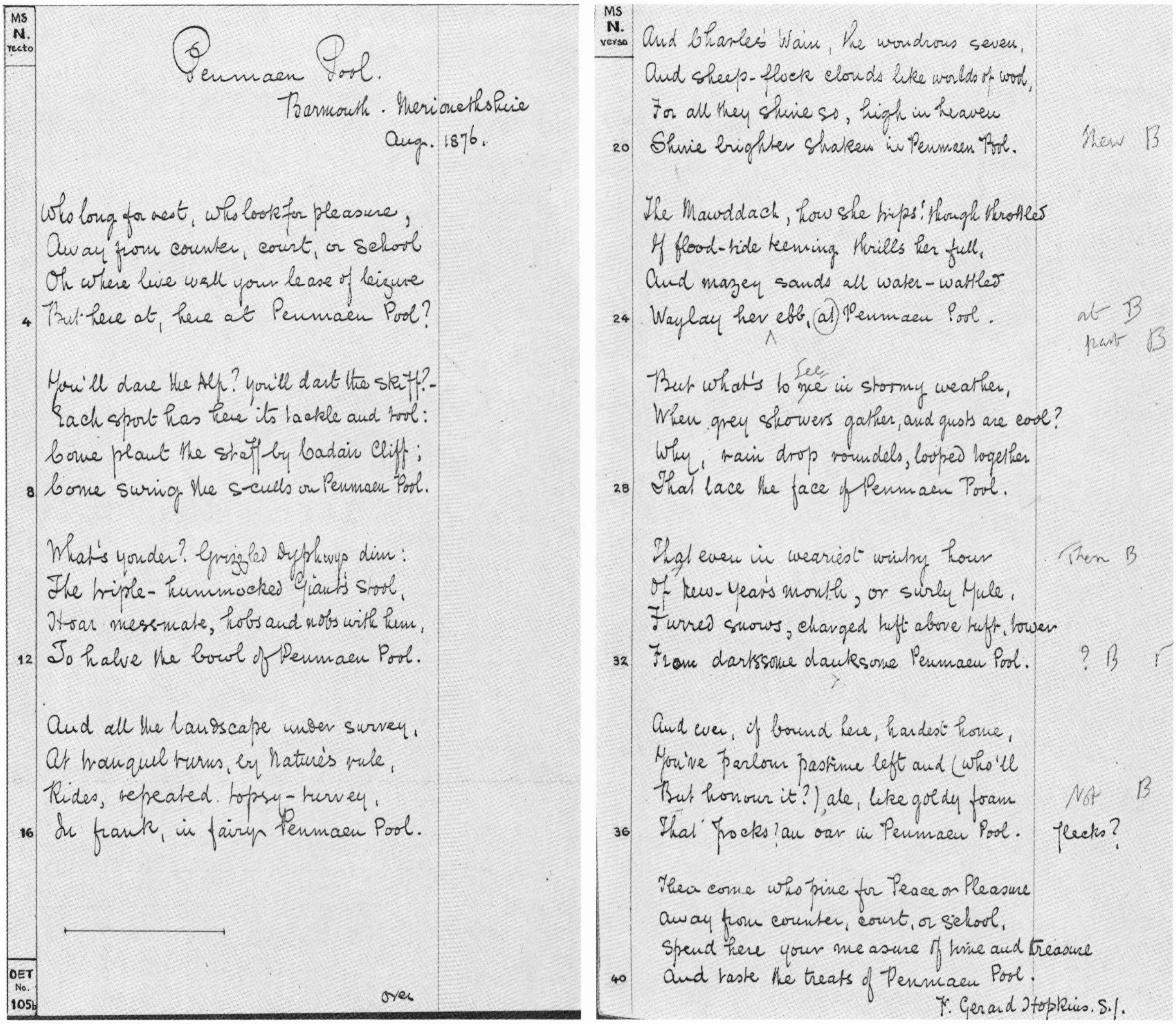

Penmaen Pool.
Barmouth. Merionethshire
Aug. 1876.

Who long for rest, who look for pleasure,
Away from counter, court, or school
Oh where live well your lease of leisure
4   But here at, here at Penmaen Pool?

You'll dare the Alp? you'll dart the skiff?—
Each sport has here its tackle and tool:
Come plant the staff by Cadair Cliff;
8   Come swing the sculls on Penmaen Pool.

What's yonder? Grizzled Dyphwys dim:
The triple-hummocked Giant's stool,
Hoar mess-mate, hobs and nobs with him,
12   To halve the bowl of Penmaen Pool.

And all the landscape under survey,
At tranquil turns, by Nature's rule,
Rides, repeated topsy-turvey,
16   In frank, in fairy Penmaen Pool.

over

And Charles's Wain, the wondrous seven,
And sheep-flock clouds like worlds of wool,
For all they shine so, high in heaven
20   Shine brighter shaken in Penmaen Pool.   Shew B

The Mawddach, how she trips! though throttles
Of flood-tide teeming thrills her full,
And mazey sands all water-wattled
24   Waylay her ebb, (at) Penmaen Pool.   at B
                                              past B

But what's to me in stormy weather,
When grey showers gather, and gusts are cool?
Why, rain drop roundels, looped together
28   That lace the face of Penmaen Pool.

That even in weariest wintry hour   Then B
Of New-Year's month, or surly Yule,
Furred snows, charged tuft above tuft, tower
32   From darksome danksome Penmaen Pool.   ? B

And ever, if bound here, hardest home,
You've parlour pastime left and (who'll
But honour it?) ale, like goldy foam
36   That frocks! an oar in Penmaen Pool.   Not B
                                                flecks?

Then come who pine for Peace or Pleasure
Away from counter, court, or school.
Spend here your measure of time and treasure
40   And taste the treats of Penmaen Pool.
                              F. Gerard Hopkins. S.J.

Plate 278   OET No. 105(b) - Penmaen Pool   (later version)

MS. N--Transcript by Fr. Francis Bacon, SJ, of a version close to B. In 36 Bacon
queries "frocks", and in the margin writes "flecks?". RB's editorial pencil (prob. 1918) records
N's departures from B: "Shine" for "Shew" (20); "her ebb, at Penmaen Pool" for "her at ebb,
past Penmaen Pool" (24); "me" for "See" (25); "That" for "Then" (29); "danksome" queried and
rejected (32); "But" for "Not" (35). The MS. is now at CH.

PLATE 279. OET 105(a). *Penmaen Pool* • 87

B.
43r

13

Penmaen Pool :

for the Visitors' Book at the Inn

Who long for rest, who look for leisure
Away from counter, court, or school
O where live well your lease of leisure
4 But here at, here at Penmaen Pool?

You'll dare the Alp? you'll dart the
     skiff? — [tool :
Each sport has here its tackle and
               the
Come, plant your staff by Cadair cliff;
               the
Come, swing your skulls on Penmaen
8   Pool.

What's yonder? — Grizzled Dyphwys dim:
                                 x
The triple-hummocked giant's stool,
Hoar messmate, hobs and nobs with him
12 To halve the bowl of Penmaen Pool.

                              sur
And all the landscape under survey,
At tranquil turns, by nature's rule,
Rides repeated topsyturvy
16 In frank, in fairy Penmaen Pool.

And Charles's Wain, the wondrous seven,
And sheep-flock clouds like worlds of
                              wool,
For all they shine so, high in heaven,
20 Shew brighter shaken in Penmaen
               Pool.

x Cadair Idris

The Mawddach, how she trips! though
                    throttled
If floodtide teeming thrills her full,
And mazy sands all water-wattled
Waylay her at ebb, past Penmaen Pool. 24

But what's to see in stormy weather,
When grey showers gather and gusts
               are cool? —
Why, raindrop-roundels looped together
That lace the face of Penmaen Pool. 28

Then even in weariest wintry hour
Of new year's month or surly Yule
Furred snows, charged tuft above tuft,
               tower
From darksome darksome Penmaen Pool. 32

               bound here
And ever, if hardest bound home,
You've parlour-pastime left and (who'll
Not honour it?) ale like goldy foam
That frocks an oar in Penmaen Pool. 36

Then come who pine for peace or pleasure
Away from counter, court, or school,
Spend here your measure of time and
               treasure
And taste the treats of Penmaen Pool. 40

          Barmouth, Merionethshire.
          Aug. 1876

OET
No.
105b

Plate 279   OET No. 105(b) - Penmaen Pool   (final version)

B.43r.--Autograph faircopy of final version, pasted into album B. Revisions in 7,8,33,
date. Slips mended in 13 ("ser"), 37 "pire".

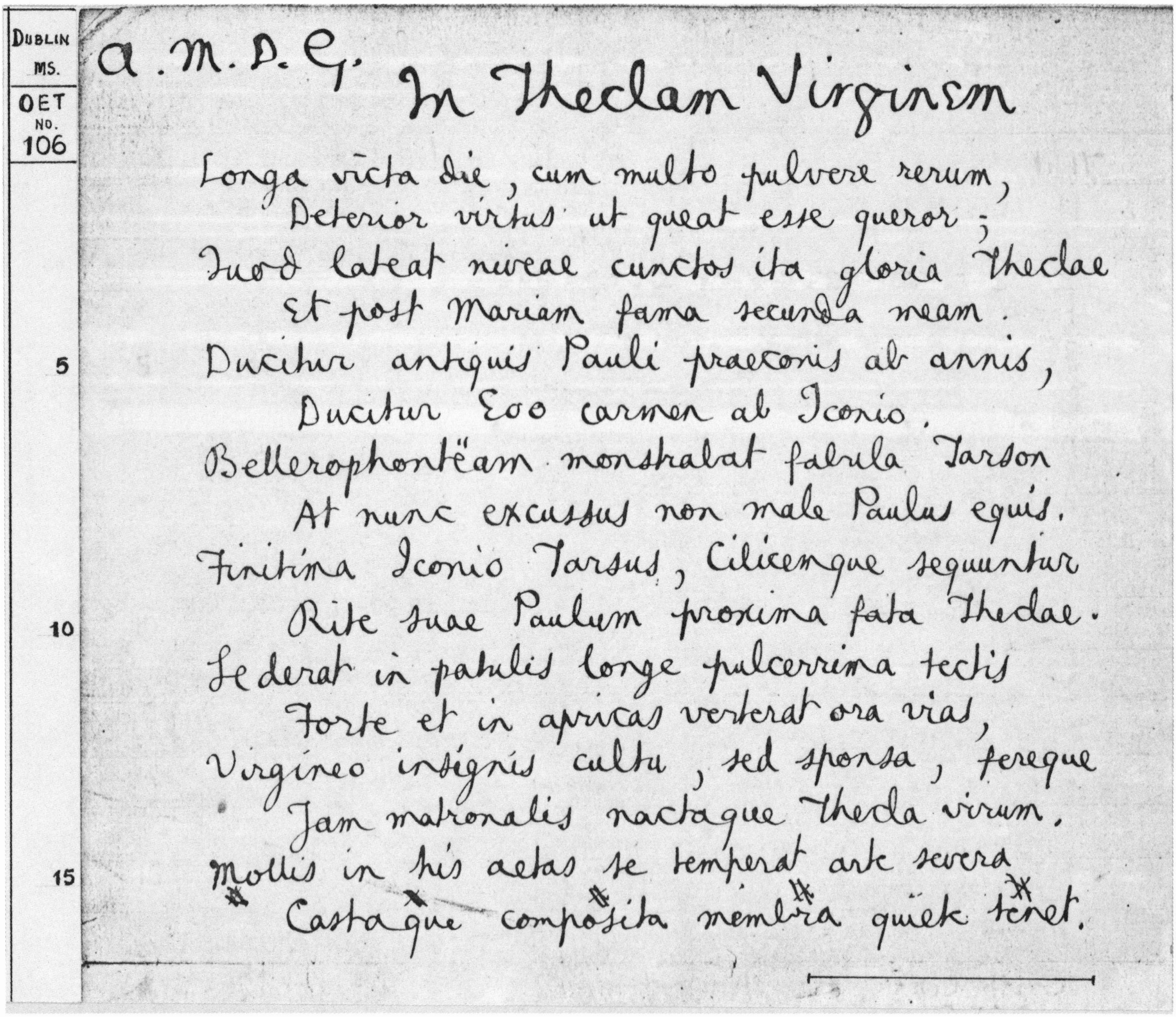

A. M. D. G.   In Theclam Virginem

Longa victa die, cum multo pulvere rerum,
  Deterior virtus ut queat esse queror;
Quod lateat niveae cunctos ita gloria Theclae
  Et post Mariam fama secunda meam.
Ducitur antiquis Pauli praeconis ab annis,
  Ducitur Eoo carmen ab Iconio.
Bellerophontëam monstrabat fabula Tarson
  At nunc excussus non male Paulus equis.
Finitima Iconio Tarsus, Cilicemque sequuntur
  Rite suae Paulum proxima fata Theclae.
Sederat in patulis longe pulcerrima tectis
  Forte et in apricas verterat ora vias,
Virgineo insignis cultu, sed sponsa, fereque
  Jam matronalis nactaque Thecla virum.
Mollis in his aetas se temperat arte severa
  Castaque composita membra quiete tenet.

Plate 280   OET No. 106: In Theclam Virginem

    Sole MS (Society of Jesus, Dublin), autograph faircopy in large writing designed to be displayed at a festival. It is a loose translation of the first twenty lines of No. 52, "St. Thecla". The English version was composed about 1864-65, but it was copied out around 1876 on a page of a double sheet to face this incomplete Latin version (see <u>Facsimiles i</u>, Plate 155). There are no revisions or corrections (a rare achievement for Hopkins), except for the deleted asterisks after 15, where he had apparently intended to end, in the middle of a couplet.

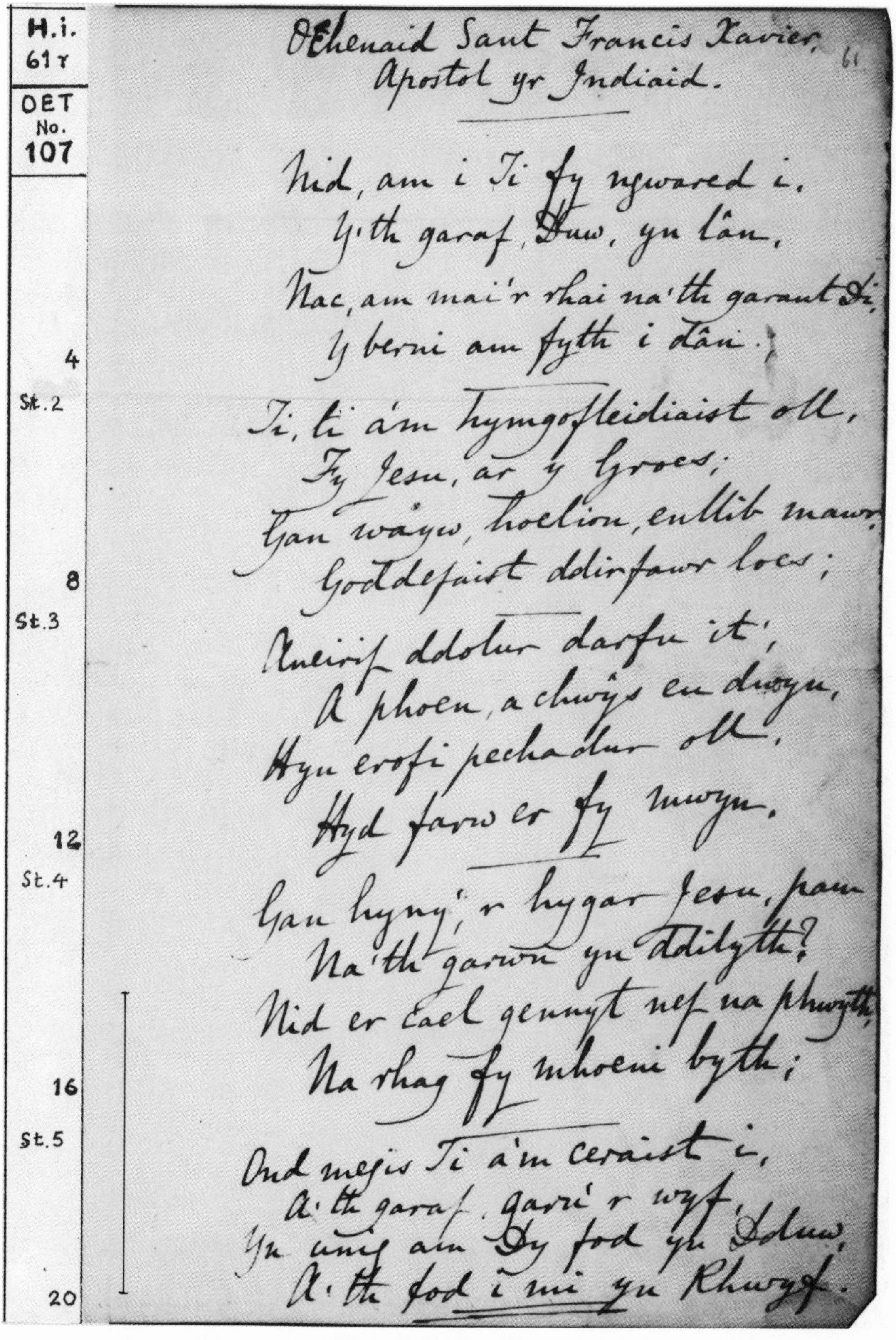

PLATE 281. OET 107. Ochenaid Sant Francis Xavier • 89

H.i.
61 r

OET
No.
107

4
St.2

8
St.3

12
St.4

16
St.5

20

Ochenaid Sant Francis Xavier,
Apostol yr Indiaid.

61

Nid, am i Ti fy ngwared i.
Y'th garaf, Duw, yn lân.
Nac, am mai'r rhai na'th garant Di,
Y berni am fyth i dân.

Ti, ti a'm hymgofleidiaist oll,
Fy Iesu, ar y Groes;
Gan waywer, hoelion, enllib mawr,
Goddefaist ddirfawr loes;

Aneirif ddolur darfu it,
A phoen, a chwys en dwyn,
Hyn erofi pechadur oll,
Hyd farw er fy mwyn.

Gan hyny'r hygar Iesu, paun
Na'th garwn yn ddilyth?
Nid er cael gennyt nef na phwyth,
Na rhag fy mhoeni byth;

Ond megis Ti a'm ceraist i,
A'th garaf, garu'r wyf,
Yn unig am Dy fod yn Dduw,
A'th fod i mi yn Rhwyf.

<u>Plate 281</u>   <u>OET No. 107: Ochenaid Sant Francis Xavier</u>

<u>H.i.61r</u> -- Transcript in an unknown hand of a translation into Welsh, attributed to Hopkins, of "O Deus, ego amo te" -- a Latin hymn long thought to be by St. Francis Xavier. Identification of the handwriting might lead to more certain ascription.

In the title, the second letter was a capital mended to a small "c". St. 1 ends with a smudged semicolon; the period formerly printed may be a mark on the original page (cf. one above the "n" just before it): no other periods or dots over the letter "i" resemble it. In 9, "it" is followed by an apostrophe and comma. The text provided by W.H. Gardner to Dr. Thomas Parry and Sir Idris Bell was defective: the punctuation errors they detected in lines 7 and 9 (<u>Poems</u>, 4th edn., p.325) are not in the MS.

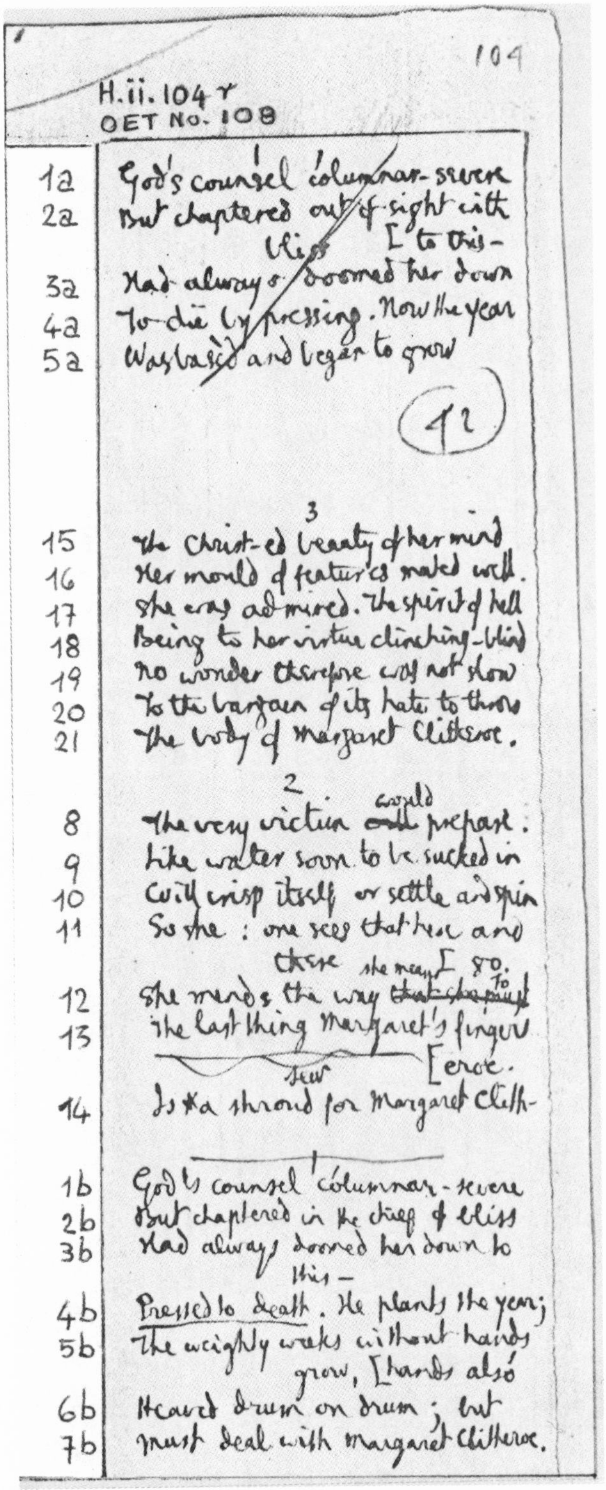

H.ii.104r
OET No. 108

1a God's counsel cólumnar-severe
2a But chaptered out of sight with
         bliss   [to this –
3a Had always / doomed her down
4a To die by pressing. Now the year
5a Was based and began to grow

(42)

3
15 The Christ-ed beauty of her mind
16 Her mould of features maked well.
17 She was admired. The spirit of hell
18 Being to her virtue clinching-blind
19 No wonder therefore was not slow
20 To the bargain of its hate to throw
21 The body of Margaret Clitheroe.

2
       would
8 The very victim ~~will~~ prepare:
9 Like water soon to be sucked in
10 Will crisp itself or settle and spin
11 So she : one sees that here and
        there she means I so.
              To
12 She mends the way ~~that she may~~
13 The last thing Margaret's finger
         sew   [eroe.
14 Is it a shroud for Margaret Clith-

1b God's counsel cólumnar-severe
2b But chaptered in the chief of bliss
3b Had always doomed her down to
        this –
4b Pressed to death. He plants the year;
5b The weighty weks without hands
          grow, [hands also
6b Heaved drum on drum ; but
7b must deal with Margaret Clitheroe.

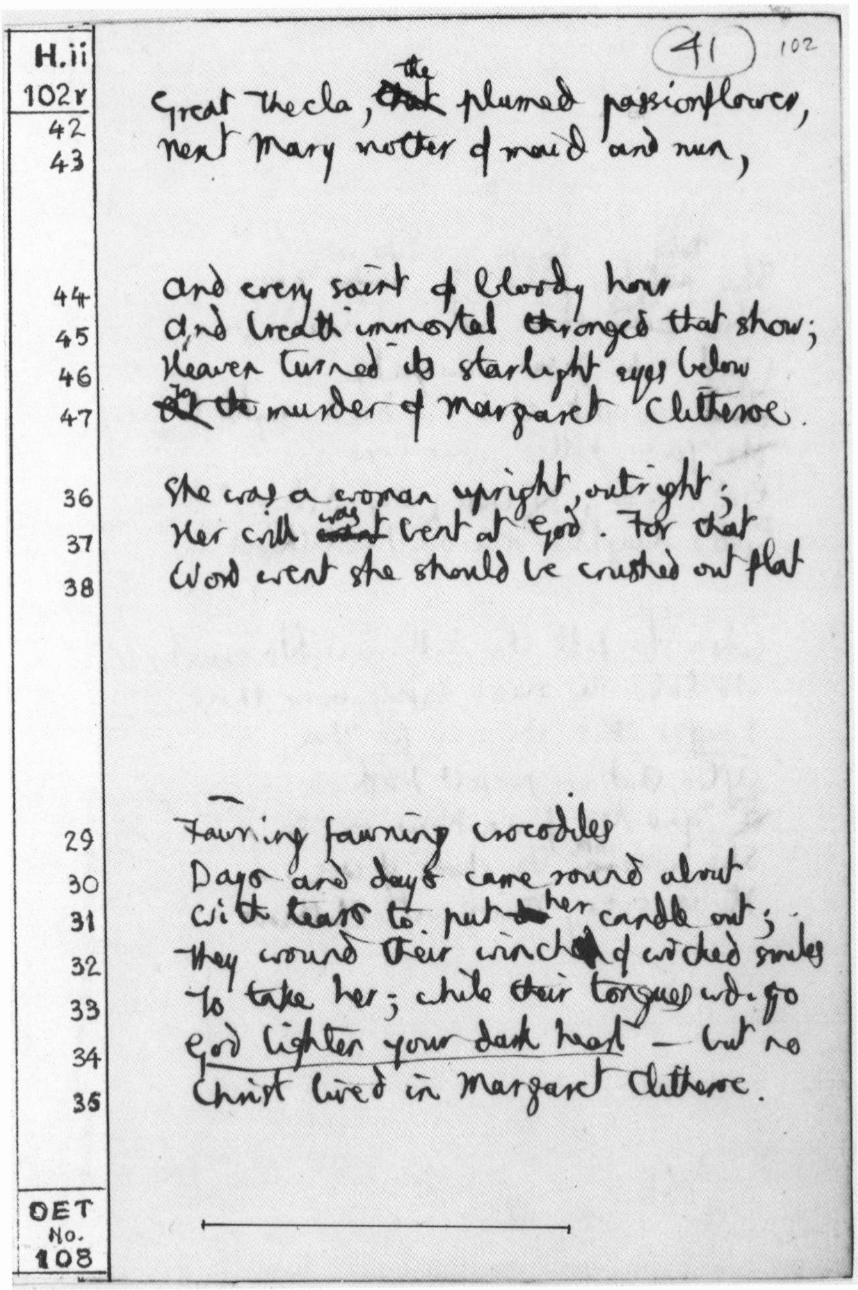

H.ii
102r

(41) 102

            the
42 Great Thecla, ~~that~~ plumed passionflower,
43 next Mary mother of maid and nun,

44 And every saint of bloody hour
45 And breath immortal thronged that show;
46 Heaven turned its starlight eyes below
47 ~~At the~~ to murder of Margaret Clitheroe.

36 She was a woman upright, outright;
          was
37 Her will ~~went~~ bent at God. For that
38 Word went she should be crushed out flat

29 Fawning fawning crocodiles
30 Days and days came round about
31 With tears to put her candle out;
32 They wound their winched wicked smiles
33 To take her; while their tongues wd. go
34 God lighten your dark heart — but no
35 Christ lived in Margaret Clitheroe.

OET No. 108

OET No. 108   [Margaret Clitheroe]

Rough autograph drafts in ink, unfinished, with only the first 3 stanzas arranged in logical sequence.

Plate 282 - MS. 1

[left] H.ii.104r. A separate strip of paper, its first st. (numbered "1"--not a stress mark on "counsel") is crossed through in ink. Deletions include: 8 will   12 that she must rev. to she means to.   After writing 12 GMH prob. drew a line across for the revision of st. 1, leaving insufficient room for 13 and 14.

[right] H.ii.102r. The poem continues on three sides of folded note-paper, of which this is the first. Deletions include: 42 that   47 At   37 went [confusion with the line below, mended to "wa"]   32 winchéd.

PLATE 283. OET 108. *[Margaret Clitheroe]* • 91

H.ii. 102v

48 The ⟨put⟩ her ⟨palms⟩ hands to, ⟨as for⟩ like in prayer;
49 They ⟨drew them⟩ out and laid them wide
50 (just like Jesus crucified);
51 ⟨and⟩ they brought their hundredweights to bear/.
52 ⟨The⟩ Jews killed Jesus long ago
53 God's son; & these (they did not know)
54 God's daughter Margaret Clitheroe.

55 When she felt the kill-weights crush
56 She told His name times-over three;
57 I suffer this she said for thee.
58 After that in perfect hush
59 for a quarter of an hour or so
60 She was with the choke of woe. —
61 It is over, Margaret Clitheroe.

H.ii. 103v

22 She caught the crying of those Three,
23 The Immortals of the ⟨age-old⟩ eternal a ring,
24 The Utterer, Uttered, Uttering,
25 and witness in her place would she.
26 She not considered whether or no
27 She pleased the Queen and Council. So
28 To the death with Margaret Clitheroe!

39 Within her womb the child was quick.
40 Small matter of that then! let him smother
41 and creak in ruins of his mother

Plate 283   OET No. 108   [Margaret Clitheroe] cont. MS. 2.

H.ii.102v: 48,49 orig. [The mended to] She put her palms to, as for prayer;/They drew [the black mark before wide is a tear.]   51 bear/   53 so   60 in

103v--Deletions: 23 age-old R   28 To mended from L   39 within orig. Th

OET No. 109   "Hope holds to Christ the mind's own mirror out". The single facsimile of this poem, which cannot be exactly dated, was in the OET assigned to Plate 299, to permit pairs of plates to face each other in the intervening poems. The redesign, with extra plates, obscures the original reason.

OET No. 110   "Murphy gives sermons so fierce and hell-fiery"; no MS of this fragment, ascribed to Hopkins by Jesuit tradition, is known.

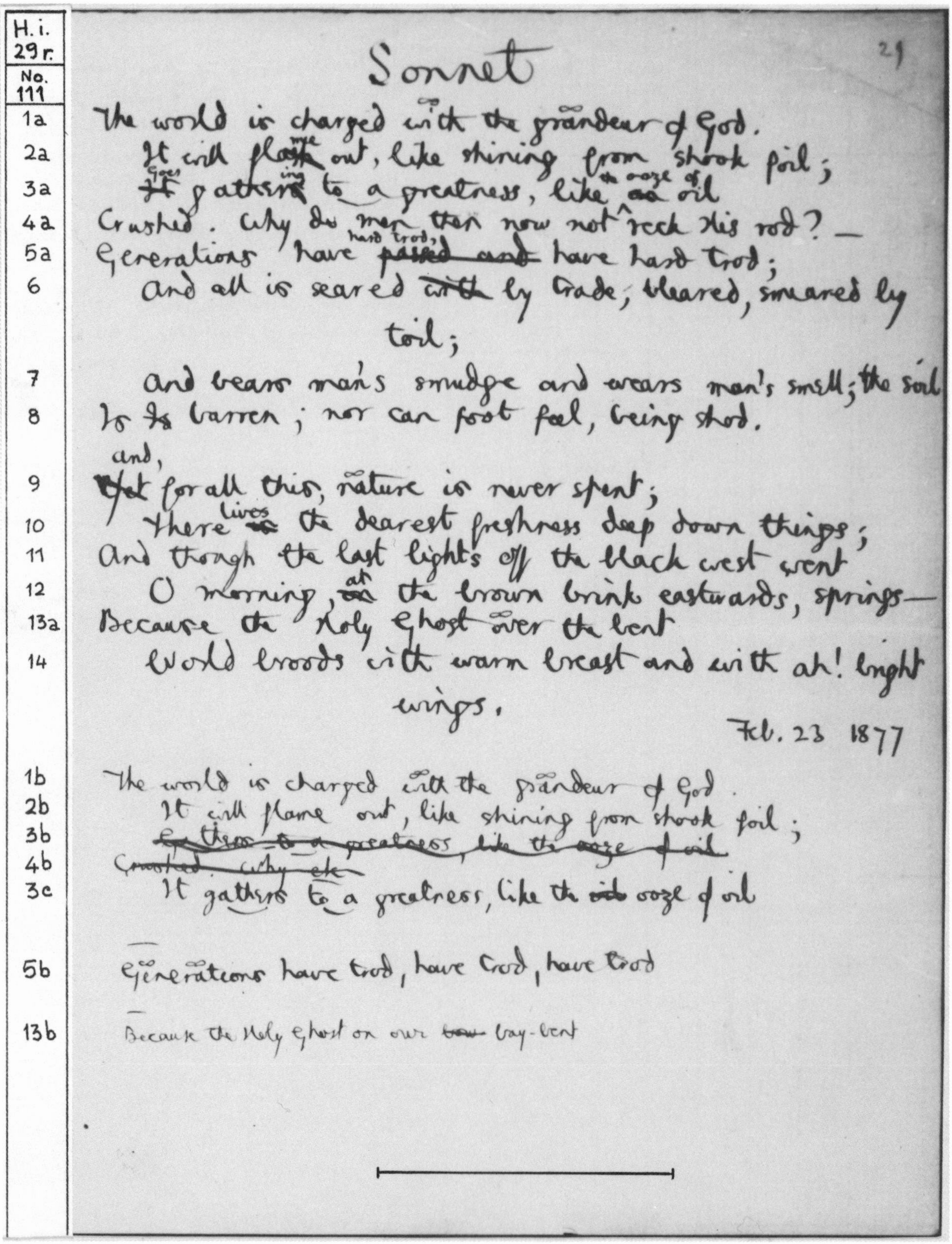

H.i. 29 r.	
No. 111	

Sonnet

1a The world is charged with the grandeur of God.

2a It will flash out, like shining from shook foil;

3a It gathers to a greatness, like the ooze of oil

4a Crushed. Why do men then now not reck his rod? —

5a Generations have passed and have hard trod;

6 And all is seared with ly trade; bleared, smeared ly

        toil;

7 And bears man's smudge and wears man's smell; the soil

8 Is is barren ; nor can foot feel, being shod.

    and,

9 Yet for all this, nature is never spent;

10 There lives the dearest freshness deep down things;

11 And though the last lights off the black west went

12 O morning, at the brown brink eastwards, springs—

13a Because the Holy Ghost over the bent

14 World broods with warm breast and with ah! bright

      wings.

                   Feb. 23 1877

1b The world is charged with the grandeur of God.

2b It will flame out, like shining from shook foil ;

3b ~~It gathers to a greatness, like the ooze of oil~~

4b ~~Crushed. Why etc~~

3c It gathers to a greatness, like the ooze of oil

5b Generations have trod, have trod, have trod

13b Because the Holy Ghost on our ~~bow~~ bay-bent

Plate 284   OET No. 111: God's Grandeur -- MS. 1 (H)

    H.i.29r -- Autograph faircopy, with revisions. Counterpoint signs on single syllables in 1a, b; 5b, 9, 13a (cf. L.i.43). Curves under words (in 3a, b, c) are slurs, not outrides--contrast H, F, and A[1] with A[2] and B. In 6 after "trade" a faint brown mark like the top of a semicolon seems erased. In 8 "Is" was del. and rewritten to correct the indentation. Some revisions: 2a flash rev. to flame   3a an oil rev. to the ooze of oil   10 is rev. to lives   12 on   13b bow-[bent] rev. to bay-bent.

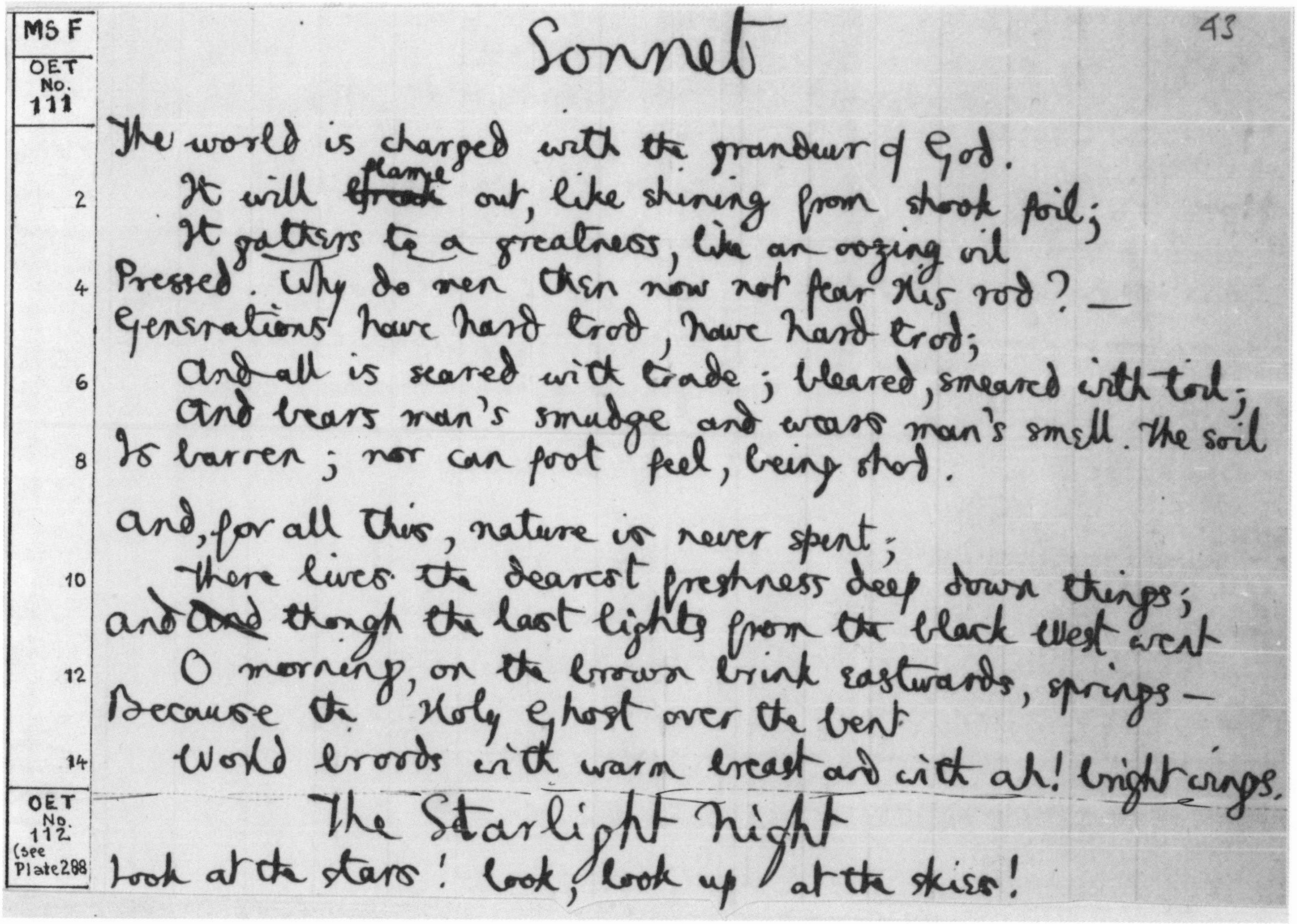

PLATE 285. OET 111. *God's Grandeur* • 93

MS F

OET NO. 111

43

Sonnet

The world is charged with the grandeur of God.
2   It will ~~break~~ flame out, like shining from shook foil;
     It gathers to a greatness, like an oozing oil
4 Pressed. Why do men then now not fear His rod? —
Generations have hard trod, have hard trod;
6   And all is seared with trade ; bleared, smeared with toil;
     And bears man's smudge and wears man's smell. the soil
8 Is barren ; nor can foot feel, being shod.

And, for all this, nature is never spent ;
10   There lives the dearest freshness deep down things ;
And ~~And~~ though the last lights from the black west went
12   O morning, on the brown brink eastwards, springs —
Because the Holy Ghost over the bent
14   World broods with warm breast and with ah! bright wings.

OET No. 112 (see Plate 288)

The Starlight Night

Look at the stars ! look, look up at the skies!

Plate 285   God's Grandeur -- MS. 2 (F)

     MS. F   (reproduced in L.iii. facing p.144, from GMH's Letters to his Family, Bodleian Lib., MS Eng. Letters, e.40, f.43). Autograph faircopy of Nos. 111 and 112, sent to his mother, for her birthday 3 March 1877: top portion only shown--see Plate 288 for bottom. Slurs (drawn below the line, where he later indicated outrides--see MS. 1) occur below "gathers" and "to a" (3). Deletions: break (2); And (11, rewritten to correct indenting). Note how the "e" in "the" is flattened to near invisibility in 13, etc.

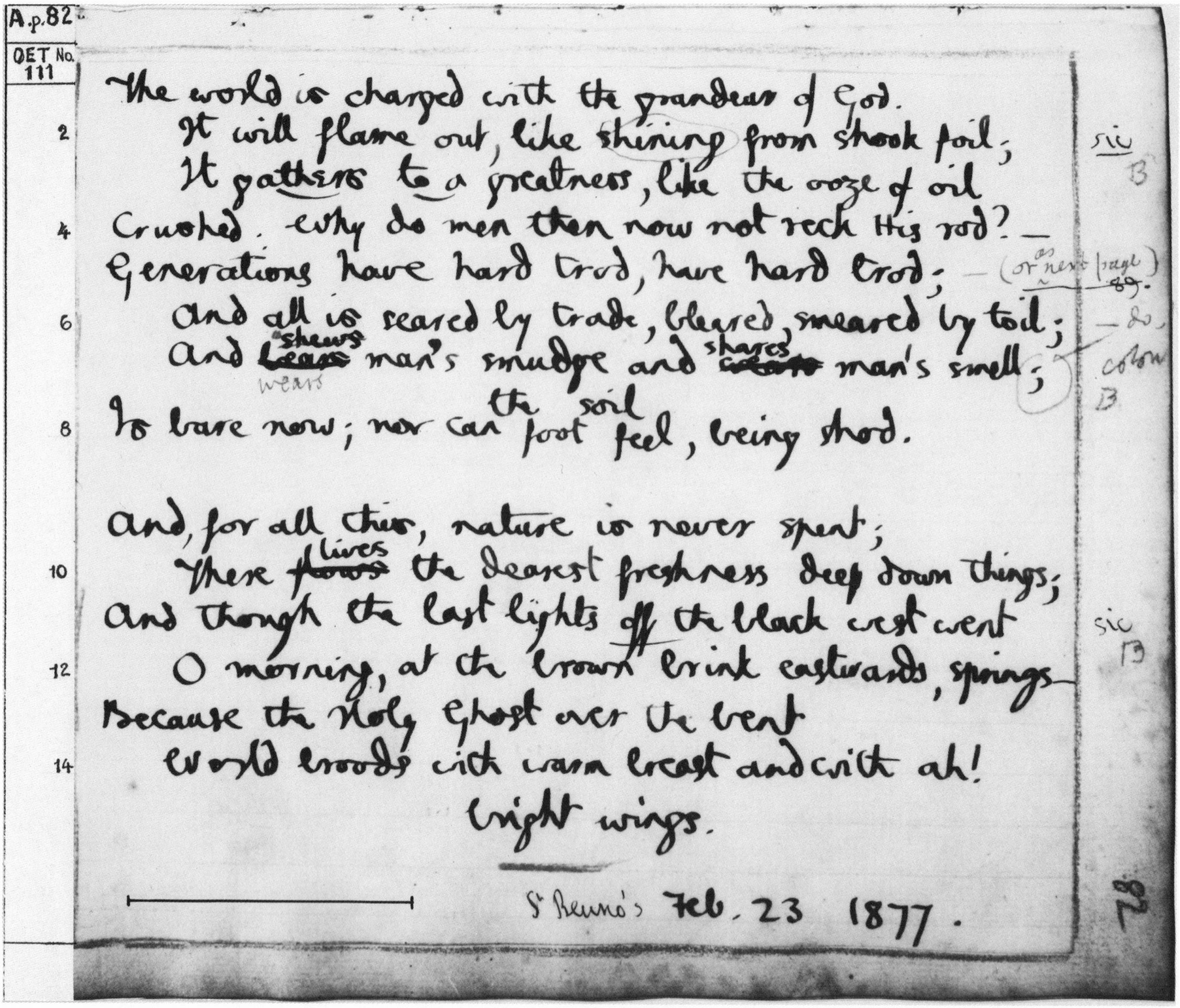

A.p.82

OET No. 111

2

4

6

8

10

12

14

The world is charged with the grandeur of God.
    It will flame out, like shining from shook foil;
    It gathers to a greatness, like the ooze of oil
Crushed. Why do men then now not reck his rod? —
Generations have hard trod, have hard trod;
    And all is seared by trade, bleared, smeared by toil;
    And wears man's smudge and shares man's smell;
Is bare now; nor can foot feel, being shod.

And, for all this, nature is never spent;
    There lives the dearest freshness deep down things;
And though the last lights off the black west went
    O morning, at the brown brink eastwards, springs
Because the Holy Ghost over the bent
    World broods with warm breast and with ah!
        bright wings.

St Beuno's Feb. 23 1877.

Plate 286   OET No. 111 : God's Grandeur -- MS. 3 (A¹)

[above] A.p.82 . -- Autograph faircopy, pasted in album A. Slurs are placed under words in 3 (see note on H).

GMH's revisions: 7 bears shews   wears shares   10 flows lives

RB's notes. (a) Red Ink (1884): 5 [after "trod"]--(or as next page) [i.e. A²] underlined in black [18] 89   6 [after "toil;"]--do [ditto]   7 cancels shews, replaces it below with wears. (b) Black Ink (1889): adds "St Beuno's" to the date   2 sic [i.e. "shining", outlined in pencil, is the reading to follow]   11 adds line under "off", sic in margin   (c) Pencil (1918?) notes that both readings marked "sic" are in B, and so is a colon to end 7.

Plate 287   OET No. 111: God's Grandeur -- MS. 4 (A²)

[opposite] A.pp.83 (title), 84 (text). -- Revised autograph. GMH made slips in indenting in:6 A[nd] del. and blotted; 12 line rewritten, also closing up the line space, "springs" compressed, del., then rewritten below. In 7 "wears" was mended to "shars", then rewritten as "shares". Note counterpoint signs on single syllables (1, 5, 9, 13); slurs over words (3)--all in ink. His comma after "smeared" (6) is added later.

RB in pencil (1918) rings "from" (11), and on the opposite page (not shown) notes "off" as "B MS correctn." and 'B has "eastward" in my hand wh. GMH left'. RB's ink below title "see last page" refers back to A¹.

PLATE 287. OET 111. *God's Grandeur* • 95

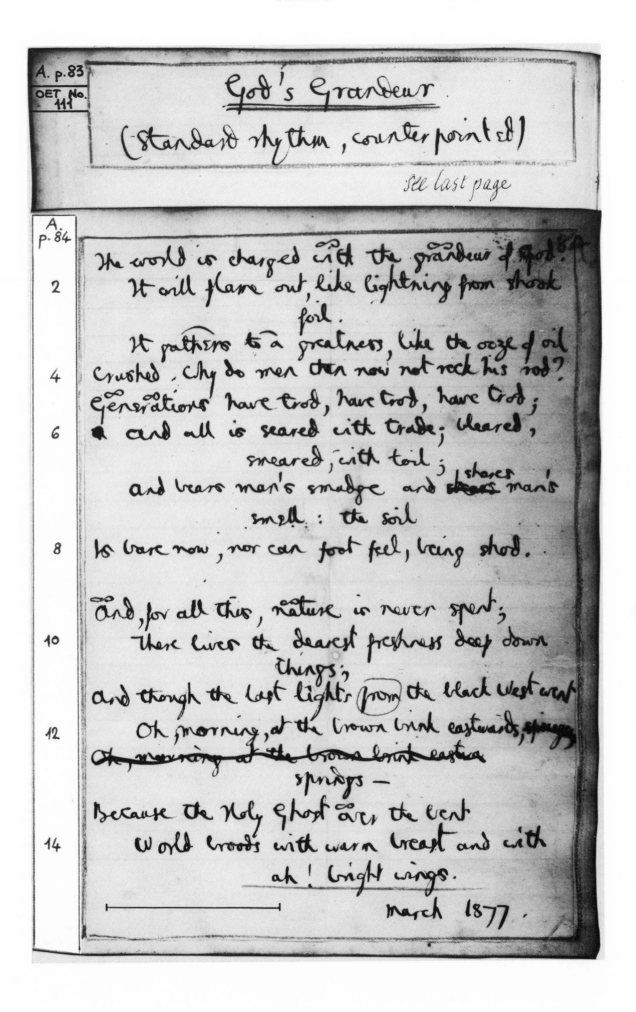

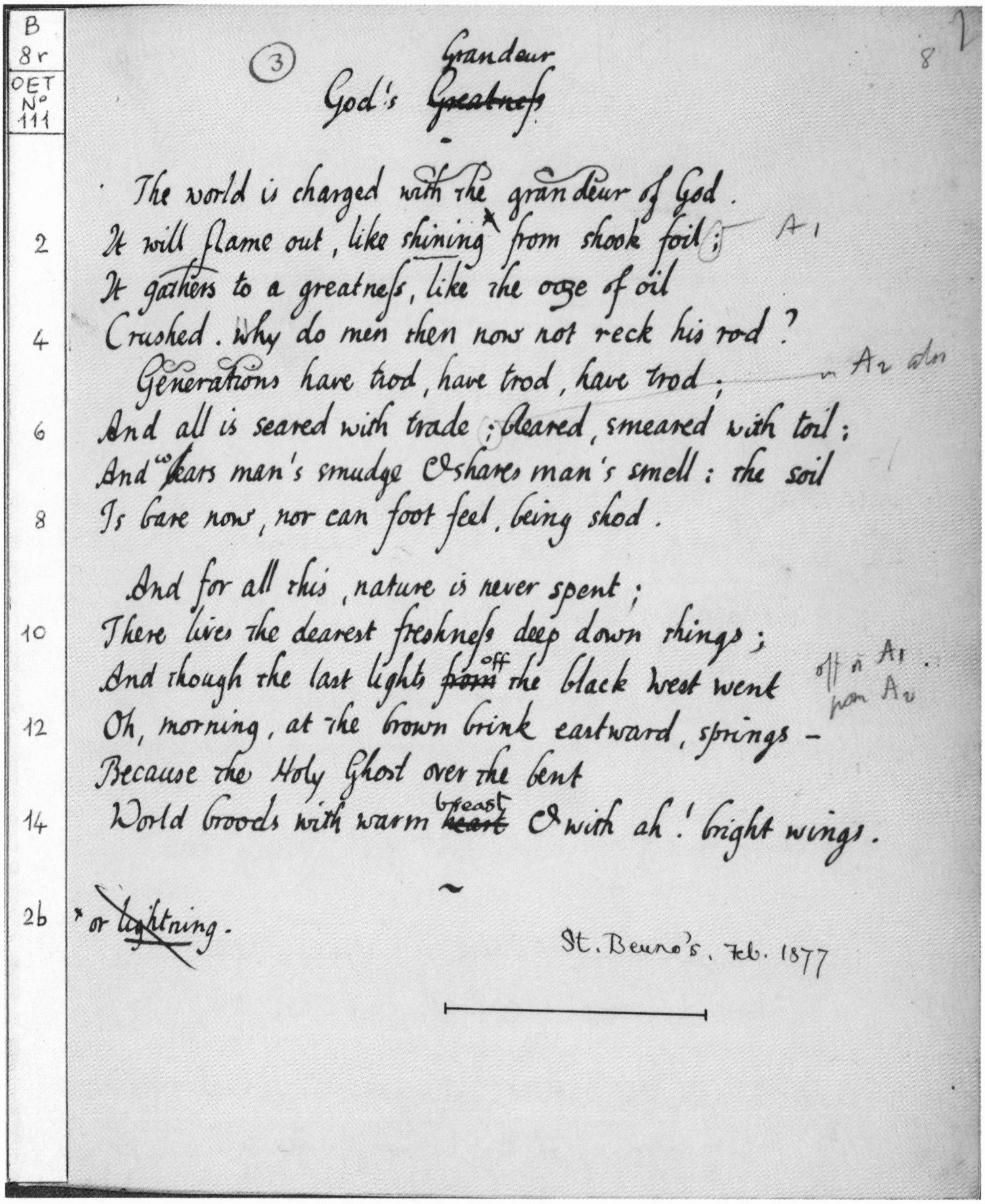

B
8 r
OET
N°
111

③   *Grandeur*

God's ~~Greatness~~

· The world is charged with the grandeur of God.
2   It will flame out, like shining* from shook foil; A₁
It gathers to a greatness, like the ooze of oil
4   Crushed. Why do men then now not reck his rod?
Generations have trod, have trod, have trod;   ⁿ A₂ also
6   And all is seared with trade; bleared, smeared with toil;
And wears man's smudge & shares man's smell: the soil
8   Is bare now, nor can foot feel, being shod.

And for all this, nature is never spent;
10   There lives the dearest freshness deep down things;
                   off
And though the last lights ~~from~~ the black West went   off ⁿ A₁
12   Oh, morning, at the brown brink eastward, springs —   ↙ from A₂
Because the Holy Ghost over the bent
                    breast
14   World broods with warm ~~heart~~ & with ah! bright wings.

~

2b   ✗ or ~~lightning~~.

St. Beuno's. Feb. 1877

Plate 287a   OET No. 111: God's Grandeur -- MS. 5 (B)

B.8r -- Transcription by RB, revised by GMH. RB corrected his own slip in the title, in different ink, now a faded brown (cf. 3 beside it). He omitted the commas after "smeared" (6, A²--a change of rhythm from the smooth first half of the line) and after "And" (9, all MSS): Both these have been restored in the OET.

GMH's ink: del. the asterisk after "shining" (2) and the alternative "lightning" at the foot; revised "bears" (7) to "wears"; "from" (11) to "off"; and RB's unauthorised "heart" (14) to "breast". He appended the date (ink). In purple pencil GMH added counterpoint signs in 1, 5 and only one slur in 3. He later added "St. Beuno's" in ink.

RB's black ink (1889) underlined "shining" (2) as the final reading. His pencil (1918) noted that his semicolon after "foil" (2) followed A¹, and the same stop after "trade" (6) followed A²; that in 11 A¹ had "off", A² "from". RB also mended in pencil his "why" (4) to "Why", and the colons ending 9 and 10 to semicolons.

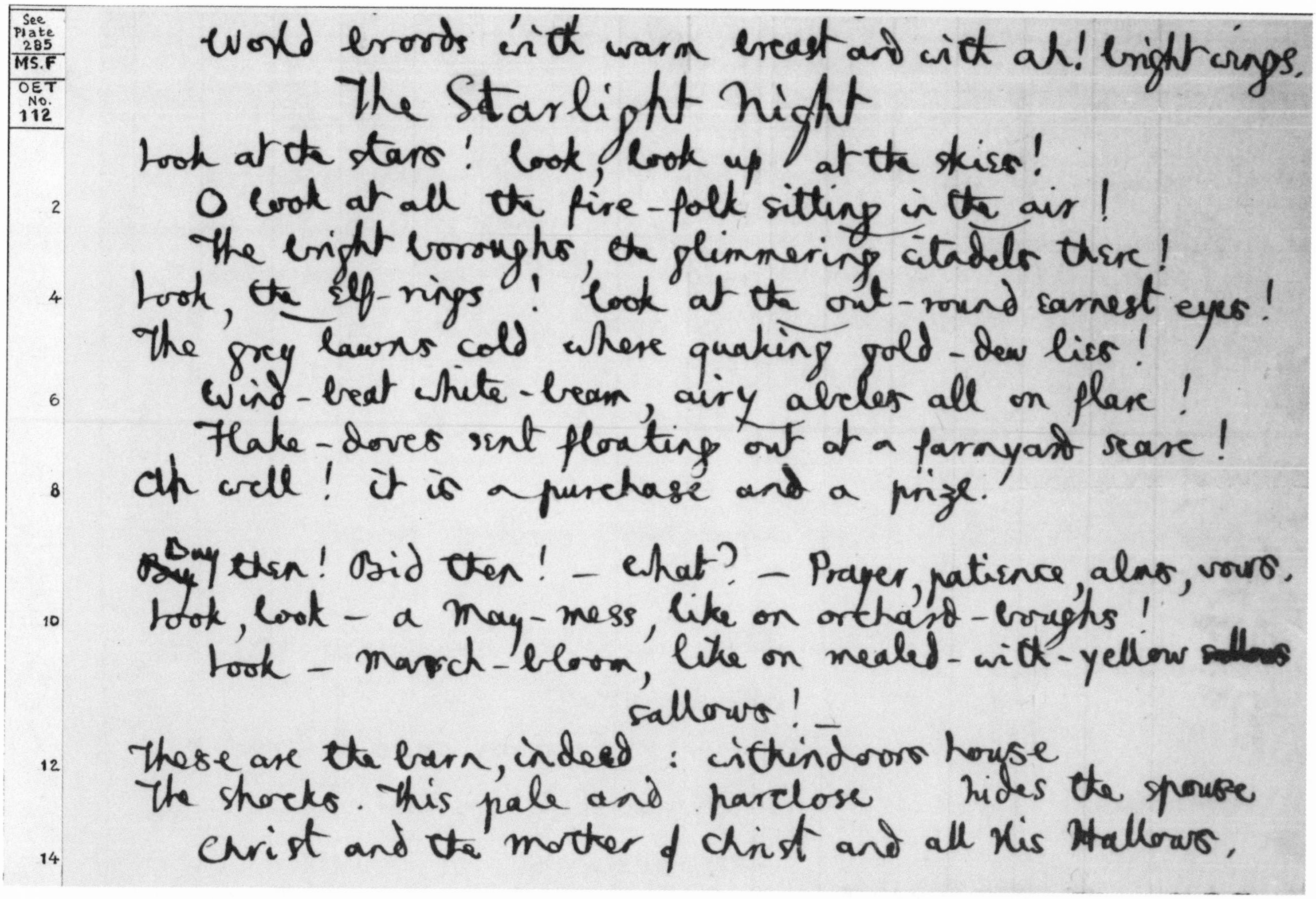

PLATE 288. OET 112. *The Starlight Night* • 97

World broods with warm breast and with ah! bright wings.

The Starlight Night

Look at the stars ! look, look up / at the skies !
     O look at all the fire-folk sitting in the air !
       The bright boroughs, the glimmering citadels there !
Look, the elf-rings ! look at the out-round earnest eyes !
The grey lawns cold where quaking gold-dew lies !
     Wind-beat white-beam, airy abeles all on flare !
       Flake-doves sent floating out at a farmyard scare !
Ah well ! it is a purchase and a prize.

Buy then ! Bid then ! — what ? — Prayer, patience, alms, vows.
Look, look — a May-mess, like on orchard-boughs !
     Look — march-bloom, like on mealed-with-yellow sallows
                    sallows ! —
These are the barn, indeed : withindoors house
The shocks. This pale and parclose   hides the spouse
     Christ and the mother of Christ and all His Hallows,

<u>Plate 288</u>   <u>OET No. 112: The Starlight Night</u> -- MS. 1 (F)

   <u>MS. F</u> -- Bodleian Library, GMH's Letters to his Family, MS. Eng. Letters, e.40, f.43. Autograph faircopy of Nos. 111 (top portion, Plate 285) and 112 (lower portion), sent to his mother, for her birthday 3 March 1877. The curves below the line in 2, 4 and 6 are not outrides (a purpose for which he later used them) but intended as slurs only. <u>Title:</u> "Se" mended to "St". <u>Deletions:</u> 9 "By" mended, del., then rewritten as "Buy"; "March" mended from "Mas"(?) (11). 11 "sallows" (del. because there was no room for the exclamation at the edge of the paper). In 13 a large space was left after "and", "parclose" being prob. added later.

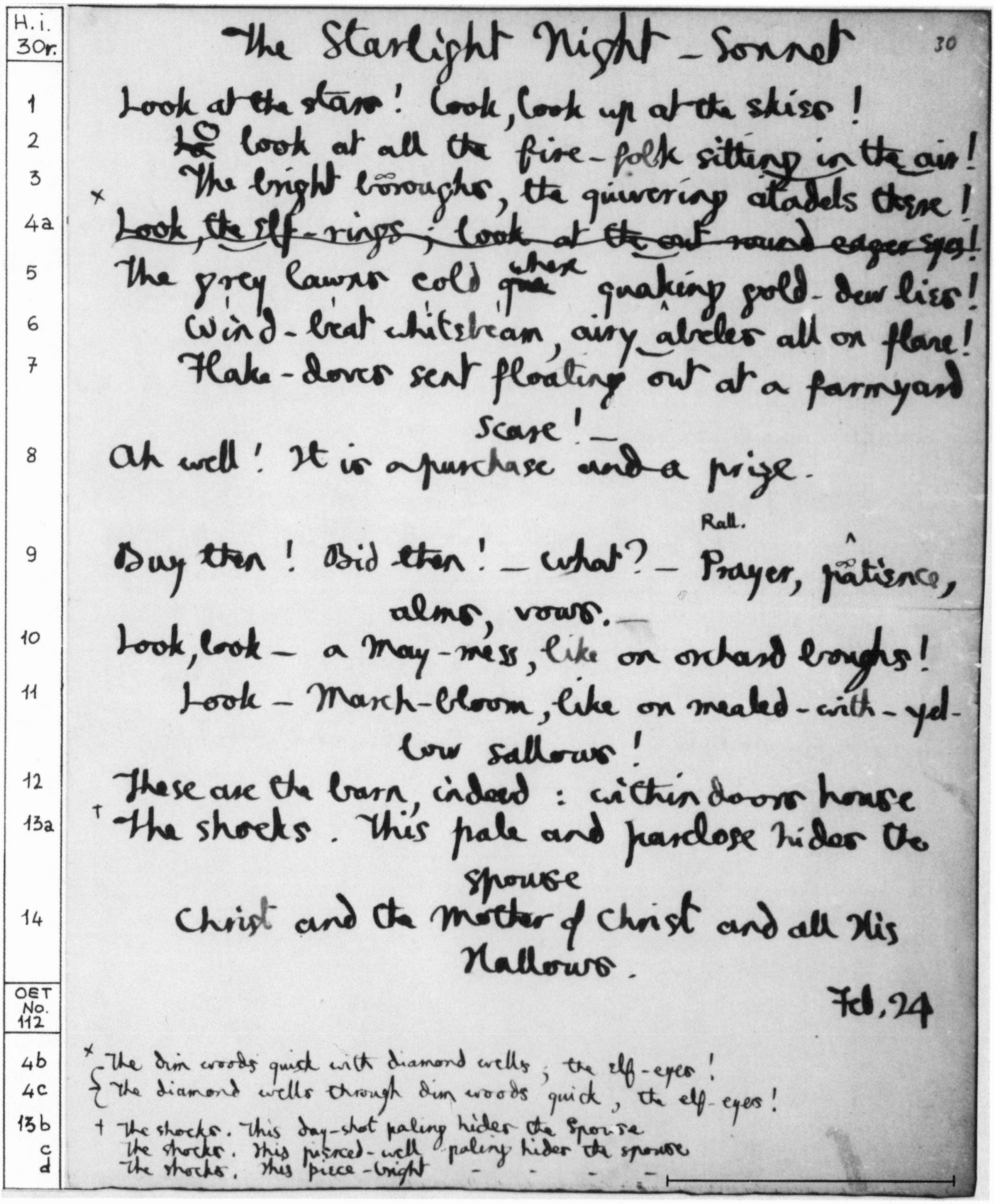

H.i. 30r.	
	The Starlight Night — Sonnet 30
1	Look at the stars ! look, look up at the skies !
2	Lo look at all the fire-folk sitting in the air !
3	× The bright boroughs, the quivering citadels there !
4a	Look, the elf-rings ; look at the out round edges sqq !
5	The grey lawns cold where quaking gold-dew lies !
6	Wind-beat whitebeam, airy abeles all on flare !
7	Flake-doves sent floating out at a farmyard scare ! —
8	Ah well ! It is a purchase and a prize.
9	Buy then ! Bid then ! — what ? — Prayer, patience, alms, vows. —
10	Look, look — a May-mess, like on orchard boughs !
11	Look — March-bloom, like on mealed-with-yel-low sallows !
12	These are the barn, indeed : within doors house
13a	† the shocks. This pale and passdoose hides the spouse
14	Christ and the mother of Christ and all His Hallows.
	Feb. 24
OET No. 112	
4b	× The dim woods quick with diamond wells ; the elf-eyes !
4c	The diamond wells through dim woods quick, the elf-eyes !
13b	† the shocks. This day-shot paling hides the Spouse
c	the shocks. This pierced-well paling hides the spouse
d	the shocks. This piece-bright — — —

Plate 288a · The Starlight Night -- MS. 2 (H¹)

H.i.30r -- Autograph faircopy on blotchy paper, with footnote revisions of 4, 13. Early type of <u>counterpoint</u> sign on the stressed syllables only of "boroughs" (3) and "patience" (9). <u>Slurs</u> (not outrides) below words in 2, 4a, 6 (contr. A², H²). Metrical marks from music: <u>staccato</u> on first 4 syllables in 6; <u>sforzando</u> (sudden stress) on "abeles" (6), "patience" (9); <u>Rall</u>[entando], slowing the second half of 9. <u>Deletions</u>: 2 Lo   5 qua.

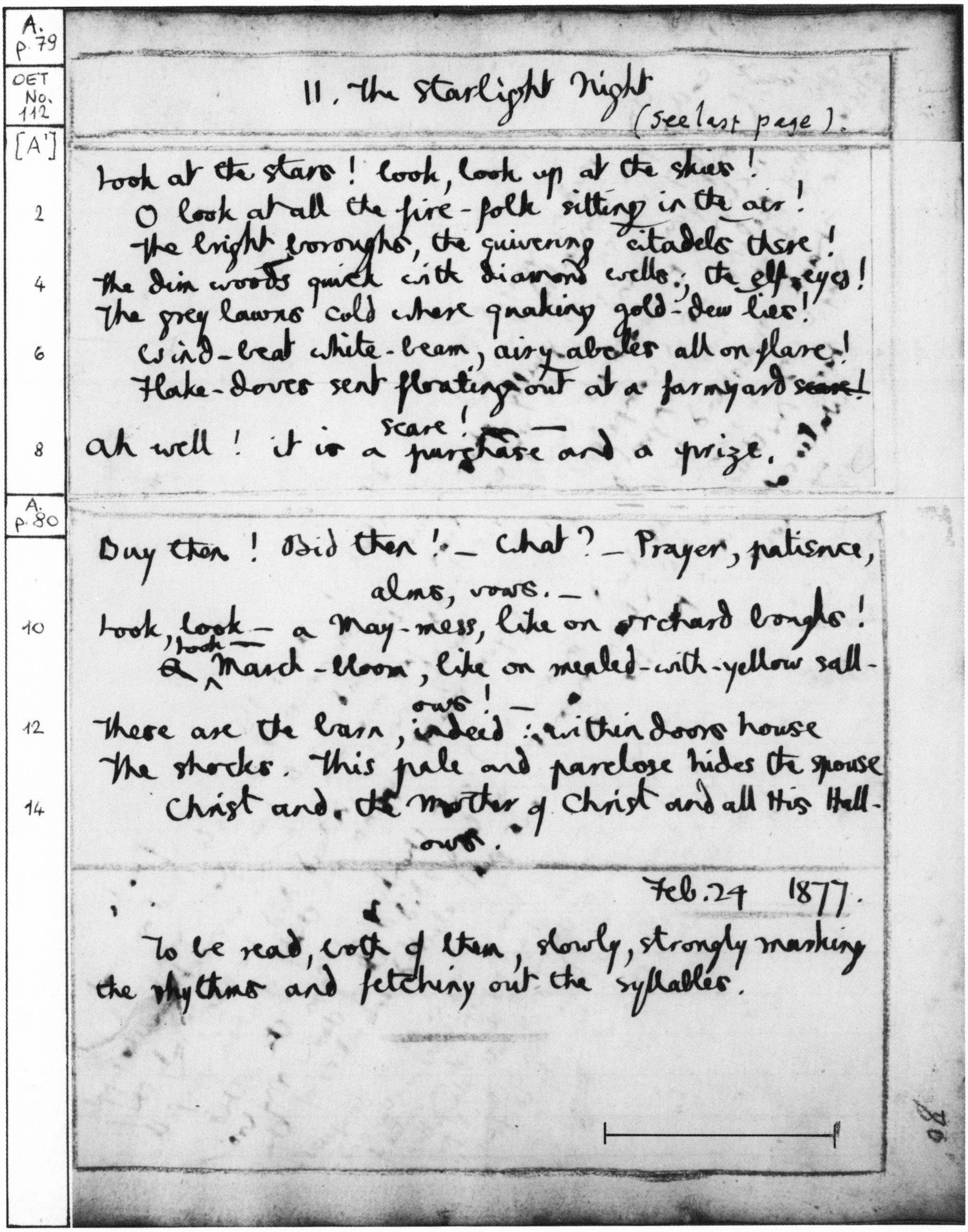

11. The Starlight Night
(see last page).

Look at the stars ! look, look up at the skies !
   O look at all the fire-folk sitting in the air !
   The bright boroughs, the quivering citadels there !
The dim woods quick with diamond wells; the elf-eyes !
The grey lawns cold where quaking gold-dew lies !
   Wind-beat white-beam, airy abeles all on flare !
   Flake-doves sent floating out at a farmyard scare !
Ah well ! it is a purchase and a prize.

Buy then ! Bid then ! — What ? — Prayer, patience,
       alms, vows. —
Look, look — a May-mess, like on orchard boughs !
   A March-bloom, like on mealed-with-yellow sall-
       ows ! —
These are the barn, indeed ; within doors house
The shocks. This pale and pareclose hides the spouse
   Christ and, the mother of Christ and all His Hall-
       ows.

Feb. 24 1877.

To be read, both of them, slowly, strongly marking
the rhythms and fetching out the syllables.

Plate 289   The Starlight Night -- MS. 3 (A[1])

   A.pp.79 (1-8), 80 (9-14). The original MS was cut into pieces by RB to be distributed artistically over the two pages. These gaps have been closed up again in the facsimile.

   Autograph faircopy, disfigured by blotches from the draft of a letter to RB written obliquely across the back. GMH's footnote (and RB's note below the title: "See last page") refer back to No. 111, "God's Grandeur", sent to RB at the same time. Fitting in the dash ending 7 prob. accounts for "scare!" being deleted. The slurs (as in F and H[1]) are again below the line.

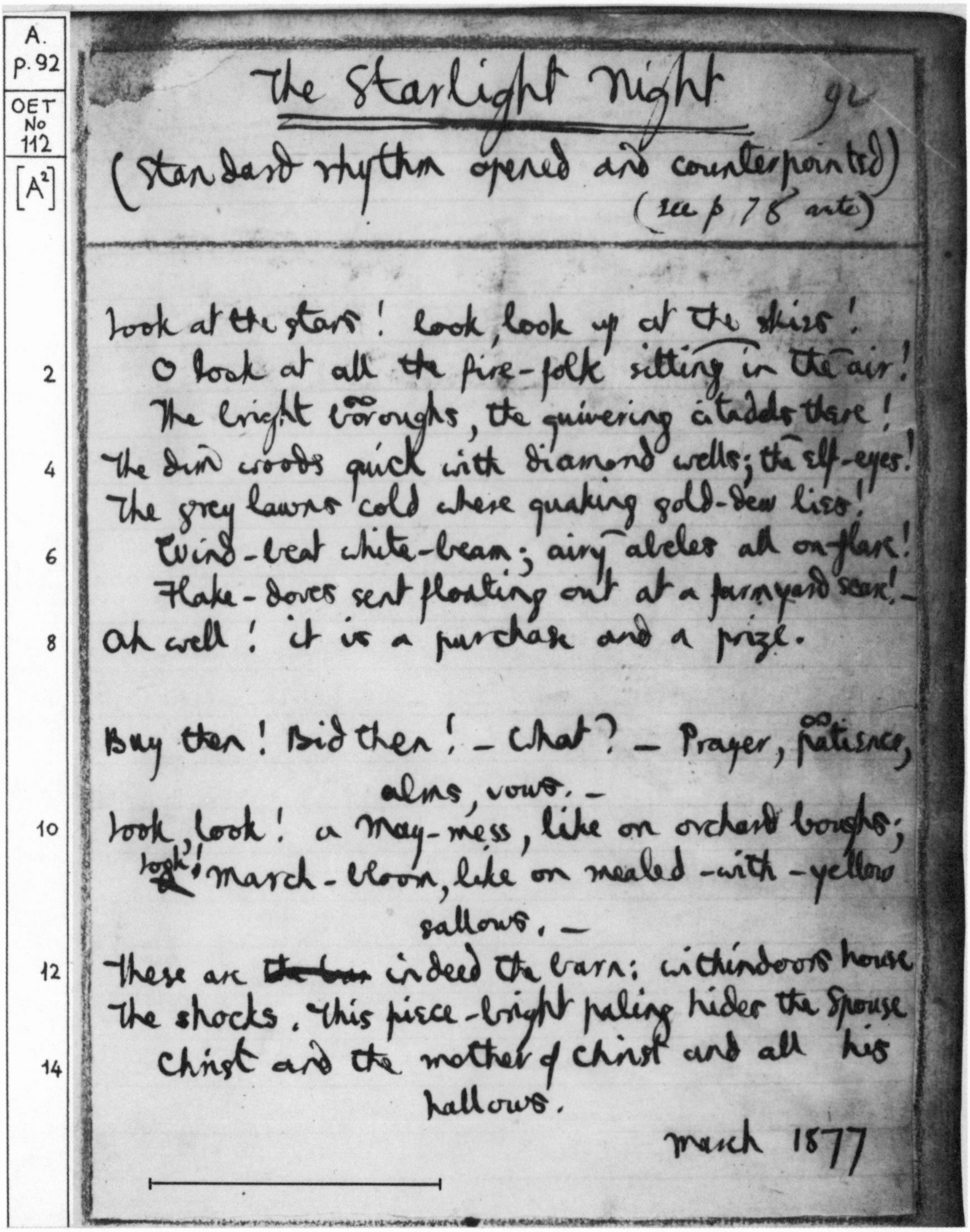

A.
p. 92

OET
No
112

[A²]

The Starlight Night

(Standard rhythm opened and counterpointed)
(see p 78 note)

Look at the stars ! look, look up at the skies !
2   O look at all the fire-folk sitting in the air !
The bright boroughs, the quivering citadels there !
4 The dim woods quick with diamond wells; the elf-eyes!
The grey lawns cold where quaking gold-dew lies !
6   Wind-beat white-beam; airy abeles all on-flare !
Flake-doves sent floating out at a farmyard scare ! —
8 Ah well ! it is a purchase and a prize.

Buy then ! Bid then ! — What ? — Prayer, patience,
alms, vows. —
10 Look, look ! a May-mess, like on orchard boughs;
Look! march-bloom, like on mealed-with-yellow
sallows. —
12 These are indeed the barn: withindoors house
The shocks. This piece-bright paling hides the Spouse
14 Christ and the mother of Christ and all his
hallows.

march 1877

Plate 290   OET No. 112: The Starlight Night -- MS. 4 (A²)

   A.p.92 -- Revised autograph faircopy, adopting variants from the foot of H¹. Slurs are now above the line (2, 4, 6), but the counterpoint signs are still cramped onto the stressed syllables. In 12 he began "the barn" before "indeed". RB's note below the title refers back to his own transcription of B², the final version: his copy was not checked by Hopkins and, since the autograph is extant, has no independent value.

(opposite) Plate 291   OET No. 112: The Starlight Night -- MS. 5 (H²)

   H.i.31r, 30v. Autograph faircopy on 31r, with rev. in 13 ("hides") and 14 ("Christ's Hallows, all Hallows"--the tail of the final "s" looks like an exclamation mark, but cf. ends of 10, 11). The variants of 3, 4, 5 on 30v (here reproduced on a larger scale) belong to about the same date: note the slurs above words in both, and the music-turns, used for counterpoint signs, over two syllables, a type found in 1879.   [Note cont. opposite]

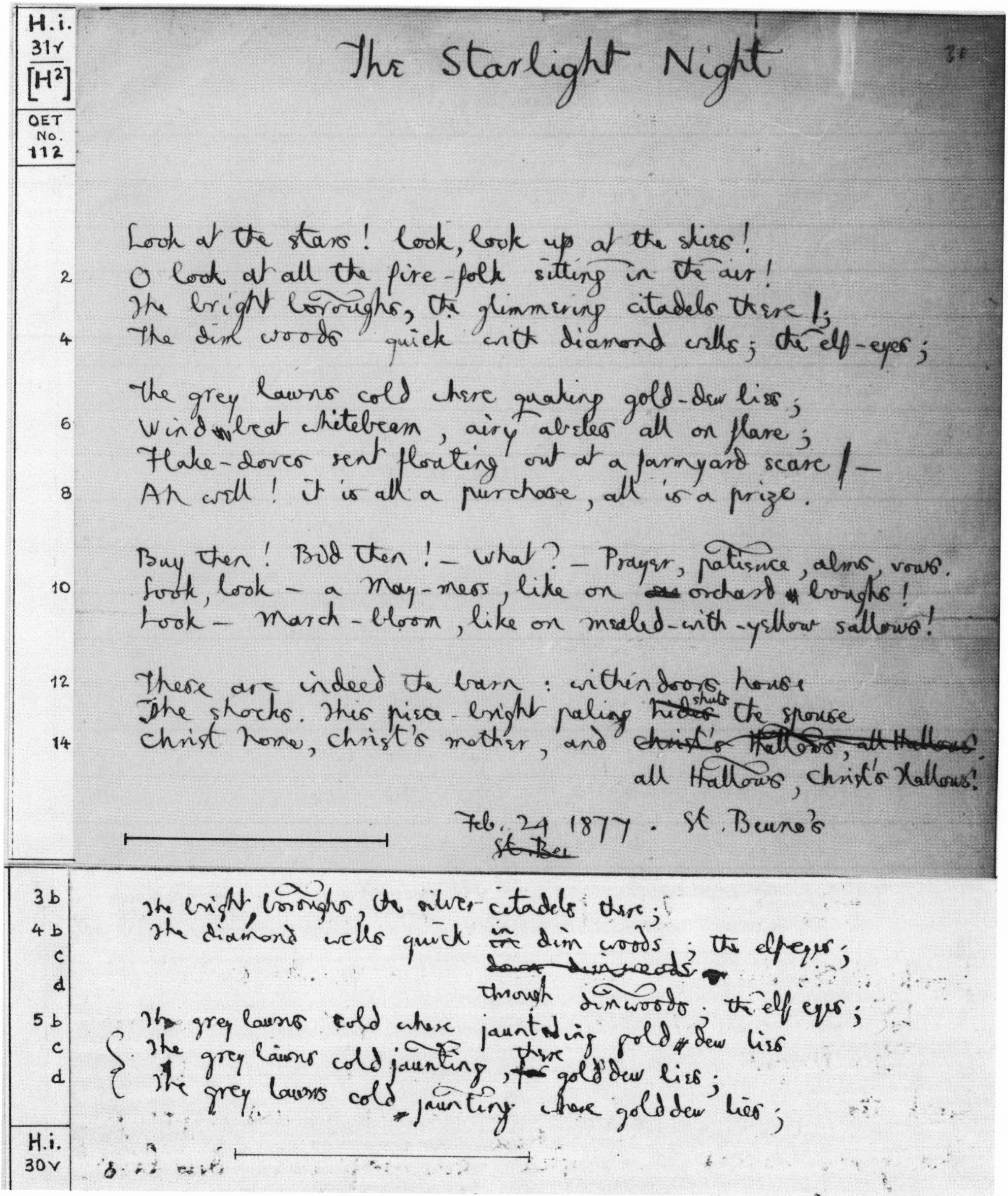

PLATE 291. OET 112. *The Starlight Night* • 101

H.i. 31r [H²] OET No. 112	

The Starlight Night

Look at the stars ! look, look up at the skies !
O look at all the fire-folk sitting in the air !
The bright boroughs, the glimmering citadels there !;
The dim woods quick with diamond wells; the elf-eyes;

The grey lawns cold where quaking gold-dew lies;
Wind-beat whitebeam, airy abeles all on flare;
Flake-doves sent floating out at a farmyard scare !—
Ah well ! It is all a purchase, all is a prize.

Buy then ! Bid then !— what ?— Prayer, patience, alms, vows.
Look, look — a May-mess, like on orchard boughs !
Look — March-bloom, like on mealed-with-yellow sallows !

These are indeed the barn : within doors house
The shocks. This piece-bright paling shuts the spouse
Christ home, christ's mother, and christ's hallows, all hallows!
                     all Hallows, Christ's Hallows!

Feb. 24 1877 . St. Beuno's

3b 4b c d 5b c d	the bright boroughs, the silver citadels there ; The diamond wells quick in dim woods ; the elf-eyes; down dimwoods through dimwoods. the elf eyes ; The grey lawns cold where jaunting gold-dew lies The grey lawns cold jaunting there gold dew lies ; The grey lawns cold jaunting where golddew lies ;
H.i. 30v	

The variants are confused by blots showing through the paper from 30r; thus in 3b there is a blot like a comma after "bright".

Deletions include: exclamations ending 3a, 7; hyphens in "wind-beat" (6), after "orchard" (10), and in "gold-dew" (5b). The hyphen in "elf-eyes" (4b) is elusive. Note the homonym "oar" before "orchard" (10). In 4c after "down dimwoods" the comma is lost in a blot. In 5b "jaunted" is rev. to "jaunting". In 5c, d "golddew" may be meant for one word, though there is no join. Comma del. after "cold" (5d).

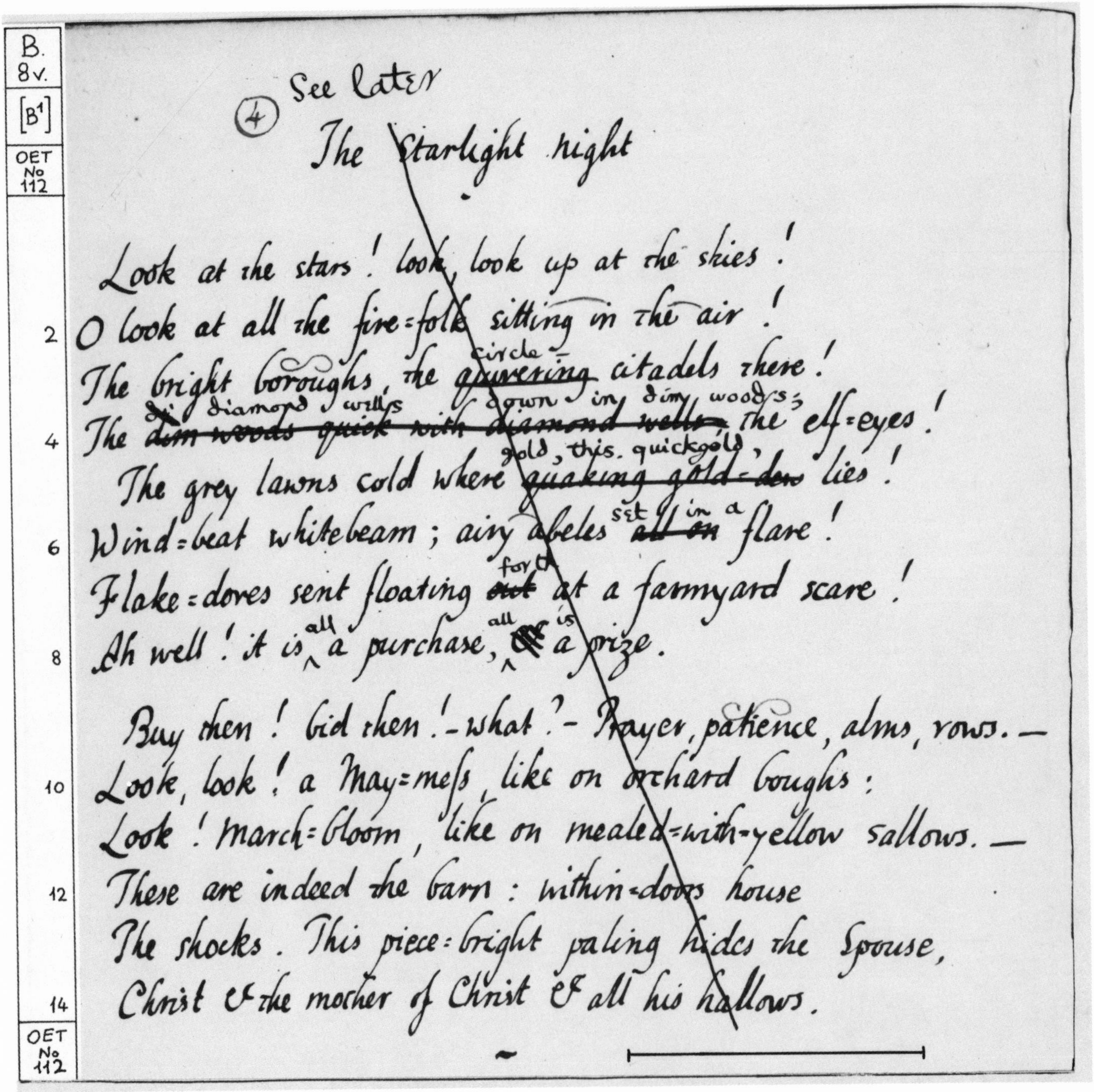

④ See later

The Starlight night

Look at the stars ! look, look up at the skies !
2 O look at all the fire=folk sitting in the air !
   The bright boroughs, the <del>quivering</del> circle= citadels there !
                    the diamond wells   down in dim woods;
4 The <del>dim woods quick with diamond wells</del> the elf=eyes !
                                gold, this quickgold
   The grey lawns cold where <del>quaking gold=dew</del> lies !
                                      set in a
6 Wind=beat whitebeam ; airy abeles <del>all on</del> flare !
                          forth
   Flake=doves sent floating <del>out</del> at a farmyard scare !
          all   all or is
8 Ah well ! it is ᴧ a purchase, ᴧ a prize.

   Buy then ! bid then !—what ?—Prayer, patience, alms, vows.—
10 Look, look ! a May=mess, like on orchard boughs :
   Look ! march=bloom, like on mealed=with=yellow sallows.—
12 These are indeed the barn : within=doors house
   The shocks. This piece=bright paling hides the Spouse,
14 Christ & the mother of Christ & all his hallows.

OET
No
112

Plate 291a   OET No. 111: The Starlight Night -- MS. 6 (B¹)

B.8v. Transcript of A² by RB. In 9 RB copied GMH's "What" (u.c., all MSS) as "what" (ℓ.c.; cf. No. 101, st. 25:6).
GMH partly revised it (not noticing the ℓ.c. "what") and then crossed it through, adding "See later", a reference to
B² on f.27v. GMH marked slurs and counterpoint signs in purple pencil (2, 3, 6, 9), and in 8 an ink comma after
"purchase". In 4 note the lower half of the semicolon after RB's "wells" (not a stress on "quickgold").

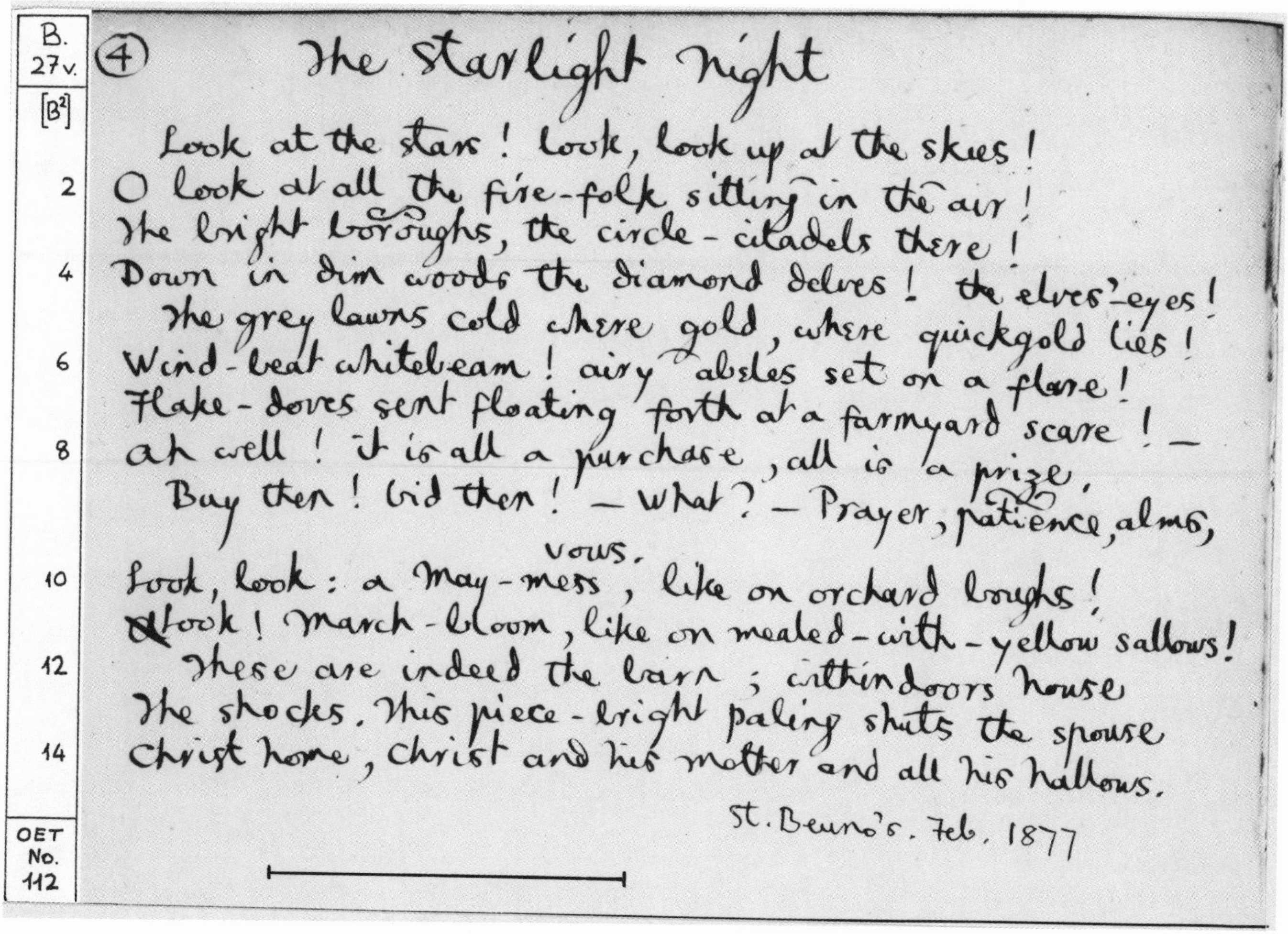

B. 27v. ④	**The Starlight Night**
[B²]	Look at the stars ! look, look up at the skies !
2	O look at all the fire-folk sitting in the air !
	The bright boroughs, the circle-citadels there !
4	Down in dim woods the diamond delves ! the elves'-eyes !
	The grey lawns cold where gold, where quickgold lies !
6	Wind-beat whitebeam ! airy abeles set on a flare !
	Flake-doves sent floating forth at a farmyard scare ! —
8	Ah well ! it is all a purchase, all is a prize.
	Buy then ! bid then ! — What ? — Prayer, patience, alms,
	vows.
10	Look, look : a May-mess, like on orchard boughs !
	Look ! March-bloom, like on mealed-with-yellow sallows !
12	These are indeed the barn ; withindoors house
	The shocks. This piece-bright paling shuts the spouse
14	Christ home, Christ and his mother and all his hallows.
OET No. 112	St. Beuno's. Feb. 1877

Plate 291b   OET No. 112: The Starlight Night -- MS. 7 (B²)

    B.27v. Final revised autograph inscribed in album B in 1884. In 11 he began with a reversion to the reading del. in

A¹ and A² ("A March-bloom"). The metrical marks are in ink, but the date seems later. Note the different sonnet layout

(no line spaces, but the opening lines of the quatrains and tercets all indented).

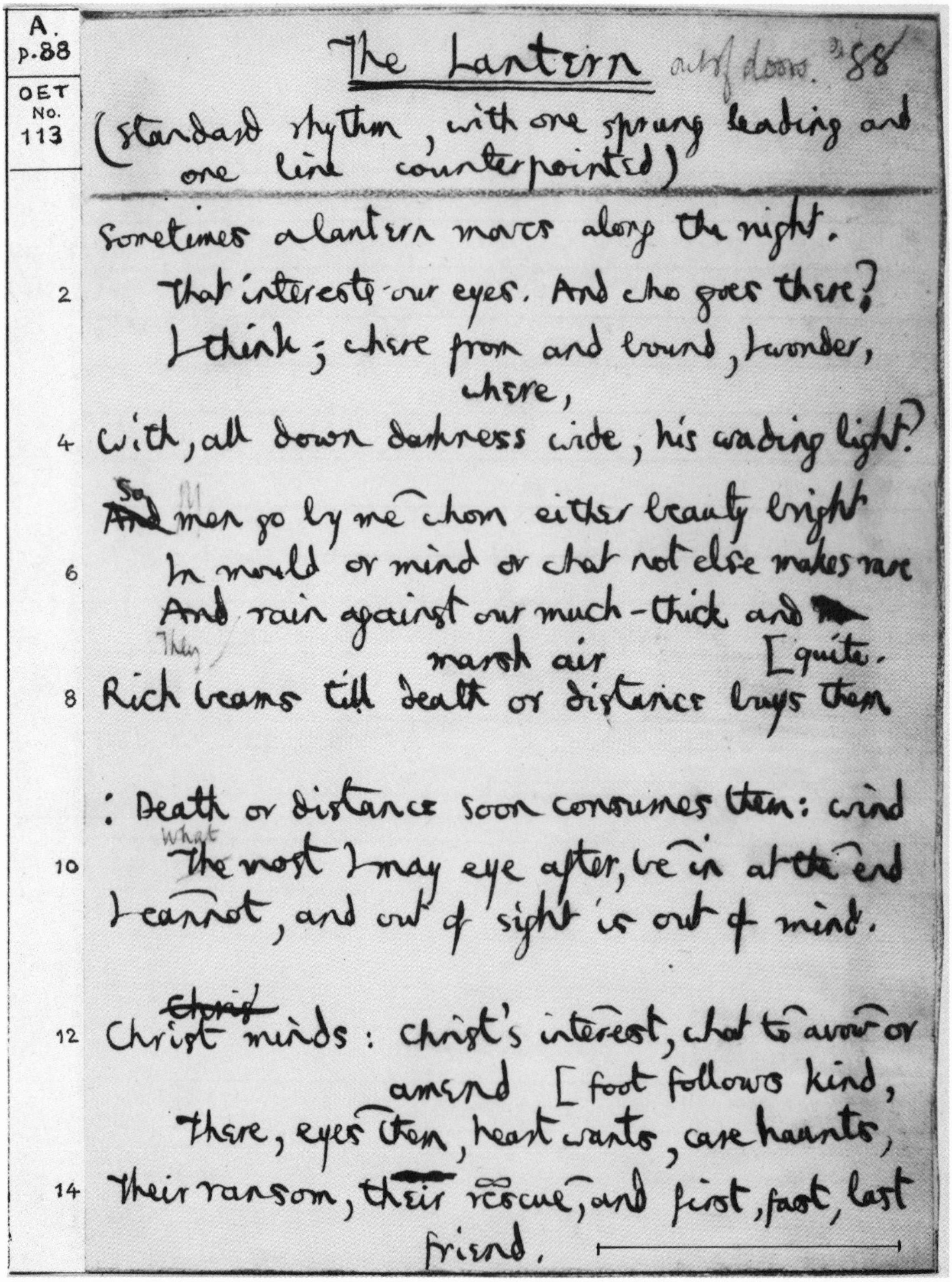

A.
p.88
 	
OET
No.
113
	<u>The Lantern</u> out of doors ³⁸⁸
	
	(standard rhythm, with one sprung leading and
	one line counterpointed)
	
	Sometimes a lantern moves along the night.
	   That interests our eyes. And who goes there?
	   I think; where from and bound, I wonder,
	            where,
	With, all down darkness wide, his wading light?
	
	       So
	And men go by me whom either beauty bright
	   In mould or mind or what not else makes rare
	And rain against our much-thick and ~~M~~
	   They
	            marsh air [quite.
	Rich beams till death or distance buys them
	
	: Death or distance soon consumes them: wind
	   What
	      The most I may eye after, be in at the end
	I cannot, and out of sight is out of mind.
	
	~~Christ~~
	Christ minds: Christ's interest, what to avow or
	            amend [foot follows kind,
	   there, eyes them, heart wants, care haunts,
	their ransom, their rescue, and first, fast, last
	         friend.

Line numbers in left margin: 2, 4, 6, 8, 10, 12, 14

Plate 292   OET No. 113: The Lantern out of doors -- MS. 1

A. p.88--autograph faircopy, with GMH's change in 5 ("So" for "And"). In 7 "M[arsh]" is deleted. In 2 the final query was originally a comma. Note the great colon before 9 (giving a "sprung leading"). In the final tercet the indentation (used at this date by GMH to mark b and d rhymes) was begun correctly (with the del. "Chris"), but put wrong by rewriting. In 14, a counterpoint sign over "their" was del. and moved to "rescue" (contrast stresses in B).

RB's red ink copies from B changes made by GMH to the title, and 5, 7, 10, but not the revised punctuation. On p.87 (not shown) he copied the footnote in B.

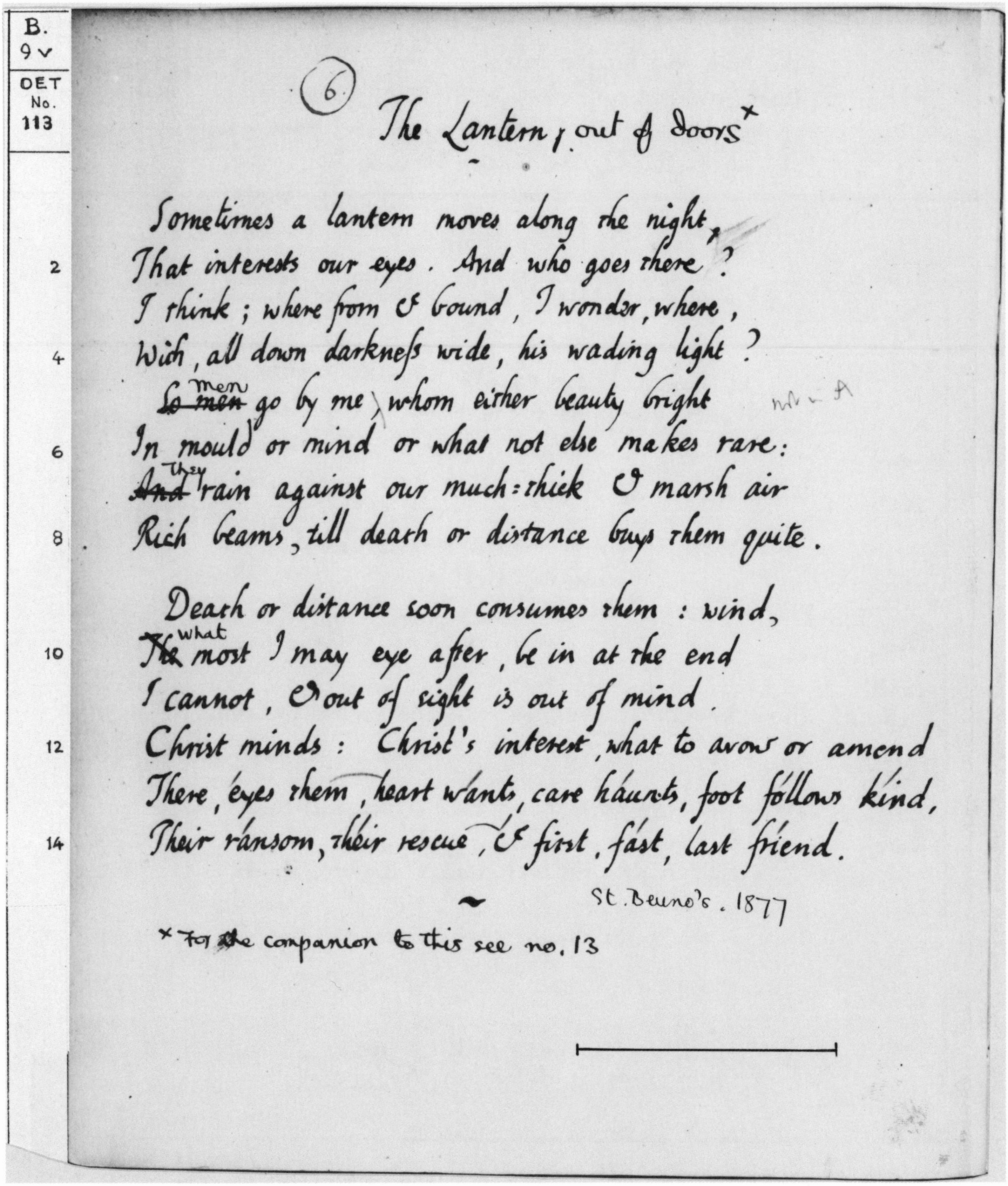

PLATE 293. OET 113. *The Lantern out of doors* • *105*

B.
9 v

OET
No.
113

⑥

The Lantern, out of doors ˣ

Sometimes a lantern moves along the night,

2 That interests our eyes. And who goes there?

I think; where from & bound, I wonder, where,

4 With, all down darkness wide, his wading light?
men
So men go by me, whom either beauty bright   not in A

6 In mould or mind or what not else makes rare:
they
And rain against our much=thick & marsh air

8 Rich beams, till death or distance buys them quite.

Death or distance soon consumes them : wind,
what
10 The most I may eye after, be in at the end

I cannot, & out of sight is out of mind.

12 Christ minds : Christ's interest, what to avow or amend

There, eyes them, heart wants, care haunts, foot follows kind,

14 Their ransom, their rescue, & first, fast, last friend.

⁓   St. Beuno's. 1877

ˣ For the companion to this see no. 13

—

Plate 293   OET No. 113: The Lantern out of doors -- MS. 2

   B. 9 verso. Transcript by RB, who prob. inserted the comma after 'me' (5), which in 1918 he del. in pencil, noting "not in A". There is a smudged period after "night" (1), not a comma (I rev. the text in 1970).

   GMH added "out of doors" to the title (with a footnote); put commas after "beams" (8), and "wind" (9), strengthened one after "ransom" (14) and perhaps added the colon after "rare" (6, because he had revised 7). He added "St. Beuno's. 1877" later. GMH's stress marks in 13, 14 are in purple pencil, as is the slur in 13, but the slur in 14 is in ink. The companion poem referred to in the footnote is OET No. 133 (see Plates 342-5).

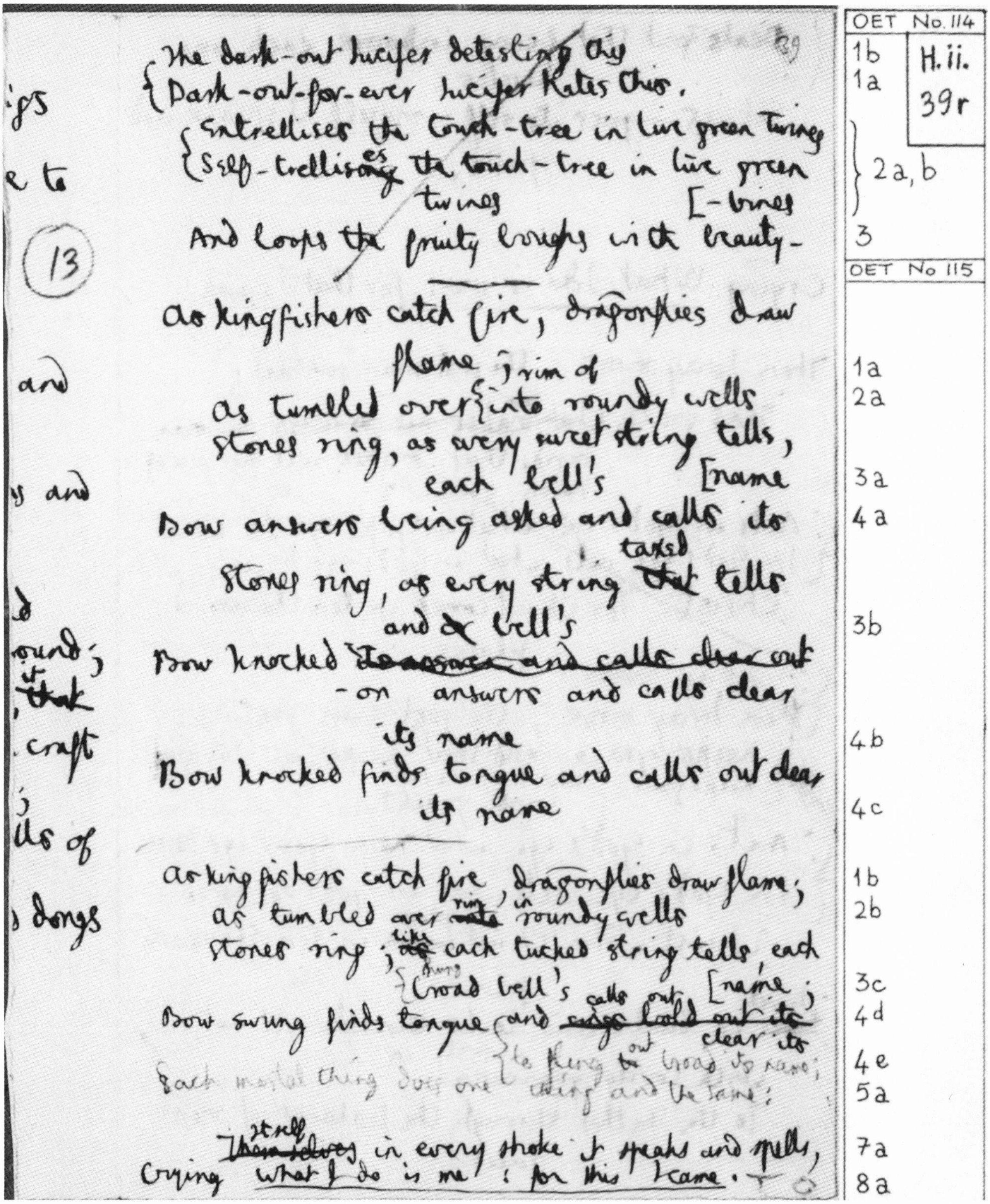

Plate 294   OET No. 114: The dark-out Lucifer detesting this

H.ii.39r. Autograph draft, in ink, deleted in pencil; the only surviving fragment (of a sonnet?). The words in the left margin, kept to provide a hinge, may belong either to this poem or to No. 115 (? [r]ound/[s]ound; [te]lls of; dongs) or to another unidentified poem. The large 13 in a circle is in pencil.

OET No. 115: "As kingfishers catch fire"

H.ii.39r. Autograph, sole surviving draft. Deletions include: 3b or   4b its answer and calls clear out   2b into 3c as   4d sings bold out its   4e br[oad]   Pencil additions: 3c hung [bracketed above broad]   4e to fling br broad out its name;   5a e[mended to]Each mortal thing does one thing and the same: Bottom right TO [Turn Over].

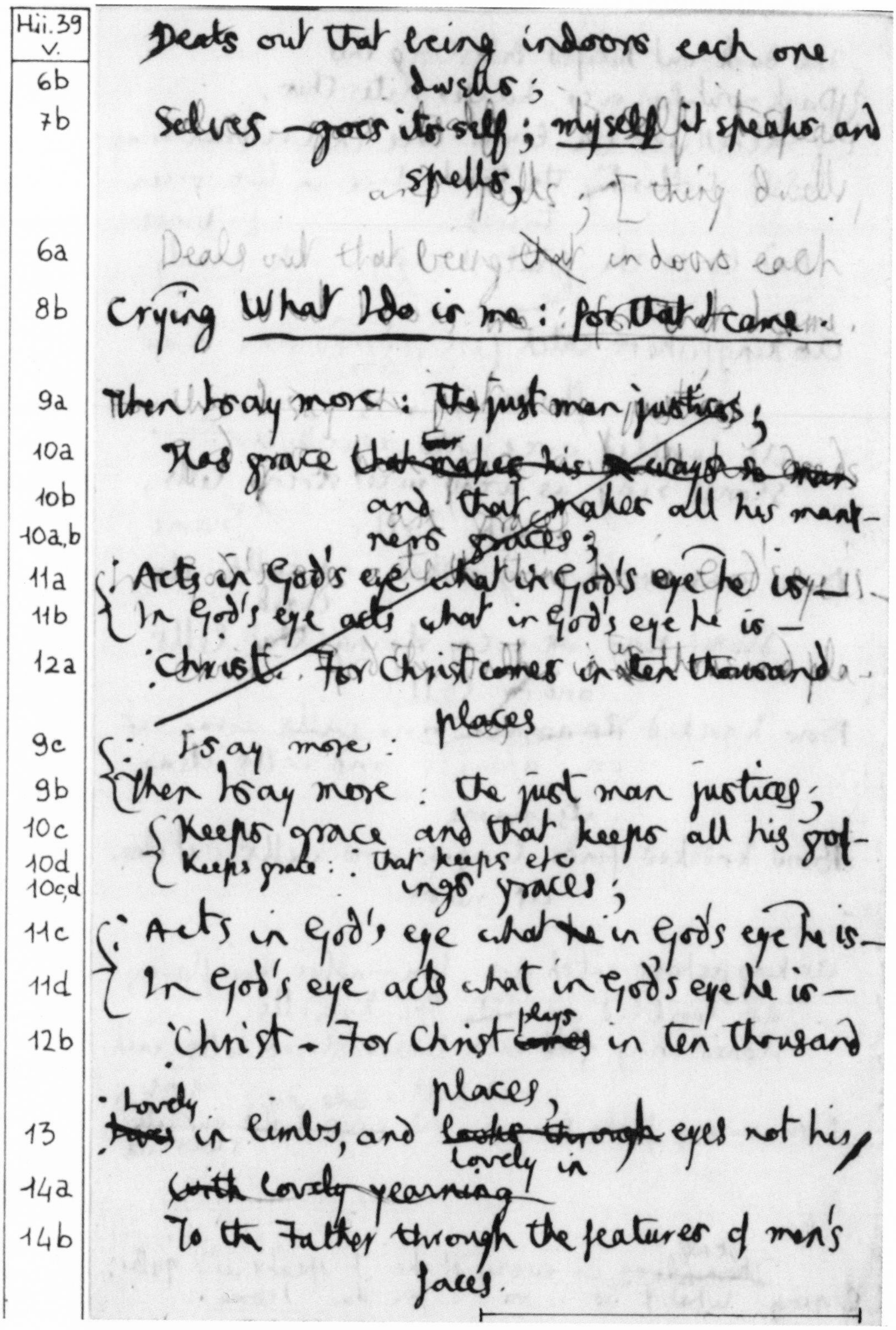

PLATE 295. OET 115. "As kingfishers catch fire" • *107*

Plate 295 OET No. 115 (cont): "As kingfishers catch fire" -- MS. 2

H.ii.39v. Autograph draft cont.. Pencil versions (except for 6a, these are beneath the ink) of the lines numbered:
7b Selves--goes itself: its Self it speaks and spells; 6a Deals out that being that indoors each thing dwells, 8b Crying [no slur, rest as ink]. 9a For this I say the just man justices; 10a, 11a, 12a God gives him grace and all his deeds are graces; In God's eye acts the thing he in God's eye is--/Christ. God the Father in ✗ ten thousand places [end of pencil versions].

Deletions in ink: 9a to 12a crossed through   10a that makes ʒur[ns?] his ɱ[anners] ways so man[ners graces] 11c he 12b dash replaced by period after first "Christ"   13 Lives   looks through   comma after "his" 14a With lovely yearning.

Great colons open 9c, 11a, 11c, 12a, 12b, 13 [before "Lives", but revision, "Lovely", is simply counterpointed]. Another is in 10d.

H.ii.
71 r.

OET
No.
116

Ⓨ 71

A. M. D. G.

Ad Reverendum Patrem
Fratrem Thomam Burke O. P.
Collegium S. Beunonis
invisentem

1   Ignotum spatiari horto, discumbere mensis,
         Et nova miralar sacra litare virum,
3   Simplicibus propior quam nos candore columbis
         Ille erat et qualis veste referret avem,
5   Mox ut quaesivi : Monacho quod nomen et ordo
         Iui velit ad nostros unicus esse lares ;
7   Pura caput tonsum cui velat lana cucullo
         Et cadit ad medium cui toga pura pedem,
9   Nescio quod duplex a tergo, a pectore peplum est,
         Atque terit laevum magna corona latus ?
11 Respondent : Haec vox toto clamantis in orbe
         Perque hominum Domino corda parantis iter.
13 Huic fuit Oceanus submissis utilis undis,
         Audiit occidua hunc, hunc oriente plaga.
15 Sed ~~non est~~ monachus non est verum est ex fratri-
         bus unus,
         Iuem pater agnoscit stelliger ille suum ;
17 Doctus Aquinatis reserare oracula Thomae,
         Si tamen est illo nunc quod in ore latet,

Plates 296, 297   OET No. 116: Ad Rev. Pat. Fr. Thomam Burke -- MSS 1 and 2

H.ii.71r.v. Autograph faircopy. Slips corrected: 15 non est   21 in 23 Praeterea [obscured by stain]   24 Dux simul ... dubiae 25 Si[c?--begun a line too soon?] mended to At.

There is no need in 19 to print "Godatus" for "Gobatus" [3rd edn. note, p.271, 4th. edn. 332, reproduced O A p.349].

OET identifies "Gobatus" as George Gobat (1600-79), a Jesuit theologian.

PLATE 297. OET 116. *Ad Rev. Pat. Fr. Thomam Burke* • 109

Quem tam Gudinus, Gobatus, tamque Goretus,
   Tam Cajetanus perspicuum esse jubent,

21 Jamdudum ~~ita~~ innumeri patientem interpretis et quem
   torqueat in sensus, nec mora, quisque suos,

23 ~~Praeterea~~ teneris fuit hic tironibus olim
      Ductor.
  ~~Dux simul~~ et ~~dubiae~~ ~~inmetae~~ candida norma viae.

25 At non omnis in his, vel, si placet, omnis in his est,
   Sic tamen in magnis ut levis esse queat,

27 Intermiscet enim cum sacris ludicra curis,
   Nec vox nec facies constet ut una viro.

29 Haec et plura movent atque addunt nomen, at illud
   Non tulit aut aegre nostra Camoena tulit;

31 Talem ego nunc hominem multum salvere juberem
   Ancipitem sed me scrupulus unus habet;

33 Num sese velit ille a me laudarier Anglo,
   Toto qui circo sternit in orbe meos.

35 Quidquid erit, passim mea dat Querenida salutem:
   Huic det et aversam solvat amore sinum.

37 Quodque etiam possit plebi prodesse fideli,
   Muneris id nostro debeat ille solo.

Apr. 23 1877

L. D. S.

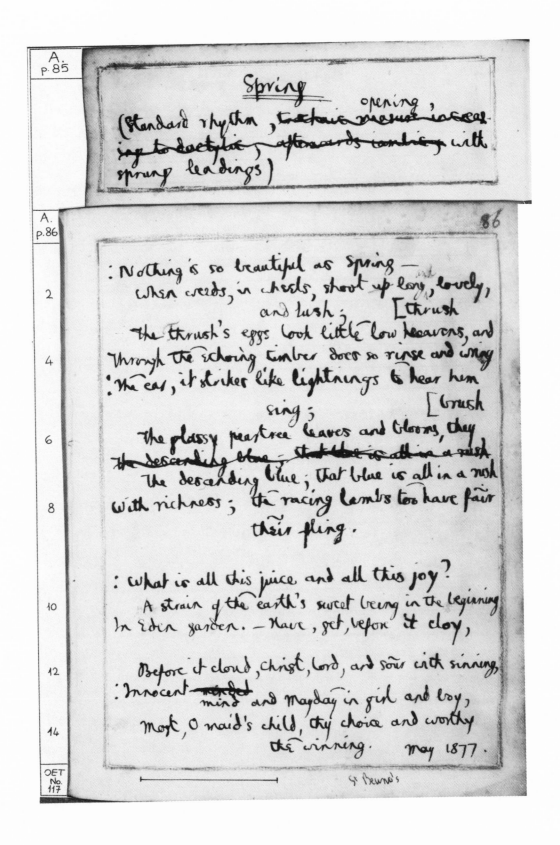

Plate 298   OET No. 117: Spring -- MS. 1 (A)

A.p.85 (title and metrical note, here restored to their place above the text), and p.86 (text). Autograph faircopy, with GMH's deletions in the metrical note ("trochaic measure increasing to dactylic, afterwards iambic;"). He forgot to indent 7, so deleted and rewrote it. 13 originally "Innocent-minded". Note great colons (ink) opening 1, 5, 9, 13. In 3 he added an extra "e" to "heavens": both his paper and his pen were inferior, and the first "e" was upset by a fibre in the sheet. The slurs and three circumflexes (8, 12) are all in ink.

RB, copying from GMH's revisions in B (Plate 301) (easily compared by holding up the intervening sheet), deleted "up" (2) and "The" (3), inserted "and" (2) and changed "t" to "T" in "thrush" (3), all in red ink. He did not cross out the commas before and after "lovely" (2). He later (1889) added "St. Beuno's" in black ink.

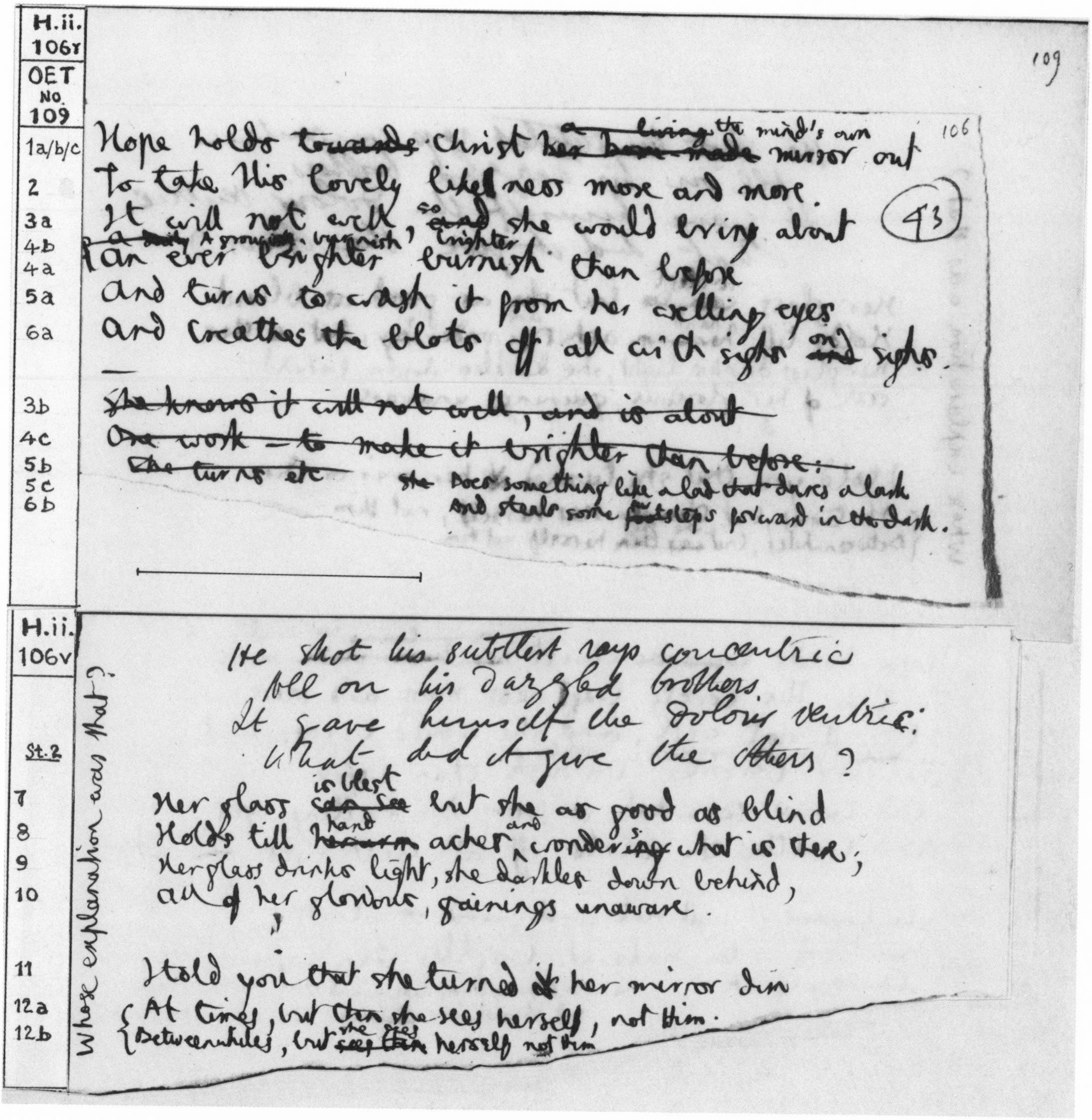

PLATE 299. OET 109. "Hope holds to Christ" • 111

Plate 299   OET No. 109: "Hope holds to Christ the mind's own mirror out"

[Note: The single MS of this poem which cannot be dated exactly, is introduced here, out of numerical sequence, to enable pairs of intervening MSS to face each other.]

H.ii.106r.v. Autograph draft on a roughly torn scrap of scribbler paper. Above the second stanza on the verso is a quatrain in an unknown hand, not attributed to Hopkins.

a living

Deletions include: 1 towards...her home-made   2 like [??]   4b A [?] daily 6b foot few   7 can see 8 orig. her arm aches, wondering   10 [smudges below "her" and after "glorious"]   11 it 12b sees then [below "not" the top of a letter torn off seems like italics].

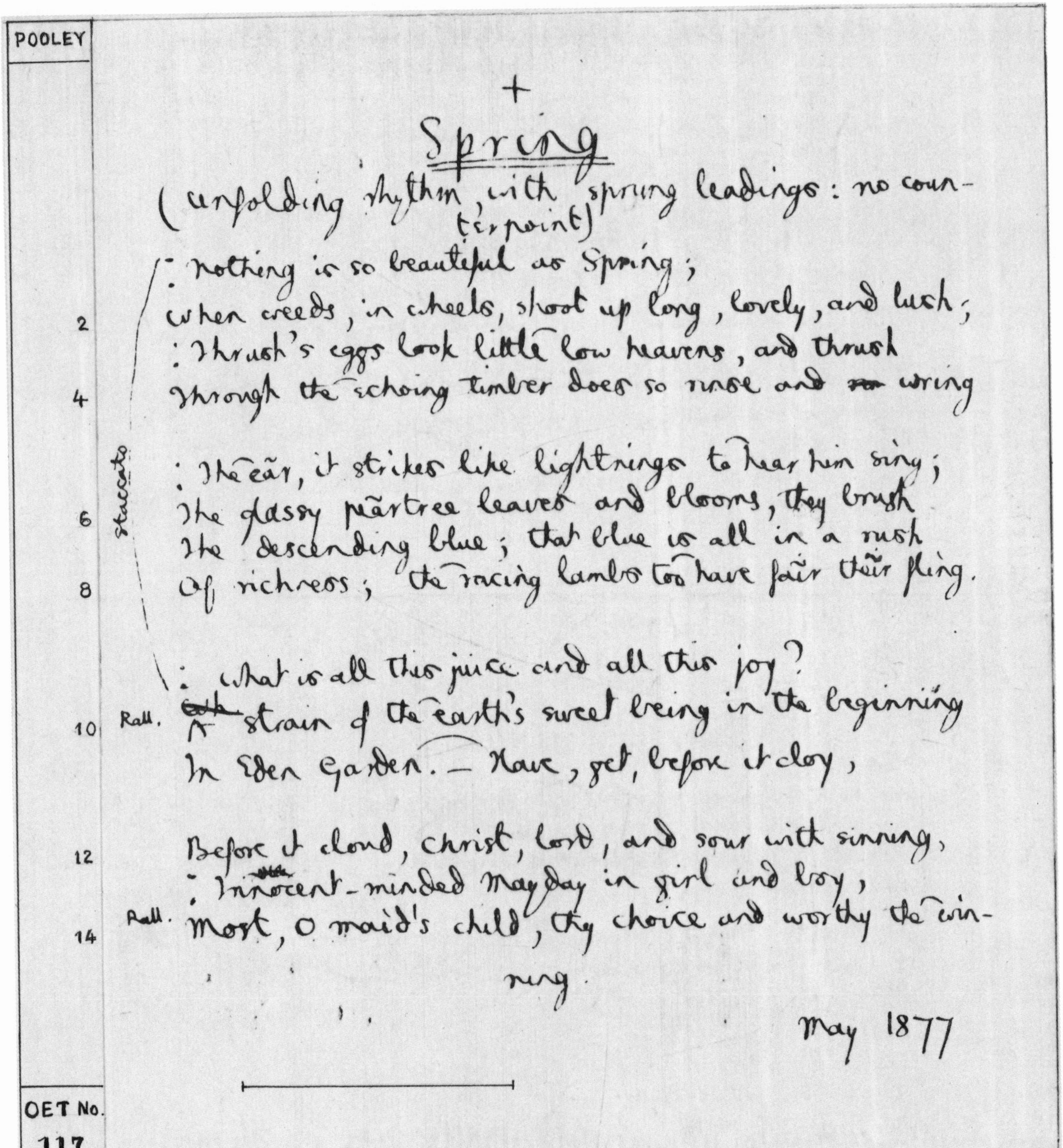

POOLEY

+

Spring

(unfolding rhythm, with sprung leadings: no counterpoint)

: nothing is so beautiful as Spring;

2 when weeds, in wheels, shoot up long, lovely, and lush;
: Thrush's eggs look little low heavens, and thrush

4 Through the echoing timber does so rinse and ~~so~~ wring

: The ear, it strikes like lightnings to hear him sing;

6 The glassy peartree leaves and blooms, they brush
The descending blue; that blue is all in a rush

8 Of richness; the racing lambs too have fair their fling.

\: What is all this juice and all this joy?

10 ~~Wh[at]~~ A strain of the earth's sweet being in the beginning
In Eden garden. — Have, get, before it cloy,

12 Before it cloud, Christ, lord, and sour with sinning,
: Innocent-minded Mayday in girl and boy,

14 Most, O maid's child, thy choice and worthy the winning.

May 1877

staccato

Rall.

Rall.

OET No.
117

Plate 300   OET No. 117: Spring -- MS. 2 (P)

Pooley MS. -- One of three autograph faircopies of poems found by Christabel, Lady Pooley, GMH's niece, in a portable desk inherited from his sister Grace. Lady Pooley sent me photographs in Aug. 1964, and later allowed me to examine her MSS. in her home and describe them in the Month (N.S. 33:6, June 1965, 347-50). The other poems were "In the Valley of the Elwy" (on the verso, No. 119, Plate 305) and "The Sacrifice" (No. 139, Plate 374).

The marginal directions were probably intended to assist Grace in setting the poem to music. Deletions: 4 rin[g] (homonym for "wring")   9 "Wh[at]" (rewritten above and to right to leave space for great colon)   13 slur mended and deleted (the first bar would have three notes).

Note great colons opening 1, 3, 5, 9, 13 (cf. the "sprung leadings" in the metrical note); and circumflexes on "ear" (5), "pear" (6), "fair", "their" (8)--see L.i.43.

PLATE 301. OET 117. *Spring* • *113*

B
9r

(5.)

Spring.

Nothing is so beautiful as spring —
When weeds, in wheels, shoot long & lovely & lush ;
The Thrush's eggs look little low heavens, & thrush
Through the echoing timber does so rinse & wring
The ear, it strikes like lightnings to hear him sing ;
The glassy pear tree leaves & blooms, they brush
The descending blue ; that blue is all in a rush
With richness ; the racing lambs too have fair their fling.

What is all this juice & all this joy ?
A strain of the earth's sweet being in the beginning
In Eden garden. — Have, get before it cloy,
Before it cloud, Christ, lord, & sour with sinning,
Innocent mind & may-day in girl & boy,
Most, O maid's child, thy choice & worthy the winning.

St. Beuno's. 1877

OET
No.
117

Plate 301   OET No. 117: Spring -- MS. 3 (B)

  B.9 recto. Transcript of A by RB with many deviations. He crossed out the comma after "choice" while the ink was wet (14).

  Errors corrected by GMH are: 1 "spring." to "spring--" (the period can be seen with infrared)   2 "lush:" to "lush;"   5 "lightenings" to "lightnings"   8 "full" to "fair"   14 "child" to "child,"   GMH added ink slurs in 5, 8, and strengthened RB's semicolons. He revised 2, 3, trying to match RB's writing: his caret after "long" (2) hides RB's comma. Later he added "St. Beuno's. 1877".

  RB's pencil (c.1918) changed "pear-tree" (6) into one word by deleting his double hyphen and adding a slur meaning "close up".

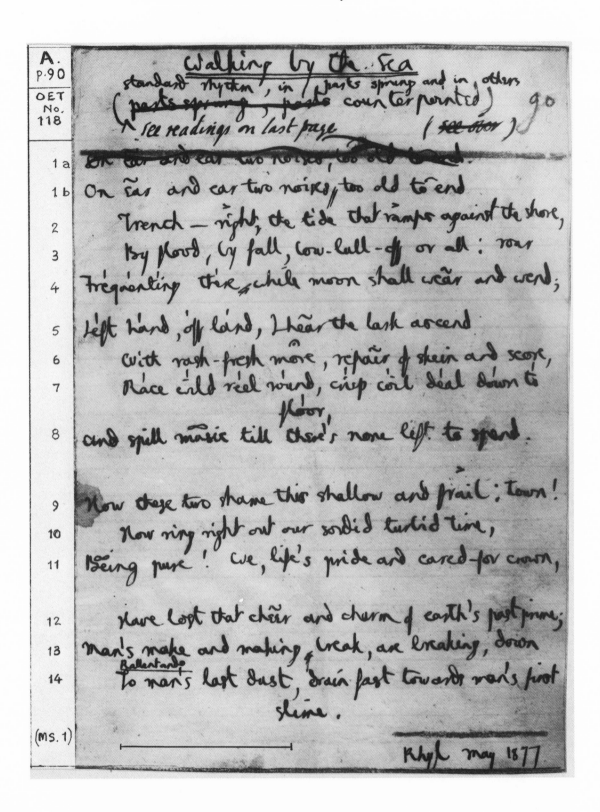

Earlier title (changed in 1884): Walking by the Sea.

A.p.90. Autograph faircopy of original version. GMH deleted 1a and rewrote it a line lower (omitting the slur over "too old"): cf. notes on Plate 306 for the first line of the "Windhover" being rewritten. Perhaps RB had asked him to leave a specified space between the title and first line: cf. RB's request for a particular size of paper (L.i.109). Deletions: Metrical note, "parts sprung, parts"; commas after "noises" (1b), "there" (4), "making" (13).

Metrical marks (all in ink): *circumflexes* on "ear" (1, first only), "wear" (4), "hear" (5), "repair" (6), "cheer" (12); contrast *counterpoint* on "music" (8), "Being" (11)--see L.i.43; *sforzando* signs on "right", "ramps" (2), "frail" (9); *dwell mark* on "more" (6); *rallentando* on 14; *great colons* in 3, 9; *staccato* on first four syllables in 4 and in 5, on all ten in 7.

RB's note "(see over)" was replaced by "see readings on last page", reproduced as Plate 303b. For convenient comparison, MS. 3 is placed opposite as Plate 303.

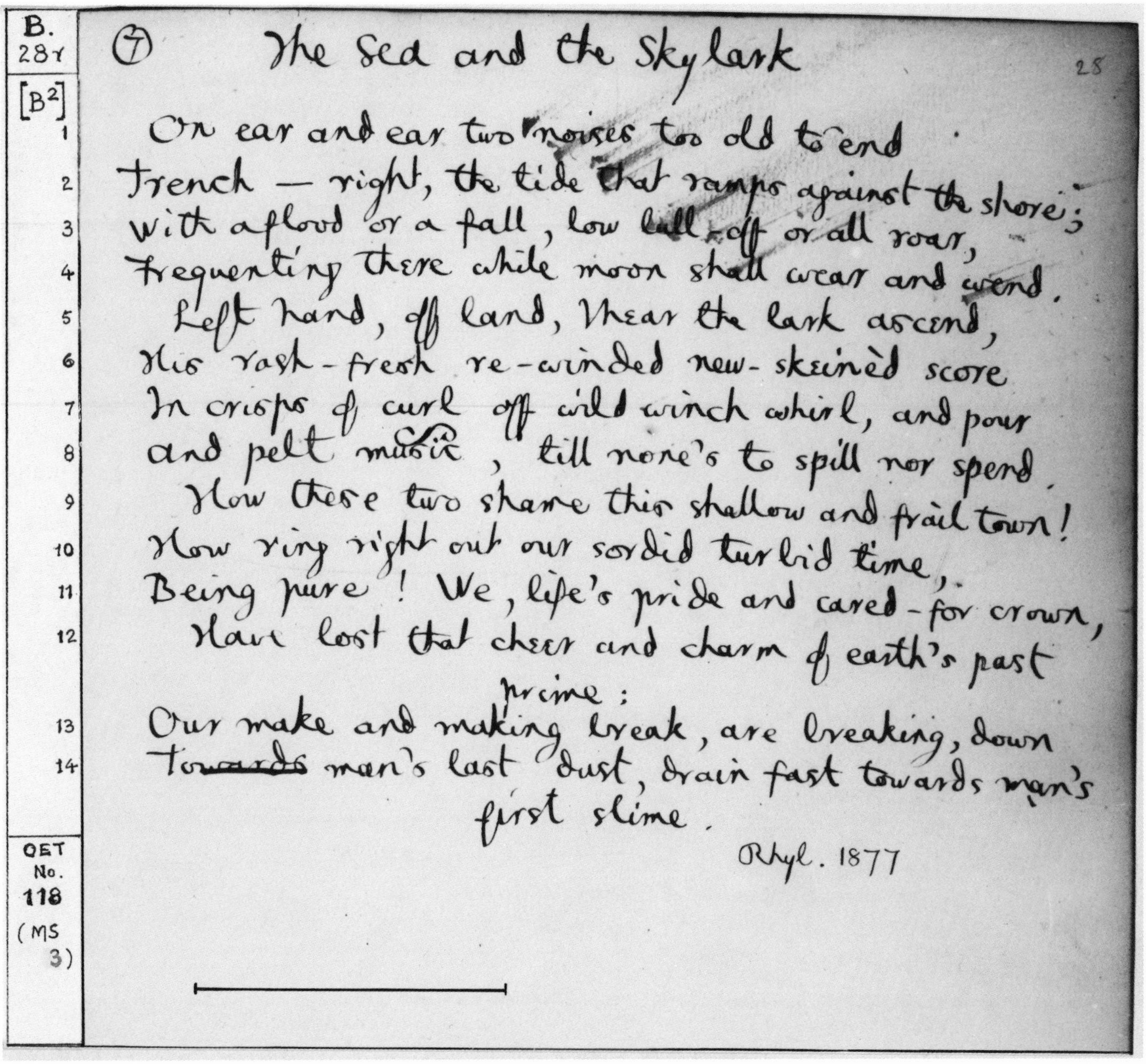

PLATE 303. OET 118. *The Sea and the Skylark* • 115

⑦ The Sea and the Skylark

On ear and ear two noises too old to end
Trench — right, the tide that ramps against the shore;
With a flood or a fall, low lull-off or all roar,
Frequenting there while moon shall wear and wend.
    Left hand, off land, I hear the lark ascend,
His rash-fresh re-winded new-skeinèd score
In crisps of curl off wild winch whirl, and pour
and pelt music, till none's to spill nor spend.
    How these two shame this shallow and frail town!
How ring right out our sordid turbid time,
Being pure! We, life's pride and cared-for crown,
    Have lost that cheer and charm of earth's past
                prime:
Our make and making break, are breaking, down
Towards man's last dust, drain fast towards man's
                first slime.

                        Rhyl. 1877

Plate 303   OET No. 118: The Sea and the Skylark -- MS. 3 (B²)

B.28r. Autograph faircopy of a revised version, written on a page in album B which was apparently already smudged

(e.g. 1-4, 14 below "man's"). There is only one counterpoint, "music" (8), and one slur (1), both in ink. In 14 "Towards"

is changed to "To". GMH accepted from B.10r (MS. 2) RB's period after "wend" (4) instead of his own semicolon.

A.p.89

Note on lines 6 & 7 of "Walking by the Sea". **More** is a midline rhyme to *score*, as *round* is meant to mark *down* in the next line. "**Rash-fresh**
"**-more** ("it is dreadful to explain these things in cold blood) means a headlong
" & exciting new snatch of his singing, resumption by the lark of song, which by
" turns he gives over & takes up again all day long, & this goes on, the sonnet
" says, through all time without ever losing its first freshness, being a thing both
" new & old. **Repair** means the same thing, renewal, resumption. The
" **skein** & **coil** are the lark's song, which from his height gives the impression
" of something falling to the earth, & not vertically quite, but trickingly or
" wavingly, something as a skein of silk ribbed by having been tightly wound)
" on a narrow card, or a notched holder, or as fishing=tackle or twine un=
" winding from a **reel** or winch, or as pearls strung on a horsehair: the laps
" or folds are the notes or short measures & bars of them. The same is called
" a **score** in the musical sense of score & this score is " writ upon a liquid
" sky trembling to welcome it ", only not horizontally. The lark in wild glee
" **races the reel round**, paying out or dealing out & down the turns of the
" skein or **coil** right to the earth **floor**, the ground, where it lies in a heap,
" as it were or rather is all wound off on to another winch, reel, bobbin, or
" spool in Fancy's eye by the moment the bird touches earth & so is ready for
" a fresh unwinding at the next flight. **Crisp** means almost crisped, namely
" with notes". | 82

MB **Readings from later MS. Aug 1884.**
3. With a flood or a fall, low lull-off or all roar,
6. His rash-fresh rewinded newskeined score
7. In crisps of curl off wild winch whirl, & pour
8. And pelt music, till none's to spill or spend.
13. Our make & making break, are breaking, down

Plate 303a   OET No. 118: The Sea and the Skylark -- MS. 4 (A)

A.p.89. This page from album A, facing MS. A of the poem, is reproduced as an example of the interest which Bridges evinced in the interpretation of Hopkins's more difficult poems. He stimulated the priest's poetic flow by responding in detail to his verse with shrewd, often appreciative though sometimes exasperated and baffled, comments. When the author replied with an exposition (as of No. 118 in a letter of 26 Nov. 1882, L.i.163-4, which RB cites on the page above), he often copied out extracts, or entered cross-references to the letter concerned. His request for an explanation led Hopkins to make a major revision. Not many people in the 1880s could have predicted that within half a century Hopkins's letters to Bridges would be published in full with annotations.

Bridges also tried to make album A a reasonably full and accurate source of Hopkins's poetry by entering the author's revisions, usually in red or black ink in the autograph itself, or when the changes were extensive, with a note of them on an adjacent page, or a complete transcription. Where, thanks largely to Bridges' later efforts, the autograph itself has survived, these copies have no authority and are not reproduced in the Facsimiles. In other cases, above all for "The Wreck of the Deutschland", the solicitude of Bridges has saved a masterpiece from vanishing without trace.

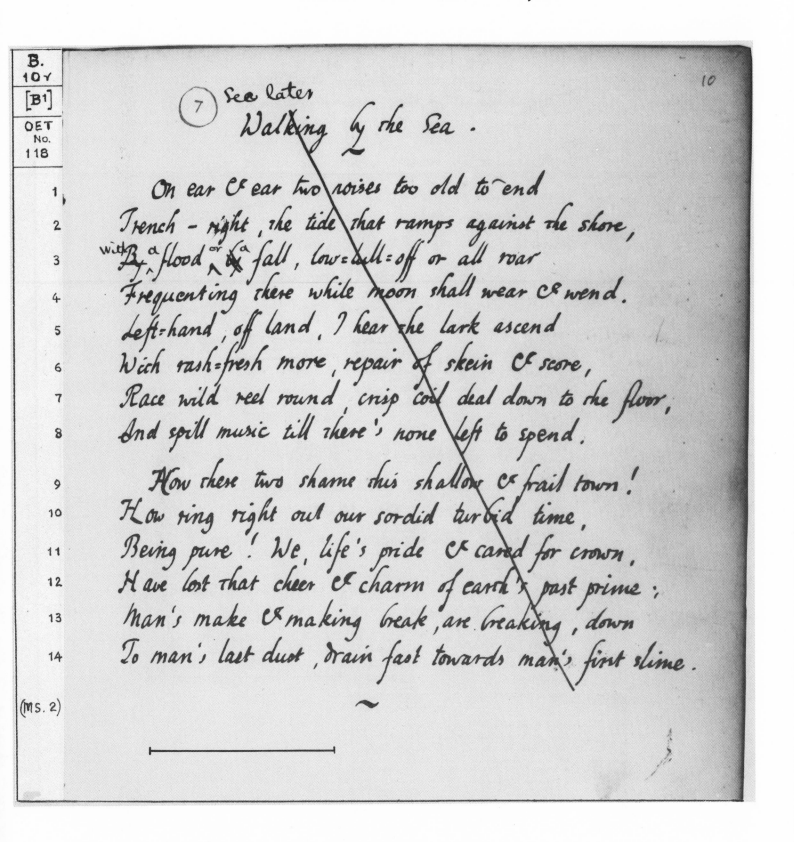

⑦ See later

Walking by the Sea .

On ear & ear two noises too old to end
Trench - right, the tide that ramps against the shore,
With By a flood or by a fall, low=lull=off or all roar
Frequenting there while moon shall wear & wend.
Left=hand, off land, I hear the lark ascend
With rash=fresh more, repair of skein & score,
Race wild reel round, crisp coil deal down to the floor,
And spill music till there's none left to spend.

How these two shame this shallow & frail town !
How ring right out our sordid turbid time,
Being pure ! We, life's pride & cared for crown,
Have lost that cheer & charm of earth's past prime ;
Man's make & making break, are breaking, down
To man's last dust, drain fast towards man's first slime .

~

(MS. 2)

Plate 303b   OET No. 118: The Sea and the Skylark -- MS. 2 (B[1])

Earlier title: Walking by the Sea

    B.10r. Transcript by RB of the original version (A.p.90) where GMH's "How" in 9, and still more in 10, looks like "Now", so RB had to mend "Now" to "How" in 9.

    GMH began to revise it, changing "By flood, by fall," (3), and adding a slur in purple on "to end" (1); then he decided to rewrite 6-8 entirely in view of RB's perplexities, alluded to in L.i.163-4 (26 Nov. 1882). He therefore crossed the whole transcript through and wrote "See later"--a reference to B.28r (Plate 303).

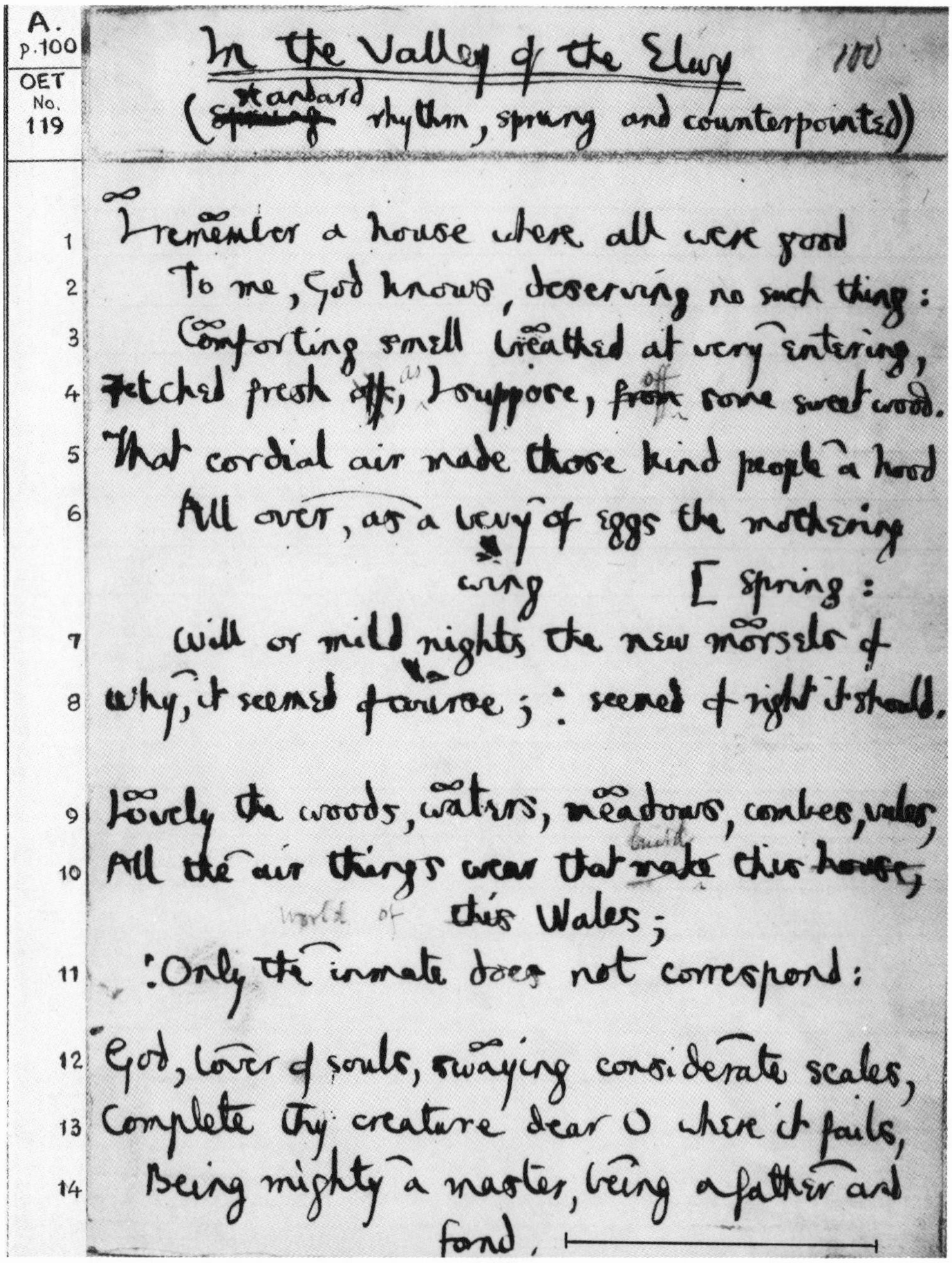

A.
p.100

OET
No.
119

In the Valley of the Elwy   100

(~~spining~~ ^standard^ rhythm, sprung and counterpointed)

1 I remember a house where all were good
2   To me, God knows, deserving no such thing :
3   Comforting smell breathed at very entering,
4 Fetched fresh ^(as)^ off, I suppose, from some sweet wood.
5 That cordial air made those kind people a hood
6   All over, as a bevy of eggs the mothering
                    wing   [spring :
7   Will or mild nights the new morsels of
8 why, it seemed of course ; : seemed of right it should.

9 Lovely the woods, waters, meadows, combes, vales,
10 All the air things wear that ^built^ make this house,
        world of this Wales ;
11   : Only the inmate does not correspond :

12 God, lover of souls, swaying considerate scales,
13 Complete thy creature dear O where it fails,
14 Being mighty a master, being a father and
                    fond .

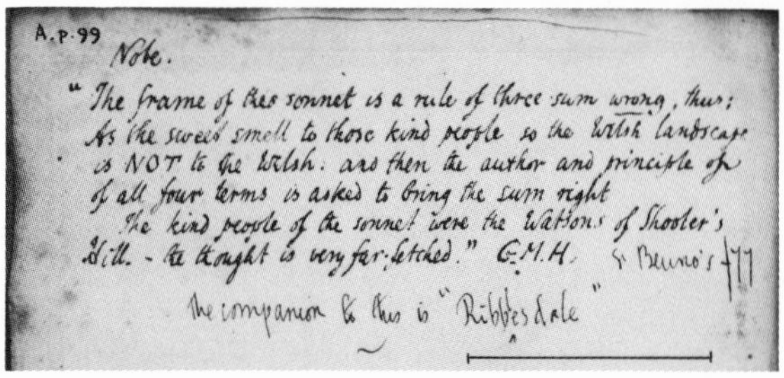

A.p.99 Note.
" The frame of this sonnet is a rule of three sum wrong, thus :
As the sweet smell to those kind people so the Welsh landscape
is NOT to the Welsh. and then the author and principle of
of all four terms is asked to bring the sum right
The kind people of the sonnet were the Watsons of Shooter's
Hill. - the thought is very far-fetched." G.M.H. St Beuno's '77

the companion to this is "Ribblesdale"

<u>Plate 304</u>   <u>OET No. 119: In the Valley of the Elwy</u> -- MS   1   (A)

    <u>A.p.100</u>. Autograph faircopy. GMH's <u>Deletions</u>: (metrical note) "Sprung"   earlier sforzando sign over "wing" (6) and "course" (8)--inverted "V". Note the great colon in 8 and preceding 11; also the counterpoint signs in 1, 3, 7, 9, 12.

    <u>RB's red ink</u> in 4, 10 copies GMH's revisions in B: in 4, by adding "as" after "off," and not deleting that comma (as GMH did in B) he did not need to insert one after "fresh". In 10 he carefully del. the comma after "house", which GMH had left in B.

    <u>A.99</u>. On the page facing this autograph, A.p.99, RB copied from GMH's explanatory letter of April 8 1879 (L.i.76). The additions ("St. Beuno's" and "The companion to this is 'Ribblesdale'") are in the backward sloping black ink of 1889.

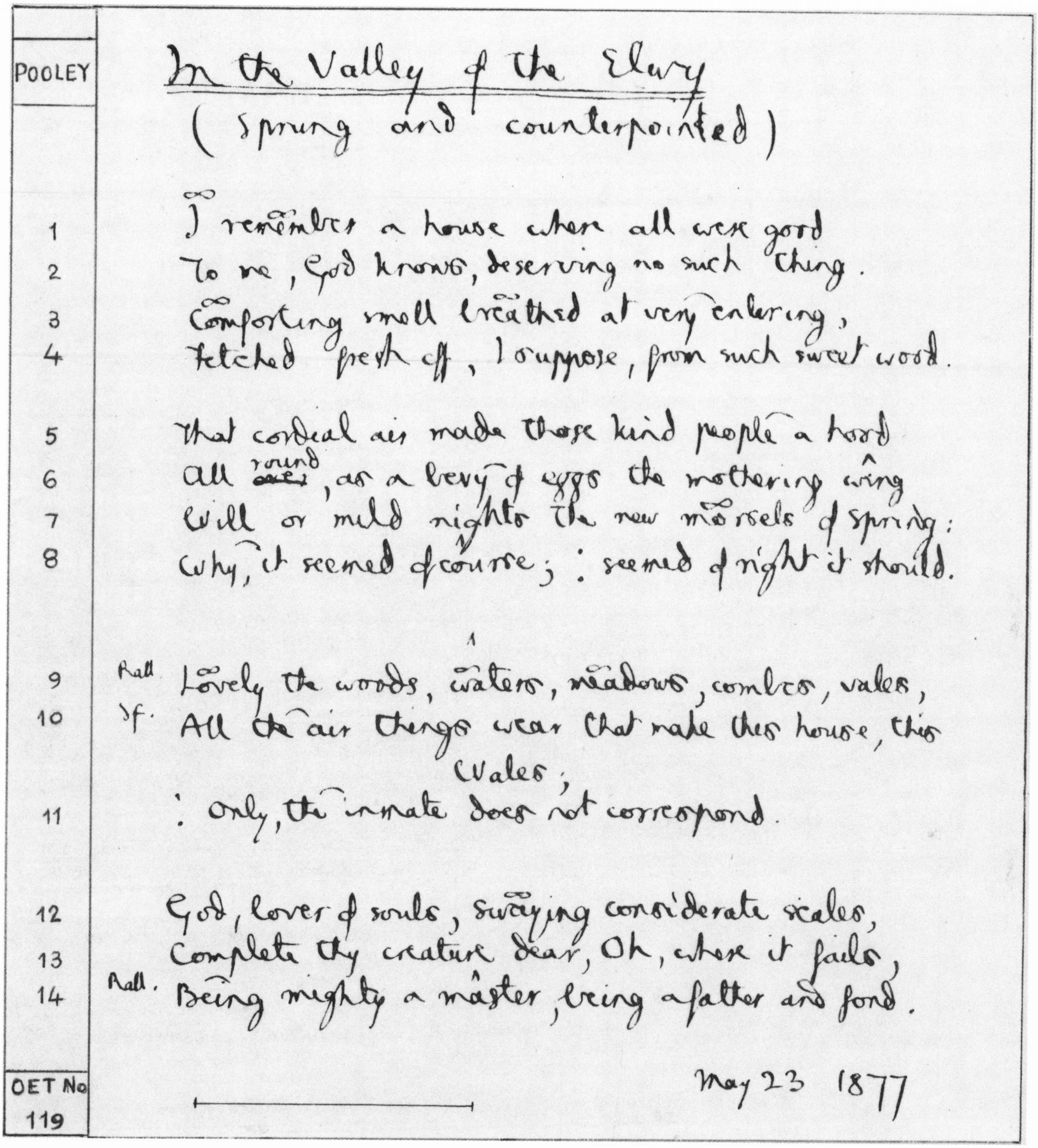

PLATE 305. OET 119. *In the Valley of the Elwy* • 119

In the Valley of the Elwy
(Spring and counterpointed)

1   I remember a house where all were good
2   To me, God knows, deserving no such thing.
3   Comforting smell breathed at very entering,
4   Fetched fresh off, I suppose, from such sweet wood.

5   That cordial air made those kind people a hood
6   All round, as a bevy of eggs the mothering wing
7   Will or mild nights the new morsels of spring:
8   Why, it seemed of course; : seemed of right it should.

9   Lovely the woods, waters, meadows, combes, vales,
10   All the air things wear that make this house, this
               Wales;
11   : Only, the inmate does not correspond.

12   God, lover of souls, swaying considerate scales,
13   Complete thy creature dear, Oh, where it fails,
14   Being mighty a master, being a father and fond.

May 23 1877

<u>Plate 305</u>   <u>OET No. 119: In the Valley of the Elwy</u> -- MS. 2 (P)

   <u>Pooley MS</u> -- Autograph faircopy, one of three poems sent by GMH to his sister Grace; it was found by Lady Christabel Pooley in 1964. She sent me photographs, invited me to her home in Surrey to examine the MSS, and allowed me to describe them in an article "Gerard and Grace Hopkins", The <u>Month</u> (N.S. 33:6, June 1965, 347-50). This autograph is on the verso of "Spring" (No. 117--the third poem was No. 139, Plate 374).

   This MS and the Pooley MS of "Spring" (Plate 300), have musical annotations presumably intended to help Grace in setting them to music. Note the sforzando signs (an inverted V) over "course" (8), "waters" (9), and "master" (14), and the "sf." preceding 10; also "Rall[entando]" before 9 and 14. In the metrical description, "s" is mended to "t" in "counterpointed". In 5 the ink slur over "people a" is mended in pencil. This MS provided for the first time an exact date for the first composition of the sonnet. In 4 "such" (for "some" in A and B) may be due to dittography from 2: GMH was an absent-minded transcriber, or relied upon an imperfect memory.

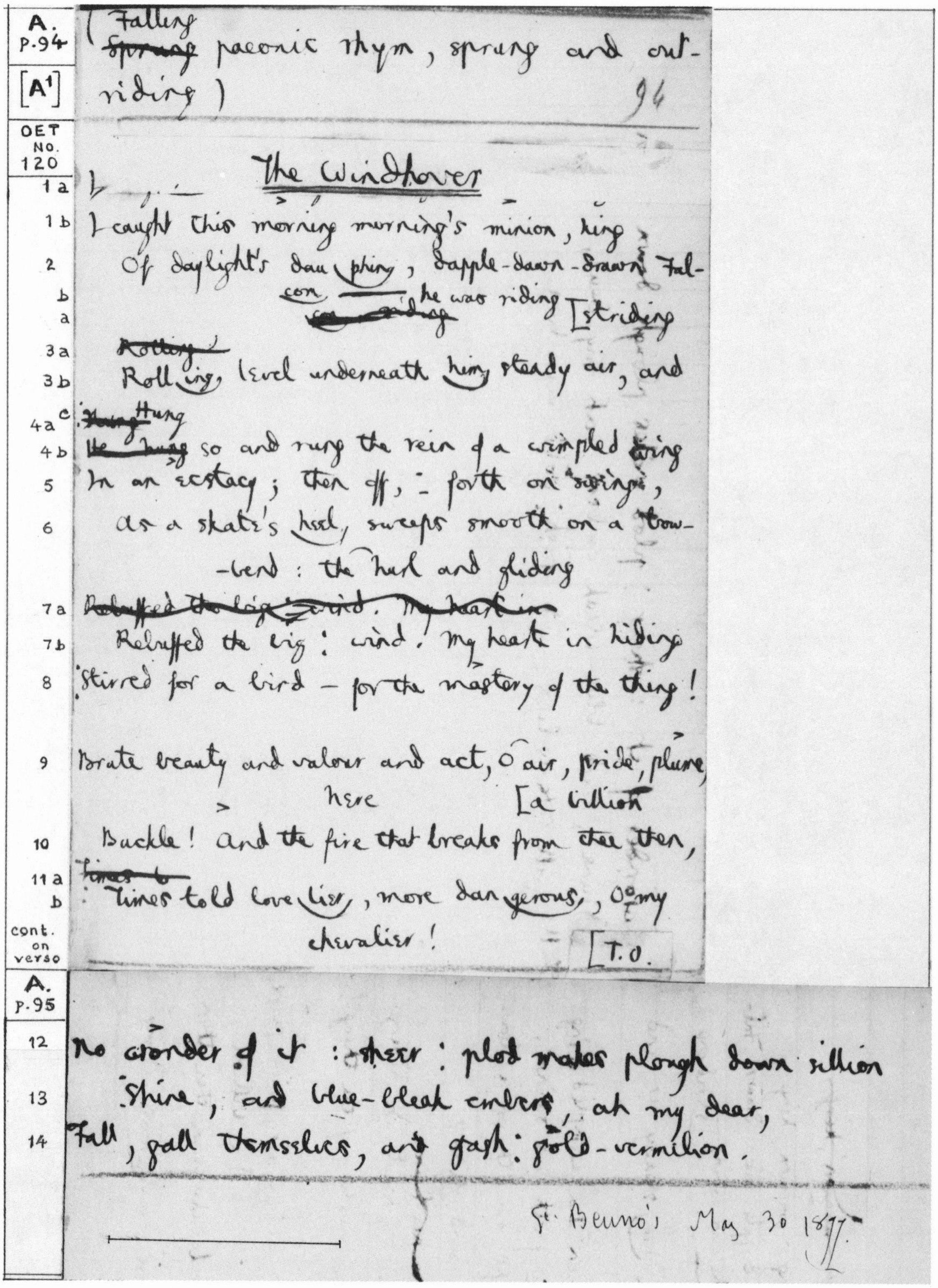

A. p.94 [A1]

(Falling ~~Sprung~~ paeonic rhym, sprung and outriding) 94

OET No. 120

The Windhover

I caught this ~~morning~~ morning's minion, king-
Of daylight's dauphin, dapple-dawn-drawn Fal-
con, he was riding [striding
Rolling level underneath him steady air, and
Hung so and rung the rein of a wimpled wing
In an ecstacy; then off, forth on swing,
As a skate's heel sweeps smooth on a bow-
-bend: the hurl and gliding
~~Rebuffed the big wind. My heart in~~
Rebuffed the big: wind. My heart in hiding
Stirred for a bird – for the mastery of the thing!

Brute beauty and valour and act, O air, pride, plume,
here [a billion
Buckle! and the fire that breaks from thee then,
~~Times to~~
Times told lovelier, more dangerous, O my
chevalier!
cont. on verso [T.O.

A. p.95

No wonder of it: sheer: plod makes plough down sillion
Shine, and blue-bleak embers, ah my dear,
Fall, gall themselves, and gash: gold-vermilion.

St. Beuno's May 30 1877

Plate 306 OET No. 120: The Windhover -- MS. 1 (A^1)

A.pp.94 (1 to 11), 95 (12-14, at right angles down the back, visible as blotches on the ends of 1-11). In this facsimile they are attached below. -- Autograph, intended as a faircopy of the earliest version, but revised during transcription. See Plate 309a and the notes opposite it for analysis of 1-5. In the metrical note "Sprung" is del.: that "rhythm" was misspelt and not corrected shows the poet's haste and preoccupation with the surging development of a masterpiece.

GMH's slips, deletions and revisions lost him so much space that he reached the bottom of his sheet with three lines yet to add. His decision to write these sideways down the back made it impossible for RB to display the whole of this great sonnet on a single opening. No doubt meaning to indent lines rhyming b and d, he slipped up in 7a (del. and rewritten, but 11a may have been del. in error); also 12, 13 and 14 (corrected in A^2, Plate 308). Great colons before 4a and 4c, 8, 11b and 13 give them sprung openings (surely one is missing before 3b?). Other great colons are in 5, 7a, 7b, 12 and 14. The sforzando signs (a V pointing right) include one on "minion" (1b). There are seven outrides. The hooked end of the outride under "Rolling" (3b) could be misread as a comma.

RB in 1889 added the date ("May", misread as "Maj" by some).

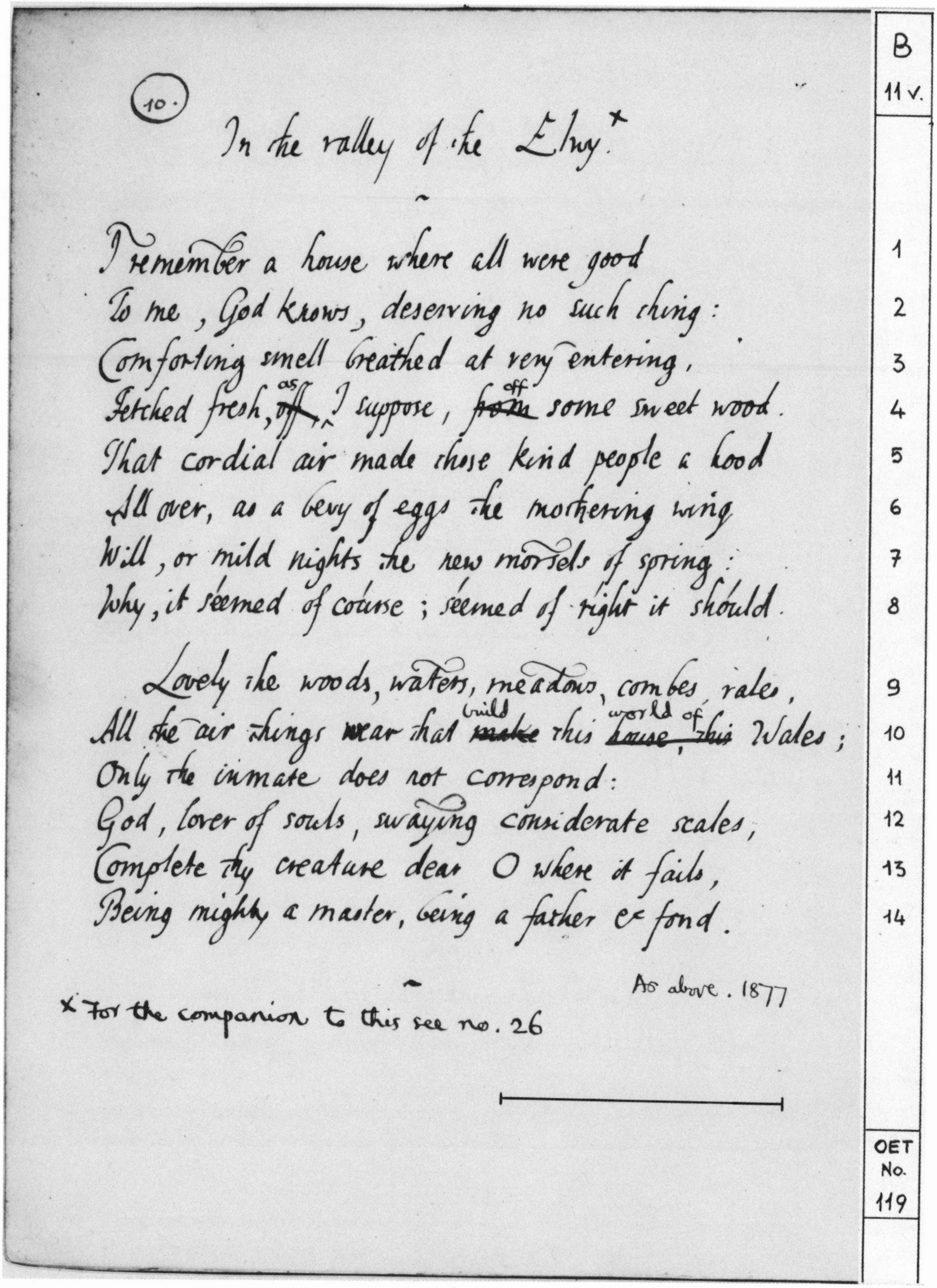

PLATE 307. OET 119. *In the Valley of the Elwy* • 121

B
11 v.

⑩·

In the valley of the Elwy.*

I remember a house where all were good   1
To me, God knows, deserving no such thing: 2
Comforting smell breathed at very entering,   3
Fetched fresh, *as* off, I suppose, ~~from~~ *off* some sweet wood.   4
That cordial air made those kind people a hood   5
All over, as a bevy of eggs the mothering wing   6
Will, or mild nights the new morsels of spring: 7
Why, it seemed of course; seemed of right it should.   8

    Lovely the woods, waters, meadows, combes, vales,   9
All the air things wear that ~~make~~ *build* this ~~house, this~~ *world of* Wales;   10
Only the inmate does not correspond: 11
God, lover of souls, swaying considerate scales,   12
Complete thy creature dear O where it fails,   13
Being mighty a master, being a father & fond.   14

As above. 1877

x For the companion to this see no. 26

OET
No.
119

Plate 307   OET No. 119: In the Valley of the Elwy -- MS. 3 (B)

B.11 verso. Copy of A transcribed by RB in album B: the two MSS may be compared by raising the intervening sheet. RB may have been responsible for the comma after "Will" (7), an improvement.

GMH revised 4 (adding the comma after "fresh" to replace one he had del. after "off") and 10: he had already sent RB the correction of "make" to "build this world of Wales" on March 27 1883 (L.i.178). He inserted in ink counterpoint signs in 1, 7, 9 and a slur in 10; but used purple pencil for the counterpoint in 12, the slur in 3, and five stresses in 8. The star after the title, with its footnote, and the date appear to have been added later, on two different occasions.

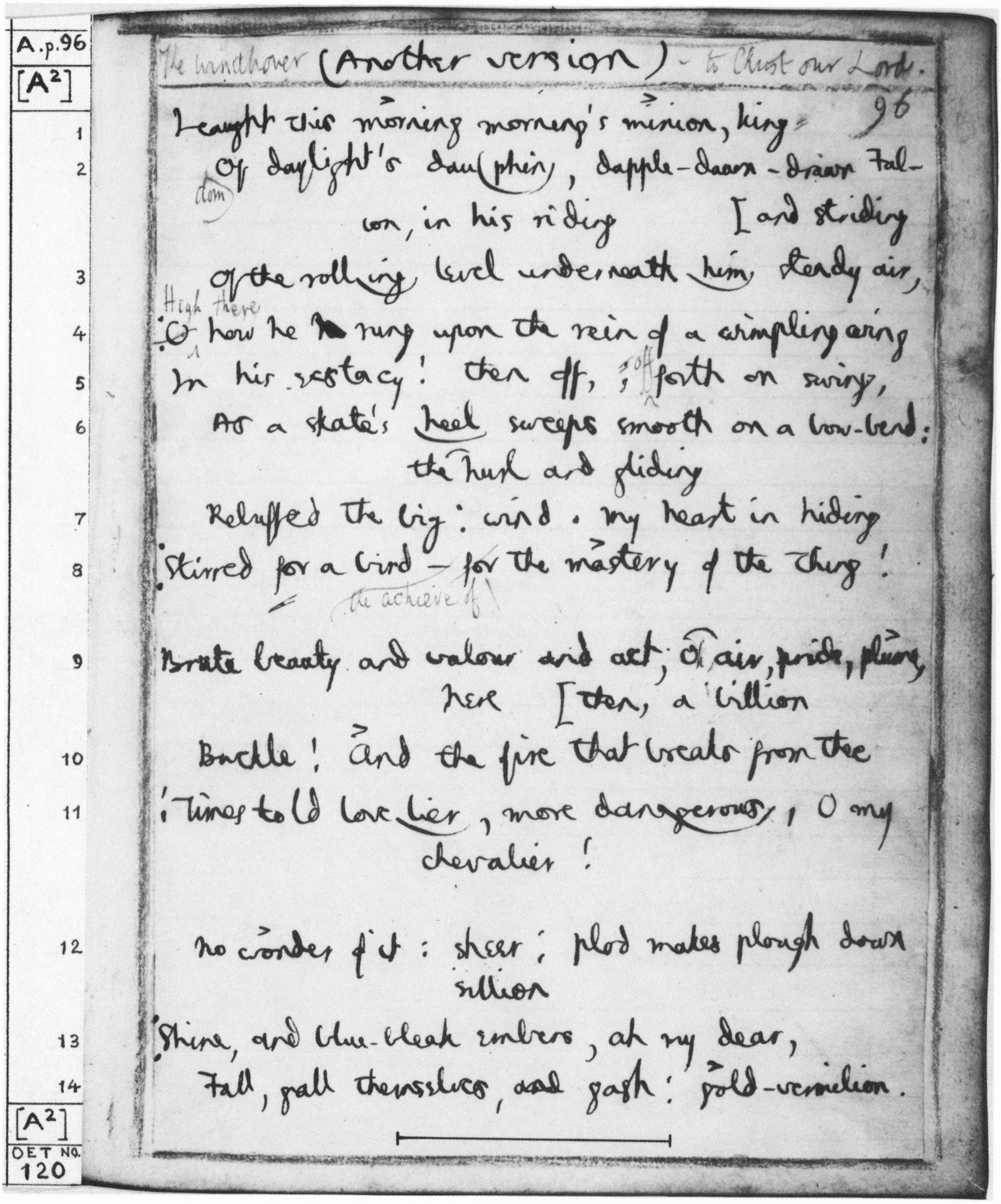

A.p.96
[A²]

The Windhover (Another version) — to Christ our Lord.   96

1 I caught this morning morning's minion, king-
2 dom of daylight's dauphin, dapple-dawn-drawn Falcon, in his riding   [and striding
3 Of the rolling level underneath him, steady air,
4 High there! O how he [*hung*] rung upon the rein of a wimpling wing
5 In his ecstacy! then off, ; off forth on swing,
6 As a skate's heel sweeps smooth on a bow-bend: the hurl and gliding
7 Rebuffed the big: wind. My heart in hiding
8 Stirred for a bird — for the mastery of the thing! [the achieve of
9 Brute beauty and valour and act, oh air, pride, plume,
   here   [then, a billion
10 Buckle! And the fire that breaks from thee
11 Times told lovelier, more dangerous, O my
    chevalier!
12 No wonder of it: sheer; plod makes plough down
    sillion
13 Shine, and blue-bleak embers, ah my dear,
14 Fall, gall themselves, and gash: gold-vermilion.

[A²]
OET NO. 120

Plate 308   OET No. 120: The Windhover -- MS. 2 (A²)

A.p.96 -- Autograph faircopy of a revised version, prob. written in the summer of 1877. Changes in 1-5 can be studied on Plate 309a. In 5 "an ecstacy" became "his ecstacy". Above "beauty" (9) a stray ink dot is struck through lightly with two brown ink strokes meeting in a V: this is not a sforzando sign. GMH would certainly have headed his MS "The Windhover", above "Another version", but in album A, where A² was mounted next to A¹, cutting off the title to fit in a MS too tall for the page could create no ambiguity.

RB's red ink (1884) copies, from GMH's revisions in MS. B, the extended title, and changes in ℓℓ. 1, 2, 4, 5, 8 and 9, but not 10. Contrast the analysis of these three MSS, based only on photocopies, in PMLA 82, no. 5(Oct. 1967), 465-8.

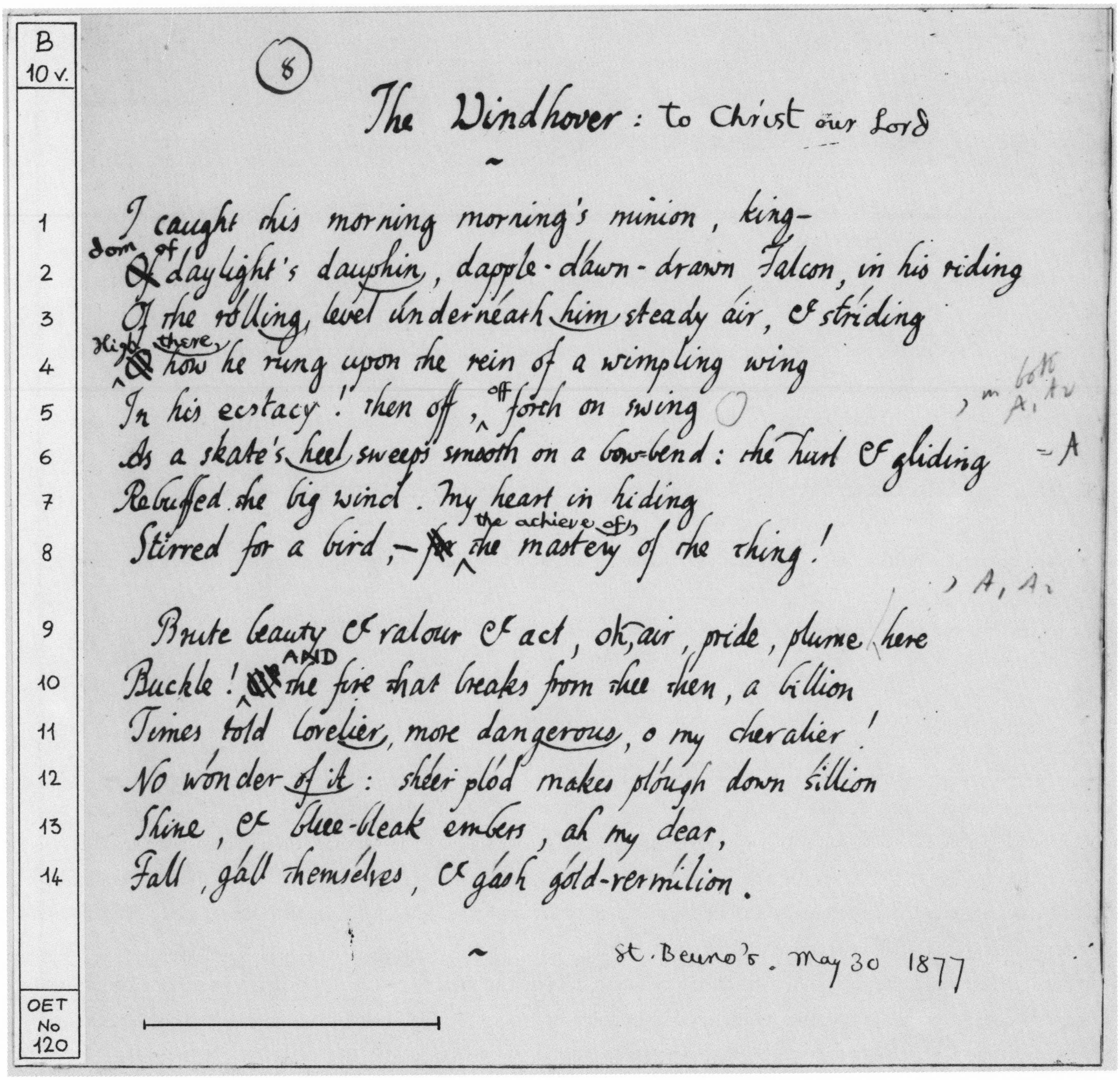

PLATE 309. OET 120. *The Windhover* • *123*

B
10 v.

(8)

The Windhover : to Christ our Lord

1 I caught this morning morning's minion, king-
dom of
2 Of daylight's dauphin, dapple-dawn-drawn Falcon, in his riding
3 Of the rolling, level underneath him steady air, & striding
High there,
4 how he rung upon the rein of a wimpling wing
5 In his ecstacy! then off, off forth on swing
6 As a skate's heel sweeps smooth on a bow-bend: the hurl & gliding   —A
7 Rebuffed the big wind. My heart in hiding
the achieve of,
8 Stirred for a bird, — the mastery of the thing!

9 Brute beauty & valour & act, oh, air, pride, plume, here
AND
10 Buckle! the fire that breaks from thee then, a billion
11 Times told lovelier, more dangerous, o my chevalier!
12 No wonder of it: sheer plód makes plough down sillion
13 Shine, & blue-bleak embers, ah my dear,
14 Fall, gall themselves, & gash gold-vermilion.

St. Beuno's. May 30 1877

Plate 309   OET No. 120: The Windhover -- MS. 3 (B)

    MS.B.10v. RB's transcript from A², inscribed in album B (1883). He omitted the metrical marks, substituted ampersands for "and" as usual (3, 6, 9, 10, 13, 14, in seven places, not simply in the celebrated 10th line); and "o" for "O" in 9 and 11. Only 9 is indented.

    GMH in 1884 revised 1, 2, 4, 5, 8, 9 ("o air" became "oh, air"), 10 (ampersand changed to "AND"). In ink, he added the slur in 6, six outrides from A², along with new ones in 12 and in his revisions to 4, 8. After "bird" (8) he strengthened the dash and seems to have added or strengthened the comma. In purple pencil, he inserted metrical stresses (one in 2, five each in 3, 12, and 14). Before sending album B on to Patmore, he extended the title (": to Christ our Lord"), using a different pen. After receiving album B back from RB as a gift GMH added the date.

    RB, when editing <u>Poems</u>, 1st. edn. in 1918, used pencil to draw in the margin a circle after "swing" (5), noting that "in both A₁ A₂" there was a comma he had overlooked in transcription. After "plume" (9) he pencilled a caret with ", A₁ A₂". The note at the end of 6 ("=A", i.e., "hyphen in A") refers to the double hyphen, like an equals sign, which he then pencilled in between "bow" and "bend". His edn. corrected all three omissions.

Plate 309a   OET No. 120: The Windhover -- 1-5 in A^1, A^2 and B.

(top) A^1--A.p.94. (Earliest version). 1a was hurriedly deleted, along with its two sforzando signs, and rewritten with no material changes as 1b. The title had to be cut off to allow the text of lines 1-11 to fit the page: it was guarded into the album. The title was pasted over 1a before RB drew a red border down the right edge. All that is still visible of 1a, to the left of the title and below it, are the opening "I" and the tails of four "g"s (which on WHG's microfilm appeared as strange metrical marks for 1b). The first ending to 2 was "Fal-con, riding". In 3a "Rolling" was del. and rewritten with a space before the outride "ing". As no line space would be left after 3, the first version of 4 must be "Hung" preceded by a great colon (4a); then came "He hung" (4b), and finally a reversion to "Hung" (4c).

(middle) A^2--A.p.95. (Second version). A true faircopy, no longer disturbed by the ardours of composition. The red ink revisions copied by RB, from B (1884), belong of course to the final version. Note that "Falcon" (2) has no outride here or in B. The changes from "--he was riding" to "in his riding", and the addition "Of the" before "rolling", allow the kestrel to glide more smoothly up to the hover in 4. The del. before "rung" (4) is "h[ung]". But the onset of the hover itself has now been obscured: in A^1 "Hung so and rung the rein of a wimpled wing/In an ecstacy; then off, forth on swing" was obviously all a description of the most striking feature of the windhover's flight, its hanging in the air with rapid rippling wings. A^2 opens the way to the common misapplication of line 4 to the kestrel's great looping circles, inappropriately compared by critics to the rigid disciplining of a horse through being made to run in a circle, tethered to a long rope held at its centre by a trainer: who could believe that the horse was "In an ecstacy"? The revision of ℓ.4 in B breaks the glide of the kestrel more dramatically with "High there," as he rises slightly to begin the hover.

(bottom) B.10v. (Final version). The new title emphasises the Lordship of Christ. Because A^1 and A^2 might be easily misunderstood as hailing the windhover as the king of daylight (a description more appropriate to the "dayspring from on high," the "Lord of light"), the poet makes clear that the kestrel is only the dauphin, a type of Christ. GMH's inventive addition of "-dom" to "king", leaving the first syllable to rhyme, avoided having to revise the echoing rhymes in 4, 5 and 8 ("wing", "swing" and "thing"--the b rhymes, of course, are two syllabled, "riding", "striding", "gliding", "hiding" though some have imagined the octave as all a rhymes). In 5 the extra "off" helps to mark the end of one movement (the wings vibrating in the hover) and start of another--the splendid ease of the falcon's sweep down wind and round again into it, mastering the strong gusts. We misunderstand the windhover's flight pattern if we do not recognise the sudden change of activity represented by "then off, off forth on swing".

A¹
A. p.94

The Windhover

1a

1b I caught this morning morning's minion, king

2   Of daylight's dauphin, dapple-dawn-drawn Fal-

b   con ——————— ~~the was riding~~ he was riding [striding

a

3a ~~Rolling~~

3b Rolling, level underneath him steady air, and

4a ᶜ ~~Hung~~ Hung

4b ~~He~~ ~~hung~~ so and rung the rein of a crimpled wing

5   In an ecstacy; then off, – forth on swing,

A
p.96

[A²]   The windhover (Another version) – to Christ our Lord.   [A²]

1   I caught this morning morning's minion, king–   96

2   Of daylight's dauphin, dapple-dawn-drawn Fal-
dom
    con, in his riding   [and striding

3   Of the rolling, level underneath him steady air,

    High there
4   : O how he ~~no~~ rung upon the rein of a crimpling wing

5   In his ecstacy! then off, ꞏ off forth on swing,

B
10 v.

⑧

The Windhover : to Christ our Lord

1   I caught this morning morning's minion, king–

dom
2   of
    Of daylight's dauphin, dapple-dawn-drawn Falcon, in his riding

3   Of the rolling, level underneath him steady air, & striding

    High there
4   ᣔ how he rung upon the rein of a wimpling wing

5   In his ecstacy! then off, ᐧ off forth on swing

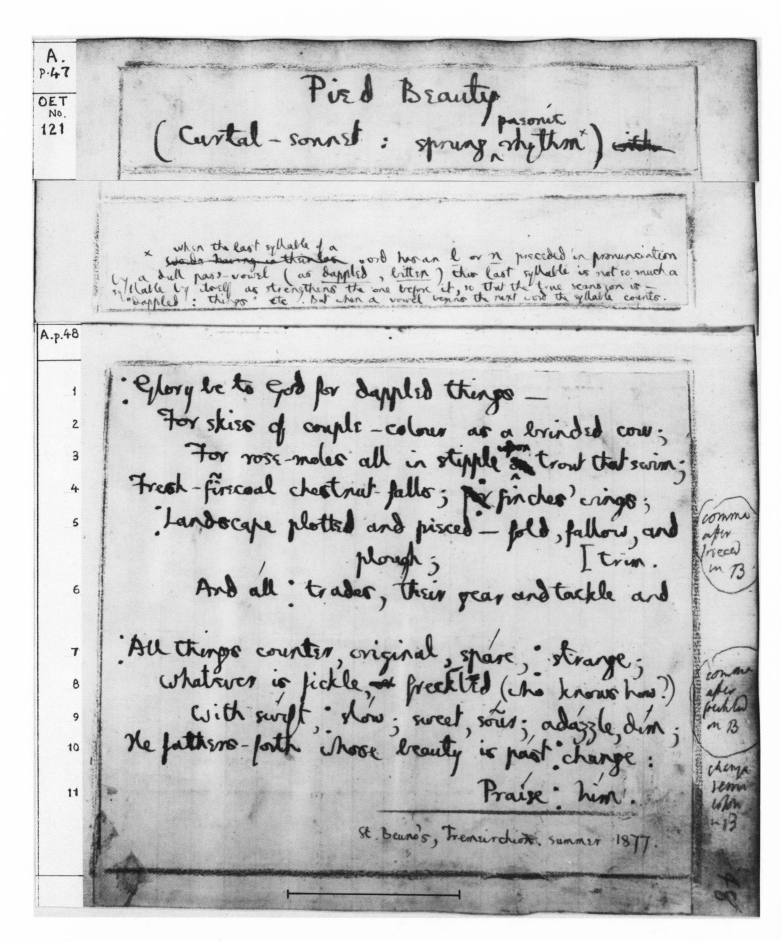

Plate 310   OET No. 121: Pied Beauty -- MS. 1 (A)

A.pp.47-48. Autograph faircopy. GMH's footnote to "sprung paeonic rhythm" (the closing bracket obscures a comma, before the del. "with"): "[Words having in their las all del.]. When the last syllable of a word has an *l* or *n* preceded in pronunciation [not "punctuation" as in L.i.56, n.] by a dull pass-vowel (as dappled, bitten) this last syllable is not so much

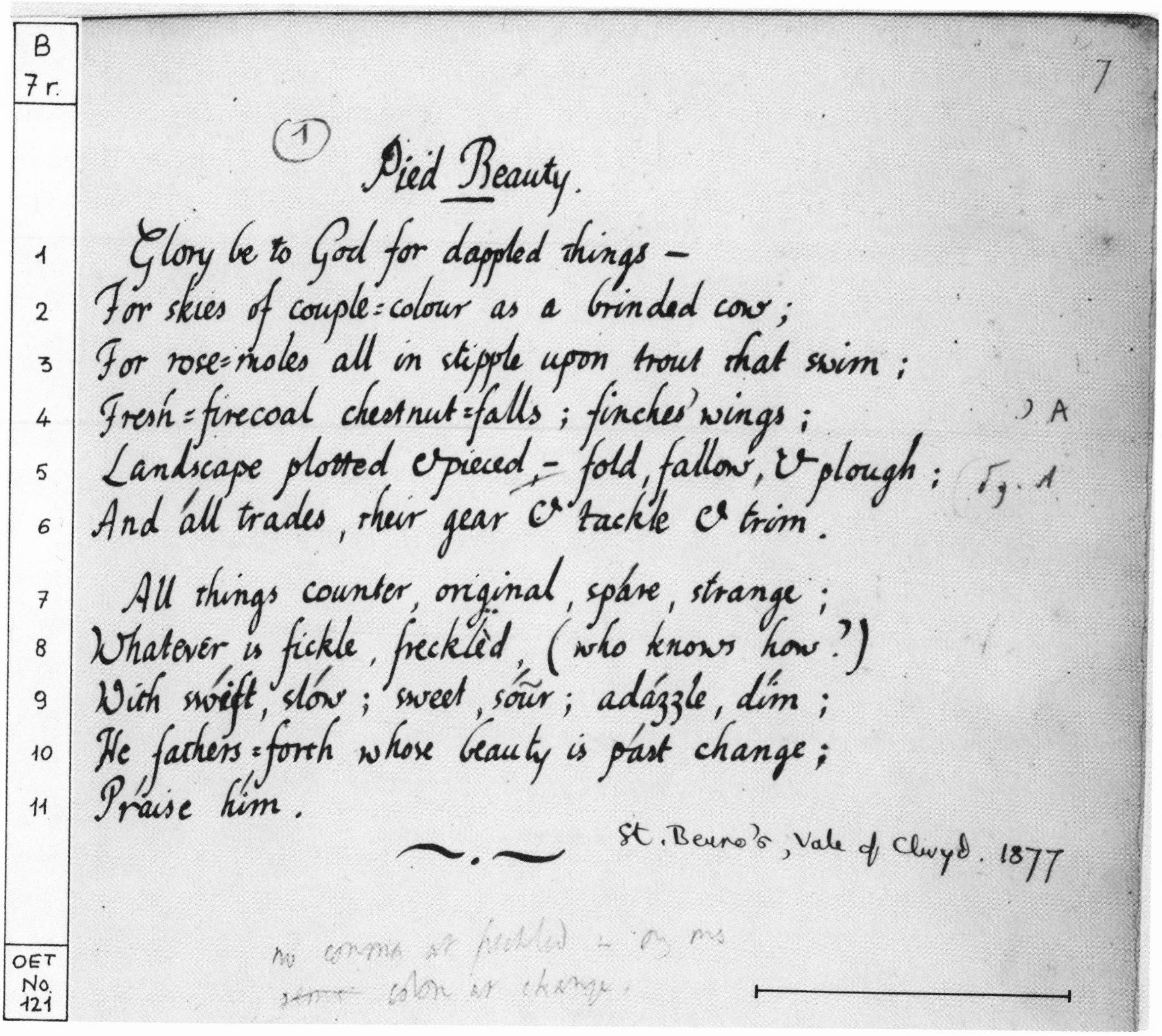

PLATE 311. OET 121. *Pied Beauty* • 127

B
7 r.

① *Pied Beauty.*

1 Glory be to God for dappled things –
2 For skies of couple=colour as a brinded cow ;
3 For rose=moles all in stipple upon trout that swim ;
4 Fresh=firecoal chestnut=falls ; finches' wings ;   ) A
5 Landscape plotted ᴐpieced – fold, fallow, ᴐplough ; [ᴐ .A]
6 And all trades, their gear ᴐtackle ᴐtrim .

7 All things counter, original, spare, strange ;
8 Whatever is fickle, frecklèd, (who knows how ?)
9 With swíft, slów ; sweet, sóur ; adázzle, dím ;
10 He fathers=forth whose beauty is past change ;
11 Práise hím .

~ . ~   St. Beuno's, Vale of Clwyd . 1877

no comma at freckled + ... ms
... colon at change .

OET
No.
121

---

a syllable by itself as strengthens the one before it, so that the true scansion is--'dappled: things' [great colon intended--contr. L.i.56, n.]. But when a vowel begins the next word the syllable counts". Great colons precede 1, 5, 7, and occur in 4, 6, 7, 9, 10, 11. Circumflexes on "fire" (4), "sour" (9). <u>Deletions</u>: 3 on 4 for [replaced by a great colon] 8 or [also diaeresis and grave accent on 2nd syllable of "freckled"]. GMH added the date later.

RB's black ink (1889) adds stress marks from B in 6, 7, 9, 10, 11. His pencil (1918) notes in the margin that B has commas after "pieced" (5) and "freckled" (8), and a semicolon after "change" (10) [it is, however, really a smudged colon].

Plate 311   OET No. 121: Pied Beauty -- MS. 2 (B)

B.7r. Copy of A inscribed in album B by RB. After "change" (10) a colon has been smudged, making it look like a semicolon (even to RB). In 9 RB wrote "sweet" <u>before</u> "slow", then mended his slip to "swift".

GMH added (1884) in purple pencil ten stresses in 6, 7, 9, 10, 11; both a diaeresis and a grave accent on the 2nd syllable of "freckled" (8); and a circumflex on "sour" (9). The date he appended in ink later.

RB's pencil (1918), on the authority of the autograph in A, adds an apostrophe after "finches" (4), and a comma after "fallow" (5); he deletes the comma after "pieced" (5)--see his marginal notes. At foot RB notes other stops in A: "no comma at freckled in orig. MS [semi <u>del.</u>] colon at change."

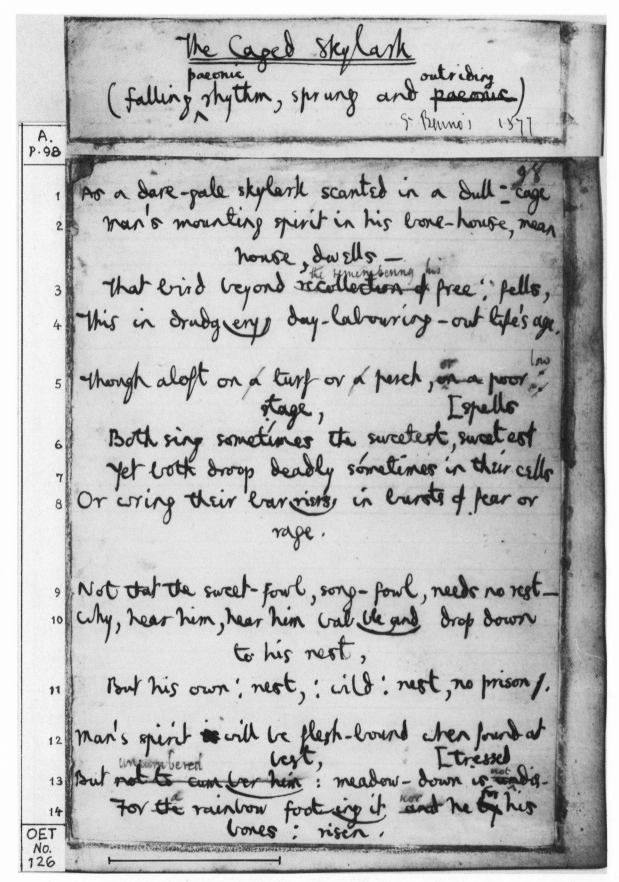

Plate 312   OET No. 122: The Caged Skylark -- MS. 1 (A)

A.pp.97 (title) and 98 (poem). Autograph faircopy. For this plate the title has been restored to the top of the sheet. All metrical marks are in the same ink as the text. Note the great colons in 1, 3, 5, 11 (three), 14; outrides (one in 10 has been mended to include "and"); stresses in 6 ("sometimes") and 7 ("sómetimes"). Deletions by GMH: metrical note "paeonic"   11 colon after "prison"   12 "is"   14 "by"   Note that there is no comma after "drudgery" (4), only a double-tailed outride.

RB's red ink (1884) copies from B GMH's revisions in 3, 5, 13, 14. His black ink (1889) inserts the date at the top. His pencil on p.97 (not shown) notes opposite 13, 14 "Correction is from a letter Aug. 8 1877" (see Plate 313a) but he has really followed B ("But" makes better sense in 13 than L's "And").

PLATE 313. OET 122. *The Caged Skylark* • 129

B
11 r.

⑨ The caged skylark

1 As a dare-gale skylark scanted in a dull cage, *no comma in orig*

2 Man's mounting spirit in his bone-house, mean house, dwells —

3 That bird beyond ~~recollection of~~ the remembering his free fells;

4 This in drudgery, day-labouring-out life's age.

5 Though aloft on ✗ turf or ✗ perch ✗✗ ✗✗✗ or poor low stage *orig has , — orig has no stop*

6 Both sing sometimes the sweetest, sweetest spells,

7 Yet both droop deadly sometimes in their cells

8 Or wring their barriers, in bursts of fear or rage.

9 Not that the sweet-fowl, song-fowl, needs no rest —

10 Why, hear him, hear him babble & drop down to his nest,

11 But his own nest, wild nest, no prison.

12 Man's spirit will be flesh-bound, when found at best,

13 But ~~not to cumber him~~ uncumbered : meadow-down is not distressed

14 For ~~the~~ a rainbow footing it nor ~~he~~ he for his bones risen.

St. Beuno's. 1877

Plate 313   OET No. 122: The Caged Skylark -- MS. **3** (B)

B.11r -- Copy of MS. A transcribed in album B by RB. <u>Bridges</u> omitted the comma after "stage" (5), but added one after "it" (14); he was prob. responsible for changing "fells," to "fells;" (3--not an improvement). Originally 1 read "sky-lark" and 4 "drudgery--". In 12 the comma after "Flesh-bound" looks like a later intrusion;   it is not in either autograph (A or L), nor in K and was not accepted by RB or the first four Oxford edns. Examining it under high magnification and infrared I could find no clear evidence of GMH's pen or ink. As I prefer the rhythm of this musical line without the comma, I have not restored it in the <u>OET</u>. Catherine Phillips introduces it in OA, so readers have a choice.

<u>GMH revised</u> 3, 5, 13, 14; he added ink outrides (including one in his revision in 13); and thirteen stresses in purple: note one on "his" in the revised 3 (this probably downgrades the stress thrown on "free" in A by the great colon). GMH seems to have added commas after "cage" (1), "spells" (6), and reinforced the comma after "drudgery" (4); but he did not restore the comma after "stage" (5), where it does not suit his revision. He added the date after receiving album B back from RB in August 1884.

<u>RB's pencil (1918)</u> notes in the margin some departures from the "orig[inal]" (i.e., A) in punctuation: "no comma" [after "cage" (1)]   "orig has ," [after "stage" (5)]   "orig has no stop" [after "spells" (6)].

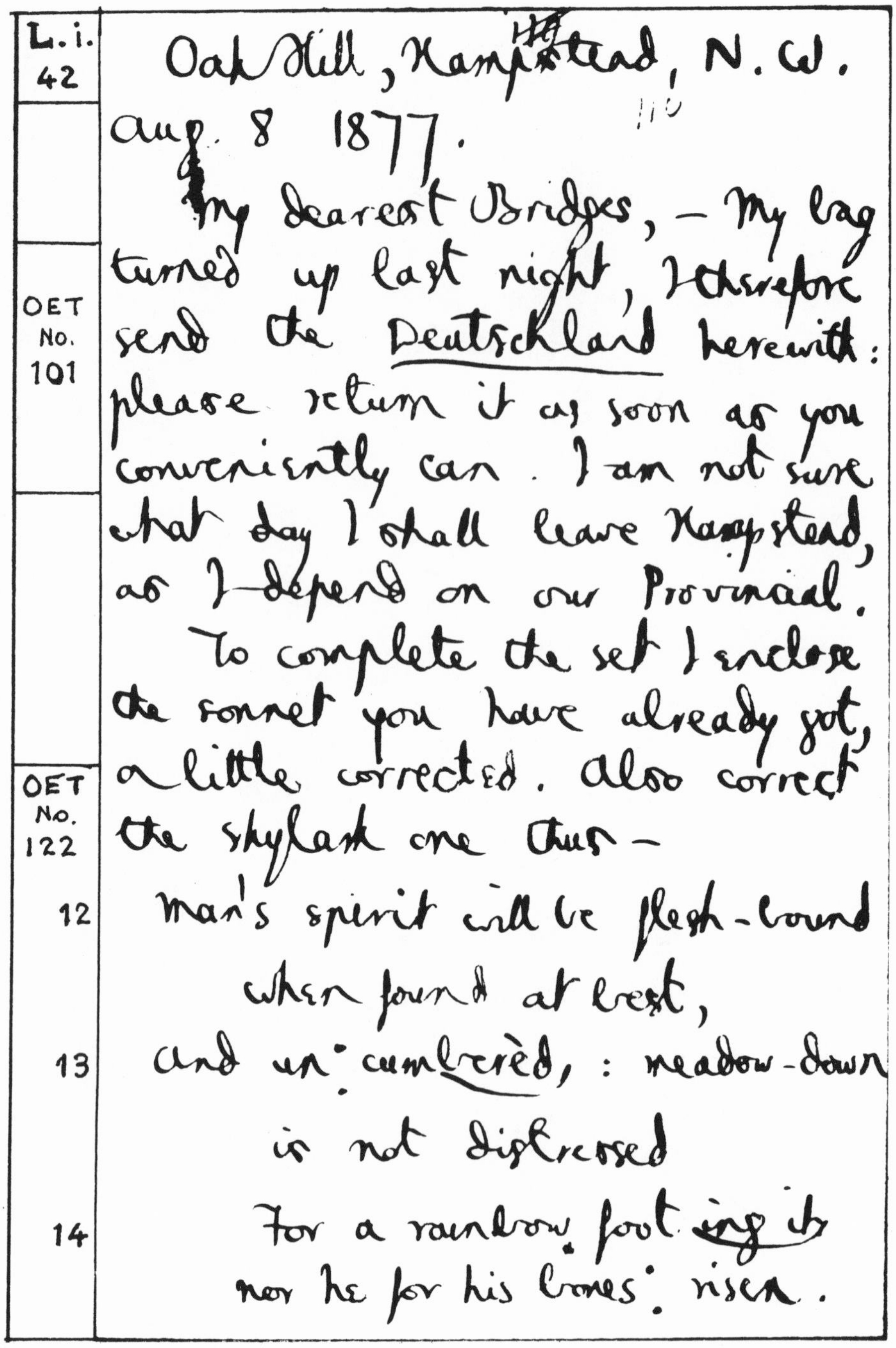

L.i. 42	Oak Hill, Hampstead, N. W. Aug. 8 1877.
OET No. 101	My dearest Bridges, — My bag turned up last night, I therefore send the <u>Deutschland</u> herewith: please return it as soon as you conveniently can . I am not sure what day I shall leave Hampstead, as I depend on our Provincial. To complete the set I enclose the sonnet you have already got, a little corrected. Also correct
OET No. 122	the skylark one thus —
12	Man's spirit will be flesh-bound when found at best,
13	And un·cumber̀ed, : meadow-down is not distressed
14	For a rainbow footing it nor he for his bones: risen .

Plate 313a   OET No. 122: The Caged Skylark -- MS. 2 (L)

L.i.42 -- Autograph revision of 13, 14, in a letter to RB written Aug. 8 1877 from his parent's home in Hampstead, London. There are no changes in 12 (still no comma after "flesh-bound"). In 13 "And" seems less appropriate than "But" (="And yet"): RB did not copy this into A, nor did GMH revert to "And" in correcting B. On the early part of the letter, of particular interest to students of his poetic MSS, see the Introduction. The ink blotch below the date is from a heavily blacked-out word before "sleep" (L.i.43) on the verso. Note with the two outrides how he begins from both ends in turn, producing the confusing illusion of a comma.

MS. K — Aug: 1877. The Skylark. G.M.H. — OET NO. 122

1 As a dare-gale sky-lark scanted in a dull cage
2 Man's mounting spirit in his bone-house, mean house,
3 That bird beyond recollection of free: fells, dwells—
4 This in drudgery, day-labouring-out life's age.
5 Though aloft on a turf or a perch or a poor stage
6 Both sing sometimes the sweetest, sweetest spells
7 Yet both droop deadly sometimes in their cells
8 Or wring their barriers, in bursts of fear or rage.

9 Not that the sweet-fowl song-fowl needs no rest—
10 Why hear him, hear him, babble and drop down to his nest,
11 But his own nest, wild-nest, no prison—
12 Man's spirit will be flesh-bound when found at best,
13 But not to cumber him: meadow-down is undistressed
14 For the rainbow footing it; and he for his bones: risen.

H.i. 32 r.	
OET No 124	

Heart's   Hurrahing.

~~Sonnet~~ in Harvest   32

(sprung and outriding rhythm ; no counterpoint)

Summer ends now.

1   ~~It is harvest~~ : now, barbarous in beauty, the stooks
                                            rise   [behaviour

2   Around ; up above, what wind-walks ! what lovely

3a   Of silk-sack clouds !   ~~never~~   have   swan-wing-whiter   ever   or
                                                            wavier   rall.

4a   Meal-drifts moulded ʃand melted across˙ skies.

5   I walk, I lift up, lift up the heart and the eyes,

6   ~~From~~ Down all that glory in of the heavens to glean our Sa-

7b   And, eyes, ˙heart, what looks, what viour, ;   [or a

7a   ~~O heart, and eyes or heart~~   never gave you

8a   ~~Tongue prist, per such overwhelming replies~~
      Real love's-welcoming , loud greetings, rounder replies ?

c   ˙: Rapturous love's-greetings of realer, of rounder replies ?

9   And the azurous, ~~strong~~ grand hills are his world-wielding

                     shoulder   [-sweet ! —

10   majestic , — as a stallion stalwart , very-violet-

11   These things, these things were here and but the
                                            beholder

12   Wanting ; which two when they once˙ meet,

13a   The heart ˙: rears ˙: wings , ˙ ~~beats them~~ bolder,

14   And hurls for him , ˙O half hurls earth for him, off under his feet.
                              Vale of Clwyd ~~aug~~ Sept. 1 1877

H.i. 32 v.	

3b Of silk-sack clouds ! No swan-wing-whiter or wavier
4b Meal-drifts moulded and melted ever across˙ skies.

13b   The heart ˙: rears ˙: wings ˙cold ʃand colder

PLATE 315. OET 123. "Matchless mercy" and "To him who ever thought" • *133*

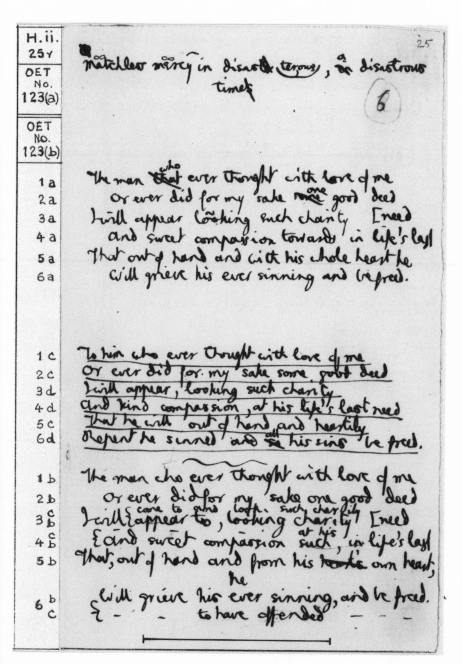

Plate 315   OET No. 123(a): "Matchless mercy"

H.ii.25r -- Autograph fragment. Note the counterpoint signs (figure-of-eight on the accented syllable only of the reversed foot), slur, and outride (the last syllable of "disaster" was deleted and rewritten after a space to make room for the outride--at first this ended with the "r", its tail easily mistaken for a comma; then it was extended when he changed to "disast(e)rous," forgetting to delete the "e"). Other deletions: "O" (above the beginning of the line), "in", final "s".

OET No. 123(b): "To him who ever thought"

H.ii.25r. -- Autograph drafts (top and bottom, with b-rhymes indented) and faircopy (middle, no indenting--cf. No. 124), with italics because these are the words of Christ (cf. No. 101, st. 11). Deletions: 1a that   2a some   6d so   5b heart's   . In 3a the circumflex on "looking" is a slip for a counterpoint sign (see his warning to RB not to confuse them, L.i.43).

Plate 314   OET No. 124: Hurrahing in Harvest -- MS. 1 (H)

[opposite] H.i.32r [ℓℓ. 1-14] and v[more revisions]. Autograph, faircopy of an early version of 1-12, with later revisions in smaller grey writing. Great colons open 4a, 7a, 8a,b and c, and 12; they occur in 1, 4a and b, 7b, 9, 12, 13a (three), 13b (three, a fourth cancelled after "bold"). Note music sign "rall." over "melted" (4a), slowing the rest of the line (r[all.] del. before "across", 4a). Thirteen outrides, three stresses (12) and four slurs are all in ink.

Deletions include: 4a (after "moulded") "e[ver]"   6 "From"   "of in"   Saviour,;   7a ": O eyes, O heart, and eyes or [heart del.] tongue" all del. "never"..."or a"   8a ": [Tongue, print del.] Print or pen such overwhelming replies.--" all del. 8c "love's-greetings"   10 "-sweet!..." [dots mended to dash]   13a "wings, beats them bolder,"   Date: Aug.

A. **P. 45** **OET** **No.** **124**	*Hurrahing in Harvest :* Sonnet (sprung and outriding rhythm : no counter- point . Take notice that the outriding feet are not to be confused with paeons, though sometimes the line might be scanned either way. the first strong syllable in an outriding foot has always a great stress and after the outrider follows a short pause . the paeon is easier and more flowing)

1 Summer ends now ; now, barbarous in beauty, the stooks
                rise   [views

2 Around ; up above, what wind-walks ! what lovely beha-
3 Of silk-sack clouds ! { have wilder, wilful-, swan-wing whiter ever or }
           ever wavier rall.
4 : Meal - drifts moulded and melted across : skies ?
       /GMH (B)

| **A. p. 46** | |

5 I walk, I lift up, I lift up the heart, and the eyes,
6 Down all that glory of the heavens to glean our Sa-
         viour ;   [you a
7 And, eyes and heart, what looks, what lips yet gave
8a ~~Rapturous love's greeting of realer, rounder replies~~
 b ~~: Realer love's welcoming, loud greetings, rounder replies?~~
 c : Rapturous, love's greeting of realer, of rounder replies?
9 And the azurous hung hills are his world - wielding
         shoulder
10 Majestic, — as a stallion stalwart, very-violet-sweet ! _
11 These things, these things were here and but the beholder
12 : Wanting ; which two when they once : meet,
13 The heart : rears : wings : bolder and bolder
14 And hurls for him, : O half hurls earth for him, off under his feet.
           Vale of Clwyd Sept. 1 1877.

<u>Plate 316</u>   <u>OET No. 124: Hurrahing in Harvest</u> -- MS. 2 (A)

    <u>A. pp. 45 (1-4) and 46 (5-14)</u>. Autograph faircopy. GMH's additional metrical note reads: "Take notice that the outriding feet are not to be confused with dactyls or paeons, though sometimes the line might be scanned either way. The ~~first~~ strong syllable in an outriding foot has always a great stress and after the outrider follows a short pause. The paeon is easier and more flowing)". There are <u>autograph changes</u> in: 3 "<u>never</u> have"   6 "<u>of</u> in"   7 "<u>lip</u> looks" H 8a [whole line del.]   " <u>:</u> Rapturous love's greeting of [rounder <u>del</u>.] realer, rounder replies?"   8b " <u>:</u> <u>Realer</u> love's welcoming, loud greetings, rounder replies?" all del., replaced with 8c.

    Great colons open lines 4, 8a, b and c, and 12, and occur in 1, 4, 9, 12, 13 (three). Ink stresses in 1 (five), 3 (silk, clouds, swan, white, wav--but the apparent X above "wing" comes from the crossing of GMH's upstroke to dot his <u>i</u> and RB's 1918 pencil comma after his red ink "wilder"), 5 (five) 12 (five).

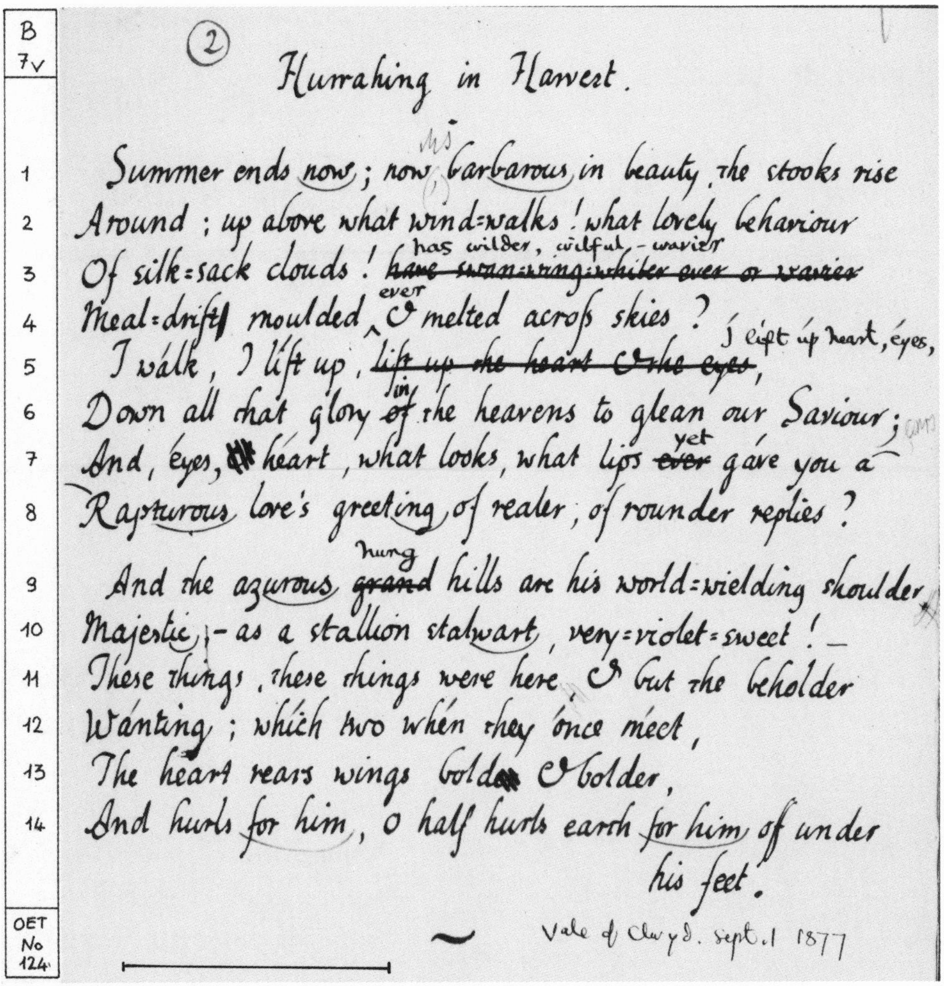

PLATE 317. OET 124. *Hurrahing in Harvest* • 135

Plate 317   OET No. 124: Hurrahing in Harvest -- MS. 3 (B)

[above] B.7v -- copy of A inscribed in album B by RB. He added in ink a stress on "gave" (7) to show it was part of the rhyme with "Saviour". He missed some commas--e.g. before "barbarous" (1), after "above" (2)--and was prob. responsible for adding others: "shoulder," (9); "Majestic," (10); and the final stop in 13. The change in 6 from "of" to "in" was due to RB's noticing GMH's obscure correction in A.

GMH in ink revised 3 and 4 ("has" and "drifts" however were changes after Aug. 1884); also 5, 7 (he del. the ampersand, added a comma before it and changed "ever" to "yet"). He used broken slurs to show that the rhyme ending 7 included the R of "Rapturous" (8). In 9 "grand hung", 13 "bolder". In purple pencil GMH added twelve stresses, and nine outrides. His date is in later ink (after Aug. 1884).

RB's pencil (1918) adds before "barbarous" (1) the comma he had omitted, noting "MS"; in 6 changes "Saviour:" to "; GMH"; deletes commas he had added after "shoulder" (9), "Majestic" (10), "here" (11); adds a dash after "sweet!" (10).

Plate 316 cont.   OET No. 124: Hurrahing in Harvest -- MS. 2 (A)

RB's red ink (1884, copying GMH's revisions in B) in 3 crosses out "have swan-wing-whiter ever or", and replaces them with "have wilder, wilful-" but RB bracketed the new version with the old one, an indication that he rather preferred the old. His red ink in 4 adds "ever"; in 5 adds "I" after the first "up", then deletes and encloses in parentheses "the" along with "and the". In 7 "ever" becomes "yet"; 9 grand hung; 13 "bolder and".

The MS is further complicated by RB's editorial pencil (1918) which caught up with GMH's later changes in B, made after 1884. In 3 (already a maze of corrections), RB crosses out in pencil his own red ink "have", pencilling "has" in the margin. In 4 the "s" is del. in "drifts" with the note below it "GMH (B)". In 5 he corrects an omission in his red ink changes by adding a pencilled comma after "heart".

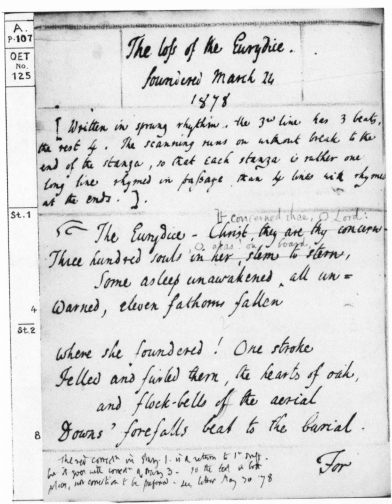

A.
p.107
OET
No.
125

St.1

4
St.2

The Loss of the Eurydice.
foundered March 24
1878

[Written in sprung rhythm. the 3rd line has 3 beats,
the rest 4. The scanning runs on without break to the
end of the stanza, so that each stanza is rather one
long line rhymed in passage than 4 lines with rhymes
at the ends.].

It concerned thee, O Lord:
The Eurydice – Christ, they are thy concern
O alas! on board.
Three hundred souls in her, stem to stern,
Some asleep unawakened, all un =
Warned, eleven fathoms fallen

Where she foundered! One stroke
Felled and furled them, the hearts of oak,
and flock-bells of the aerial
Downs' forefalls beat to the burial.

8

For

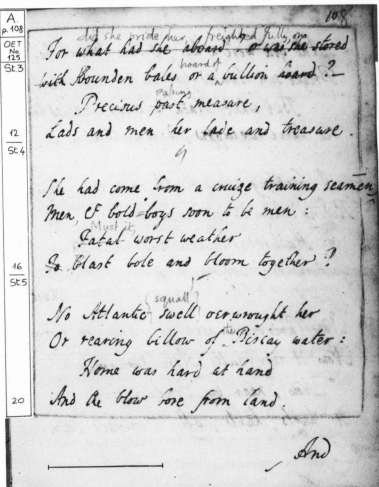

A.
p.108
OET
No.
125
St.3

12
St.4

16
St.5

20

did she pride her, freighted fully, on
For what had she aboard – or was she stored
hoard of
with Bounden bales or a bullion hoard?
Palsing
Precious past measure,
Lads and men her lade and treasure.

She had come from a cruize training seamen
Men, & bold boys soon to be men:
Must it
Fatal worst weather
So blast bole and bloom together?

squall?
No Atlantic swell overwrought her
the
Or rearing billow of Biscay water:
Home was hard at hand
And the blow sore from land.

And

L.i.
54

1

2

OET
No.
125
L.i.54
cont.

9
10

28

OET
No.
125

I see I have omitted one or
two things. If the first stanza
is too sudden it can be changed
back to what it was at first –
The Eurydice – it concerned thee,
O lord: You board –
O alas! three hundred heart.
But then it will be necessary to
write change the third stanza to
as follows, which you will hardly
approve –
Did she pride her, freighted fully, on
Bounden bales or a hoard of bullion? –
About "grimstones" you are mistaken. It is not
the remains of a rhyme to "grimstone". I could
run you some rhymes on it. You must know, we
have a Falter Grimstone in our province.

OET No. 125: The Loss of the Eurydice

MS. A: The autograph of the earlier version is now lost, but fortunately RB transcribed a copy into album A. This transcript (A. pp.107-116--left hand plates) was not checked by GMH and is certain to contain minor errors in accidentals (e.g., the metrical note should have a colon after "sprung rhythm", and 64 has no final period). Note RB's hurried stanza numbers in pencil (1918?), corrected after st. 22. Some of RB's red ink corrections were based on letters from the author sent in 1878 (see note on L.i below): others were made after album B was returned to him in 1884 with GMH's new version.

MS. B. Autograph revised version, occupying the rectos B.30-34. with 34v (right hand plates), inscribed in album B by GMH in 1884 before he sent the album on to Coventry Patmore. Faircopy, with no changes (except in 90, a comma del.). A period was omitted at the end of 60 (as RB's editorial pencil of 1918 indicates).

L.i. In letters to RB of April and May 1878, GMH quoted some early and several revised versions of certain lines. In L.i.53-4 (May 30--see Plates 318 and 324) he was reacting to criticisms and suggestions from RB. RB's footnote to A.p.107 (Plate 318, left top) shows that, as GMH had expected, RB thought some revisions were no improvements: "The red correct.[n] in stanza 1 is a return to 1st draft. but it goes with correct[n] of stanza 3. So the text in both places, not correction to be preferred. See letter May 30 '78."

Plate 318   A.pp.107-8: 13 "cruize/cruise" (see L.i.52). Red ink revisions in 1, 2, 7 ("of" rev. to "off"), 9, 10, 11, 13 (dash added after comma), 14 (orig. "Men & bold boys", "and" not del. but comma added before it), 15, 16, 17, 18.

PLATE 319. OET 125. *The Loss of the Eurydice* • 137

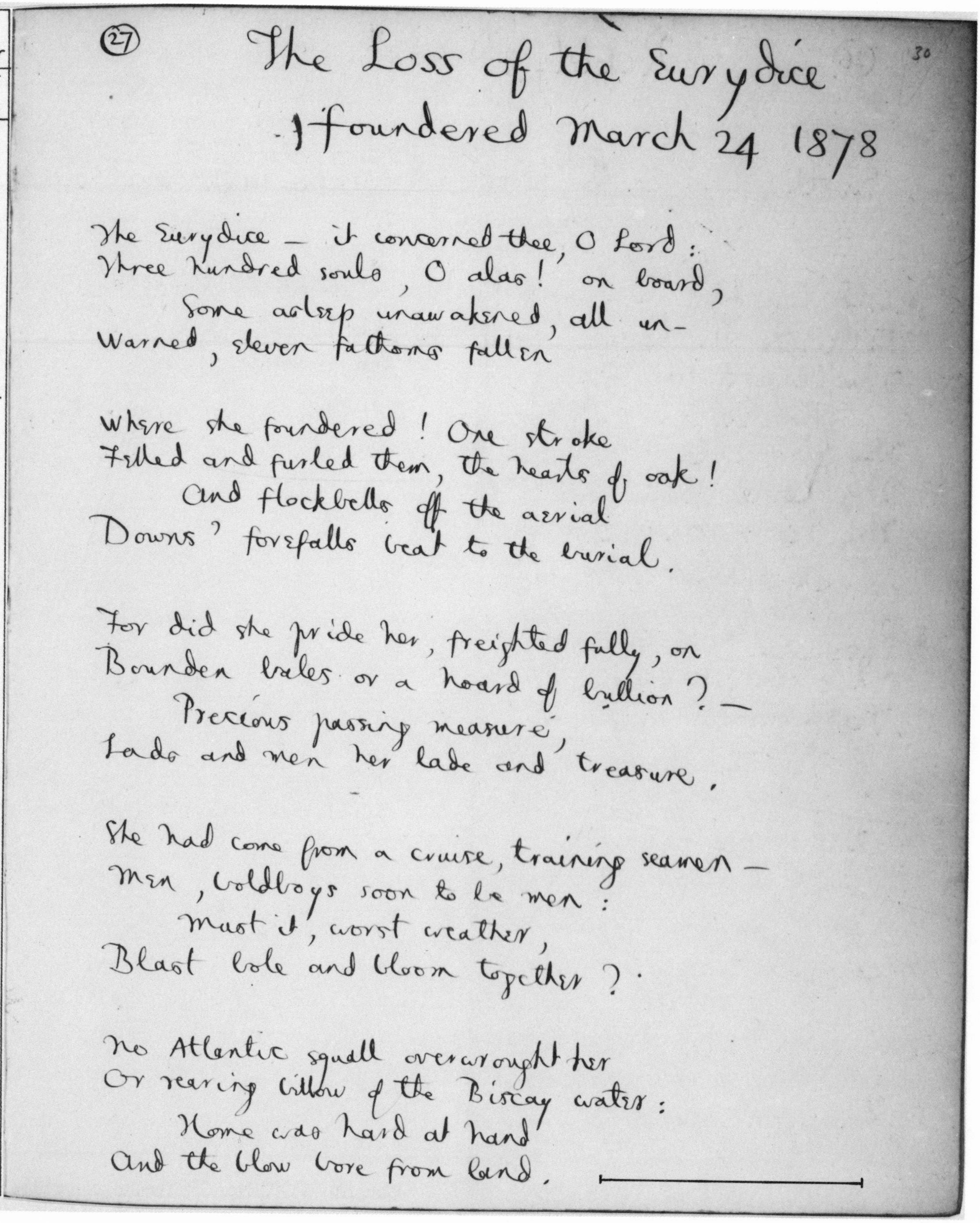

㉗

The Loss of the Eurydice
-) foundered March 24 1878

The Eurydice — it concerned thee, O Lord:
Three hundred souls, O alas! on board,
    Some asleep unawakened, all un-
warned, eleven fathoms fallen

Where she foundered! One stroke
Felled and furled them, the hearts of oak!
    And flockbells off the aërial
Downs' forefalls beat to the burial.

For did she pride her, freighted fully, on
Bounden bales or a hoard of bullion? —
    Precious passing measure,
Lads and men her lade and treasure,

She had come from a cruise, training seamen —
Men, boldboys soon to be men:
    Must it, worst weather,
Blast bole and bloom together?.

No Atlantic squall overwrought her
Or rearing billow of the Biscay water:
    Home was hard at hand
And the blow bore from land.

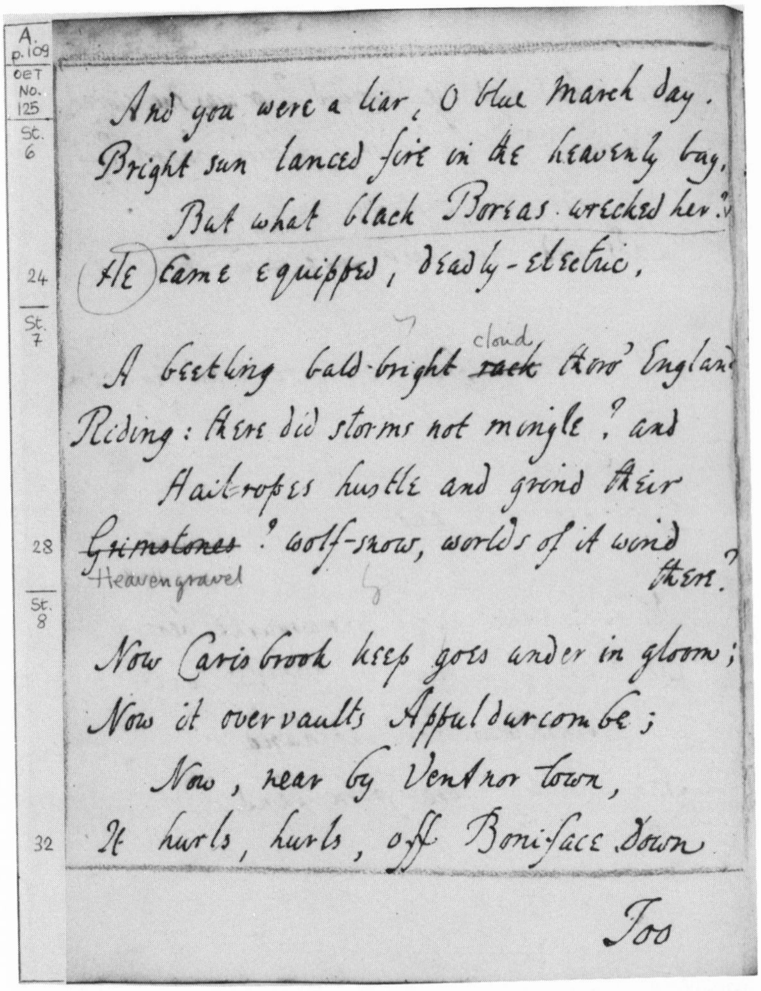

And you were a liar, O blue March day.
Bright sun lanced fire in the heavenly bay;
   But what black Boreas wrecked her?
He came equipped, deadly-electric.

              cloud
A beetling baldbright ~~rack~~ thro' England
Riding: there did storms not mingle? and
   Hailropes hustle and grind their
~~Grimstones~~? Wolf-snow, worlds of it wind
Heavengravel   there?

Now Carisbrook keep goes under in gloom;
Now it overvaults Appuldurcombe;
   Now, near by Ventnor town,
It hurls, hurls, off Boniface Down

                 Too

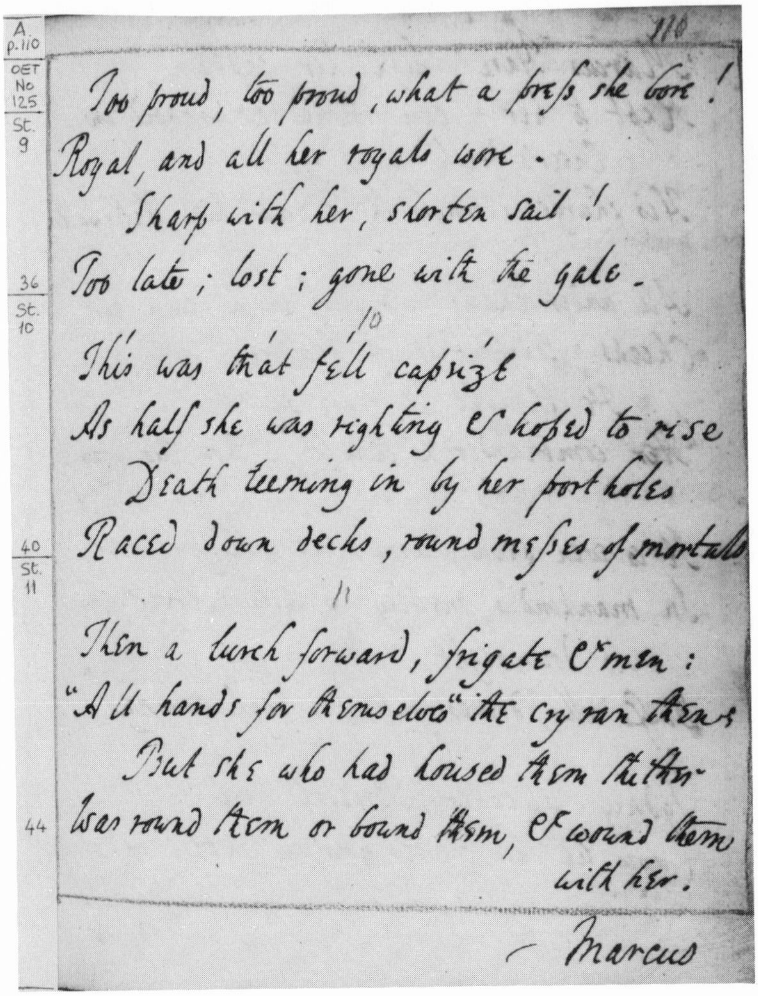

Too proud, too proud, what a press she bore!
Royal, and all her royals wore.
   Sharp with her, shorten sail!
Too late; lost; gone with the gale.

This was that fell capsize
As half she was righting & hoped to rise
   Death teeming in by her portholes
Raced down decks, round messes of mortals

Then a lurch forward, frigate & men:
"All hands for themselves" the cry ran then;
   But she who had housed them thither
Was round them or bound them, & wound them
               with her.

           — Marcus

Plate 320   OET No. 125: The Loss of the Eurydice, cont.
(lines 21-44)

     A.pp.109-110 -- The stresses in 37 are in ink contemporary with the transcription. RB's red ink corrections: 23-4 ("He" trans. to line end and "came" given u.c.), 25, 27 (double hyphen added to "Hail-ropes"), 28 (see L.i.54 reprod. on Plate 318).

PLATE 321. OET 125. *The Loss of the Eurydice* • 139

And you were a liar, O blue March day.
Bright sun lanced fire in the heavenly bay;
        But what black Boreas wrecked her? he
Came equipped, deadly-electric,

A beetling baldbright cloud thorough England
Riding : there did storms not mingle? and
        Hailropes hustle and grind their
Heavengravel? wolfsnow, worlds of it, wind there?

Now Carisbrook keep goes under in gloom;
  Now it overvaults Appledurcombe;
        Now near by Ventnor town
It hurls, hurls off Boniface Down,

Too proud, too proud, what a press she bore!
Royal, and all her royals wore.
        Sharp with her, shorten sail!
Too late; lost; gone with the gale.

This was that fell capsize.
As half she had righted and hoped to rise
        Death teeming in by her portholes
Raced down decks, round messes of mortals.

Then a lurch forward, frigate and men;
"All hands for themselves" the cry ran then;
        But she who had housed them thither
Was around them, bound them or wound them with her.

[continued next leaf

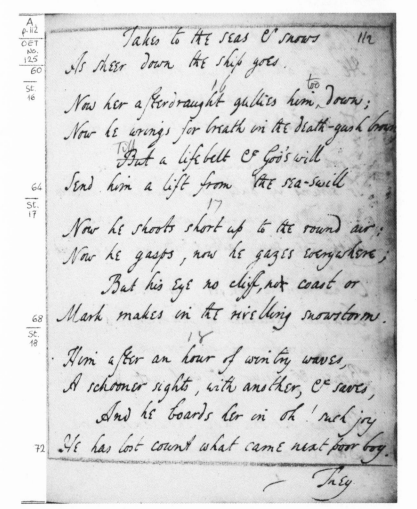

Marcus Hare, high her captain,
Kept to her,—care-drowned & wrapped in
        Cheer's death would follow
His charge through the champ-white water-in-a-wallow

All under channel to bury in a beach her
Cheeks : Right, rude of feature,
        He thought he heard say
"Her commander, & thou too, c~thou this way."

It is even seen, time's something-server
In mankind's medley, a duty-swerver,
        At downright "No or yes?"
Doffs all, drives full for righteousness.

Sydney Fletcher Bristol-bred
(low he his mates now on watery bed)

                                Takes

Takes to the seas & snows
As sheer down the ship goes.

Now her afterdraught gullies him too down;
Now he wrings for breath in the death-gush brown
        But a lifebelt & God's will
Send him a lift from the sea-swill

Now he shoots short up to the round air;
Now he gasps, now he gazes everywhere;
        But his Eye no cliff, not coast or
Mark makes in the rivelling snowstorm.

Him after an hour of wintry waves,
A schooner sights, with another, & saves,
        And he boards her in oh ! such joy
He has lost count what came next poor boy.

                                & They

Plate 322   OET No. 125: The Loss of the Eurydice, cont.
(lines 43-72)

A.pp.111, 112. In 52 there is a tiny speck above the comma following "commander"--this is not a semicolon. In 67 the r of "nor" was del. in black ink when the writing was wet.

RB's red ink corrects 48, 50 (orig. "Cheeks, [period misread?] Right rude"), 53 (hyphen del., query in margin), 61, 63.

[opposite]   Plate 323 B.32r -- 68 note "stowstorm" for "snowstorm". In 60 RB's editorial pencil notes the omission of a final period.

PLATE 323. OET 125. *The Loss of the Eurydice* • 141

Marcus Hare, high her captain,
Kept to her — care-drowned and wrapped in
　　cheer's death, would follow
His charge through the champ-white water-in-a-wallow,

All under Channel to bury in a beach her
Cheeks: Right, rude of feature,
　　He thought he heard say
"Her commander! and thou too, and thou this way?"

It is even seen, time's something server,
In mankind's medley a duty-swerver,
　　At downright "No or Yes?"
Doffs all, drives full for righteousness.

Sydney Fletcher, Bristol-bred,
(Low lie his mates now on watery bed.)
　　Takes to the seas and snows
As sheer down the ship goes

Now her afterdraught gullies him too down;
Now he wrings for breath with the deathgush brown;
　　Till a lifebelt and God's will
Lend him a lift from the sea-swill.

Now he shoots short up to the round air;
Now he gasps, now he gazes everywhere;
　　But his eye no cliff, no coast or
Mark makes in the rivelling snowstorm.

[continued next leaf

They say who saw one sea-corpse cold
He was all of lovely manly mould,
  Every inch a tar,
                our sailors
Of the best we boast seamen are.

Look, foot to forelock, how all things suit!
                                                he
Is strung by duty, is strained to beauty,
          brown
  And tawny-as-dawning-skinned
              brine et shining
With the sun, salt, et the whirling wind.

O his nimble finger, his gnarlèd grip!
Leagues, leagues of seamanship
                        these
  Slumber in his forsaken
          this
Bones, et sinew, et will not #waken.

He was but one like thousands more
Day et night I deplore

                                                My

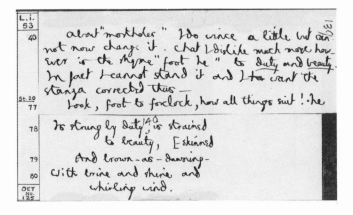

about "mortholes". I do since a little but am
not now change it. What I dislike much more how-
ever is the rhyme "foot he" to duty and beauty.
In fact I cannot stand it and I too want the
stanza corrected thus —
  Look, foot to forelock, how all things suit! — he
  Is strung by duty, is strained
                to beauty, [skinned]
  And brown-as-dawning-
  With brine and shine and
        whirling wind.

My people et born own nation,
Fast=foundering own generation.

I might let bygones be — our curse.
Of ruinous shrine no hand or, worse,
  Robbery's hand is busy to
                          shining
Dress, hoar-hallowed wells-unvisited;

I had not written a line till the
foundering of the Eurydice the other day and that
worked on me and I am making a poem —
in my own rhythm but in a measure something like Tennyson's Violet (round with maul);
S. 8 —
  they say who saw one sea-corpse cold
  Now he was of lovely manly mould,
    Every inch a tar,
  Of the best we boast seamen are.

  Look, from forelock, down to foot he,
  Strung by duty, is strained to beauty
  And russet-of-morning-skinned
  With the sun, salt, and whirling wind.

  O this his nimble finger, his gnarlèd grip!
  Leagues, leagues of seamanship
    Slumber in his forsaken
  Bones and will not, will not waken.
I have consistently carried out my rhyming system,
using the first letter of the next line to com-
plete the rhyme in the line before it.

Plate 324   OET No. 125: The Loss of the Eurydice, cont.
(lines 73-92)

A.pp.113. 114 (to line 92 only, to facilitate comparison with B). In 84 "awaken" is corr. in black ink. RB's marginal note at right angles to st. 20 was orig. in pencil, partly rephrased in black ink: it refers to the red ink changes, "correction in a letter May 30. 78--it is made for rhyme's sake." (See L.i.53, this plate, top right, and cf. B.33r). In 77 RB's red ink missed the comma after "forelock", but this is added in pencil (1918?). In A.p.113, 80, "the" had prob. been del. with an oblique pencil stroke before being crossed through horizontally in red ink. Other red rev. in 84, 92.

L.i,48 was written 2 April 1878, barely a week after news of the disaster. Of the five lines with some stresses marked, the sprung rhythm effects in three were later reduced by revision: 81-2 remained unchanged. In 79 the revisions moved towards a strength of simplicity, the drowned sailor was at first (L.i.48) "russet-of-morning-skinned", then, less romantically (A.p.113) "tawny-as-dawning-skinned", and finally (L.i.53 and B.33r) "brown-as-dawning-skinned/With brine and shine and whirling wind"--it is noticeable that he here eschews the poetic pronunciation which rhymes "wind" with "kind".

L.i.53 -- also preserves an early reading which RB had obviously challenged, "mortholes", a coinage which no doubt rhymed with "portholes" (39). GMH did change it after all for the half-rhyme "mortals".

PLATE 325. OET 125. *The Loss of the Eurydice* • 143

B.
33 r.
St. 18

72
St. 19

76
St. 20

80
St. 21

84
St. 22

88
St. 23

92

OET
No.
125

33

Him, after an hour of wintry waves,
A schooner sights, with another, and saves,
        And he boards her in Oh! such joy
He has lost count what came next, poor boy. —

They say who saw one sea-corpse cold
He was all of lovely manly mould,
        Every inch a tar,
Of the best we boast our sailors are.

Look, foot to forelock, how all things suit! he
Is strung by duty, is strained to beauty,
        And brown-as-dawning-skinned
With brine and shine and whirling wind.

O his nimble finger, his gnarled grip!
Leagues, leagues of seamanship
        Slumber in these forsaken
Bones, this sinew, and will not waken.

He was but one like thousands more.
Day and night I deplore
        My people and born own nation,
Fast foundering own generation.

I might let bygones be — our curse
Of ruinous shrine no hand, or, worse,
        Robbery's hand is busy to
Dress, hoar-hallowèd shrines unvisited;

                        [continued next leaf

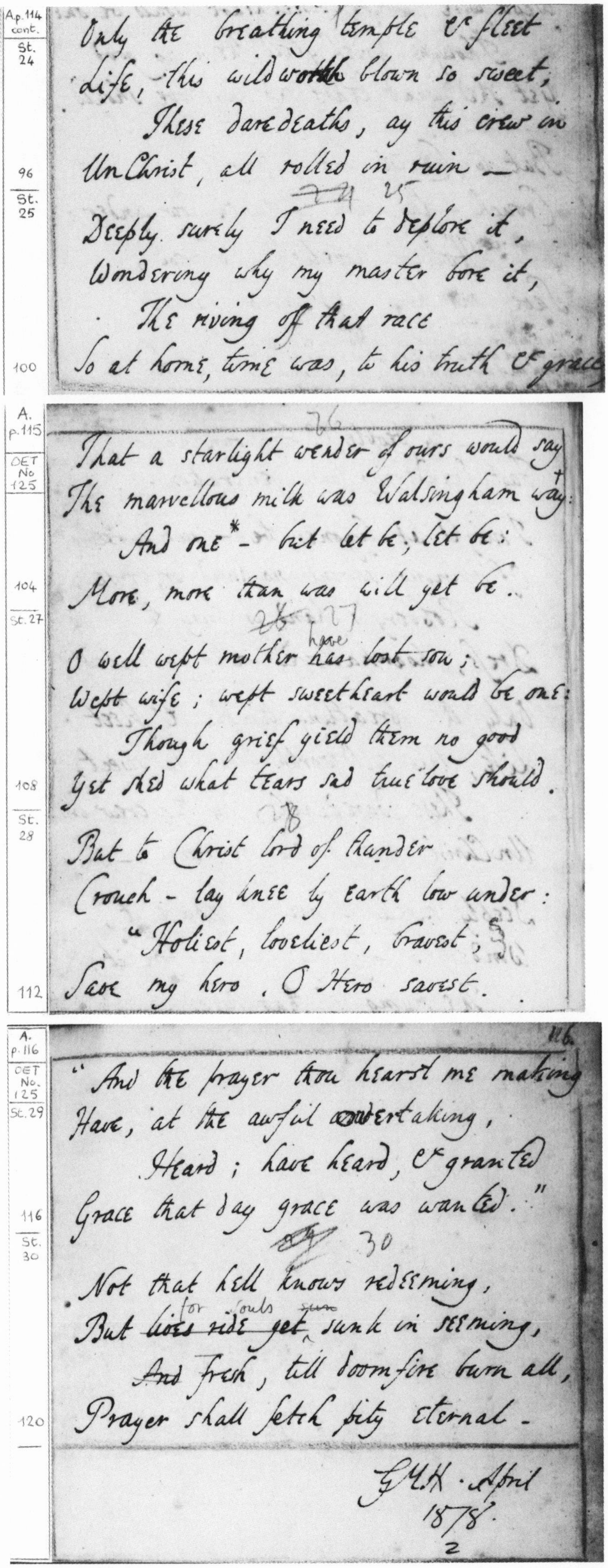

Only the breathing temple & fleet
Life, this wildworth blown so sweet,
  These daredeaths, ay this crew, in
UnChrist, all rolled in ruin—

Deeply, surely I need to deplore it,
Wondering why my master bore it,
  The riving of that race
So at home, time was, to his truth & grace

That a starlight wender of ours would say
The marvellous Milk was 'Walsingham Way':
  And one*— but let be, let be:
More, more than was will yet be..

O well wept mother has lost son;
Wept wife; wept sweetheart would be one:
  Though grief yield them no good
Yet shed what tears sad true love should.

But to Christ lord of thunder
Crouch—lay knee by earth low under:
  "Holiest, loveliest, bravest,
Save my hero, O Hero savest.

"And the prayer thou hearst me making
Have, at the awful overtaking,
  Heard; have heard, & granted
Grace that day grace was wanted."

Not that hell knows redeeming,
But for souls sunk in seeming,
  And fresh, till doomfire burn all,
Prayer shall fetch pity eternal—

G.M.H. April
1878.

Plate 325a, 325b   OET No. 125: The Loss of the Eurydice, concl. (lines 93-120)

A.p.114 (from line 93), 115, 116. In 94 "wildworth"-- a coinage prob. hard to read in the original autograph, has been mended, perhaps from "wildwork". In 114 "overtaking" has been mended from "undertaking". RB's red ink corrects from B 99 ("of" to "off"), 105 (comma after "wept" missed, as others elsewhere), 118 (final comma not del.), 119 ("And fresh" rev. to "Fresh"). Footnotes in A.pp.115, 116 (not shown): the one to line 102 is RB's own gloss--GMH in L.i.53 suggests that RB did not know the significance of Walsingham Way: "This was not only, and perhaps not originally, an english conceit. In Gallicia the Milky way [cf. RB's ℓ.c. "way" in Plate 255, OET No. 101, st. 26:6] was called, & is (?), 'El Camino de Jerusalem.' & in other provinces of Spain it is given to St James as 'el camino de Santiago.'--Chaucer has in 'The House of Fame' 430 [Bk. II.431, or 936] 'The galaxy, The which men clepe the Milky Way, For it is white: and some parfay, Callen it Watling street.' [Watling St. was said by some to run from Chester to Canterbury--see OED, para 1.] The footnote on the "one" of line 103 (Duns Scotus), is a quotation from L.i.77. At the bottom of A.p.116 is a pencilled note on 111-116, quoting L.i.78, "The words are put into the mouth...her hero." Catherine Phillips identifies the note as in the hand of Mrs. Monica Bridges.

A separate autograph fragment of the poem, revisions of sts. 29 and 30, is signed "G.M.H. April 1878 Mount St. Mary's, Spink Hill, Derbyshire". It coincides with A in st. 29 (comma after "have heard" in 115). In 118 it deletes four words in A, to read "But for souls sunk in seeming" [misquoted as "sank", HQ 5.4 (1979), 141]. In 119 the A reading "And fresh," is changed to B's "Fresh,". This MS. is now in the Hopkins Collection, Humanities Center, University of Texas at Austin. It was not among the MSS. found by Lady Pooley, and was not made available to me for reproduction.

B.
34r
St.
24

Only the breathing temple and fleet
Life, this wildworth blown so sweet,
　　These daredeaths, ay this crew, in
Unchrist, all rolled in ruin —

St.
25

Deeply surely I need to deplore't,
Wondering why my master bore it,
　　The riving off that race
So at home, time was, to his truth and grace

St.
26

That a starlight-wender of ours would say
The marvellous Milk was Walsingham Way
　　And one — but let be, let be :
More, more than was will yet be, —

St.
27

O well wept, mother have lost son;
Wept, wife ; wept, sweetheart would be one :.
　　Though grief yield them no good
Yet shed what tears sad truelove should.

St.
28

But to Christ lord of thunder
Crouch ; lay knee by earth low under :
　　" Holiest, loveliest, bravest,
Save my hero, O Hero savest.

St.
29

And the prayer thou hearst me making
Have, at the awful overtaking,
　　Heard ; have heard and granted
Grace that day grace was wanted."

[T. O.

St.
30

Not that hell knows redeeming,
But for souls sunk in seeming
　　Fresh, till doomfire burn all,
Prayer shall fetch pity eternal.

　　　　　　Mount St. Mary's, Derbyshire . April 1878

OET
No.
125

B
34
r

96

100

104

108

112

116

B
34
v

120

B
47r

a. m. d. g.　　　　　　　　　　47

The May Magnificat

May is Mary's month, and I
{ Ask myself with wonder why :
{ muse at that and
　　　Her feasts follow reason,
　　　Dated due to season —

4

Candlemas, Lady Day ;
But the Lady Month, May,
　　　Why fasten that upon her
　　　Or feast it in her honour?
　　　with a feasting

8

Is it only its being brighter
Than the most are must delight her?
　　　Is it opportunest,
　　　{ Finding flowers the soonest?,
　　　{ Finds {which the soonest?

12

Ask { herself, the mighty mother :
{　 her,　 the mighty mother,
She replies by another
{ And in reply hear this their
　　　Question : What is Spring? —
　　　Growth in every thing —

16

Flesh and fleece, fur and feather;
Grass and greenworld all together;
　　　　　　　　　　[T. O.

OET
No.
126

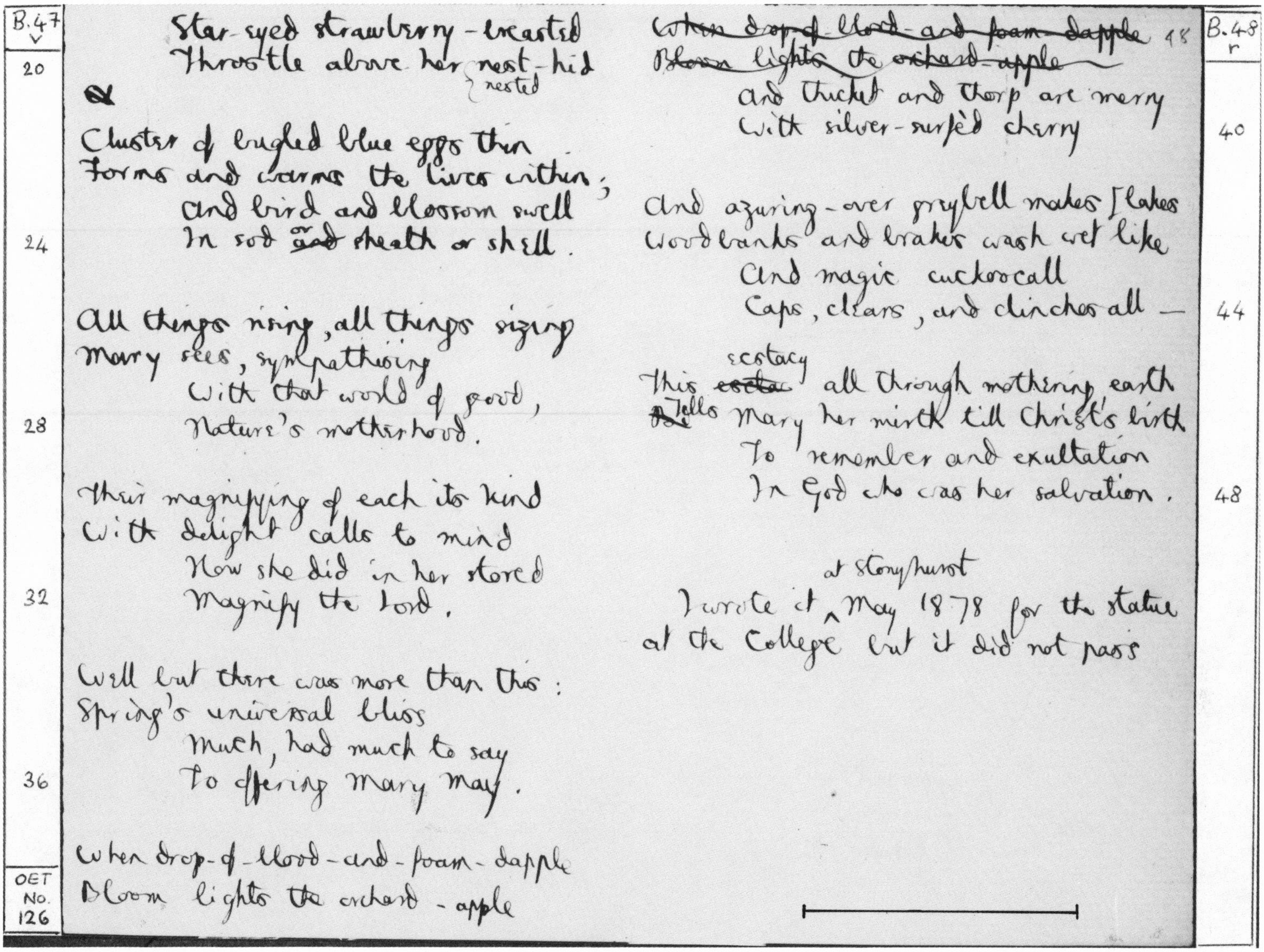

PLATE 327. OET 126. *The May Magnificat* • *147*

B.47
v

20

Star-eyed strawberry-breasted
Throstle above her nest-hid
       { nested
&

Cluster of bugled blue eggs thin
Forms and warms the life within;
    And bird and blossom swell
24
    In sod and sheath or shell.

All things rising, all things sizing
Mary sees, sympathising
28
    With that world of good,
    Nature's motherhood.

Their magnifying of each its kind
With delight calls to mind
32
    How she did in her stored
    Magnify the Lord.

Well but there was more than this:
Spring's universal bliss
36
    Much, had much to say
    To offering Mary May.

When drop-of-blood-and-foam-dapple
Bloom lights the orchard-apple

OET
No.
126

B.48
r

When drop-of-blood-and-foam-dapple 38
Bloom lights the orchard-apple
    And thicket and thorp are merry
40
    With silver-surfèd cherry

And azuring-over greybell makes [flakes
Woodbanks and brakes wash wet like
    And magic cuckoocall
44
    Caps, clears, and clinches all —

      ecstacy
This ecstac all through mothering earth
Tells Mary her mirth till Christ's birth
    To remember and exultation
48
    In God who was her salvation.

       at Stonyhurst
I wrote it May 1878 for the statue
at the College but it did not pass

<u>Plates 326, 327</u>   <u>OET No. 126: The May Magnificat</u> -- MS. 1 (B[1])

<u>B.47r (ℓℓ. 1-18), 47v (19-38), 48r (37-48)</u>. Early autograph faircopy (with later revisions and alternatives made about 1884); on three sides of a folded sheet pasted into album B. He began 5 and 21 without leaving a line space between stanzas, and copied 37, 38 twice. In 45 he corrected a misspelling ("esctac" to "ecstacy", his normal form (an acceptable 19th C. variant); in 46 he may have begun "Bids". <u>Revisions</u> include: 13, 14 "Ask her, the mighty mother,/And in reply hear this other". Sts. 1-4 are del. in pencil (probably by RB), who notes on f.49r (not shown): "The final version is written into this book earlier back p[blank]".

A.
p. 49

OET
No.
126

The May Magnificat

(Spring rhythm: four stresses in the first couplet, three in the second) (corrections from version of 1884)

[each line of / each of]

May is Mary's month, and I
~~Ask myself~~ with wonder shy:
Muse at that, and
Her feasts follow reason,
Dated due to season —

4

Candlemas, Lady Day;
But the Lady Month, May,
Why fasten that upon her
With a feasting in her honour?

8

Is it only its being brighter
Than the most are must delight her?
Is it opportunest,
~~Finding~~ flowers ~~the~~ soonest?
And *finds*

12

Ask her the mighty mother:
~~She replies by another~~
Her reply puts this other
Question : What is spring?
Growth in every thing —

16

Flesh and fleece, fur and feather;
Grass and greenworld all together;
Star-eyed strawberry-breasted
Throstle above her ~~nest-hid~~
nested

20

Cluster of bugled blue eggs thin
Forms and warms the life within
And bird and blossom swell
In sod or sheath or shell.

24

A.
p. 50

All things rising, all things sizing
Mary sees, sympathising
With that world of good,
Nature's motherhood.

28

Their magnifying of each its kind
With delight calls to mind
How she did in her stored
Magnify the Lord.

32

Well but there was more than this:
Spring's universal bliss
Much, had much to say
To offering Mary May.

36

When drop-of-blood-and-foam-dapple
Bloom lights the orchard apple
And thicket and thorp are merry
With silver-surfèd cherry

40

And azuring-over greybell makes [lakes
Wood banks and brakes wash wet like
And magic cuckoocall
Caps, clears, and clinches all —

44

This ecstasy all through mothering earth
Tells Mary her mirth till Christ's birth
To remember and exultation
In God who was her salvation.
Stonyhurst, May 1878.

48

[right margin, Monica Bridges' pencil note]
Sent with the following : "A May piece in which I see little good but the freedom of the May rhythm"

A.pp.49 (lines 1-24), 50 (lines 25-48) -- Autograph faircopy; MS here rearranged to resemble the original before RB cut the title, metrical note and two columns of verse into separate pieces to fit into album A. GMH's changes include del. of comma after "rhythm" (metrical note), and "&" (5); mending of "spring" (15) to u.c.. The italicizing of "her" (13) may be a revision. The final stop in 22 is uncertain: there is a faint dot over the comma.

RB's black ink (now faded to brown, whereas GMH's black ink is now grey) adds after the metrical note "corrections from version of 1884" (i.e., from B.30v, not noticed by RB till 1889). There were: 2 "Muse at that, and" 12 "And...finds" 14 "Her reply puts this other" 20 "nested" In 21 the del. of the "d" in "bugled" seems to be by RB: the stroke has faded to brown although it does show pen tracks like GMH's usual quills. Mrs. Monica Bridges adds in pencil up the right margin: "sent with the following. "A May piece in which I see little good but the freedom of the rhythm"" [see L.i.65]. This was incorporated in RB's 1st. edn. note, p.110.

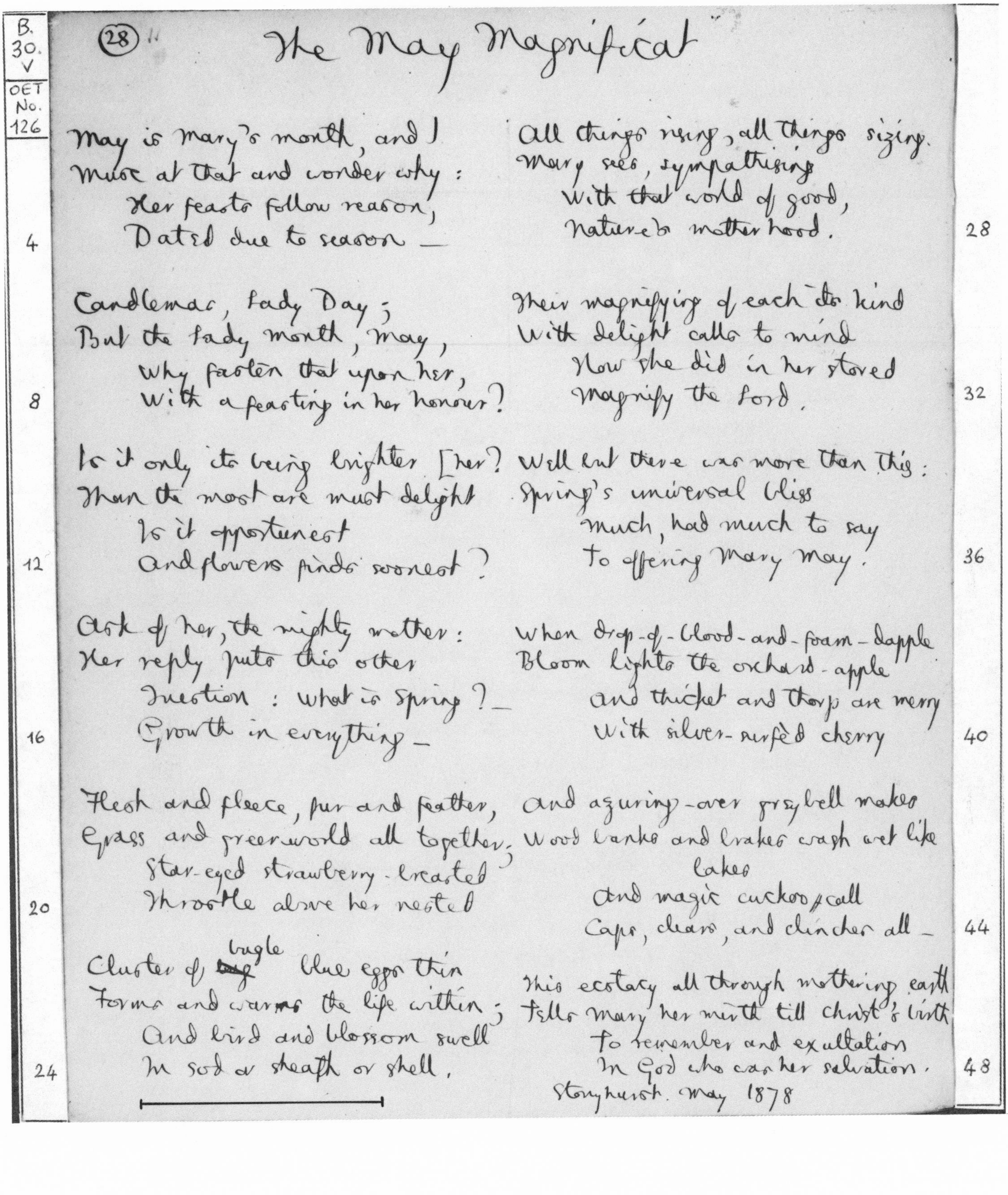

(28)

The May Magnificat

May is Mary's month, and I
Muse at that and wonder why :
   Her feasts follow reason,
   Dated due to season —

Candlemas, Lady Day ;
But the Lady Month, May,
   Why fasten that upon her,
   With a feasting in her honour?

Is it only its being brighter [her?
Than the most are must delight
   Is it opportunest
   And flowers finds soonest?

Ask of her, the mighty mother :
Her reply puts this other
   Question : what is Spring ? —
   Growth in everything —

Flesh and fleece, fur and feather,
Grass and greenworld all together ;
   Star-eyed strawberry-breasted
   Throstle above her nested

Cluster of bugle blue eggs thin
Forms and warms the life within ;
   And bird and blossom swell
   In sod or sheath or shell.

All things rising, all things sizing.
Mary sees, sympathising
   With that world of good,
   Nature's motherhood.

Their magnifying of each its kind
With delight calls to mind
   How she did in her stored
   Magnify the Lord.

Well but there was more than this :
Spring's universal bliss
   Much, had much to say
   To offering Mary May.

When drop-of-blood-and-foam-dapple
Bloom lights the orchard-apple
   And thicket and thorp are merry
   With silver-surfèd cherry

And azuring-over greybell makes
Wood banks and brakes wash wet like lakes
   And magic cuckoo call
   Caps, clears, and clinches all —

This ecstasy all through mothering earth
Tells Mary her mirth till Christ's birth
   To remember and exultation
   In God who is her salvation.

Stonyhurst. May 1878

Plate 327b   OET No. 126: The May Magnificat -- MS. 3 (B)

B.30v -- Autograph faircopy, inscribed in album B. 21 "lug" mended to "bug", then deleted and rewritten. 43 "cuckoo-call" (hyphen del., presumably implying a compound, as it is in B¹ and A).

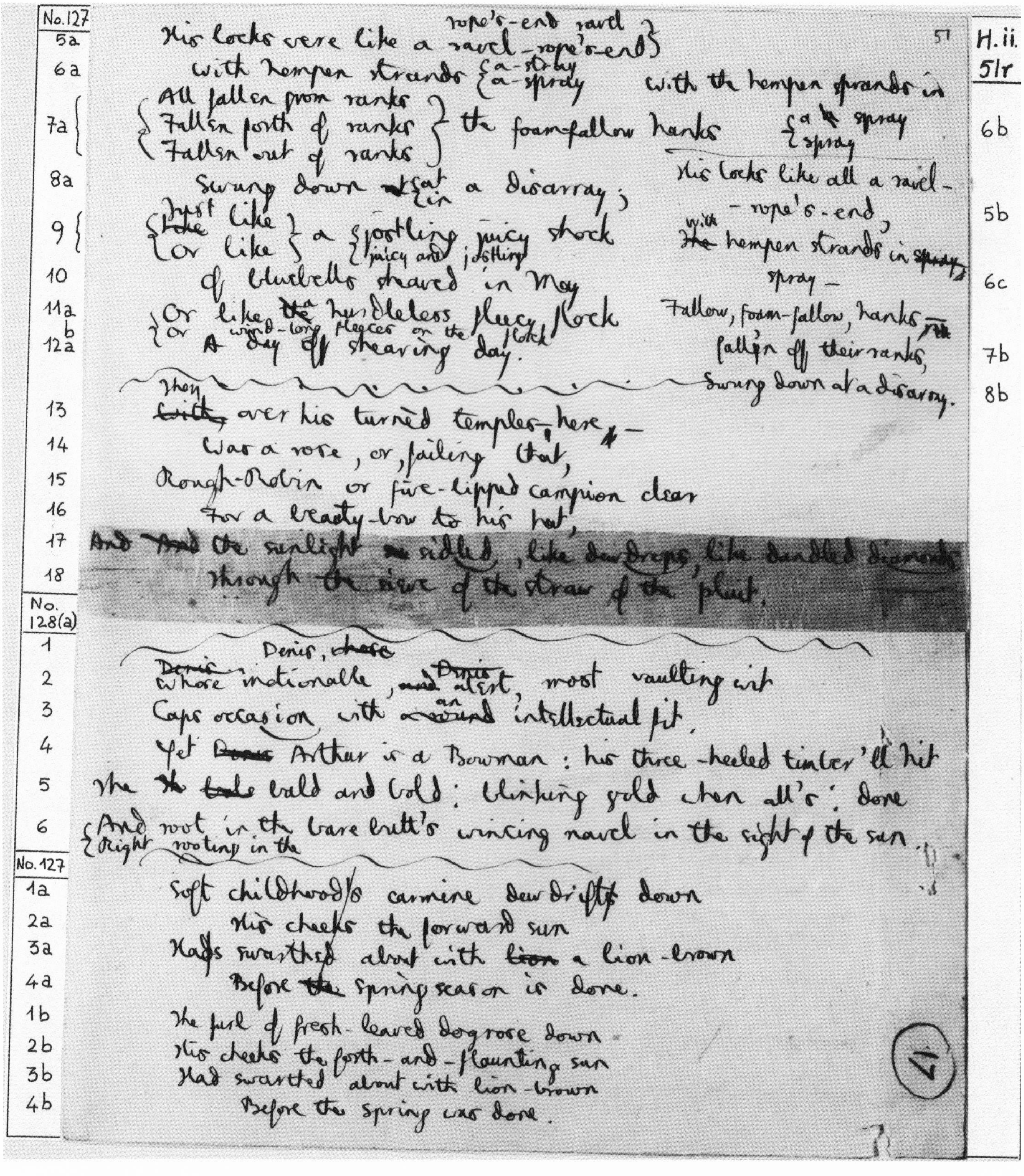

No. 127

5a His locks were like a ravel-rope's-end

rope's-end ravel

6a with hempen strands {a-str* {a-spray   with the hempen strands in

7a { All fallen from ranks }
   { Fallen forth of ranks } the foam-fallow hanks   {a * spray
   { Fallen out of ranks }   {spray

His locks like all a ravel-

8a   Swung down *that in a disarray;   - rope's-end,

9 { just like }   with
  { or like } a spotting juicy shock   the hempen strands in spray

10   of bluebells shaved in May   spray —

11a/b Or like the *needleless fleecy flock   Fallow, foam-fallow, hanks —

12a or A day off shearing day.   fallen off their ranks,

     they   Swung down at a disarray.

13   with over his turned temples here —

14   Was a rose, or, failing that,

15   Rough-Robin or five-lipped campion clear

16   for a beauty-bow to his hat,

17   And *had the sunlight *as sidled, like dewdrops, like dandled diamonds

18   through the sieve of the straw of the plait.

No. 128(a)

     Denis, whose

1   Denis, whose

2   whose motionable, and Denis alert, most vaulting wit

3   caps occasion with *an* *around intellectual fit.

4   Yet Denis Arthur is a Bowman: his three-heeled timber 'll hit

5   the *the *tall bald and bold: blinking gold when all's: done

6 { And root in the bare butt's wincing navel in the sight of the sun
   { Right rooting in the

No. 127

1a   soft childhood's carmine dew drifts down

2a   his cheeks the forward sun

3a   Has swarthed about with *lion a lion-brown

4a   Before the spring season is done.

1b   The furl of fresh-leaved dogrose down

2b   his cheeks the forth-and-flaunting sun

3b   Had swarthed about with lion-brown

4b   Before the spring was done.

Plate 328   OET No. 127: "The furl of fresh-leaved dogrose down"
                 OET No. 128(a): "Denis,/Whose motionable, alert, most vaulting wit"

H.ii.51r -- Autograph drafts, all in ink, of No. 127 in the top half and bottom quarter, and of No. 128(a) in between. The sheet (which has an early draft of No. 130 on the verso) was folded in half (note the transparent mending strip darkening lines 17, 18), so GMH may perhaps have begun on the lower half, as he did with No. 128(d).
     Deletions include: 6b "a"   6c "spray,"   7b "hanks, fallen"   8a "at"   After 12a a row of dots is deleted with a wavy ink line.   13 "With...temples, here," 17 "And" (indenting wrong) *su*
     No. 128(a) 1 Note GMH's uncertainty where to place "Denis," the only word in the first line.   5 "Th[e]" (indenting wrong). There are great colons after "bold" and "all's".

PLATE 329. OET 125. *The Loss of the Eurydice* • *151*

H.M.S. "EURYDICE."

THE

LAST FOUR DAYS

OF THE

"EURYDICE."

By CAPTAIN E. H. VERNEY, R.N.

The Profits of this Publication will be devoted to the *Eurydice* Fund.

1878.

PORTSMOUTH.
GRIFFIN & CO., 2, THE HARD,
(Publishers by Appointment to H.R.H. The Duke of Edinburgh.)
LONDON AGENTS:—SIMPKIN, MARSHALL & CO.

---

6   The "Eurydice" Commissioned.

is a water-tight deck, communicating with the lower deck only by hatchways in the middle of the ship. It is very usual to carry the main deck ports open at sea in moderate weather, because if she does ship one or two seas, no harm is done beyond wetting the deck; the water cannot get below, as there are high coamings round the hatchways, and it only runs off harmlessly through the lee scuppers. Indeed, frigates are built on purpose to fight their main deck guns, and carry their main deck ports open at sea in all reasonably fine weather.

She was a peculiarly handy ship for navigating in narrow waters—more bouyant than a brig, and safer, from her higher freeboard; her main deck ports were about five feet above the water line; her draught of water at this time was 16 feet 6 inches, rather more than it had had been formerly; her twenty-six old-fashioned guns had been removed, and she carried four 64-pr. guns of a modern pattern.

---

48   The Squall increases.

so they could not be seen far off. The wind off the shore was sharp and cutting; the Captain ordered the watch to be called to shorten sail; the ropes were manned, but not a ropeyarn must be started till the order is given. He sees the merchant vessels in the offing shortening sail betimes to the freshening gale, as shorthanded vessels must; but the *Eurydice* with her numerous and picked crew can well afford to wait till the last moment; his men have never failed him yet, and they will not fail him now: it is no rash or foolhardy spirit that makes him wait to give the order, but the experience and self-reliance of some thirty years of seafaring life.

The first puff of the coming squall is seen, and the order is given to take in the royals; the royal-yard-men are in the rigging on their way up to furl their sails when the Captain calls them down; the squall is already increasing with dangerous rapidity; and at once the order is given to shorten sail; already the studding-sails are coming in when a terrific

---

Plate 329   OET No. 125: "The Loss of the Eurydice"

See above, Plates 318 to 325b. The profits from the sale of this 63-page book were devoted to the fund for the relief of the bereaved families of the three hundred men and boys drowned in this terrible calamity.

Capt. Verney reconstructs the typical routines in a training ship. In the course of this he seeks to defend Capt. Hare from what he considers unfair charges of negligence. Page 6 describes the main deck, below which were the seamen's quarters, as made watertight so that the old gun-ports could be kept open. On p.48 he explains that naval captains habitually postponed the order to shorten sail when merchant vessels were reefing their canvas: the navy had larger and more efficient crews (and in action they had often to maintain their speed as long as possible). My copy of this interesting book formerly belonged to the Earl of Belmore.

L.i. 73 OET No. 128c	*I have two sonnets soaking, which if they shd. come to anything you shall have, and something if I'd. only seize it, on the decline of wild nature, beginning and somehow like this —*	
1	*O where is it, the wilderness,*	
2	*The wildness of the wilderness?*	
3	*Where is it, the wilderness?* *and ending —*	
	And wander in the wilderness,	4
	In the weedy wilderness,	5
	Wander in the wilderness.	6

[above] Plate 330   OET No. 128(c): "O where is it, the wilderness"

L.i.73 -- Autograph draft at the end of a long letter to RB, Feb. 22-26 1879, written from Oxford. In 2 a comma is mended to a query: GMH frequently changed his mind about the position to give his question-mark--see, e.g., drafts of OET No. 158.

[opposite] Plate 331   OET No. 128(d): "What being in rank-old nature" -- H[1], H[2], H[3]

[H[1]] H.ii.42r -- The earliest of three autograph drafts, on the lower half of a folded sheet (upper half blank: watermarked Joynson), a palimpsest at right angles to his pencil notes of paintings seen at the Royal Academy Exhibition after 6 July 1878. These entries are all decipherable: Leighton--Nausicaa--Skein [2 pictures]/Millais--Mrs. Langtry ["A Jersey Lily"]/Wyllie [no initials or title]/Yeames--Royalist 329 [No. 329 was the famous "And when did you last see your Father?"]/Watts--Britomart/Riviere--Sympathy--Victims [2 pictures]/514 Skirt[s] of a Wood (Benham)/and another by May [No.] 586/Brett--Lions/Prince's Choice (Lamont)/Haunted House (Ellis)/Herkomer--Workhouse ["Eventide--a scene in the Westminster Union"].

In the poem deletions include: 2a "such"   2b first comma (del. and rewritten)...su[ch]   3a "Say a casquèd" semicolon changed to comma   1c (separately deleted in the canc. line) have...unbound...have   1d ", earlier" Metrical marks: nine outrides, and grave accents on "casquèd" and "helvèd" (twice each).

[H[2]] H.ii.42v -- Second autograph draft, upside down on the back of H[1], blotches from which show through. Deletions include: 1e "$"...outride under "earlier"   4a "gale wet" 5a "thundering"   6a "the"   Note the great colon after "South" (4a). No comma after "nature" (1e), simply the hooked end of an outride.

[H[3]] H.ii.41v -- Third autograph draft, on a separate piece of paper. Deletions: 1f "In"   6b "with a"   Great colons follow "here" (2e), "beetle-browed" (3c), "south", "wind" (4b), and precede 6b. Punctuation at end of 1f is doubtful. RB's pencil notes "on back draft of Handsome Heart" [No. 134]: he marks it 14 beta. 7a was long mistaken for an alternative to an earlier line, the "Or" being printed in italics, but it is an alternative interpretation of the music.

PLATE 331. OET 128d. "What being in rank-old nature" • *153*

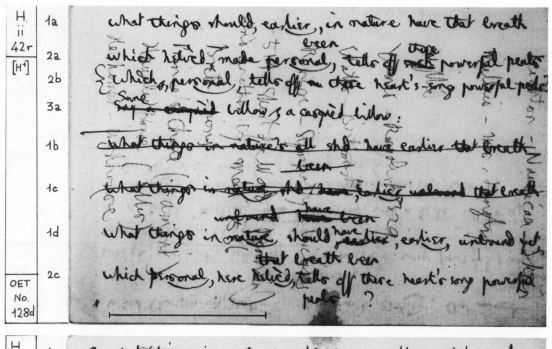

H.
ii
42r

[H¹]

OET
No.
128d

1a what things should, earlier, in nature have that breath

2a which lived made personal, tells off such powerful peals

2b Which, personal, tells off on their heart's-song powerful peals

3a Same caspied willow; a casqued billow:

1b what things in nature's all shd have earlier that breath

1c what things in natural shd have earlier unbound that breath

1d what things in nature, should earlier, unbound yet that breath been

2c which personal, here lived, tells off their heart's song powerful peals ?

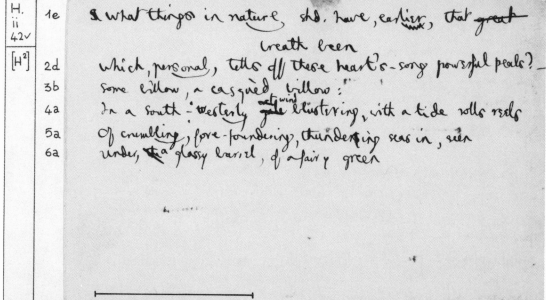

H.
ii
42v

[H²]

1e what things in nature, shd. have, earlier, that great breath been

2d which, personal, tells off these heart's-song powerful peals?

3b Some billow, a casqued billow:

4a In a south-westerly gale blustering, with a tide rolls reels

5a Of crumbling, fore-foundering, thundering seas in, seen

6a under, the a glassy barrel, of a fairy green

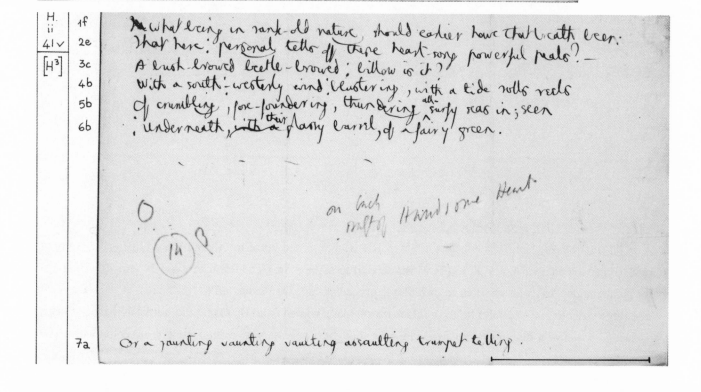

H.
ii
41v

[H³]

1f what being in rank-old nature, should earlier have that breath been:

2e that here: personal tells off these heart-song powerful peals? —

3c A lush-browed beetle-browed; billow is it?

4b With a south-westerly wind blustering, with a tide rolls reels

5b Of crumbling, fore-foundering, thundering surfy seas in; seen

6b underneath, with a glassy barrel, of a fairy green.

7a Or a jaunting vaunting vaunting assaulting trumpet telling.

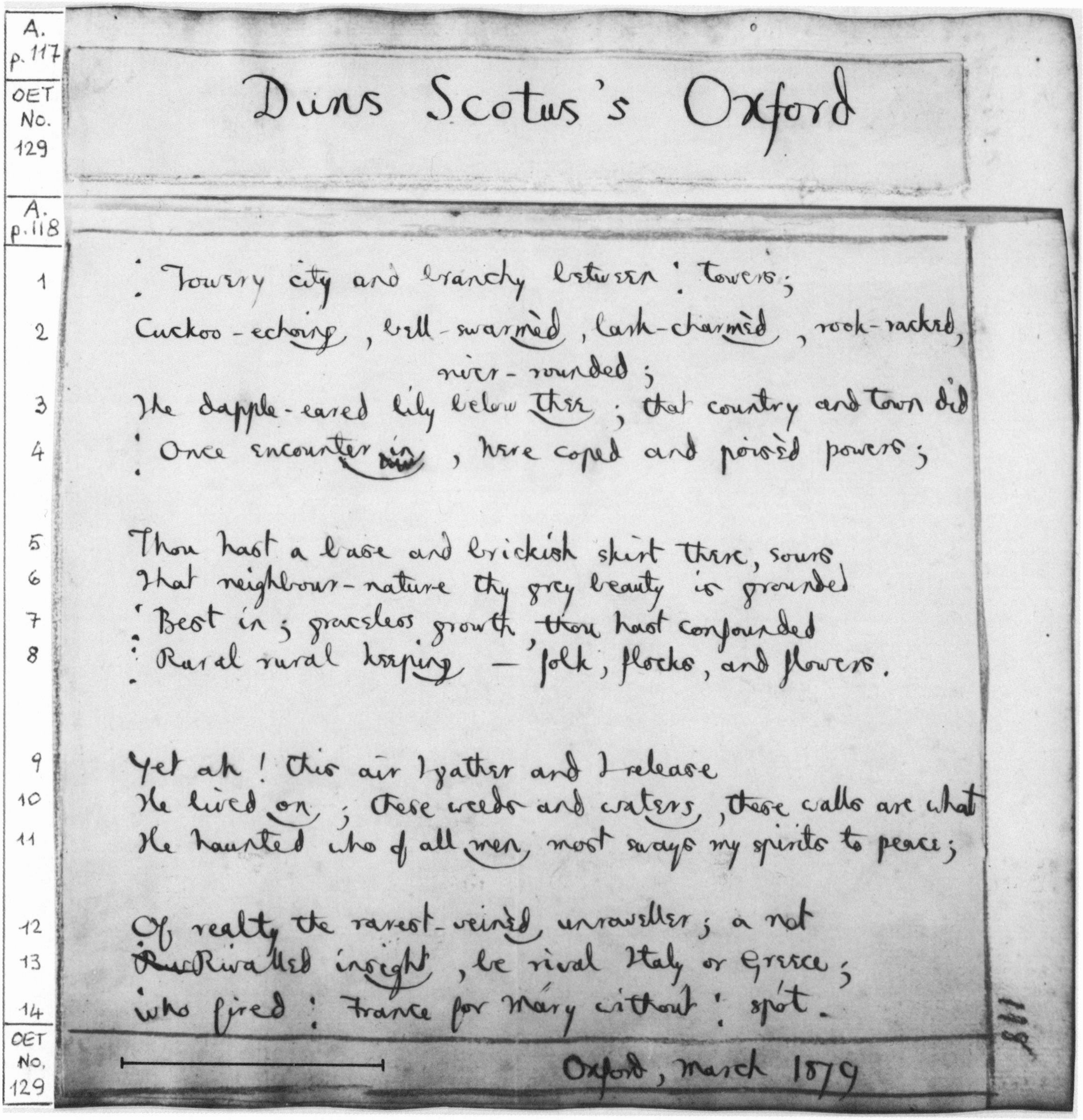

Duns Scotus's Oxford

1 : Towery city and branchy between : towers;
2 Cuckoo-echoing , bell-swarmèd , lark-charmèd , rook-racked,
river-rounded ;
3 The dapple-eared lily below thee ; that country and town did
4 : Once encounter in , here coped and posèd powers ;

5 Thou hast a base and brickish skirt there, sours
6 That neighbour-nature thy grey beauty is grounded
7 ' Best in ; graceless growth, thou hast confounded
8 : Rural rural keeping — 'folk, flocks, and flowers.

9 Yet ah ! this air I gather and I release
10 He lived on ; these weeds and waters, these walls are what
11 He haunted who of all men most sways my spirits to peace;

12 Of realty the rarest-veinèd, unraveller; a not
13 Rivalled insight , be rival Italy or Greece ;
14 : who fired : France for Mary without : spot .

Oxford, march 1879

Plate 332   OET No. 129: Duns Scotus's Oxford -- MS. 1 (A)

A.pp.117 (Title only; blank space below it left by RB is here closed up as in original MS), 118 (text). Autograph faircopy. Great colons open 1, 4, 7, 8, 13 ("Riv" was deleted to make room), and occur in 1 and 14 (twice). The outride in 4, originally under "in", was rewritten to include the preceding "er", then extended to "ter".

The three stresses in 14 seem to be RB's (black ink of 1889), copied from B: GMH did not usually place his stress on the second vowel of a diphthong, nor would he have thought it necessary to reduplicate a great colon with stresses before and after.

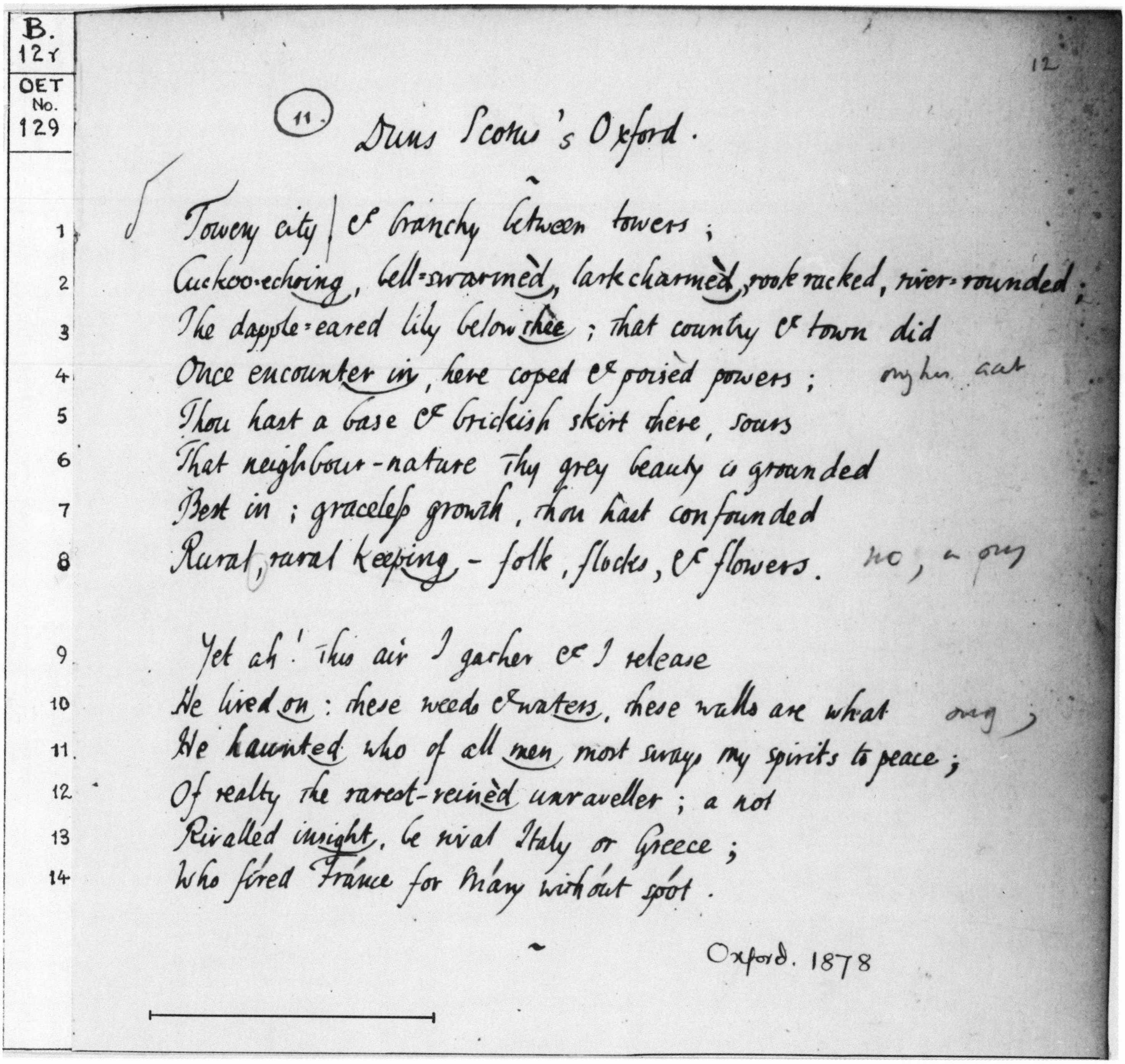

PLATE 333. OET 129. *Duns Scotus's Oxford* • 155

B.
12 r

OET
No.
129

12

(11.) *Duns Scotus's Oxford.*

1 Towery city | & branchy between towers ;
2 Cuckoo-echoing, bell-swarmèd, lark-charmèd, rook-racked, river-rounded ;
3 The dapple-eared lily below thee ; that country & town did
4 Once encounter in, here coped & poisèd powers ;   orig hs acct
5 Thou hast a base & brickish skirt there, sours
6 That neighbour-nature Thy grey beauty is grounded
7 Best in ; graceless growth, thou hast confounded
8 Rural, rural keeping, — folk, flocks, & flowers.   no, in orig

9 Yet ah ! this air I gather & I release
10 He lived on : these weeds & waters, these walls are what   orig ;
11 He haunted who of all men, most sways my spirits to peace ;
12 Of realty the rarest-veinèd unraveller ; a not
13 Rivalled insight, be rival Italy or Greece ;
14 Who fired France for Mary without spot.

Oxford. 1878

Plate 333   OET No. 129: Duns Scotus's Oxford -- MS. 2 (B)

B.12r -- Transcription of A by RB in album B. In the title he omitted the "s" after the apostrophe (added in pencil 1918); in 1 added a comma after "city" (deleted in pencil 1918); in 2 omitted hyphens after "lark" and "rook", but may have intended compound words; in 4 RB omitted the grave on "poisèd" (added in pencil 1918, with marginal note "orig has acct"); in 8 RB added a comma after the first "Rural" (ringed in pencil 1918 with note "no,,in orig"); in 10 used a colon after "on" (pencilled note, 1918, "orig;"--RB's stop might easily be read as a comma). There are no red ink corrections (RB 1884).

GMH (1884) added outrides (first two in 2 with purple pencil, elsewhere in ink); outrides in "swarmèd" and "charmèd" (2) omit the "m" which in English speech bridges both syllables (contr. A). He strengthened the grave accents in 2 (in 3 the apparent grave on "thee" is only a smudge), but overlooked the missing grave on "poisèd" (4); he prob. added commas after "charmèd" (2) and "flocks" (8). The five purple pencil stresses in 14 are certainly GMH's. The date he added later (it differs from A).

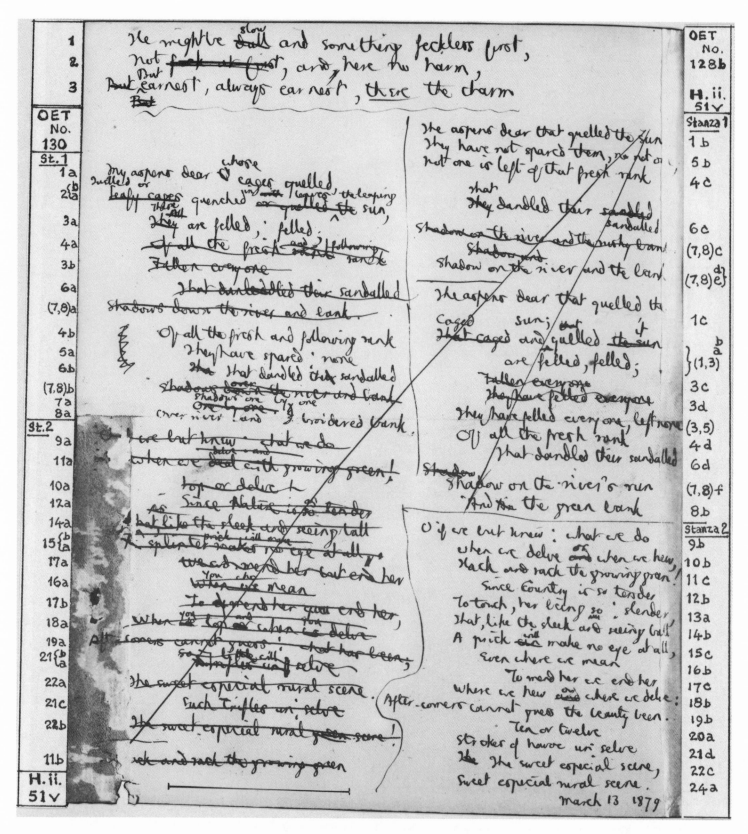

Plate 334   OET No. 128(b): "He might be slow" and Binsey Poplars

H.51v -- "He might be slow and something feckless first". Sole MS of a fragment which may be connected with OET No. 128(a) on the recto--see Plate 328. In 1 "might be" should prob. be printed as one word if it is related in sense to the hyphenated noun "might-be" (OED, "an unlikely possibility"). But OED cites no verbal use, and the mng. here seems simply (OED, "May", v.1, 5b), "He is perhaps slow". GMH's erratic penlifts in undoubted compounds and close spacing or pen glides between separate words (e.g., "Iamgall", No. 155) can create ambiguity. Cf. the crowding of "quelledthe", "andthe", "Theyhave" in "Binsey Poplars", below. Deletions include: 2 "feck at first"   3 "But/But"

Binsey Poplars. Earliest draft (H[1]), with OET Nos. 127 and 128(a) on the recto. The sheet was almost torn in two by a crease running across it where st. 2 begins in col. 2. The left edge of the lower half was lightly attached at an earlier stage to a green scrapbook sheet from which it was severed for mounting in H, but almost the complete text can be recovered. (Note cont. opposite)

PLATE 335. OET 130. *Binsey Poplars* • *157*

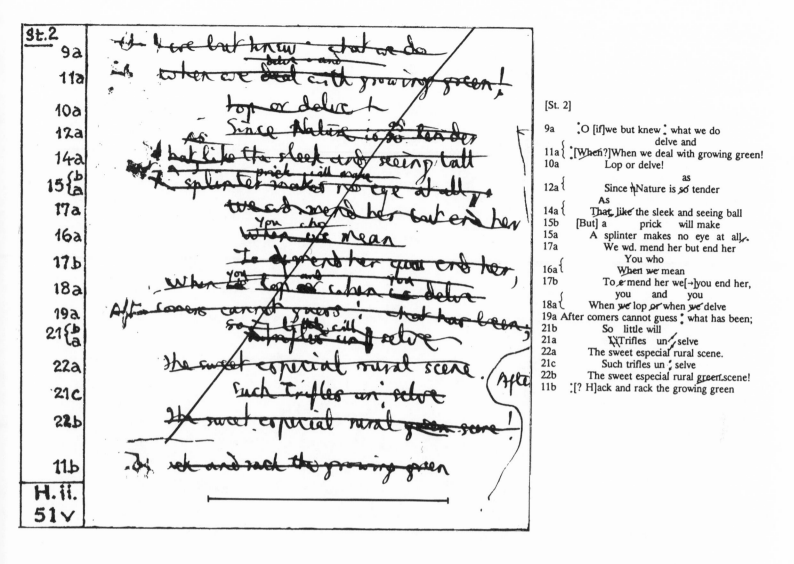

[St. 2]

9a	:O [if]we but knew : what we do
	delve and
11a {	:[When?]When we deal with growing green!
10a	Lop or delve!
	as
12a {	Since nNature is so tender
	As
14a {	That like the sleek and seeing ball
15b	[But] a prick will make
15a	A splinter makes no eye at all.
17a	We wd. mend her but end her
	You who
16a {	When we mean
17b	To emend her we[→]you end her,
	you and you
18a {	When we lop or when we delve
19a	After comers cannot guess : what has been;
21b	So little will
21a	IxTrifles un/selve
22a	The sweet especial rural scene.
21c	Such trifles un : selve
22b	The sweet especial rural green.scene!
11b	:[? H]ack and rack the growing green

Plate 334 (cont). There are three attempts at st. 1, of which the left column must be the first. When GMH found himself struggling to compose he sometimes changed the metre (as with "Brothers", L.i.106; Reader's Guide, 140), and here col. b. begins with a hum-drum abandonment of Sprung Rhythm. My marginal line nos. for st. 1 of H[1] are mere pointers to particular images in the final version which are hinted at in the drafts--e.g. 5 involves the idea of a conqueror sparing some of his brave foes, while 7 and 8 (the final "bank" is obscured in two versions) remember the shadows that used to dance on water and greenery. Their sequence (6a, 6b, etc.) is more for convenient reference than a claim to represent the stanza's tangled evolution.　　Deletions in st. 1 (i.e. top half of plate) include: (left col.) 1a "th[at?]" rev. to "whose"　2b "with" rev. to "in"　2a "or quelled the"　3a "They/All"　4a "rank" twice　6a "dan/eddled"　6b "Tha[t]" del. and rewritten to correct indentation: "the/f"　The marginal brace linking 4b, 5a and 6b, as if to preserve them for a faircopy, is del., as is another smaller brace three lines lower: both sections were further revised.　　(right col.) 5b end "o[ne]"6c "sandled"　(1, 3) "That caged and that quelled the sun"　(just before st. 2) 8b "And Aa[d]" (indenting wrong). Deletions in st. 2 (for left col. see transcription above) (right col.) 13a italics del. in "so"　15c "can"　18b "and" rev. to "or"　22c "The" del. and rewritten to correct indenting.

Plate 335　　　OET No. 130: Binsey Poplars -- enlargement of H[1] (bot. left)

　　The above first draft of st. 2 (enlarged about 130%) reveals three waves of deletion: individual words or letters within phrases were heavily blacked out; then whole lines were crossed through, probably as he rewrote them in the right-hand column; and finally the entire page, except for the revised st. 2, was seemingly discarded by the oblique lines running from the top right corner. The following transcription cannot, of course, reproduce every fine point in the MS or be completely confident about the damaged openings to lines.

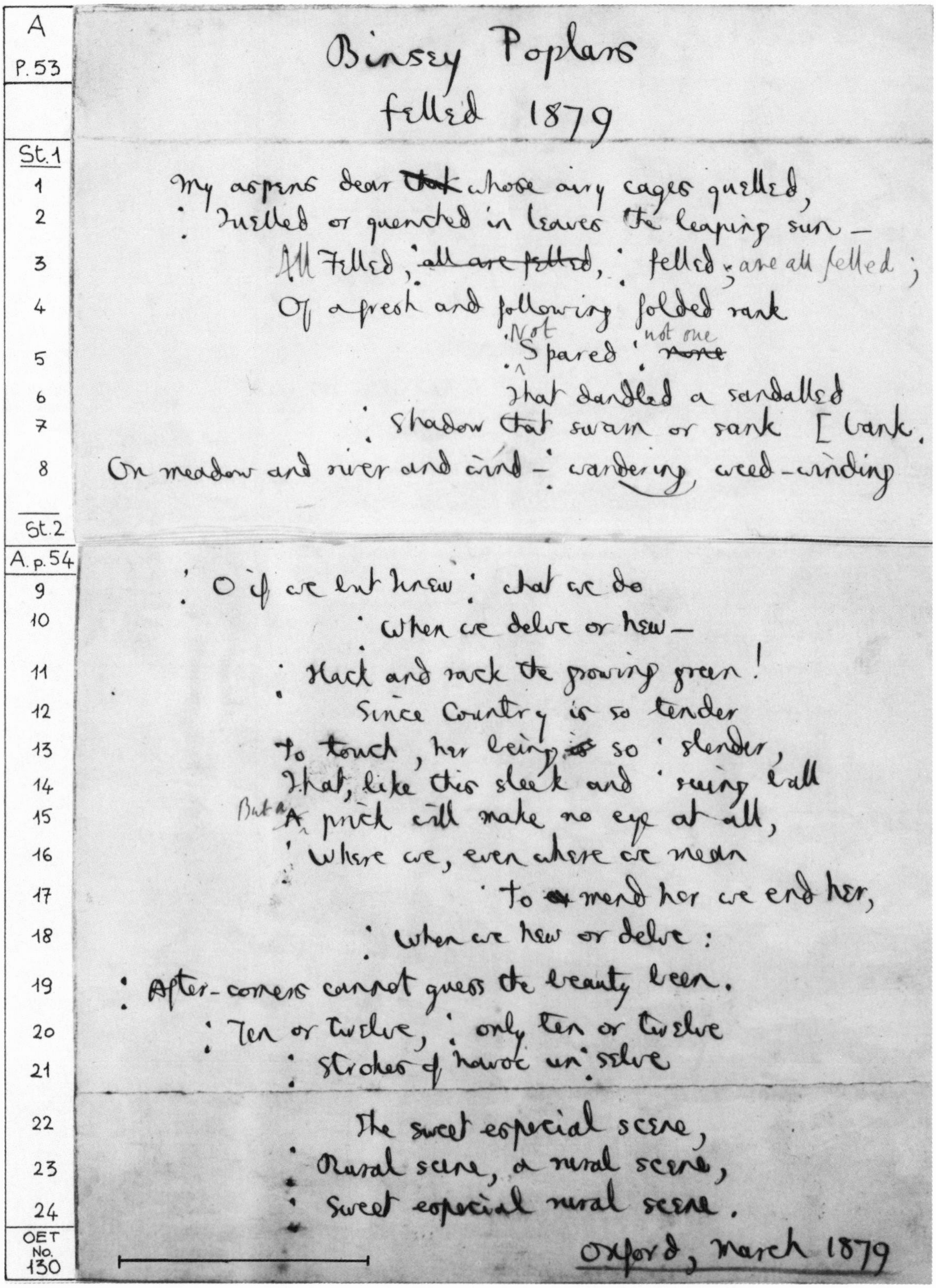

The handwritten manuscript (column markers at left):

A
P. 53

Binsey Poplars
felled 1879

St. 1

1 My aspens dear ~~that~~ whose airy cages quelled,
2 Quelled or quenched in leaves the leaping sun —
3 All Felled, all are felled, felled, are all felled;
4 Of a fresh and following folded rank
5 Not Spared, not one none
6 That dandled a sandalled
7 Shadow that swam or sank [bank.
8 On meadow and river and wind — wandering, weed-winding

St. 2
A. p. 54

9 O if we but knew what we do
10 When we delve or hew —
11 Hack and rack the growing green!
12 Since Country is so tender
13 To touch, her being is so slender,
14 That, like this sleek and seeing ball
15 But a A prick will make no eye at all,
16 Where we, even where we mean
17 to mend her we end her,
18 When we hew or delve:
19 After-comers cannot guess the beauty been.
20 Ten or twelve, only ten or twelve
21 Strokes of havoc unselve
22 The sweet especial scene,
23 Rural scene, a rural scene,
24 Sweet especial rural scene.

Oxford, March 1879

OET
NO.
130

Plate 336   OET No. 130: Binsey Poplars -- MS. 3 (A)

[Note: The MSS of "Binsey Poplars" have been so arranged that by raising the intervening sheets H[1] can be compared with H[2], and A with B.]

A.pp.53-54 -- Autograph faircopy. GMH corrected slips in 1 "that", 17 "e[nd]". GMH's autograph must be distinguished from RB's red ink in 3, 5, 13, 15, copying GMH's revisions in B. GMH wrote: 3 " ⦂ Felled, ⦂ all are felled, ⦂ felled;"   5 " ⦂ Spared ⦂ none"   13 "is" del. in red by RB   15 GMH's "A" was deleted in red ink and replaced by "But a". Great colons open 14 lines, and occur in eight other places. There is only one outride (8).

RB's red ink (1884) copied GMH's revisions in B. His pencil (1918) stressed "wind" (middle of 8).

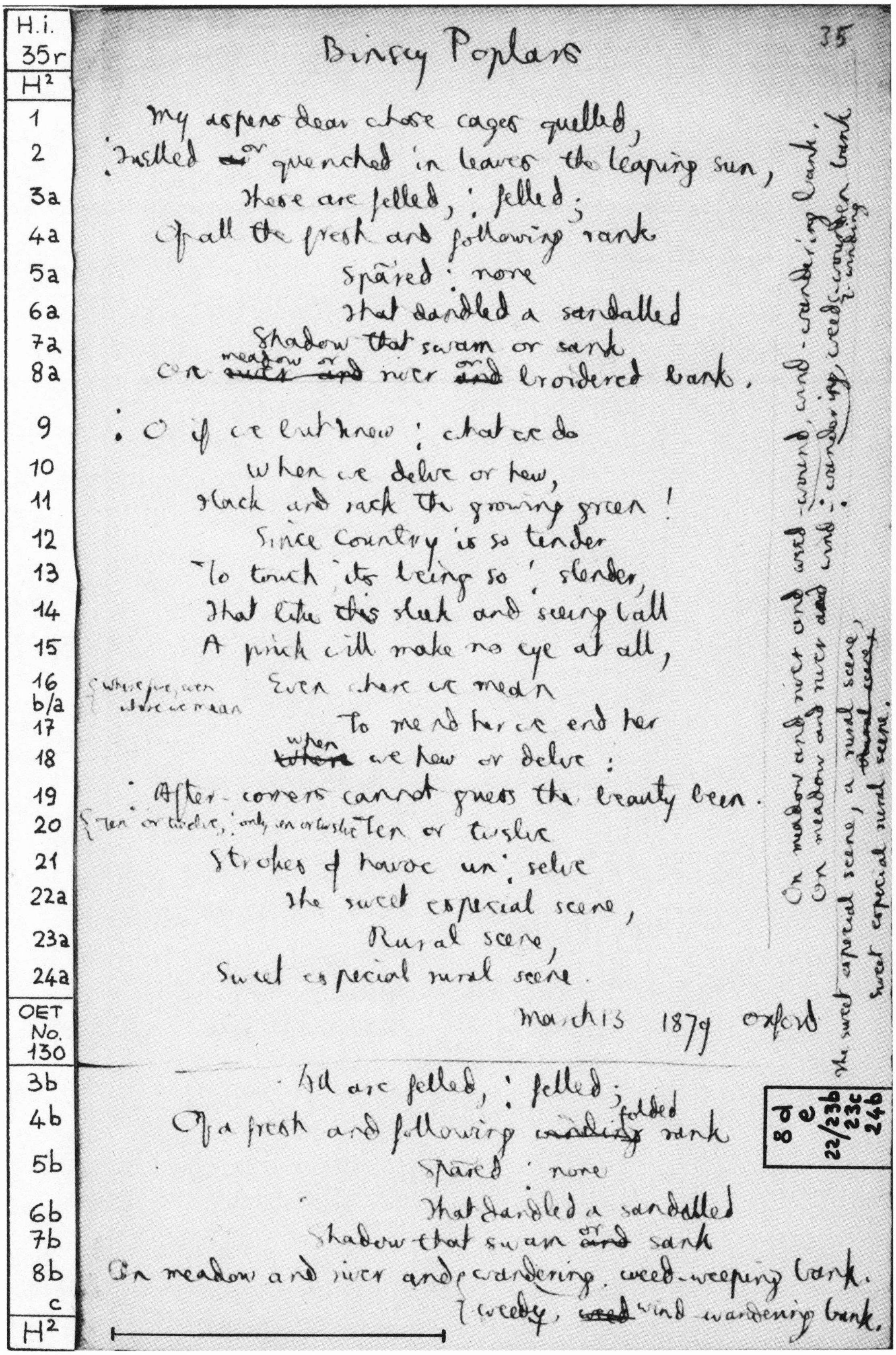

PLATE 337. OET 130. *Binsey Poplars* • *159*

Binsey Poplars 35

H.i. 35r	
H²	
1	My aspens dear whose cages quelled,
2	Justled or quenched in leaves the leaping sun,
3a	those are felled, : felled ;
4a	Of all the fresh and following rank
5a	Spared : none
6a	that dandled a sandalled
7a	Shadow that swam or sank
8a	On meadow and river and broidered bank.
9	: O if we but knew : what we do
10	when we delve or hew,
11	Hack and rack the growing green !
12	Since Country is so tender
13	To touch, its being so : slender,
14	That like this sleek and seeing ball
15	A prick will make no eye at all,
16 b/a	Even where we mean
17	To mend her we end her
18	when we hew or delve :
19	: After-comers cannot guess the beauty been.
20	Ten or twelve Ten or twelve
21	Strokes of havoc un: selve
22a	the sweet especial scene,
23a	Rural scene,
24a	Sweet especial rural scene.
	March 13 1879 oxford
OET No. 130	
3b	All are felled, : felled ;
4b	Of a fresh and following folded rank
5b	Spared : none
6b	that dandled a sandalled
7b	Shadow that swam or sank
8b	On meadow and river and gardening, weed-weeping bank.
c	Tweeby, wind wandering bank.
H²	

Plate 337   OET No. 130: Binsey Poplars -- MS. 2 (H²)

H.i.35r -- Autograph faircopy of H¹, with later marginal and footnote alternatives. It is written on the back of a printed announcement of Needlework and Language classes at St. Joseph's Convent (Plate 338). Great colons open 2, 9, 19 and occur in 3a, 5a, 9, 13, 20, 21, 3b, 5b, 8e. Deletions include: 2 "A[nd] or"   8a "river and"   18 "Where" 4b "winding"   8c "weed"   23c "Rural scene,"

The tiny revisions touching the left margin of 16 and 20 record MS. A readings. Note in 16(b) that a stress seems intended on the second "where". Circumflex on "Spared" (5a, 5b).

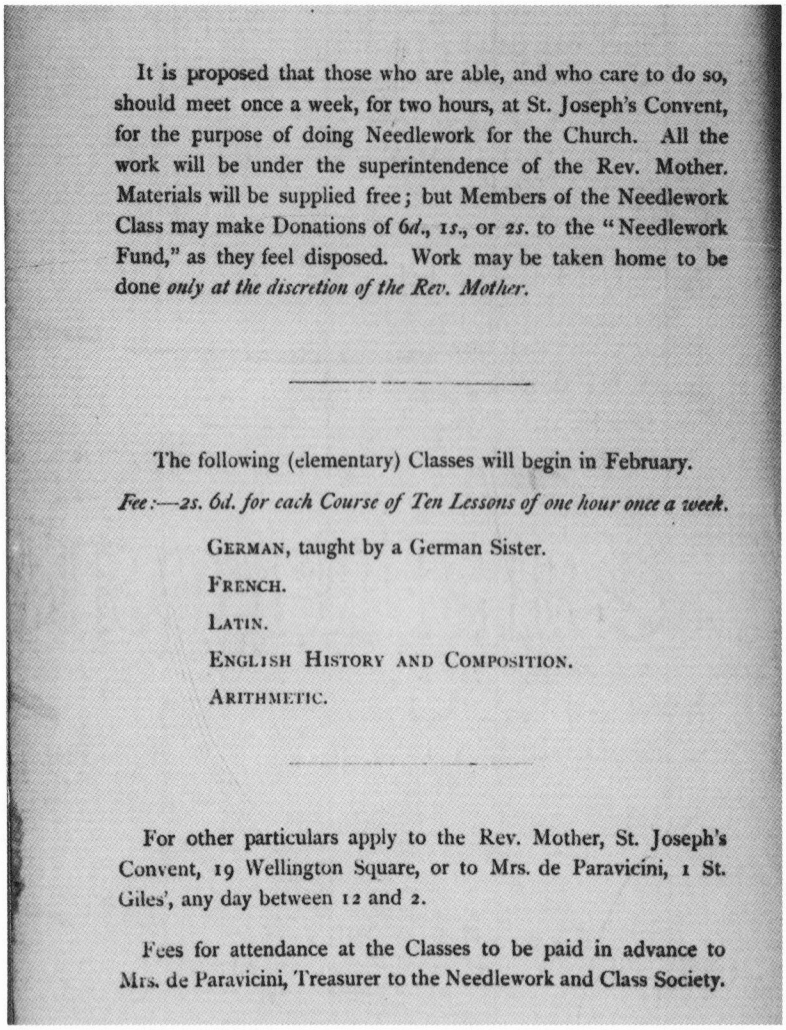

It is proposed that those who are able, and who care to do so, should meet once a week, for two hours, at St. Joseph's Convent, for the purpose of doing Needlework for the Church. All the work will be under the superintendence of the Rev. Mother. Materials will be supplied free; but Members of the Needlework Class may make Donations of *6d.*, *1s.*, or *2s.* to the "Needlework Fund," as they feel disposed. Work may be taken home to be done *only at the discretion of the Rev. Mother.*

The following (elementary) Classes will begin in February.

Fee:—2s. 6d. for each Course of Ten Lessons of one hour once a week.

German, taught by a German Sister.

French.

Latin.

English History and Composition.

Arithmetic.

For other particulars apply to the Rev. Mother, St. Joseph's Convent, 19 Wellington Square, or to Mrs. de Paravicini, 1 St. Giles', any day between 12 and 2.

Fees for attendance at the Classes to be paid in advance to Mrs. de Paravicini, Treasurer to the Needlework and Class Society.

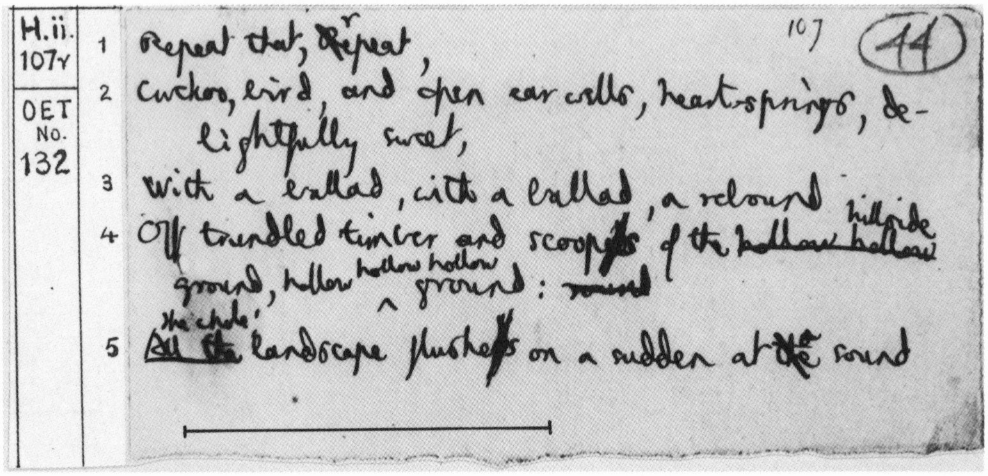

H.ii. 107v

OET No. 132

1 Repeat that, repeat,

2 Cuckoo, bird, and open ear wells, heart-springs, delightfully sweet,

3 With a ballad, with a ballad, a rebound

4 Off trundled timber and scoops of the hollow hollow hillside ground, hollow hollow hollow ground: sound

5 The whole landscape flushes on a sudden at a sound

Plate 338

[top] H.i.35v -- GMH used the back of this notice for his H^2 revision of "Binsey Poplars" (H.i.35r, Plate 337). This leaflet would have been distributed by the Oxford priests and in their churches. A leading organiser of the needlework and language classes, twice mentioned in the notice, was the wife of Baron Francis de Paravicini, who had been a brilliant contemporary of GMH's at Balliol when he was a student, and who had become Tutor of Balliol (1872-98) and classics lecturer. He and his wife (a Catholic convert) were among GMH's best friends during his second spell in Oxford: see L.iii.62-3 and J.16, 301.

[bottom] H.ii.107r -- Autograph draft, sole MS, of a fragment. The obscure great colon after "whole" (5), discovered by Catherine Phillips, assists the dating. Changes include: 4 "scooped" rev. to "scoops" 5 "All the" rev. to "The whole : landscape" and "flushed" rev. to "flushes".

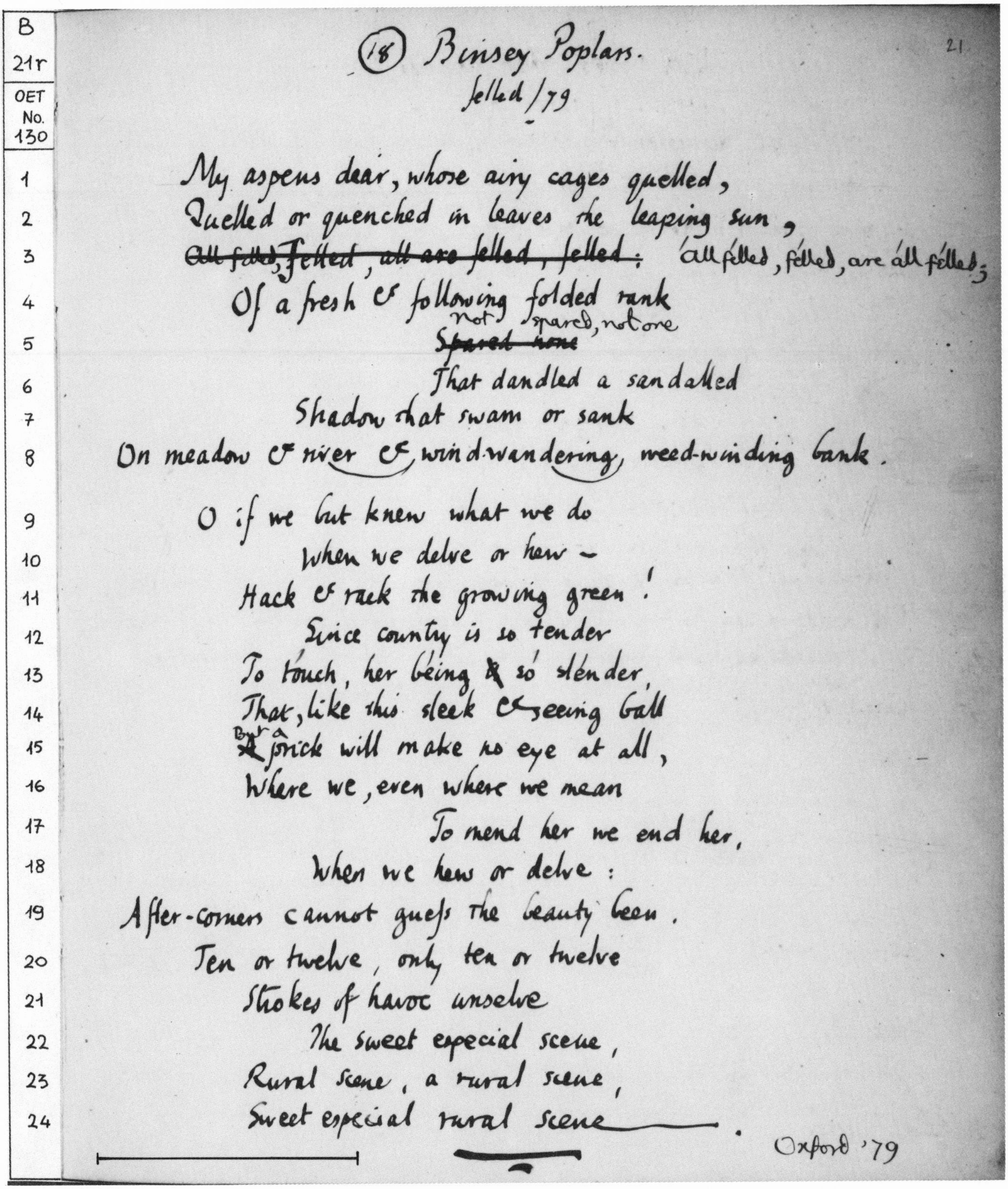

PLATE 339. OET 130. *Binsey Poplars* • 161

B	
21r	
OET No. 130	

(18) Binsey Poplars.

felled /79

1 My aspens dear, whose airy cages quelled,
2 Quelled or quenched in leaves the leaping sun,
3 ~~All fell, Felled, all are felled, felled;~~ 'All felled, felled, are all felled;
4 Of a fresh & following folded rank
5 ~~Spared none~~   not spared, not one
6 That dandled a sandalled
7 Shadow that swam or sank
8 On meadow & river & wind-wandering, weed-winding bank.

9 O if we but knew what we do
10 When we delve or hew —
11 Hack & rack the growing green!
12 Since country is so tender
13 To touch, her being ⅄ so slender,
14 That, like this sleek & seeing ball
15 But a ⅄ prick will make no eye at all,
16 Where we, even where we mean
17 To mend her we end her,
18 When we hew or delve:
19 After-comers cannot guess the beauty been.
20 Ten or twelve, only ten or twelve
21 Strokes of havoc unselve
22 The sweet especial scene,
23 Rural scene, a rural scene,
24 Sweet especial rural scene ————— .

Oxford '79

Plate 339   OET No. 130: Binsey Poplars -- MS. 4 (B)

B.21r -- Transcription of A by RB who omitted "18" from the year in the title; he added a comma after "dear" (1--accepted and strengthened by GMH); substituted a colon for the semicolon ending 3; crowded "wind wandering" into one word, then inserted a dot as hyphen; added an ornate "line-filling" to end 24.

GMH strengthened some of RB's final commas (1, 15); changed "sun--" (2) to "sun,"; tried to revise 3 by adding "All felled," on the left and mending "F" to "f", then deleted this and the whole line and rewrote it to the right with five purple pencil stresses; he rewrote 5; deleted "is" (13) and inserted four purple stresses in that line; he replaced "A" (15) with "But a". In 8 contrast the outrides with MS. A (the first was not in A, the second included "d"). GMH added the date later.

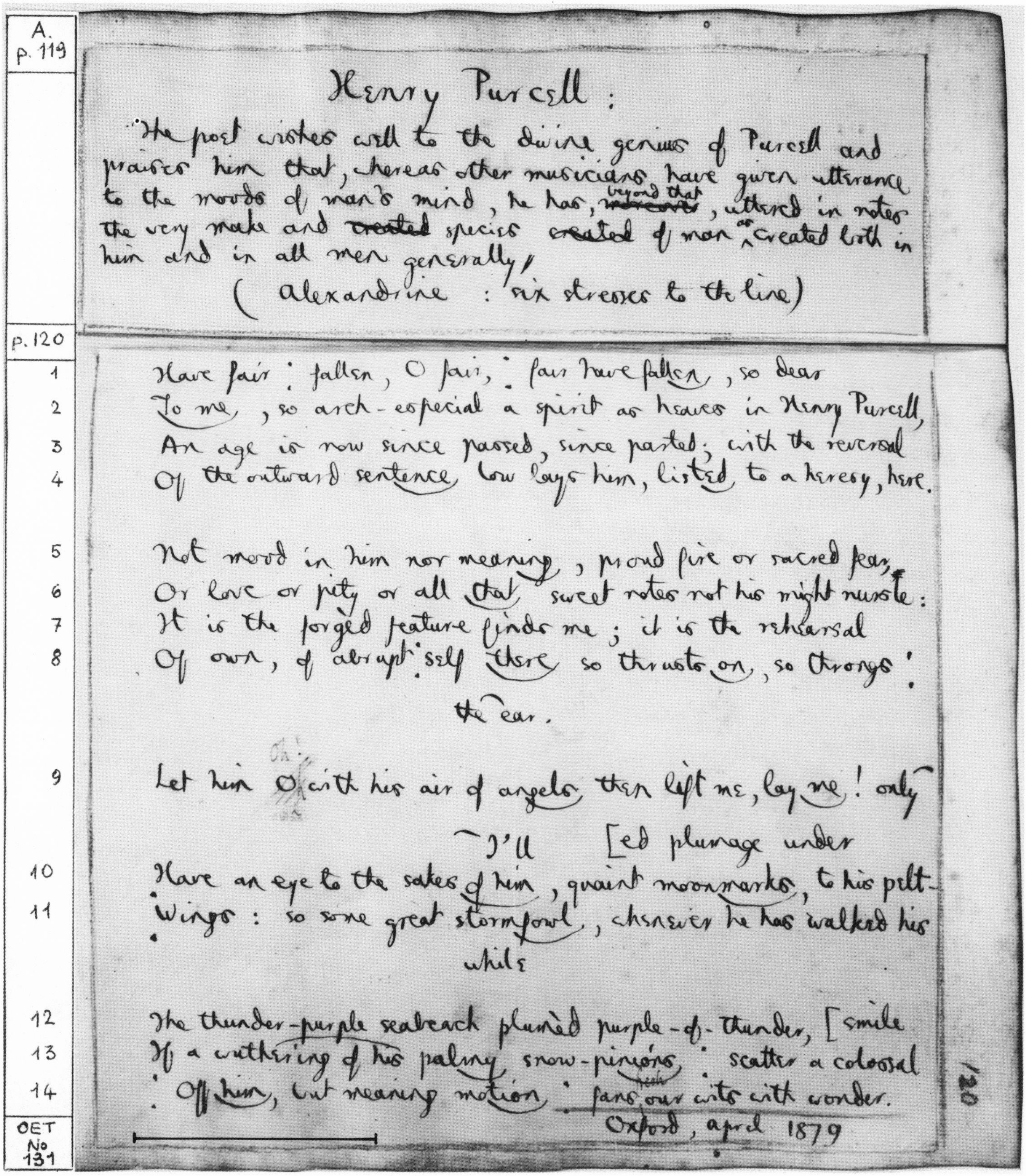

A.
p. 119

Henry Purcell :
"The poet wishes well to the divine genius of Purcell and praises him that, whereas other musicians have given utterance to the moods of man's mind, he has, ~~moreover~~ beyond that, uttered in notes the very make and ~~created~~ species ~~created~~ of man, created both in him and in all men generally/

(Alexandrine : six stresses to the line)

p. 120

1 Have fair : fallen, O fair, : fair have fallen, so dear
2 To me, , so arch-especial a spirit as heaves in Henry Purcell,
3 An age is now since passed, since passed; with the reversal
4 Of the outward sentence, low lays him, listed, to a heresy, here.

5 Not mood in him nor meaning, proud fire or sacred fear,
6 Or love or pity or all that, sweet notes not his might nursle:
7 It is the forgèd feature finds me ; it is the rehearsal
8 Of own, of abrupt self there so thrusts on, so throngs the ear.

9 Let him Oh! with his air of angels then lift me, lay me ! only I'll
   [ed plumage under
10 Have an eye to the sakes of him, quaint moonmarks, to his pelt-
11 Wings : so some great stormfowl, whenever he has walked his while

12 The thunder-purple seabeach plumèd purple-of-thunder, [smile
13 If a wuthering of his palmy snow-pinions scatter a colossal
14 Off him, but meaning motion fans our wits with wonder.

Oxford, april 1879

120

OET No 131

Plate 340   OET No. 131: Henry Purcell - MS. 1 (A)

   A.pp.119 (Title, etc.), 120 (text)--autograph faircopy mounted in album A; in the argument, three words and the final punctuation were deleted by GMH ("moreover", "created" twice). At the end of 5, a comma was del. and rewritten clear of "nursle" in the line below (6).

   RB's red ink of 1884, copying GMH's revisions in B, in 9 squeezed in "h" after "O", then deleted both letters and rewrote "Oh!" above; in 14 he inserted "fresh".

PLATE 341. OET 131. *Henry Purcell* • 163

B
12v

Henry Purcell.

1 Have fair fallen, O fair, fair have fallen, so déar
2 To me, so arch-especial a spirit as heaves in Henry Purcell,
3 An age *is* now since passed, since parted; with the reversal
4 Of the outward sentence low lays him, listed to a heresy, here.

5 Not mood in him nor meaning, proud fire or sacred fear,
6 Or love, or pity, or all that sweet notes not his might nursle:
7 It is the forgèd feature finds me; it is the rehearsal
8 Of own, of abrupt self there, so thrusts on, so throngs the ear.

9 Let him *oh!* with his air of angels, then lift me, lay me, only I'll
10 Have an eye to the sakes of him, quaint moonmarks, & his pelted
                              plumage under
11 Wings: so some great stormfowl, whenever he has walked his while
12 The thunder-purple seabeach, plumèd purple of thunder,
13 If a wuthering of his palmy snow-pinions scatter a colossal smile
14 Off him, but meaning motion fans *fresh* our wits with wonder.

Oxford. 1879

Plate 341   OET No. 131: Henry Purcell -- MS. 2 (B)

B 12v -- transcription of A by RB, as usual without any stresses or metrical signs except grave accents on "forgèd" (7) and "plumèd" (12). In 3 RB mended his slip "has" to "is", but the "h" was still faintly visible.

GMH revising B, deleted this "is" and rewrote it above. In 9, he deleted "Oh" and rewrote it above as "oh!"; and in 14 added "fresh". He used purple pencil for six stresses in 1, but ink for seventeen outrides. He added or reinforced commas after "fear" (5), "love", "pity" (6), "seabeach" (12). He later added the date.

In 11 there is a blot like a grave after "his".

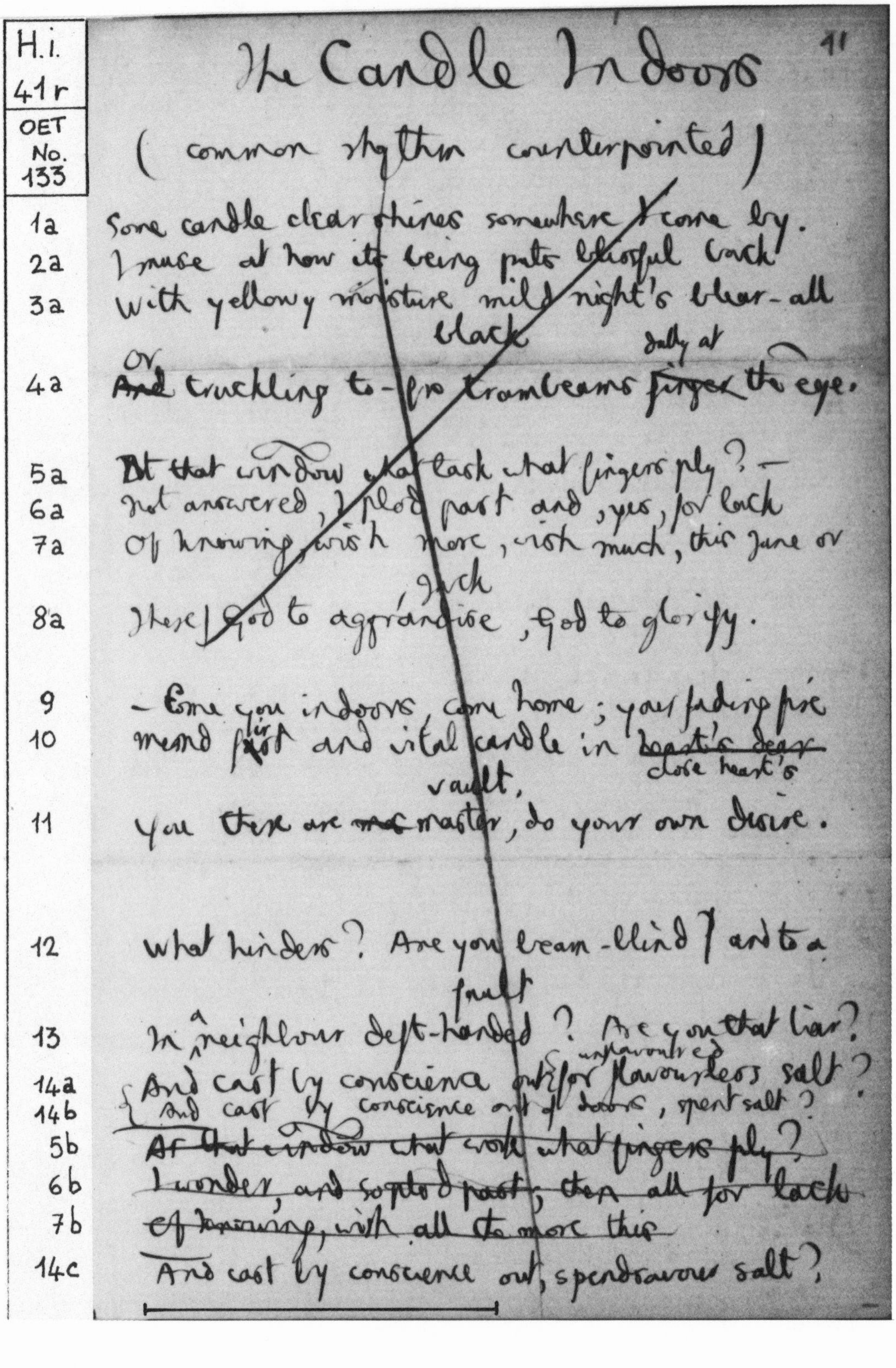

H.i. 41r

OET No. 133

The Candle Indoors 41

(common rhythm counterpointed)

1a Some candle clear shines somewhere I come by.
2a I muse at how its being puts blissful back
3a With yellowy moisture mild night's blear-all black
4a ~~And~~ Or truckling to-fro trambeams ~~finger~~ dally at the eye.

5a ~~Bt~~ At that window what task what fingers ply? —
6a Not answered, I plod past and, yes, for lack
7a Of knowing, wish more, wish much, this Jane or Jack
8a There / God to aggrandise, God to glorify.

9 — Come you indoors, come home; your fading fire
10 Mend ~~fast~~ first and vital candle in ~~heart's dear~~ close heart's vault,
11 You there are master, do your own desire.

12 What hinders? Are you beam-blind, yet to a fault
13 In a neighbour deft-handed? Are you that liar?
14a And cast by conscience out, for unfavoured flavourless salt?
14b And cast by conscience out of doors, spent salt?
5b ~~At that window what work what fingers ply?~~
6b ~~I wonder, and so plod past, then all for lack~~
7b ~~Of knowing, with all the more this~~
14c And cast by conscience out, spendsavour salt?

Plate 342 (above) and 343 (opposite) OET No. 133: The Candle Indoors -- MS. 1 (H)

H.i.41r,v--autograph faircopy of an early version, with minor revisions; followed at the foot and on the verso with successive drafts, particularly of the second quatrain. Ink deletion lines run through 1a to 8a, 5b to 7b, and (41v) 5c to 7g; pencil lines delete both pages. Quick lines of different lengths run from the left margin to mark off new revisions --after 14b, 7b; on 41 verso after 7g, 8d and 8e.

Changes include: 5a "B[y?]" mended to "At" 9 "c" mended to "Come" 10 "Mend" (like "Memd") "fast" rev. to "first" 11 "mas", obscure, so rewritten 12 orig. "blind?" between 6e and 7e "A" (perhaps for new version of 5) del. 4b long slur over "truckle at the" deleted and replaced with two short slurs marking elisions. Note the counterpoint signs on "window" (5) and "wondering" (6e to 6h).

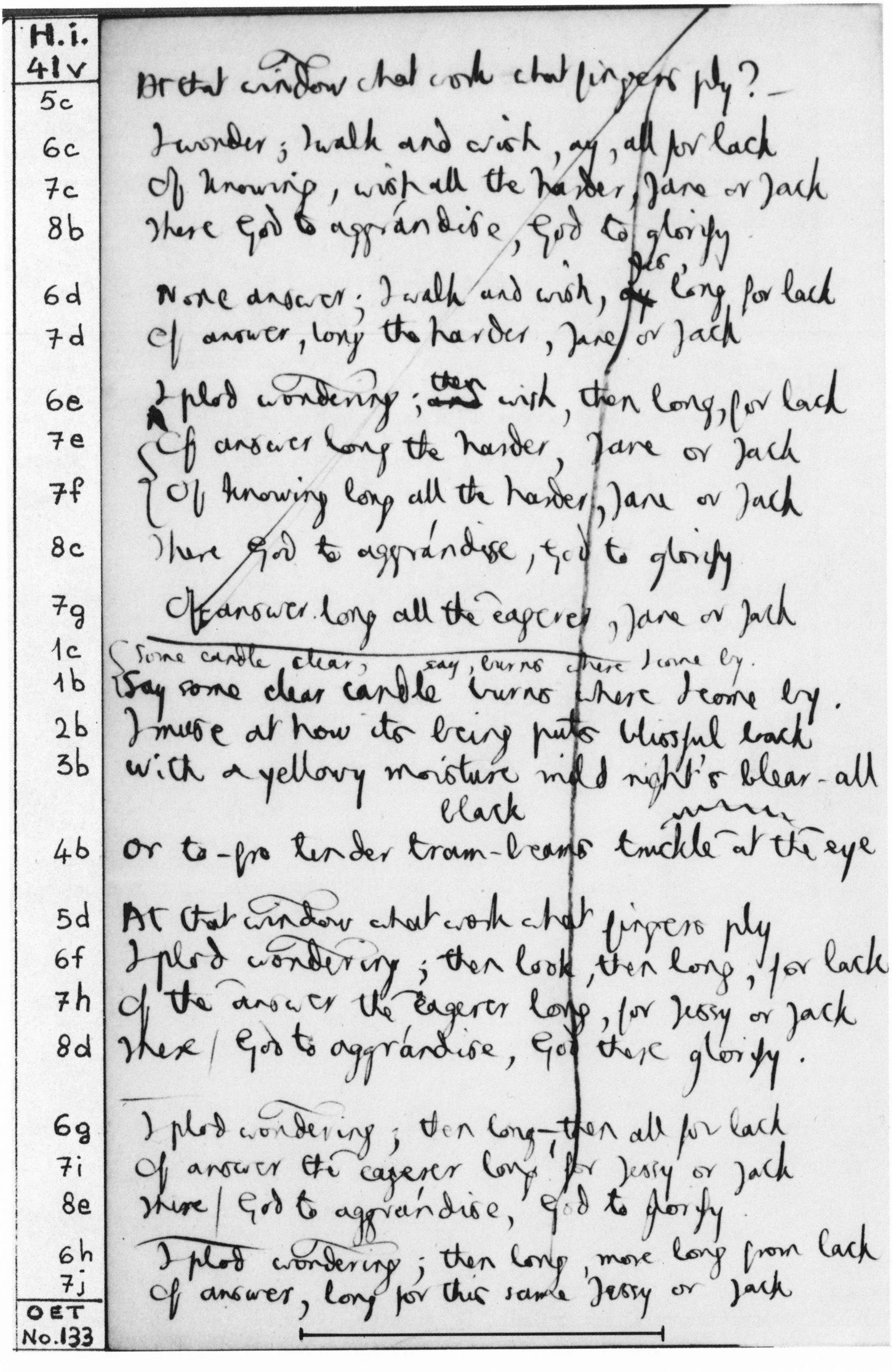

PLATE 343. OET 133. *The Candle Indoors* • 165

H.i. 41v	
5c	At that window that now that fingers ply? —
6c	I wonder; I walk and wish, ay, all for lack
7c	Of knowing, wish all the harder, Jane or Jack
8b	There God to aggrándise, God to glorify
6d	None answer; I walk and wish, ay long for lack
7d	Of answer, long the harder, Jane or Jack
6e	I plod wondering; then wish, then long, for lack
7e	Of answer long the harder, Jane or Jack
7f	Of knowing long all the harder, Jane or Jack
8c	There God to aggrándise, God to glorify
7g	Of answer. long all the eagerer, Jane or Jack
1c	Some candle clear, say, burns there I come by.
1b	Say some clear candle burns where I come by.
2b	I muse at how its being puts blissful back
3b	With a yellowy moisture mild night's blear-all black
4b	Or to-fro tender tram-beams truckle at the eye
5d	At that window that now that fingers ply
6f	I plod wondering; then look, then long, for lack
7h	Of the answer the eagerer long, for Jessy or Jack
8d	There / God to aggrándise, God there glorify.
6g	I plod wondering; then long—then all for lack
7i	Of answer the eagerer long, for Jessy or Jack
8e	There / God to aggrándise, God to glorify
6h	I plod wondering; then long, more long from lack
7j	Of answer, long for this same Jessy or Jack
OET No.133	

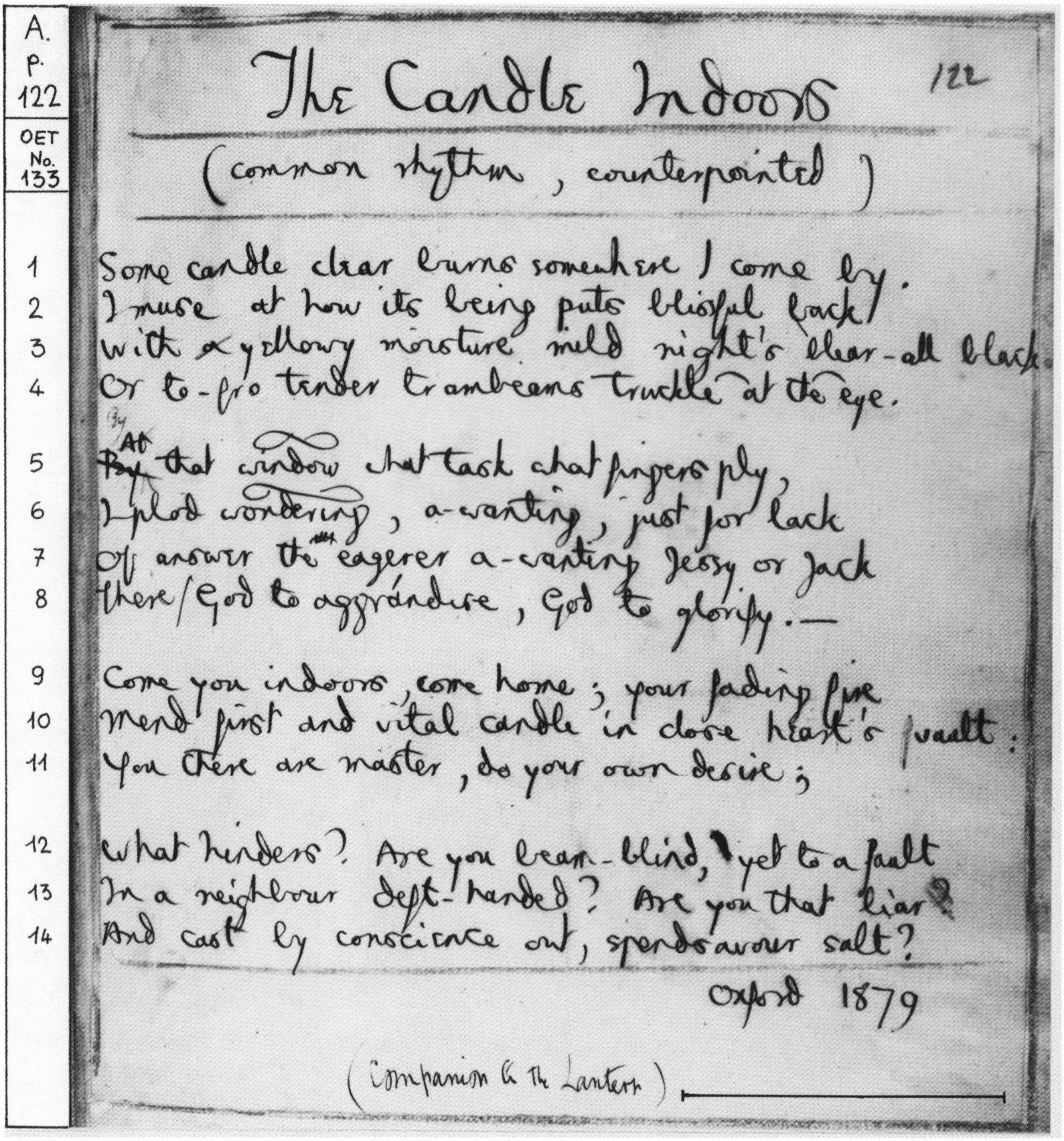

A.
p.
122

OET
No.
133

The Candle Indoors

122

(common rhythm , counterpointed)

1   Some candle clear burns somewhere I come by.
2   I muse at how its being puts blissful back
3   With a yellowy moisture mild night's blear-all black,
4   Or to-fro tender trambeams truckle at the eye.

5   At that window what task what fingers ply,
6   I plod wondering, a-wanting, just for lack
7   Of answer the eagerer a-wanting Jessy or Jack
8   There/God to aggrándise, God to glorify.—

9   Come you indoors, come home; your fading fire
10 Mend first and vital candle in close heart's vault:
11 You there are master, do your own desire;

12 What hinders? Are you beam-blind, yet to a fault
13 In a neighbour deft-handed? Are you that liar
14 And cast by conscience out, spendsavour salt?

Oxford 1879

(Companion to the Lantern)

Plate 344   OET No. 133: The Candle Indoors -- MS. 2 (A)

A.p.122--autograph faircopy. Changes by GMH: 5 "By" rev. to "At"   7 slur del.   10 "f" before "vault" (confusion with "fault" ending 12) partly erased   11 final semicolon clarified   12 query after "blind" begun and del. (as in H 12a).

RB's red ink (1884), copying GMH's revisions in B, in 3 del. "a", in 5 restores "By", in 13 del. query after "liar". RB's black ink (1889) notes at the foot "(Companion to the Lantern)", i.e., No. 113.

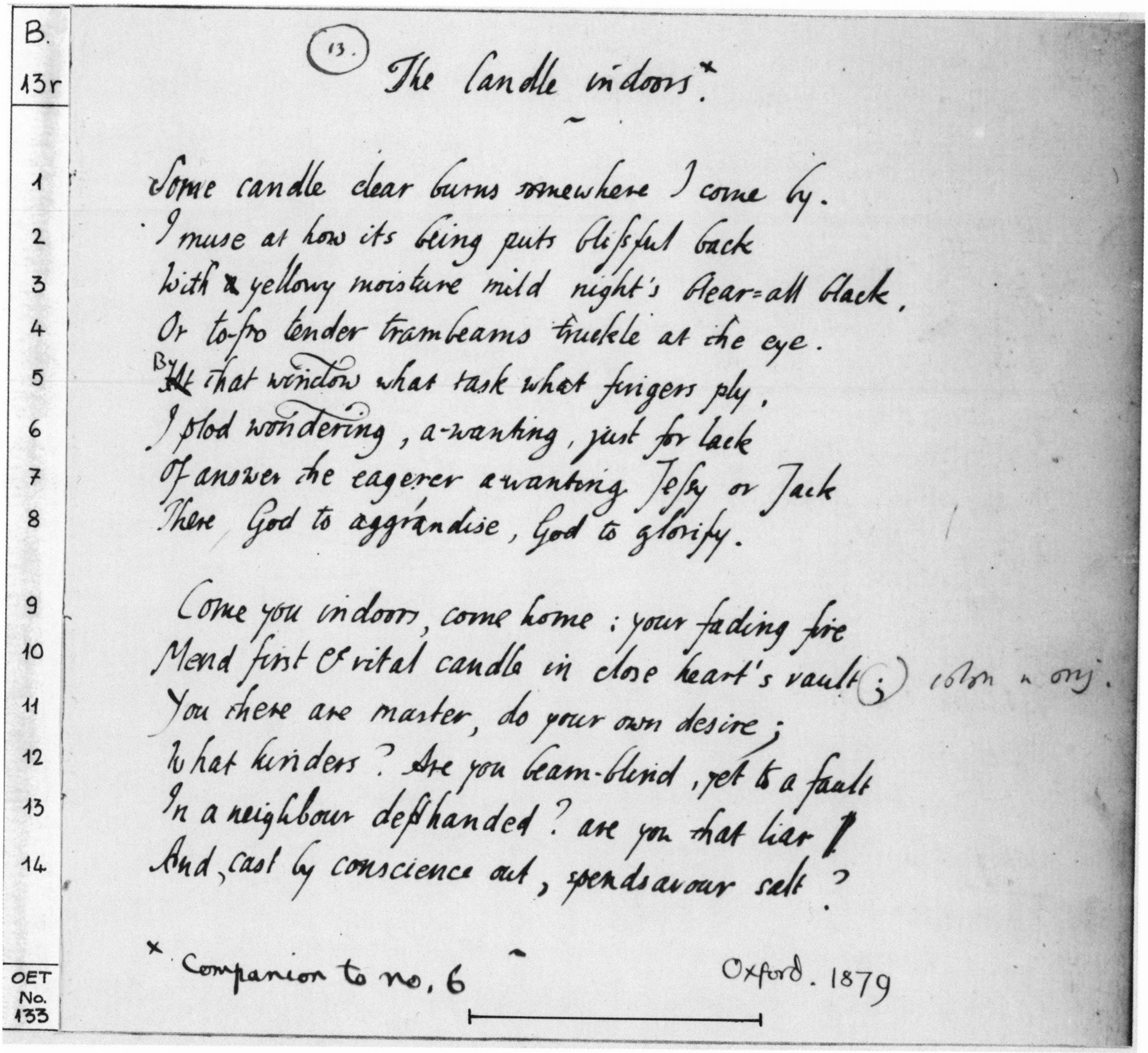

PLATE 345. OET 133. *The Candle Indoors*   •   *167*

B.
13r

(13.)

The Candle indoors*

1 Some candle clear burns somewhere I come by.
2 I muse at how its being puts blissful back
3 With a yellowy moisture mild night's Bear=all black.
4 Or to-fro tender trambeams truckle at the eye.
5 By that window what task what fingers ply,
6 I plod wondering, a-wanting, just for lack
7 Of answer the eagerer a-wanting Jessy or Jack
8 There, God to aggrándise, God to glorify.

9 Come you indoors, come home : your fading fire
10 Mend first & vital candle in close heart's vault(;) colon in orig.
11 You there are master, do your own desire ;
12 What hinders ? Are you beam-blind, yet to a fault
13 In a neighbour deft handed ? are you that liar
14 And, cast by conscience out, spendsavour self ?

* Companion to no. 6   Oxford. 1879

Plate 345   OET No. 133: The Candle Indoors -- MS. 3 (B)

   B.13r--transcription of A by RB on a page of album B marked with little ink flecks, like small grave accents (see, e.g., 4 "truckle", "the", 5 "what"). In 8 the oblique stroke after "There" is made like a faint straight comma. RB's deviations include: 3 comma added after "black"   13 "deft handed" (no hyphen: intended as one word?) "are" for "Are".

   GMH revised it in 3 "a" del.   5 "At" rev. to "By"   13 query del. after "liar". He added ink counterpoint signs in 5, 6; and stressed "aggrandise" (8) in purple pencil. He changed the colon after "vault" (10) to ";" [RB in 1918 mistook this deviation from A for his own slip, noting in pencil "colon in orig", which he restored in the 1st. edn.]. GMH also probably introduced the comma after "And" (14). He later added the footnote to the title and the date.

   RB's pencil (c. 1918) clarified the final semicolon in 11 (orig. like the punctuation after "home" in 9, it might have been either a colon or semicolon).

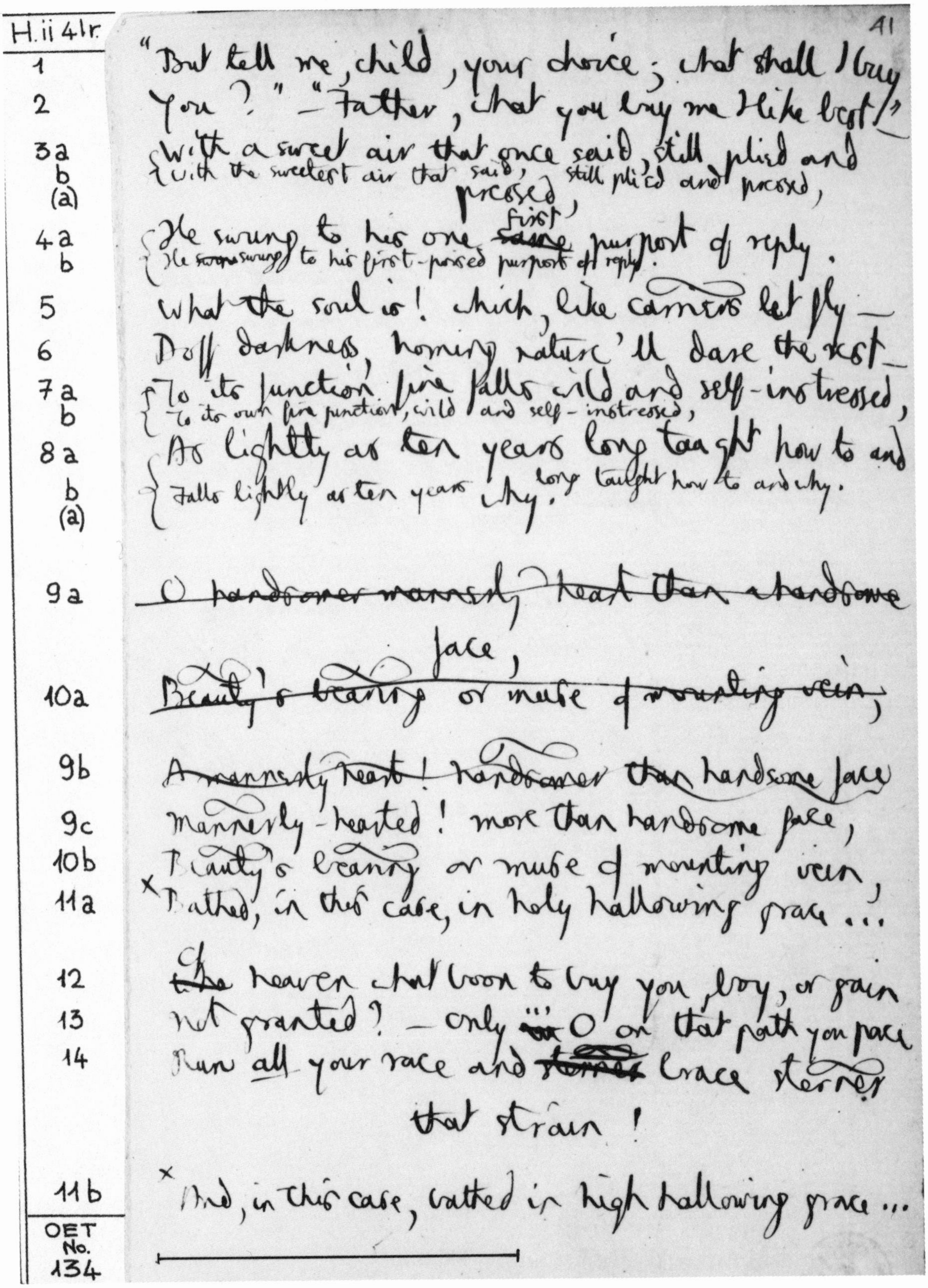

H.ii 41r — 41

1 "But tell me, child, your choice; what shall I buy
2 you?" — "Father, what you buy me I like best!"
3a {With a sweet air that once said, still plied and
b {with the sweetest air that said, still plied and pressed,
(a) pressed,
4a {He swung to his one first purport of reply.
b {He soon swung to his first-poised purport of reply.
5 What the soul is! which, like carriers let fly —
6 Doff darkness, homing nature 'll dare the rest —
7a {To its function fine falls wild and self-instressed,
b {To its own fine function, wild and self-instressed,
8a {As lightly as ten years long taught how to and
b {Falls lightly as ten years why, long taught how to and why.
(a)

9a O handsomer mannerly heart than a handsome
face,
10a Beauty's bearing or muse of mounting vein,
9b A mannerly heart! handsomer than handsome face
9c Mannerly-hearted! more than handsome face,
10b Beauty's beauty or muse of mounting vein,
11a X Bathed, in this case, in holy hallowing grace ...

12 Of heaven what boon to buy you, boy, or gain
13 not granted? — only O on that path you pace
14 Run all your race and crace steerer
that strain!

11b X And, in this case, bathed in high hallowing grace ...

OET No. 134

Plate 346   OET No. 134: The Handsome Heart -- MS. 1 (H)

H.ii.41r--(with final draft of No. 128d on verso) autograph, begun as a faircopy of the octave, then drafts of 9, 10, the rest already close to final form. Later came revisions with a finer pen to 3, 4, 7, 8. <u>Changes</u> include: 4b "swin swung" 9a "than a" (?) [A]   12 "Wha[t]"   13 "..." mended to dash, then del., and "..." added above. <u>Note</u> 9a tilted slur between "mannerly" and "heart" (cf. 9b); 14 "<u>all</u>" (italics).

PLATE 347. OET 134. *The Handsome Heart* • 169

*The Handsome Heart : 124
    at a Gracious Answer*

"But tell me, child, your choice; what shall I buy
You?"—"Father, what you buy me I like best".
With the sweetest air that said, still plied and pressed,
He swung to his first poised purport of reply.

What the soul is! which, like carriers let fly—
Doff darkness, homing nature knows the rest—
To its own fine function, wild and self-instressed,
Falls light as ten years long taught what and why.

Mannerly-hearted! more than handsome face,—
Beauty's bearing or muse of mounting vein,
All, in this case, bathed in high hallowing grace...

Of heaven what boon to buy you, boy, or gain
Not granted?—Only ... O on that path you pace
Run all your race, O brace sterner that strain!

Oxford 1879

Plate 347   OET No. 134: The Handsome Heart -- MS. 2 (A¹)

A.p.124--autograph faircopy of pentameter version, cut into sections (title, octave, two tercets) and spaced out for mounting in album A. In 9, 10 u.c. <u>M</u>s intended for "More" and "Muse". <u>Changes</u>: 4 orig. "own"   5 "heart" rev. to "soul" [this was crossed through in pencil by RB because it seemed to require a change in the title: he pencilled "heart" in huge letters on A.p.123].   9 final comma del.   13 dash replaced by three dots.

In 8 <u>RB's pencil</u> (1918) writes "how" below "what". In <u>Poems</u> 1st. edn. he printed "how to" (from H).

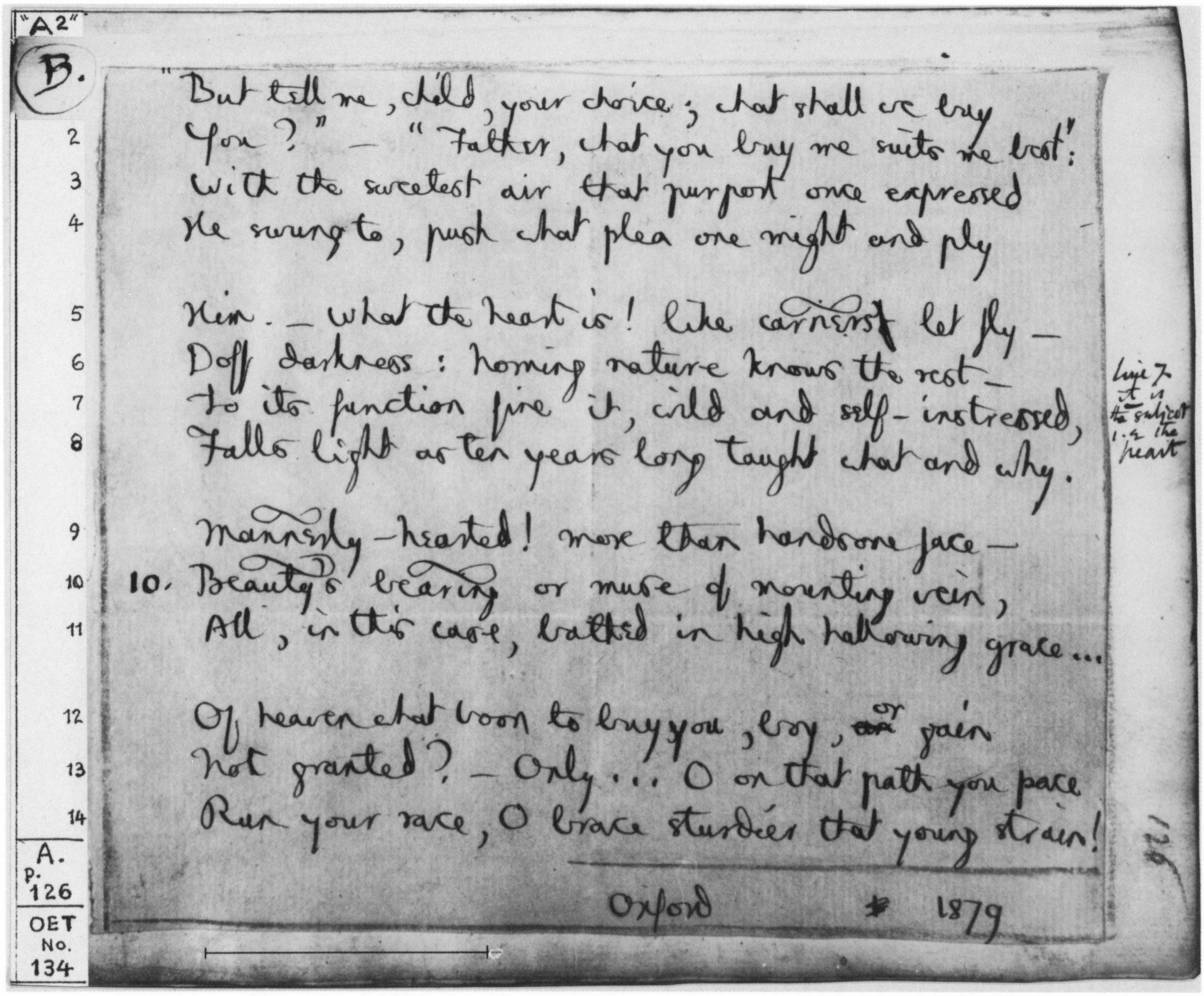

"A2"

B.

"But tell me, child, your choice; what shall we buy
You?" — "Father, what you buy me suits me best!"
With the sweetest air that purpose once expressed
He swung to, push what plea one might and ply

Him. — What the heart is! like carriers let fly —
Doff darkness: homing nature knows the rest —
To its function fine it, wild and self-instressed,
Falls light as ten years long taught what and why.

Mannerly-hearted! more than handsome face —
10. Beauty's bearing or muse of mounting vein,
All, in this case, bathed in high hallowing grace...

Of heaven what boon to buy you, boy, or gain
Not granted? — Only... O on that path you pace
Run your race, O brace sturdier that young strain!

Oxford   1879

line 7 it is the subject i.e the heart

Plate 348   OET No. 134: The Handsome Heart -- MS. 3 (A²)

A.p.126--revised pentameter autograph, on blue paper. Deletions: 5 "carriers's"   12 "buy;" (comma--inserted through

confusion with "boy,"--covered up with "you")   "an[d]".

In the right margin RB notes "line 7 *it* is the subject i.e the heart". He numbers line 10 in the left margin.

PLATE 349. OET 134. *The Handsome Heart* • 171

"B¹"

B.13v

OET
No.
134

See later

(14·)

The Handsome Heart

(at a gracious answer)

1 But tell me child your choice ; what shall I buy
2 You ? — Father what you buy me I like best —
3 With the sweetest air that said, still plied expressed
4 He swung to his first poised purport of reply
5 what the heart is ! like carriers let fly —
6 Doff darkness : homing nature knows the rest —
7 To its function fine it, wild & self mistressed,
8 Falls light as ten years long taught what & why.

9 Mannerly-hearted ! more than handsome face —
10 Beauty's bearing or muse of mounting vein,
11 All, in this case, bathed in high hallowing grace —
12 Of heaven what boon to buy you, boy, or gain
13 Not granted ? Only ... O on that path you pace
14 Run your race, O brace sturdier that young strain.

In above lines 3 & 4 & 5 shd read

3 + + air that purport once expressed
4 He swung to. push what plea one might, & fly
5 Aim. — What the heart is] etc

Plate 349   OET No. 134: The Handsome Heart -- MS. 4 (B¹)

B.13v--No editor has yet found any of the five autograph versions wholly satisfactory. This is RB's transcription into album B of his preferred blend of A¹ and A². The first quatrain is from A¹, with the quotation marks omitted and the punctuation varied. The rest is from A², with the omission at the beginning of 5 of the "Him.--" spilling over from the first quatrain.

RB's footnote begins: "In above lines 3 and 4 & 5 shd read"--he quotes A² from "air" to the middle of 5. This correction still avoids the A² version of 1 and 2.

GMH crossed the whole page through and wrote at the top "See later", i.e., B.28v.

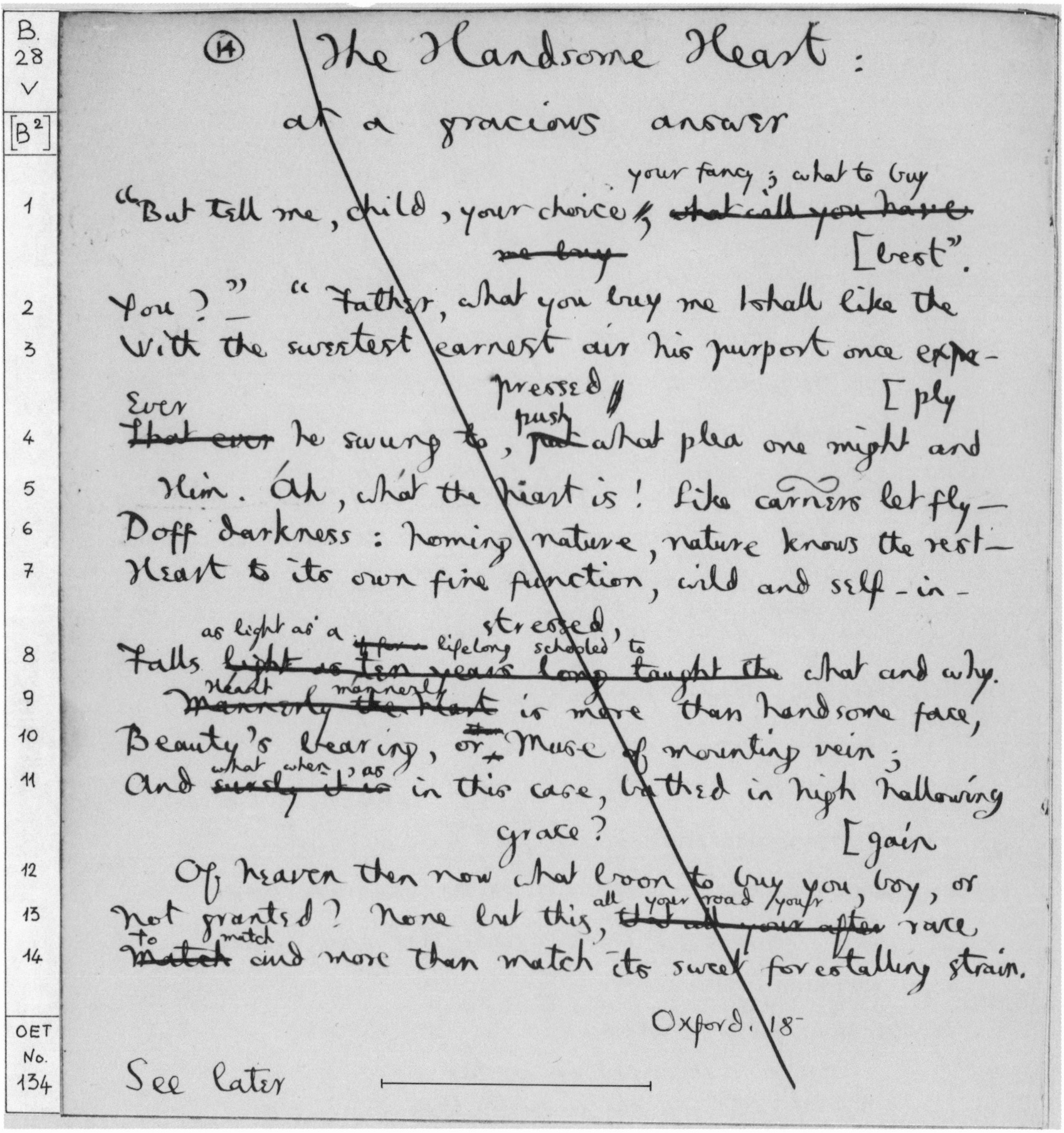

B.
28
v

[B²]

1

2

3

4

5

6

7

8

9

10

11

12

13

14

OET
No.
134

⑭ The Handsome Heart :

at a gracious answer

your fancy ; what to buy
"But tell me, child, your choice // ~~that call you have~~
~~me buy~~   [best".

You ? " " Father, what you buy me I shall like the
With the sweetest earnest air his purport once expe-
                        pressed //   [ply
Ever   push
~~That ever~~ he swung to, ~~put~~ what plea one might and
Him. Ah, what the heart is ! Like carriers let fly —
Doff darkness : homing nature, nature knows the rest —
Heart to its own fine function, wild and self - in -
        as light as a   stressed,
Falls ~~light as ten years~~ ~~lifelong~~ schooled to ~~taught the~~ what and why.
        Heart   mannerly
~~Mannerly the Heart~~ is more than handsome face,
Beauty's bearing, or ~~than~~ Muse of mounting vein ;
        what when , as
And ~~surely it is~~ in this case, bathed in high hallowing
                        grace ?   [gain
Of heaven then now what boon to buy you, boy, or
                        all your road your
not granted ? None but this, ~~that all your~~ after race,
to   match
~~Match~~ and more than match its sweet forestalling strain.

                                        Oxford. 18—

See later |———————————|

Plate 350   OET No. 134: The Handsome Heart -- MS. 5 (B²)

B.28v--autograph faircopy of a version lengthened into Alexandrines, inscribed in album B.   GMH subsequently revised it, then crossed it through in ink with a cross-reference ("See later") to B.35v. He could not remember the year of composition. Changes include: 1 "choice," 3 "expr [word badly divided] ;" 4 "put" rev. to "push" 8 "as ten years" rev. "as if for a" 10 "than" del. with its caret.

Purple pencil is used in 5 for stresses and counterpoint, and in 9 for stresses on "Héart mánnerly".

PLATE 351. OET 134. *The Handsome Heart* • 173

B.
35
V

[B³]

1
2
3
4
5
6
7
8
9
10
11

12
13
14

OET
No.
134

The Handsome Heart:
at a gracious answer

"But tell me, child, your choice, | your fancy; what to buy
You?"—"Father, what you buy me | I shall like the best".
With the sweetest earnest air | his purport, once expressed,
Ever he swung to, push | what plea I might and ply
Him. Ah, what the heart is! | Like carriers let fly—
Doff darkness: homing nature, | nature knows the rest—
Heart to its own fine function, | wild and self-instressed,
Falls as light as, di life-long, | schooled to what and why.
Heart mannerly | is more than handsome face,
Beauty's bearing or | muse of mounting vein;
And what when, as in this case, | bathed in high hallowing
grace?—
Of heaven then now what boon | to buy you, boy, or gain
not granted? None but this, | all your road your race
to match and more than match | its sweet forestalling
strain.

Oxford 1879

Plate 351   OET No. 134: The Handsome Heart -- MS. 6: B³

B.35v--autograph faircopy of B² as revised (28v), with caesural marks (ink) added, and a few minor changes (e.g.,

3, 8). The seven stresses (5, 9, 11) are in ink; so is the counterpoint (5) and the dwell or pause on "bathed" (11). In 8

"Fallás" ran two words together: "à̜ life-long".

RB ringed and linked the seven echoing "what"s (see Poems, 1st. edn. p.113).

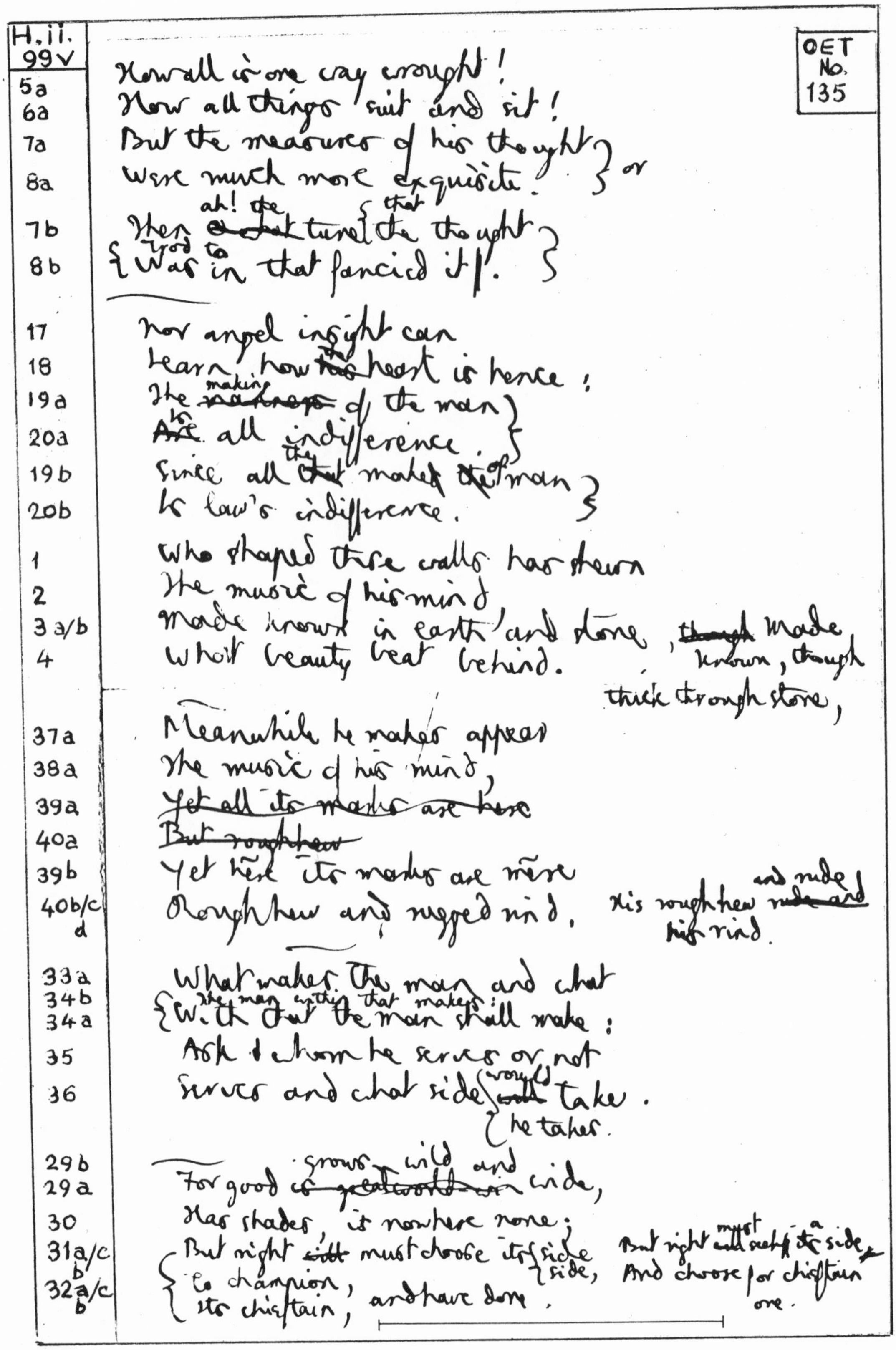

		OET No. 135
H.ii. 99v		
5a	How all is one way wrought!	
6a	Now all things suit and sit!	
7a	But the measures of his thought	
8a	Were much more exquisite. } or	
7b	Then ah! the that turned the thought }	
8b	{ Was god to in that fancied it! }	
17	Nor angel insight can	
18	Learn how his heart is hence;	
19a	The making of the man }	
20a	Are all indifference. }	
19b	Since all they makes the man }	
20b	Is law's indifference. }	
1	Who shaped these walls has hewn	
2	The music of his mind	
3 a/b	Made known in earth and stone, though Made,	
4	What beauty beat behind. known, though	
	thick through stone,	
37a	Meanwhile he maker appears	
38a	The music of his mind,	
39a	Yet all its marks are here	
40a	But roughhew	
39b	Yet here its marks are mere	
40b/c d	Roughhew and rugged rind. His roughhew and rude his rind.	
33a 34b 34a	What makes the man and what { With that the man shall make: they may within that makes	
35	Ask whom he serves or not	
36	Serves and what side would take. he takes.	
29b 29a	For good is grows wild and wide,	
30	Has shades, is nowhere none;	
31a/c b	But right will must choose its side, But right must seek its side,	
32a/c b	{ To champion, side, And choose for chieftain { its chieftain, and have done. one.	

Plate 352　　　<u>OET No. 135</u>:　"<u>Who shaped these walls has shewn</u>" formerly entitled "<u>On a Piece of Music</u>"

　Autograph draft of stanzas for an untitled poem which compares a masterwork of architecture to an inspired piece of music. The stanzas are on two separate pieces of paper, one the back of a letter from Walter Pater (see Plate 354). They are not in any logical sequence: note on 99v the short division lines between sts. to mark a break in continuity. My numbering of the lines, in an order quite different from the 4th. edn., is an attempt to show the flow of thought: it is not claimed as definitive. The return at the end to the opening is found in the poem by RB which GMH took as his model ("Will Love again awake"), and the lengthening of some final lines will be found in OET Nos. 127 and 141.

　H.ii.99v. Note the circumflexes in 39b over "here" and "mere". The division stroke over "Meanwhile" (37a) is not a counterpoint sign. <u>Deletions</u> include 7b "O what"　8b "it!"　18 "his" replaced by "the" (crossbar to "t" makes "the" seem deleted)　19a "manners"　37a to 40b del. in pencil (prob. by a later editor).　35 after "Ask" the beginning of a "w" (?) is del. with a vertical stroke　29a "is greatworld-wi[de]" (i.e. universal?)　31c "will seeks its side,"

H.ii.100r--autograph draft of further sts.. The verso (Plate 354) redrafts *ll*.5 to 8. Deletions include: 39d "Thou[gh]" 41a "His" del. and rewritten closer to the margin to indicate that the line had an extra stress (as 42 has also) "blossoms" revised to "blooms" 9a "All" 15a "did but" replaced with "drew", then with "worked" 16a "draw" 10c "Like air" del. and rewritten in left margin (10d) to save rewriting parts of 10b 12b "Tha[t]" 23a "n[ot]" mended to "unfound" (notice the hyphens before and after "unfound") 26 "re" mended to "Re" 27 "glue" prob. orig. "blue" (dittography from 25).

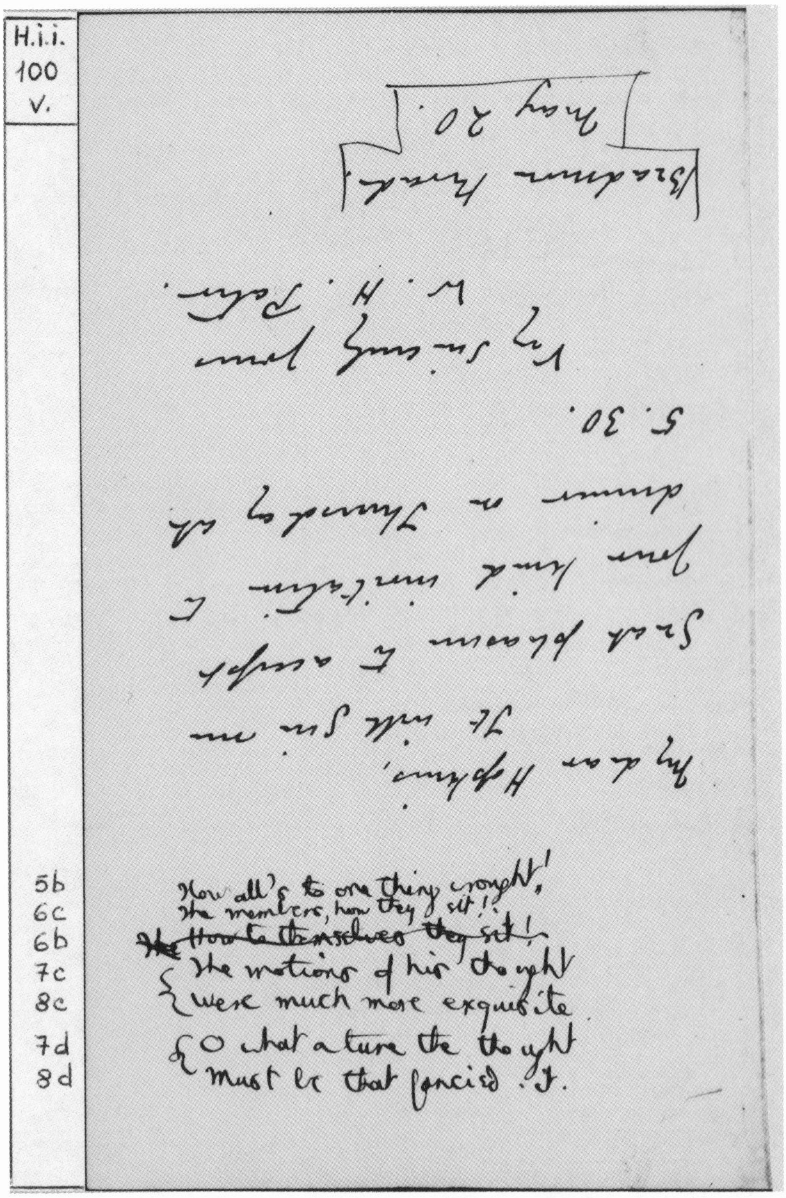

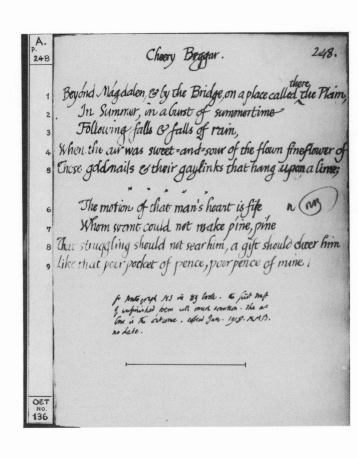

Cheery Beggar.

1 Beyónd Mágdalen, & by the Bridge, on a place called the Plain,
2 In Summer, in a burst of summertime
3 Following falls & falls of rain,
4 When the air was sweet=and=sour of the flown fineflower of
5 These gold-nails & their gay links that hang upon a lime;

6 The motion of that man's heart is fife
7 Whom want could not make pine, pine
8 That struggling should not sear him, a gift should cheer him
9 Like that your pocket of pence, poor pence of mine.

[left margin numbers:]
5b
6c
6b
7c
8c
7d
8d

How all's to one thing wrought!
the members, how they sit!!
~~The How in themselves they sit!~~
⟨ The motions of his thought
⟨ were much more exquisite
⟨ O what a tune the thought
⟨ must be that fancied it.

Plate 354   OET No. 135: "Who shaped these walls" -- formerly [On a Piece of Music]) -- MS. 3

[left] H.ii.100v. Autograph redraft of 5-8 upside down, above a letter from Walter Pater, dated Bradmore Road, May 20 [1879]: "My dear Hopkins,/It will give me great pleasure to accept your kind invitation to dinner on Thursday at 5.30." In the stanza the marginal "The" below 6b, larger than the rest of the writing, may have been the first attempt at the stanza.

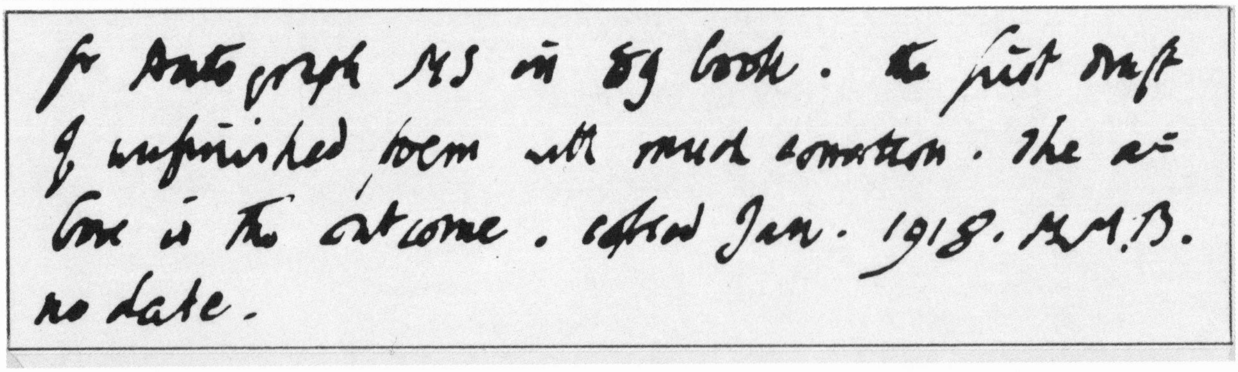

[right] A.p.248--transcription in the ornate hand of RB's wife, (Mary) Monica Bridges, of "Cheery Beggar", the final version extracted from H.ii.27r (Plate 355). She was an expert in calligraphy, much influenced by the Italianized gothic script of the sixteenth century. Although this MS has no authority (indeed it introduced into edns. 1 to 3 the error "fineflower" for "fineflour" in 4) it shows her participation in preparing the first Hopkins edn.. Her misreading of GMH's badly scrawled "fine" as "fire" is thoroughly understandable: RB corrected her slip in the margin. RB's note (enlarged below the other MSS) illustrates his casual use of *l.c.* after a period, as in some MS. B transcriptions, including the "Wreck". He describes the transcript as "fr[om] Autograph MS in 89 book [i.e. MS. H]. the first draft of unfinished poem with much correction. The above is the outcome. copied Jan. 1918. M.M.B. no date."

The final period (9) is smudged.

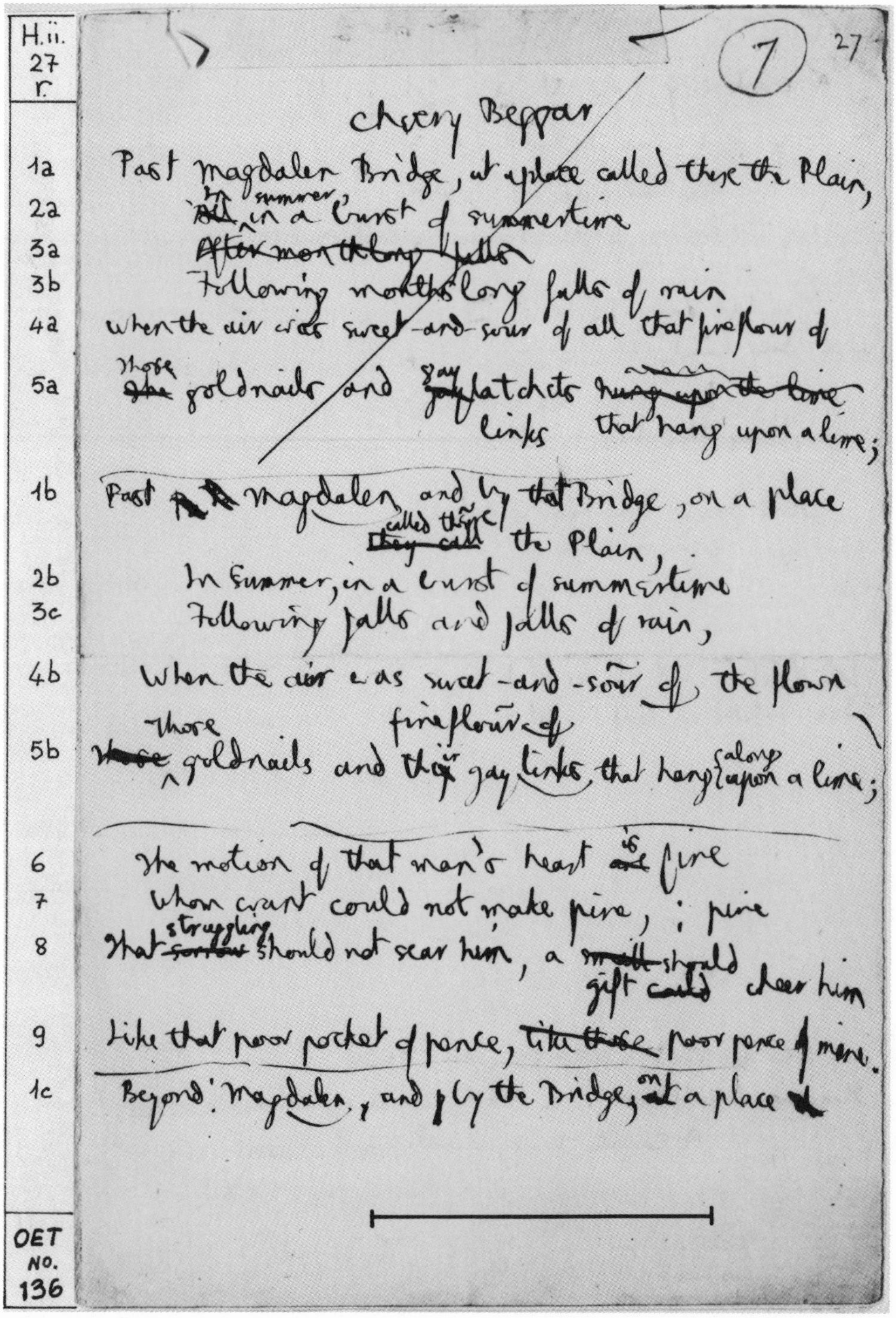

PLATE 355. OET 136. *Cheery Beggar* • 177

H.ii.27r

Cheery Beggar

1a Past Magdalen Bridge, at a place called there the Plain,
2a in a burst of summertime
3a After monthlong
3b Following monthslong falls of rain
4a when the air was sweet-and-sour of all that fireflour of
5a those goldnails and gay latchets
        links   that hang upon a lime;

1b Past Magdalen and by that Bridge, on a place
        called there
        the Plain,
2b In Summer, in a burst of summertime
3c Following falls and falls of rain,
4b When the air was sweet-and-sour of the flown
5b those goldnails and their gay links, that hang along upon a lime;
        fireflour of

6   the motion of that man's heart is fire
7   whom want could not make pine, : pine
8   that sorrow struggling should not sear him, a gift could cheer him
9   like that poor pocket of pence, like those poor pence of mine.
1c Beyond Magdalen, and by the Bridge, at a place

OET NO. 136

Plate 355   OET No. 136: Cheery Beggar

H.ii.27r--autograph, unfinished draft, sole manuscript, with an early draft of No. 137 on the verso. 3a, 3b intend 'monthlong ', 'monthslong ' as one word. Deletions, changes include: 5a "gaylatchets" del. and rewritten to make "gay" a separate word (?)   1b "Pa[st]" del. twice to correct indentation   2b "summer" mended to "S"   4b "ar" mended to "air"   5b "Those" [indentation wrong?] "they" mended to "their"   1c "Magdalen, and [?]" "place th[at]". Note the circumflexes (ink) in 1b, 4b (2); great colons in 7 and 1c; and outrides in 1b, 4b, 5b and 1c.

An early draft of the next poem is on the verso.

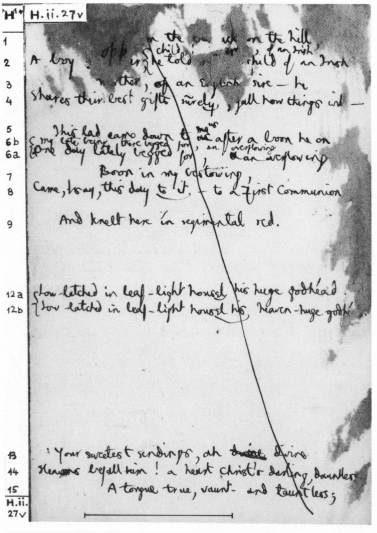

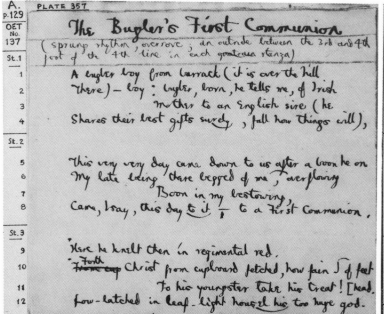

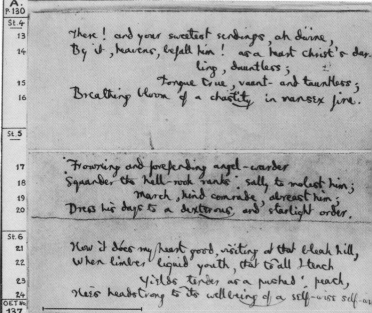

Plate 356   OET No. 137:   The Bugler's First Communion -- MS. 1 (H[1])

[left]   H.ii,27v--autograph, earliest draft, on the verso of No. 136, damaged by having been at first thought worthless and pasted face down onto salmon-pink paper: parts of this still obscure some words; other pink pieces as they were removed lifted fragments of the text. RB's "opp[osite]" is written on the obscuring pink, and therefore does not concern this poem. Still recoverable from 1-3 are:

1   "A buglerboy from the barrack on the hill,

2   A boy:bugler, {child, * * * me, of an Irish / he told me, the child of an Irish

3   Mother, [an mended to] of an English sire -- he"

6a "L" mended to "One"..."th[?] rev. to "an"   Note the ink stresses on "in" (9) and "godhéad." (12a and b). In 14 "dauntless" is followed by a semicolon.

Plate 357   OET No. 137: The Bugler's First Communion -- MS. 3 (A.pp.1,2)

[Above]   A.pp.129, 130--autograph faircopy of the text after it had been drafted in MS. H[2] (opposite and on next two right-hand facsimile pages). Deletions, changes by GMH include: 8 comma del. below dash   10 "From cup"   12 "L" in "Low" reinforced. Great colons in or before 2, 9, 17, 18, 23; stresses on "in" (9), "does" (21). Before being mounted in album A, st. 5 was at the top of a new sheet, and in the album has a larger space above it. The MS. A versions are reproduced on left-hand pages to facilitate comparison with MS. B versions on right-hand pages (Plates 367, 369).

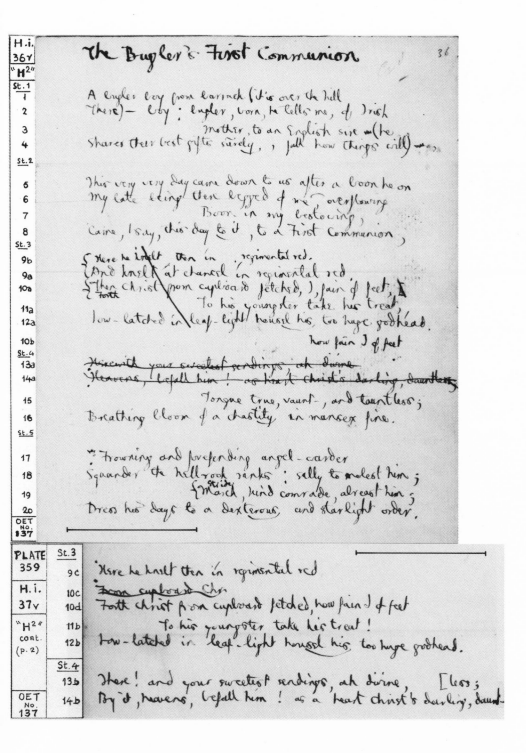

Plate 358   OET No. 137: The Bugler's First Communion -- MS. 2 (H[2] p.1)

[top]   H.i.36r--the beginning of another autograph draft (1-20). The first four pages (36r,v, 37r,v) form a large double sheet of blue paper, watermarked "R. BARNARD 1876". Deletions, changes include: 3, 4 dashes replaced by parentheses   9a the stroke above "at" is not a stress, but the start of a letter (? "h[ere]") crossed through.   10a (end) square bracket del., prob. intended for the rev. 10b, which was added below the stanza instead.   17 "F[rowning]" begun, then del. to make room for the great colon. Note the great colons in or before 2, 14a, 17, 18; and stresses on "in" (9a,b) and "godhéad" (12a).

RB's pencil (1918) notes above st. 1 that he has collated the readings (cf. H.i.44r, version of "Brothers", OET No. 143, Plate 384).

Plate 359: MS. 2 cont. (H[2] p.2)

[bottom]   H.i.37v--autograph second draft, cont. (revision of 9-14). There is no clear final punctuation to 9c: a great colon opens it.

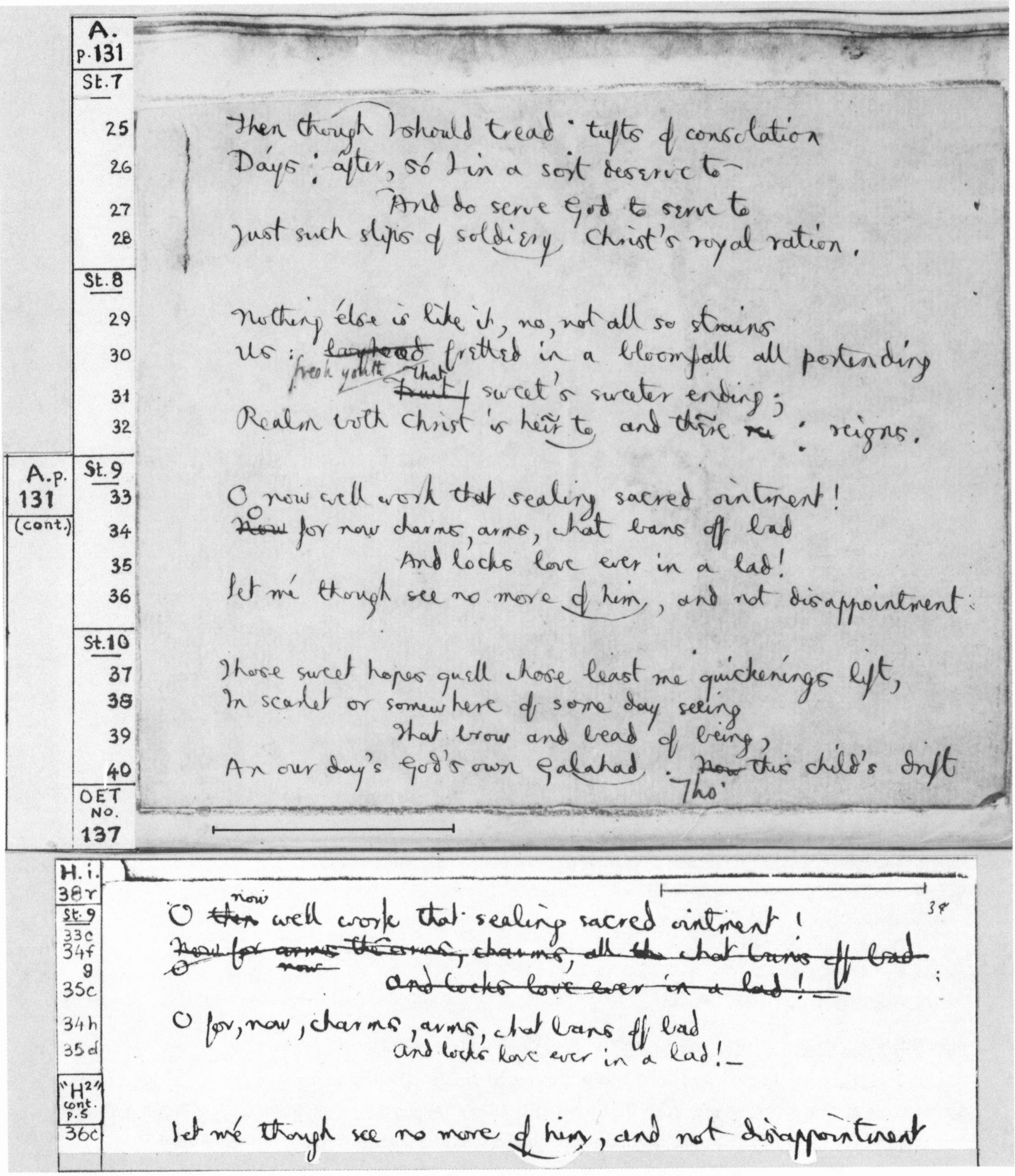

A. p·131 St.7	
25	Then though I should tread · tufts of consolation
26	Days · after, só I in a sort deserve to—
27	And do serve God to serve to
28	Just such slips of soldiery, Christ's royal ration .
St.8	
29	Nothing élse is like it, no, not all so strains
30	Us : fresh youth that frettèd in a bloomfall all portending
31	Fruit/ sweet's sweeter ending ;
32	Realm both Christ is heir to , and there ru · reigns.
A.p. 131 (cont.) St.9	
33	O now well work that sealing sacred ointment !
34	Now for now charms, arms, what bans off bad
35	And locks love ever in a lad !
36	let mé though see no more of him, , and not disappointment :
St.10	
37	Those sweet hopes quell whose least me quickenings lift,
38	In scarlet or somewhere of some day seeing
39	that brow and bead of being,
40	An our day's God's own Galahad · now this child's drift Tho'
OET NO. 137	

H. i. 38ʳ St.9 33c 34f 9 35c	O then now well work that sealing sacred ointment ! Now for arms the arms , charms, all the what bans off bad now and locks love ever in a lad !
34 h 35 d	O for, now, charms, arms, what bans off bad and locks love ever in a lad !—
"H²" cont. p.5 36c	let mé though see no more of him, and not disappointment

Plate 360   OET No. 137: The Bugler's First Communion -- MS. 3 cont. (A.p.3)

[top]   A.p.131--autograph faircopy, cont. (25-40). GMH's deletions, changes include: 31 "Fruit/" rev. to "That" 32 "rei[gns]" del. to leave room before the word for a great colon   34 "Now" del. (cf. H² readings below, 34f).   Note great colons in 25, 26, 32; stresses on "else" (29), "me" (36).

RB's red ink (1884) enters in 30 and 40 GMH's revisions in B, but he changes "Though" to "Tho "

Plate 361   MS. 2 cont. (H² p.5)

[bottom]   H.i.38r (top stanza only, reproduced here to provide another draft of st. 9). See notes on Plate 365. 34f "Now for [arms del.] the arms, charms, all [the del.] what bans off bad" all del.

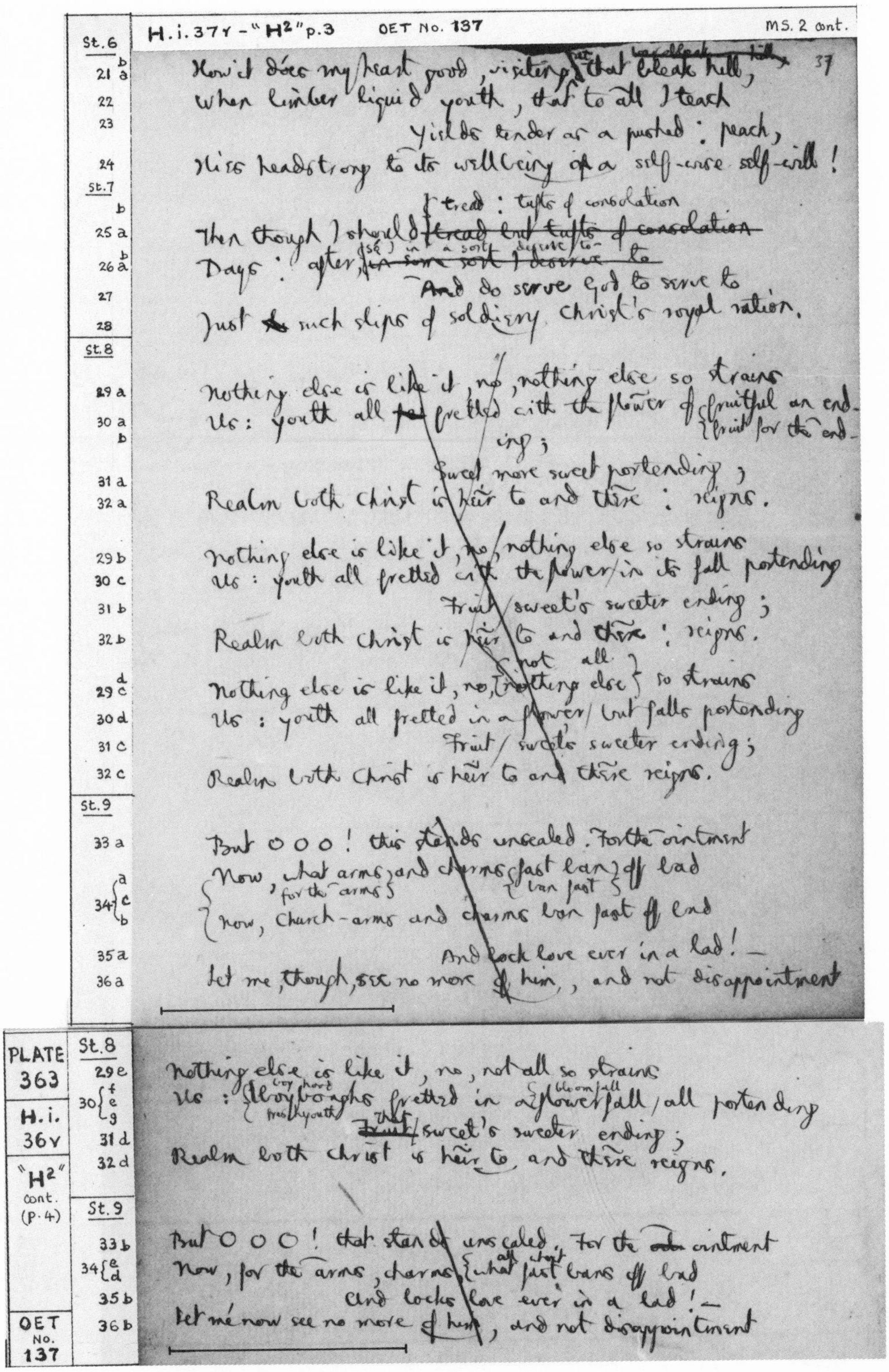

Plate 362 OET No. 137: The Bugler's First Communion -- MS. 2 cont. (H^2 p.3)

[top] H.i.37r--autograph second draft, cont. (21-36). Deletions, changes include: 21b after "visiting" the bracket joining alternatives is del. because he rejected the version "barebleak hill," 24 "on" mended to "of" 25a,b, and 26a,b brackets del. 28 "sli[ps]" 30a "fe" Note great colons in 23, 25b, 26a, 32a,b; stresses on "does" (21a) "so" (26b); broken slur linking 26b and 27 "to/And"; virgules after "flower" (30c,d), "Fruit" (31b,c). In 26b the interlineation reads "so I in a sort deserve to" (half slur, linking with second half slur on "And" (27). St. 7 is shown enlarged on Plate 366 (top)

Plate 363 MS. 2 cont. (H^2 p.4)

[bottom] H.i.36v--autograph second draft, cont. (29-36). Deletions, changes include: bracket joining 30e and f del. 30f "boy hood" one word intended, but letters in 30e interfered, as with 30g "fres hyouth". In 30e and f "flowerfall" and "bloomfall" are bracketed--virgules after "flowerfall" and "Fruit" (31d). 33b "oit[ment]" del., not "oil" 34e "all what". Note stress on "me" (36b). This page is shown enlarged on Plate 366 (middle).

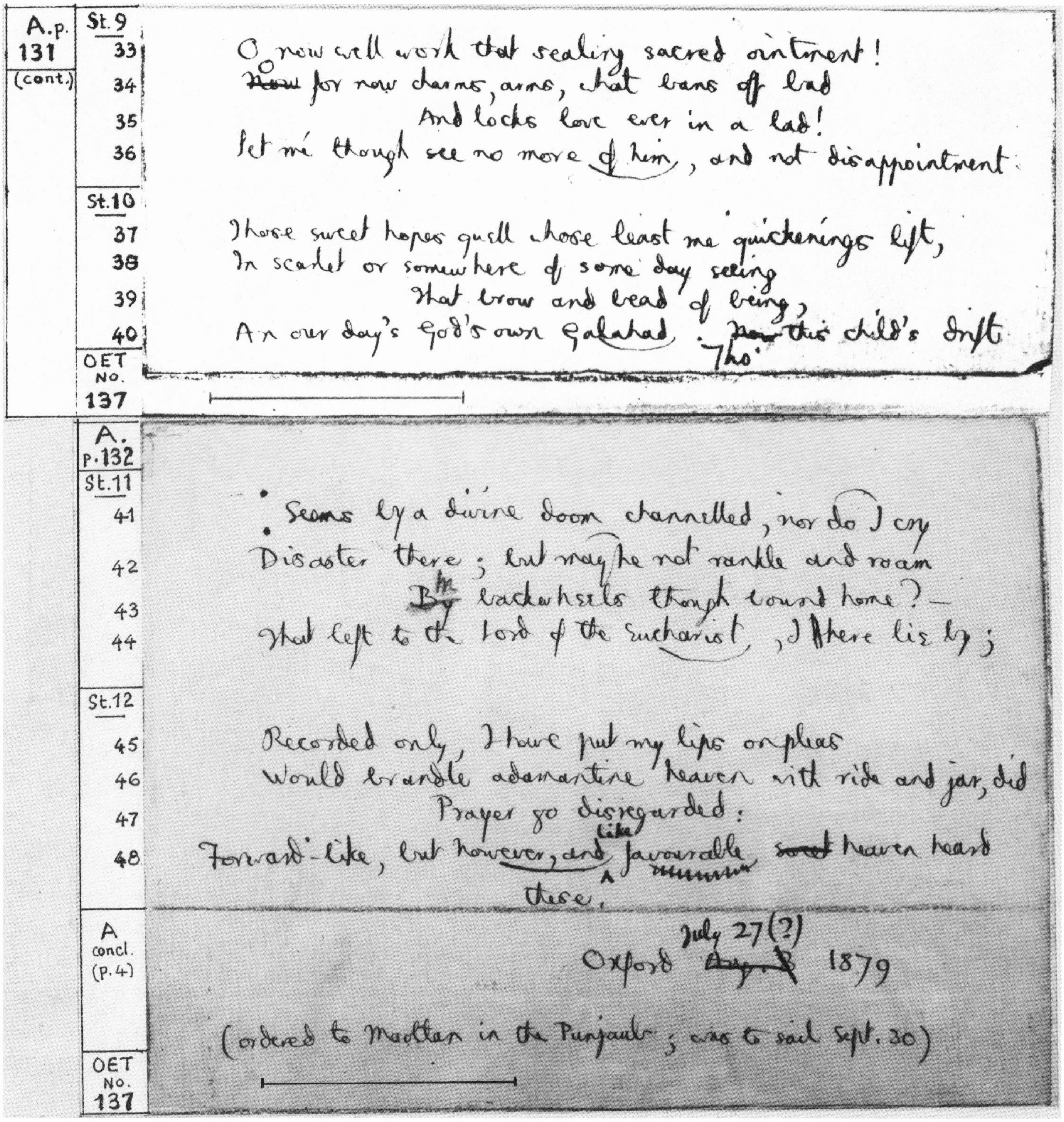

A.p. 131 (cont.)	St.9	
	33	O now well work that sealing sacred ointment!
	34	How for now charms, arms, that bans off bad
	35	And locks love ever in a lad!
	36	Let me though see no more of him, and not disappointment
	St.10	
	37	Those sweet hopes quell whose least me quickenings lift,
	38	In scarlet or somewhere of some day seeing
	39	That brow and bead of being,
	40	An our day's God's own Galahad. now this child's drift Tho'
OET NO. 137		

A. P.132	St.11	
	41	: Seems by a divine doom channelled, nor do I cry
	42	Disaster there; but may he not rankle and roam
	43	By backwheels though bound home? —
	44	That left to the Lord of the Eucharist, I there lie by;
	St.12	
	45	Recorded only, I have put my lips on pleas
	46	Would brandle adamantine heaven with ride and jar, did
	47	Prayer go disregarded:
	48	Forward-like, but however, and like favourable sweet heaven heard there.
A concl. (P.4)		Oxford July 27(?) Aug 8 1879
		(ordered to Mooltan in the Punjaub; was to sail Sept. 30)
OET NO. 137		

Plate 364   OET No. 137: The Bugler's First Communion -- MS. 3 cont. (A.pp.3,4)

[top] A.p.131--lower half, repeated from Plate 361 for comparison with H.i.38r. See notes on that plate.

[bottom] A.p.132--autograph faircopy, cont. (41-48). GMH's deletions, changes include: 44 "I" linked with "here"

(cf. 45, "I" linked with "have") del. and rewritten separately to avoid being mistaken for "there"   48 revision in darker

ink, perhaps simultaneously revised in H², 48 (opposite).   Great colon precedes 41.

RB's red ink (1884) records in 43 GMH's revision in B.

PLATE 365. OET 137. *The Bugler's First Communion* • 183

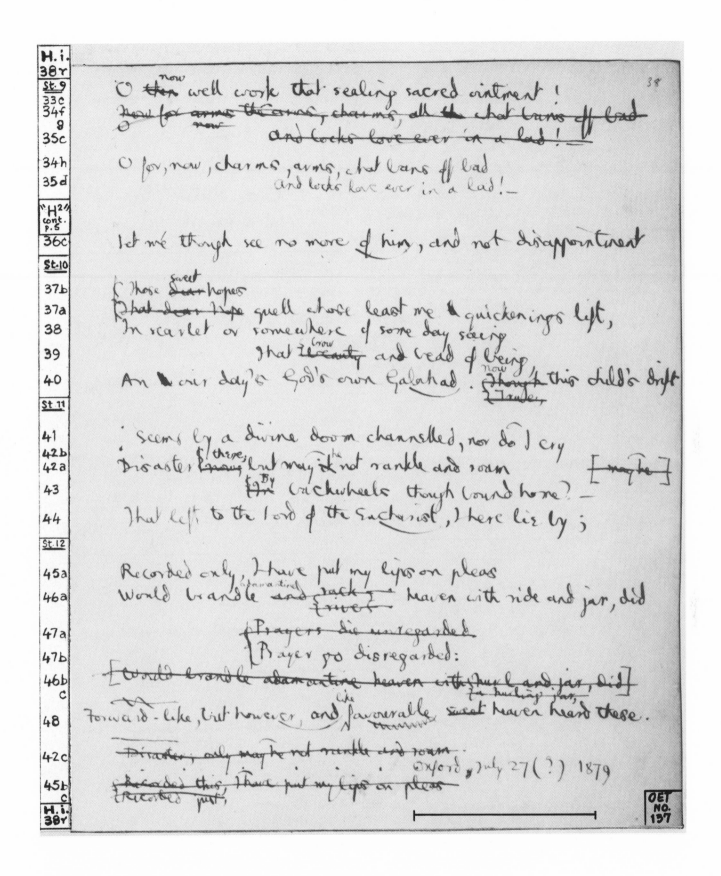

Plate 365   OET No. 137: The Bugler's First Communion -- MS. 2 cont. (H² p.5)

   H.i.38r--autograph second draft, concl. (33-48), on a separate sheet of blue paper (Britannia watermark). For st. 9 see notes on Plate 361. Deletions, changes include: 37b "dear" rev. to "sweet"   37a "me ¢"   40 "An ½[our?--homophone] "True," 42a,b bracket linking "now; there;" del.   43, 46a, 47a,b brackets del.   46a great colon del. after "rack/rive" 47a "die unregarded." 46b "hurl and jar, / a hurling jar,"   48 outride del. under "favourable."   45b,c "Recorded this,/...just," "Oxford,"

   St. 12 is shown enlarged on Plate 366 (bottom).

A. p.131 St.7 25 26 27 28	Then though I should tread · tufts of consolation Days : after, só I in a sort deserve to— And do serve God to serve to Just such slips of soldiery, Christ's royal ration.

PLATE
363
 	
H.i.
36v
 	
"H²"
cont.
(P.4)
	St.8
	29 e
	30 {f
	  {e
	  {g
	31 d
	32 d
	
	St.9
	
	33 b
	34 {e
	  {d
	35 b
		Nothing else is like it , no, not all so strains
		us : {boy bugle boughs fretted in a flower fall , all portending
		     {sweet's sweeter, ending ;
		Realm both Christ is heir to, and their reigns,
		
		But O O O ! that stand of unsealed, for the ointment
		Now, for the arms, charms {what just bans off bad
		   And locks love ever in a lad !—
		Let me now see no more of him, and not disappointment

OET No. 137	36 b	

St 12
 	
45a
46a
 	
47a
47b
46b
  c
48
 	
42c
45h
  c
H.i.
38r
	Recorded only, I have put my lips on pleas
	Would brandle adamantine heaven with ride and jar, did
	
	{Prayers die unregarded
	{Prayer go disregarded:
	[Would brandle adamantine heaven with ride and jar, did]
	Forward-like, but however, and like favourable sweet heaven heard these.
	
	Disaster; only may he not rankle and roam.
	Recorded this, I have put my lips on pleas Oxford, July 27(?) 1879

PLATE 367. OET 137. *The Bugler's First Communion*   •   185

B
24
r

23

The Bugler's First Communion.

St.
1

1 A bugler boy from barrack (it is over the hill
2 There)— boy bugler, born, he tells me, of Irish
3   Mother to an english sire (he
4 Shares their best gifts surely, fall how things will),

St.
2

                    very
5 This very day came down to us after a boon he on
6 My late being there begged of me, overflowing
7   Boon in my bestowing,
8 Came, I say, this day to it — to a First Communion.

St.
3

9 Here he knelt then in regimental red.
10 :Forth Christ from cupboard fetched, how fain I of feet
11   To his youngster take his treat!
12 Low-latched in leaf-light housel his too huge godhead.

St.
4

13 There! and your sweetest sendings, ah divine,
14 By it, heavens, befall him! as a heart Christ's darling, dauntless;
15   Tongue true, vaunt- & tauntless;
16 Breathing Bloom of a chastity, in mansex fine.

OET
No.
137

Plate 367   OET No. 137: The Bugler's First Communion -- MS. 4 (B.p.1)

B.24r--RB's transcription of A (1-16), inscribed in album B. Among RB's deviations, he began "English" (3) with *l*.c.; he omitted the second "very" (5--this was added by GMH); he substituted a small colon to open 10 instead of a great colon to open 9. "There" (13) and "Tongue" (15--orig. "Town") had to be rewritten. The blot below "Christ" (10) is an offset from B. 23 verso; note the vertical smudge in 16 before "mansex".

In checking B, GMH added the second "very" (5); two slurs: the one after "he " (3) shows that "Irish" in the line above rhymes with "sire (he/Sh[ares]". He also inserted outrides in the fourth line of each stanza.

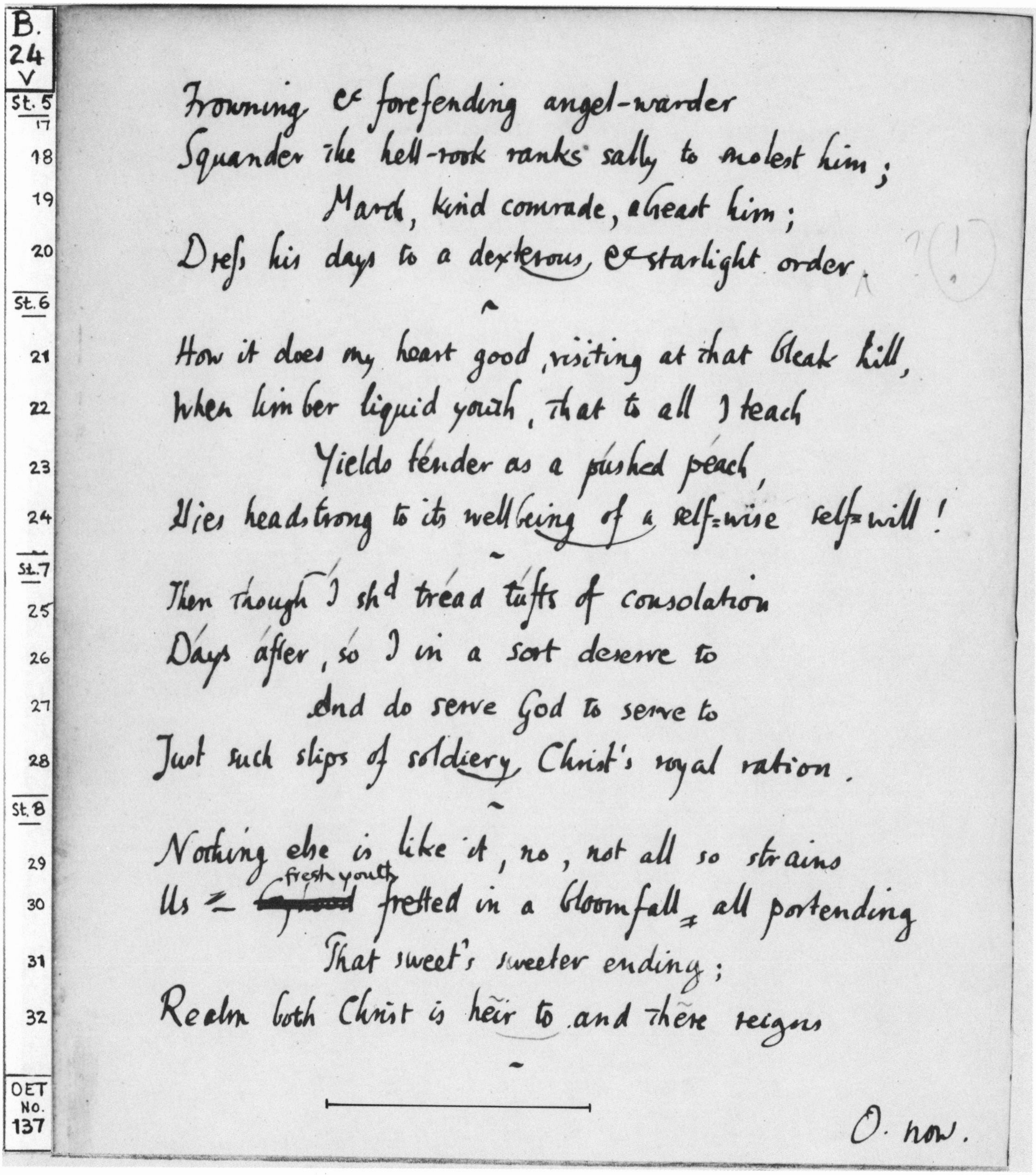

B.
24
v

St. 5
17

Frowning & forefending angel-warder

18 Squander the hell-rook ranks sally to molest him;

19 March, kind comrade, abreast him;

20 Dress his days to a dexterous, & starlight order.

St. 6

21 How it does my heart good, visiting at that bleak hill,

22 When limber liquid youth, that to all I teach

23 Yields tender as a pushed peach,

24 Hies headstrong to its wellbeing of a self-wise self-will!

St. 7

25 Then though I sh^d tread tufts of consolation

26 Days after, so I in a sort deserve to

27 And do serve God to serve to

28 Just such slips of soldiery, Christ's royal ration.

St. 8

29 Nothing else is like it, no, not all so strains

30 Us = ~~fresh youth~~ fretted in a bloomfall, all portending

31 That sweet's sweeter ending;

32 Realm both Christ is heir to and there reigns

OET
NO.
137

O. now.

Plate 368   OET No. 137: The Bugler's First Communion -- MS. 4 cont. (B.p.2)

B.24v--transcription of A by RB, cont. (17-32). RB's slips include: 30 insertion of a comma after "bloomfall" (del by RB while still wet); 32 no period after "reigns". His inkwell was running dry towards the end of the poem (e.g. 31 and f.25r).

GMH revised 30 "Us : boyhood" to "Us--freshyouth" (clearly one word in H², 30g, Plate 363). He added outrides in ink to 20, 24, 28, but in purple pencil to 32; the nine stresses in 23, 25, 26 and the circumflexes in 32 are also in purple pencil. He strengthened the semicolon ending 18.

RB's pencil (1918) queries the period ending 20 and suggests it should be an exclamation mark (see his note, Poems, 1st. edn. p.112).

PLATE 369. OET 137. *The Bugler's First Communion* • 187

O now well work that sealing sacred ointment!
O now for charms, arms, what bans off bad
      And locks love ever in a lad!
Let me though see no more of him, & not disappointment

Those sweet hopes quell whose least me quickenings lift,
In scarlet or somewhere of some day seeing
      That brow & bead of being,
An our day's God's own Galahad. Now this child's drift

Seems by a doom divine channelled, nor do I cry
Disaster there; but may he not rankle & roam
      In backwheels, though bound home? —
That left to the lord of the Eucharist, I here lie by;

Recorded only, I have put my lips on pleas
Would brandle adamantine heaven with ride & jar, did
      Prayer go disregarded:
Froward-like, but however, & like favourable heaven heard
        these.

Oxford. 1879

Plate 369   OET No. 137: The Bugler's First Communion -- MS. 4 concl. (B.p.3)

B.25r--transcription of A by RB, concl. (33-48). RB's slips include: 34 "O now for" (missed by GMH in revision: RB's pencil, 1918, notes this as a mistake of copyist, "Copy wrong/MS has <u>for now</u>"); in 48 "Froward" for "Forward" (missed by RB and GMH himself!): yet the 1st. edn. was correct. This page lacks the ornaments between stanzas.

    <u>GMH revised</u> 40 "Now" to "Though"; and 43 "By" to "In" (prob. adding comma after "backwheels"); and corrected in 41 the misplacement of "doom" by RB. (RB's pencil note, 1918, began "doom", then mended it to "ditto", i.e. mistake of copyist, as with ℓ.34). GMH prob. added the comma after "however" (48). GMH's purple pencil marked five stresses in 36, 41, but the outrides were in ink. He inserted the date later.

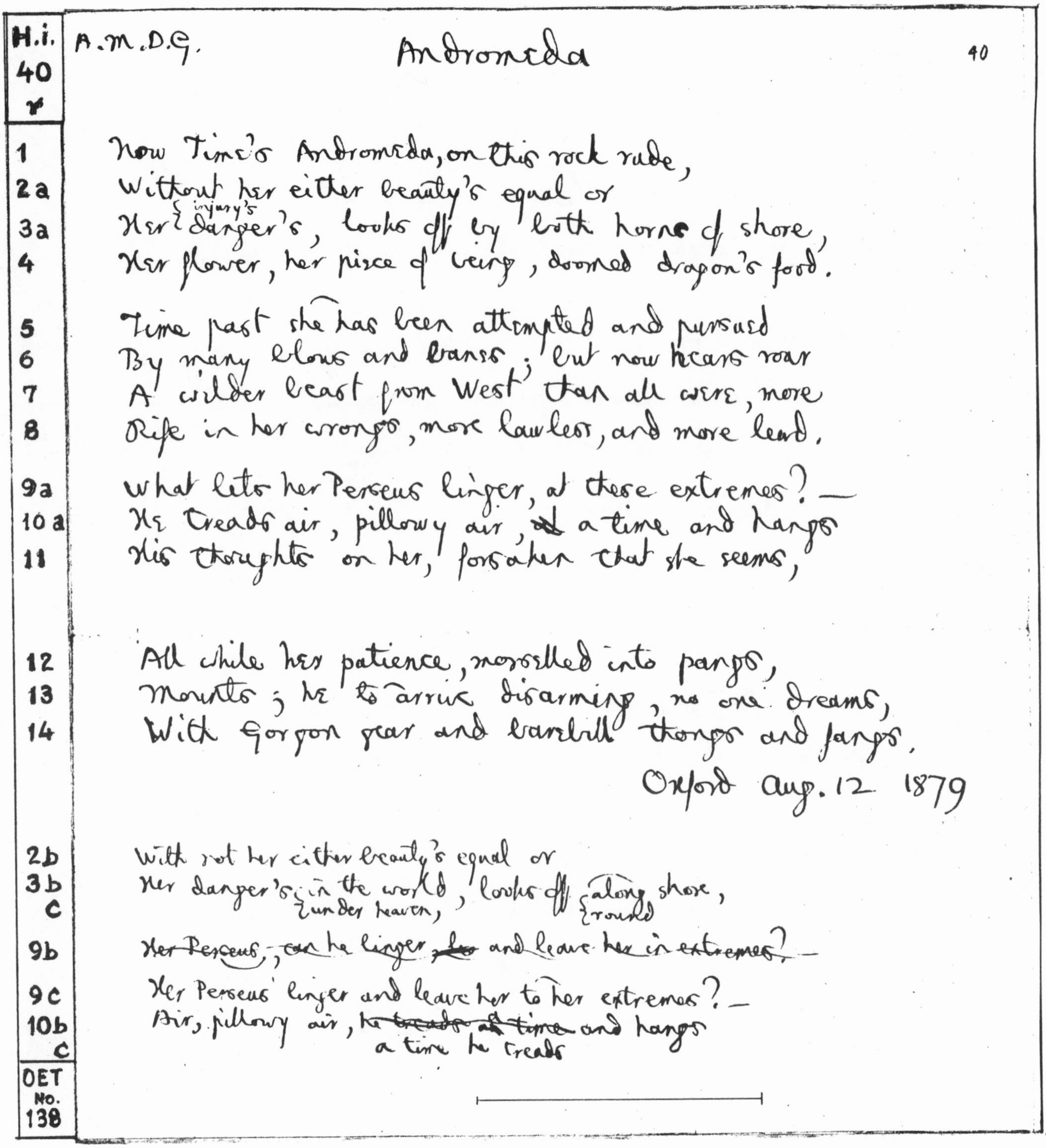

H.i. 40 r	A.M.D.G.　　　　　　Andromeda　　　　　　　40

1　Now Time's Andromeda, on this rock rude,

2a　Without her either beauty's equal or

3a　Her ⟨injury's⟩ danger's, looks off by both horns of shore,

4　Her flower, her piece of being, doomed dragon's food.

5　Time past she has been attempted and pursued

6　By many blows and bans; but now hears roar

7　A wilder beast from West than all were, more

8　Rife in her wrongs, more lawless, and more lewd.

9a　What lets her Perseus linger, at these extremes? —

10a　He treads air, pillowy air, at a time and hangs

11　His thoughts on her, forsaken that she seems,

12　All while her patience, morselled into pangs,

13　Mounts; he to aurora disarming, no one dreams,

14　With Gorgon gear and bublll thongs and fangs.

　　　　　　　　　　　Oxford Aug. 12 1879

2b　With not her either beauty's equal or

3b　Her danger's in the world, looks off {along shore,
c　　　　　{under heaven,　　　　　　{round

9b　Her Perseus, or he linger, and leave her in extremes? —

9c　Her Perseus linger and leave her to her extremes? —

10b　Air, pillowy air, he treads at a time and hangs
c　　　　　　　a time he treads

OET No. 138

Plate 370　OET No. 138: Andromeda -- MS. 1 (H)

H.i.40r--autograph, begun as a faircopy, on blue paper with Britannia watermark (cf. H.i.38r, No. 137). Deletions,

changes include: 6 "rears" mended to "hears"　10a "at" (dittography from 9a)　9b "linger, lea[ve]"　10b "treads an[d?]"

Note outride under "Perseus" (9b). 14 "W" in "With" mended to emphasise u.c.

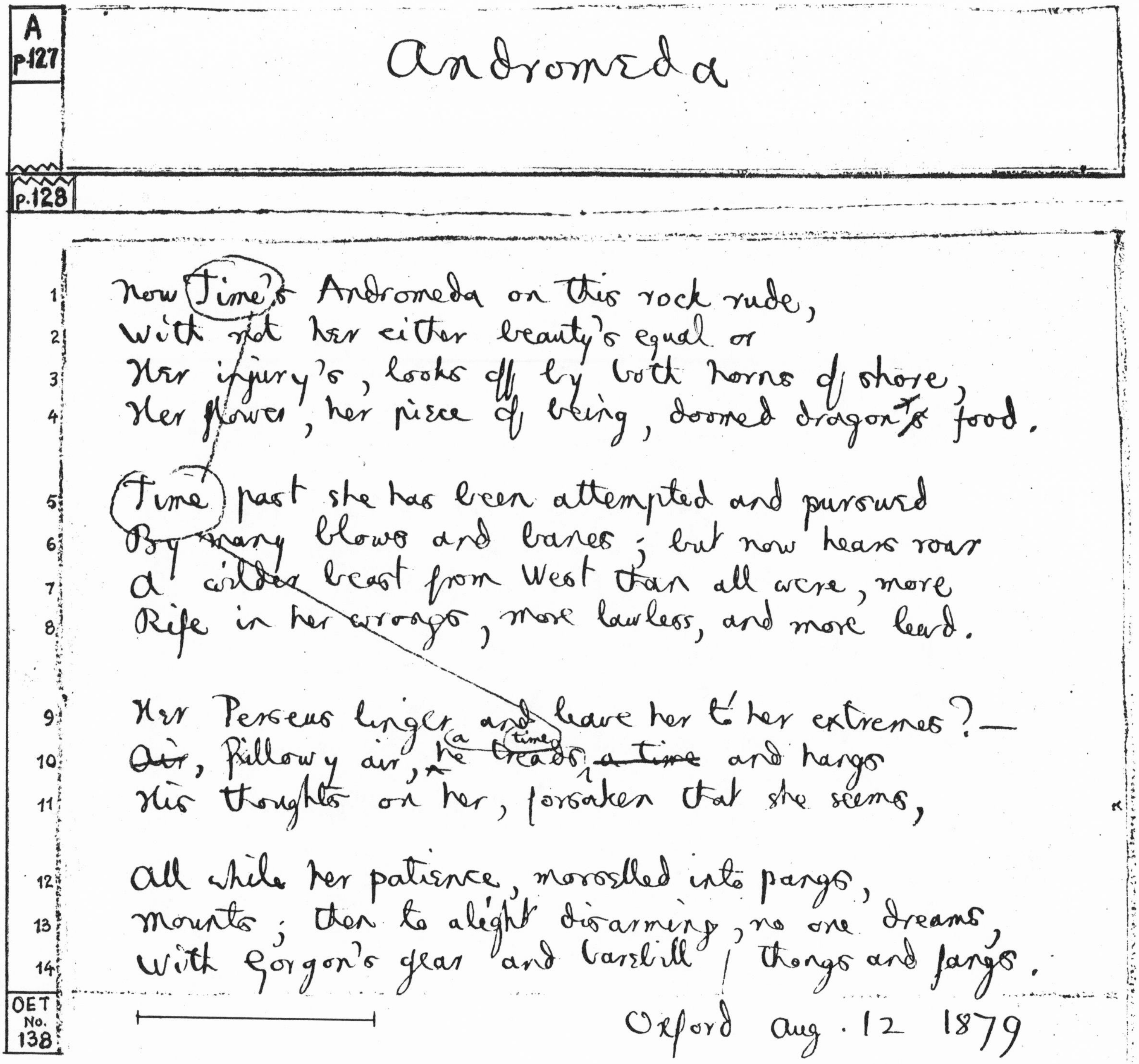

PLATE 371. OET 138. *Andromeda* • *189*

Andromeda

1 Now Time's Andromeda on this rock rude,
2 With not her either beauty's equal or
3 Her injury's, looks off by both horns of shore,
4 Her flower, her piece of being, doomed dragon's food.

5 Time past she has been attempted and pursued
6 By many blows and bares; but now hears roar
7 A wilder beast from West than all were, more
8 Rife in her wrongs, more lawless, and more lewd.

9 Her Perseus linger and leave her to her extremes? —
10 Air, pillowy air, he treads a time and hangs
11 His thoughts on her, forsaken that she seems,

12 All while her patience, morselled into pangs,
13 Mounts; then to alight disarming, no one dreams,
14 With Gorgon's gear and barebill / thongs and fangs.

Oxford Aug. 12 1879

Plate 371   OET No. 138: Andromeda -- MS. 2 (A)

A, pp.127 (title only, rest blank, here closed up), 128 (text)--autograph faircopy, cut and mounted in A. In 10 he

transposed "a time" by del. it, and rewriting it above "he treads" with a caret before "he". Note the stress on "to" (9).

RB's red ink (1884), copying GMH's revisions in B, del. apostrophe s in "dragon's" (4), and in 10 del. "Air", mended

l.c. "p" in "pillowy" to "P", del. GMH's caret (but not the comma beside it) and transposed the interlined "a time" back

to its old place (GMH, as often, had reverted to an earlier version).

RB's pencil (c. 1918) looped and joined "Time's" (1), "Time" (5) and "time" (10).

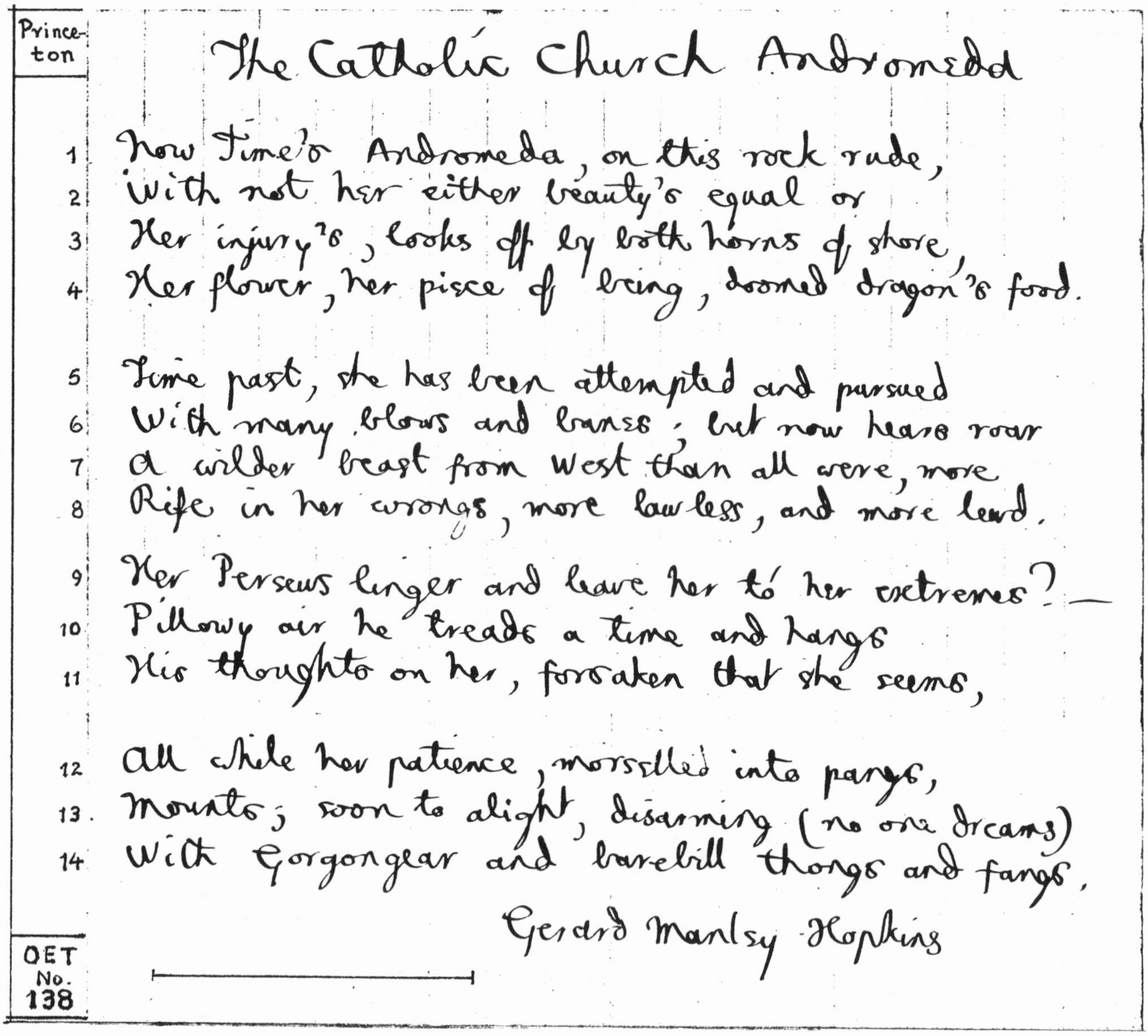

Princeton

The Catholic Church Andromeda

1 Now Time's Andromeda, on this rock rude,
2 With not her either beauty's equal or
3 Her injury's, looks off by both horns of shore,
4 Her flower, her piece of being, doomed dragon's food.

5 Time past, she has been attempted and pursued
6 With many blows and bans; but now hears roar
7 A wilder beast from West than all were, more
8 Rife in her wrongs, more lawless, and more lewd.

9 Her Perseus linger and leave her to her extremes? —
10 Pillowy air he treads a time and hangs
11 His thoughts on her, forsaken that she seems,

12 All while her patience, morselled into pangs,
13 Mounts; soon to alight, disarming (no one dreams)
14 With Gorgongear and barebill thongs and fangs.

Gerard Manley Hopkins

OET
No.
138

Plate 372   OET 138: Andromeda -- MS. 3 (Princeton)

Princeton--autograph faircopy, extraordinary in being signed in full (without "SJ", for reasons given to Dixon later over No. 139, in L.ii.140); acquired by Princeton University in 1985 with the Robert H. Taylor Collection. The explicit title, now for the first time disclosed, explains what had long mystified me, for this was the copy sent to Hall Caine.

Canon Dixon in March 1881 sent Hall Caine two Hopkins sonnets ("The Starlight Night" and a Skylark poem-- either 118 or less likely the "Sprung and paeonic" "Caged Skylark"), for publication in Caine's forthcoming Sonnets of Three Centuries (1882), if Hopkins could be persuaded to permit it. So far from entreating his friends to promote the publishing of his poetry, Hopkins in 1879 had, in great agitation, forbidden Dixon to arrange the printing of his "Loss of the Eurydice" in a Carlisle newspaper (L.ii.28,31). Yet on this occasion, within a week he sent Caine his "Andromeda" and two other poems (L.ii.47, L.i.127-132), no doubt with the consent of his Liverpool Rector. The changed title, "The Catholic Church Andromeda", provides the clue: as a priest he was seizing the chance of furthering his cause by awakening pity for the sufferings of his Church. But Caine was offended by Hopkins's laxity of form, as was his friend D.G. Rossetti when consulted, and he rejected the sonnets. Bridges offered to try to persuade Caine to accept "Andromeda", but Hopkins dismissed this out of hand (L.i.132).

The Princeton MS has the following unique readings (the deviations are underlined): Title, 5 "Time past," 6 "With many" 13,14 "soon to alight, disarming (no one dreams)/With Gorgongear and barebill thongs"

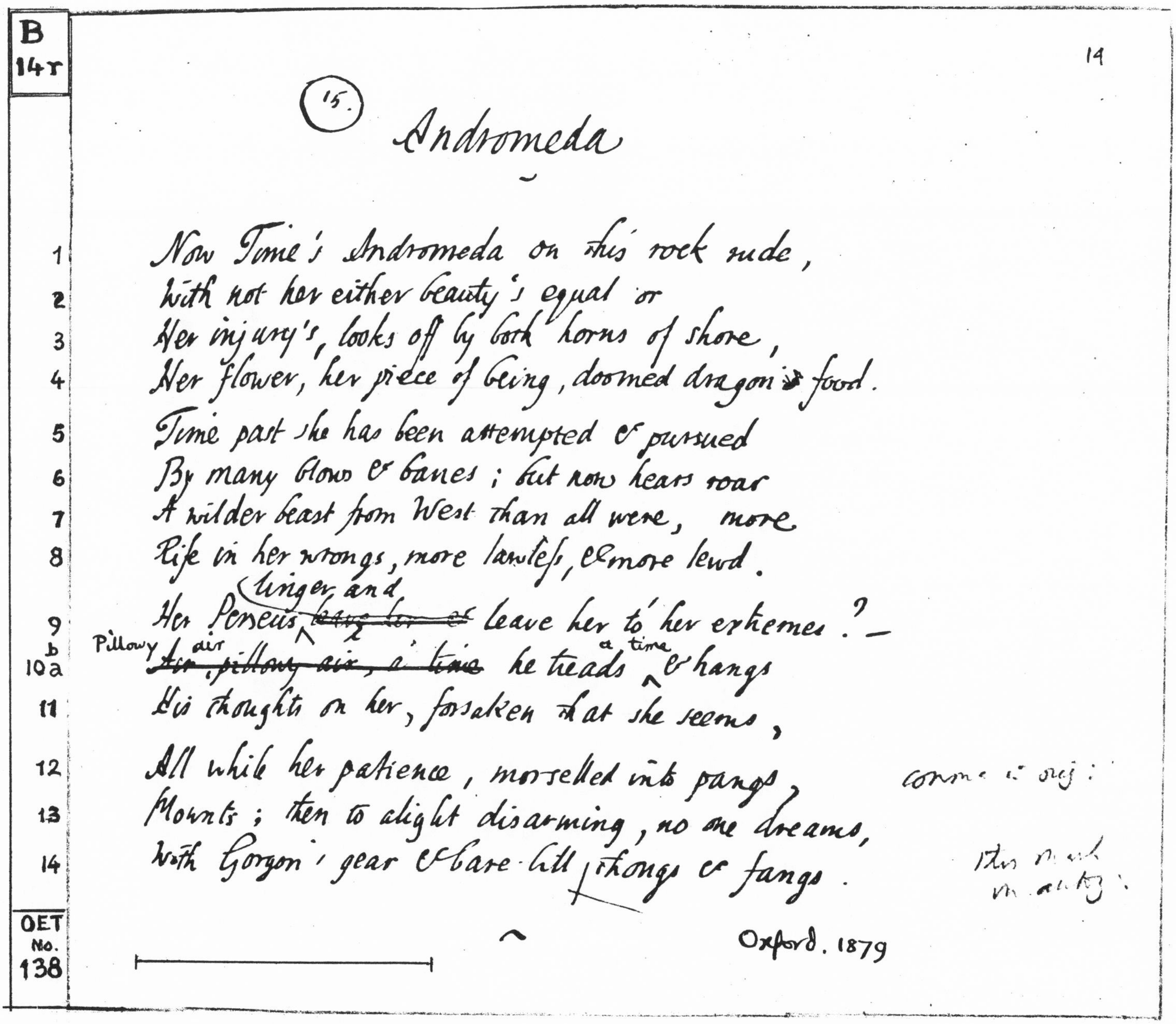

B
14r

14

(15.)

Andromeda

1 Now Time's Andromeda on this rock rude,
2 With not her either beauty's equal or
3 Her injury's, looks off by both horns of shore,
4 Her flower, her piece of being, doomed dragon's food.

5 Time past she has been attempted & pursued
6 By many blows & banes ; but now hears roar
7 A wilder beast from West than all were, more
8 Rife in her wrongs, more lawless, & more lewd.

linger and
9 Her Perseus, ~~hang her or~~ leave her to her extremes ?—
b
10 a Pillowy of air ~~his pillowy air, a time~~ he treads a time & hangs
11 His thoughts on her, forsaken that she seems ,

12 All while her patience , morselled into pangs ,
13 Mounts ; then to alight disarming, no one dreams,
14 With Gorgon's gear & bare-bill thongs & fangs .

comma in orig:

this mark
in autog:

Oxford. 1879

OET
No.
138

Plate 372a   OET No. 138: Andromeda -- MS. 4 (B)

B.14r--transcription of A by RB, inscribed in album B.   RB omitted "linger and" (9), but immediately corrected his slip, placing his caret below the del. "leave". The stress in 9 on "to", and the virgule in 14 were probably put in by RB, copying A. In 14 note his minute apostrophe s after "Gorgon" and mere dot for a hyphen in "bare-bill" (one word in A).

In revising B GMH either del. the apostrophe s after "dragon" (4) himself or approved RB's deletion: (there are four other apostrophes in 1, 2, 3 and 14). GMH also added a firm caret in 9 after "Perseus" and a second cancel line through "leave her &"; he clarified the commas after "her" and "seems" (11), and later added the date.

RB's pencil (c. 1918) added a comma after "pangs" (12)--which he had overlooked in copying A, and which GMH had not restored--with a marginal note "comma in orig:". RB drew attention to the virgule after "bill" (14), noting "this mark in autog:" The pencil stroke through the virgule is not intended to delete it.

H.i. 39r	
1	The dappled die-away
2	Cheek and wimpled lip,
3	The gold-crisp, the airy-grey
4	Eye, all in fellowship —
5	This, all this, beauty blooming,
6	This, all this, freshness fuming,
7	Give God while worth consuming.
St.2	Both
8	~~He~~ thought and thew now bolder
9	And told by nature: Tower,
10	head ~~When head~~ that leapt, heart, hand, her~~s~~ and shoulder
11	~~Beat~~ and breathe in power —
12	This pride of prime's enjoyment
13	O take for tool, not toy-meant
14	And hold at heaven's employment.
St.3	
15a	and The vault the scope and schooling
16a	And mastery in the mind,
17 {b,a,c}	Silk-ashed and ~~The silk, ~~ kept from cooling; Silk-ashed, ~~into core not~~ cooling,
18a	And ripest under rind
19a	what ~~This~~ life half lifts the latch of,
20a	What hell stalks towards the snatch of,
21a	Your offering, with despatch, of!
19b	what death now lifts the latch of,
20b	what hell steals near the snatch of,
21b	The surrender, with despatch of!
39v	
15b	The vault and scope and schooling
16b	And mastery in the mind,
17 {e,d}	In Silk-ashed ~~kept from~~ ~~will be not~~ cooling,
18b	And ripest under rind —
19c	what death dare lift the latch of,
20c	what hell hopes soon the snatch of,
21c	Your offer, with despatch, of!
OET No. 139	Oxford 1879

Plate 373   OET No. 139: Morning, Midday, and Evening Sacrifice -- MS. 1 (H)

H.i.39r,v--autograph faircopy, followed by rev. of 19-21; then st. 3 was further revised on the verso, and 15a to 21b on recto were crossed through with an ink line. Other deletions and changes include: 15a ", the" rev. to "and"   17a "ask" (slip for "ash")   17b "Silk-ashed and"   17c "Silk-ashed, its but core not cooling,". This is repeated in 17d, where it is rev. again: " -ashed, but core not" are del.; "Silk" is left u.c. in spite of the insertion of "In" before it.   18b "ripeness" rev. to "ripest". Note that on the recto in 17a the final stop after "cooling" is a comma, though a speck above it on the paper seems to convert it into a semicolon.

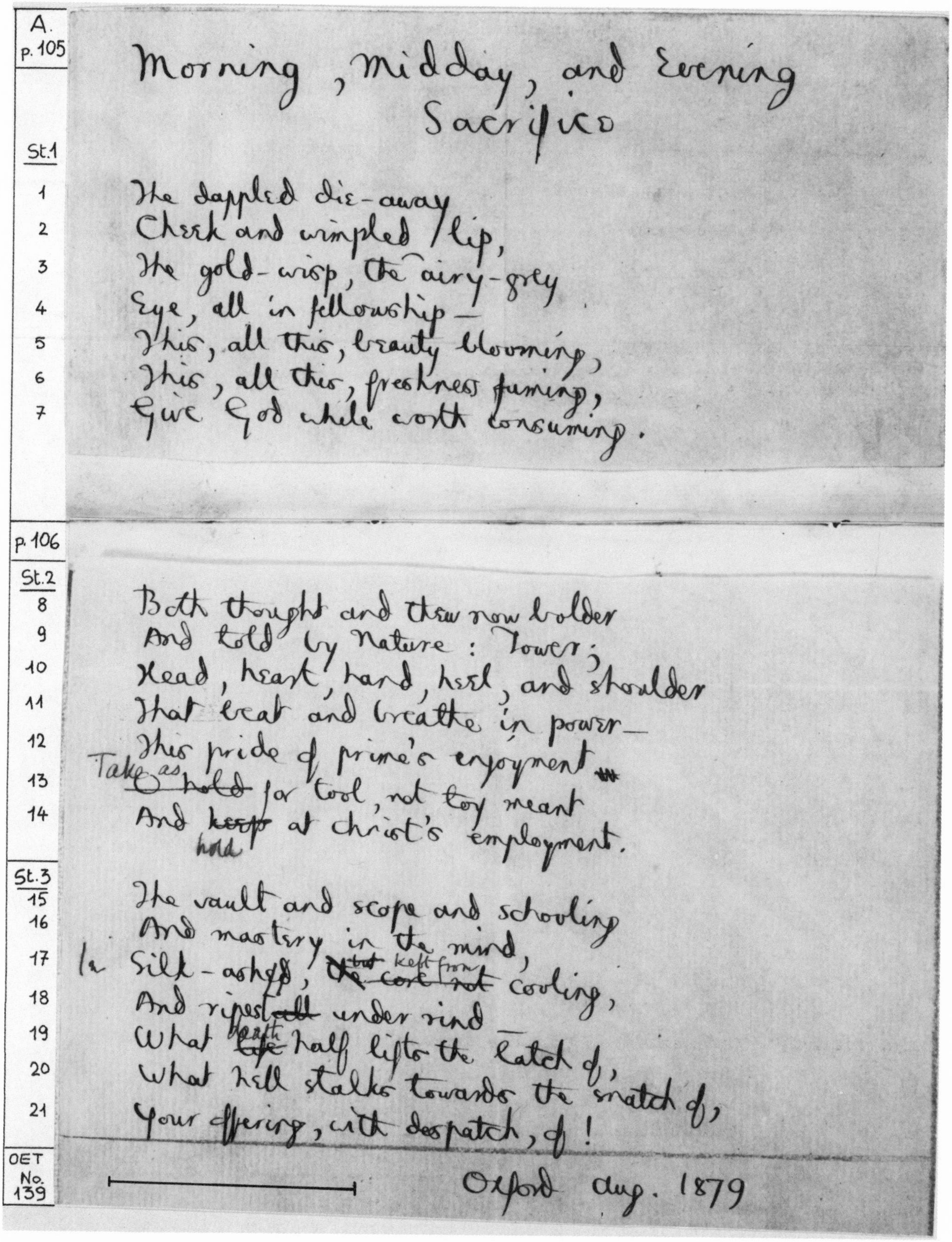

A. p. 105	
St.1	
1	The dappled die-away
2	Cheek and wimpled lip,
3	The gold-wisp, the airy-grey
4	Eye, all in fellowship—
5	This, all this, beauty blooming,
6	This, all this, freshness fuming,
7	Give God while worth consuming.

p. 106	
St.2	
8	Both thought and thew now bolder
9	And told by Nature: Tower;
10	Head, heart, hand, heel, and shoulder
11	That beat and breathe in power—
12	This pride of prime's enjoyment
13	Take as ~~hold~~ for tool, not toy meant
14	And ~~keep~~ hold at Christ's employment.
St.3	
15	The vault and scope and schooling
16	And mastery in the mind,
17	In silk-ashes, ~~the core not~~ but kept from cooling,
18	And ripest under rind—
19	What ~~life death~~ half lifts the latch of,
20	What hell stalks towards the snatch of,
21	Your offering, with despatch, of!

| OET No. 139 | |

Oxford Aug. 1879

Plate 373a OET No. 139: Morning, Midday, and Evening Sacrifice -- MS. 2 (A)

A.105-06--autograph faircopy on blue paper, cut up and mounted in album A. Changes by GMH: 12 "enjoyment ⨍" 17 "the but" 18 "all"

RB's red ink copies from B GMH's revisions: 13 "∅ hold Take as" 14 "keep hold" 17 "ashed, but core not In...kept from" 19 "life death"; but he disliked the rev. in 20 and did not copy it.

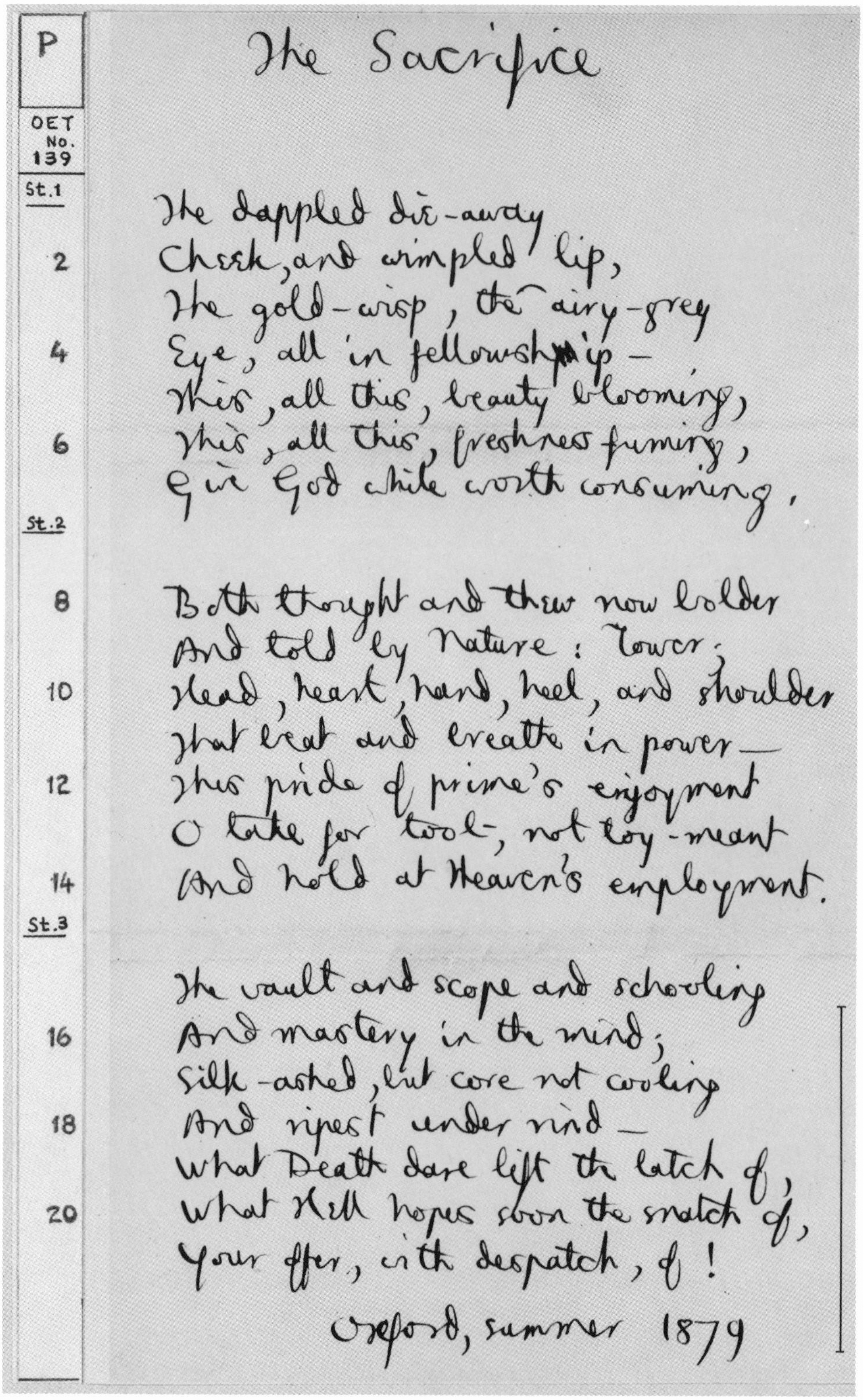

The Sacrifice

P	
OET No. 139	
St.1	The dappled die-away
2	Cheek, and wimpled lip,
	The gold-wisp, the airy-grey
4	Eye, all in fellowship —
	This, all this, beauty blooming,
6	This, all this, freshness fuming,
	Give God while worth consuming,
St.2	
8	Both thought and thew now bolder
	And told by Nature: Tower;
10	Head, heart, hand, heel, and shoulder
	That beat and breathe in power —
12	This pride of prime's enjoyment
	O take for tool, not toy-meant
14	And hold at Heaven's employment.
St.3	
	The vault and scope and schooling
16	And mastery in the mind;
	Silk-ashed, but core not cooling
18	And ripest under rind —
	What Death dare lift the latch of,
20	What Hell hopes soon the snatch of,
	Your offer, with despatch, of !

Oxford, summer 1879

Plate 374 OET No. 139: Morning, Midday, and Evening Sacrifice -- MS. 3 (P)

Pooley MS -- one of three autographs sent to GMH's sister Grace. See notes to Plates 300 and 305 for their discovery in 1964. All three were subsequently purchased by the Humanities Research Center, University of Texas,-- see note to Plates 325a and b.

This is the only autograph entitled: "The Sacrifice" but see Plate 374a for MS. K. Slips corrected in: 4 "fellowship" 12 "enjoyment". Note the two hyphens in 13: the first was overlooked in the list of variants from the final text, HQ 5.4, 1979, 141, along with other variants in 2 and 20. Unlike other poems sent to Grace (Nos. 117, 119) this MS bears no musical notations to encourage her to set it to music, probably because GMH had set it himself (L.i.92, J.490).

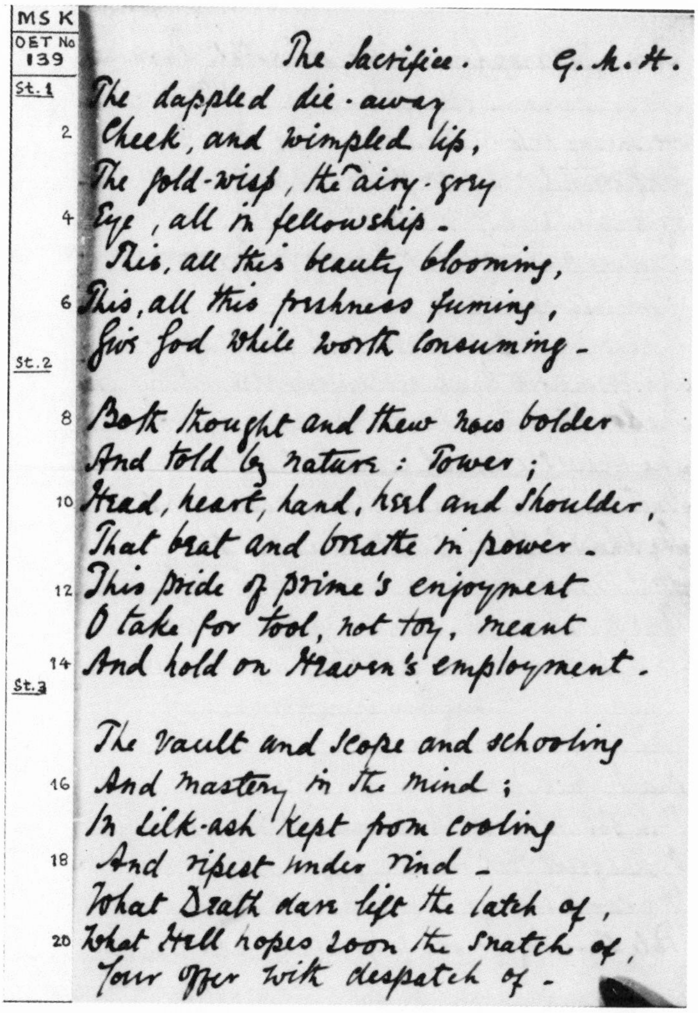

MS K
OET No 139

St. 1

The Sacrifice.   G. M. H.

The dappled die-away
2 Cheek, and wimpled lip,
The pold-wisp, the airy-grey
4 Eye, all in fellowship -
'Tis, all this beauty blooming,
6 This, all this freshness fuming,
Gives God while worth consuming -

St. 2

8 Both thought and thew now bolder
And told by nature: Tower;
10 Head, heart, hand, heel and shoulder,
That beat and breathe in power -
12 This pride of prime's enjoyment
O take for tool, not toy, meant
14 And hold on Heaven's employment.

St. 3

The vault and scope and schooling
16 And mastery in the mind;
In silk-ash kept from cooling
18 And ripest under rind -
What Death dare lift the latch of,
20 What Hell hopes soon the snatch of,
Your offer with despatch of -

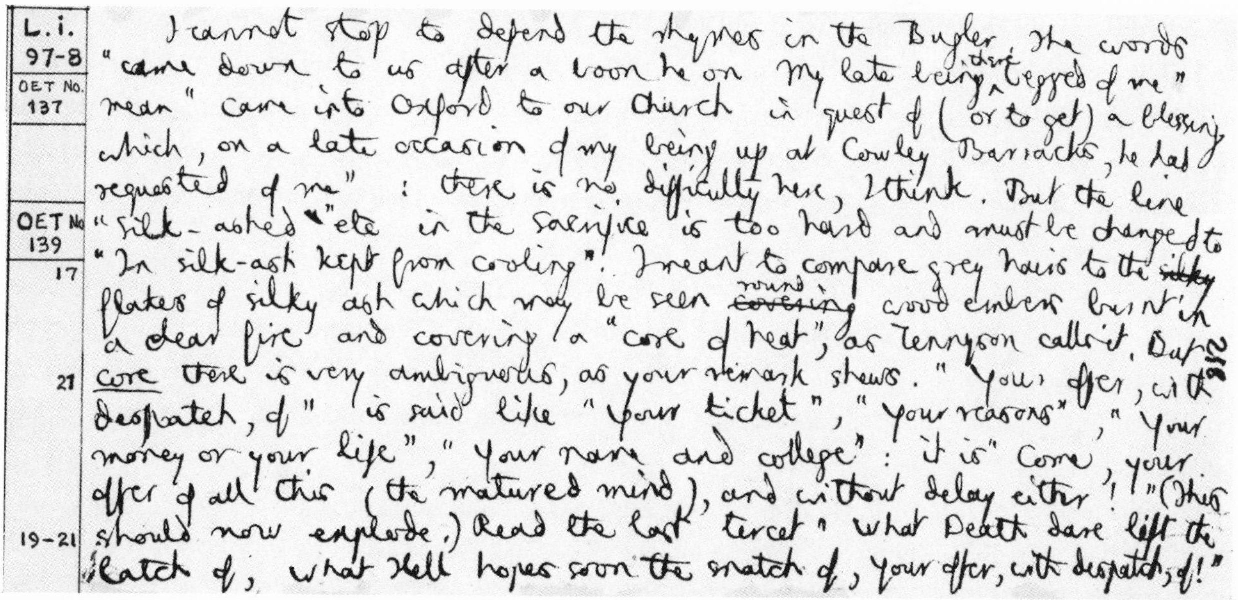

L. i.
97-8
OET No. 137
OET No. 139
17
21
19-21

[handwritten letter:] I cannot stop to defend the rhymes in the Bugler. The words "came down to us after a boon he on my late being... begged of me" mean "came into Oxford to our church in quest of (or to get) a blessing which, on a late occasion of my being up at Cowley Barracks, he had requested of me": there is no difficulty here, I think. But the line "silk-ashed" etc in the Sacrifice is too hard and must be changed to "In silk-ash kept from cooling". I meant to compare grey hairs to the silky flakes of silky ash which may be seen round covering wood embers burnt in a clear fire and covering a "core of heat", as Tennyson calls it. But core there is very ambiguous, as your remark shews. "Your offer, with despatch, of" is said like "your ticket", "your reasons", "your money or your life", "your name and college": it is "Come, your offer of all this (the matured mind), and without delay either!" (This should now explode.) Read the last tercet "what Death dare lift the latch of, what Hell hopes soon the snatch of, your offer, with despatch, of!"

Plate 374a   OET No. 139: Morning, Midday, and Evening Sacrifice -- MSS. 4 (L) and 7 (K)
    [top] MS. K--transcript made by GMH's mother Kate, Mrs. Manley Hopkins, in her Commonplace Book. Although its title is the same as the autograph sent to his sister Grace (Plate 374), it differs from that version most strikingly in 17 (the first and last reading of the draft in H, Plate 373) and in having "on" instead of "at" in 14: other deviations might have been attributed to oversights, e.g., punctuation in 5, 6, 10, 13). GMH might have copied the poem out for his mother from memory during some visit to his home. For other transcripts by Kate see Plates 313b, 384, 425, 436.

    [bottom] L.i.97-8--autograph letter to RB, begun Oct. 22, 1879; the end, including this para., dated Nov. 18. In a footnote to the printed Letters of GMH to RB (1935) Abbott says "The last three lines became:/'What life half lifts the latch of,/What hell stalks towards the snatch of,/Your offering, with despatch, of!'" But this was the earlier version, taken from A, which GMH wanted changed. RB disliked the emended tercet (see his marginal comments on Plate 375), and the text Abbott quotes became that of Poems 1st. to 3rd. edns. (1919-1967).

D²
L.ii.
132
OET No. 139
2
5
OET No. 141

[first,] the one you quote, might stand by itself. If so the text should be something about first fruits: there must be several that would do, but I think of none just now. The second line had better be "Cheek and the wimpled lip" and the count made up to six. And the stopping "This, all this, beauty" etc. is cumbrous: it is better "This, all this beauty." I have nothing else to send, but something new might strike me. There is a 3-stanza piece made at a wedding that possibly might do, but I rather think not: it is too personal and, I believe, too plain spoken.

Sutcliffe Bibliog. Eng.Prov SJ		
OET No. 139		
St.1		
2		
4		
6		
7+		

208. HOPKINS, GERARD MANLEY   B 1844;
e 1868 ; d 1889

1. In : The Bible Birthday Book. Arranged
by the Rev. Canon [Richard Watson]
Dixon. (Routledge) 1887. 32°. For
May 25th prints :
  This dappled die-away
  Cheek and wimpled lip,
  The gold-wisp, the airy-grey
  Eye, all is fellowship—
  This, all this beauty blooming,
  This, all this freshness fuming,
  Give God, while worth consuming,
    Only for this one day.
Perhaps the earliest quotation of his poetry.

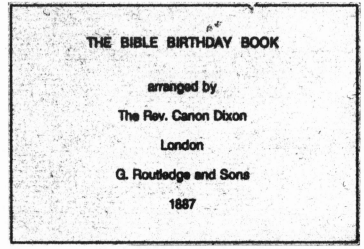

THE BIBLE BIRTHDAY BOOK

arranged by

The Rev. Canon Dixon

London

G. Routledge and Sons

1887

Plate 374b   OET No. 139: Morning, Midday, and Evening Sacrifice -- MS. 6 (D)

[top left] [D] L.ii.132--autograph letter from GMH, June 30 1886, in reply to a request from Canon R.W. Dixon (June 21, L.ii.130) for permission to use "The dappled die-away...consuming" (i.e., st. 1) and any other poetry GMH could offer, in his Bible Birthday Book: this provided for each day of the year a biblical text and some lines of verse. Dixon had been given the stanza by RB during a recent visit to Yattendon. GMH agreed, and the st. was printed under 25 May with the text: "As for the oblation of the first-fruits, ye shall offer them unto the Lord. Leviticus ii.12" (L.ii.130, n.2).

[top right] Bibliography of the English Province of the Society of Jesus, 1773-1953, ed. Edmund Felix Sutcliffe, SJ, Manresa Press, 1957, p.82, item 208. This is the only known full citation of the stanza as it appeared in print under May 25: it varies from all autographs in: 1 "This" for "The" (anticipating 5 and 6), 4 "is" for "in" (a misprint?), and the surprising new final line, repeating the a-rhyme and intended to urge the daily surrender of beauty to God (not merely on one's birthday).

[bottom] Please be on the look-out for this Volume--The Bible Birthday Book; arranged by...Canon Dixon. London, G. Routledge and Sons, 1887. 252 pp. 16° (British Library 3128.aa.3). This was the only copy known in any British or North American library. It was still in the B.L. about 1955, when James Sambrook analysed the poets quoted in it by Dixon, in order to gauge Dixon's width of reading. Sambrook calls it a "very tiny book": he copied only the first line of the GMH stanza. By the sixties, when Tom Dunne and I both wanted to examine it, the B.L. had mislaid it. Dunne organised searches through the British National Central Library and antiquarian booksellers; Fr. Alfred Thomas published an appeal in Notes and Queries, Fr. Tony Bischoff investigated American libraries and alerted booksellers on this continent. No trace of it has appeared. The B.L. description of it as 16mo can be reconciled with Sutcliffe's 32mo if the tiny book was either Crown 16mo (about 9.5 cm x 12.7) or Imperial 32mo (about 14 cm x 9.5), but whether upright or (as I suspect) oblong we do not know. A 32mo book can be as small as 6.5 cm x 9.5, roughly the size of the rectangle above. Scores of copies probably survive in old rectories or attics, or shops selling old furniture, if only we knew where to look.

PLATE 375. OET 139. *Morning, Midday, and Evening Sacrifice* • *197*

(19) Morning , Midday & Evening Sacrifice . . .

The dappled die-away
Cheek & wimpled lip,
The gold-wisp ,the airy-grey
Eye ,all in fellowship —
This , all this, beauty blooming ,
This , all this, freshness fuming,
Give God while worth consuming.

a letter t Dixon June 30 86
inserts the before wimpled
wh. I take

Both thought & thew now bolder
And told by nature Tower ;
Head ,heart ,hand ,heel, & shoulder
That beat & breathe in power —
This pride of prime's enjoyment

Take as ~~A hold~~ for tool, not toy meant
~~And keep at Christ's employment~~ and hold at Christ's employment.

The vault & scope & schooling
And mastery in the mind,
~~Silk-ashed, but core not cooling,~~ In silk-ash kept from cooling
And ripest under rind —
What ^(death) ~~life~~ half lifts the latch of,
What hell ~~stalks~~ ^(hopes) ~~towards~~ ^(soon) the snatch of,
Your offering, with despatch, of !

I reject . RB.

stet RB

Oxford. 1879

Plate 375   OET No. 139: Morning, Midday, and Evening Sacrifice -- MS. 5 (B)

B.21v--RB's transcription of A, inscribed in album B. In 18 RB del. his slip, a hyphen in "under rind".

GMH revised 13, 14 (first merely changing "at" into "for"), 17 (his new version omitted the final comma), 19 and 20. He later added the date.

RB's pencil (1918) brackets 19 and 20 with a note on GMH's revisions there: "I reject. RB."; and his red ink (prob. also 1918) underlines the deleted "stalks towards" (20) and notes in red with an X in the left margin, "stet RB".

In Poems, 1st. edn., RB reverted to A for 19 and 20, with a note p.112; I restored the text in the 4th. edn.. RB's pencil opposite 2 notes: "a letter to Dixon June 30 86 inserts the before wimpled wh. I take" (though he eventually decided to omit it in the 1st. edn.). RB did not record in the margin that the same letter deleted the comma after the second "this" in 5 (and by implication in 6), changes he incorporated in the 1st. edn.

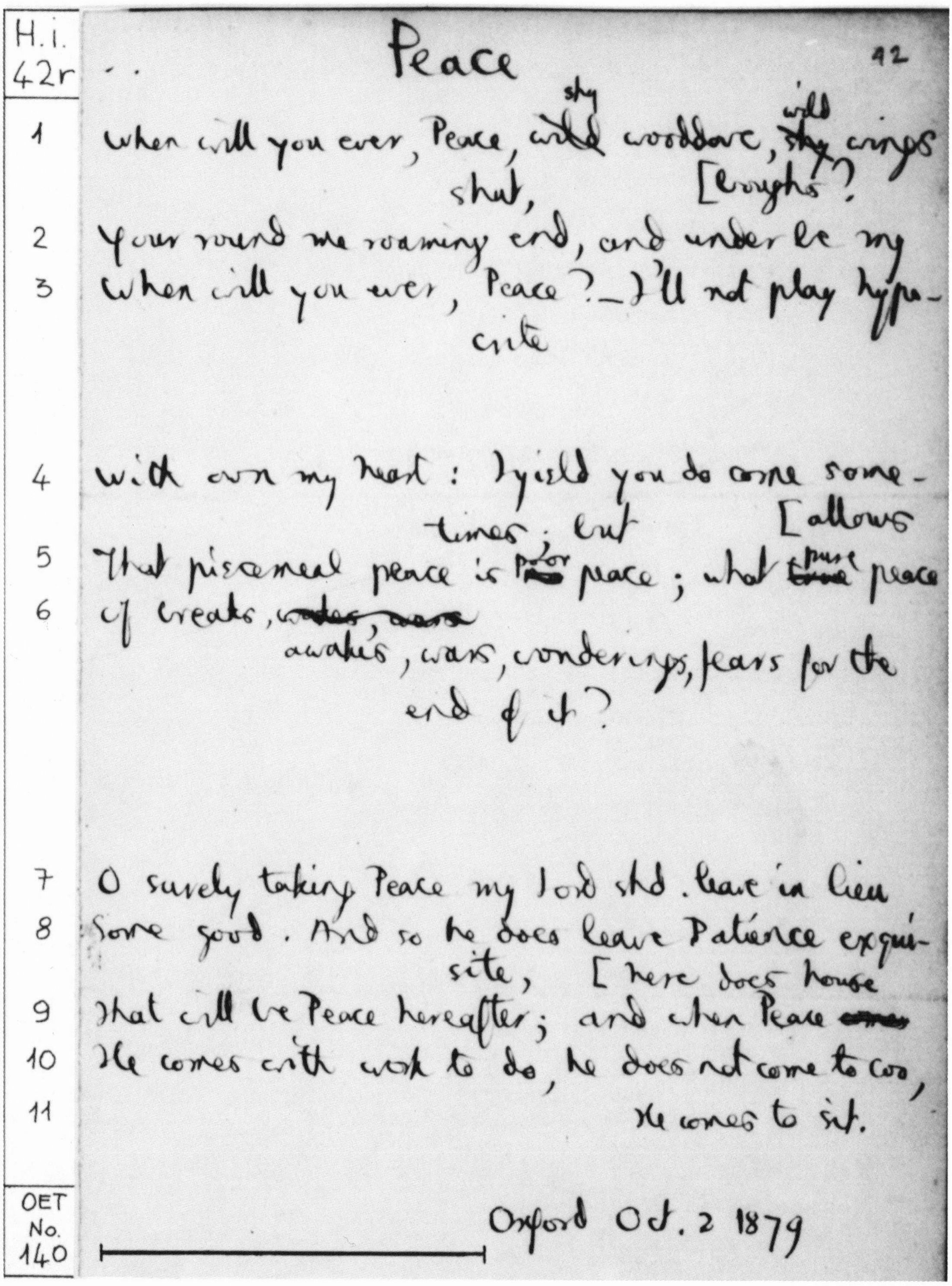

H.i. 42r		
	Peace	42
1	When will you ever, Peace, wild wooddove, shy wings shut, [roughs?	
2	Your round me roaming end, and under be my	
3	When will you ever, Peace? — I'll not play hypo- crite	
4	With own my heart: I yield you do come some- times; but [allows	
5	That piecemeal peace is no peace; what pure peace	
6	of creaks, wakes awakes, wars, wanderings, fears for the end of it?	
7	O surely taking Peace my lord shd. leave in lieu	
8	Some good. And so he does leave Patience exqui- site, [here does house	
9	That will be Peace hereafter; and when Peace comes	
10	He comes with work to do, he does not come to coo,	
11	He comes to sit.	
OET No. 140	Oxford Oct. 2 1879	

Plate 376 OET No. 140: Peace -- MS. 1 (H)

H.i.42r--autograph early version, with some revisions. Deletions include: 5 no...true   6 wakes, wars   9 comes.

Note in 8 that the dot over "i" in "Patience" and "exquisite" could be mistaken for stresses. The layout uses line spaces

to separate the units of the curtal sonnet, GMH's practice in 1879: no indenting.

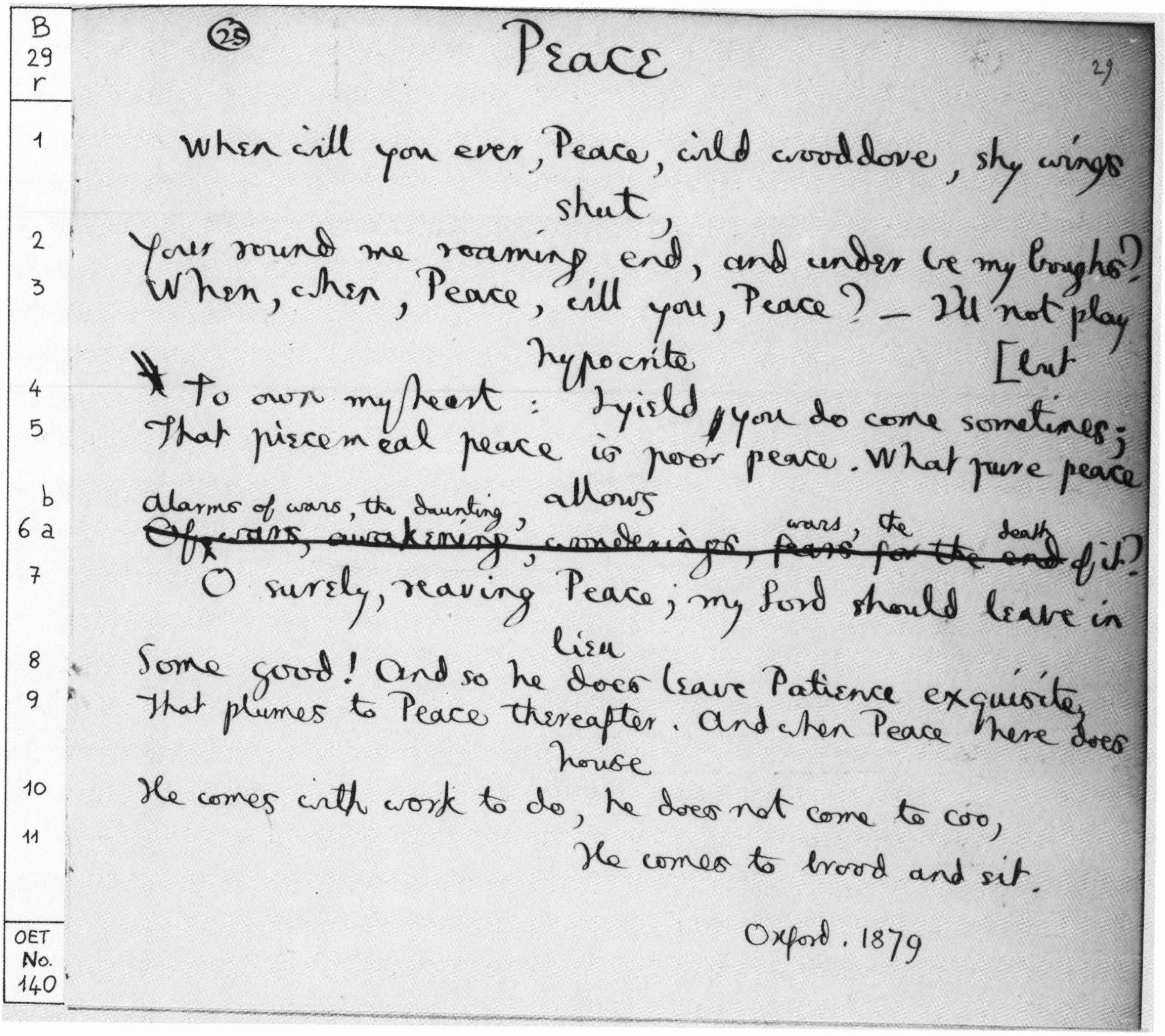

PLATE 377. OET 140. *Peace* • *199*

PEACE

When will you ever, Peace, wild wooddove, shy wings
    shut,
Your round me roaming end, and under be my boughs?
When, when, Peace, will you, Peace? — I'll not play
                hypocrite   [but
✻ to own my heart: I yield, you do come sometimes;
That piecemeal peace is poor peace. What pure peace
    Alarms of wars, the daunting, allows
    ~~Of wars, awakening, condensings, fears for the end of it?~~ wars, the death
    O surely, reaving Peace; my Lord should leave in
                lieu
Some good! And so he does leave Patience exquisite,
That plumes to Peace thereafter. And when Peace here does
              house
He comes with work to do, he does not come to coo,
    He comes to brood and sit.

          Oxford. 1879

Plate 377   OET No. 140: Peace -- MS. 2 (B)

B.29r--autograph faircopy, inscribed in album B in 1884, before it was sent to Patmore (the note in L.i.196 wrongly identifies the curtal sonnet as "Peace"). The units were marked by his then current practice of indenting their beginnings, without line spaces (1, 4, 7--he forgot in 4, and so deleted his first "T"). The comma after "yield" (4) was deleted after the ink had dried: it was in fact still the reading when RB received album B back from Patmore in Aug. 1884. GMH replied to RB's criticism "If you do not like 'I yield, you do come sometimes'...will 'I yield, you foot me sometimes' do?" (L.i.196, Aug. 24 1884). The comma after "Of" (6a) seems distracted, as the one after "daunting" (6b, in the middle of a phrase) certainly is.

H.i.
43
r

13

1b ⸬ God with worship hang your head,
1a ⸬ God hang his worship on your head,
2b
2a ⸬ Groom, and ~~bless you~~, bride, ⸱the your bed
3a With lissome scions /sweet ⸱ scions
4a ~~Out of hallowed bodies bred,~~
4b Out of here ÷ hallowed bodies bred.

5a ⸬ Each be other's /comfort kind
6a And deep ⸬ deeper than divined,
7a Divine ⸱ charity, dear ⸬ charity
8a ~~Ever bind you, fast ⸬ bind.~~
  b Fast ⸬ bind you / ever, fast ⸬ bind.

9a Then let the March ⸬ tread our ears, !
10a ~~⸬ But I to him⸱ turn in tears~~
11a That ⸬ wedlock, ⸱this ⸬ wonder wedlock,
12a ~~Crowned ⸱ with immortal years.~~
  b Deals ⸬ triumph and immortal years.

                    Leigh Oct. 21 1879

1c ⸬ God with worship hang your head,
2c ⸬ Groom, and grace you, bride, your bed
3b With lissome scions, sweet scions
4c out of hallowed ⸬ bodies bred.

5b ⸬ Each be other's comfort kind ⸬
6b ⸬ Deep, ⸬ deeper than divined,
7b Divine ⸬ charity, dear ⸬ charity
8c ⸬ fast you ever, fast ⸬ bind .
9b Then let the march ⸬ tread our ears !
10b ⸬ I to him⸬ turn with tears

43 v

11b ⸬ Who to wedlock, his ⸬ wonder wedlock,
12c Deals ⸬ triumph and immortal years.

                    Bedford Oct. 21 1879

OET
No.
141

PLATE 379. OET 141. *At the Wedding March* ● *201*

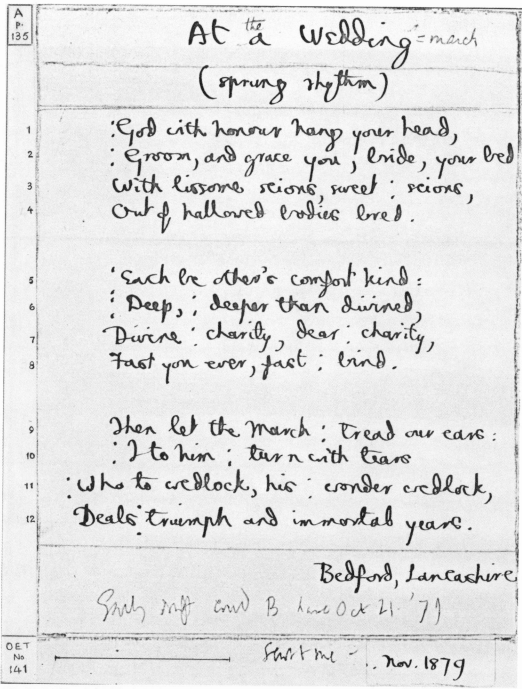

At ~~the~~ a Wedding=march
(sprung rhythm)

1 :God with honour hang your head,
2 :Groom, and grace you, bride, your bed
3 With lissome scions, sweet: scions,
4 Out of hallowed bodies bred.

5 'Each be other's comfort kind:
6 :Deep,: deeper than divined,
7 Divine: charity, dear: charity,
8 Fast you ever, fast: bind.

9 Then let the march: tread our ears:
10 :I to him: turn with tears
11 :Who to wedlock, his: wonder wedlock,
12 Deals: triumph and immortal years.

Bedford, Lancashire

Early draft and B have Oct 21 '79

Start me -- . Nov. 1879

OET No 141

Plate 378   OET No. 141: At the Wedding March -- MS. 1 (H)

[opposite]   H.i.43r,v--autograph draft on a roughly torn scrap of paper: GMH told Dixon the poem was "made at a wedding" (L.ii.132), and though he may well have composed it in his head, the scrap of paper with its tiny writing may have been pressed into use shortly after the wedding register was signed. It began as a faircopy of the whole poem: then each stanza was revised and made to end with a 5-stress line. This was then del. in ink, and followed by a faircopy (the last 2 *ll.* are on the verso), which in turn is del. in pencil, but is nevertheless close to the final text. "Leigh" (after 12b) and "Bedford" (after 12c) both refer to the parish of Bedford Leigh. Note the great colons in every line except 1a, 4a, 3b, 4c: in 6b one was widened--a third dot appears below. In 8c "Ea[ch?]" is deleted; in 9a "ears," becomes "ears!" in 12a "Crowns" becomes "Crowned".

Plate 379   OET No. 141: At the Wedding March -- MS. 2 (A)

[above]   A.p.135--autograph faircopy, pasted into album A. The date is on a separate piece of the page, cut off from beside "Lancashire".

RB's red ink (1884) altered the title in response to GMH's revision in B, also adding a hyphen. His purple pencil note (c. 1918) at the foot says "Early draft and B have Oct. 21 '79/Sent to me" [June 1880]

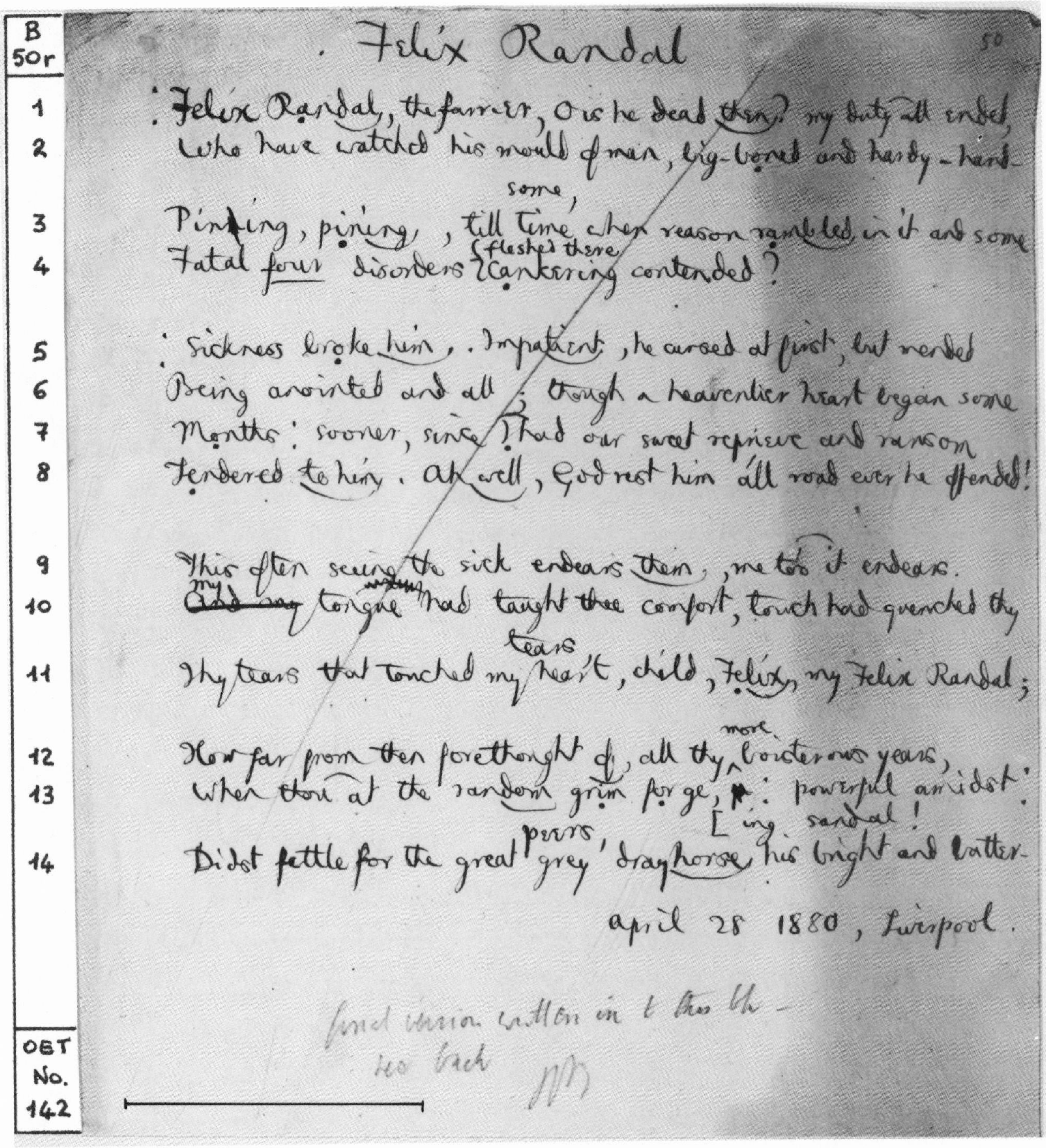

Felix Randal

B
50r
50

1 . Felix Randal, the farrier, O is he dead then? my duty all ended,
2 Who have watched his mould of man, big-boned and hardy – handsome,
3 Pining, pining, , till time when reason rambled, in it and some
4 Fatal four disorders {fleshed there} {cankering} contended?

5 . Sickness broke him . Impatient , he cursed at first, but mended
6 Being anointed and all ; though a heavenlier heart began some
7 Months : sooner, since I had our sweet reprieve and ransom
8 Tendered to him . Ah well, God rest him all road ever he offended!

9 This often seeing the sick endears them , me too it endears.
10 My tongue had taught thee comfort, touch had quenched thy
                                                              tears
11 Thy tears that touched my heart, child, Felix, my Felix Randal;

12 How far from then forethought of, all thy more boisterous years,
13 When thou at the random grim forge , : powerful amidst
                                        Long sandal!
14 Didst fettle for the great grey peers drayhorse, his bright and batter-

                                         April 28 1880, Liverpool.

   final version written in to this bk –
   –see back

Plate 380   OET No. 142: Felix Randal -- MS. 1 (B[1])

(B[1]) B.50r--autograph faircopy, which was pasted into album B later than Aug. 1884. Because the sonnet had six-foot lines, and was both sprung and outriding, GMH attempted to clarify the stresses, but used three different ways: (a) great colons (which at the beginning of a line are followed by a stress, and within a line have a stress before and after)--cf. MS. A; (b) stresses, on "all" (8), "too" (9); (c) black balls, here under twelve syllables (see L.i.109)--none in this MS seem intended as white balls, though some show a little white. In addition "four" (4) is in italics.

GMH corrected a slip in 3 "PinNing" and in 13 del. "ϸ[owerful]" because he had not left enough room for the great colon before it. In 10 he rev. "And my" to "My" and so del. the slur on "tongue had".

RB's pencil (1918) crossed out the poem, noting "final version written in to this bk--/see back/RB"

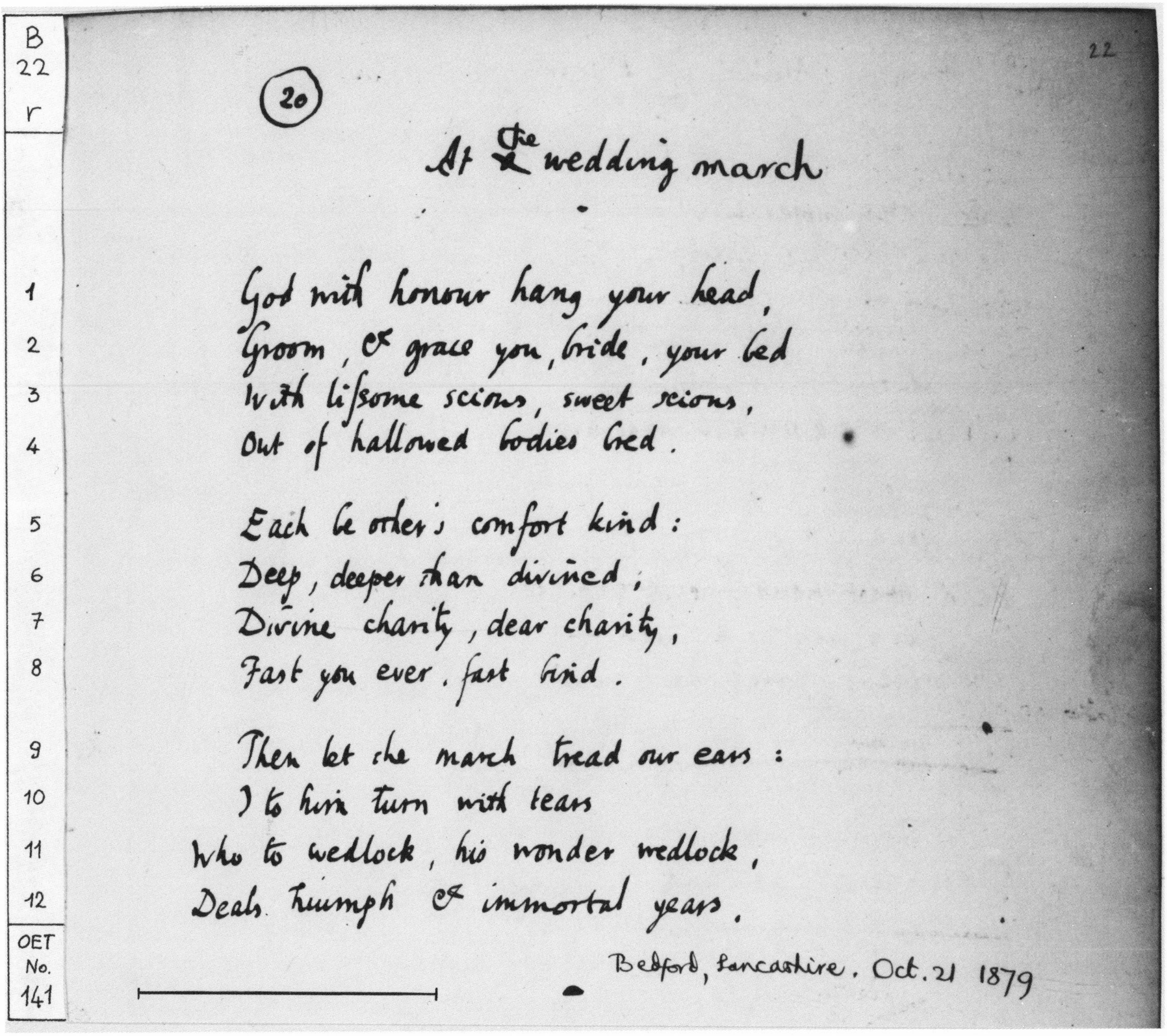

PLATE 381. OET 141. *At the Wedding March* • 203

㉒

⟨20⟩

At the wedding march

God with honour hang your head,
Groom, & grace you, bride, your bed
With lissome scions, sweet scions,
Out of hallowed bodies bred.

Each be other's comfort kind:
Deep, deeper than divined;
Divine charity, dear charity,
Fast you ever, fast bind.

Then let the march tread our ears:
I to him turn with tears
Who to wedlock, his wonder wedlock,
Deals triumph & immortal years.

Bedford, Lancashire. Oct. 21 1879

Plate 381   OET No. 141: At the Wedding March -- MS. 3 (B)

B.22r--RB's transcription of A in album B. GMH altered the title from "At a wedding" to "At the wedding march",

and later added the date. In 6 a slight flaw makes the comma after "divined" look like a semicolon.

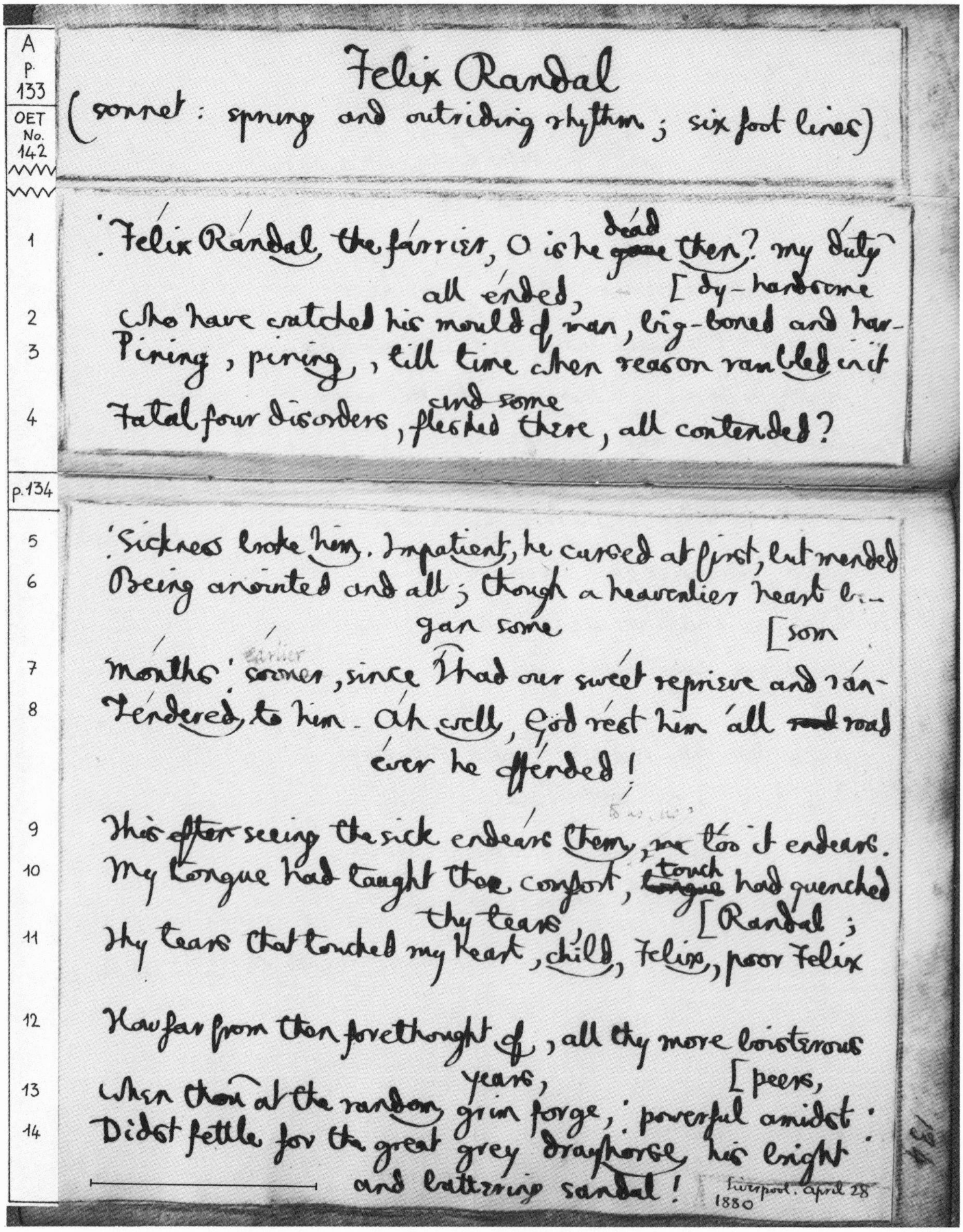

Plate 382   OET No. 142: Felix Randal -- MS. 2 (A)

A.pp.133 (title, 1-4), 134 (5-14)--autograph faircopy, with revision in 1 from "gone" to "dead". Slips corrected by GMH: in 8 "rood", perhaps a phonetic spelling of a common pronunciation of "road" in Lancashire; in 10 "thee" is blotted and "tongue" was an absent-minded confusion with the first half of the line. The stresses on "all" (8) and "too" (9) are GMH's; so is the date, squeezed in with a different pen before he sent the autograph to RB on 23 June 1880. Great colons open 1 and 5, and occur after "Months" (7), "forge", "amidst" (13).

RB's red ink (1884) in 7 and 9 copies GMH's revisions in B[2], though in 7 he omits the new outride and in 9 del. the comma after "them" which GMH had overlooked. RB's black ink adds most of GMH's stresses from B[2], including two on his own red ink corrections: as usual RB is less particular about the letter on which the stress falls (e.g. in 1 on two consonants, and in 9 on the second vowel of a diphthong).

PLATE 383. OET 142. *Felix Randal* • 205

B
14
V

16   Felix Randal.

1   Félix Rándal, the fárrier, O is he déad then,? my dúty all énded,
2   who have watched his mould of man, bigboned & hardy-handsome
3   Pining, pining, till time when reason rambled in it, and some
4   Fatal four disorders, fleshed there, all contended?
5   Sickness broke him. Impatient, he cursed at first, but mended
6   Being anointed & all; tho' a heavenlier heart began some
7   Months earlier, since I had our sweet reprieve & ransom
8   Téndered to him. Ah well, God rést him áll road he éver offénded!

9   This often séeing the sick endéars them, to us, us too it endéars.
10 My tongue had taught thee comfort, touch had quenched thy tears,
11 Thy tears that touched my heart, child, Felix, poor Felix Randal;
12 How far from then forethought of, all thy more boisterous years,
13 When thou at the random grim forge, powerful amidst peers
14 Didst fettle for the great grey drayhorse his bright & battering sandal!

1880

Plate 383   OET No. 142: Felix Randal -- MS. 3 (B²)

(B²) B.14v--transcription of A by RB, inscribed in album B: his slip in 8 ("ever he" reversed) was corrected by GMH. Note the rather small "o" in 1 (cf. No. 120, B.10v, 9 and 11). In 6 "though" is abbreviated as "tho'" (cf. No. 101, sts. 5:6 and 7:7, B transcript). The comma after "forge" (13) is a very faint brown. In 14 the peculiar "t" in "great" seems a slip of the pen.

GMH revised "sooner" (7) to "éarlier"; del. "often" (9) and rev. "them, me" (leaving the comma by oversight); he added outrides in ink, (some differing from those in A and B¹); also the date. He inserted stresses in purple pencil in 1, 7, 8, 9, including two on his revisions.

MS K		OET No. 143
	Brothers. G.M.H.	
1	How lovely is love in brothers!	1
2	Dropped, locked in one another's	2
3	Being, I have watched this well,	3
4	As once my fortune fell -	4
5	Our Shrovetide plays drew on	5, 6
6	And a part was picked for John,	7
7	The young one. Fear and joy	8
8	Run in a revel in the elder boy -	9
9	Now the night came - All	10
10	The company was down the hall -	11
11	Henry by the wall	12
12	Beckoned one beside him -	13
13	So there I sat and eyed him,	14
14	His eye upon the play, but my play	15
15	Turned on tender byplay -	16, [17, 18] 19
16	He blushed, he bit his lip,	20
17	And droove with a diver's dip	21
18	Clasped hands down through clasped knees,	22
19	And with such marks as these	22
20	Told with what heart's stress	23
21	He hung on Jack's success -	24
22	Now Jack was brass : bold :	25
23	He had no work to hold	26
24	His heart up at the strain.	27
25	Nay, roguish ran the vein -	28
26	Two tedious acts were past	29
27	And Jack's cue come at last	30
28	When Henry, all heart-forsook,	31
29	Dropped eyes and dared not look.	32
30	But when that imp saw tongue,	33
31	And how the hall : rung!	34
32	O Harry, in his hands he flung	35
33	His tear-tricked cheeks of flame	36
34	For fond love and sweet shame -	37
35	Ah Nature framed in fault,	38
36	There's comfort then, there's salt;	39
37	Poor nature, base and blind	40
38	Dearly thou canst be kind -	41 [42 43]

Plate 384   OET No. 143: Brothers -- MS. 1: K

 K--transcription of a missing autograph made in her Commonplace Book, on two pages, by GMH's mother Kate, Mrs. Manley Hopkins. This represents the earliest surviving version, in 38 lines instead of 43. GMH was reworking the poem in August 1880 when he was at home in Hampstead (see date on Plates 388, 389). No MSS. of a still earlier form have survived, "written in stanzas in Wordsworth's manner" during the summer of the previous year (see L.i.86, 106). Line numbers in the right margin indicate the lineation of the final version.

 Queries, errors of copy. As usual Kate, though her pen could make points over an "i" or in an exclamation, commonly used a short dash instead of a period (4, 7, 8, 9, 10, 12, 15, 21, 25, 34, 38, but periods are found in 24, 29). In 3 after "Being" the original may have had an ambiguous comma/period where a period is clearly needed. Great colons are copied as ordinary colons in 22 ("brass : bold", not differentiated from the conventional colon which follows) and 31 ("hall : rung"). In 18 there is no grave to make two syllables of "clasped" (the transcript given me for the OET was in error). In 14 Kate prob. orig. miscopied the first "play" as "stage". In 31 "how" is mended, perhaps where the autograph had been revised. The transcription is a valuable record of an earlier version. For other transcripts by Kate see 313b, 374a.

 [opposite]   Plate 385   OET No. 143: Brothers -- MS. 2 - enlargement

 [H] H.i.44r--enlargement of lines 10 to 39, where there are most variants. See Plate 386 for the whole MS. with annotations.

PLATE 385. OET 143. *Brothers* • 207

(Rotated manuscript page — Hopkins's draft of "Brothers," with numbered lines in the left margin and variant readings keyed in the right margin.)

10	·Now the night come, all
11	·The company thronged the hall;
12	·Henry, by the wall,
13	·Beckoned me beside him,
14a	to [. . .] with him
15a	·came where called, and eyed him
16	·mean whiles, so that my play
17a	·Turned on tender byplay.
18a	And [. . .] his thought were Jack.
18b	The [. . .] thoughts all
19a	He smiled, blushed, bit his lip;
20	·drove with a diver's dip,
21	Clasped hands down through clasped knees,
22a	And with such signs as these
23a	Told see with what heart's stress
24a	He hung [. . .]'s success.
25	was brass: told
26	He had no work to hold
27	His heart up at the strain:
28	Nay, roguish ran the vein.
29a	Two tedious acts were past
30a	And Jack's cue given at last,
31b	when [. . .] all heart forsook,
31a	Dropped eyes and dared not look.
32	There! the hall rung,
33a	Young dog, he did give tongue
34a	And how the hall rung;
33b	But Harry, in his hands he has flung
35a	His tear-tricked cheeks of flame
36	For fond love and for shame.
37	Ah nature, framed in fault,
38	There's comfort then, there's salt.
39	[. . .]

Right-margin variants:

14c	Or . . . . eyed him
15b	mean whiles, so that my play
17c / 17d	For, all wrung on love's rack
18c / 18d / 18e	all jeoparded in Jack, / smiles, blushes, and bit his lip, / in Jack
19b	
17e	(= for the lad, all on love's rack
18f	wrung, all wrapped in Jack)
22b	By many a mark like these
23b	Saying with what heart's stress
24b	he hung on the imp's success.
29b	Two tedious acts were past
30b	Jack's call and cue at last;
31c	When Henry, heart-forsook,
33d / 34d	Young dog
34c	Dog, he did give tongue!
33e / 33f	And how the hall rung!
34b / 33f	Dog, he did give tongue!
35b / 35c	But Harry—in his hands he has flung
H.i. 44ᵛ	

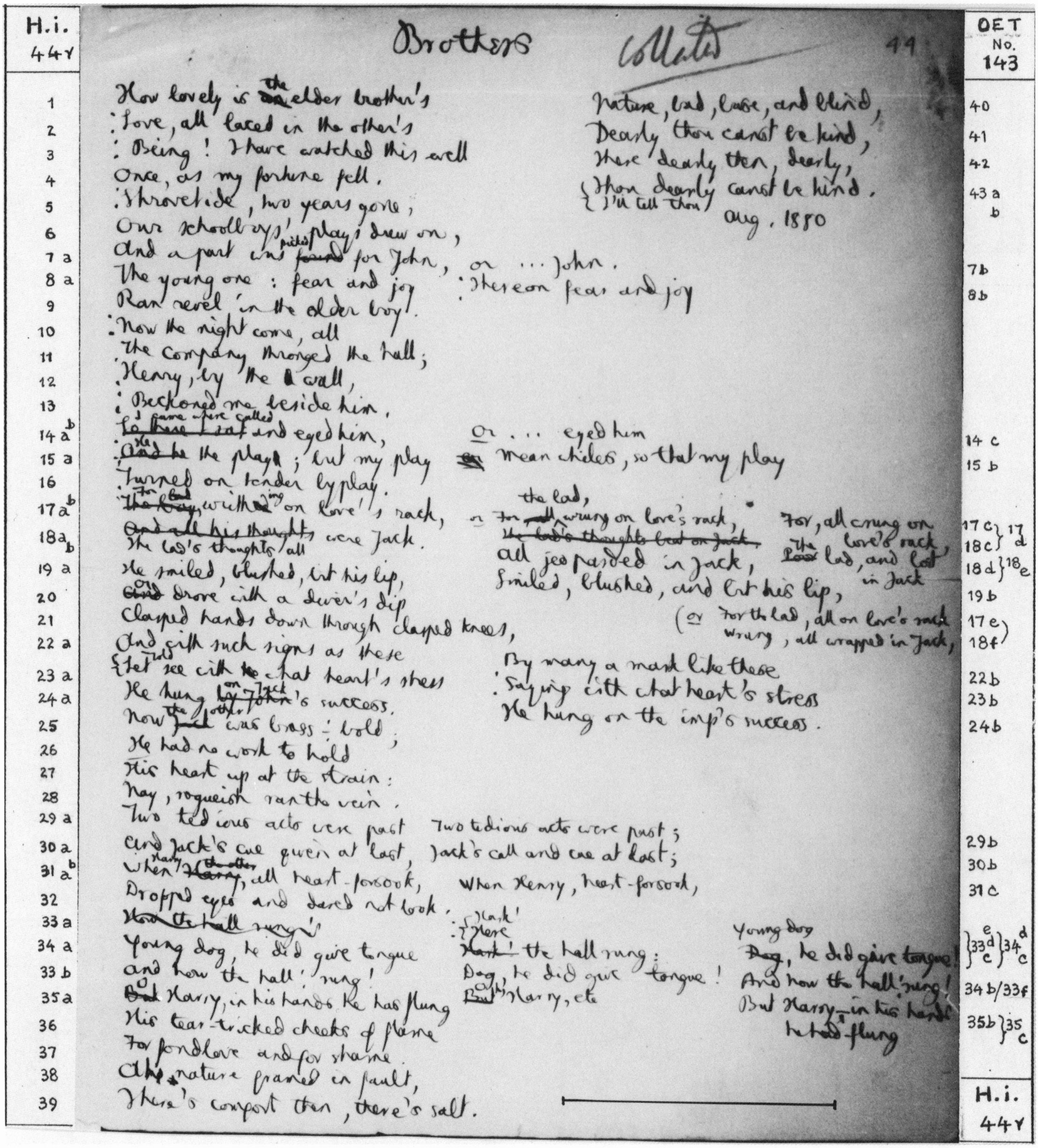

Plate 386　　OET No. 143:　Brothers -- MS. 2 (H)

H.i.44r--complete autograph version, with many revisions and marginal alternatives. (See Plate 385 for enlargement of some lines.) Note the great colons, opening eleven lines and occurring in others. Deletions, changes include: 1 "an"
7a, 8a "found" rev. to "picked"　"John,"　7b, 8b "John./ Thereon..."　9 "elder" mended to "older"　12 ╳ wall　14a "So there I sat" rev. to "I came where called"　15a orig. "And he the plays" [there was a double bill--see Plate 393]　15b "or" del. "Mean whiles" (two words)　16 Great colon before "Turned"　17 "The boy [or "lad"] writhed on love's rack" then "The boy, writhing..." then "For writhing..."　17c "For, all wrung" then "For the lad, wrung"　23a "Let see [bracketed with "Told"] with he[art's?]　33a "rung!"　35b "But Oh,"　35c "But Harry,--" (Note in the MSS the oscillation between "But"/"O"/"Oh Harry")　38 "O na" mended to "Ah, nature"

RB's purple pencil (1918) notes beside the title that this version has been "Collated"

PLATE 387. OET 143. *Brothers*   •   209

Brothers

How lovely is the elder brother's
Love, all laced in the other's
Being! I have watched this well
Once, as my fortune fell.
Shrovetide, two years gone,

Our schoolboys' plays drew on
And a part was picked for John
The young one: fear, joy
Run a revel in the elder boy.
Now the night come, all
Our company thronged the hall;
Henry, by the wall,
Beckoned me beside him;
I came where called and eyed him
And the play, though my play
Turned most on tender byplay.
For wrung all on love's rack,
And lost, my lad, in Jack,
Smiled, blushed, and bit his lip,
Or drove, with a diver's dip
Clutched hands down through clasped knees —
True tokens tricks like those;
Old telltales with what stress
He hung on the imp's success.
Now the other was brass-bold:
He had no work to hold
His heart up at the strain;
Nay, roguish ran the vein.
Two tedious acts were past;
Jack's call and cue at last;
When Henry, heart-forsook,
Dropped eyes and dared not look.
Hark! the hall rang.
Dog, he did give tongue!
But Henry — in his hands he has flung
His tear-tricked cheeks of flame
For fond love and for shame.

Ah nature, framed in fault,   Dearly, thou canst be kind —
There's comfort then, there's salt;   There dearly then, dearly
Nature, bad, base, and blind,   I'll cry thou canst be kind.
                                                                Hampstead. aug. 1880

Plate 387   OET No. 143: Brothers -- MS. 4 (D¹)

D. pp.80-81--autograph faircopy sent to Canon Dixon, along with No. 144, 16 Jan. 1881--see L.ii.174-5. Changes, etc. include: 17 "a[l]"   18 "And" rev. to "All"   34 "Dog!,"   37 "lov[e]" dittography from three words earlier.

The poem interested both Dixon and Bridges sufficiently to lead to various suggestions for improvement. Dixon "objected to the first four lines" while RB's criticisms began after that point (L.i.118). See Plate 391 (top) for GMH's letter of April 1881 to Dixon about the revisions he had made: Bridges was not satisfied and wanted the original version restored.

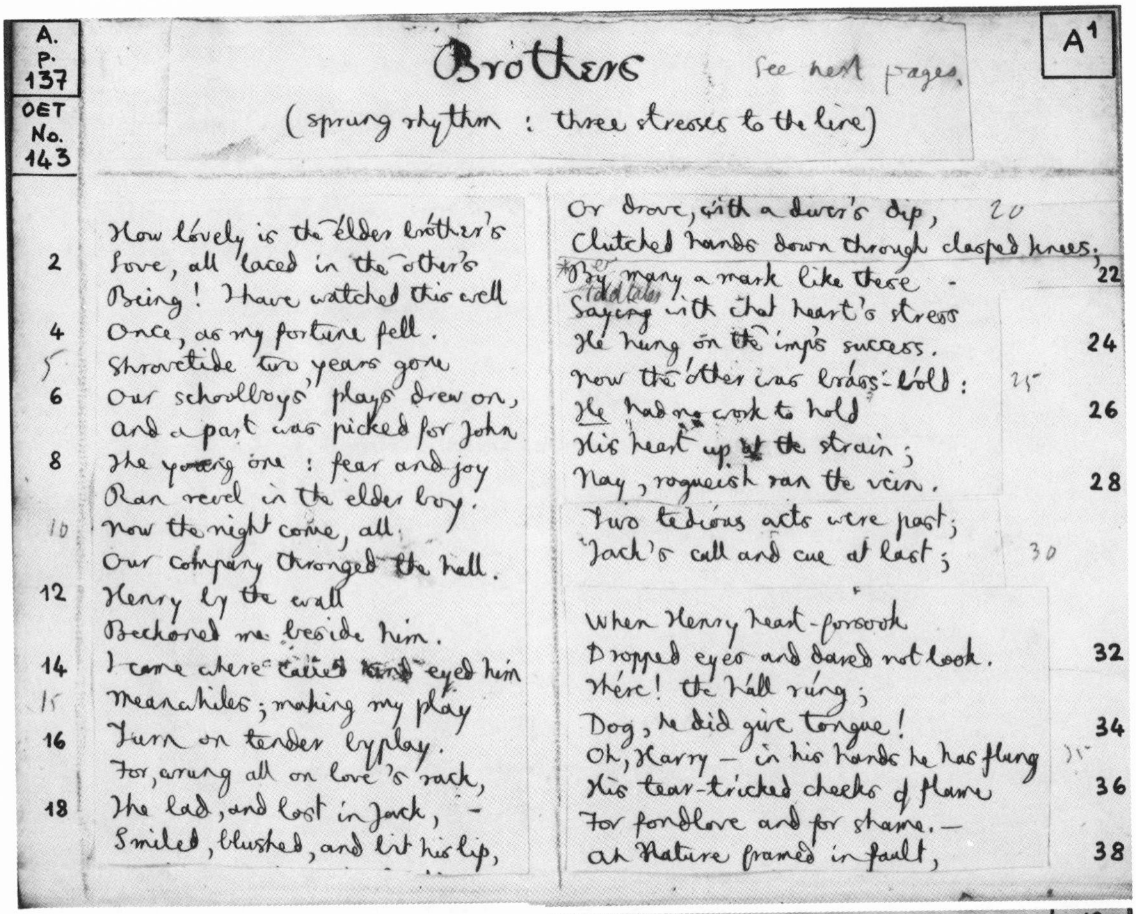

Brothers

(sprung rhythm : three stresses to the line)

How lovely is the elder brother's
2 Love, all laced in the other's
Being! I have watched this well
4 Once, as my fortune fell.
5 Shrovetide two years gone
6 Our schoolboys' plays drew on,
and a part was picked for John
8 The young one : fear and joy
Ran revel in the elder boy.
10 Now the night come, all;
Our company thronged the hall.
12 Henry by the wall
Beckoned me beside him.
14 I came where called and eyed him
15 Meanwhiles; making my play
16 Turn on tender byplay.
For, wrung all on love's rack,
18 The lad, and lost in Jack, —
Smiled, blushed, and bit his lip,

Or drove, with a diver's dip, 20
Clutched hands down through clasped knees;
By many a mark like these - 22
Saying with that heart's stress
He hung on the imp's success. 24
Now the other was brass-bold: 25
He had no crook to hold 26
His heart up at the strain;
Nay, roguish ran the vein. 28
Two tedious acts were past;
Jack's call and cue at last; 30

When Henry heart-forsook
Dropped eyes and dared not look. 32
There! the hall rung;
Dog, he did give tongue! 34
Oh, Harry — in his hands he has flung 35
His tear-tricked cheeks of flame 36
For fondlove and for shame. —
ah Nature framed in fault, 38

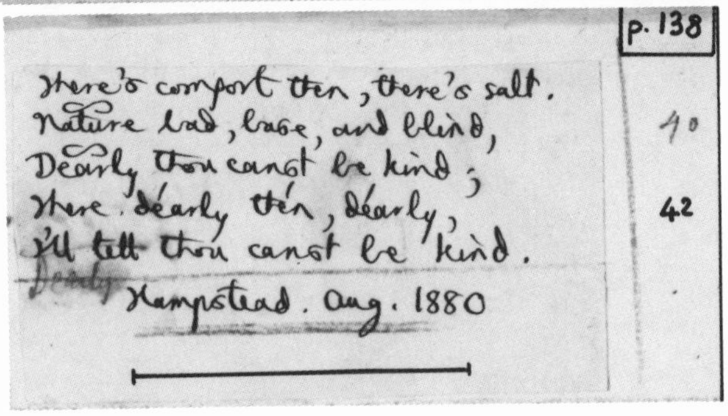

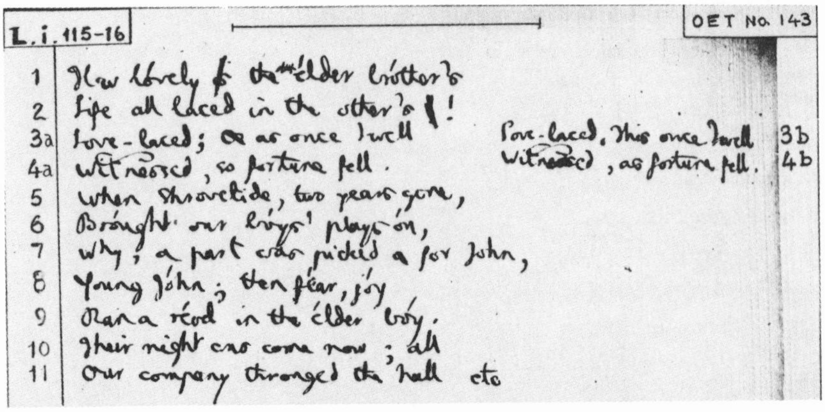

L.i. 115-16   OET NO. 143

1 How lovely of the elder brother's
2 Life all laced in the other's !
3a Love-laced; or as once I well
4a Witnessed, so fortune fell.   Love-laced. This once I well   3b
                                          Witnessed, as fortune fell.   4b
5 When shrovetide, two years gone,
6 Brought our boys' plays on,
7 why; a part was picked a for John,
8 Young John; then fear, joy
9 Ran a revel in the elder boy.
10 Their night was come now; all
11 Our company thronged the hall   etc

P. 138

There's comport then, there's salt.
Nature bad, base, and blind, 40
Dearly thou canst be kind;
there dearly then, dearly, 42
I'll tell thou canst be kind.

Hampstead. Aug. 1880

Plate 388   OET No. 143: Brothers -- MSS. 3 (A¹) and 5 (L)

(A¹) A.pp.137-138--autograph faircopy, prob. handed to RB while GMH was visiting his parents in Aug. 1880: by 5 Sept. he had already revised it (L.i.106, 109). RB cut it into six pieces and rearranged them for pasting into album A (tops of 20 are visible below 19, while 29, 30 are on a separate strip). At some stage another sheet (prob. not A², which has no thin patches) was gummed over it with a dark adhesive, traces of which remain on 8-14, 24-27. In 8 and 27 "young" and "at" are not del., and there is a gum mark, not punctuation, after "all" (10). In 26 "He" is underlined in ink. In 38 "nature" was mended to "N". Stress marks are in original ink (1, 25, 33; possibly on "with" in 20, though this is not confirmed by other MSS.

RB's red ink noted beside title: "See next pages" (i.e. A²), and he drew a line after 21 with an asterisk (see A²-- opposite--for the asterisk at the bottom of the left hand column and the top of it for that note:"hence read from version on last page", i.e. from A¹. He therefore records (1884) in red ink in A¹ GMH's revisions to B from 22 onwards: 22 "By &" for "And"   23 "Saying Told tales"   43 "I'll tell Dearly" (written below the line, across red pencil border). RB's pencil numbers every fifth line.

[bot. left] L.i.115-116 (MS Letters to Bridges, i.358)--draft revision of 1-11, found among GMH's papers after his death, on the back of part of a discarded letter to RB dated Jan. 23 [1881]. Note the stress marks in 6 (and cf. interim correction in B.22v). Changes include: 1 "is" and slur del.   2 "," [?]   3a orig. prob. "laced. On[ce?]"   7 "a" del.

PLATE 389. OET 143. *Brothers* • 211

Brothers

(sprung rhythm, three feet to the line; lines not overrove); and free-ended and reversed or counterpointed rhythm allowed in the first foot)

Hampstead. Aug. 1880

As revised Feb 1841 or January

※ hence read from version on last page

×† And many a mark like these

How lovely the elder brother's
Life all laced in the other's!
Love-laced — what once I well
Witnessed, so as fortune fell.
When Shrovetide, two years gone,
Our schoolboys' plays brought on,
Why, a part was picked for John,
Young John; then fear, then joy
Ran a revel in the elder boy.
Now night was come; all
Our company thronged the hall;
Henry, by the wall,
Beckoned me beside him:
I came there called, and eyed him
And the play; though my play
Turned most on tender byplay.
For, wrung all on love's rack,
All lost, my lad, in Jack,
Smiled, blushed, and bit his lip;
Or drove, with a diver's dip,
Clutched hands through clasped knees — ※

Truth's tokens tricks like these, ×
Told tell tales, with what stress
He hung on the imp's success.
Now the other was brass-bold:
He had no work to hold
His heart up at the strain;
Nay, roguish ran the vein.
Two tedious acts were past;
Jack's call and cue at last;
When Henry, heart-forsook,
Dropped eyes and dared not look.
Eh, how all rung!
Young dog, he did give tongue!
But Harry — in his hands he has
flung
His tear-tricked cheeks of flame
For fond love and for shame.
Ah nature, framed in fault,
There's comfort then, there's salt;
Nature, bad, base, and blind,
Dearly thou canst be kind;
There dearly then, dearly,
I'll cry thou canst be kind.

22
24
26
28
30
32
34
36
38
40

Plate 389   OET No. 143: Brothers -- MS. 6 (A²)

   (A²) A.pp.139-140--autograph faircopy of revised version, cut up and rearranged (the date had to be cut off below 43 and pasted under the title). Deletions by GMH: (metrical note) "overrove"   28 "rogueish" (see RB's note on B, Plate 391, concerning the omission of the "e", an 18th C. spelling)   33 "the" [hall etc.]   42 "th"[?]   Note GMH's three stresses in each of 2 (not, of course, on "in"), 8, 9, 15, 25, 33, 42. Many lines could be read as four-stress (e.g., 8, 9, 25).

   When RB in 1884 tried to transfer to an autograph GMH's revisions to the A¹ text which he had copied into MS. B, he found that these were in the first half of the poem extensive and closer to A² than to A¹. For lines 1-21 therefore he tried to make the A² text coincide with B (i.e. A¹) as revised by GMH, but at the bottom of the left column RB placed a red ink asterisk, referring to the red ink note at the top of that column: "hence read from version on last page" (i.e. A¹). Observe the revisions in 2, 4, 6, 7, 8, 9, 10, 15, 16, 18, 21 ("down", grave accent added to "clasped"), 22 (whole line del. and rewritten above), 23 (TOld tell tales"). RB failed to note changes in punctuation, and as the Introduction points out, he slipped up in line 10, telescoping the casting and rehearsals into a single day.   For RB's red-ink corrections in the second half see notes on Plate 388.

   RB's pencil (c. 1918) below the date notes that this version is "As revised Feb 1881 or January"--it was sent him in a letter begun 26 Jan., finished 8 Feb.. A further note below this (not shown on plate) was erased. RB also numbered every fifth line.

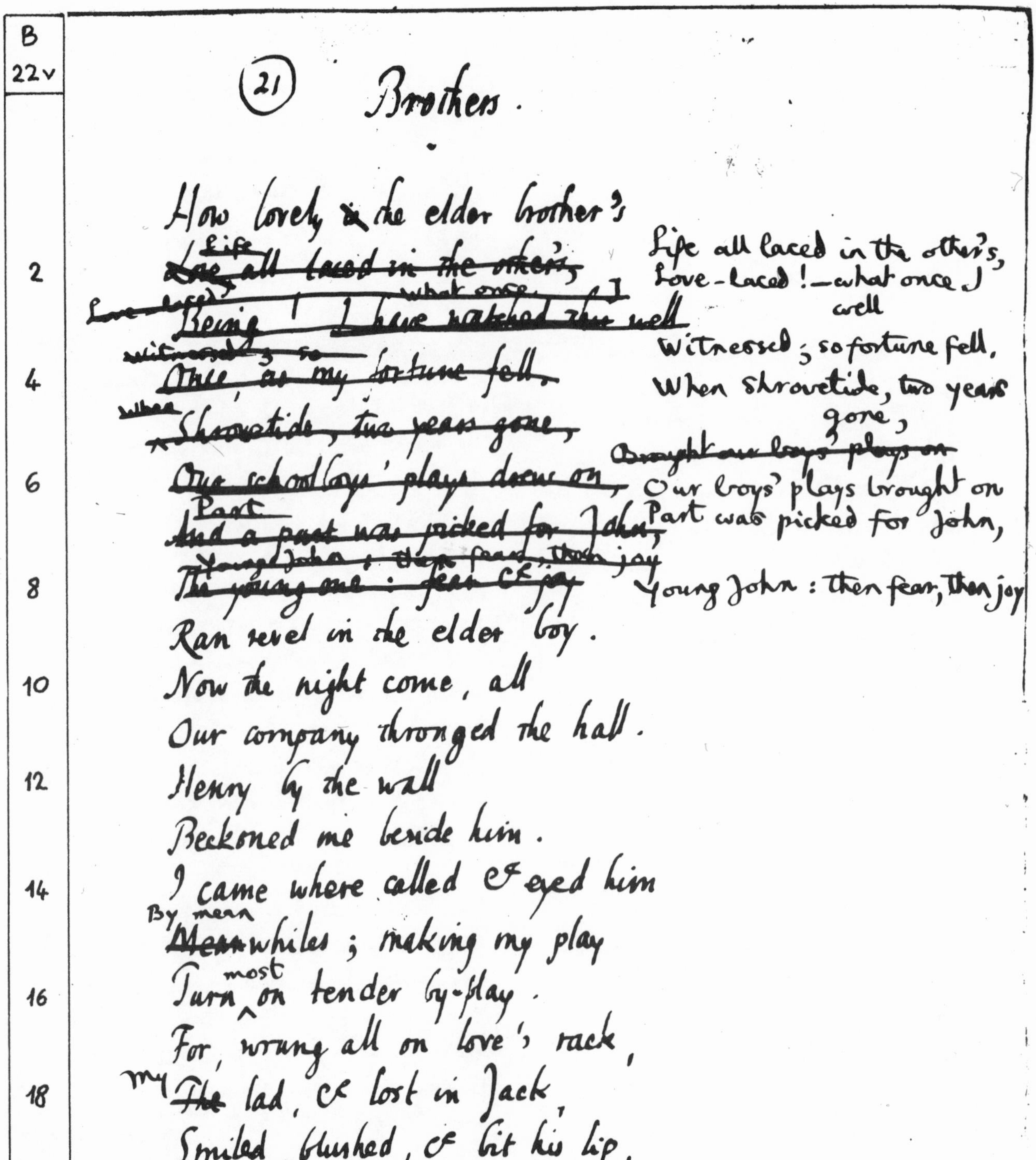

B
22v

(21) *Brothers.*

How lovely is the elder brother's

2 ~~Life all laced in the other's,~~ Life all laced in the other's,
   ~~Love-laced ! I have watched this well~~ Love-laced !—what once I
   Being   what once I well

4 ~~Once, as my fortune fell,~~ Witnessed; so fortune fell.
   when When shrovetide, two years
   ~~Shrovetide, two years gone,~~ gone,

6 ~~One schoolboys' plays down on,~~ Brought our boys' plays on
   Part Our boys' plays brought on
   ~~And a part was picked for John,~~ Part was picked for John,

8 ~~Young John: then fear, then joy~~ Young John : then fear, then joy
   ~~The young one: fear & joy~~

   Ran revel in the elder boy.

10 Now the night come, all
   Our company thronged the hall.

12 Henry by the wall
   Beckoned me beside him.

14 I came where called & eyed him
   By mean
   ~~Meanwhiles~~ ; making my play

16 Turn on tender by-play .
   most

   For, wrung all on love's rack,

18 my
   ~~The~~ lad, & lost in Jack,
   Smiled, blushed, & bit his lip.

20 Or drove, with a diver's dip,
   Clutched hands thro' claspèd knees ;

Plates 390, 391   OET No. 143: Brothers -- MSS. 7 (D²) and 8 (B)

[opposite]   (D²). Redraft of 1-4, in a letter to Dixon dated April 6 1881 (printed L.ii.49). The counterpoint signs are carelessly placed; 2, 3 orig. "other's--/Love-laced!"

[above top] B.22v (and oppos.) B.22v, 23r--transcription of A¹ by RB in album B. Plate 390 shows 1-21 full size; Plate 391 repeats these on a smaller scale along with 22-42, on a right-hand page to facilitate comparison with earlier left-hand plates. In 21 RB omitted "down" (presumably because the line had too many feet), a change GMH accepted--though it was prob. GMH who added the grave on "clasped". In 26 RB did not italicize "He". In 42 RB del. his own comma before "then" (a slip).

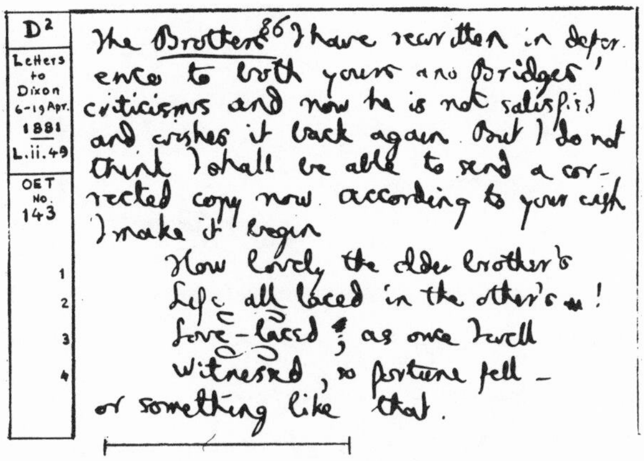

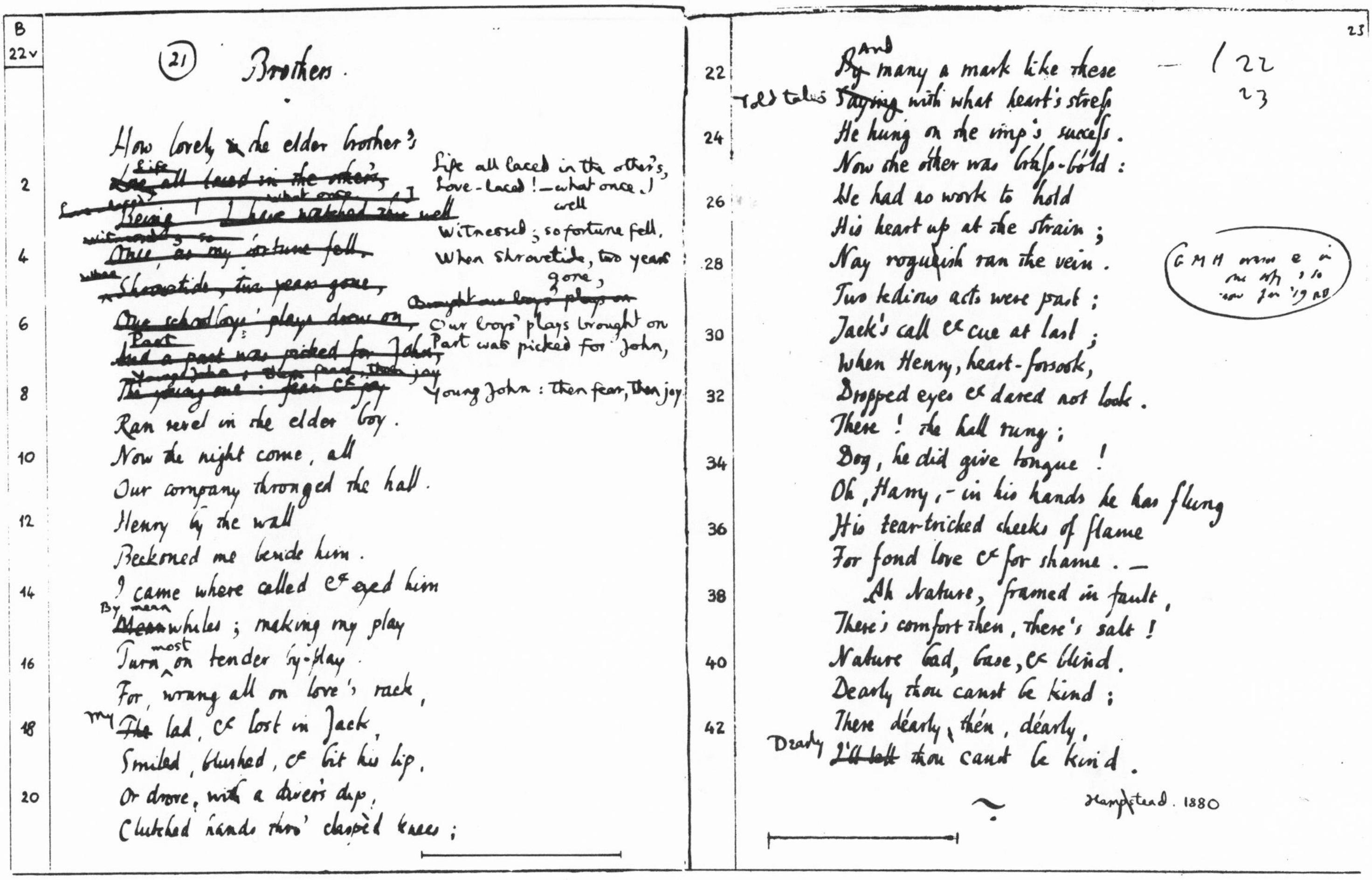

PLATE 391. OET 143. *Brothers* • 213

GMH at first interlined his revisions (except for 6, rewritten in right margin: "Brought our boys' plays on"), adding final commas for 2, 5, 7, and another after "Shrovetide" (5). His ink had dried when he decided to del. 2-8 (old and new) and to rewrite them all in the margin. He made verbal changes in 15, 16, 18, 22, 23, 43. He strengthened or inserted various stops, etc., elsewhere, e.g.: 1 "brother's" (apostrophe)   15 "whiles;"   27 "strain;"   30 "last;"   38 "Nature," (not in A[1])   40 "bad, base," (yet GMH left unchanged the period in mid-sentence after "blind")   He added three stresses in 25 and in 42, and in 39 seems to have changed "salt." to "salt!". He later added the date, but coming back to it afterwards he struck through "Hampstead" (perhaps because so much revision was carried out elsewhere).

RB notes (Jan. 1919) opposite "rogueish" (28): "GMH erases e in one copy I so now". He also numbered the troublesome lines 22, 23 in the margin.

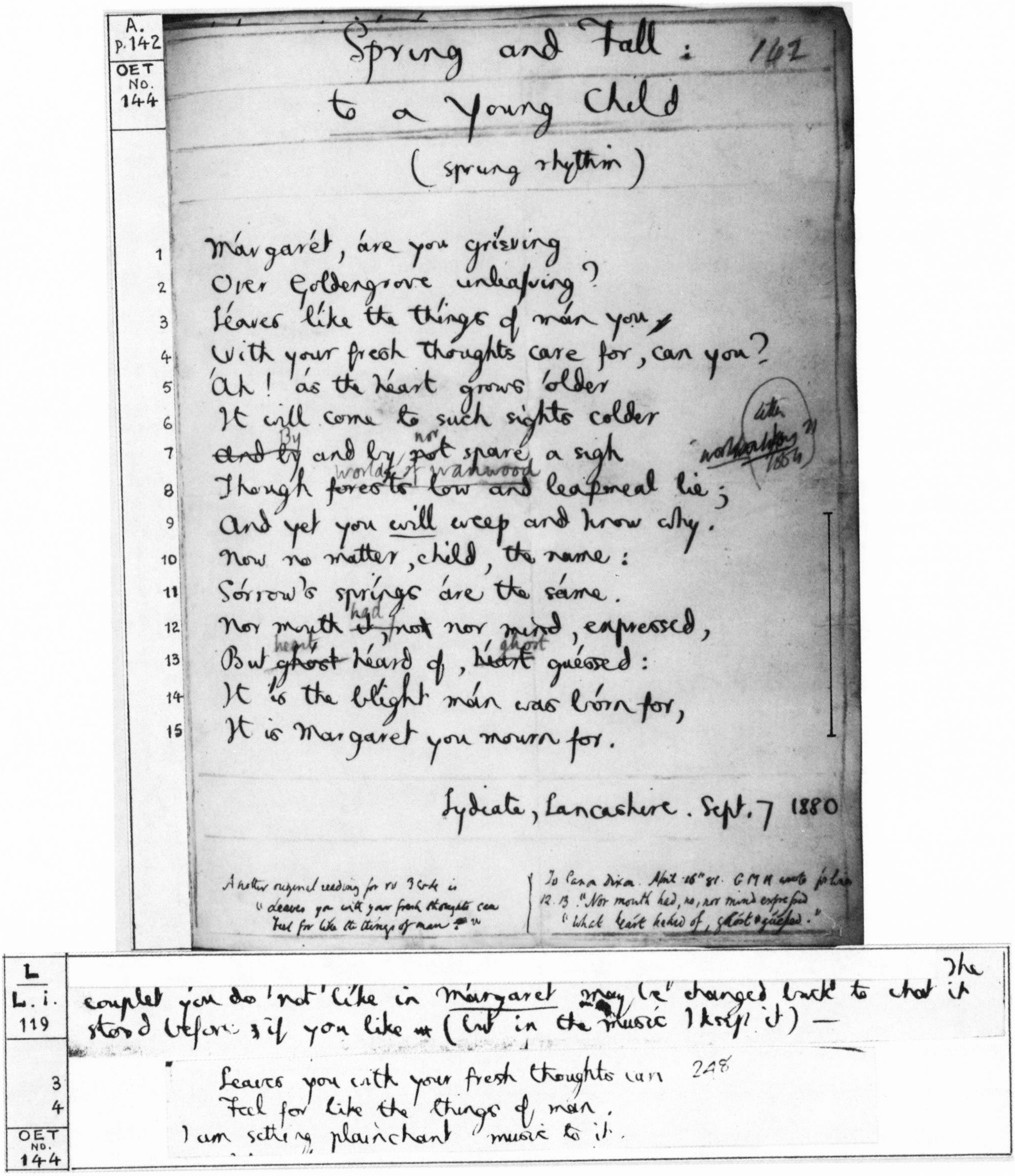
A. p.142

OET No. 144

Spring and Fall: 162

to a Young Child

(sprung rhythm)

Márgarét, áre you gríeving
Over Goldengrove unleafving?
Léaves like the things of mán you,
With your fresh thoughts care for, can you?
Áh! ás the héart grows ólder
It will come to such sights colder
And by By and by nor not spare, a sigh
Though forests low and worlds of wanwood leafmeal lie;
And yet you will weep and know why.
Now no matter, child, the name:
Sórrow's springs áre the sáme.
Nor mouth it had not nor mind, expressed,
But ghost heart héard of, héart ghost guéssed:
It is the blight mán was bórn for,
It is Margaret you mourn for.

Lydiate, Lancashire. Sept. 7 1880

worlds (letter Aug 21 1884)

Another original reading for vv 3 and 4 is "Leaves you with your fresh thoughts can Feel for like the things of man?"

To Canon Dixon. April 16th '81. GMH wrote for lines 12.13. "Nor mouth had, no, nor mind expressed "What heart heard of, ghost guessed."

L. L. i. 119

The couplet you do 'not' like in Márgaret may be changed back to what it stood before: if you like (but in the music I keep it) —

3 Leaves you with your fresh thoughts can 248
4 Feel for like the things of man.
I am setting plainchant music to it.

OET No. 144

Plate 392 OET No. 144: Spring and Fall -- MSS. 1 and 3 (A,L)

[top] A.p.142--autograph faircopy; metrical marks in same ink; "will" (9) underlined. Changes made by GMH are: 2 "unleafving" (3) "you," 12 "it, not nor mind" [cf. MS. D].

RB's red ink [1884] copies from GMH's revisions to B in: 8 "world of wanwood" ["s" in "worlds", omitted from B at first by GMH, added to A later by RB in black ink: RB pencils in margin a note "worlds (letter Aug 21 1884)"--"worlds" was also inked on top of the date]; 12-13 "it had" [comma not del. after "expressed", and "But" not changed to "What"]. At the foot RB adds (black ink): 'Another original reading for vv [verses] 3 and 4 is "Leaves you with your fresh thoughts can/Feel for líke the thíngs of man?"'. Beside it: 'To Canon Dixon. April 16th [6-19th] 81. GMH wrote for lines 12.13. "Nor mouth had, no, nor mind expressed/What heárt heárd of, ghóst guéssed."'

[bottom] L.i.119 (MS Letters to Bridges, i.247-8). GMH's letter to Bridges 26-7 Jan. 1881, after agreeing with some of RB's criticisms of "Brothers" (No. 143), quotes the orig. of 3, 4, a draft which has not survived.

PLATE 393. OET 143. *Brothers* • 215

A. M. D. G.

Mount St. Mary's College,

SHROVETIDE—1878.

"A MODEL KINGDOM:"

A Burlesque in one Act.

KING CHRONONHOTONTOLOGOS
    (a *sovereign* worth a *crown*) .... H. HOPKINS.
GENERAL BOMBARDINIAN
    (commanderissimo-in-chief) ... H. BROUGHTON.
ALDIBORONTIPHOSCOPHORNIO (a swell at Court)... W. CARTER.
RIGDUM-FUNNIDOS (a swell*er ater* courti*er*) ...... J. MARSLAND.
EUKNAYMIDOS (Captain of no *h*army)................ R. KERNAN.
SALPINGOPHALOS (Herald husband to)
    Sal Pingophale) .... J. BROADBENT.
SKINDALAMOPHRASTES (a right learned doctor) ... JN. WILSON.
PHARMACOPOIETES (a fast friend of the doctor,
    and more *stewdious*) . J. BRAMLEY.
CAPTAIN OF THE BODY-GUARD .... J. EDGE.
ROYAL BODY-GUARD .... R. WORDEN.
MARSHAL OF RECRUITS................................. J. McMAHON.
DRUM MAJOR .... J. GUDGEON.
BIG-DRUMMER .... J. ATKINSON.
CYMBALS .... D. CROSS.
TRIANGLE .... J. EDGE.
TRUMPETERS TWO .... { J. COONEY.
                 { G. PARGETER.
SAPPER AND MINER.................................. R. HOLDEN.
SCOTTISH LEGION................................... H. TREVOR.
IRISH BRIGADE...................................... M. FANNING.
ETHIOPIAN RESERVE .... J. KITCHIN.
TURKISH LEVY .... S. IMPERIALE.

LORDS, ATTENDANTS, FLUNKEYS, SERVANTS, SCULLIONS,
"BOOTS," "BUTTONS," PUNS, HORSES, ETC., ETC.

Scene—IN QUEERROUMANIA.

L. D. S.

A. M. D. G.

Mount St. Mary's College,

SHROVETIDE—1878.

"MAURICE, THE WOOD-CUTTER:"

A Melodrama in two Acts—BY C. A. SOMERSET.

PRINCE LEOPOLD .... D. CROSS.
BARON LIEBHEIM (Leopold's favourite) .... J. HART.
COUNT HARTENSTEIN................................ H. HOPKINS.
STEFFEN (An old peasant) .... J. MARSLAND.
MAURICE, THE WOOD-CUTTER)
    (Son to Steffen) .... A. DE VERE HAVERS.
HANS (friend to Maurice) .... W. CARTER.
DOMINIE STARRKOPF (Schoolmaster) .... J. EDGE.
GLANDOFF (Attendant on Count Hartenstein) ...... J. COONEY.
LYNX (Grand Usher at the Palace) .... JN. WILSON.
CAPTAIN MANHOOF .... F. FERGUSON.
RIEGEL (Prison Keeper).............................. J. BROADBENT.
BOLTZEN (Turnkey to Riegel) .... F. COUPE.
FRITZ (about 10 years old) } Sons to Maurice { J. ATKINSON.
ERNEST (about 9 years old) }   { S. IMPERIALE.

GUARDS, OFFICERS OF JUSTICE, ATTENDANTS.
PEASANTS, ETC.

L. D. S.

Plate 393   **OET No. 143: Brothers** -- The Playbills

    Fr. Francis Keegan, SJ, when he was teaching at Mount St. Mary's College, the scene of the story, discovered that the play was A Model Kingdom (adapted from a celebrated one act musical burlesque, with six scenes, by Henry Carey, 1734, Chrononhotonthologos--the Jesuit spelling shed an h), and that the bold young actor was apparently J. Broadbent, the herald in this production. The burlesque was a favourite at Stonyhurst (presented there in the Christmas holidays of 1851, 1875 and 1881). The "two tedious acts" alluded to in the poem (ℓ.29) formed the first play in the double-bill, a two-act melodrama, Maurice, the Wood-cutter, which in its non-Jesuit form had parts for 2 women, 12 men, 1 boy, plus supers, with 5 interior and 4 exterior scenes: any delays during numerous changes of scenery may have helped to make the "serious" play drag. The original play-bills, preserved at Mount St. Mary's College, have been described to me as printed in red and black on soft, rough yellow paper, a background which defeated earlier photocopiers. See the Hopkins Quarterly, 6.1, Spring 1979, 11-34, and my Reader's Guide, 140-141. For Jesuit play production traditions at Stonyhurst, see Percy Fitzgerald's Stonyhurst Memories (London: 1895), esp. chapters v, vii and xx.

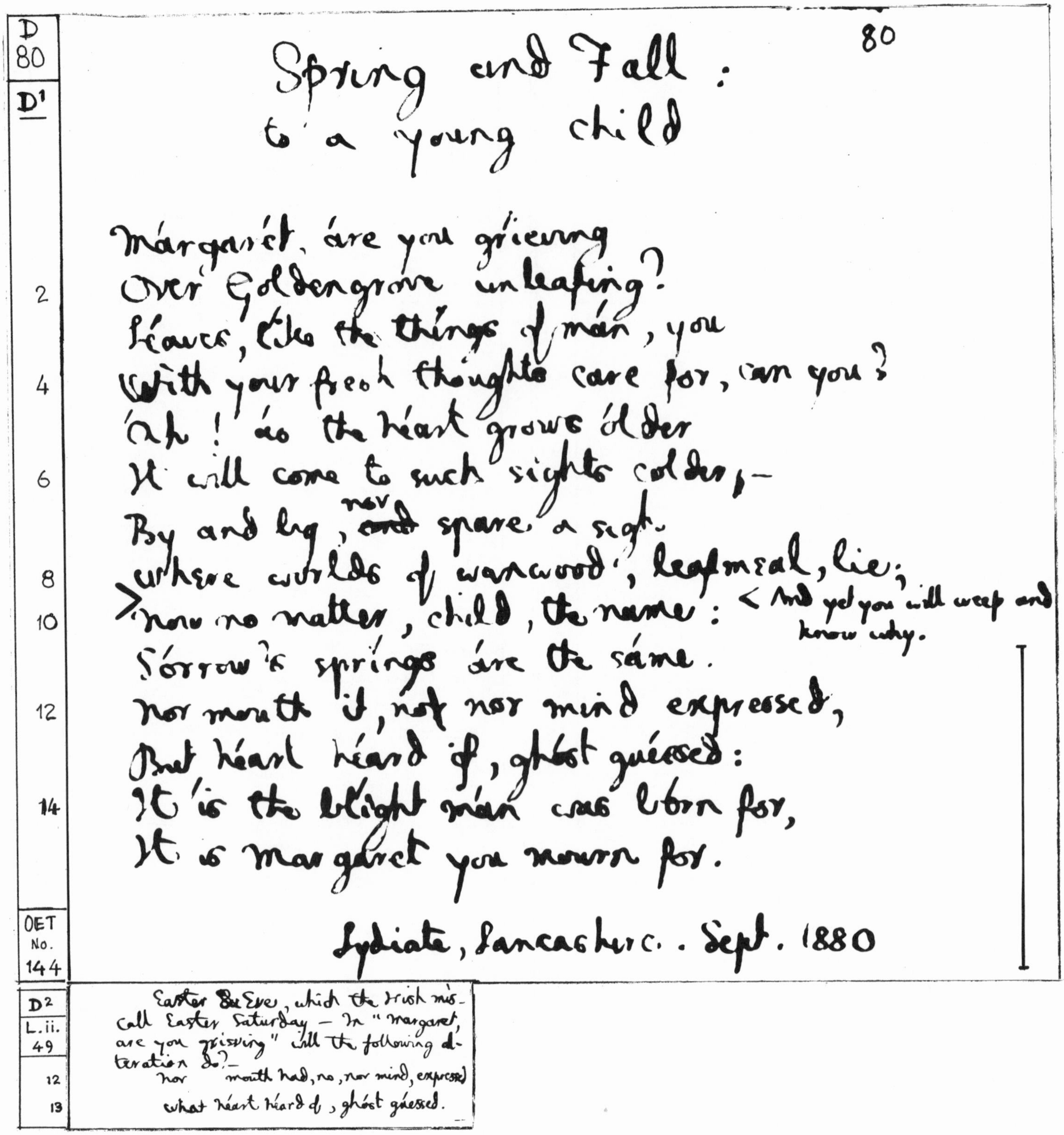

D
80

D¹

80

Spring and Fall :
to a young child

Márgarét, áre you gríeving
Over Goldengrove unleafing?
Léaves, like the things of mán, you
With your fresh thoughts care for, can you?
Áh! as the heart grows older
It will come to such sights colder,—

By and by, ~~and~~ ⁿᵒʳ spare a sigh.

2

4

6

> whére worlds of wanwood, leafmeal, lie;
Now no matter, child, the name : < And yet you will weep and know why.
Sórrow's springs are the same.
Nor mouth it, not nor mind expressed,
But heart heard of, ghost guéssed:
It is the blight mán was born for,
It is margáret you mourn for.

8
10

12

14

Lydiate, Lancashire. . Sept. 1880

OET
No.
144

D²
L.ii.
49

12
13

Easter Eve Eve, which the Irish mis-
call Easter Saturday — In "margaret,
are you grieving" will the following alteration do?—
nor   mouth had, no, nor mind, express)
what heart heard of, ghost guessed.

<u>Plate 394</u>   <u>OET No. 144: Spring and Fall</u> -- MSS. 2 and 4 (D¹ and D²)

[top]   D¹ (p.80)--autograph faircopy sent to Dixon along with No. 143 (Plate 387). <u>GMH's changes</u>: 6 "colder,-"
7 "~~and~~ nor"   9 line omitted, added in margin.   12 "it, not nor"   <u>Note</u> numerous stresses.

[below]   D²--L.ii.49, Letters to Dixon, 6-19 April 1881. Dixon greatly admired the poem, but suggested (L.ii.44, 24 Jan. 1881) that in 12, 13 the second line should be in common rhythm: "But heart heard of it, ghost guessed." This was GMH's inspired reply.

PLATE 395. OET 144. *Spring and Fall*   •   217

B
23 V

(22).

Spring & Fall:
to a young child.

Margaret, are you grieving
2   Over Goldengrove unleaving?
Leaves, like the things of man, you
4   with your ~~clear~~ fresh thoughts care for, can you?
Ah! as the heart grows older
6   It will come to such sights colder

       By   nor
~~And by & by, not~~ spare a sigh   Though worlds of wanwood leafmeal
8   ~~Though forests low & leaf=meal lie~~,   lie;
And yet you will weep & know why.
10   Now no matter, child, the name:
Sorrows springs are the same.

          had, no
12   Nor mouth ~~it~~, nor mind, expressed,   } see also confirmed
  what heart   ghost   in letter to RWD
~~But ghost~~ heard of, ~~heart~~ guessed: Ap 6 '81.
14   It is the blight man was born for,
It is Margaret you mourn for.

                   near Liverpool. 1881

2

OET
No.
144

Plate 395   OET No. 144: Spring and Fall -- MS. 5 (B)

    B.23v--transcription of A by RB, who corrected his own slips: 4 "clear"   12 "no" interlined after "it,"   In 8 RB hyphenated "leaf-meal" and in 9 he did not italicize "will" (stress in ink prob. added by GMH).

    GMH in revising added commas in 3, 4 after "Leaves" "man" "care for"   Other changes include: 7 "And by" rev. to "By" "not" rev. to "nor"   8 (margin) orig. "world"--"s" squeezed in later (see L.i.196)   12 "it" rev. to "had"   final comma del. (cf. A, final comma in 3)   13 Note that GMH's purple pencil stresses fall on two words in his revision.

    The date (added later) is wrong ("1881" for 1880). He did not add the apostrophe to "Sorrows" (11), but prob. inserted the stress on 'will' (9).

    RB's marginal note on 12, 13 reads: "see also confirmed in letter to RWD [Dixon] Ap 6 '81."

Vol. 1.2
July
1881

OET
NO.
145

34 *THE STONYHURST MAGAZINE*

*VERSIONS OF DRYDEN'S EPIGRAM
ON MILTON*

[THE following versions were made by boys on occasion of an examination. That which comes last is from an older pen.]

Three poets in three distant ages born,
Greece, Italy, and England, did adorn.
The first in loftiness of thought surpassed,
The next in majesty, in both the last.
The force of Nature could no farther go,
To make a third she joined the other two.

Dryden.

I.

Diverso terni florebant tempore vates
  Graius hic, ille Italus, tertius Anglus erat.
Eminet ingenio primus, gravitate secundus,
  Tertius at donis præstat utrique suis.
Promere nil majus potuit Natura creatrix;
  Externi nostro dos utriusque datur.

P. L.

II. *Philip Langdale.*

Hellados, Ausoniæ, nostræque Britannidis, ævo
  Diverso, vates tres viguere decus.
Sublimi ingenio Graius, gravitate Latinus
  Est melior: laudem noster utramque rapit.
Nec vires proferre ultra Natura valebat:
  Juncta itaque Angligenæ dona utriusque dedit.

H. C. J.

Henry John.

THE STONYHURST MAGAZINE 35

III.

Primum Argos, tum Roma, et deinde Britannia—
  vates
  Tempore diverso tres peperere sibi,
Primo magniloquæ est altæ sententia mentis,
  Lingua alter versus nobiliore canit.
Majorem nequiit Natura creare; priores,
  Tertius ut fieret, miscuit illa duos.

C. A. N.

IV. *C. Newdigate.*

Tres tria sæcla ferunt vates; hunc Hellas, at illum
  Italia, extremum terra Britanna parit,
Altior est animis primus, numerisque secundus,
  Tertius egregium nomen utrinque gerit.
Tantæ molis erat magnum generare poetam
  Hoc tantum potuit jungere Diva duos.

H. K.

V. *Henry Keating.*

Ævo diversi tres et regione poetæ
  Hellados, Ausoniæ sunt Britonumque decus.
Ardor in hoc animi, majestas præstat in illo,
  Tertius ingenio junxit utrumque suo.
Scilicet inventrix cedens Natura labori
  "Quidquid erant isti" dixerat "unus eris."

G. H.

Gerard Hopkins SJ.

---

52 COWPER'S WORKS.

I have often wondered that Dryden's illustrious epigram on Milton,† (in my mind the second best that ever was made) has never been translated into Latin, for the admiration of the learned in other countries. I have at last presumed to venture upon the task myself. The great closeness of the original, which is equal, in that respect, to the most compact Latin I ever saw, made it extremely difficult.

Tres tria, sed longè distantia, sæcula vates
  Ostentant tribus è gentibus eximios.
Græcia sublimem, cum majestate disertum
  Roma tulit, felix Anglia utrique parem.
Partubus ex binis Natura exhausta, coacta est,
  Tertius ut fieret, eonsociare duos.

Plate 396   Milton (Dryden's epigram translated into Latin)
     In this epigram (1688) Dryden compares the world's three greatest epic poets, Homer, Virgil and Milton.
     i. Stonyhurst Magazine, Vol. 1, no. 2, July 1881, 34-5. No MS. The reproduction is from the editorial files in Stonyhurst, which give the composers' names: I. Philip Langdale; II. Henry C. John, as sports news on the same page reveals, was an outstanding batsman and bowler in "London" (as distinct from Stonyhurst) cricket. He matriculated with General Hons. in 1879 and later became a merchant in Karachi, India. III. C.A. Newdigate, who matriculated in 1881. At the time of the Stonyhurst Centenary Record he was Master of Rhetoric in his old school (1890-93). IV. Henry Keating. V. Gerard Hopkins, SJ.

     Ross Kilpatrick is reminded of his own Oxbridge teachers of Latin composition by the way GMH frees himself from the sort of close rendering which is liable to restrict, and to produce unnatural Latin: he achieves an unexpected ending by making Nature address Milton directly in simple words--the only one to do so. He is not afraid to use English words derived from the Latin ones where they seem the nearest equivalent ("poetae" and "majestas" are lighter than "vates" and "gravitate"). H.C.J.'s composition "would do for a 17th century epitaph: GMH sounds like Ovid" (R.K.).
     ii. William Cowper, letter to Rev. Wm. Unwin, from Olney, July 11, 1780, in Cowper's Works, ed. T.S. Grimshawe, London, Wm. Tegg, 1851, p.52. This version is added for the diversion of classical scholars.

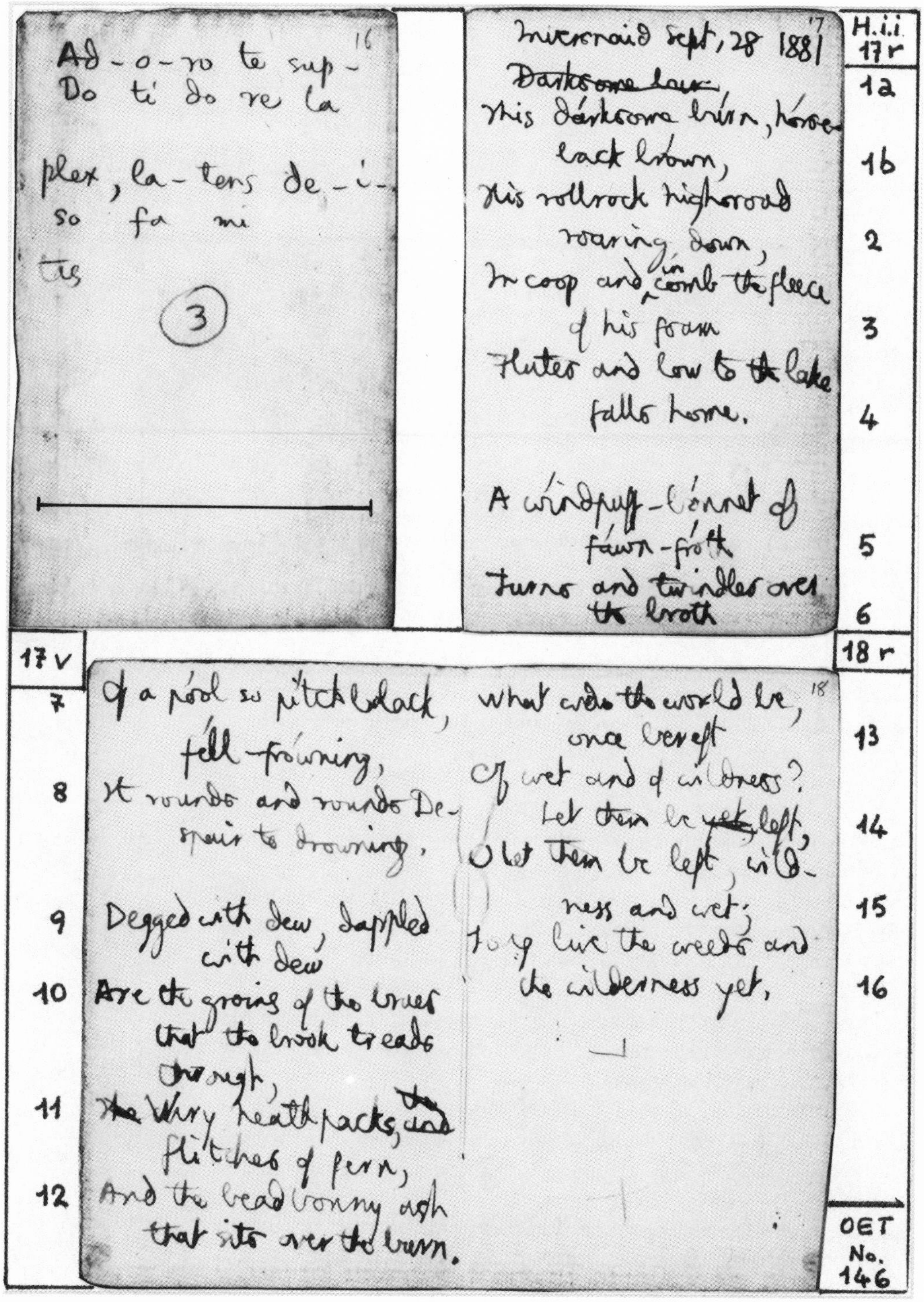

PLATE 397. OET 146. *Inversnaid* • *219*

Manuscript facsimile (H.ii.17r, 18r, 17v):

H.ii.17r (left panel):

Ad – o – ro te sup –
Do ti do re la

plex, la – tens de – i –
so   fa   mi

tis

③

H.ii.17r (right panel):

Inversnaid Sept, 28 1881

~~Darksome bur~~,
This darksome burn, horse-
back brown,
His rollrock highroad
roaring down,
In coop and in comb the fleece
of his foam
Flutes and low to the lake
falls home.

A windpuff-bonnet of
fáwn-fróth
Turns and twindles over
the broth

line numbers: 1a, 1b, 2, 3, 4, 5, 6

17v:

Of a pool so pitchblack,
fell-frówning,
It rounds and rounds De-
spair to drowning,

Degged with dew, dappled
with dew
Are the groins of the braes
that the brook treads
through,
The wiry heathpacks,
flitches of fern,
And the beadbonny ash
that sits over the burn.

line numbers: 7, 8, 9, 10, 11, 12

18r:

What would the world be,
once bereft
Of wet and of wildness?
Let them be ~~yet~~ left,
O let them be left, wild-
ness and wet;
Long live the weeds and
the wilderness yet,

line numbers: 13, 14, 15, 16

OET No. 146

Plate 397   OET No. 146: Inversnaid -- H

H.ii.16r ('Adoro te supplex'--tonic solfa tune; see No. 100),

17r.v. 18r--sole autograph of 'Inversnaid', both written in pages taken from a tiny notebook 56 x 88 mm. Deletions, etc.: 1a "Darksome bur[n]"   11 "The w[mended to] Wiry...and/the"   13 "What wi[ll?]" mended to "wd."   14 "yet," [his mind slipped to 16]   Note the periods like commas ending 8, 16. Some appreciative comments on the poem, written in pencil by readers, have been erased below 16.

PLATE 398

OET No. 147

The Song of Chaucer's Clerk of Oxenford, "*Angelus ad Virginem.*"

EVERY student of Chaucer will remember his description of the Clerk of Oxenford in "The Milleres Tale," in whose chamber

> All about there lay a gay sautrie,
> On which he made on nightes melodie,
> So swetely that all the chambre rong :
> And "*Angelus ad Virginem*" he song,
> And after that he song the kinge's note :
> Full often blessed was his merrie throte.

The "kinge's note" was the national anthem of the time, the stirring martial song which was sung at the head of the forces before battle, like the song of Roland at the Battle of Hastings. But the sacred song which he sang first of all, the "Angelus ad Virginem," has been lost for centuries, and it is only a few weeks since that it was discovered among the manuscripts of the British Museum by a zealous student and learned antiquarian, the Rev. H. Combs. It was found among the Arundel MSS (248), and is written in a small but beautifully clear hand. Of the date we shall have a word to say presently. One inaccuracy runs through it, that the Anglo-Saxon þ, or *th*, is repeatedly written for *h*. Otherwise it is careful and fairly correct. Probably the transcriber in copying it from an old MS. did not advert to the spelling of the words, but copied on uncritically from the original.

The collection of Arundel MSS. in the British Museum is well known to every English antiquarian. Many of them passed into the hands of the Arundels from the famous Sir Henry Savile, who was Warden of Merton College, Oxford, and Provost of Eton, in the reign of James the First, and founded the Savile professorships in his own University. The MS. with which we are

Plates 398-407b   OET No. 147: Angelus ad Virginem

The Month, vol. 44, Jan. 1882, 100-111: "The Song of Chaucer's Clerk of Oxenford, 'Angelus ad Virginem'." In the Miller's Tale (line 3216), Chaucer mentions the sacred song of the Angel to the Virgin as being sung by the poor scholar of Oxford. This song was a paraphrase in Middle English, made c. 1300, of a medieval Latin sequence on the Annunciation. All knowledge of it had disappeared for centuries when, towards the end of 1881, the Rev. H. Combs found a copy in the British Museum Library (Arundel MS. 248, f. 154a, still its only known source). He mentioned his discovery to the philologist F.J. Furnivall (founder of the Early English Text Society and the Chaucer Society, etc.), and also to Fr. Richard Clarke, SJ, both of whom decided to publish it. Clarke, a former Fellow of St. John's, Oxford, until he became a Catholic, had studied theology at St. Beuno's College along with Hopkins: in a letter of March 2 1876 to his mother Hopkins mentions that he and Clarke were one of only two pairs who reached Moel Fammau on a long walking expedition (L.iii.137). Clarke had just taken over as editor of the Jesuit magazine The Month, and decided to rush out an article on the song for his first number, Jan. 1882. Furnivall examined the Latin and M.E. more carefully and published an edition, with a facsimile of the MS, in a volume for the Chaucer Society, 1st. series, No. 73, pp.695-6: it did not appear until 1885.

Hopkins in 1881-82 was making his Tertianship (or second Novitiate) at Manresa House, Roehampton, close to London. He wrote to his mother about the find on Christmas Eve 1881 (L.iii.161). Along with the Latin and the Middle English there was "a modernisation of the latter..., made originally by me but altered since, perhaps not altogether for the better. The footnotes on the old english [i.e., Middle English] are mostly by me." As none of his drafts have survived it is impossible to determine exactly what sentences are his, but I draw attention to some which seem to have his special flavour.

PLATE 399. OET 147. Angelus ad Virginem   •   *221*

The Song of Chaucer's Clerk of Oxenford.   101

concerned was one of this number. It was given to Savile by his father-in-law,[1] Thomas Foxcroft of Christall. On fol. 4 is written—

Liber Henrici Savil junioris, ex dono Thomæ Foxcroft de Christall.

And on fol. 73, the following doggerel—

> Thomas Bromhead is my name,
> And with my hand I wratt the same.

And on fol. 94, in the same hand—

Thomas Brumead of Bromley within the paris of Ledes, gentleman.

All of these are in a hand of the time of James the First.

From the above data we gather that the MS. came from Bromley, near Leeds, and by some means passed into the possession of the Foxcrofts, who handed it on to Savile. Now Bromley belonged to the domain of Kirkstall, where was the well known Cistercian monastery. We may therefore reasonably conjecture that our MS. was in the possession of that monastery at the time of its suppression, when its literary treasures were scattered about the surrounding country.

So far for its origin. The MS. is a 4to, on vellum. It is written by various hands, and dates from the reign of Edward the First. It contains some very suggestive notes on the Sunday Gospels, treatises entitled *Liber de doctrina dicendi et tacendi*, *Liber consolationum*, &c., as well as a number of beautiful hymns, of which we give a verse or two before passing on to the one which now immediately concerns us. On fol. 154 *b* is a sequence relating to St. Mary Magdalen—

> Spei vena, melle plena
> Collaudatur Magdalena
>   Cordis, oris jubilo,
> Per quam reis innotescit
> Vitæ via, ac patescit
>   Lapsis reparatio.
> Forma patens pœnitendi
> Et exemplar resurgendi
>   Datur ista miseris ;
> Quæ commissa pie flevit,
> Et per fletum abolevit
>   Cuncti noxam criminis.

[1] Peacock's List of Yorkshire Roman Catholics, p. 2, note.

102 *The Song of Chaucer's Clerk of Oxenford,*

On fol. 155 is a hymn to our Lady, which begins as follows—

> Ave, virgo virginum, parens Genitoris,
> Salve, lumen luminum, radius splendoris,
> Salve, flos convallium, stella veri roris,
> > Nostra spes in te.

On fol. 133, one in more serious strain—

> Memorans novissima, cogitans futura,
> Quam horrida, quam aspera sit mortis hora dura,
> Quod secundum merita post mortem redditura
> Sit justis, et reprobis tortura.

But the reader who cares to examine further will find in the printed Catalogue of the Arundel MSS. all that he requires.

What is specially interesting to us is the date of the present hymn. It was evidently a popular melody in Chaucer's time (1350), and was chosen by him as the best representative of the religious hymn or song or lay then prevalent. This gives it a peculiar value. It belongs to a time when Church music was under the patronage of kings. Richard Cœur de Lion was celebrated throughout Europe for his passionate love of music, and under the succeeding kings it flourished none the less. John of Peckham, who was consecrated Archbishop in 1279, wrote pious Latin hymns to be sung in the churches.[2] John of Hoveden (or Howden), chaplain to Eleanor of Castile, Queen of Edward the First, was himself a skilful musician and the author of many hymns on the Passion, the Blessed Sacrament, our Lady, &c. We cannot exactly determine how many years before the time of Chaucer our hymn was written,[3] but we have certain data from which we may form a reasonable conjecture.

Among the pieces in the same MS., Arundel 248, is a translation or adaptation, a part of which corresponds almost exactly to the *Stabat Mater*. Now the *Stabat Mater* was in all probability the work of Jacopo de Benedictis, who lived under Pope Boniface (1294—1303). This would bring the date of the MS. quite to the close of the thirteenth century. It is how-

---

[2] "Hic Johannes carminum erat dictator egregius" (Tanner's *Bibliotheca*, p. 585). One of these hymns commenced—

> Ave vivens hostia, veritas et vita.

Another is a sequence to the Blessed Trinity, beginning—

> Deum Trinum Adoremus
> Tres in uno.

[3] "Johannes Hovedenus fuit musicæ sacræ addictissimus" (Tanner, *Ibid.* p. 415).

MONTH
vol.44
p.103

OET
No.
147

End
of
Introd.

"Angelus ad Virginem."   103

ever possible that the *Stabat Mater* may have been previously in circulation in a shorter form, and therefore no conclusion can be absolutely drawn from the similarity between the two pieces. But there is no doubt that our hymn must have been in circulation some fifty years at least before the middle of the fourteenth century. It had had time to be quoted as a representative of its class and as a familiar ditty. If it is really subsequent to the *Stabat Mater*, its rapid spread is not to be wondered at. Its extreme beauty and elegance would soon give it a wide circulation, and the music accompanying it is excellently suited to the words. It is indeed a treasure which Mr. Combs has discovered, exceedingly interesting to the antiquarian, but of a very special interest to the Catholic.[4]

[4] For those who take an interest in the scansion of mediæval hymns we subjoin the following analysis of the Latin metre :

Each of the 5 verses contains 10 lines, of which 1 and 3 are trochaic, the rest iambic. The trochaic lines are technically called trochaic dimeters catalectic, consisting of 3½ feet—

án - ge | lús ad | vír - gi | ném ‖

Of the iambic lines, 2 and 4 and 9 are iambic dimeters catalectic, consisting like the trochaic lines of 3½ feet—

sùb ín | trans ín | con - clá | ve ‖

5 and 6 are dimeters catalectic, *i.e.*, consist of a full 4 feet—

a - vé | re - gí | na vír | gi - núm ‖

8 and 10 are dimeters brachycatalectic, *i.e.*, are a foot short of the double metre, or consist of 3 feet—

sa - lú | tem | hóm | i - núm ‖

While 7 is a trimeter catalectic, or 5½ feet—

con - cí | pi - és | et pá | ri - és | in - táct | a ‖

The feet, whether trochees or iambi, are of course the accentual feet of popular poetry.

The English metre reproduces the Latin exactly, as will be found when allowance has been made for the *e* of inflection, which is sounded or dropped freely. In the English, however, there is this curious addition. The 8th and 10th lines of each stanza have in the Latin a peculiar grace of cadence, due to the way in which, though consisting properly of three (accentual) iambic feet of two syllables, they naturally fall into two feet of three syllables (mostly dactylic feet), and so give rise to a counterpoint rhythm. It was not possible to reproduce this grace in the English, owing to the shortness of the words, which are much more often monosyllables than in Latin. In compensation the translator has aimed at another effect : in each 8th and 9th line he seems to have supplied mid-line rhymes, at the 3rd syllable of the line, and by this means also of necessity changed the rhythm, breaking the line up into two shorter lines of three syllables each, and giving at the break or place of meeting the kind of rhythmic effect called *antispastic* or reversing. This may have been suggested to him by the phrasing of the music at this place. Thus he has : Flésh of *thée,* | máiden bríght, ‖ mánkind *frée* | fór to máke —'All man*kín*' | wórth ybóught ‖ Thórough *thí[ne]* | swéet childíng—Thát I *síth* | hís will is ‖ Máiden *wíth* | óuten láw — Whére through *ús* | cáme God wón ‖ Hé bought *ús* | óut of pain —'Us give *fór* | thíne sáke ‖ Hím so *hére* | fór to sérven.

---

a

b

c

Plate 401   OET No. 147: Angelus ad Virginem -- End of Introduction

The Month, p.103.   (a) The MS sets out each stanza continuously, without the usual line layout. Although the Month decided to arrange the poem into 10-line stanzas, Hopkins in his modernised version subdivided the seventh line of each into three, having skilfully imitated the rhyming device in the Latin and, in effect, converting the 10-line format into 12-line units. He appears, therefore, to have anticipated the decision of F.J. Furnivall, a professional linguist, whose 12-line stanzas have been approved by later editors: in the Latin the Month's seventh line is now always split to provide end-rhymes, e.g., "Concipies/Et paries/Intacta."   (b) The variable sounding or dropping of the final e in Chaucer is mentioned by GMH in a letter to Bridges of 5-13 Sept. 1880 (L.i.108).   (c) Since GMH had imparted an unorthodox and prosodic meaning to the music term "counterpoint", readers of the Month are unlikely to have understood his suggestion that two different rhythms might be generated simultaneously in the mind.

MONTH Vol.44 p.104	104 *The Song of Chaucer's Clerk of Oxenford,*	FURNIVALL line nos.	
OET NO. 147	LATIN VERSION OF THE THIRTEENTH CENTURY.[5]	St.1	
St.1			
1	Angelus ad Virginem	1	
2	Subintrans in conclave,	2	
3	Virginis formidinem	3	
4	Demulcens inquit "Ave!	4	
5	Ave! Regina Virginum,	5	
6	Cœli terræque Dominum	6	
7	Concipies et paries intacta	7/8/9	
8	Salutem hominum,	10	
9	Tu porta cœli facta,	11	
10	Medela criminum."	12	
St.2		St.2	
1	"Quomodo conciperem,	1	
2	Quæ virum non cognovi?	2	14
3	Qualiter infringerem	3	
4	Quod firma mente vovi?"[6]	4	16
5	"Spiritus Sancti gratia	5	
6	Perficiet hæc omnia:	6	18
7	Ne timeas, sed gaudeas secura,	7/8/9	
8	Quod castimonia	10	22
9	Manebit in te pura,	11	
10	Dei potentia."	12	24
St.3		St.3	
1	Ad hæc virgo nobilis	1	
2	Respondens inquit ei:	2	26
3	"Ancilla sum humilis	3	
4	Omnipotentis Dei	4	28

[5] In the MS. each stanza is written continuously: in all other respects the above reproduction is exact. The full stops and colons are employed by the scribe to mark off the lines, not the sense; and are sometimes omitted.

[6] These lines show the general acceptance in England, at the time this hymn was written, of the fact of our Lady having vowed her virginity to God previously to the Incarnation. It is true that it is a necessary consequence of her words in the Gospel, for if she had simply stated the fact of her being a virgin at the time of the Angel's visit, his natural answer would have been, as the French preacher, Le Jeune, well puts it, "Vous ne connaissez point d'homme, mais vous en pourrez connaître." But it is satisfactory to find that the explicit belief is proved to have existed among our Catholic ancestors so generally as to find its way into a popular song.

PLATE 403. OET 147. Angelus ad Virginem • 225

MONTH Vol. 44 / OET NO. 147	"*Angelus ad Virginem.*" 105	FURNIVALL line nos.	
St.1	ENGLISH VERSION OF THE THIRTEENTH CENTURY.	**St.1**	
1	Gabriel fram evene king	1	
2	sent to þe maide swete :	2	
3	broute þire blisful tiding : [7]	3	
4	and faire þe gan hire grete[n].	4	
5	heil be þu ful of grace arith.	5	
6	for godes sone þis euene lith.	6	
7	al for mannes loven wile man bicomen and taken	7/8/9	
8	fles of þe maiden brith	10	
9	maken fre for to maken	11	
10	Of senne and devles mith.	12	
Sr.2		**St.2**	
1	Mildeliche im gan andsweren	1	
2	þe milde maiden þanne.	2	14
3	wiche wise sold ichs beren	3	
4	child with huten manne.	4	16
5	þangle seide ne dred te nout.	5	
6	þurw þoligast sal ben iwrout	6	18
7	þis ilche þing. war of tiding ichs bringe.	7/8/9	
8	al manken wrth ibout [8]	10	22
9	þur þi swete chiltinge :	11	
10	and hut of pine ibout. [9]	12	24
St.3		**St.3**	
1	Wan þe maiden understud	1	
2	and þangles wordes herde.	2	26
3	mildeliche with milde mud.	3	
4	to þangle þie andswerde.	4	28

[7] The accentuation *blissfill tidîng* is no licence. All compound words, even words compounded with suffixes like *ly* or *ness*, have in verse a variable accent in old English. The accent is also often found on the last syllable of words ending in *ing* or *er*.

[8] This seems to be *All mankind worth ybought*, All mankind becomes bought, comes to be redeemed.

[9] Probably *ibrout* (brought) ought to be read here.

Plate 403   OET No. 147: Angelus ad Virginem -- Middle English Paraphrase

The text of the Middle English (or old English as it is here called) with which Hopkins was confronted was defective in a number of places. As the editor of the Month pointed out (p.100), the medieval transcriber had frequently mistaken "h" in the original MS for "þ" (thorn, th). This was sometimes corrected (e.g., in 26 MS has "þerde") but it was left in 4, 28 and (Plate 405) in 39, 47, 53 and 60. Combs's transcription was also sometimes in error: in 11 the first "maken" should be "manken" (mankind), as GMH realised; in 24 (by dittography from 22) "ibout" was written for "ibrout" (see note 9).

MONTH Vol. 44		The Song of Chaucer's Clerk of Oxenford,	FURNIVALL line nos.	
St. 3 cont		106	St. 3 cont.	
5		Tibi cœlesti nuntio,	5	
6		Tanti secreti conscio	6	30
7		Consentiens, et cupiens videre	7/8/9	
8		Factum quod audio	10	34
9		Parata sum parere	11	
10		Dei consilio."	12	36
St. 4			St. 4	
1		Angelus disparuit,	1	
2		Et statim puellaris	2	38
3		Uterus intumuit	3	
4		Vi partus salutaris ;	4	40
5		Quo circumdatur utero	5	
6		Novem mensium numero.	6	42
7		Post exiit, et iniit conflictum,	7/8/9	
8		Affigens humero[10]	10	46
9		Crucem, qui dedit ictum	11	
10		Soli mortifero.	12	48
St. 5			St. 5	
1		Eja, Mater Domini,	1	
2		Quæ pacem reddidisti	2	50
3		Angelis et homini	3	
4		Cum Christum genuisti,	4	52
5		Tuum exora filium,	5	
6		Ut se nobis propitium	6	54
7		Exhibeat, et deleat peccata	7/8/9	
8		Præstans auxilium,	10	58
9		Vita frui beata	11	
10		Post hoc exilium. Amen.	12	60

[10] There is probably here an allusion to the Crusaders, or at all events the cross worn by them was in the mind of the writer, as the introduction of our Lord's fighting the fight with the cross upon his shoulder as the badge of the conflict needs some motive to render it natural and suitable to the passage.

OET No. 147

MONTH Vol.44	"*Angelus ad Virginem.*" 107	FURNIVALL line nos.	
St.3 cont		St.3 cont.	
5	hur lordes þeumaiden iwis.	5	
6	ics am þat her abouen is.	6	30
7	aneftis[11] me fulfurthed be þi sawe.	7/ 8/ 9	
8	þat ics sithen his wil is :	10	34
9	maiden withhuten lawe :[12]	11	
10	of moder haue þe blis.	12	36
St.4		St.4	
1	Þangle wente awei mid þan	1	
2	al hut of hire sichte.	2	38
3	and þire wombe arise gan.	3	
4	þurw þoligastes miche [*sic*].	4	40
5	in hire was crist biloken anon	5	
6	suth god soth man ine fleas and bon.	6	42
7	and of her fleas iboren was at time.	7/ 8/ 9	
8	warþurw us kam god won.[13]	10	46
9	þe bout us hut of pine	11	
10	and let im for us sloy [? slon].	12	48
St.5		St.5	
1	Maiden moder makeles[14]	1	
2	of milche ful ibunden	2	50
3	bid for hus im þat þe ches :	3	
4	at wam þu grace funde.	4	52
5	þat þe forgiue hus senne and wrake.	5	
6	and clene of euri gelt us make.	6	54
7	and eune blis wan hure time is to steruen :	7/8/9	
8	hus giue for þine sake	10	58
9	him so her for to seruen	11	
10	þat þe us to him take.	12	60

[11] Aneftis. Derived from the prefix an—and eft or æft=after. An adverb akin to anentis, anent=respecting, relating to.

[12] *Withouten law*, contrary to the general law of humanity. The Blessed Virgin was not at this time without law in the sense of being free of a husband, for her so-called espousals were in fact marriage.

[13] *Where through us came God won*. Perhaps: Through whom God came to be won over, reconciled, to us,—or, came to be one with us.

[14] Although there is a German word *makel*, a spot, and its derivative *makellos*, immaculate, yet *makeles* would seem to be nothing but *matchless*, from *make* the older form of *mate*.

OET No. 147

Plate 405   OET No. 147: Angelus ad Virginem -- Middle English Paraphrase, cont.

    Other mistakes made by Combs or the medieval scribe were: 31 "aneftis" for "anenttis" (note 11, presumably by Hopkins, reaches the meaning, as his translation--Plate 407--also does). In 40 the editor adds "[sic]" after "miche", a slip for "mithe", which Hopkins correctly translates as "might"; and in 48 after "sloy" the editor has "[? slon]". For the medieval scribe's "Þ" instead of "h" in 39, 47, 53 and 60 see note to Plate 403. Note 13 (to line 46) should read "Whereby good hope came to us". On Note 14 see OET, p.427 for the Hopkinsian slant it reveals.

MONTH Vol. 44	108	*The Song of Chaucer's Clerk of Oxenford,*		
OET No. 147				
		We insert for the benefit of our readers who are not skilled in the old English forms, a modernized version. We have kept the quaintness of the original so far as the necessities of metre and of clearness permitted.		
St.1				
	1	Gabriel, from heaven's king		
	2	Sent to the maiden sweet,		
	3	Brought to her blissful tiding		
	4	And fair 'gan her to greet.		
	5	"Hail be thou, full of grace aright!		
	6	For so God's Son, the heaven's light,		
	7	Loves man, that He | a man will be | and take	7/8/9	
	8	Flesh óf thee, maiden bright,	10	
	9	Mankind free for to make		
	10	Of sin and devil's might."	12	
St.2				
	1	Gently tó him gave answér		
	2	The gentle maiden then :	14	
	3	"And in what wise should I bear		
	4	Child, that know not man?"	16	
	5	The angel said : "O dread thee nought.		
	6	'Tis through the Holy Ghost that wrought	18	
	7	Shall be this thing | whereof tidíng | I bring:		
	8	Lost mánkind shall be bought	22	
	9	By thy sweet childbearíng,		
	10	And back from sorrow brought."	24	
St.3				
	1	When the maiden understood		
	2	And the angel's words had heard,	26	
	3	Mildly, of her own mild mood,		
	4	The angel she answéred :	28	
	5	"Our Lord His handmaiden, I wis,		
	6	I am, that here above us is :	30	

Plate 406   OET No. 147: Angelus ad Virginem -- Modernised Version

Though Hopkins made the original modernisation of the Middle English version, his work was subsequently altered, "perhaps", as he modestly suggested, "not altogether for the better" (L.iii.361). In line 7 of each stanza he manages to produce rhymes in imitation of the Latin and the M.E.. These were no doubt intended as end rhymes, and modern versions print line 7 in three separate lines.

PLATE 407. OET 147. Angelus ad Virginem • 229

MONTH Vol.44	*"Angelus ad Virginem."* 109
St.3 cont	
7	As touching me | fulfillèd be | thy saw ;
8	That I, since His will is, 34
9	Be, out of nature's law
10	A maid with mother's bliss." 36
St.4	
1	The angel went away thereon
2	And parted from her sight 38
3	And straightway she conceived a Son
4	Through th' Holy Ghost His might. 40
5	In her was Christ contained anon,
6	True God, true man, in flesh and bone ; 42
7	Born óf her too | when time was due; | who then
8	Redeemed us for His own, 46
9	And bought us out of pain,
10	And died for us t' atone. 48
St.5	
1	Fillèd full of charity,
2	Thou matchless maiden-mother, 50
3	Pray for us to him that He
4	For thý love above other, 52
5	Away our sin and guilt should take,
6	And clean of every stain us make 54
7	And heaven's bliss, | when our time is | to die,
8	Would give us for thy sake ; 58
9	With grace to serve him by
10	Till He us to him take. Amen. 60
OET NO. 147	

"*Angelus ad Virginem.*"   III

in - tac - ta   Sa - lu - tem ho - mi-num.

Tu,   por - ta   cœ - li . . fac - - ta

Me - de - - - la cri - - - mi - num.

Plates 407a, 407b   OET No. 147: Angelus ad Virginem -- Original Music

The Month, pp.110-111. Writing to his mother on Christmas Eve 1881 Hopkins remarked that the music to the "Angelus ad Virginem" was "quite easy to read to anyone that knows a little about plainsong"--his own favourite form of liturgical chant. "The music is interesting from its great age besides being striking and pretty;" it was being "harmonised by the organist at Farm Street," the chief Jesuit church in London (L.iii.161). A week later, New Year's Day 1882, when Hopkins had seen that issue of The Month, he expressed his disappointment: "I am sorry to say that you must put no trust in the music headed 'original'. The Thirteenth Century composer if he saw it wd. scarcely know it and would not acknowledge it for his own. What a thing it is that even in publishing an antiquity, a piece of music every note interesting and precious from its date, people must change, adulterate, and modernise! If the editor of the Month were a musician he would have been aware of this and would not have allowed it, at all events without warning the reader. The effect of the original is totally lost by the change for instance

from   to

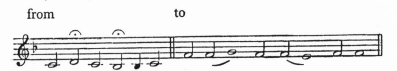

The first is characteristic, fresh, and quaint; the second a platitude. The true original is in the 7th Mode, the Young Men's Mode or Angelic Mode, the natural scale of G, and I had wanted Grace to see the effect. But now it is all a mess" (L.iii.162-3).

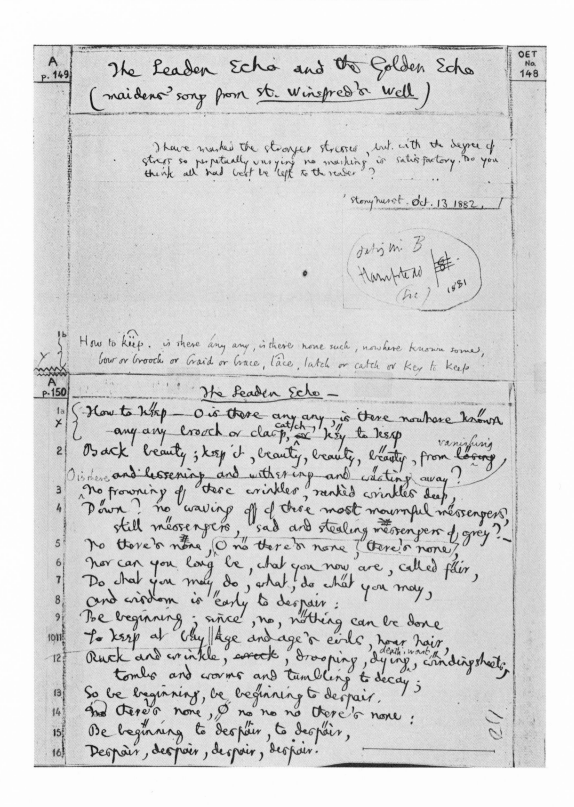

Plate 408   OET No. 148: The Leaden Echo and the Golden Echo -- MS. 1 - A(1)

A.pp.149-150 (ℓℓ. 1-16), [cont. on Plates 410, 412, 414]--autograph faircopy. GMH's changes: 1 "or/, catch,"
4 "stealing mĕssengers"   5 "nŏne"

RB's red ink (1884) copies from B GMH's revisions: 1a whole ℓ. del. and new one written (1b) on p.149
2 "losing/vanishing [six more words del.]...away?"   3 "O is there" added before "No" [u.c. kept]   5 "there's none"
transposed without comma to precede "O"   10, 11 divided into two lines, with double stroke after "bay", and "age"
mended to "Age"   12 "Ruck" (? bad u, transcribed into B by RB as "Rank") mended to a clear "Ruck"   "wreck"
"death's worst," added   14 "No" mended to "O"   "none, Ŏ"

RB's black ink (1889) on p.149 adds (below GMH's date "Stonyhurst. Oct. 13 1882") "Hampstead/81/1881". RB's
pencil, c. 1918, adds "dating in B (sic)".

PLATE 409. OET 148. *The Leaden Echo and The Golden Echo* • 233

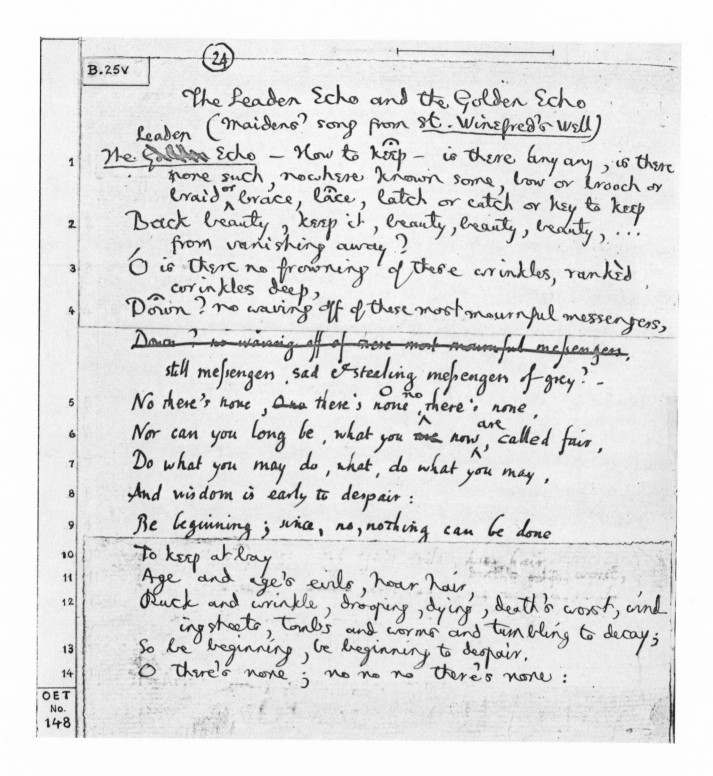

Plate 409   OET No. 148: The Leaden Echo and the Golden Echo -- MS. 2 - B(1)

B.25v (lines 1-14), first of four pages [cont. on Plates 411, 413, 415]--transcription of A by RB in album B, revised by GMH, who covered over RB's transcription of the title and 1-3 and 10-14 with two pieces of paper on which he had rewritten them and the first half of 4.

RB's transcription (invisible) follows A, exc. for ℓ.c. in title and in the first heading (for 1-16) "The golden echo" (corrected to "The leaden echo" by RB)--the same slip made by GMH when rewriting it. In 10-14 (invisible below GMH's second strip) RB had in 12 "Rack" (mended to "Ruck" by GMH), and in 14 "O no, no, no," (three commas added).

Other Revisions by GMH: none to RB's transcription of title and 1-3 (hidden beneath GMH's upper strip)   4 first half del. and rewritten with pause mark on "Down"   5 "O no" transposed   6 RB's slip corrected ("are" misplaced) 9 semicolon strengthened   In RB's copy of 10-14 (invisible beneath GMH's lower strip), he left 10, 11 as one line but put a pause mark on "bay"   12 "wreck"   after "dying" he added "death's self, worst,"   14 "No/Oh" "none, Ø no"

The Golden Echo —   Spáre!

There ís one, yes I have one (High there!) ((;))
Only not within seeing of the sun,
Not within the singeing of the strong sun,
Tall sun's tinging, or treacherous the tainting of
      the earth's air,

Somewhere elsewhere there is ah well where! one,
One. yes I cán tell such a key, I do know such a place,
Where whatever's prizèd and passes of us, everything that's
      fresh and fast flying of us, seems to us sweet of us
      and swiftly away with, done away with, undone,
Undone, done with, soon done with and yet dearly and
      dangerously sweet
Of us, the wimpled-water-dimpled, not-by-morning-match-
      èd face,
The flower of beauty, fleece of beauty, too too apt to ah!
      to fleet,
Never fleets móre, fastened with the tenderest truth
To its own best being and its loveliness of youth: it is an
      everlastingness of, O it is an all youth!

Plate 410   OET No. 148: The Leaden Echo and the Golden Echo -- MS. 1 - A(2)

A.p.151 (ℓℓ. 17-29)--autograph faircopy cont. from Plate 408. GMH's changes: 21 "tainting" (slip?)   22 "ah/well"

27 "ah/!"

RB's pencil (c. 1918) in 18 rings the final comma and substitutes a semicolon [from B].

PLATE 411. OET 148. *The Leaden Echo and The Golden Echo* • 235

B. 26r

26

15 Be beginning to despair, to despair,

16 Despair, despair, despair, despair.

17 [The Golden Echo]   Spare!

18 There is one, yes I have one ('hush there!),

19 Only not within seeing of the sun.

20 Not within the singeing of the strong sun,

21 Tall sun's tingeing, or treacherous the tainting of the earth's air,

22 Somewhere elsewhere there is (ah well where!) one,   [much]

23 One. Yes I can tell such a key, I do know such a place,

24 Where whatever's prized & passes of us, everything that's fresh
     & fast flying of us, seems to us sweet of us & swiftly
     away with, done away with, undone,

25 Undone, done with, soon done with, & yet dearly & dangerously
     sweet   wimpled=

26 Of us, the water-dimpled, not-by-morning-matchèd face,

27 The flower of beauty, fleece of beauty, too too apt to, ah!
     to fleet,

28 Never fleets more, fastened with the tenderest truth,

29 To its own best being & its loveliness of youth: it is an
     everlastingness of, o it is an all youth!

30 Come then, your ways & airs & looks, locks, maidengear,
     gallantry & gaiety & grace,

OET
No.
148

winning

Plate 411   OET No. 148: The Leaden Echo and the Golden Echo -- MS. 2 - B(2)

B.26r (lines 15-30)--second of four pages: transcription of A by RB, cont. In 26 he interlined "wimpled-" which he had left out.

GMH's changes: 17 "The golden echo" mended to u.c. G, E   Punctuation altered or clarified in 15, 18 (final semicolon), 24, 25, and 27   In 22 the parentheses were GMH's (RB del. them in pencil in 1918, thinking they must have been his own, with a note "del. bracket")   Metrical pause marks and circumflexes were added in 23, 25 and 28, but the pause mark on "Come" (30) was changed to a single stress.

RB's pencil (c. 1918) in 22 also rings for deletion the first comma (not in A).

Come then, your ways and airs and looks, locks, maidengear, gallantry and gaiety and grace,
Winning ways, airs innocent, maiden/manners, sweet looks,
   loose locks, long locks, love locks, gay gear, going gall-
   ant, girlgrace —
Resign them, sign them, seal them, send them, motion them
   with breath,
and with sighs soaring, soaring sighs, & deliver
Them; beauty-in-the-ghost, deliver that now, early now,
   long before death
Give beauty back, beauty, beauty, beauty, back to God
   beauty's self and beauty's giver.
See; not a hair is, not an eyelash, not the least lash
   lost; every hair
Is, hair of the head, numbered.   Volti.

Plate 412   OET No. 148: The Leaden Echo and the Golden Echo -- MS. 1 - A(3)

A.p.152 (lines 30-37)--autograph faircopy cont. from Plate 410. [See Plate 414 for conclusion.]

GMH's changes: 31 "maiden/manners"--compound was split into two words while the ink was wet.   33 "ø"

35 "beauty's giver"--the apostrophe s is smudged, not del.   Note the pause mark over "sighs" in 33, sometimes used as

sf.. In 30 the apparent apostrophe s or stress on the s in "looks" is from the tail of the y cut off from "youth" (29--

bottom of Plate 410): RB had to cut the autograph in a wavy line between 29 and 30 to avoid ascenders and descenders:

he could not paste it over the hinge of album A. In 36 after "See" a colon is prob. intended (cf. "dot" over "with" in 33).

RB's red ink (1884), copying from GMH's revisions in B: 34 "that now/it".

RB's black ink at the bottom of p.152 writes "Volti" (Turn over). RB's pencil (c. 1918) in 33 rings the comma after

"soaring sighs" and notes in margin "del.?" [RB had omitted this comma in B and GMH had not reinstated it.]

PLATE 413. OET 148. *The Leaden Echo and The Golden Echo* • 237

B. 26v	OET NO. 148	
31		Winning ways, airs innocent, maiden manners, sweet looks, loose locks, long locks, lovelocks, gaygear, going gallant, girlgrace —
32		Resign them, sign them, seal them, send them, motion them with breath,
33		And with sighs soaring, soaring sighs deliver
34		Them ; beauty-in-the-ghost, deliver ~~that now~~ it, early now, long before death
35		Give beauty back, beauty, beauty, beauty, back to God beauty's self & beauty's giver.
36	) A	See, not a hair is, not an eyelash, not the least lash lost ; every hair
37		Is, hair of the head, numbered .
38	⊃ A	Nay, what we had, light-handed left in surly the mere mould
39		Will have waked & have waxed & have walked with the wind what while we slept,
40		This side, that side hurling a heavy headed hundredfold
41		What while we, while we slumbered.
42		O then, weary then why sh^d we tread ? O why are we so haggard at the heart, so care-coiled, carekilled, so fagged, so fashed, so cogged, so cumbered,
43 End of 26v		When the thing we freely forfeit is kept with fonder a care,

<u>Plate 413</u> <u>OET No. 148: The Leaden Echo and the Golden Echo</u> -- MS. 2 - B(3)

<u>B.26v (31-43)</u>--RB's transcription of A, cont.. In 40 "heavyhanded" was RB's slip (confused with 38--prob. corrected by GMH). In 42 stress on "why" is prob. RB, strengthened by GMH.

<u>GMH's changes:</u> 34 "that now, /it,"   38 "had" interlined. Note GMH's metrical marks in 33, 43 and his characteristic commas in 40, 42 ("O then,").

<u>RB's pencil</u> in 36 notes that he copied as "See," A's "See;" [but I think GMH intended "See:"] and in 38 notes he omitted a comma after "Nay".

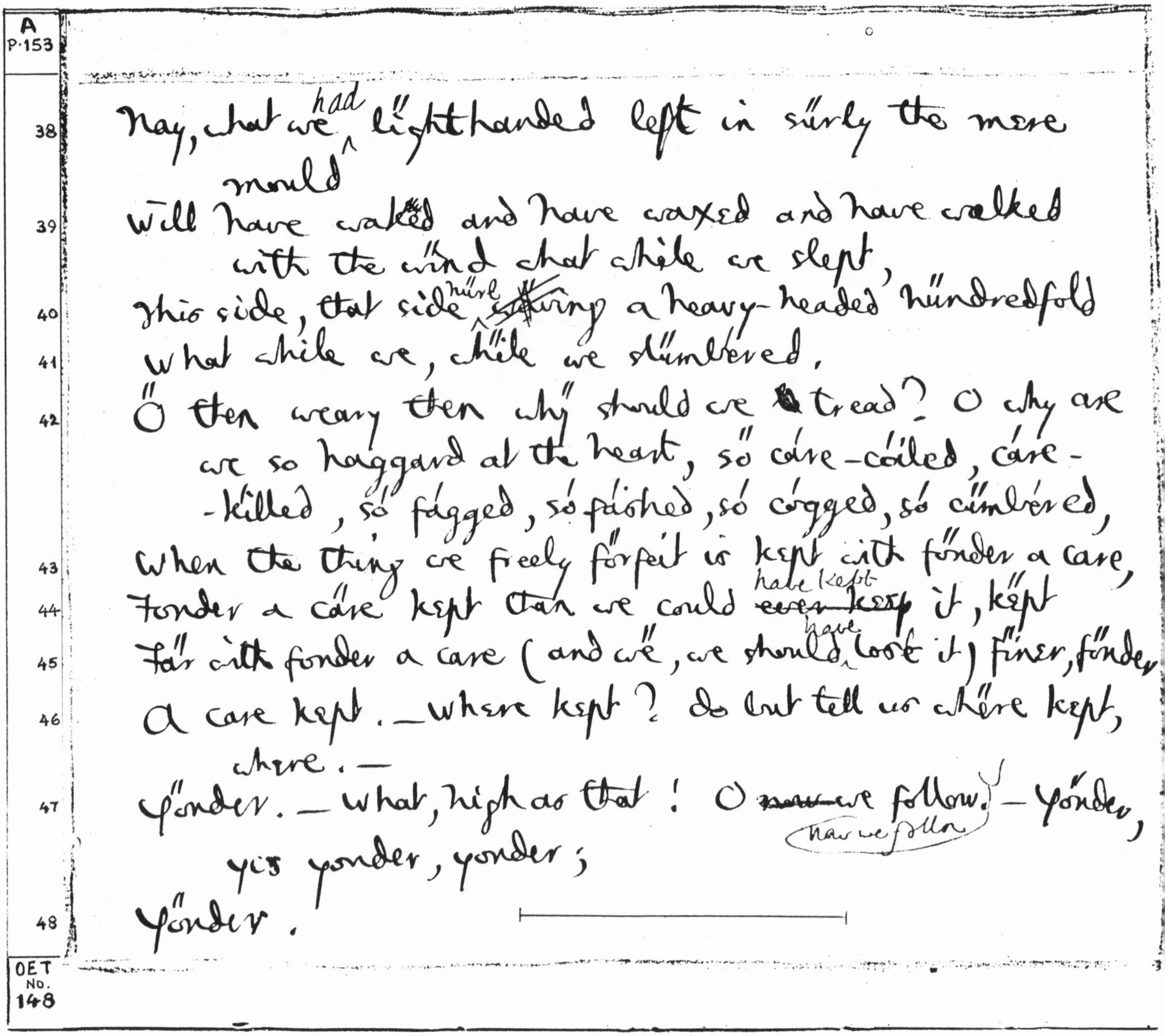

Plate 414   OET No. 148: The Leaden Echo and the Golden Echo -- MS. 1 - A(4)

A.p.153 (lines 38-48, the end)--autograph faircopy cont. from Plate 412. GMH's changes: 39 "waked" grave deleted

"whele" [anticipating "we"?] mended to "while" 40 "wav" del. rev. to "hurl[ing]" 42 "ℓℯ [?] tread" Note the single

and double stresses in 42.

RB's red ink (1884), copying from GMH's revisions in B: 38 adds "had" 44 "ever keep/have kept" 45 "should

lose" changed to "should have lost" 47 "O now we follow." RB adds "now we follow".

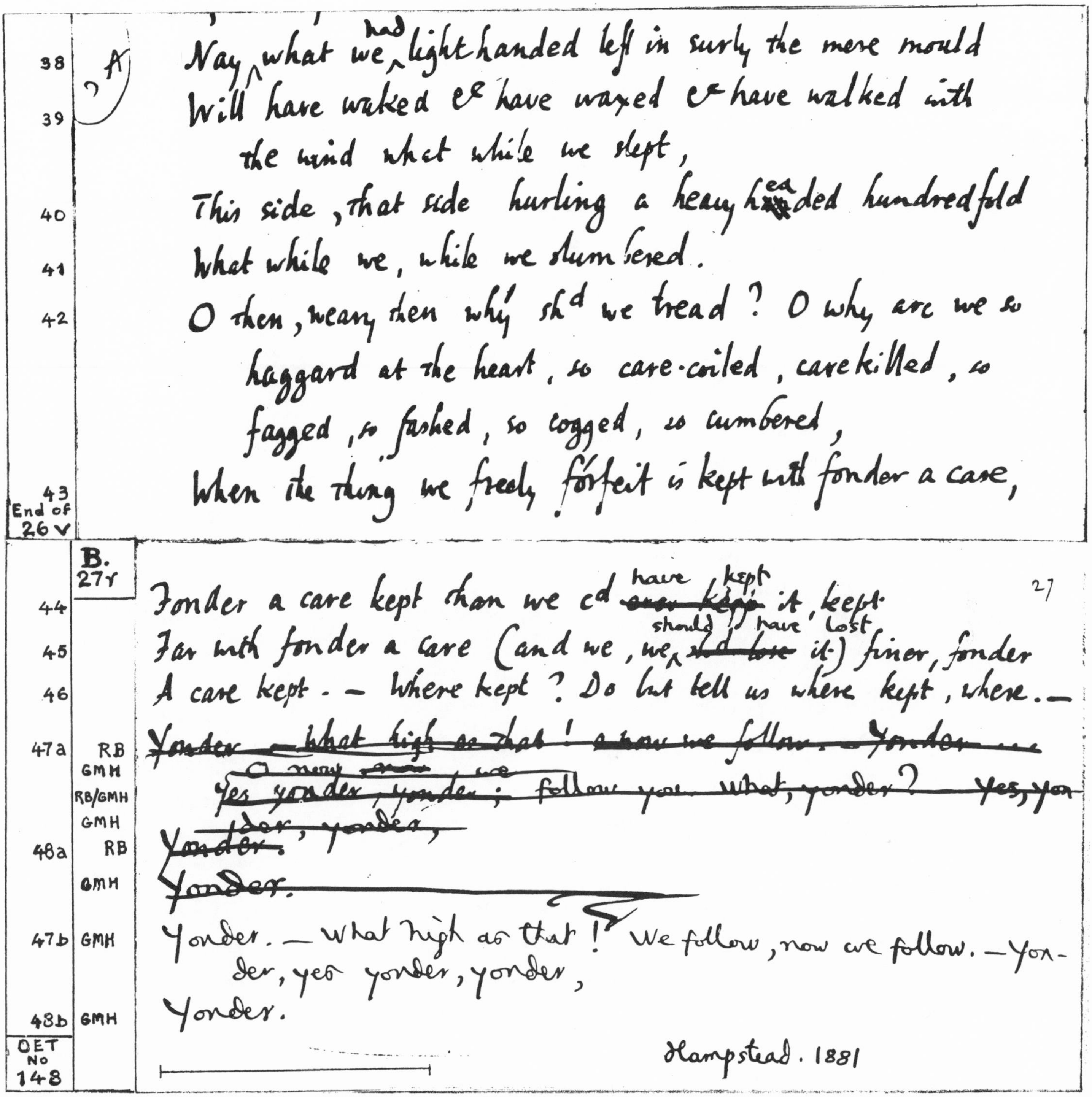

PLATE 415. OET 148. *The Leaden Echo and The Golden Echo* • 239

38	Nay, what we had light-handed left in surly the mere mould
39	Will have waked & have waxed & have walked with the mind what while we slept,
40	This side, that side hurling a heavy-headed hundredfold
41	What while we, while we slumbered.
42	O then, weary then why shd we tread ? O why are we so haggard at the heart, so care-coiled, care-killed, so fagged, so fashed, so cogged, so cumbered,
43 End of 26 v	When the thing we freely forfeit is kept with fonder a care,

B. 27r	27
44	Fonder a care kept than we cd ~~over keep~~ it kept. (have kept)
45	Far with fonder a care (and we, we, ~~shd lose~~ it.) finer, fonder (should have lost)
46	A care kept. — Where kept ? Do but tell us where kept, where. —
47a RB GMH RB/GMH GMH	~~Yonder — what high as that ! o now we follow. Yonder~~ ~~O now now we~~ ~~Yes yonder, yonder; follow you. what, yonder ? Yes, you-~~ ~~der, yonder,~~
48a RB GMH	~~Yonder.~~ ~~Yonder.~~
47b GMH	Yonder. — What high as that ! We follow, now we follow. — Yon- der, yes yonder, yonder,
48b GMH	Yonder.
OET NO 148	Hampstead. 1881

Plate 415   OET No. 148:   The Leaden Echo and the Golden Echo -- MS. 2 - B(4)

B.26v (lines 38-43 only, repeated from Plate 413 to facilitate comparison with A--see notes below Plate 413); B27r (lines 44-48)--conclusion of RB's transcription of A.

GMH's changes: 44 "ever keep [smudged]/have kept"   45 "shd lose/should have lost"   47a, 48 GMH first del. after "that!" RB's "o now we follow.--Yonder...Yes, yonder, yonder;/Yonder." (which deviated from A in accidentals), and revised it as: "O now, now we follow you. What, yonder? Yes, yonder, yonder,/Yonder." He then del. all RB's and his own 47-48 and rewrote them below. The date, added later, may refer to an interim version, begun at Hampstead a year earlier than MS. A--see OET, p.429, on the Composition of the poem.

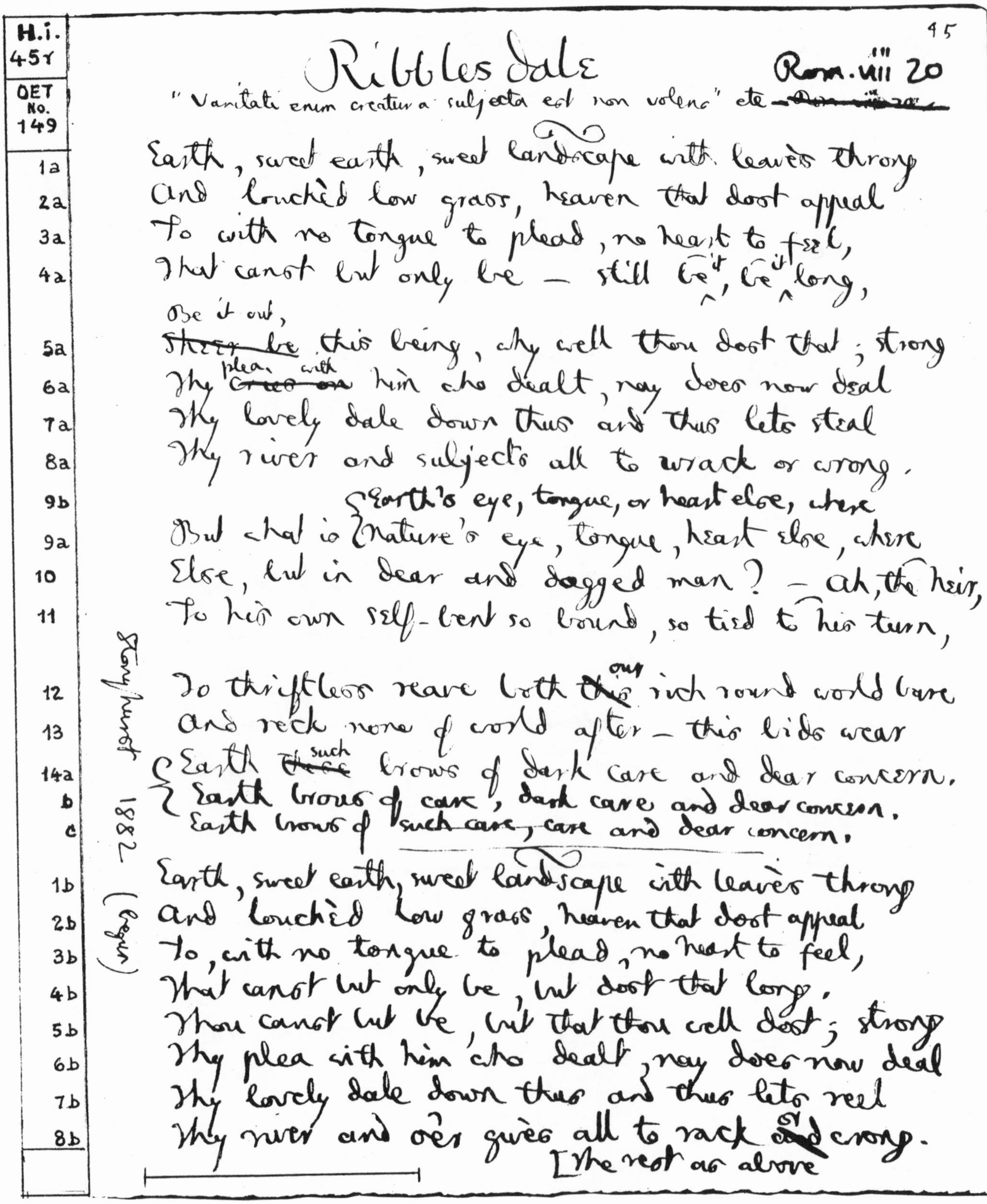

H.i. 45r	45
OET NO. 149	

Ribbles dale   Rom. viii 20

"Vanitati enim creatura subjecta est non volens" etc ~~Rom. viii 2.~~

1a Earth, sweet earth, sweet landscape with leavès throng

2a And louchèd low grass, heaven that doot appeal

3a To with no tongue to plead, no heart to feel,

4a That canot but only be — still be it, be it long,

Be it out,

5a ~~There be~~ this being, why well thou doot that; strong

6a Thy ~~plea with~~ ~~cries on~~ him who dealt, nay does now deal

7a Thy lovely dale down thus and thus lets steal

8a Thy river and subjects all to wrack or wrong.

9b   ⌠Earth's eye, tongue, or heart else, where

9a But what is ⌡Nature's eye, tongue, heart else, where

10 Else, but in dear and dogged man? — ah, the heir,

11 To his own self-bent so bound, so tied to his turn,

12 To thriftless reave both the^{our} inch round would bare

13 And reck none of world after — this bids wear

14a ⌠Earth ~~these~~^{such} brows of dark care and dear concern.

b ⌡Earth brows of care, dark care and dear concern.

c Earth brows of ~~such care~~, care and dear concern.

1b Earth, sweet earth, sweet landscape with leavès throng

2b And louchèd low grass, heaven that doot appeal

3b To, with no tongue to plead, no heart to feel,

4b That canot but only be, but doot that long.

5b Thou canot but be, but that thou well doot; strong

6b Thy plea with him who dealt, nay does now deal

7b Thy lovely dale down thus and thus lets reel

8b Thy river and oèr gives all to rack and wrong.

[the rest as above

Stonyhurst 1882 (begun)

Plate 416   OET No. 149: Ribblesdale -- MS. 1 (H)

H.i.45r--autograph draft in faded brown ink, with line spaces after 4, 8, 11; revised in the blacker ink used for the faircopy of the octave at foot. The epigraph, squeezed in below the title, reads: "'Vanitati enim creatura subjecta est non volens" etc--Rom. viii.20' (reference blotted and rewritten above). Changes include: 6a "cries on/plea with"   10 "degged" [cf. No. 146, ℓ.9] mended to "dogged"   14c, the final revision, was written on top of the division line originally drawn under the completed sonnet: "such care, care" is not del. Another dividing line was added before the revision at the foot (1b to 8b)--the ink ran into it from the counterpoint sign on "landscape" (1b).

PLATE 417. OET 149. *Ribblesdale* • 241

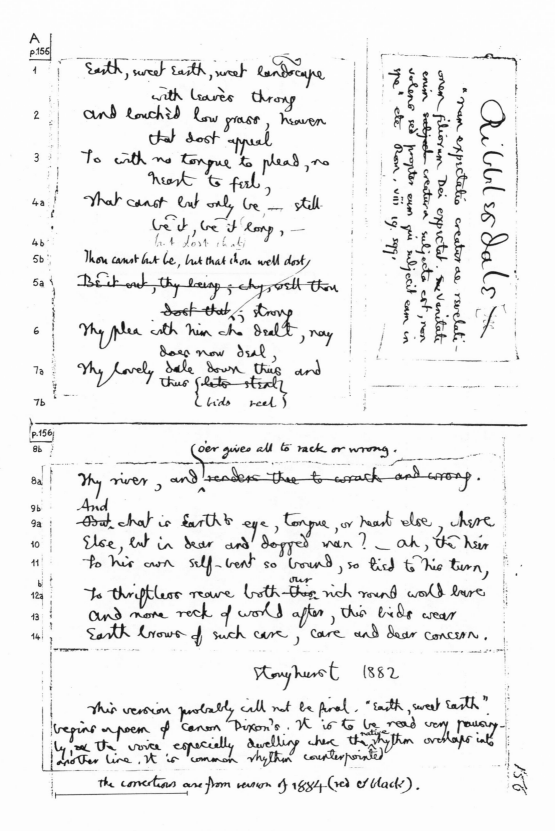

Plate 417   OET No. 149: Ribblesdale -- MS. 2 (A)

   A.pp.155-56--autograph faircopy, on two sheets 11 cm. x 17.3 cm., (title plus 1-7 on first, rest sideways on second) cut up to fit album A. Changes by GMH: epigraph "Sú" "subject"   7a "dale" mended   9a "earth's" mended to "E".

   RB's red ink (1884) corrects it from the autograph version in B: beside title "[See" in red, del. by RB in black ink 4a "Still be it, be it long," replaced by 4b and "long" with new stops before and after: ", but dost that long--"

   RB's black ink (not backward sloping, so perhaps also 1884) del. 5a except "; strong" before which his caret leads up to his copy in 5b of GMH's B version.   Also in black ink RB deleted words in 7a, 8a, 9a and 12a, replacing them with 7b and 8b (both written on the album pages themselves), 9b "And" and 12b "our". His footnote in black ink, "The corrections are from version of 1884 [i.e., B] (red and black).", does not explain why or when he changed from red to black.

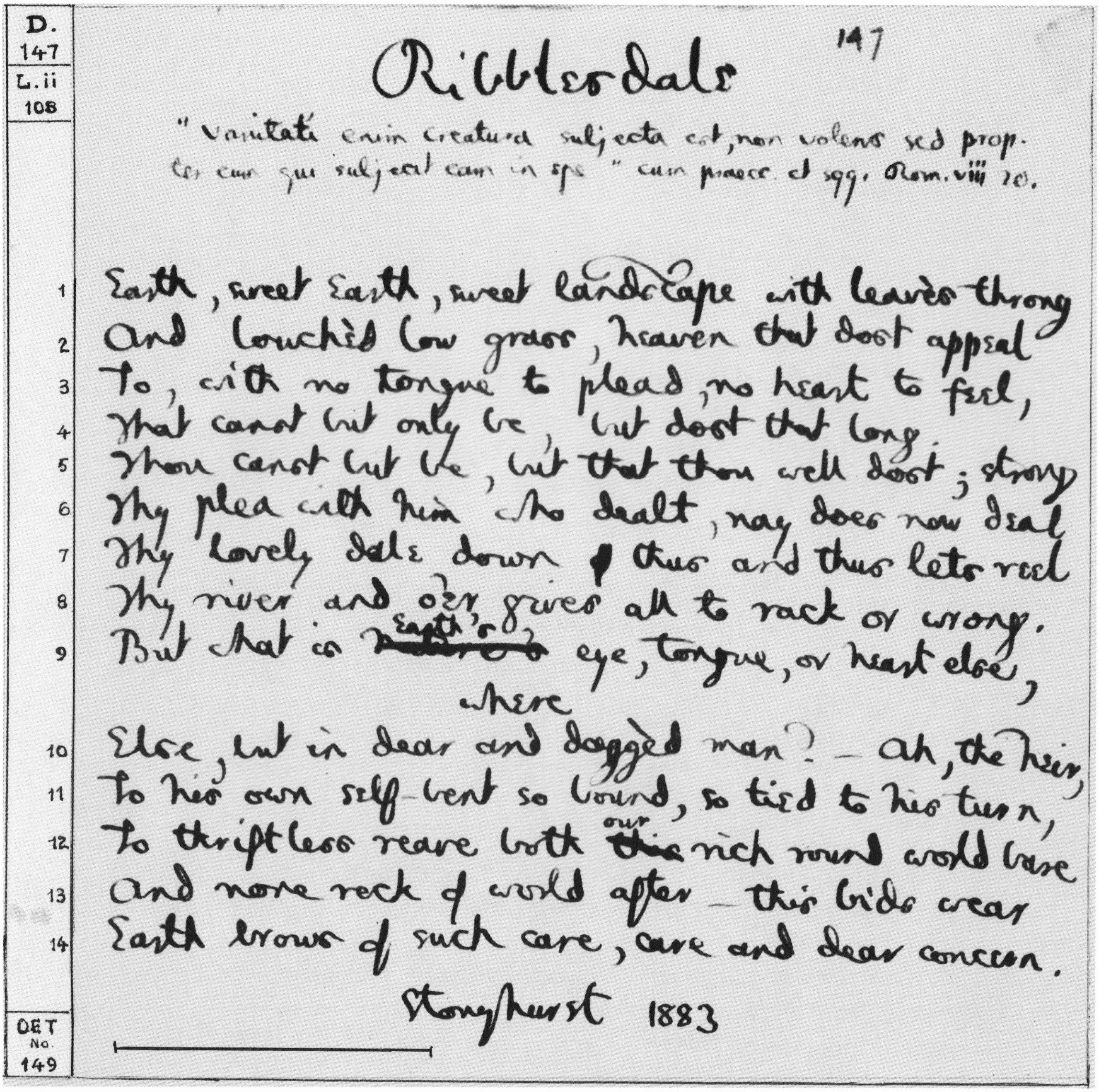

D.
147

L. ii
108

Ribblesdale

"Vanitati enim creatura subjecta est, non volens sed prop-
ter eum qui subjecit eam in spe " cum praec. et sqq. Rom. viii 20.

1 Earth, sweet Earth, sweet landscape with leavès throng
2 And louchèd low grass, heaven that doest appeal
3 To, with no tongue to plead, no heart to feel,
4 That canst but only be, but doest that long;
5 Thou canst but be, but that thou well doest; strong
6 Thy plea with him who dealt, nay does now deal,
7 Thy lovely dale down thus and thus bids reel
8 Thy river and o'er gives all to rack or wrong.

9 But what is ~~Nature's~~ Earth's eye, tongue, or heart else,

where
10 Else, but in dear and dogged man? — Ah, the heir,
11 To his own self-bent so bound, so tied to his turn,
                                        our
12 To thriftless reave both ~~this~~ rich round world bare
13 And none reck of world after — this bids wear
14 Earth brows of such care, care and dear concern.

Stonyhurst 1883

OET
No.
149

Plate 418   OET No. 149: Ribblesdale -- MS. 3 (D)

D.p.147--autograph faircopy sent to Dixon (see L.ii.108).   Changes (all by GMH):   7 /\[? "and thus"]
9 "Nature's/Earth's" 12 "this/our"

Epigraph: "Vanitati enim creatura subjecta est, non volens sed propter eum qui subjecit eam in spe" cum praec.
et sqq. Rom. viii 20.

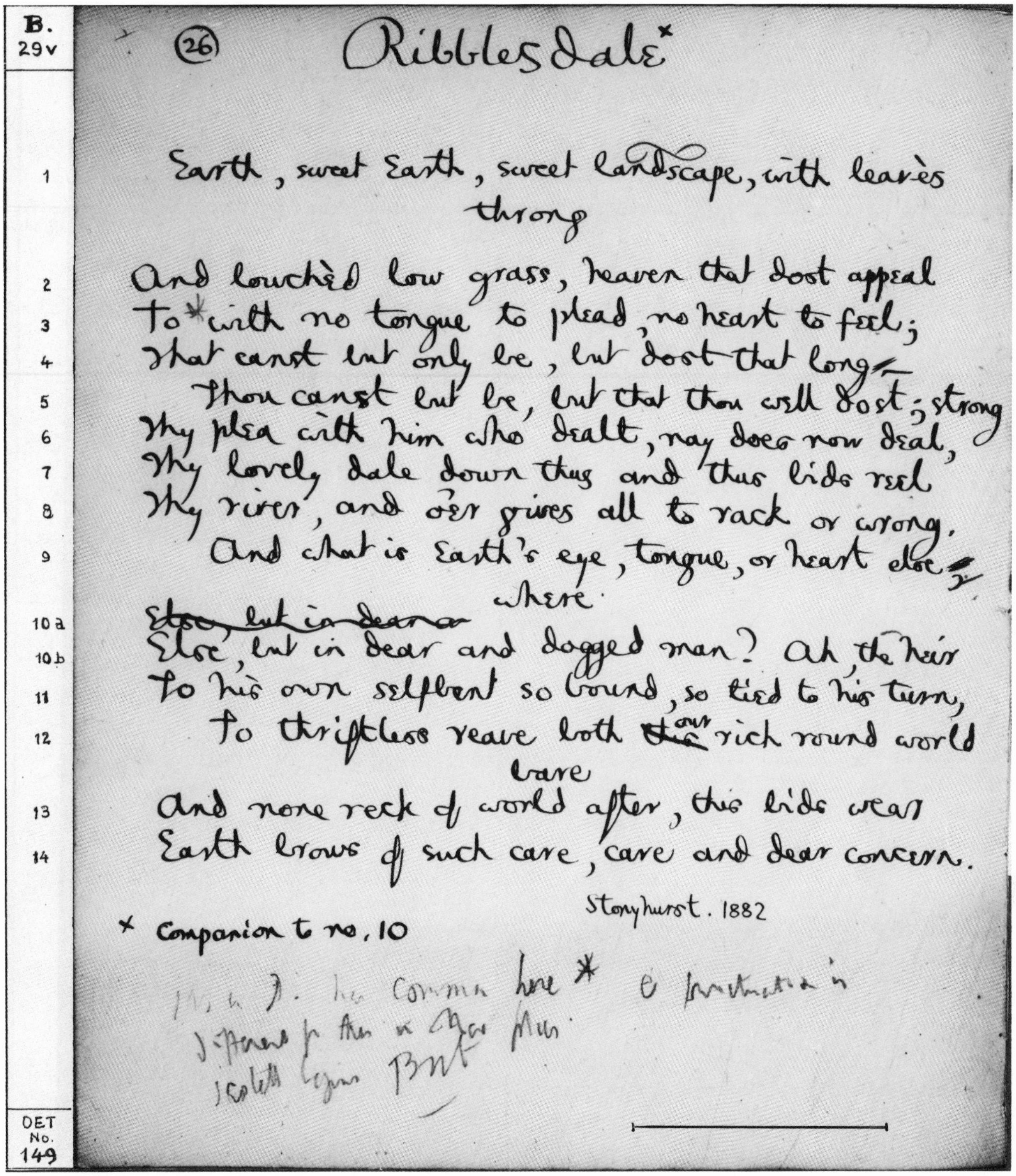

PLATE 419. OET 149. *Ribblesdale* • 243

B.
29v

(26) *Ribblesdale* ×

1 Earth, sweet Earth, sweet landscape, with leavès
throng

2 And louchèd low grass, heaven that doot appeal
3 To ×with no tongue to plead, no heart to feel;
4 That canst but only be, but doot that long—
5 Thou canst but be, but that thou well doot; strong
6 Thy plea with him who dealt, nay does now deal,
7 Thy lovely dale down thus and thus bids reel
8 Thy river, and o'er gives all to rack or wrong.
9 And what is Earth's eye, tongue, or heart else
where.

10a ~~Stoo, but in deana~~
10b Else, but in dear and dogged man? Ah, the heir
11 To his own selfbent so bound, so tied to his turn,
12 To thriftless reave both this/our rich round world
bare
13 And none reck of world after, this bids wear
14 Earth brows of such care, care and dear concern.

Stonyhurst. 1882

× Companion to no. 10

MS in D. has comma here × & punctuation is
different for this in other places.
Sestett begins But

Plate 419   OET No. 149: Ribblesdale -- MS. 4 (B)

B.29v--autograph faircopy, inscribed in album B, with footnote: "Companion to No. 10" [i.e., "In the Valley of the Elwy", No. 119].

Changes by GMH: 3, 5 prob. orig. colons, changed to semicolons   4 "long |--"   9 "else | ," [the period was heavily deleted, and the comma below it del. with one stroke which GMH then tried to erase]   10a overlooking the end of 9 he began 10 too high, so del. it.   12 "this/our"

GMH's counterpoint (1) and slur (10b) are in purple pencil. He added the date subsequently.

RB's pencil asterisk after "To" (3) links with his pencilled footnote: "MS in D. has comma here * and punctuation is different fr[om] this in other places./ Sestett begins But"

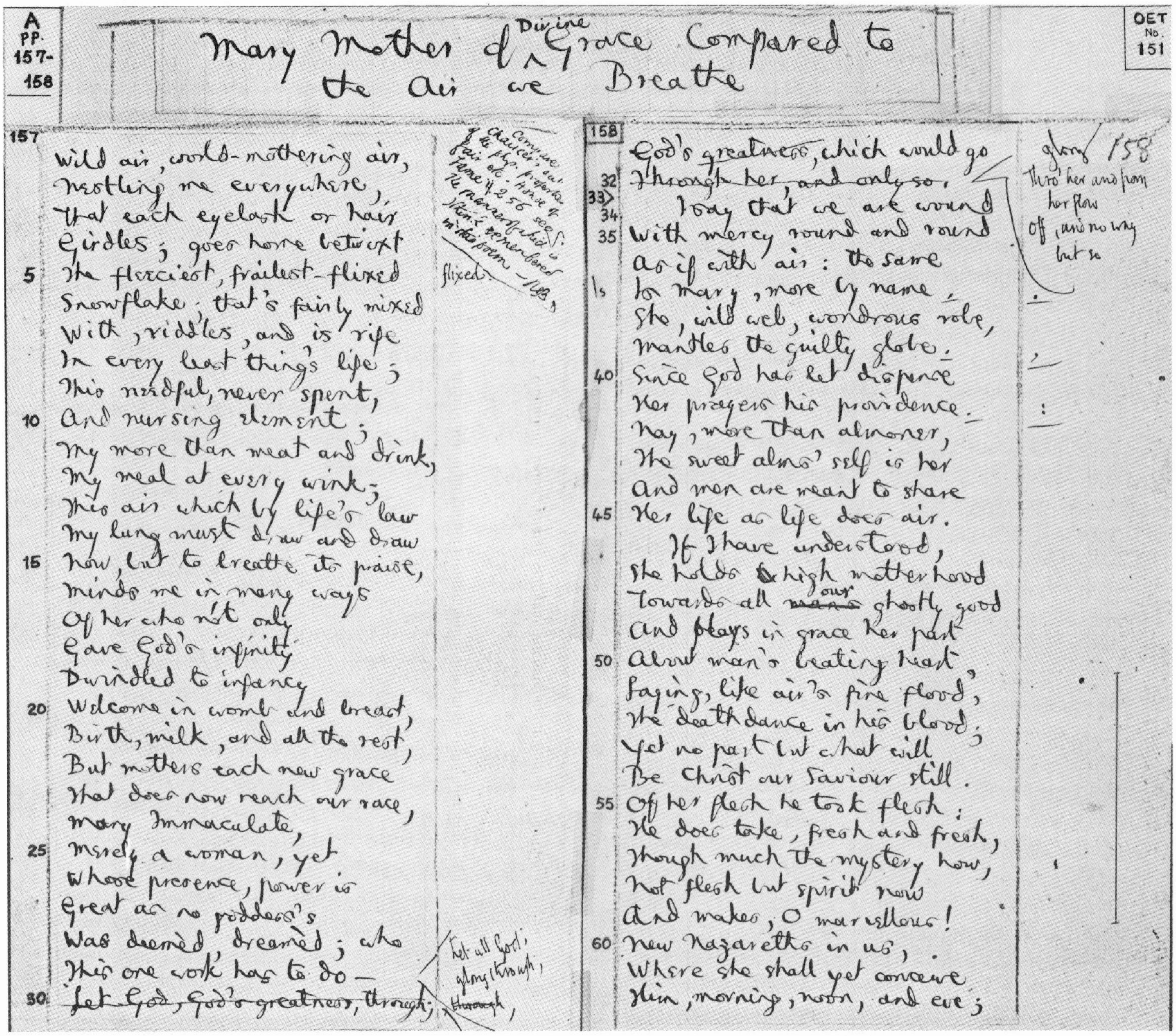

Mary Mother of ^Divine Grace Compared to
the air we Breathe

(handwritten poem, left column, p.157:)

Wild air, world-mothering air,
nestling me everywhere,
that each eyelash or hair
girdles; goes home betwixt
5 The fleeciest, frailest-flixed
Snowflake; that's fairly mixed
With, riddles, and is rife
In every least thing's life;
This needful, never spent,
10 And nursing element;
My more than meat and drink,
My meal at every wink,
This air which by life's law
My lung must draw and draw
15 Now but to breathe its praise,
minds me in many ways
Of her who not only
Gave God's infinity
Dwindled to infancy
20 Welcome in womb and breast,
Birth, milk, and all the rest
But mothers each new grace
That does now reach our race,
Mary Immaculate,
25 Merely a woman, yet
Whose presence, power is
Great as no goddess's
Was deemèd, dreamèd; who
This one work has to do —
30 Let God, God's greatness, through;

(margin note top middle:) Compare Chaucer's acct. of the phys. properties of air etc House of Fame ii 256 see. The manner of which is I think remembered in the poem — RB

(margin:) flixed ↗

(bottom margin:) Let all God's / glory through; through,

(handwritten poem, right column, p.158:)

God's greatness, which would go
32 Through her and only so,
33 >
34 I say that we are wound
35 With mercy round and round
As if with air: the same
Is Mary, more by name,
She, wild web, wondrous robe,
mantles the guilty globe,
40 Since God has let dispense
Her prayers his providence,
Nay, more than almoner,
The sweet alms' self is her
And men are meant to share
45 Her life as life does air.
If I have understood,
She holds high motherhood
Towards all ^our ghostly good
And plays in grace her part
50 About man's beating heart,
Laying, like air's fine flood,
The death dance in his blood;
Yet no part but what will
Be Christ our Saviour still,
55 Of her flesh he took flesh:
He does take, fresh and fresh,
Though much the mystery how,
Not flesh but spirit now
And makes, O marvellous!
60 New Nazareths in us,
Where she shall yet conceive
Him, morning, noon, and eve;

(margin note top right:) glory 158 / Thro' her and from / her flow / Of, and no way / but so

---

Plate 420   OET No. 151: The Blessed Virgin compared to the Air... -- MS. 1 - A(1)

A.pp.157-158--autograph faircopy (ℓℓ.1-62), originally in two columns with no space between them, with the title on top. To mount it in album A, RB had to cut off the title and paste that vertically down the left margin, and he separated the columns by about 60 cm. to avoid the hinge. For this plate the original layout has been partially restored.

GMH's changes include: title, "Divine" added   47 "ℓ high"   48 "man's/our" written on top of apostrophe 49 "bears" mended to "plays"

RB's black ink (1889) clarifies in the margins difficult words: 5 "flixed."   37 "Is"   51 [hidden in this plate by reduction of left margin] "laying". He copies GMH's revisions in B: 30 "through;" changed to "through," before noticing the revised wording.   31, 32; he adds the new line (33). Beside 37, 39, 41, RB notes discrepancies between the stops he underlines and those in B (though surely in A the final stop in 37 must be meant as a period).

RB's note (top, middle) reads: "Compare Chaucer's acct. [account] of the phys[ical] properties [o]f air etc. House of Fame ii.256 seq. The manner of which is I think remembered in this poem--RB"

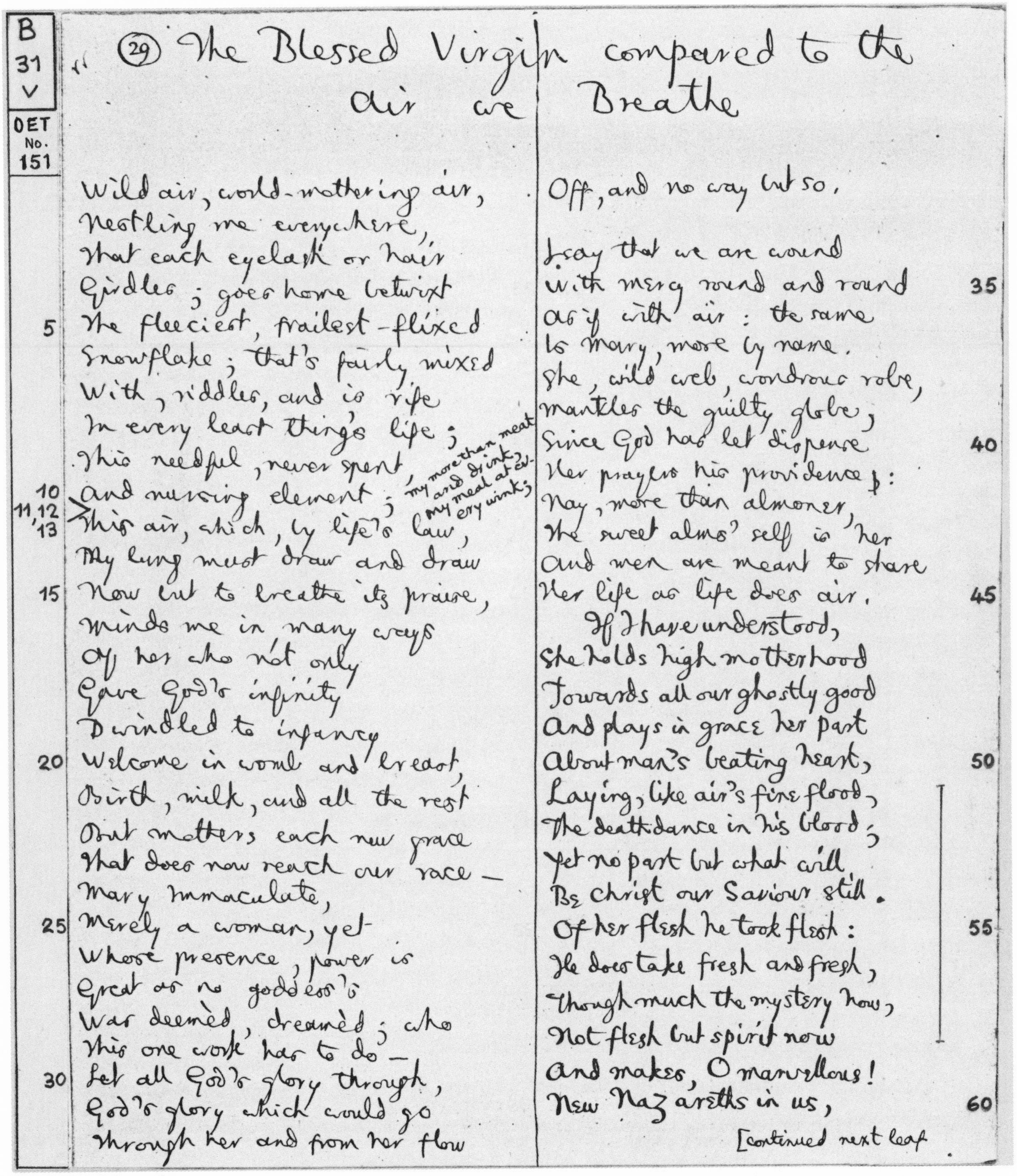

B
31
V

OET
No.
151

"㉙ The Blessed Virgin compared to the
Air we Breathe

Wild air, world-mothering air,
Nestling me everywhere,
That each eyelash or hair
Girdles; goes home betwixt
5 The fleeciest, frailest-flixed
Snowflake; that's fairly mixed
With, riddles, and is rife
In every least thing's life;
This needful, never spent,
10 And nursing element;   *my more than meat and drink, my meal at ev-ery wink;*
11,12
13 This air, which, by life's law,
My lung must draw and draw
15 Now but to breathe its praise,
Minds me in many ways
Of her who not only
Gave God's infinity
Dwindled to infancy
20 Welcome in womb and breast,
Birth, milk, and all the rest
But mothers each new grace
That does now reach our race —
Mary Immaculate,
25 Merely a woman, yet
Whose presence, power is
Great as no goddess's
Was deemèd, dreamèd; who
This one work has to do —
30 Let all God's glory through,
God's glory which would go
Through her and from her flow

Off, and no way but so.

I say that we are wound
With mercy round and round   35
As if with air: the same
Is Mary, more by name.
She, wild web, wondrous robe,
Mantles the guilty globe,
Since God has let dispense   40
Her prayers his providence:
Nay, more than almoner,
The sweet alms' self is her
And men are meant to share
Her life as life does air.   45
      If I have understood,
She holds high motherhood
Towards all our ghostly good
And plays in grace her part
About man's beating heart,   50
Laying, like air's fine flood,
The deathdance in his blood;
Yet no part but what will
Be Christ our Saviour still.
Of her flesh he took flesh: 55
He does take fresh and fresh,
Though much the mystery how,
Not flesh but spirit now
And makes, O marvellous!
New Nazareths in us,   60

[continued next leaf

Plate 421   OET No. 151: The Blessed Virgin compared to the Air... -- MS. 2 - B(1)

B.31v--autograph copy (ℓℓ.1-60), of RB's transcriptions of A (now lost) inscribed by GMH in album B up to 45 before the album was sent to Patmore. When he later completed 46 to the end (in ink over pencil, clearer in B 32v, e.g., lines 61, 92), he added in the margin 11, 12, omitted in error (a pencil note by RB, probably drawing attention to the omission, has been erased). In 14 "My" is mended from "N[ow?" cf. 15]   41 "providence �:" The ink and writing change after line 45.

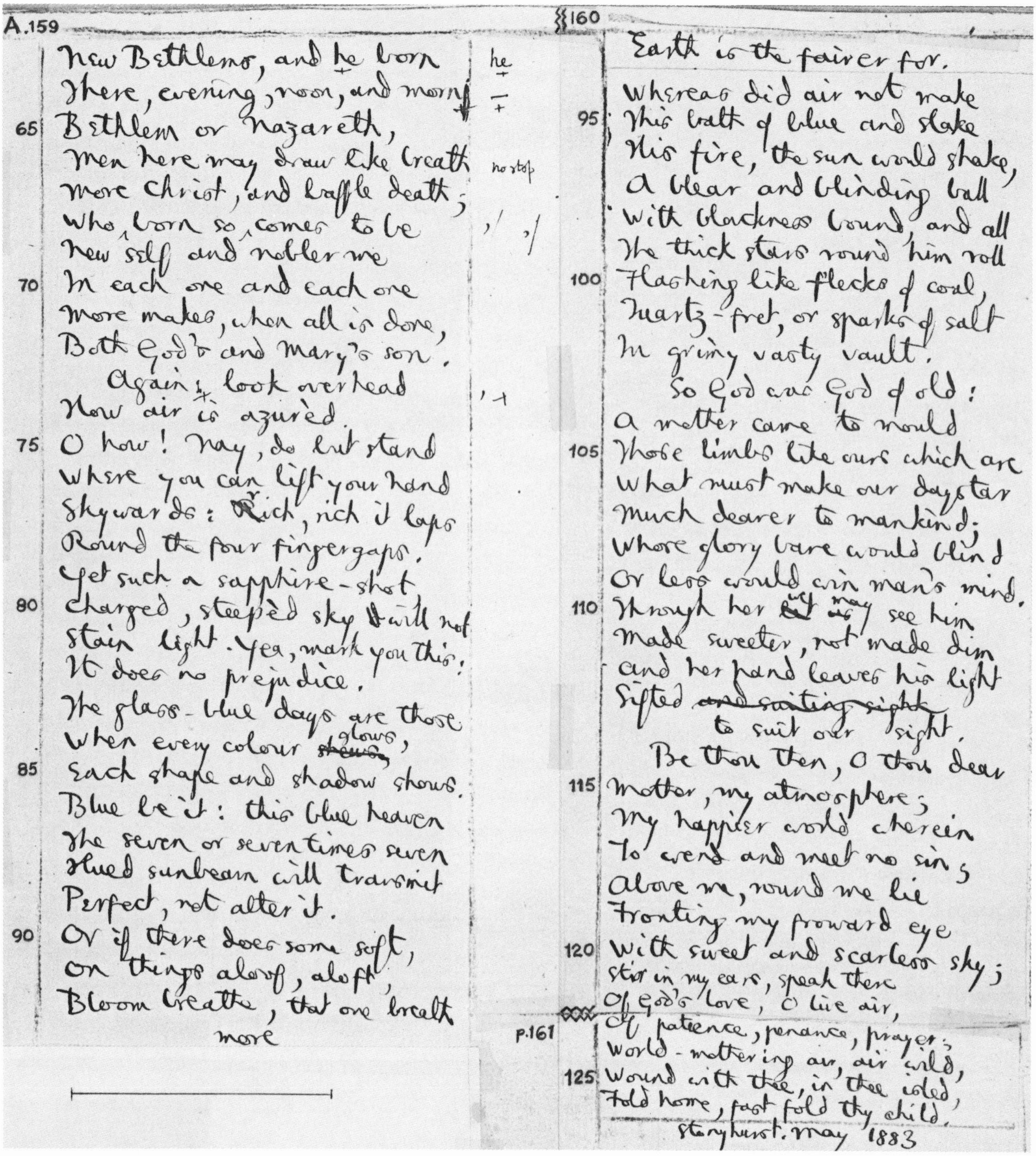

A.159

§160

New Bethlems, and he born
There, evening, noon, and morn—
65 Bethlem or Nazareth,
Men here may draw like breath
More Christ, and baffle death;
Who, born so, comes to be
New self and nobler me
70 In each one and each one
More makes, when all is done,
Both God's and Mary's son.
    Again, look overhead
How air is azurèd;
75 O how! nay, do but stand
Where you can lift your hand
Skywards: rich, rich it laps
Round the four fingergaps.
Yet such a sapphire-shot,
80 Charged, steepèd sky will not
Stain light. Yea, mark you this:
It does no prejudice.
The glass-blue days are those
When every colour glows,
85 Each shape and shadow shows.
Blue be it: this blue heaven
The seven or seven times seven
Hued sunbeam will transmit
Perfect, not alter it.
90 Or if there does some soft,
On things aloof, aloft,
Bloom breathe, that one breath more
    he
    —
    +
    +
    no stop
    ,/ ,/
    ,↑

Earth is the fairer for.
Whereas did air not make
95 This bath of blue and slake
His fire, the sun would shake,
A blear and blinding ball
With blackness bound, and all
The thick stars round him roll
100 Flashing like flecks of coal,
Quartz-fret, or sparks of salt,
In grimy vasty vault.
    So God was God of old:
A mother came to mould
105 Those limbs like ours which are
What must make our daystar
Much dearer to mankind;
Whose glory bare would blind
Or less would win man's mind.
110 Through her we may see him
Made sweeter, not made dim,
And her hand leaves his light
Sifted to suit our sight.
    Be thou then, O thou dear
115 Mother, my atmosphere;
My happier world, wherein
To wend and meet no sin;
Above me, round me lie
Fronting my froward eye
120 With sweet and scarless sky;
Stir in my ears, speak there
Of God's love, O live air,
Of patience, penance, prayer:
World-mothering air, air wild,
125 Wound with thee, in thee isled,
Fold home, fast fold thy child.

Stonyhurst. May 1883

p.161

Plate 422   OET No. 151: The Blessed Virgin compared to the Air... -- MS. 1 - A(2)

A.pp.159-161--autograph faircopy, cont.. The original grey sheet, too large for album A, was cut in four: there was originally so little space between the columns that parts of the last letters in 66 and 80 can be seen before 98 and 112; 93 had to be cut off at the bottom of the left column, 123-126 pasted on p.161.

GMH's changes: 64 "morn,..." [? RB has also del. it and changed his marginal two dots to a dash]   77 "Skywards. Rich" altered to "Skywards: rich"   80 "d[oes?] will"   84 "shews" (dittography from 85)   110 "let us"   113 "and suiting sight"

RB's black ink (1889) notes that "he" (63, RB's underlining) is correct (see note on the B version)   66 "no stop" (B has a smudge which could be taken as a period or dash)   68 RB adds two carets where B has commas   73 "Again :" colon blotted--RB places "X" beside it and again in margin, noting that B has a comma.

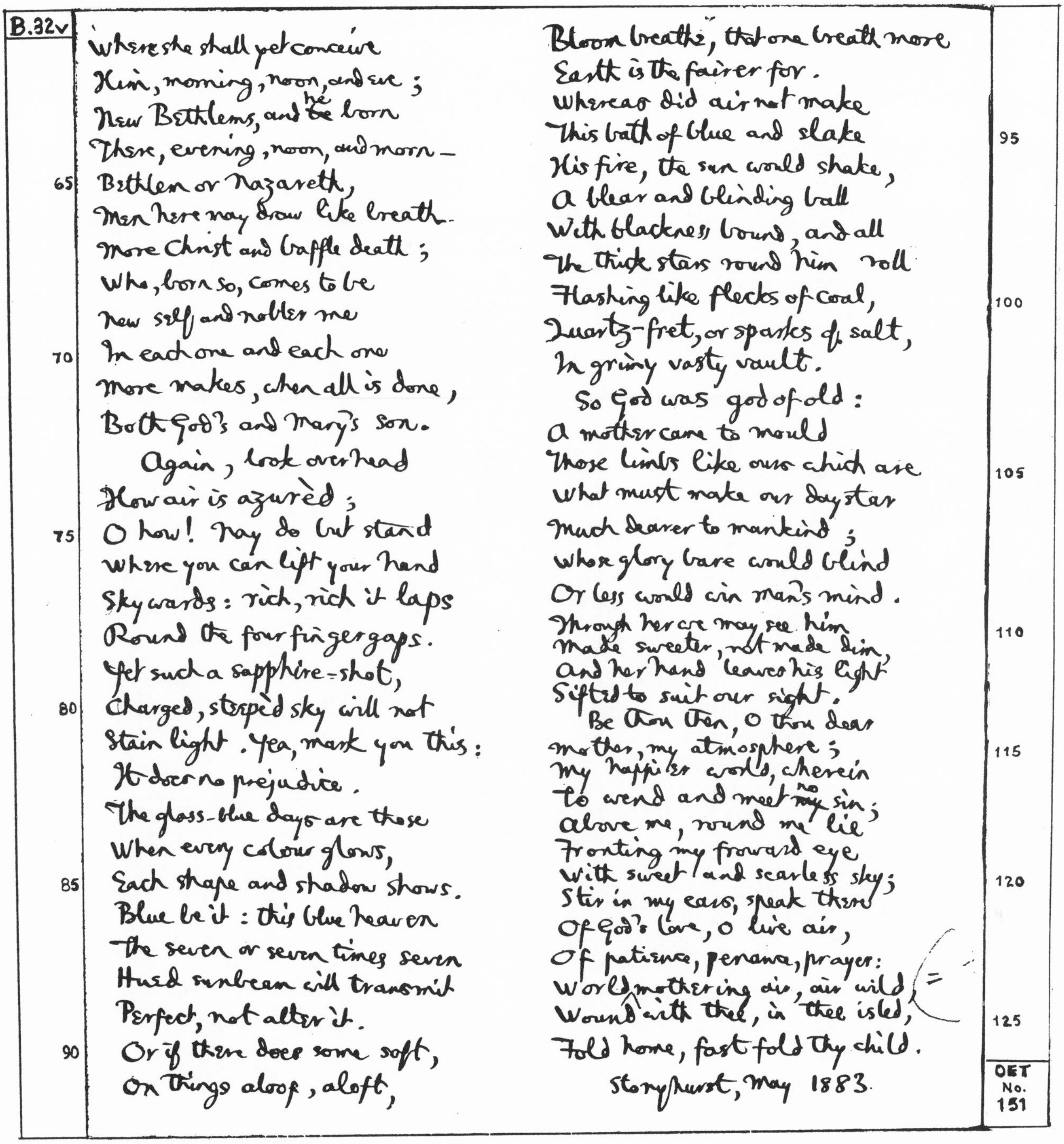

B.32v

Where she shall yet conceive
Him, morning, noon, and eve;
New Bethlems, and he born
There, evening, noon, and morn—
65 Bethlem or Nazareth,
Men here may draw like breath
More Christ and baffle death;
Who, born so, comes to be
New self and nobler me
70 In each one and each one
More makes, when all is done,
Both God's and Mary's son.
　Again, look overhead
How air is azurèd;
75 O how! nay do but stand
Where you can lift your hand
Skywards: rich, rich it laps
Round the four finger gaps.
Yet such a sapphire-shot,
80 Charged, steepèd sky will not
Stain light. Yea, mark you this:
It does no prejudice.
The glass-blue days are those
When every colour glows,
85 Each shape and shadow shows.
Blue be it: this blue heaven
The seven or seven times seven
Hued sunbeam will transmit
Perfect, not alter it.
90 Or if there does some soft,
On things aloof, aloft,

Bloom breathe, that one breath more
Earth is the fairer for.
Whereas did air not make
This bath of blue and slake　95
His fire, the sun would shake,
A blear and blinding ball
With blackness bound, and all
The thick stars round him roll
Flashing like flecks of coal,　100
Quartz-fret, or sparks of salt,
In grimy vasty vault.
　So God was god of old:
A mother came to mould
Those limbs like ours which are　105
What must make our daystar
Much dearer to mankind;
Whose glory bare would blind
Or less would win man's mind.
Through her we may see him　110
Made sweeter, not made dim,
And her hand leaves his light
Sifted to suit our sight.
　Be thou then, O thou dear
mother, my atmosphere;　115
My happier world, wherein
To wend and meet no sin;
Above me, round me lie
Fronting my froward eye
With sweet and scarless sky;　120
Stir in my ears, speak there
Of God's love, O live air,
Of patience, penance, prayer:
World-mothering air, air wild,
Wound with thee, in thee isled,　125
Fold home, fast fold thy child.
　Stonyhurst, May 1883.

OET No. 151

Plate 423　OET No. 151: The Blessed Virgin compared to the Air... -- MS. 2 - B(2)

B.32v--autograph faircopy, cont.. In 63 RB's transcription of A, which GMH was copying, probably read "be", not "he" (an easy mistake in this context): GMH caught the slip later. GMH first copied the lines in pencil, traces of which can still be seen (e.g., 61, 64, 70-80, 83, 90, 91, 103, 106). In 117 "my" was prob. dittography from "me" in 118. The date seems to have been copied with the text.

RB at 124 notes in pencil that A hyphenates "world-mothering" [as both A and B do in 1]; in B it is clearly intended as one word (cf. 77, "Sky/wards", 78 "fin/ger/gaps", 106 "day/star").

Vol.i. No.9 Mar. 1883

OET No. 150a

162 *THE STONYHURST MAGAZINE*

A. p. 306

OET No. 150 b,c

A TRIO OF TRIOLETS

No. 1—Λέγεταί τι καινόν;

" No news in the *Times* to-day,"
Each man tells his next-door neighbour.
He, to see if what they say,
" No news in the *Times* to-day,"
Is correct, must plough his way
Through that : after three hours' labour,
" No news in the *Times* to-day,"
Each man tells his next-door neighbour.

No. 2—Cockle's Antibilious Pills

" When you ask for Cockle's Pills,
Beware of spurious imitations."
Yes, when you ask for every ill's
Cure, when you ask for Cockle's Pills,
Some hollow counterfeit that kills
Would fain mock that which heals the nations.
Oh, when you ask for Cockle's Pills
Beware of heartless imitations.

No. 3—"The child is father to the man"
(*Wordsworth*)

" The child is father to the man."
How can he be ? The words are wild.
Suck any sense from that who can :
" The child is father to the man."
No ; what the poet did write ran,
" The man is father to the child."
" The child is father to the man!"
How *can* he be ? The words are wild.

BRAN

No. 2—Cockle's Antibilious Pills

" When you ask for Cockle's Pills,
Beware of spurious imitations."
Yes, when you ask for every ill's
Cure, when you ask for Cockle's Pills,
Some hollow counterfeit that kills
Would fain mock that which heals the nations.
Oh, when you ask for Cockle's Pills
Beware of heartless imitations.

No. 3—"The child is father to the man"
(*Wordsworth*)

" The child is father to the man."
How can he be ? The words are wild.
Suck any sense from that who can :
" The child is father to the man."
No ; what the poet did write ran,
" The man is father to the child."
" The child is father to the man!"
How *can* he be ? The words are wild.

BRAN

These verses are by Father Hopkins, they were for some private magazine . He sent me when I lived in London a number of comic verses which I did not preserve. R.B.

Plate 424   OET No. 150: A Trio of Triolets -- No MSS.

[left]   Stonyhurst Magazine, Vol. 1, No. 9, March 1883, p.162. If any MSS survived GMH's death, they may have been destroyed by RB as unfit to stand beside his serious poetry--see note by RB in H.ii.125r, quoted OET p.xxxi.

[right]   A.p.306--a copy of Nos. 2 and 3 of the Trio (150b and 150c), which GMH sent RB. See L.i.190 (GMH to RB, 7 March 1884): "I shall also enclose, if I can find, two triolets I wrote for the Stonyhurst Magazine, for the third was not good, and they spoilt what point it had by changing the title." RB's sharp editorial eye (and pencil) observed that in No. 3, line 7, the exclamation (by the naive protagonist) should be transposed ("tr") to after the quotation marks (where it has been moved in the OET). RB's note runs: "These verses are by Father Hopkins. They were for some private magazine. He sent me when I lived in London a number of comic verses which I did not preserve. R.B." RB included the third triolet in Poems, 1st. edn., p.87.

See OET commentary, p.434.

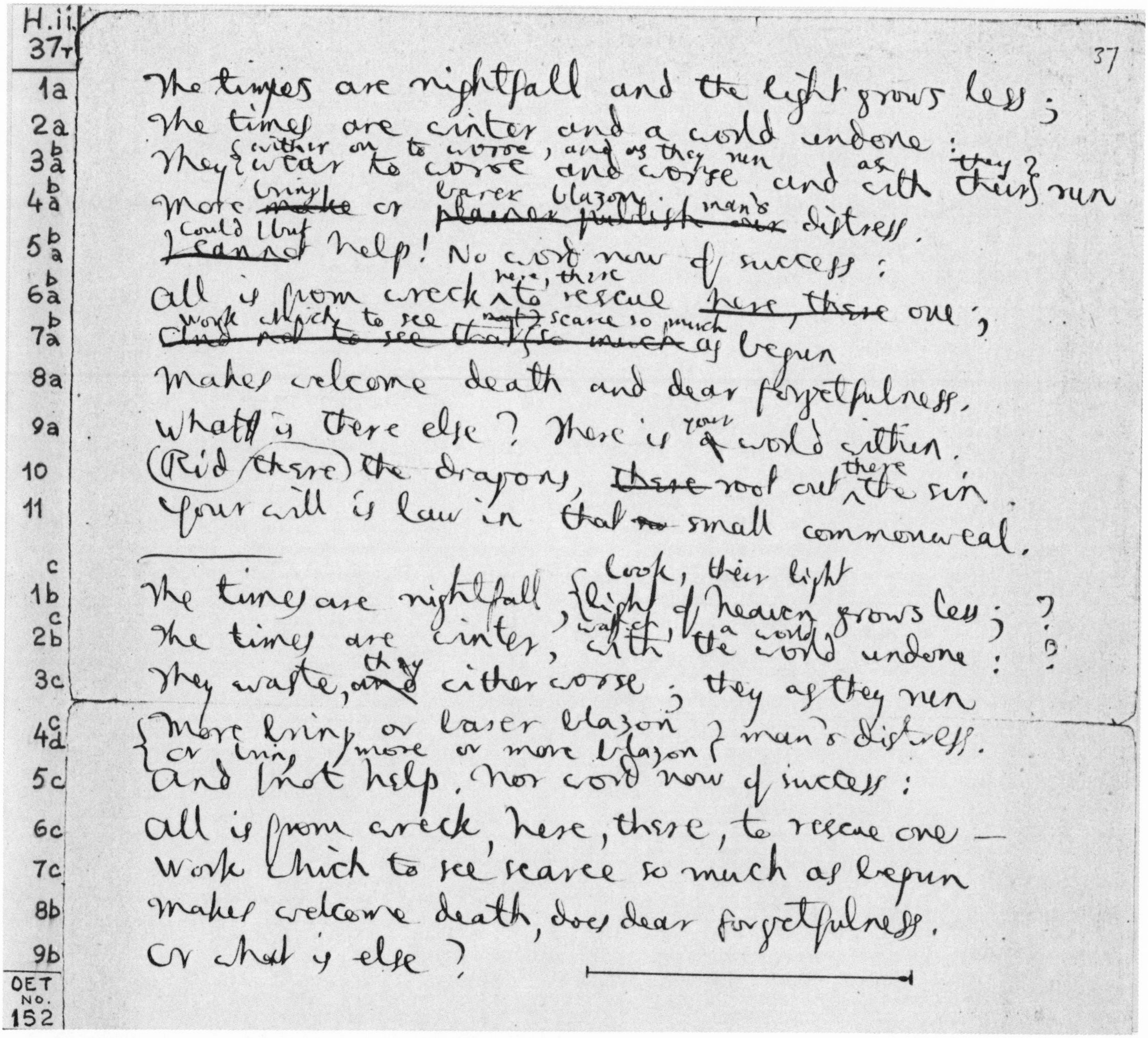

PLATE 425. OET 152. "The times are nightfall" • 249

H.ii.
37r — 37

1a The times are nightfall and the light grows less;
2a The times are winter and a world undone:
3b/a They wither on to worse, and as they run / They wear to worse and worse and as theirs run
4b/a More bring or barer blazon plainer publish man's distress.
5b/a I cannot help! No word now of success:
6b/a All is from wreck, here, there one; into rescue here, there one;
7b/a Work which to see scarce so much as begun / And not to see that so much as begun
8a Makes welcome death and dear forgetfulness.
9a What is there else? There is your world within.
10 (Ride there) the dragons, there root out there the sin.
11 Your will is law in that small commonweal.

c
1b/c The times are nightfall, look, their light / light of heaven grows less;
2b/c The times are winter, watch, with a world undone:
3c They waste, they either worse; they as they run
4c/d More bring or barer blazon / or bring more or more blazon man's distress.
5c And I not help. Nor word now of success:
6c All is from wreck, here, there, to rescue one —
7c Work which to see scarce so much as begun
8b Makes welcome death, does dear forgetfulness.
9b Or what is else?

OET NO. 152

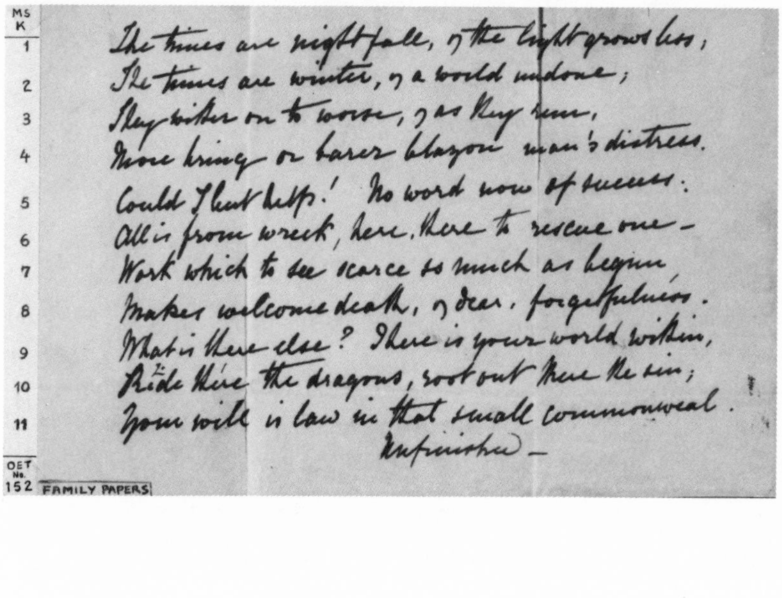

MS K

1 The times are nightfall, of the light grows less;
2 The times are winter, of a world undone;
3 They wither on to worse, of as they run,
4 More bring or barer blazon man's distress.
5 Could I but help! No word now of success:
6 All is from wreck, here, there to rescue one —
7 Work which to see scarce so much as begun,
8 Makes welcome death, of dear, forgetfulness.
9 What is there else? There is your world within,
10 Ride there the dragons, root out there the sin;
11 Your will is law in that small commonweal.
Unfinished —

OET No. 152 FAMILY PAPERS

Plate 425 — OET No. 152: "The times are nightfall" -- H and K

[top] H.ii.37 recto--sole autograph, draft of an unfinished sonnet, with the octave revised. Changes, deletions include: 1a squeezed "e" in "times" del. 4a "More make or plainer publish our" 7a "And not to see that so much as begun" rev. as 7b "Work which to see not so much as begun", and finally "Work which to see scarce so much as begun" 9a What's...a/your 11 sw small 3c "and/they" (written across the d, so that e seems to be deleted). Note GMH's queries as to which of the alternatives--1b or c, 2b or c ("watch, a world")--to select: the query at the end of 2 might be mistaken for a "B". In 2c the "h" of the interlined "watch" melds into the "h" of "with" below it.

[below] K. Family Papers--transcription from the autograph by GMH's mother, Mrs. Kate Hopkins. She either did not see, or chose not to follow, the lower half of the MS. Note the misreading in 10: "Ride there" with "2" and "1" above to indicate the transposition. Although this transcript has no authority, with many departures in punctuation, it is reproduced to help the evaluation of her reliability where (as in No. 143) she copied a version which has since been lost.

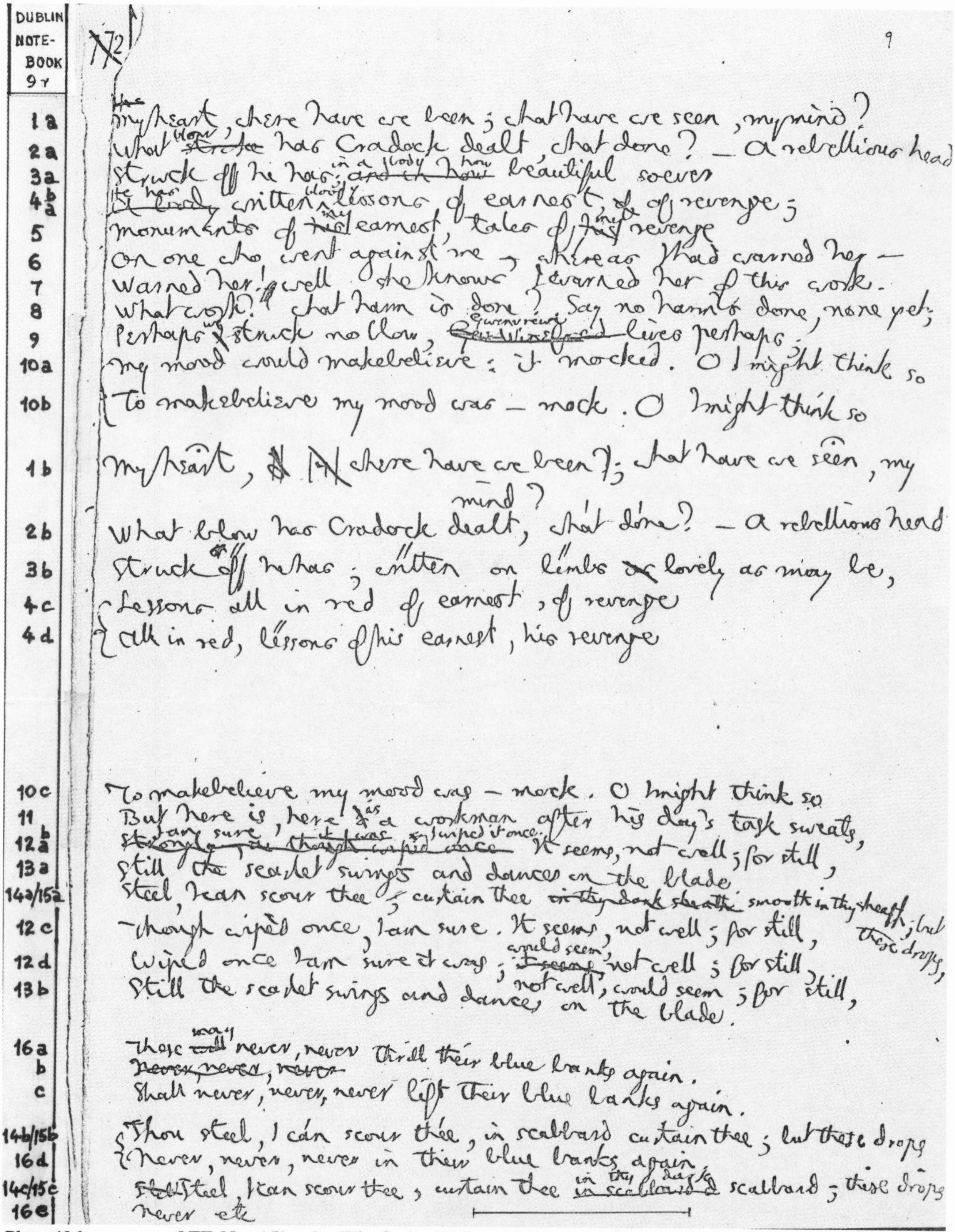

DUBLIN NOTE-BOOK 9r

9

1a My heart, where have we been; what have we seen, my mind?
2a What blow ~~stroke~~ has Cradock dealt, what done? — A rebellious head
3a Struck off he has; in a body ~~and oh how~~ how beautiful soever
4b/a He has ~~It lively~~ written blood lessons of earnest, of revenge;
5 monuments of ~~his~~ my earnest, tales of ~~his~~ my revenge
6 On one who went against me, whereas I had warned her —
7 Warned her! well she knows I warned her of this work.
8 What work? what harm is done? Say no harm's done, none yet;
9 Perhaps we struck no blow, ~~Gw Winefred~~ Gwenvrewi lives perhaps;
10a my mood would makebelieve: it mocked. O I might think so
10b To makebelieve my mood was — mock. O I might think so

1b My heart, where have we been? what have we seen, my mind?
2b What blow has Cradock dealt, what done? — A rebellious head
3b Struck off he has; written on limbs ~~as~~ lovely as may be,
4c Lessons all in red of earnest, of revenge
4d All in red, lessons of his earnest, his revenge

10c To makebelieve my mood was — mock. O I might think so
11 But here ~~'s~~ is, here is a workman after his day's task sweats,
12a/b ~~Strongly, a though wiped once~~ I am sure ~~it was~~ I wiped it once. It seems, not well; for still,
13a Still the scarlet swings and dances on the blade.
14a/15a Steel, I can scour thee, curtain thee ~~in thy dark sheath~~ smooth in thy sheath; but these drops,
12c though wiped once, I am sure. It seems, not well; for still,
12d Wiped once I am sure it was; ~~It seems~~ would seem, not well; for still,
13b Still the scarlet swings and dances on the blade. not well, would seem; for still,

16a these ~~will~~ may never, never thrill their blue banks again.
b ~~Never, never, never~~
c Shall never, never, never lift their blue banks again.
14b/15b Thou steel, I can scour thee, in scabbard curtain thee; but these drops
16d Never, never, never in their blue banks again
14c/15c ~~Stel~~ Steel, I can scour thee, curtain thee ~~in scabbard d~~ in thy dark scabbard; these drops
16e never etc

Plate 426 OET No. 152: St. Winefred's Well -- MS. 1: Dub.[1]

[Dub.[1]] Dublin Note-book 9r--earliest autograph draft. Deletions include: 1a "~~Whe~~[re]"--part hidden by stub of a page with examination marks torn out 2a "stroke" 7 "~~,~~well" 9 "~~I~~/we" "~~Gw Winefred~~/Gwenvrewi" 1b minim [for minim rest? no pitch is indicated] and quaver rest, both del.. If these were part of ℓ.1, they might indicate a pause, the silent second half of a dipody; but they might be unconnected. 3b "off" double stress del. and restored "~~as~~" 11 "here~~'s~~/is" 12a "Strongly, ~~a~~ though wiped once/I am sure ~~it was~~ I wiped it once 14a, 15a"~~;~~ , curtain thee in ~~thy dark sheath~~" 16a ~~will~~/may 14c, 15c "~~Stel...in scabbard~~ d[ark?]/in thy dark scabbard" The verso is blank.

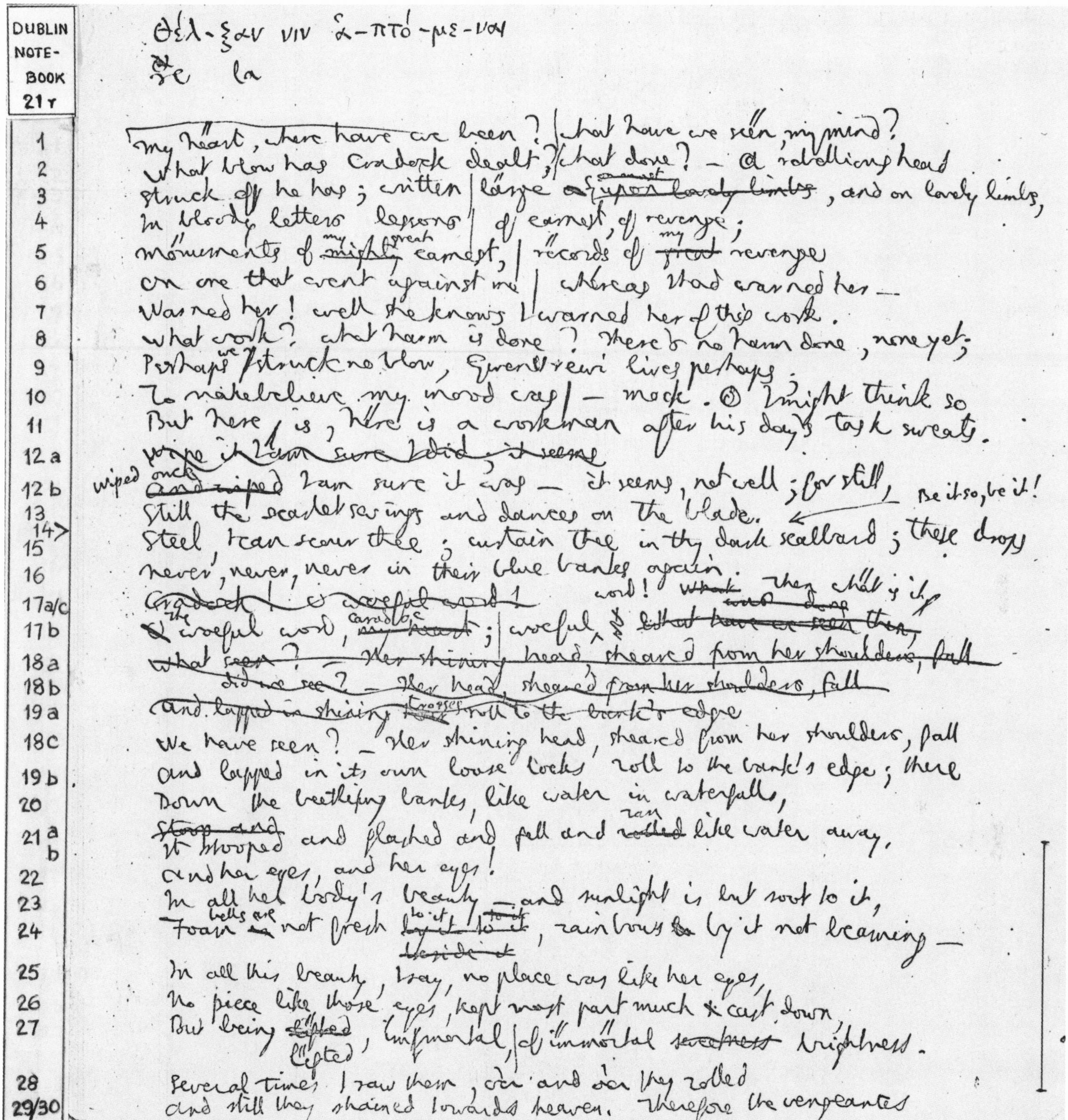

PLATE 427. OET 153. *St. Winefred's Well* • 251

DUBLIN
NOTE-
BOOK
21 r

Θελ-ξαν νιν ὡ-πτό-με-ναι
ᾷ ᵈ la

1   My heart, where have we been? What have we seen, my mind?
2   What blow has Cradock dealt? What done? — A rebellious head
3   struck off he has; written | large ~~upon lovely limbs~~, and on lovely limbs,
4   In bloody letters lessons | of earnest, of revenge;
5   monuments of ~~mighty~~ ᵐʸ ~~earnest~~ ᵍʳᵉᵃᵗ, records of ~~great~~ ᵐʸ revenge
6   on one that went against me | whereas I had warned her —
7   Warned her! well she knows I warned her of this work.
8   What work? what harm is done? There is no harm done, none yet;
9   Perhaps ʷᵉ I struck no blow, Gwenvrewi lives perhaps.
10 To make-believe my mood was — mock. ⊙ I might think so
11 But here, is, here is a workman after his day's task sweats.
12a ~~wipe it I am sure I did, it seems~~
    wiped ᵒⁿᶜᵉ
12b ~~and wiped~~ I am sure it was — it seems, not well; for still, Be it so, be it!
13 Still, the scarlet swings and dances on the blade. ←
14/15 Steel, I can scour thee; curtain thee in thy dark scabbard; these drops
16 never, never, never in their blue banks again.
17a/c ~~Cradock! O woeful word 1~~   word! ~~what~~ they shall; if
17b I woeful word, ᶜᵃⁿᵈᵒᵇᵉ ᵐʸ ~~heart~~; woeful, & ~~what have we seen then~~,
18a ~~what seen? — Her shining head sheared from her shoulders, fall~~
18b ~~did we see? — Her head, sheared from her shoulders, fall~~
19a ~~and lapped in shining tresses roll to the bank's edge~~
18c We have seen? — Her shining head, sheared from her shoulders, fall
19b and lapped in its own loose locks roll to the bank's edge; there
20 Down the beetling banks, like water in waterfall,
21a ~~Stoop and~~
21b ~~It stooped~~ and flashed and fell and ~~rolled~~ ʳᵃⁿ like water away,
22 and her eyes, and her eyes!
23 In all her body's beauty — and sunlight is but soot to it,
24 ~~Foam is~~ not fresh ~~to it to it~~ ᵇᵉˡˡˢ ᵃʳᵉ, rainbows ~~be~~ by it not beaming —
    ~~beside it~~
25 In all this beauty, I say, no place was like her eyes,
26 No place like those eyes, kept most part much & cast down,
27 But being ~~lifted~~ ˡⁱᶠᵗᵉᵈ, immortal, of immortal ~~sweetness~~ brightness.
28 Several times I saw them, o'er and o'er they rolled
29/30 and still they shined towards heaven. Therefore the vengeance

Plate 427   OET No. 152: St. Winefred's Well--MS. **2**: Dub.²

[Dub.²] Dublin Note-book 21r--autograph revised draft, on a page below a transcription of Pindar's fourth Nemean Ode, ℓℓ.1-3 (prescribed for Royal Univ. MA, 1884-86), with GMH's melody in tonic solfa (last few words at the top of plate). Deletions include: 2 "dealt,?"   "a" mended to "A"   3 "on upon/on most   9 "I/we...Gwen1 [o?]" mended to "Gwenvrewi"   17a "Cradock! O woeful word!"   17b "O/The woeful word, my heart/Caradoc; woeful/ word! [w mended to] What have we seen then,/What was done [then,]"   19a "shining hair/tresses"   24 "Foam is/Foambells are...by it to it/to it...rainbow b[eams?]" changed to "rainbows"   27 "lifted/lifted, im/mortal," [misplaced caesura?]   MS ends in mid-sentence; verso has meditation notes, Dec. 20 [1884--see S.257]

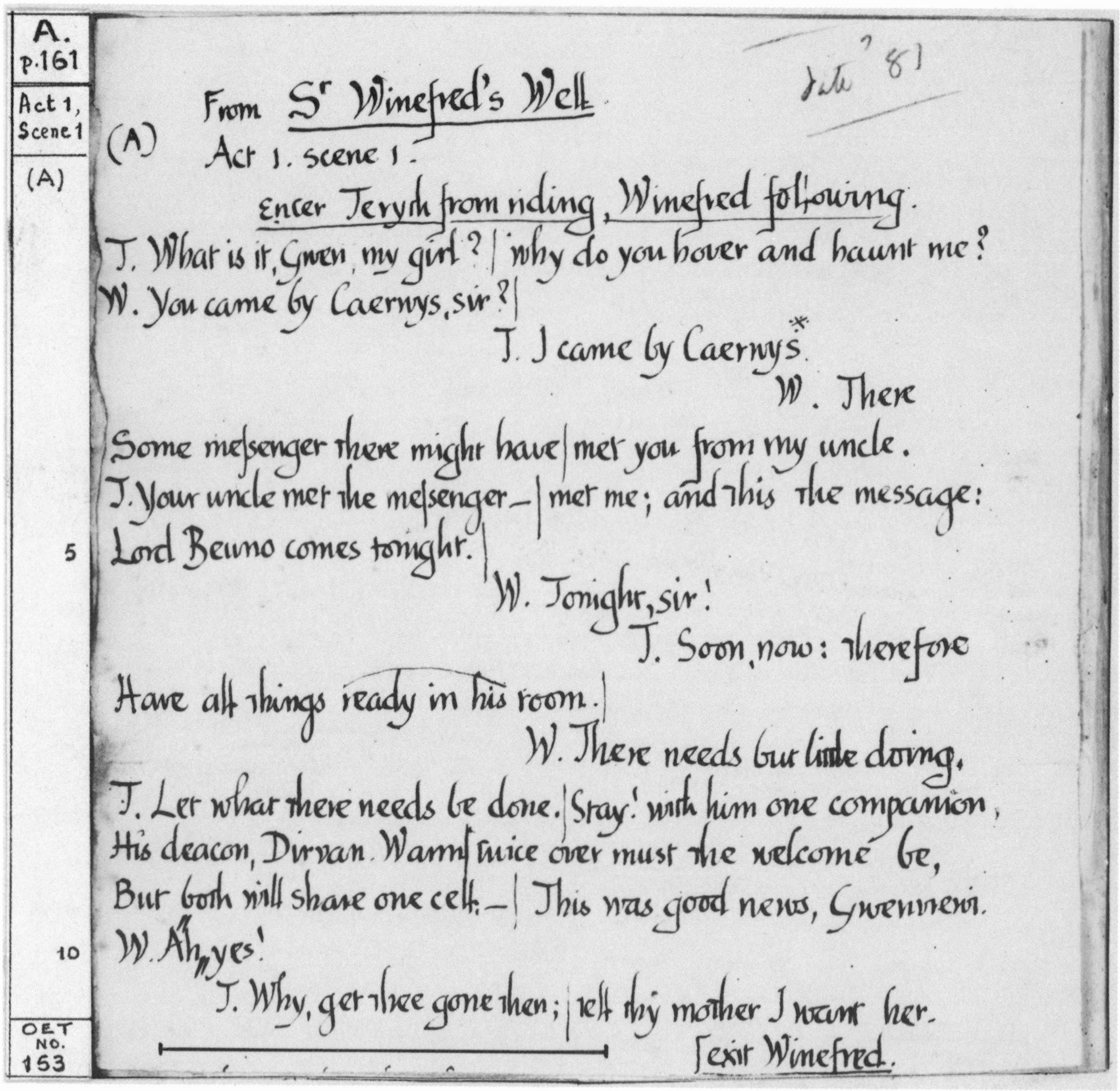

A.
p.161

Act 1,
Scene 1

(A)

OET
NO.
153

(A)

From S⟨r⟩ Winefred's Well

date '81

Act 1. scene 1.

Enter Teryth from riding, Winefred following.

T. What is it, Gwen, my girl? | why do you hover and haunt me?

W. You came by Caernys, sir? |

T. J came by Caernys.*

W. There

Some messenger there might have | met you from my uncle.

T. Your uncle met the messenger — | met me; and this the message:

5 Lord Beuno comes tonight. |

W. Tonight, sir!

T. Soon, now: therefore

Have all things ready in his room. |

W. There needs but little doing.

T. Let what there needs be done. | Stay! with him one companion,

His deacon, Dirvan. Warm twice over must the welcome be,

But both will share one cell. — | This was good news, Gwennvewi.

10 W. Ah, yes!

T. Why, get thee gone then; | tell thy mother J want her.

[exit Winefred.

Plates 428 [above] **and 429** [opposite]   OET No. 153: St. Winefred's Well -- MS. 3 (1,2)

A.pp.161-162 (Act I, Scene 1)--the first two of the seven-page transcription by Mrs. RB (Monica Bridges), in fine Italic script, of an unfinished autograph (now lost) loaned to RB by GMH. RB noted (Poems, 1st. edn., 122) that the text might "contain copyist's errors". One is in 10 where the double stress below "Ah" must belong to "Why" (on which H places it). Again in 24 "There", as RB pencils in the margin, must have been "I here": in this Italic script u.c. "I" and "T" are very similar (cf. Plate 430, 10 and 15). In 12 ", the deeper" has been partially mended to ". The deeper" (obviously correct). Below "thoughts" (24) can be read "ears" (? fears). In 2 the asterisk after "Caerwys" refers to the footnote at the bottom of Monica Bridges's first page (after 17): the asterisk was cut off during the process of mounting the pages in album A. RB's "date '81" (pencil beside the title) applies only to No. 148, the final chorus, "The Leaden Echo and the Golden Echo".

PLATE 429. OET 153. *St. Winefred's Well*   •   253

A.
P.162

162

No man has such a daughter. | The fathers of the world
Call no such maiden "mine", | The deeper grows her dearness
And more and more times laces | round and round my heart,
The more some monstrous hand | gropes with clammy fingers there,
15 Tampering with those sweet vines, | draws them out, strains them, strains them;
Meantime some tongue cries "What, Teryth! | what, thou poor fond father!
How when this bloom, this honeysuckle, | that rides the air so rich about thee,
: In english pronounced Caris, like heres

Is all, all sheared away, | thus!" Then I sweat for fear.
Or else a funeral. | and yet 'tis not a funeral,
20 Some pageant which takes tears | & I must foot with feeling that
Alive or dead my girl | is carried in it, endlessly
Goes marching thro' my mind. | What sense is this? It has none.
This is too much the father; | nay the mother. Fanciful!
There forbid my thoughts to fool themselves with fears.
Enter Gwenlo.

? There

OET NO. 153

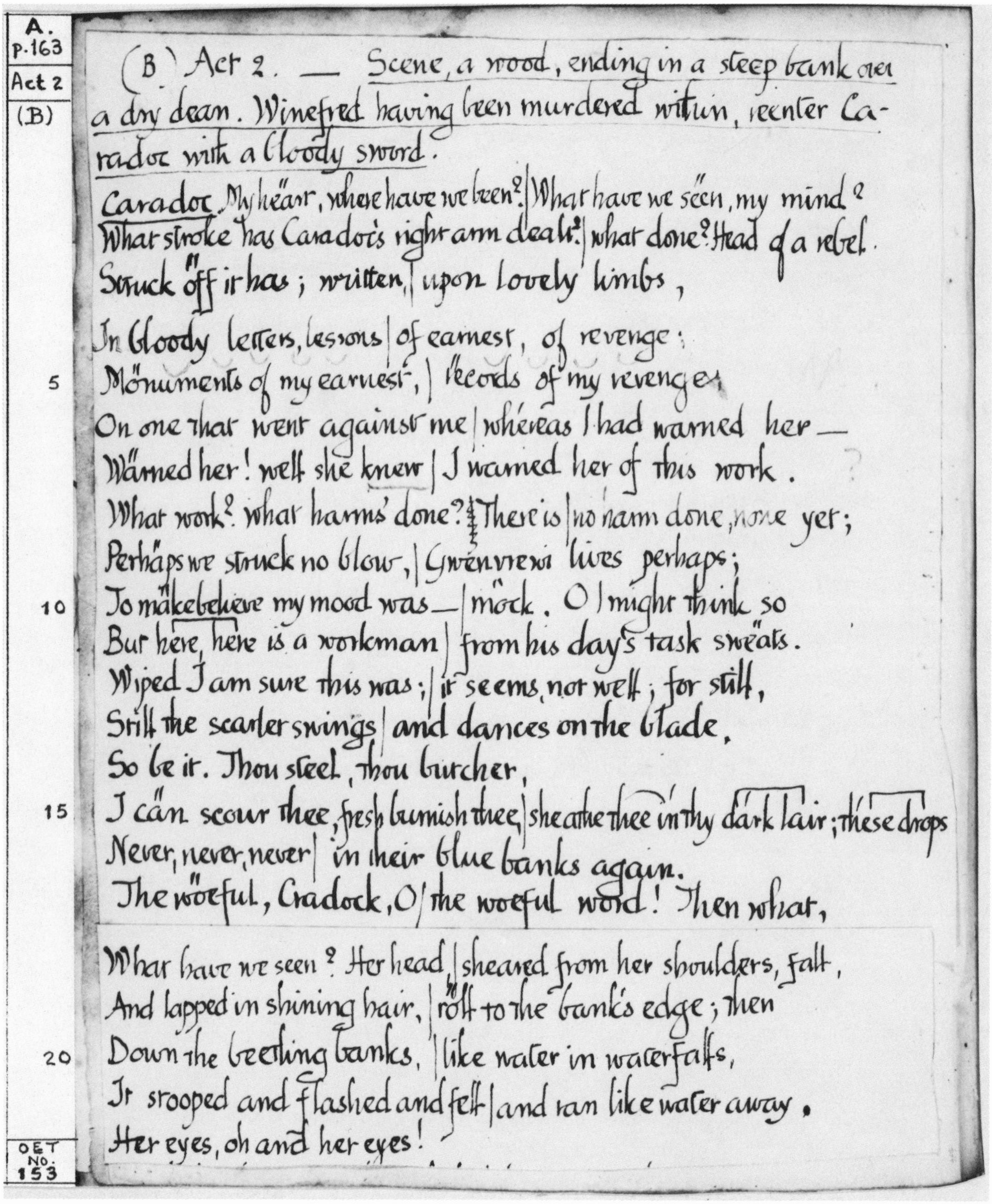

A.
p.163
Act 2
(B)

(B) Act 2. — Scene, a wood, ending in a steep bank over
a dry dean. Winefred having been murdered within, reenter Caradoc with a bloody sword.

Caradoc. My heart, where have we been? | What have we seen, my mind?
What stroke has Caradoc's right arm dealt? | what done? Head of a rebel.
Struck off it has ; written, | upon lovely limbs ,

In bloody letters, lessons | of earnest, of revenge :
5 Monuments of my earnest , | Records of my revenges
On one that went against me | whereas I had warned her —
Warned her! well she knew | I warned her of this work .   ?
What work? what harm's done? ‡ There is | no harm done, none yet ;
Perhaps we struck no blow, | Gwenvrewi lives perhaps ;
10 To makebelieve my mood was — | mock . O I might think so
But here, here is a workman | from his day's task sweats .
Wiped I am sure this was ; | it seems, not well ; for still,
Still the scarlet swings | and dances on the blade .
So be it. Thou steel, thou butcher,
15 I can scour thee, fresh burnish thee | sheathe thee in thy dark lair ; these drops
Never, never, never | in their blue banks again.
The woeful, Cradock, O | the woeful word! Then what,

What have we seen ? Her head | sheared from her shoulders, fall,
And lapped in shining hair, | rolt to the bank's edge ; then
20 Down the beetling banks, | like water in waterfalls,
It stooped and flashed and fell | and ran like water away .
Her eyes, oh and her eyes !

OET
NO.
153

Plate 430 [above] and 431 [opposite]   OET No. 153: St. Winefred's Well -- MS. 3 (cont.): A (3,4)

A.pp.163-164--Mrs. RB's transcription cont.. In 5 dittography marred the final punctuation because two successive lines ended with "revenge": she copied ";" from 4, then, realising her slip, extended the final "e" in 5 to absorb its period and tried to erase the comma--the autograph therefore prob. had no stop at the end of 5. In 36 "Honouring" shows ink over some pencil: no period can be intended to follow it (from a flaw in the autograph?). In 40 "now" (from 41) was first mended to "nor," then del., and "nor" rewritten beside it.

RB's pencil in 5 marks two runs of four light syllables. In 7 he queries "knew" (which assumes realisation of Winefred's death) because Dub.[1] and Dub.[2] have "knows", but "knew" fits 1-4 better.

PLATE 431. OET 153. *St. Winefred's Well* • 255

In all her beauty, and sunlight to it is a pit, den, darkness, 164

Foamfalling is not fresh to it, rainbow by it not beaming,

25 In all her body, I say, no place was like her eyes,

No piece matched those eyes kept most part much cast down

But, being lifted, immortal, of immortal brightness.

Several times I saw them, thrice or four times turning;

Round and round they came and flashed towards heaven: O there,

30 There they did appeal. Therefore any vengeances

Are afoot; heaven-vault fast purpling portends, & what first lightning

Any instant falls means me. And I do not repent;

I do not and I will not repent, not repent.

.The blame bear who aroused me. What I have done violent

35 I have like a lion done, lionlike done,

Honouring. an uncontrolled royal. wrathful nature,

Mantling passion in a grandeur, crimson grandeur.

Now be my pride then perfect, all one piece. Henceforth

In a wide world of defiance Caractor lives alone,

40 Loyal to his own soul, laying his own law down, no law ~~now~~ nor

Lord now curb him for ever O daring! O deep insight!

What is virtue? Valour; only the heart valiant.

And right? Only resolution; will, his will unwavering

Who, like me, knowing his nature to the heart home, nature's business,

45 Despatches with no flinching . But will flesh, O can flesh

Second this fiery strain? Not always; O no no!

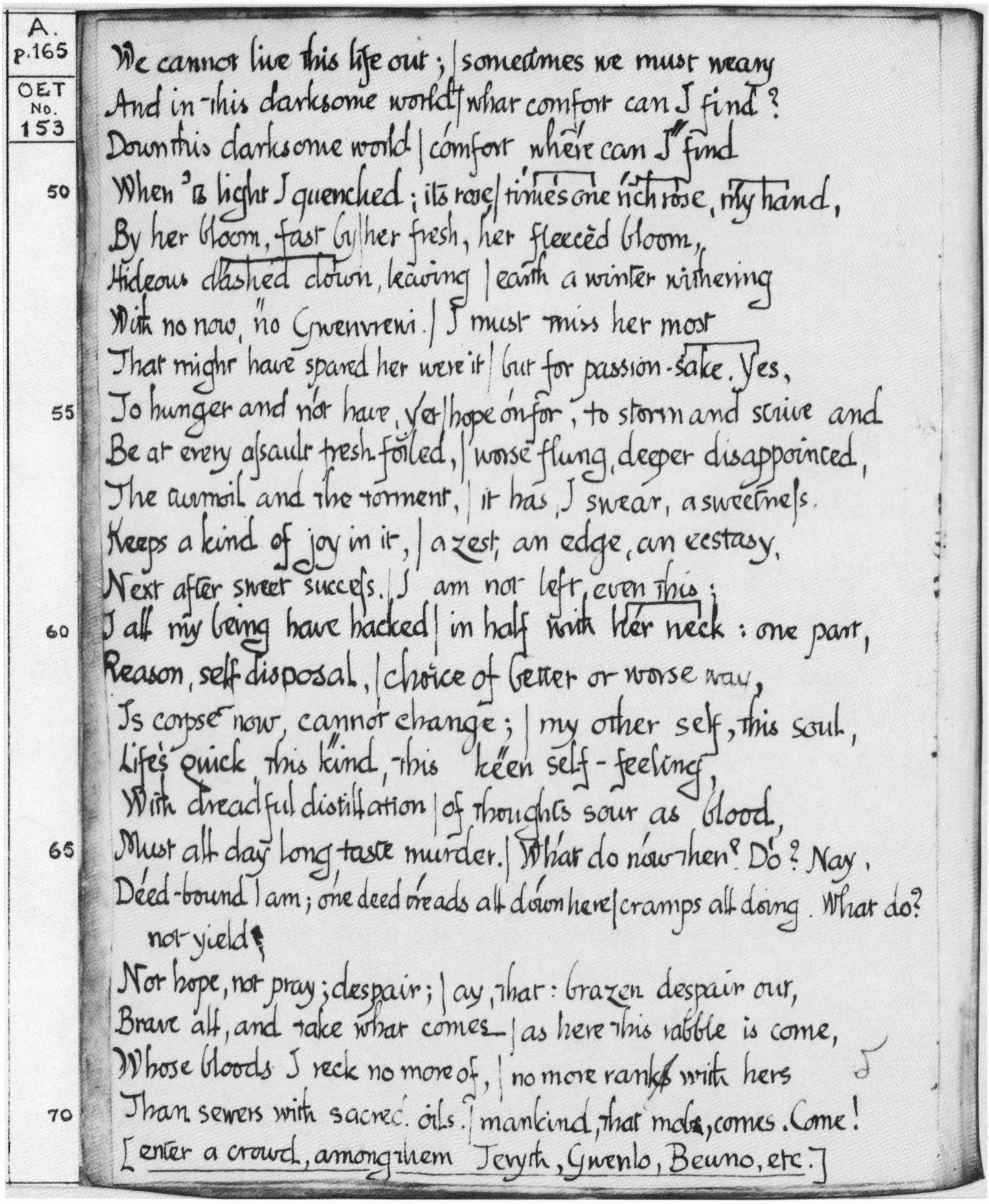

A.
p.165

OET
No.
153

We cannot live this life out; | sometimes we must weary

And in this darksome world | what comfort can I find?

Down this darksome world | comfort where can I find

50 When 'tis light I quenched; its rose | times one rich rose, my hand,

By her bloom, fast by her fresh, her fleecèd bloom,

Hideous dashed down, leaving | earth a winter withering

With no now, no Gwenvrewi. | I must miss her most

That might have spared her were it | but for passion-sake. Yes,

55 To hunger and not have, yet | hope on for, to storm and strive and

Be at every assault fresh foiled, | worse flung, deeper disappointed,

The turmoil and the torment, | it has, I swear, a sweetness.

Keeps a kind of joy in it, | a zest, an edge, an ecstasy,

Next after sweet success. | I am not left, even this;

60 I all my being have hacked | in half with her neck: one part,

Reason, self-disposal, | choice of better or worse way,

Is corpse now, cannot change; | my other self, this soul,

Life's quick, this kind, this keen self-feeling,

With dreadful distillation | of thoughts sour as blood,

65 Must all day long taste murder. | What do now then? Do? Nay,

Deed-bound I am; one deed treads all down here | cramps all doing. What do?

     not yield?

Nor hope, not pray; despair; | ay, that: brazen despair out,

Brave all, and take what comes | as here this rabble is come,

Whose bloods I reck no more of, | no more ranks with hers

70 Than sewers with sacred oils. | mankind, that mob, comes. Come!

[enter a crowd, among them Teryth, Gwenlo, Beuno, etc.]

Plates 432 [above] and 433   OET No. 153: St. Winefred's Well -- MS. 3 (cont.): A (5,6)

A.pp.165-166--Mrs. RB's transcription cont.. In 50 "times" was prob. not meant to have two stresses (and syllables). In Act II, 66, the final stop under the blots is obscure: prob. an exclamation del., changed to a comma. In 69 RB has del. the s of "ranks", but in 70 the s of "mobs" was obscurely del. in black ink by the copyist. The l.c. m of "mankind" after a period is explained by GMH's dwarf u.c. m (e.g. l.1 in Dub.[1]).   In C.5 "Of" is mended to "Or".

In C.8, RB inserted hyphens (and prob. the very faint comma after "cough"): all these are reproduced in H. In 12 the ornate r in "Dry" led to the H misreading "Day". In 17 the seraph of d in "recorded" was mistaken for a period in H.i.59r, the parenthesis being omitted: this led to the printing of a period in all editions till 1985.

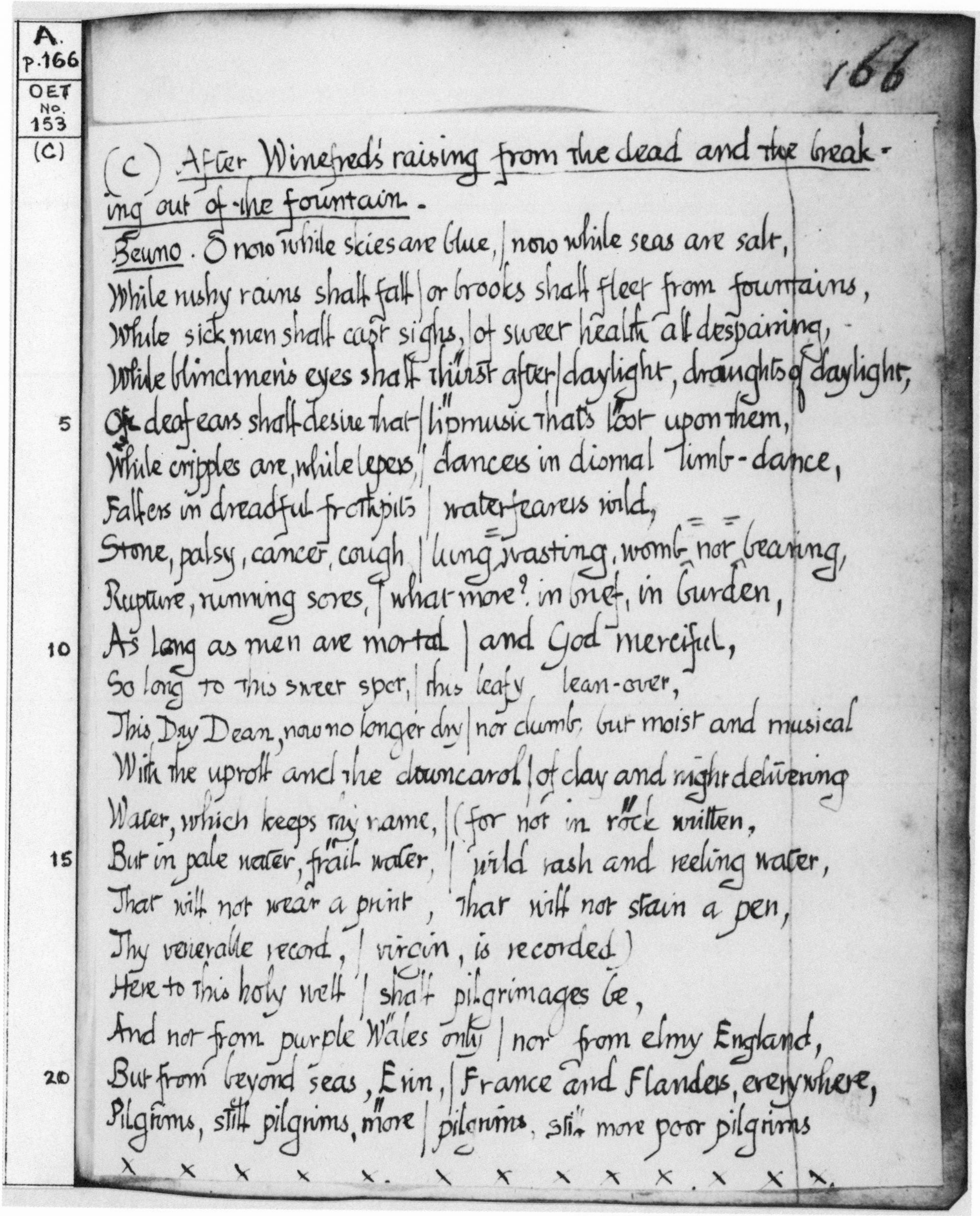

PLATE 433. OET 153. *St. Winefred's Well* • 257

A.
p.166

OET
No.
153

(C)

166

(C) After Winefred's raising from the dead and the breaking out of the fountain.

Beuno. O now while skies are blue, | now while seas are salt,
While rushy rains shall fall | or brooks shall fleet from fountains,
While sick men shall cast sighs, | of sweet health all despairing,
While blindmen's eyes shall thirst after | daylight, draughts of daylight,
5 Or deaf ears shall desire that | lip music that's lost upon them,
While cripples are, while lepers, | dancers in dismal limb-dance,
Fallers in dreadful frothpits | waterfearers wild,
Stone, palsy, cancer, cough | lung wasting, womb not bearing,
Rupture, running sores, | what more? in brief, in burden,
10 As long as men are mortal | and God merciful,
So long to this sweet spot, | this leafy lean-over,
This Dry Dean, now no longer dry | nor dumb, but moist and musical
With the uproll and the downcarol | of day and night delivering
Water, which keeps my name, | (for not in rock written,
15 But in pale water, frail water, | wild rash and reeling water,
That will not wear a print, | that will not stain a pen,
Thy venerable record, | virgin, is recorded)
Here to this holy well | shall pilgrimages be,
And not from purple Wales only | nor from elmy England,
20 But from beyond seas, Erin, | France and Flanders, everywhere,
Pilgrims, still pilgrims, more | pilgrims, still more poor pilgrims

x x x x x x. x x x x x x. x x x.

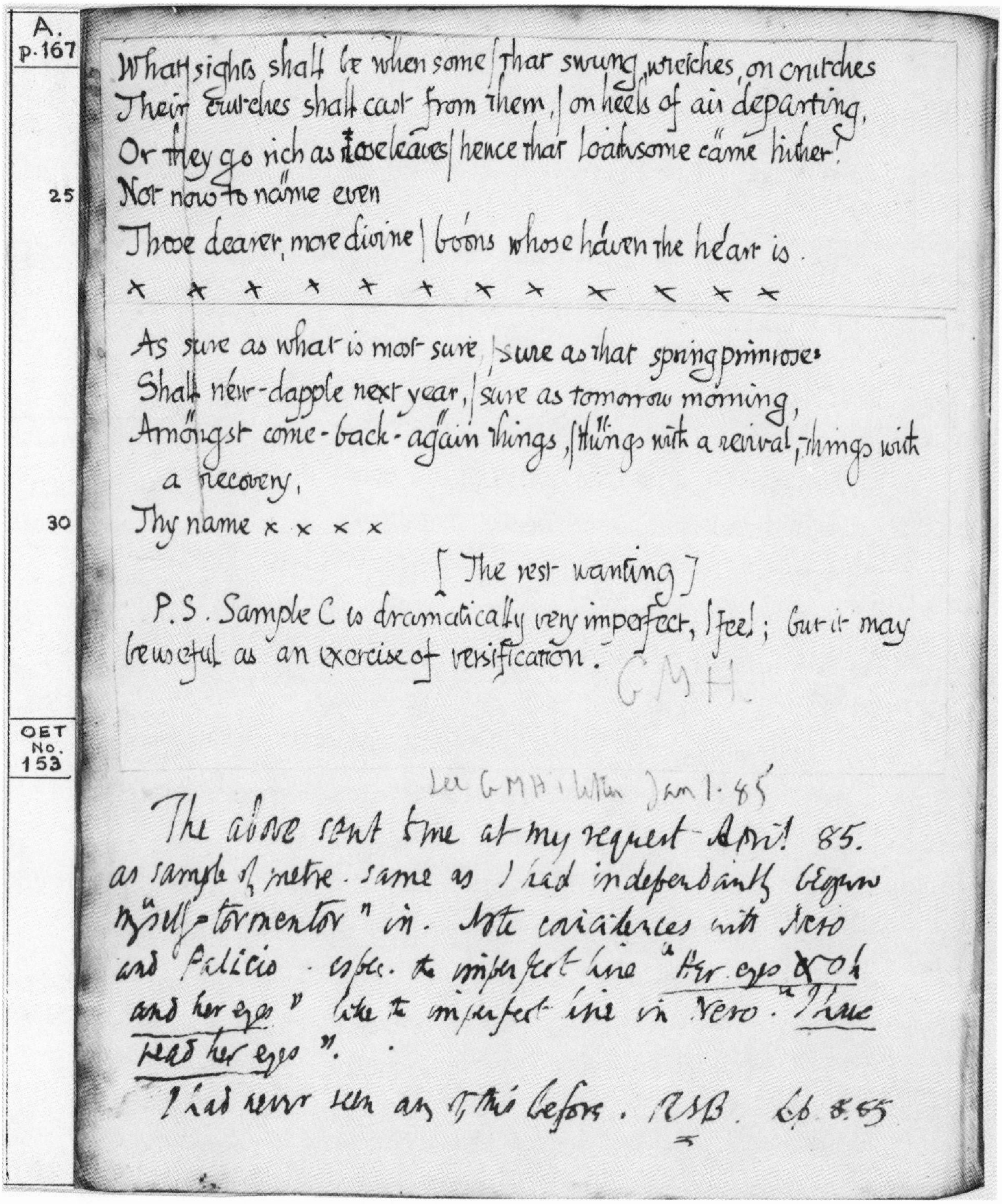

A.
p.167

What sights shall be when some / that swung wretches, on crutches
Their crutches shall cast from them, / on heels of air departing,
Or they go rich as roseleaves / hence that loathsome came hither!
25　Not now to name even
Those dearer, more divine / boons whose haven the heart is.

× × × × × × × × × × × × ×

As sure as what is most sure, / sure as that spring primrose·
Shall new-dapple next year, / sure as tomorrow morning,
Amongst come-back-again things, / things with a revival, things with
a recovery,
30　Thy name × × × ×

[The rest wanting]

P.S. Sample C is dramatically very imperfect, I feel; but it may
be useful as "an exercise of versification.

GMH.

See GMH's letter Jan 1·85

The above sent to me at my request. April 85.
as sample of metre. same as I had independantly begun
myself-"tormentor" in. Note coincidences with Nero
and Felicio. espec. the imperfect line "Her eyes & oh
and her eyes " like the imperfect line in Nero. "I have
read her eyes".

I had never seen any of this before. RSB. &c. 8.65

OET
No.
153

Plate 434 [above]　　OET No. 153: St. Winefred's Well -- MS. 2: A (7)

A.p.167--conclusion of Mrs. RB's transcription. RB has added GMH's initials in pencil to the P.S., and "See GMH's letter Jan 1. 85 [L.i.203]." His ink notes the [mild] coincidence between GMH's half-line (B, ℓ.22) and a half line in his own Nero, Part One (ℓ.2167, Act. IV.4) "I have read her eyes", which GMH had seen in MS. [the contexts are utterly different].

Plates 435, 436 [opposite, and over]　　OET No. 153: St. Winefred's Well -- MS. 4: H (1 to 9) = **K**

H.i.52r--copy of Mrs. RB's transcription in A, made by GMH's mother, Mrs. Kate Hopkins, who was 68 when her son died. Occupying the rectos of 52 to 60, it is reproduced on a smaller scale since it has no authority and shows some confusion. She mistook vertical mid-line caesuras for obliques marking the start of a new line with a capital letter, but her practice was irregular. Her e seldom has a loop, like an i without the dot.

Errors in 54r (e.g.) include: in the setting of Act 2 "dry dean" copied as "dry dam" (reversing the sense); "Winifred" misspelt thus throughout; RB's pencil line below "knew" (7) taken as italics; "make" (10) as "mak "; 15 (second half) metrical marks badly copied; 17 "woeful" given the alternative spelling "woful". Similar errors occur in other folios.

PLATE 435. OET 153. *St. Winefred's Well* • 259

H.i.
52r
OET
No.
153
Act 1
Sc.1
(A)

52

From St. Winefred's Well.

(A) Act 1. Scene 1
enter Teryth from riding, Winefred following.

T. What is it Gwen, my girl?
Why do you hover & haunt me?
W. You came by Caerwys, sir?
                                                    Pronounced
                                                    Cárus.
        I came by Caerwys.
                                            W. There
Some messenger might have met you from my uncle.
T. Your uncle met the messenger —
Met me; & this the message:
Lord Bruno comes tonight.
                                    W. Tonight, sir!
                                            T. Soon now: therefore
Have all things ready in his room.
                                    W. There needs but little doing.
T. Let what there needs be done.
        Stay! with him one companion,
His deacon, Dirvan. Warm
Twice over must the welcome be,
But both will share one cell. —
        This was good news, Gwenvrewi.
W. Ah, yes!
T. Why get thee gone then; / tell thy mother I want her.
                                            exit Winefred

H.i.
53r
OET
No.
153

53

No man has such a daughter.
The fathers of the world
Call no such maiden 'mine'.
The deeper grows her dearness
And more & more times laced
Round & round my heart,
The more some monstrous hand
Gropes with damning fingers there,
Tampering with those sweet lines,
Draws them out, strains them, strains them;
Meantime some tongue cries 'What, Teryth!
What, thou poor fond father!
"How when this bloom, this honeysuckle
That rides the air so rich about thee,
Is all, all sheared away
Thus!" then I sweat for fear.
Or else a funeral, / & yet 'tis not a funeral;
Some pageant which takes tears
And I must foot with feeling that
Alive or dead my girl / is carried in it, endlessly
Goes marching through my mind.
What sense is this? It has none.
This is too much the father; / nay, the mother. Fanciful
There forbid my thoughts / to fool themselves with fears.
                                    enter Gwenlo

H.i.
54r
OET
No.
153
Act 2
(B)

(B) Act 2 — Scene, a wood, ending in a steep bank
over a dry dean. Winefred, having been murdered
within, enter Caradoc with a bloody sword.

Caradoc. My heart, where have we been?
        What have we seen, my mind?
What stroke has Caradoc's right arm dealt?
        What done? Head of a rebel
        Struck off it has; written / upon bossy limbs,
In bloody letters, lessons / of earnest, of revenge;
Monuments of my earnest, / records of my revenge;
On one that went against me, / whereas I had warned her—
Warned her! well she knew / I warned her of this work.
What work? what harm's done? There is /
                                    no harm done, none yet;
Perhaps we struck no blow, / Gwenvrewi lives perhaps;
To make believe my mood was — / Nay now. O I might think so
But here is a workman / from his day's task sweats.
Wiped I am sure this was; / It seems not well; for still
Still the scarlet swings / and dances on the blade.
So it is. Thou steel, thou butcher,
I can scour thee, fresh burnish thee
Sheathe thee in thy dark lair; these drops
Never, never, never / in their blue banks again.
The woful, Caradoc, O / the woful word! then what

H.i.
55r
OET
No.
153

55

What have we seen? Her head
Sheared from her shoulders, fall,
And lapped in shining hair,
Roll to the bank's edge: then
Down the beetling banks, / like water in waterfalls,
It stooped & flashed & fell / & ran like water away.
Her eyes, oh and her eyes!
In all her lovely beauty & sunlight
To it is a pit, den, darkness,
Foam falling is not fresh to it
Rainbow by it not beaming,
In all her body, I say, / no place was like her eyes,
No piece matched those eyes,
Kept most part much cast down
But being lifted, immortal, / of immortal brightness
Several times I saw them, / thrice or four times turning;
Round & round they came
And flashed towards heaven: O there.
There they did appeal. / Therefore airy vengeances
Are afoot; heaven's vault fast purpling
Portends & what first lightning —
Any instant falls means me. / And I do not repent;
I do not & I will not / Repent, not repent.
The blame bear who aroused me.
What I have done violent

OET No. 153 – Act 2 – (B) cont.: Transcription of MS.A by Mrs. Kate Hopkins

35 I have like a lion done / Lionlike done,
Honouring an uncontrolled / Royal wrathful nature
Mantling passion in a grandeur / Crimson grandeur
Now be my pride then perfect, / All one piece. Henceforth
In a wide world of defiance / Caradoc lives alone,
40 Loyal to his own soul, laying / his own law down, no law
Lord now curb him for ever. / O daring! O deep insight! now
What is virtue? Valour; / only the heart valiant.
And right? Only resolution; / Will, his will unwavering
Who, like me, knowing his nature
To the heart's behoof, / nature's business,
45 Despatches with no flinching. / But will flesh, O can flesh
Second this fiery strain? / not always; O no no!
We cannot live this life out; / sometimes we must weary
And in this darksome world / What comfort can I find
When 'tis light I quenched,
Down this darksome world / comfort where can I find
50 When 'tis light I quenched; its rose, / time's one rich rose, my hand
By her bloom, fast by her fresh her fleecèd bloom,
Hideous dashed down, leaving / earth a winter withering
With no now, no Gwenvrewi. / I must miss her most
That might have spared her, me it
But for passion-sake – Yes,
55 To hunger and not have, yet / Hope on for, to storm and strive and
Beat every assault fresh foiled, / Worse flung deeper disappointed

---

The aidle of the torment / It has I swear, a sweetness,
Keeps a kind of joy in it, / A zest, an edge, an ecstasy,
Next after sweet success. / I am not left even this;
60 I all my being have hacked / In half with their neck: one part,
Reason, self-disposal, / choice of better or worse way,
Is corpse now, cannot change; / My other self, this soul,
Life's quick, this kind, this keen self-feeling,
With dreadful distillation / Of thoughts sour, as blood,
65 Must all day long taste murder.
What do now then? Do? Nay,
Deed-bound I am; one deed treads all down here
Cramps all doing. What do? Not yield
Not hope, not pray, despair; / Ay, that: brazen despair out,
Brave all and take what comes – / As here this rabble is come,
70 Whose bloods I reck no more of, / No more rank with theirs
Than sewers with sacred oils. / Mankind, that mobs, comes, come!
(enter a crowd. Teryth, Gwenlo, Beuno &c

Cont. in left column—(C)   End of (B)-Act 2

(C) After Winifred's rising from the dead & the breaking out of the fountain.

Beuno. O now while skies are blue
Now while seas are salt,
While rushy rains shall fall
Or brooks shall fleet from fountains,
While sick men shall cast sighs,
Of sweet health all despairing,
While blind men's eyes shall thirst, after
Daylight, draughts of daylight,
Or deaf ears shall desire that
Lip-music that's lost upon them,
5 While cripples are, while lepers,
Dancers in dismal limb-dance,
Fallers in dreadful froth-pits
Waterfearers wild,
Stone, palsy, cancer, cough,
Lung-wasting, womb-not-bearing,
Rupture, running sores,
What more? in brief, in sum,
10 As long as men are mortal, / And God merciful,
So long to this sweet spot, / This day dear, this happy haunt-over
This Dayspring, now no longer dry
Nor doubt, but moist and musical
With the uproll of the downcarol

Of clay or night-delivering
Water, which keeps thy name
For not in rock written,
But in pale water, frail water,
15 Wild rash of reeling water,
That will not wear a print,
That will not stain a pen,
Thy venerable record / virgin is recorded.
Here to this holy well / Shall pilgrimages be
And not from purple Wales only
20 Nor from elsewhere England,
But from beyond seas, Erin,
France or Flanders, everywhere,
Pilgrims, still pilgrims, more pilgrims, still more poor pilgrims.
What sights shall be when some
That swung, wretches, on crutches,
Their crutches shall cast from them
On heels of air departing,
25 Or they go rich as rose-leaves
Hence that loathsome came hither!
Not now to name even
Those dearer, more divine / Boons whose haven the heart is
× × + × ×

As sure as what is most sure
Sure as that spring primroses
Shall new-dapple next year,
Sure as tomorrow morning,
Amongst come-back-again things,
Things with a revival, / things with a recovery,
30 Thy name ××× The rest wanting

PLATE 437. Sonnets of Desolation   •   *261*

PLATE 438 H.ii. 29 verso (really the recto) ▶	No. 158 To what serves Mortal Beauty Plate 450	No. 159 "[Carrion Comfort]" Plate 456	
PLATE 439 H.ii. 29 recto (really the verso) ▶		No. 159 "[Carrion Comfort]" (cont) Plate 457	No. 160 "[The Soldier]" Plate 458
PLATE 440 H.ii. 31 recto ▶	No. 171 Tom's Garland (first draft) Plate 492	No. 159 "[Carrion Comfort]" (lines 11,12) Plate 492	No. 157 "No worst" (lines 1-7) Plate 447
PLATE 441 H.ii. 31 verso ▶		No. 159 "[Carrion Comfort]" (rev. lines 1-10) Plate 459	No. 157 "No worst" (lines 8-14) Plate 447a
PLATE 442 H.ii. 35 recto ▶	No. 170 "[Ashboughs]" Plate 490	No. 154 "To seem the stranger" Plate 445	No. 155 "I wake and feel" (lines 1-8) Plate 446a
PLATE 443 H.ii. 35 verso ▶	No. 162 "Patience, hard thing" Plate 462	No. 163 "My own heart" Plate 463	No. 155 "I wake and feel" (lines 9-14) Plate 446a
PLATE 444 H.ii. 33 recto ▶	No. 170 "[Ashboughs]" (revised) Plate 491	No. 163 "My own heart" (rev. of ll. 13,14) Plate 463	

<u>Plate 437</u>   <u>Sonnets of Desolation -- MSS with Two or More Poems</u>

There are seven MSS. which have drafts or faircopies of more than one of the poems Hopkins wrote in Ireland. Special perplexities confront scholars who attempt to arrange the poems of 1884-1889 in a chronological sequence. It is therefore important to examine any interlocking which may occur in such MSS. as these seven (set out above in the first column), especially when dated drafts are scattered among them ("To what serves Mortal Beauty?", and the sonnet commonly called "The Soldier") or which can be accurately placed in time through his letters or the dates given to other versions of them ("Tom's Garland").

In the following seven plates I have reproduced these as units, necessarily on a smaller scale. The diagram above analyses their contents (follow the arrows across the page), and identifies the subsequent plate on which the MS. of each poem will be found full scale or enlarged. Moreover, each segment of a larger MS., when it reappears, is printed in context, displaying the end of the preceding poem and/or the beginning of the next. Detailed annotations will be found under the separate pieces.

One further fact is important: Bridges noted that the page he numbered "10" (now classified as H.ii.33 recto--the verso is blank and so it is pasted onto f.34r) was originally part of the sheet he numbered "11" (now H.ii.35 recto and verso): the interrelationship of the pages shown on the last three lines of my diagram should also be borne in mind.

H. ii. 29 v

OET NO. 158

A

1 a/b To what serves mortal beauty ; dangerous, which ['say] dance- {sends / sets} / danc-
2 a/b {To the blood — the O-seal — that so face; powder plург the form ing blood
3 Mán Purcell tune' lets tread to ? this it does : keeps warm
4 a/b men's thoughts of what things be, that good — where a glance with means
5 Gather more may than gaze me out of countenance.
6 Those lovely lads once , wetfresh windfalls of war's storm,
7 a × Now does   our true sire Gregory, gleaned from the swarm should father have amongs
8 a Of Rome then ? Great God — nations dealt that day's dear chance. Sts england
9 b Was man lid love, lid worship, block or barren stone? noble side man fore had worshipt block in common stone:
10 b Our law is love what are loveliest, were all known, was worthiest
11 b most worth love, men's selves. Self flashes off frame and face. world's loveliest
12 What do then ? how meet beauty ? Merely meet it; own
13 Home at heart heaven's sweet gift ; then leave it, let it alone
14 Yea wish that though, wish all , God's better beauty, grace. thát it

7 c ✻ Now does st. Gregory, father, have gleaned among the swarm
8 b † Dear god dealt that golden, or golden chance.

Aug. 23 '85

H. ii. 29 v

OET NO 159

B   No. 159

1 b Out, carrion comfort , despair ! not, I'll not feast on thee;
1 a Despair, out, carrion sweetness, off ! not feast on thee
2 a Not untwist, slack they may be, my last strands of man
3 a nor cry, for all I am weary, I can no more : I can —
4 a Can hold on, hope for comfort ; hopes not wish not to be.
5 a O yet thou terrible
5 b Yet why, thou terrible, wouldst thou rock ν rude on me
6 a with wring-earth tread; launch lion-foot on me ? Why wouldst thou scan thy
7 a with darksome devouring eyes my bruisèd bones or fan
8 a In turns of tempest me heaped here, me frantic to avoid and flee ?
9 b/a Why ? for my chaff ν fly ; my grain ν lie , clear and sheer . That might
10 a Nay , in the toil and coil, because I kissed the rod
11 b/a Nay from the storm my heart stole joy , could shout, cheer. Hand rather
12 {But cheer whom
12 a {Cheer whom then ? ν the hero whose force there flung me, whose foot trod
13 a me — or me that fought him ? which ? — I know this night, this year
14 a Of darkness done, that I wretch wrestled, turning with God.

12 c But cheer whom ? The hero whose force flung me, whose foot trod heaven
13 b me — or me that fought him ? O which . this night, this dark year
14 b Now done I know that I wretch wrestled, turning with God.

9 c Why ? that my chaff might fly ; my grain lie , clear and sheer.
10 b Nay , in the toil, coil, because I kissed the rod —
11 c Hand rather — my heart from storm stole joy lo! could laugh, cheer —

12 d Cheer whom then ? The hero whose heavenforce, there flung me, foot there trod
13 c me — or me that fought him ? which one ? is each one ? That night, that dark year,
14 c Done now, I know that I wretch wrestled, turning with god.

B 2

1 c Not, I'll not, carrion comfort, despair, not feast on thee; O
2 b Not untwist, slack they may be, my last strands of man
3 b nor cry, for all we are weary, I can no more . I can ;
4 b Can hold on, hope for daylight, not choose not to be.
5 c Yet, O thou terrible, why wouldst thou rude on me scan
6 b thy wring-earth tread rock, launch thy lion foot ? Why wouldst thou so

PLATE 439. MSS with Several Poems (159, 160)   •   263

H.ii.29ʳ | No. 159 cont.

6c / d My wring-earth right foot rock? launch a lion hand or no? scan
   launch thy lion head? and scan

7b With darksome devouring eyes my bruisèd bones and fan—

8b turns of tempest!— me heaped there, me frantic, to avoid thee and flee?

9d why? that my chaff might fly; my grain lie, sheer and clear.

10c nay in all that toil, that coil, because I kissed the rod,

11d Hand rather, my heart lo! lapped strength, stole joy, give a

11f / e { give a laugh could
         { had a laugh, laugh, a, } cheer . .

12e Cheered whom though? the hero whose heaven-handling flung me, foot trod

13d me? or me that fought him? O which one? or each one? That night,
      that year

14d Of darkness done, now with done with, I wretch wrestled in wrestle

14e / f Of now done of darkness I wretch a wrestle wrong with great God.
        lay wrestling with (my God !)
        my God.

No. 160

1a C Yes. Why do we, seeing of a soldier, bless him? bless
2b / a Our redcoats, our tars? Both these, the being the greater part, greater part,
3c / b No better indeed than they
       Our frail clay, nay but foul clay.
       No better indeed than they | and. Here it is: the heart,
       since,

4 so proud, to call the calling manly, gives a guess

5 that, hopes that, makesbelieve, the men must be no less;

6a It fancies; it p deems; dears the artist after his art;

7a And feigns it finds as sterling all as all is smart

8 and scarlet wear the spirit of war there express

9a mark Christ our King. He knows war, served this soldiering
      through;

1b why seeing a soldier

10a He of all can reave a rope best. | there he bides in bliss

11a now, and seeing somewhere some man | do all that man can do,

12a For love he leans forth, needs | his neck must fall on, kiss,

13a and cry " O Christ-done deed! so God-made flesh does too:

14a / b Were I come o'er again " to cries it could be this."
        cries | Christ "it should
        Clongowes Aug. 1885

6b × It fancies, & feigns, deems, dears the artist after his art; (?)

7b/c/d # to fain to find (or and's fain to find or and fain will find)

9b If Christ, that our world's warfare once went through,

10b and knows what soldiering's now, being in bliss.

11b sees where some man does all that man can do,

12b He needs must fall his neck and kiss

13b And cries" O good deed done! so God does too:

14c Could Christ come o'er again I should be this"

H. ii. 31r
OET No. 159, l. 11
OET No. (9) 171
OET No. 171
OET No. 159 line 12
H. ii. 31r cont.
OET No. 157

31

Hand rather, my heart lo! lapped strength, stole joy, would
laugh,   cheer.

(Earl of Tom)

1 the garlanded with squat and surly steel,   (A)
2 the fallow bootel navvy has piled his pick
3 And rips out rockfire homeforth — sturdy Dick;
4 tom Heart-at-ease, that's all now for his meal
5 Sure, 's bedf. Be his lot low, handily he swings it — feel
6 That ne'er need hunger, should be seldom sick, [thick
7 Seldomer heartsore : that treads through, prickproof,
8 thousands of thorns, thoughts. And, in commonweal
9 I little reck lacklevel if all had bread :
10 Country if honour in all us.

heer clown though? the hero whose heaven-handling flung me,
                              foot trod

(Pitched past pitch of grief.

1 c\d No worst, there is none : ?grief past pitch of grief,   (B)
                            fore
2 b More pangs at pitch pangs schooled will wilder wring
2 c At fore pangs more pangs schooled will wilder wring

                O there
1 a b Worst! No worst, is none. grief past grief   top, grief
2 a And more pangs, schooled at fore pangs, wilder wring.

1 e No worst, there is none. Pitched past pitch of grief,
2 d More pangs will, schooled at forepangs, wilder wring.
3 Comforter, where, where is the your comforting?
4 Mary, mother of us, where is your relief?
5 My cries leave heave herds-long; huddle in a main, a chief-
6 Woe, wórld-sorrow; on an áge-old ánvil wince and sing —
7 Then lull, then leave off. Fury had shrieked "No ling-

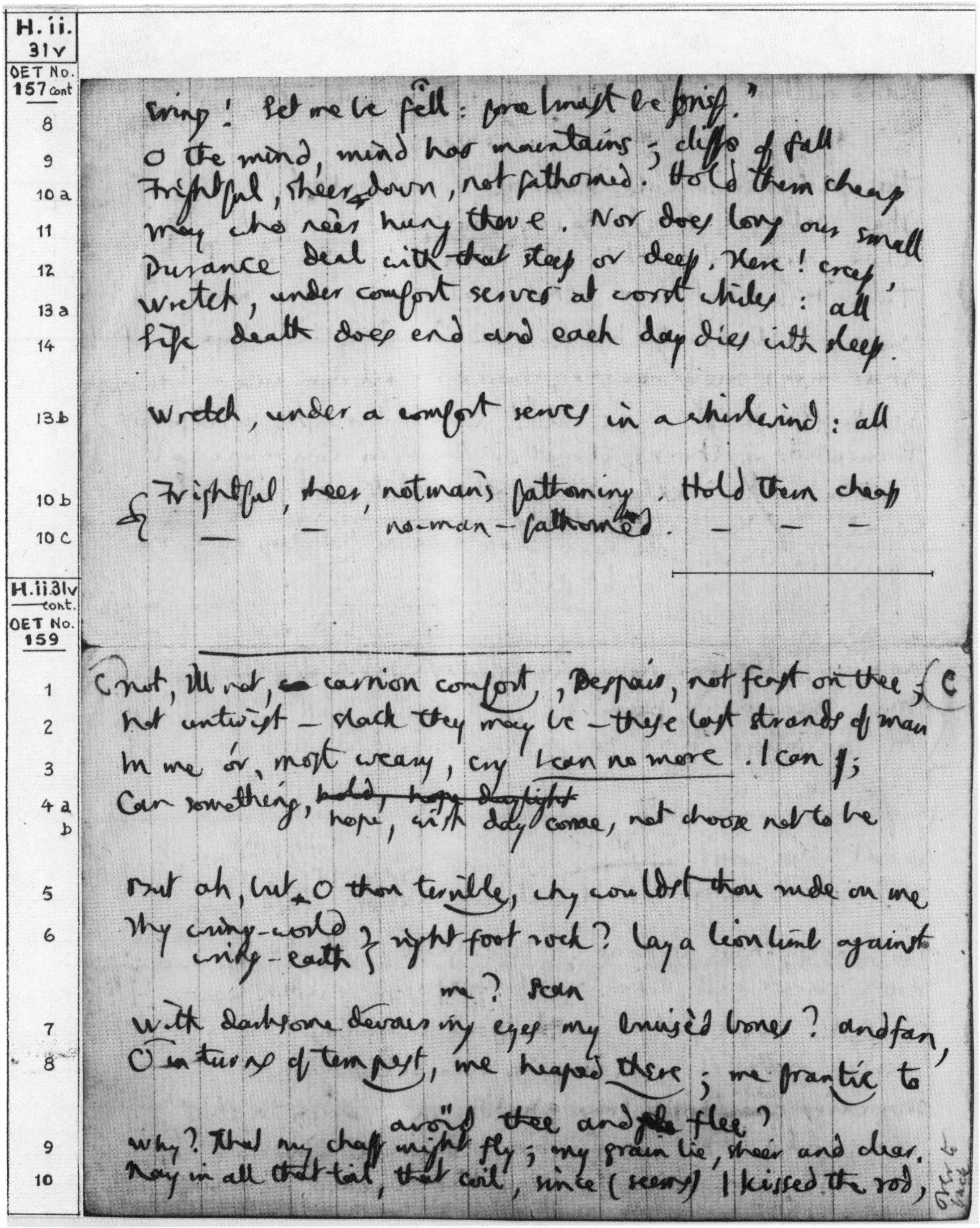

PLATE 441. MSS with Several Poems (157, 159) • 265

H. ii.
31v

OET No.
157 cont

8
9
10 a
11
12
13 a
14

13.b

10 b
10 c

...ing! Let me be fell: force I must be brief."
O the mind, mind has mountains; cliffs of fall
Frightful, sheer, down, not fathomed. Hold them cheap
may who ne'er hung there. Nor does long our small
Durance deal with that steep or deep. Here! creep,
Wretch, under comfort serves at worst while: all
Life death does end and each day dies with sleep.

Wretch, under a comfort serves in a whirlwind: all

& Frightful, sheer, not man's fathoming. Hold them cheap
—   —   no-man — fathomed . —   —   —   —

H.ii.31v
cont.

OET No.
159

1
2
3
4 a
  b

5
6

7
8

9
10

Not, I'll not, carrion comfort, Despair, not feast on thee;
not untwist — slack they may be — these last strands of man
In me ór, most weary, cry I can no more. I can;
Can something, hold, hope, day light
              hope, with day come, not choose not to be.

But ah, but O thou terrible, why wouldst thou rude on me
Thy wring-world
    wring — earth } right foot rock? lay a lionlimb against
                      me? scan
with darksome devouring eyes my bruisèd bones? and fan,
O in turns of tempest, me heaped there; me frantic to
                avoid thee and flee?
why? That my chaff might fly; my grain lie, sheer and clear.
Nay in all that toil, that coil, since (seems) I kissed the rod,

H.ii 35ʳ · **OET NO. 170**

11

35

1 Not of all my eyes see, wandering on the world,
2 Is anything a milk to the mind so, so sighs deep
3 Poetry to it, as a tree whose boughs break in the sky,
4 Say it & saying sighs; whether on a December day and pied
5 they are or their clammyish lashtender combs creep
6 Apart wide and they nestle at heaven most high.
7 they touch: their wild charm-swung talons sweep
8 the smouldering enormous winter-welkin. spring
9 melts blue and snowwhite through a thousand ring-
10 Ers: then they are old Earth groping towards that steep
11 Heaven once Earth childed by.

End of OET No. 170

OET NO. 154

1 To seem the stranger lies my lot, my life
2 among strangers. Father and mother dear,
3 Brothers and sisters are in Christ not near
4 And he my peace / my parting, sword and strife.
5 England, whose honour O all my heart woos, wife
6 to my creating thought, would neither hear
7 me, were I pleading, plead nor do I: I wear-
8 y of idle a being but by where wars are rife.
9 I am in Ireland now; now I am at a third
10 Remove. Not but in all removes I can
11 Kind love both give and get. Only that word

12 a Wisest my breast holds breeds from heaven some ban
13 b Of silence or of death.

12c Wisest my heart breeds dark
heaven's dark ban
13e Bars or hell's spell thwarts. thought
hoarded unheard

This to hoard unheard
or
Wisest my heart breeds
13¹/₄ / 12d dark heaven's baffling ban
Bars etc.

End of No. 154

14 a Heard unheeded
This to hoard unheard
b Heard unheeded, leaves me a lonely began.

OET NO. 155

1 I wake and feel the fell of dark, not day,
2 What hours, O what black hours we have spent
3 this night! what sights you, heart, saw; ways you went!
4 And more must, in yet longer light's delay.
5 With witness I speak this. But where I say
6 Hours I mean years, mean life. And my lament
7 Is cries countless, cries like dead letters sent
8 To dearest him that lives alas! away.

End of H.ii 35ʳ

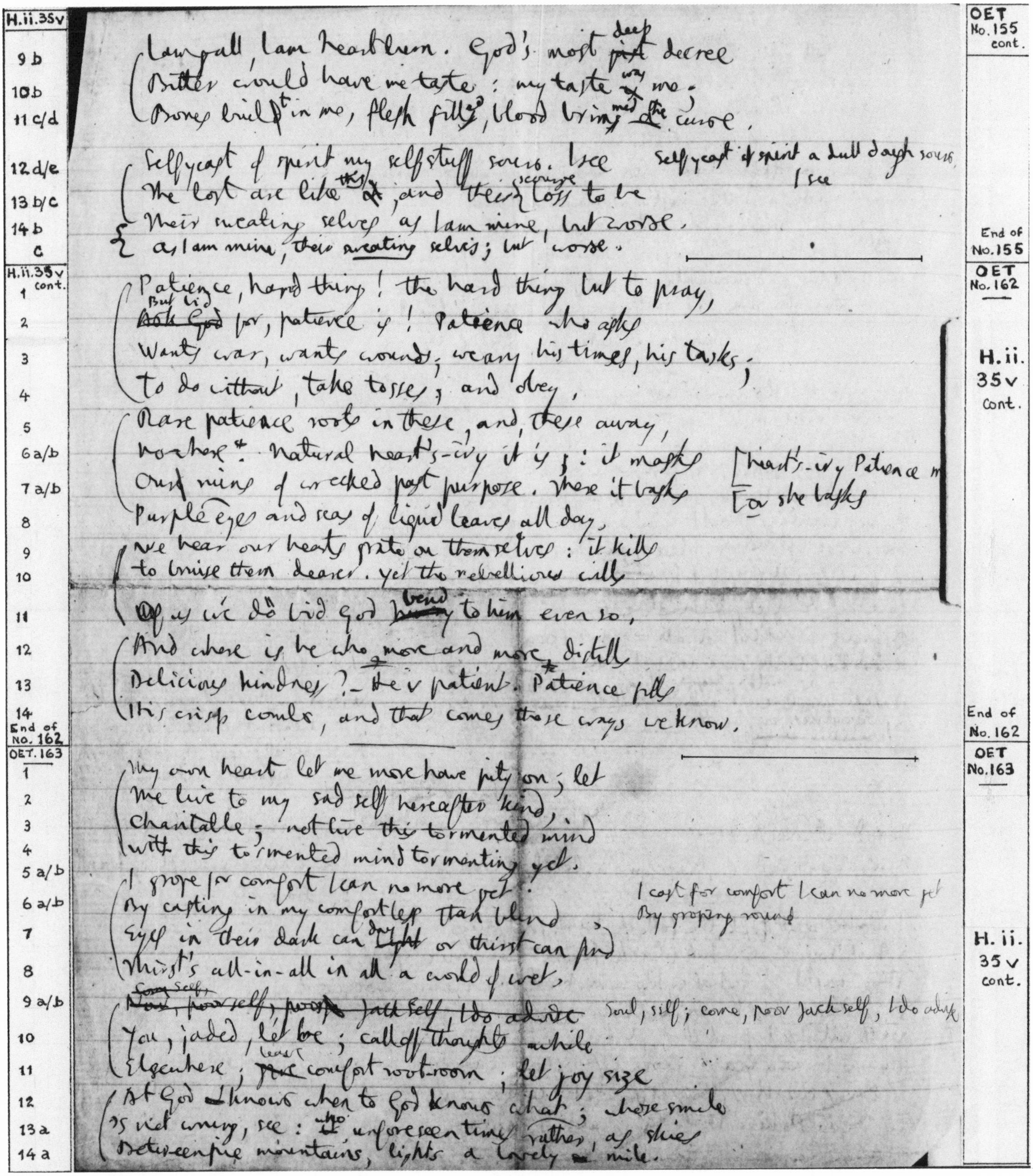

PLATE 443. MSS with Several Poems (155, 162, 163) • 267

H.ii.35v

OET
No. 155
cont.

9 b
10 b
11 c/d

Lawgall, I am heartburn. God's most deep decree
Bitter would have me taste: my taste was me.
Bones built in me, flesh filled, blood brimmed the curse.

12 d/e
13 b/c
14 b
c

Selfyeast of spirit my selfstuff sours. I see   Selfyeast of spirit a dull dough sours,
The lost are like this, and their loss to be   I see
Their sweating selves as I am mine, but worse.
As I am mine, their sweating selves; but worse.

End of
No. 155

H.ii.35v
cont.

OET
No. 162

1
2
3
4

Patience, hard thing! the hard thing but to pray,
But bid God for, patience is! Patience who asks
Wants war, wants wounds; weary his times, his tasks;
To do without, take tosses, and obey.

5
6 a/b
7 a/b
8
9
10

Rare patience roots in these, and these away,
Nowhere. Natural heart's-ivy it is; it masks   [Heart's-ivy Patience m
Our ruins of wrecked past purpose. There it basks   [or she basks
Purple eyes and seas of liquid leaves all day,
We hear our hearts grate on themselves: it kills
To bruise them dearer. Yet the rebellious wills

H.ii.
35v
Cont.

11
12
13
14

Of us we do bid God bend to him even so,
And where is he who, more and more, distils
Delicious kindness? — He is patient. Patience fills
His crisp combs, and that comes those ways we know.

End of
No. 162

OET. 163

OET
No. 163

1
2
3
4
5 a/b
6 a/b
7
8

My own heart let me more have pity on; let
Me live to my sad self hereafter kind,
Charitable; not live this tormented mind
With this tormented mind tormenting yet.
I grope for comfort I can no more yet   I cast for comfort I can no more yet
By casting in my comfortless than blind   By groping round
Eyes in their dark can day or thirst can find
Thirst's all-in-all in all a world of wet,

H.ii.
35 v
cont.

9 a/b
10
11
12
13 a
14 a

Now, poor self, poor Jackself, I do advise   Soul, self; come, poor Jackself, I do advise
You, jaded, let be; call off thoughts awhile
Elsewhere; leave comfort rootroom; let joy size
At God knows when to God knows what; whose smile
Is not wrung, see; who, unforeseen times rather, as skies
Betweenpie mountains, lights a lovely mile.

H.ii.33r	34

No.163

13b 's not rining, see you; unforescentir of rather — ay skies
14b Between pie mountains —

No.170

1b Not of all my eyes of see, wändering along of world,
2b Is anything a milk to the mind so, so sighs deep
3b Poetry to it, as a tree whose boughs break in the sky.
4b Say it is "ashboughs: whether on a December day and furled
5b Fast or they in clammyish lashtender combs creep
6b Apart wide and new-nestle at heaven most high.
7c/7b They touch heaven, talons on it; how their talons sweep
8b The smouldering enormous winter welkin! Spx May
9b Melts blue and snowwhite through them, a fringe and fray
10b Of greenery: it is old earth's groping towards the deep
11b Heaven Mow she childs us ly.

7d They touch, they, talons on it, hovering on it; here, these hurled,
7.ii With talons sweep

8c The smouldering enormous crater, welkin. Eye,
8.ii b/a with But more cheer when may
9c Melts blue and snowwhite through their fringe and fray
10d/c Of greenery and old earth gropes for, at the steep
11c Heaven whom she childs us ly.
d Heaven with it whom she childs
e thing ly.

OET No. 170

10 & 11 were one sheet

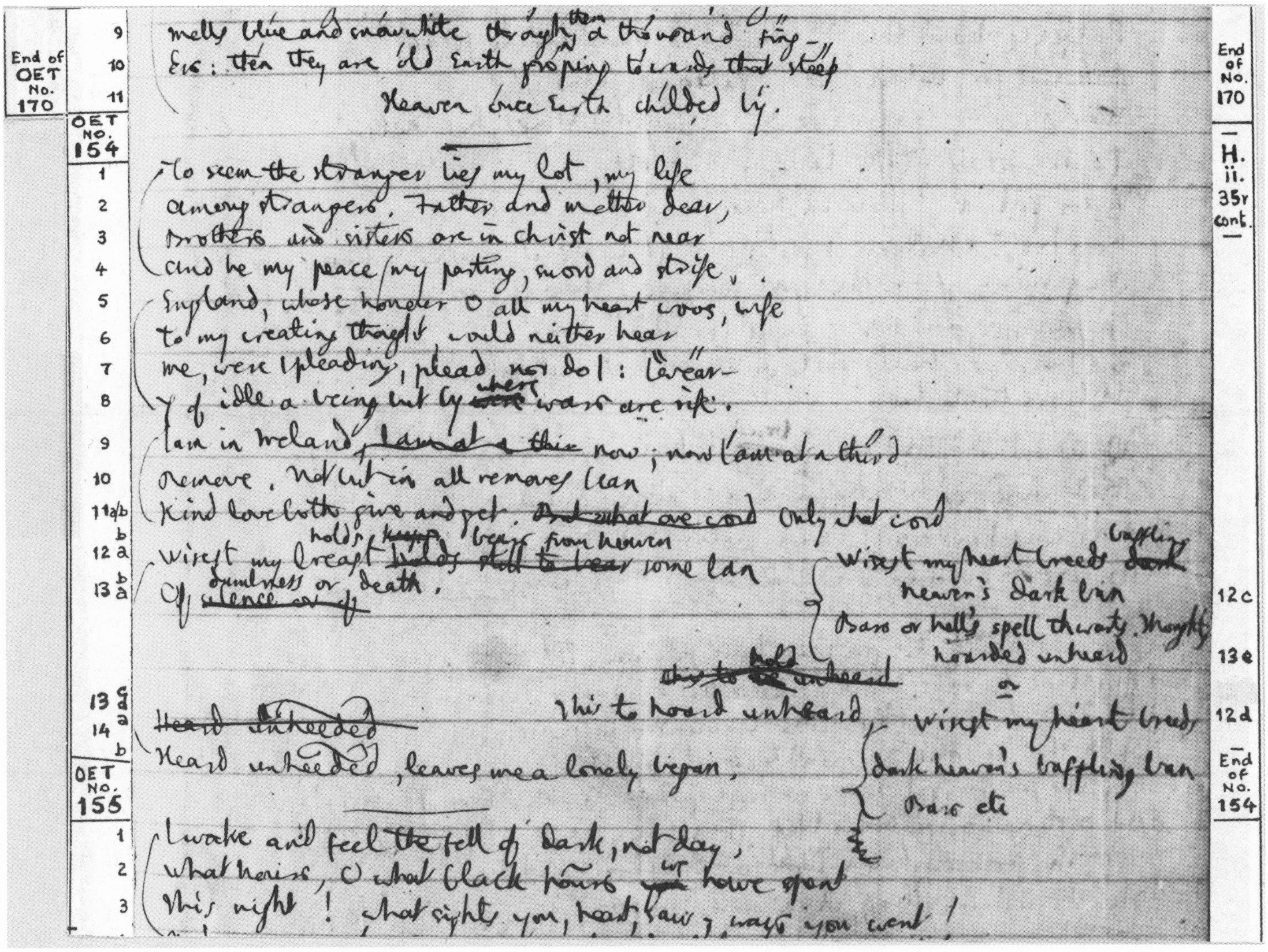

PLATE 445. OET 154. "To seem the stranger" • 269

Plate 445   OET No. 154: "To seem the stranger lies my lot" -- MS. H.ii

H.ii.35r--sole MS, autograph, faircopy of octave, draft of sestet; on a page below No. 170, and above No. 155. Even where a word is split between lines, GMH normally begins the line with a capital (cf. "fing-/Ers", No. 170, ℓ.9, top of this plate); in 8 the wide open fork and the loop on the upper right is a typical u.c. "Y". In 7 the double grave falls on "I", double full stress on "wear-". Deletions include: 8 "were" (not immediately corrected) 9 ", I am at a thir[d]"

11-14 Successive revisions (some overlapping) appear to be: "But what one word/Wisest my breast holds still to bear some ban/Of silence or of" rev. as "Only what word/Wisest my breast keeps holds bears from heaven some ban/Of dumbness or death. (13c) this [*l.c.* t, partly mended to u.c.?] to be hold unheard/(14a) Heard unheeded" [the counterpoint is shortened by deleting the part above "un" with two strokes--this is not a double grave] 13c and 14a then del. and 13d and 14b substituted. The alternatives touching the right margin (12c to 12d) come last. If "Thoughts hoarded unheard" (13e) had been finally adopted 14b would have been changed to "leave".

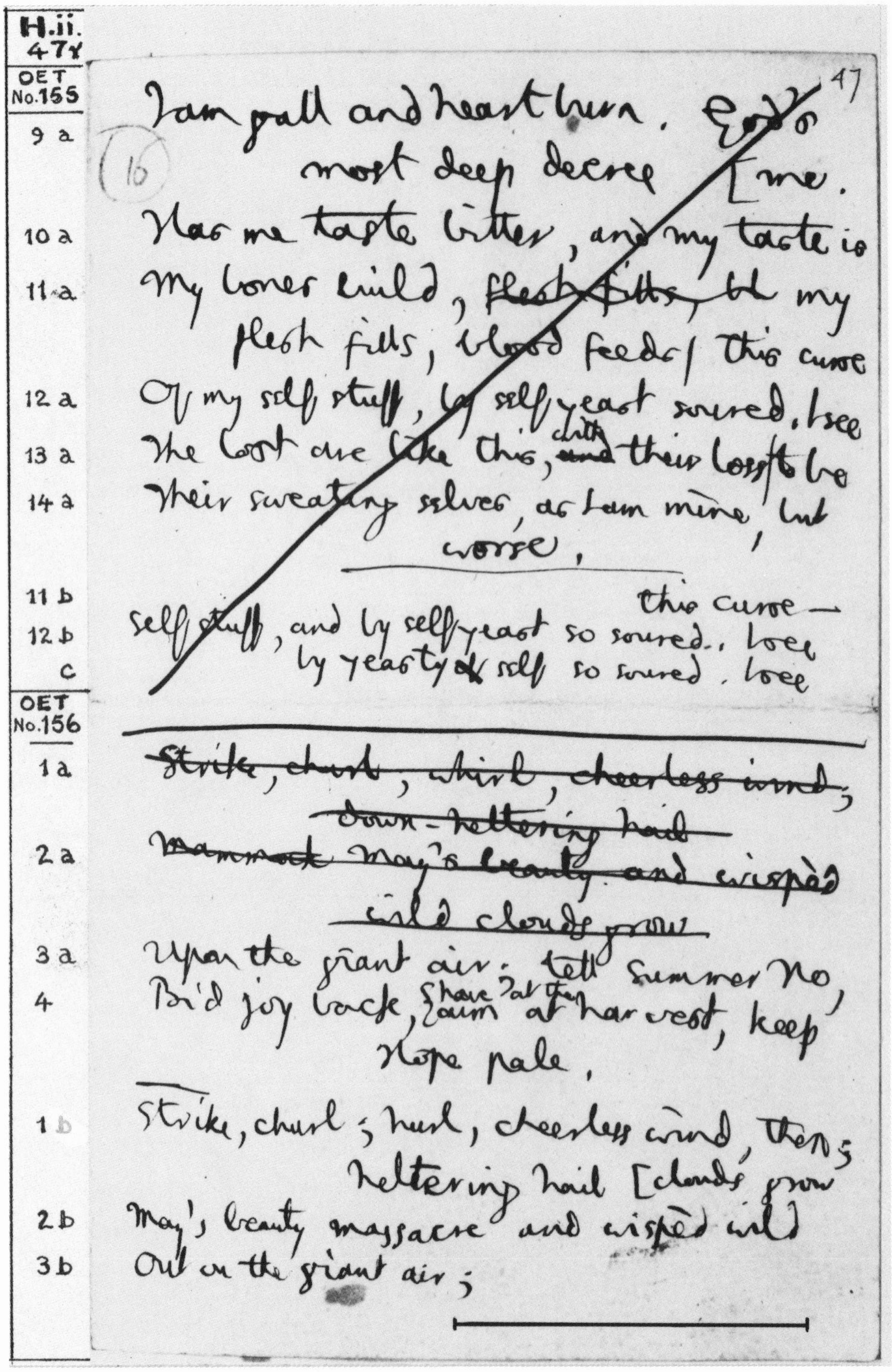

H.ii.
47r

OET
No.155

9 a

(16)

10 a

11 a

12 a

13 a

14 a

11 b

12 b

c

OET
No.156

1 a

2 a

3 a

4

1 b

2 b

3 b

47

I am gall and heart burn. God's
most deep decree [me.
bitter woud me taste bitter, and my taste is
My bones build, flesh fills, bl my
flesh fills, blood feeds/ this curse
Of my self stuff, by self yeast soured. I see
The lost are like this, and their loss to be
their sweating selves, as I am mine, but
worse,

this curse —
self stuff, and by self yeast so soured. I see
by yeasty of self so soured. I see

Strike, churl, whirl, cheerless wind,
down-heltering hail
Mammock May's beauty and crisped
wild clouds grow
Upon the giant air: tell summer No,
Bid joy back, shame at harvest, keep
hope pale.

Strike, churl; hurl, cheerless wind, then
heltering hail [clouds grow
May's beauty massacre and crisped wild]
Out on the giant air;

Plate 446   OET No. 155: "I wake and feel the fell of dark" -- MS. 1: H[1]

[upper half] H.ii.47r--autograph draft of the sestet only, del. in ink. Separate deletions include: 11a "flesh fills, bl[ood]" 12c "yeast of self" rev. to "yeasty self" (y squeezed in).

Note in 11a "feeds/" the stroke is a virgule (cf. No. 138, ℓ.14), but in 13a "loss/to be" the stroke seems merely to separate words run together, not for punctuation. Periods in 12a, 14a might be mistaken for commas.

No. 156: "Strike, churl" -- sole MS.

[lower half] sole autograph. The deleted lines include 1a "churl;"   2a "Mammock"

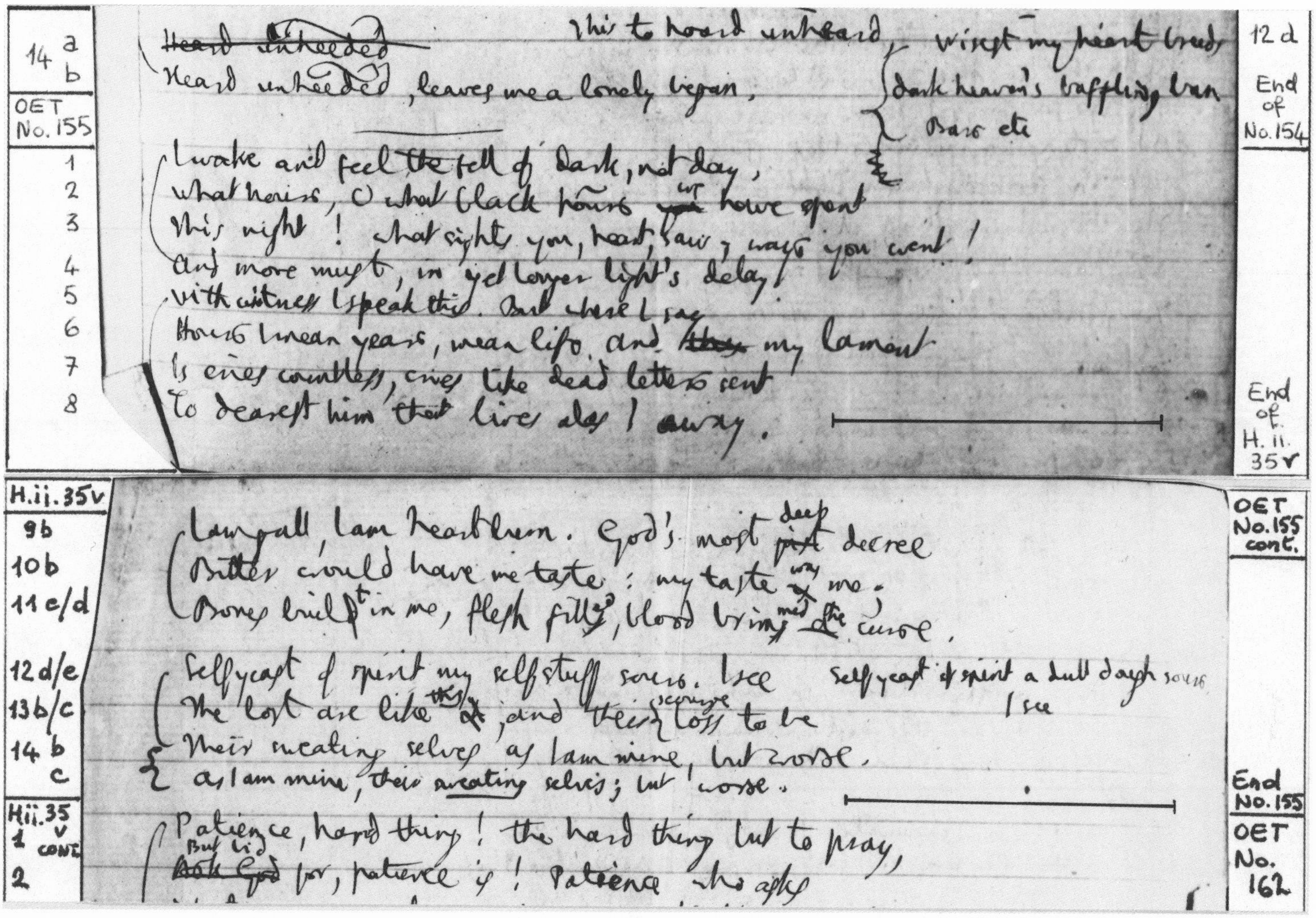

Plate 446a   OET No. 155: "I wake and feel the fell of dark" -- MS. 2: H²

H.ii.35r (*ll*.1-8), 35v (9-14)--autograph faircopy of whole sonnet, with later alternatives for 12, 13, and 14.
Some obscure stops follow: 1 "day" period (cf. dot above i in "This", 3, and final stop in 14b)   3 "saw" stop
looks like a smudged semicolon (which does not suit the syntax); prob. meant as a comma (cf. comma shapes
forming the lower halves of semicolons in Plate 446, No. 156, 1a "wind;" and 1b "then;" also cf. Plate 459, No.
159, 1, "thee;" comma below period).   After "delay" (4) the period is lost in the tail of the y in "ways": there is
a flaw like a point below it.   Note that 14c was interpolated after the usual short dividing line between sonnets had
been drawn: "sweating" is not italicised.   The slightly greater line space after 11c/d is an anomaly.   Deletions
include: 2 "you"   6 "this"   9b "just"   10b "is"   11c/d "build/t ...fills/ed...brims/med a/the"   13b/c "it/ths"
["this" intended, only the dot of the i present].

	9	1, little reck lacklevel if all had tread:
OET No. 171	10	Country, if honour is all us ...
OET No. 159 line 12		...eer chom though? the hero whose heaven-handling fling me, foot trod
H.ii.31r cont.		
OET No. 157	1c/d	No worst, there is none : grief past pitch of grief, ⟨Pitched past pitch of grief.
	2b	More pangs at ~~fore~~ pangs schooled will wilder wring
	2c	At fore pangs more pangs schooled will wilder wring
	1a b	Worst! No worst; ~~no there~~ O there is none . Grief past grief
	2a	And more pangs, schooled at fore pangs, wilder wring .
	1e	No worst, there is none . Pitched past pitch of grief,
	2d	More pangs will, schooled at forepangs, wilder wring .
	3	Comforter, where, where is the your comforting ?
	4	Mary, mother of us, where is your relief ?
	5	My cries ~~come~~ leave herds-long ; huddle in a main, a chief
	6	Woe, world-sorrow ; on an age-old anvil wince and sing —
	7	then lull, then leave off . Fury had shrieked "No ling-

Plates 447, 447a   OET No. 157: "No worst, there is none." -- Sole Autograph

H.ii.31 recto--sole autograph of "No worst", (1-7). Cont. on 31v. We cannot be sure of the order in which the drafts of 1 and 2 were written. GMH is likely to have left enough space below the first draft of "Tom's Garland" for its completion as a normal 14-line sonnet; on these grounds, and because it is least like the final version (1e), the line here marked 1a is probably where he began. After writing 2a he used part of the space above for 1c to 2c (a marginal bracket, all but the ends hidden by the stub hinge, is here roughly dotted in). Only after completing folio 31v did he add No. 159, ℓ.12 between two transverse lines.

Deletions include: 2b "at pan[gs]" (the f of "fore" runs through it)   1a/b "No worst; [semicolon becomes comma] no ℓ [or b]" mended to "there/O there"   3 th[y]   5 Come   In 6 the apparent V over "wince" (copied as such by RB in A.p.222, and as a circumflex in Harris, Inspirations Unbidden) is due to a stress mark (one of five in that line) meeting the dot over the i drawn like a grave (cf. "will" in 2b and "mind" in 9).

RB's pencil "B" beside 1c refers to his note (not reproduced) on the opposite page "Only copy of 'No worst.' This turns over".

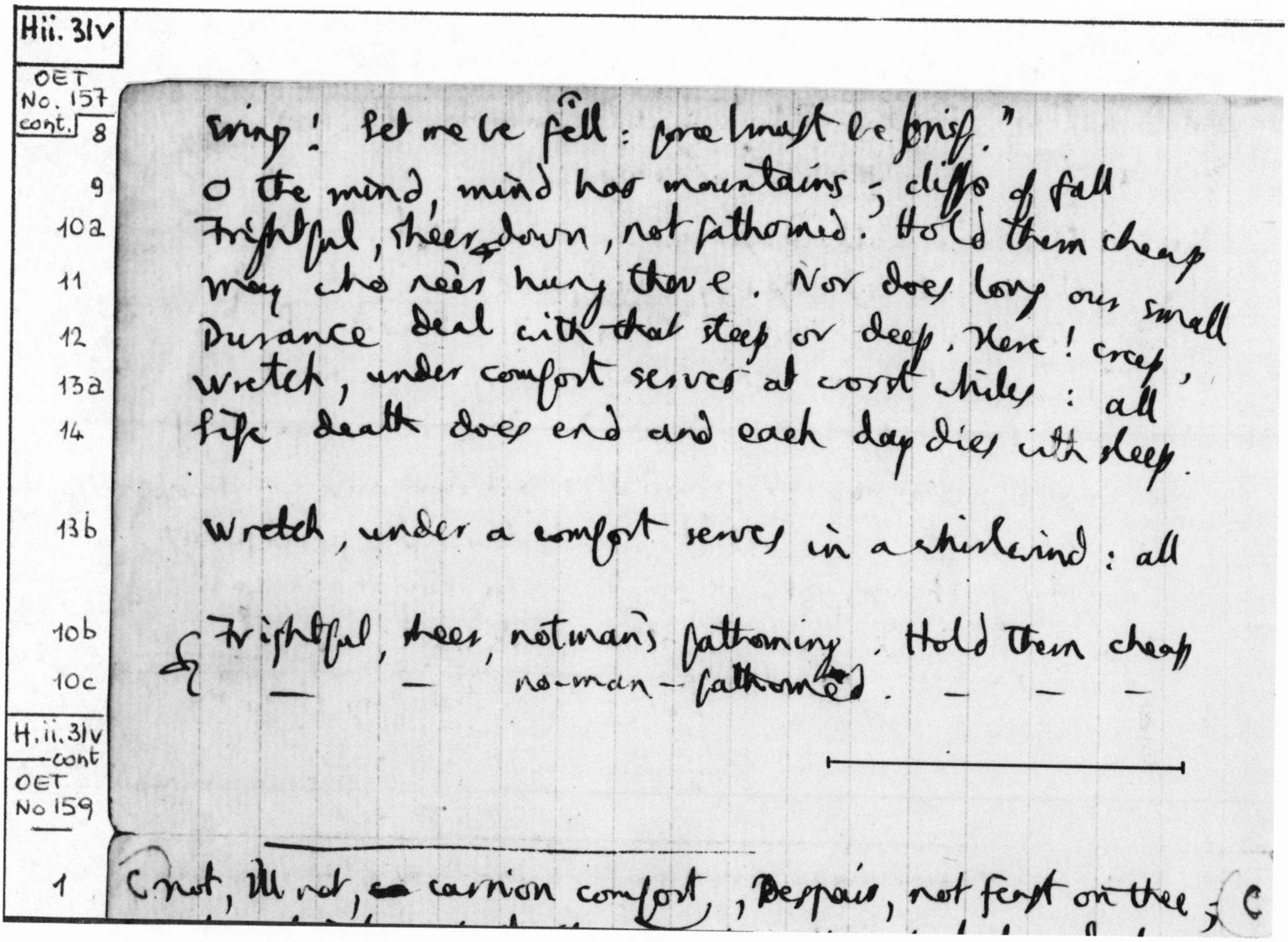

Hii. 31v

OET
No. 157
cont.

8   ering! Let me be fell: force I must be brief."

9   O the mind, mind has mountains; cliffs of fall

10a   Frightful, sheer, down, not fathomed. Hold them cheap

11   may who neer hung there. Nor does long our small

12   Durance deal with that steep or deep. Here! creep,

13a   wretch, under comfort serves at worst while: all

14   Life death does end and each day dies with sleep.

13b   Wretch, under a comfort serves in a whirlwind: all

10b   Frightful, sheer, not man's fathoming . Hold them cheap
10c   —— — no-man — fathomèd . — — — —

H.ii.31v
cont
OET
No 159

1   C not, Ill not, carrion comfort, Despair, not feast on thee; C

Plate 447a   <u>OET No. 157</u>: <u>"No worst, there is none"</u> -- sole autograph, cont.

     <u>H.ii.31v</u>--ℓ ℓ.8-14. Line 8, though beginning in the middle of a word ("ling/ering"), is characteristically given an initial capital ["E"]. <u>Changes</u> include: 8 "grief" mended to "brief"   10a "sheer," 10b "no" changed to "not" (t squeezed in; "not man's" intended as two words)   10c "fathomèd" (grave del.).

H.ii. 23v	
1a	To what serves mortal beauty ? dangerous ; which lets dance
2a	Dull blood. Face featurable ; prouder sinewy form
3a	than Purcell 's music treads it & moves to . this it does : keeps warm
4a	man's knowledge that things are ; that good is — which one clean glance
5a	may gather, more than staring out of countenance.
6a	those lads, those lovely wildfresh windfalls of war's storm,
7a	why else did father Gregory single from the swarm
8a	Of Rome ? O god's great angels dealt him that day's chance !
12a	then what do ? how meet beauty ? merely meet it ; own
13a	at heart home heaven's sweet gift ; then leave it, let it alone ;
9b 2	There is no law of fair loving truly heart, stock, or barren stone ;
10a	We are bid love that which is most lovely were it known,
11a	man. Beauty is like one fresh rose blown in a withering place .
12b	then what do ? how meet beauty ? merely meet it ; own
13b	At heart home heaven's sweet gift ; then leave it, let it alone ;
14a	yet wish it, yea wish all, god 's better beauty, grace.
3b	Than Purcell 's music treads to . this it does : keeps warm
4b	man's knowledge that things are , what good is — there a glance
5b	more gather may than staring out of countenance.
6b	those lads, those lovely wildfresh windfalls of war's storm,
7b	why how else did father Gregory single from the swarm
8b	Of Rome ? Dear god's great angels drew and dealt the chance
c	{ him that day's chance
9c	We are not bid love nor worship stock or barren stone ; { block
OET No 158	
10b	Our law is / love that is most lovely, were it known,
11b	most worth love, man's self. self flashes from frame or face.
9d	Was man bid love, bid worship block or barren stone ?
10c	Our law is / love that are most lovely, were that known,
11c	Best worth love, men's selves, self flashes off frame and face.
12c	then what do ? how meet beauty ? merely meet it ; own
13c	Home at heart heaven's sweet gift etc
H.ii. 23v cont.	

(marginal note, right side, vertical:) I have a femivel veneri] his sonnet in Gerard's own writing

(bottom:) saw

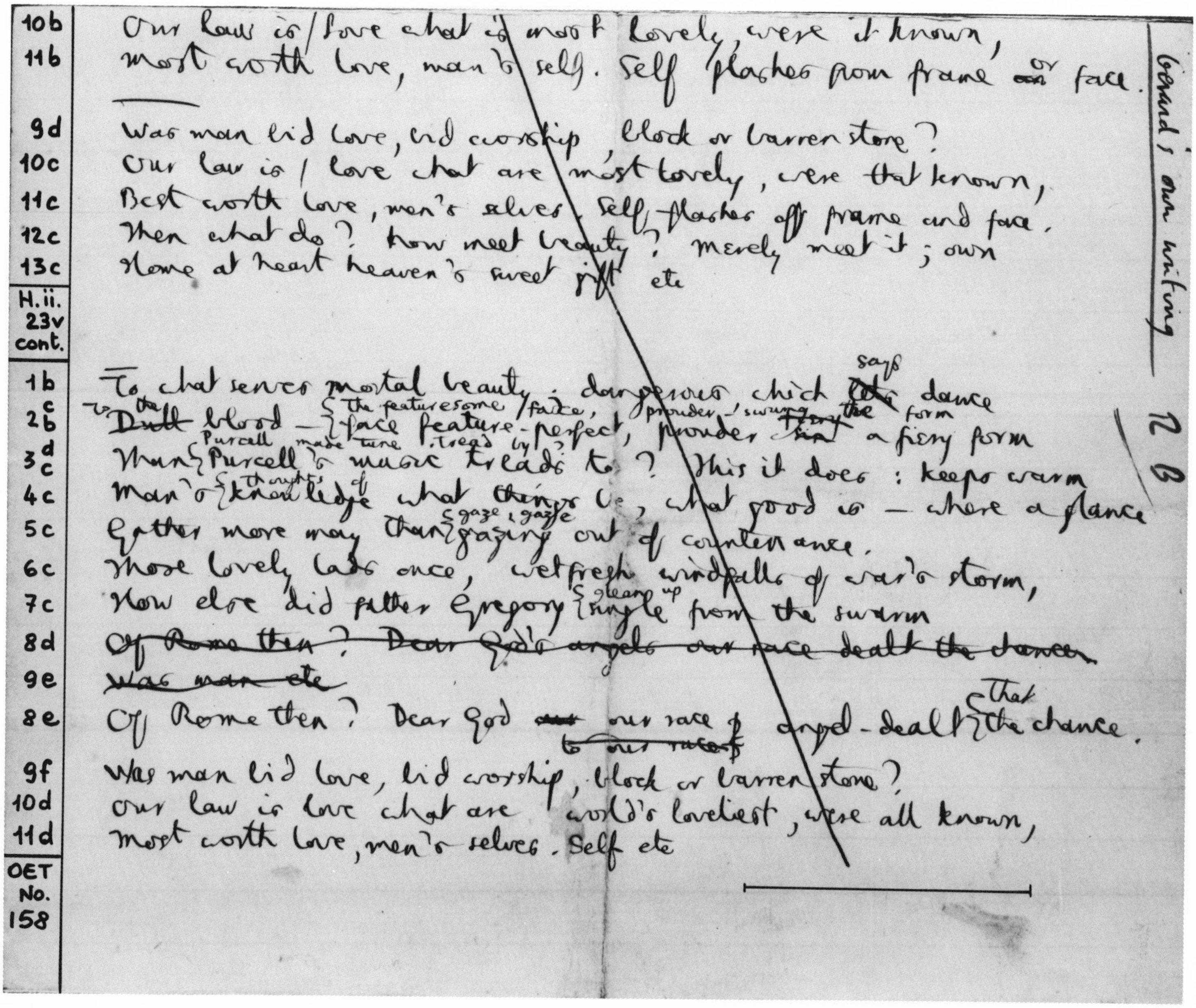

PLATE 449. OET 158. *To what serves Mortal Beauty?* • 275

(right margin, vertical:) Gerard's own writing

(right margin:) RB

Line labels (left margin): 10b, 11b, 9d, 10c, 11c, 12c, 13c, H.ii. 23v cont., 1b, 2c, 3d, 4c, 5c, 6c, 7c, 8d, 9e, 8e, 9f, 10d, 11d, OET No. 158

Plates 448 and 449   OET No. 158: To what serves Mortal Beauty? -- MS. 1: H¹

[opposite and above--the plates overlap] H.ii.23v--earliest autograph draft (on the back of drafts of No. 161). Vertical and horizontal folds have damaged some of the writing. Some words were written in pencil first, e.g. "gather" (5a), "windfalls" (6a). The deletion of 12a, 13a, 8d, 9e, and of the whole page, is in ink.

Changes include: 1a "W[hat?]"   2a "Tamé...Fe[atur?]"   3a "warms" 4a "good is/One clear"   5a "M[o]kay" 8a "In" mended to "Of"   9b "for"   9a "W" [begun] mended to "There"   11a "ạ/one" "fa[?]withering 4b "ø[ne?]" mended to "a glance"   8b "o" mended to "Of"   11b "an[d]/or"   10c "w" mended to "lovely"   2c "fiery"   "a" mended to "the form"   2b "sin[ewy?]"   8d "chance."   8e "our our"...bracket del. In 7c "glean up" is bracketed above "single".

RB has noted in red ink along the right margin: "I have a finished version of this sonnet in Gerard's own writing RB"

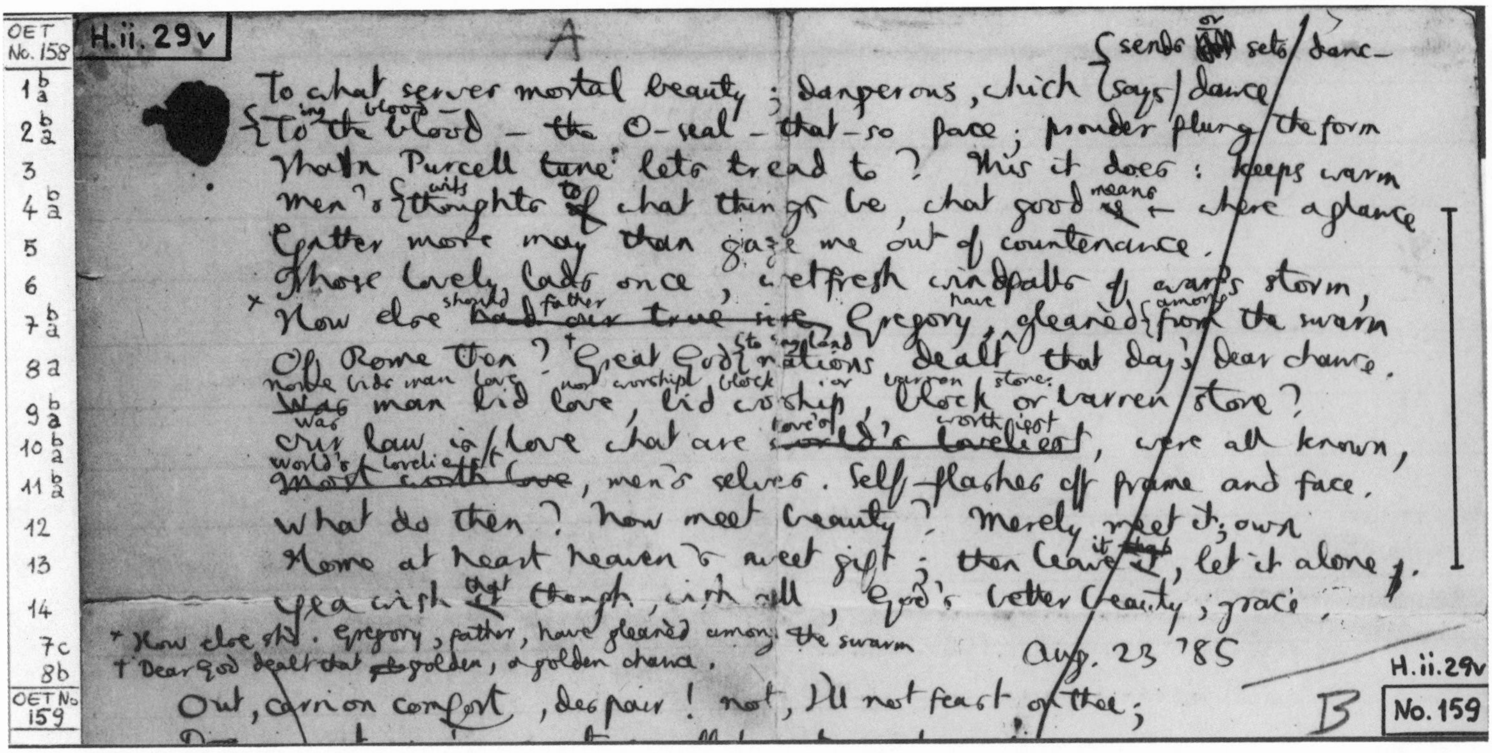

Plate 450   OET No. 158: To what serves Mortal Beauty? -- MS. 2: H²

H.ii.29v (actually the true recto)--autograph revised draft (now much creased), del. in ink; followed by drafts of No. 159 (see Plate 456), which continue on the other side; then comes No. 160 (Plate 458).

Deletions include: 1b "sends (or)/or"   3 "Than"   4a "is"   7a "sire, Gregory,"   13 "it/that" "alone."   14 "wish it/that"   8b "gl"

Note the "x" before 7b and the dagger in 8a, referring to revisions at the foot (7c and 8b).   9b reads "None bids man love nor worship block or barren stone:"

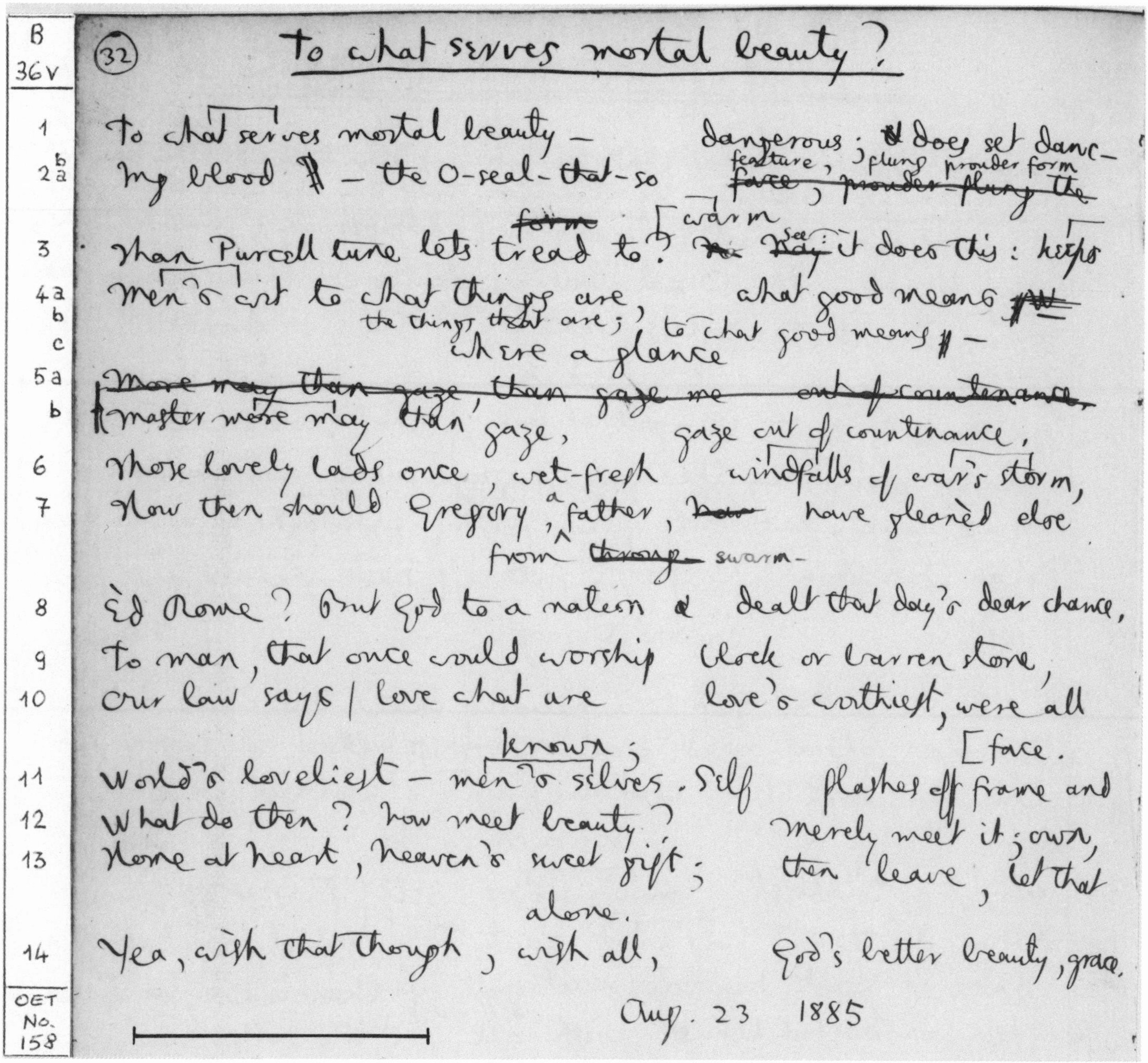

PLATE 451. OET 158. *To what serves Mortal Beauty?* • 277

Plate 451   OET No. 158: To what serves Mortal Beauty? -- MS. 3: B

B.36v--autograph faircopy inscribed in album B, with slips corrected in black ink: e.g. 1 "th[? at]" 2a "blood⸮" Words were begun in spaces meant to replace caesural strokes, in 3 "Na", 7 "hav", 8 "d" 4a "means\ W" rev. to "means;" then "means--" (the stroke below "W" is a dash, not an indication of italics).

The faircopy was later revised, with alternatives added in grey ink, some of them being later del. in brown ink. Revisions include: 2b "feature,...form" 3 "Nay/See :" 4b "means;--" 5a del. of orig. line and of the marginal bracket equating it with an alternative version 7 "a" added before "father" "throng-" changed in brown ink to "swarm-" (to restore the rhyme--see L.i.291, dated Sept. 25 1888).

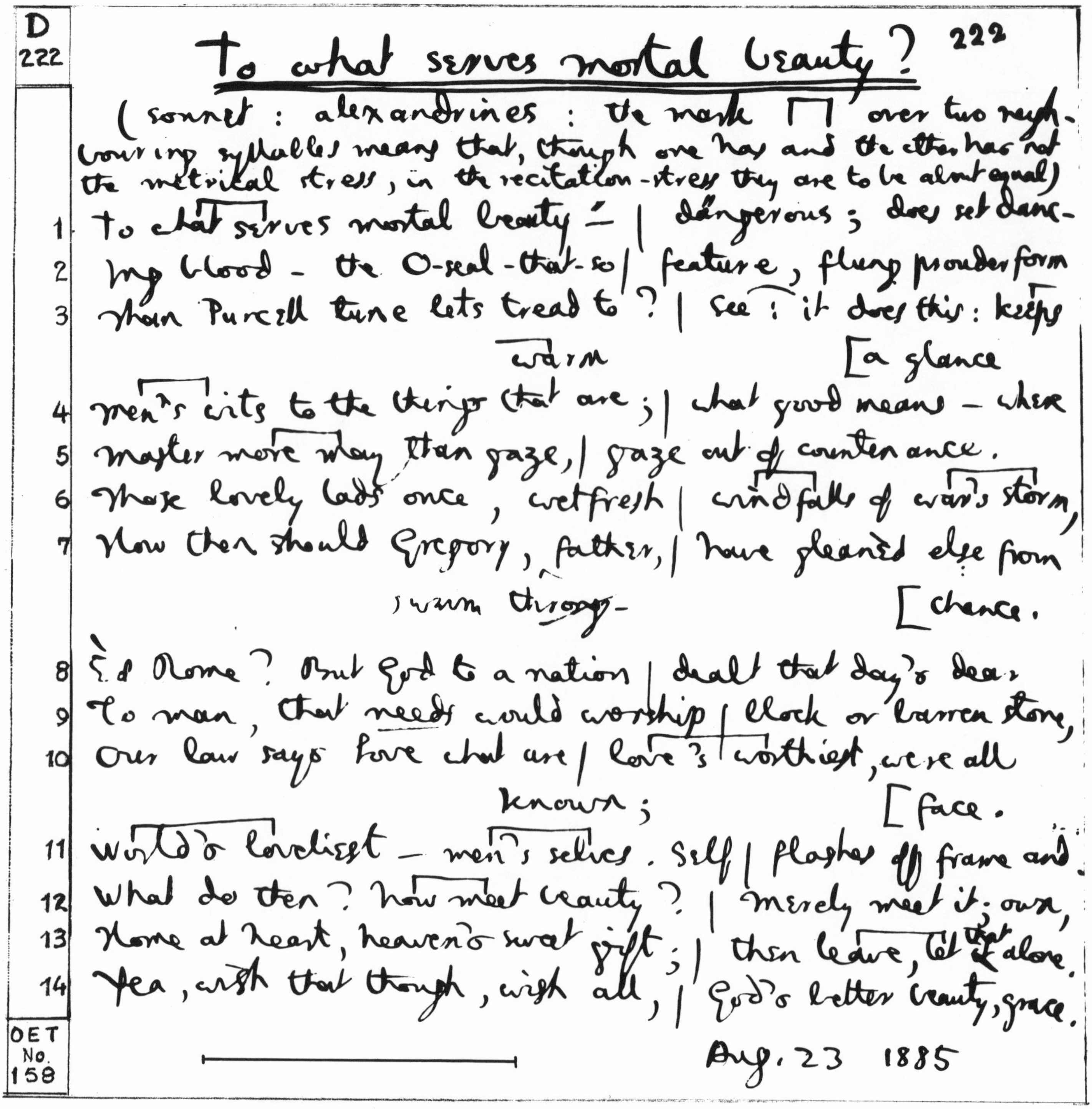

D 222

222

To what serves mortal beauty?

(sonnet : alexandrines : the mark ⊓ over two neighbouring syllables means that, though one has and the other has not
the metrical stress, in the recitation-stress they are to be about equal)

1 To what serves mortal beauty = | dángerous ; does set danc-
2 ing blood — the O-seal-that-so | feature, flung prouder form
3 than Purcell tune lets tread to ? | See : it does this : keeps
warm
[a glance
4 men's wits to the things that are ; | what good means — where
5 master more may than gaze, | gaze out of countenance.
6 Those lovely lads once, wet-fresh | windfalls of war's storm,
7 Now then should Gregory, father, | have gleanèd else from
swarm throng-
[chance.
8 Ś. d Rome ? But God to a nation | dealt that day's dear
9 To man, that needs could worship | block or barren stone,
10 Our law says love what are | love's worthiest, were all
known ;
[face.
11 world's loveliest — men's selves. Self | flashes off frame and
12 What do then ? how meet beauty ? | merely meet it ; own,
13 Home at heart, heaven's sweet gift ; | then leave, let that alone.
14 Yea, wish that though, wish all, | God's better beauty, grace.

Aug. 23 1885

OET No. 158

Plate 452   OET No. 158: To what serves Mortal Beauty? -- MS. 4: D

D.p.222--autograph faircopy sent to Dixon. Transcription printed in L.ii.129 (where "see" in 3 should be given u.c.).
Changes: 1 after "beauty" the deletion is probably the start of a caesura or possibly the beginning of a question mark (cf. H[1]).   13 "it/ that"

RB's pencil in 7 places a caret before "father" (where A and B have "a"); he also changes "throng- " to "swarm" (as GMH asked him to do with A, L.i.291); in 9 he underlines "needs", which he chose for the text of Poems, 1st. edn., instead of "once" (the reading of A, B).

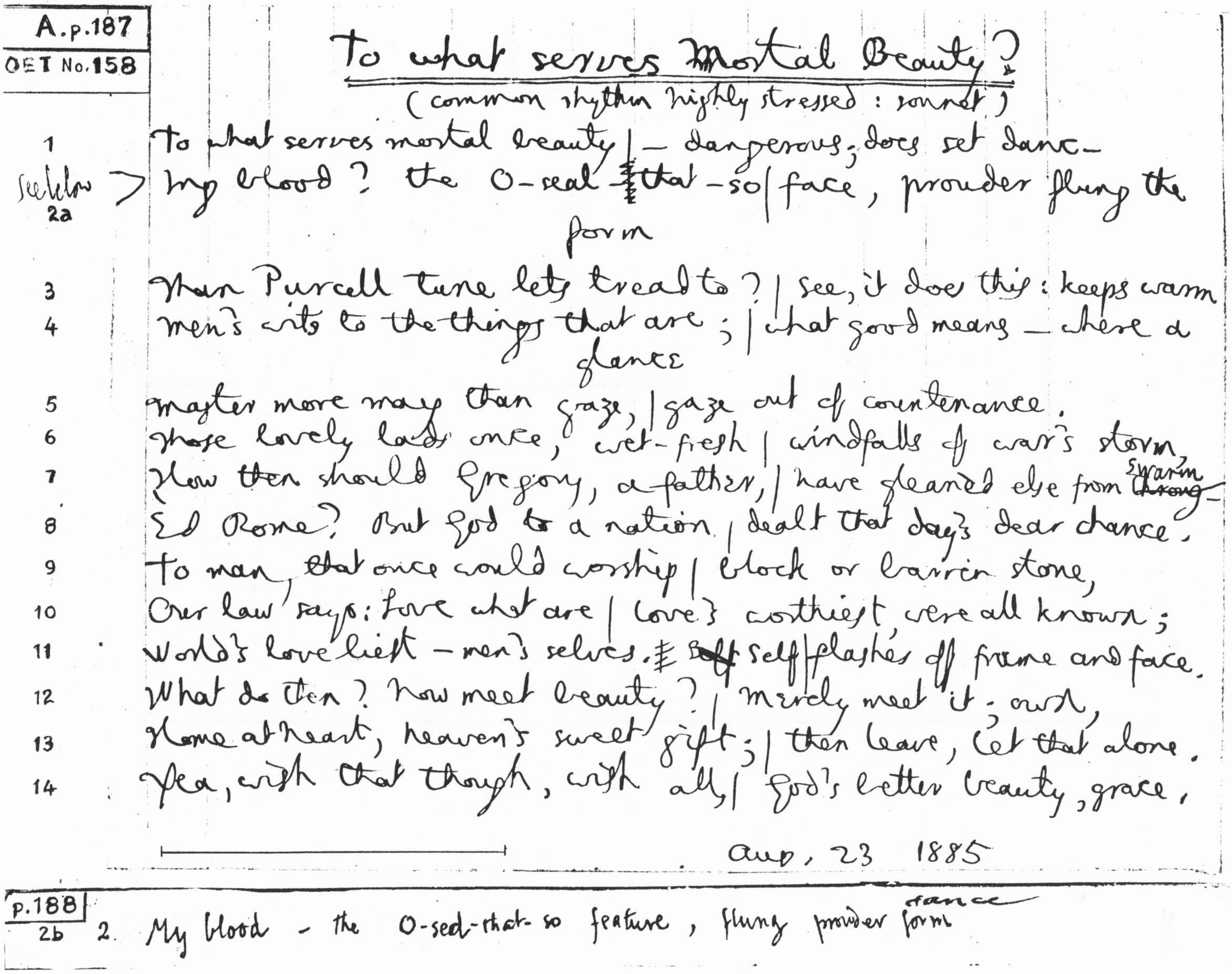

PLATE 453. OET 158. *To what serves Mortal Beauty?* • 279

A.p.187
OET No.158

To what serves Mortal Beauty?

(common rhythm highly stressed : sonnet)

1   To what serves mortal beauty | — dangerous; does set danc-
    [see below] 2a   ing blood? the O-seal-that-so | face, prouder flung the
          form
3   than Purcell tune lets tread to? | see, it does this: keeps warm
4   men's wits to the things that are ; | what good means — where a
          glance
5   master more may than gaze, | gaze out of countenance.
6   Those lovely lads once, wet-fresh | windfalls of war's storm,
7   How then should Gregory, a father, | have gleaned else from swarm-
          ed Rome? But God to a nation, | dealt that day's dear chance.
8
9   To man, that once could worship | block or barren stone,
10 Our law says: Love what are | love's worthiest, were all known;
11 World's loveliest — men's selves. Self flashes off frame and face.
12 What do then? how meet beauty? | Merely meet it; own,
13 Home at heart, heaven's sweet gift; | then leave, let that alone.
14 Yea, wish that though, wish all, | God's better beauty, grace,

                        Aug, 23 1885

p.188
2b   2. My blood — the O-seed-that- so feature , flung prouder dance form

---

Plate 453   OET No. 158: To what serves Mortal Beauty? -- MS. 5: A

A.p.187 (text of sonnet), 188 (RB's note of a revised 2)--autograph faircopy, sent along with No. 174 (the bottom of the g of "Aug." will be found at the top of its A MS., plate 504). Changes include: Title was at first copied in ℓ.c., as in MSS. B, D, "mortal beauty".   2a caesural stroke from 1 shortened   11 "selves.↗[caesura del. by RB?] Seft [? cf. "gift", H¹, 13c] mended to "Self", then deleted.

RB's black ink (1889): in 7 corrects "throng-" to "swarm" (forgetting the hyphen) as GMH had asked in L.i.291; in 9 RB adds a comma after "man"; opposite 2a he adds "See below", and on p.188 he copies the revision of 2 in B, misreading (a rare failing in RB) GMH's "[danc-]/Ing" as "My". A later editor (Charles Williams?) notes above RB's line that 1 would then have to end with "dance" (as in earlier versions), not "danc-". RB printed the line correctly in Poems, 1st. edn., p.61.

Note. Plates 454 and 455, allocated to No. 158 in the OET, were not found necessary and have therefore been omitted. Many additional plates have been allocated to other poems.

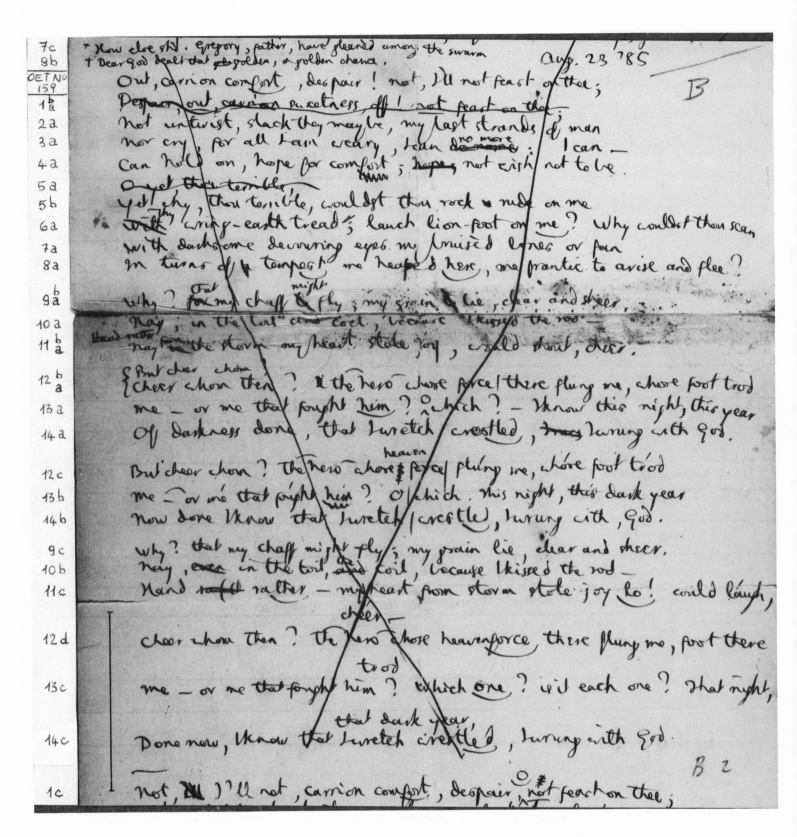

Plate 456   OET No. 159; "Not, I'll not, carrion comfort, Despair..." -- MS. 1 H¹(1)

H.ii.29 verso (really the recto)--earliest autograph draft (1a to 14c), following revised draft of No. 158; the redraft at the foot (1c to 6b) is cont. on 29r, where it is followed by the sole autograph of No. 160. The sheet has three horizontal folds or tears, and one vertical, damaging the writing. Line spaces may have been intended after 8a, 11a.

Deletions include: 1a "Despair, out," (no italics for "out", only the start of a wavy del. line)   "not" in italics   3a "can do no mo[re?]"   4a outride under "[com]fort"   "hope;"   5b "a rude"   8a "of a"   11a "Nay in"   12a "then? [blot]"   14a "I rung"   12c caesural mark del.   11c "rath" [parenthesis in place of outride] 13c "which" mended to "W".   Note the caesural marks in 12a, 12c (one del.), 13b, 14b. In 6a "lauch" is a slip for "launch"; in 11c there is a stress on "chéer".

RB's pencil shows this poem starting at "B", with a full revision at "B²".

PLATE 457. OET 159. "Not, I'll not, carrion comfort" • 281

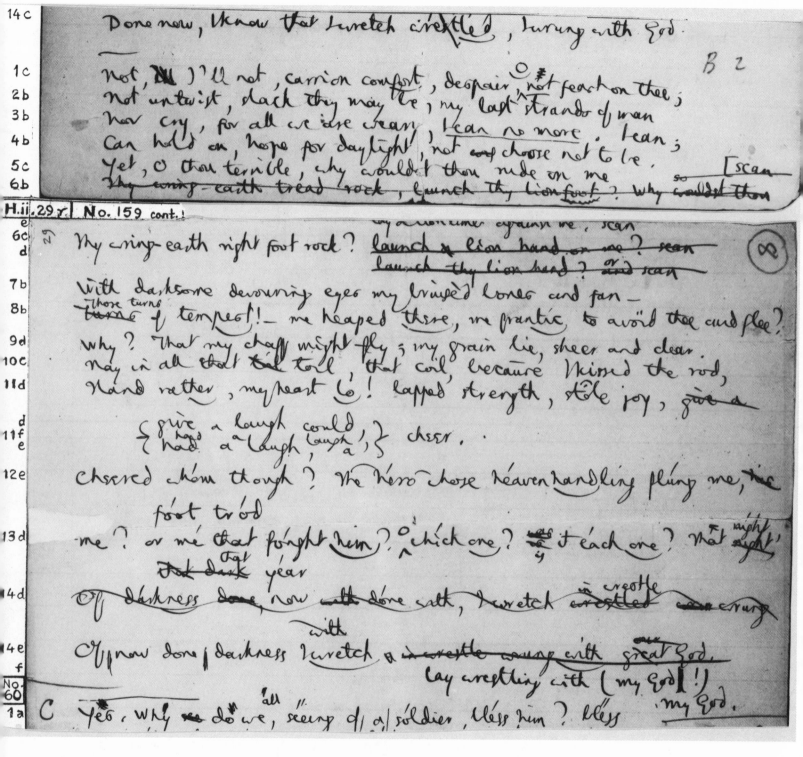

Plate 457   OET No. 159: "Not, I'll not, carrion comfort, Despair -- MS. 2: H¹ (2)

H.ii.29v (cont., redraft, lines 1c to 6b); 29r (really the verso, continuation of redraft from 29v).

29 verso (bottom). 1c "Not, c[arrion?]" mended to "I'll" then del.   stress on third "not" changed to italics.   4b "wis[h]   In 6b "Why wouldst thou scan" was rev. as "Why so scan", then the whole line was del.

29 recto. The revision in the top line is partly covered by the paper hinge attaching it to the album: "lay a lionlimb against me, scan". Deletions include: 10c "toil" (obscured by "chaff" in line above, so rewritten)   12e "his"   13d "is/was/is"   "that [acute del.] night, night," (acute shifted to noun)   14d note the outride under the deleted "darkness" (shifted in rev. 14e to "wretch").   14d "wrin[g]"   14e "Of, now done,...wretch" followed by beginning of "W[rung? or wrestled?]"   14f "(my God!)"

Note also diaeresis on "avoid" (8b) and in 11d comma placed after "could" instead of "laugh" (as in 11e and f).

For MS. 3 see Plate 459.

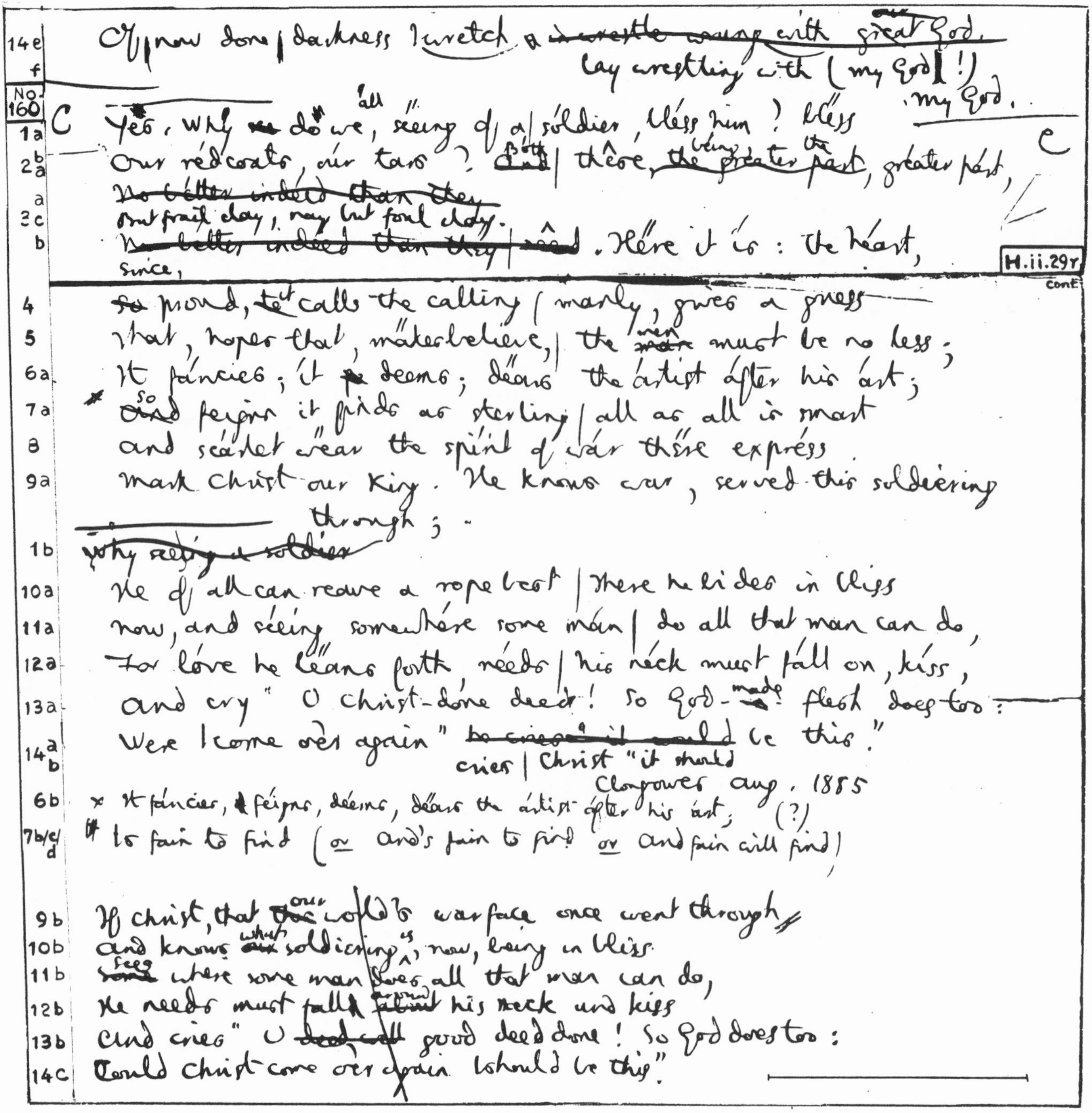

Plate 458   OET No. 160: "Yes. Why do we all, seeing of a soldier..." -- H

H.ii.29r--sole autograph draft, following a revised draft of No. 159 (Plate 457). The sheet has split in half at the fold after 3b, and is badly creased vertically. The sonnet is in Alexandrines, occasionally expanded to seven stresses (marked in 2b, 3b, 6b: see L.i.212 for theory). Note that caesural divisions are wanting in 3c, 6a, 8, 9a, 13a, 6b. After drafting the octave, GMH drew a short dividing line (like the one above "Yes. Why" in 1a) and began revising it, but wrote only 1b before inserting 9a above it and completing the sestet. The status of the footnote revisions 6b and 7b, c, d is thrown in doubt by the del. of the x beside 7a and 7b, and the insertion of a query following 6b. A further revision at the bottom was discarded--the sestet rewritten in five-stress lines.

Changes include: 1a double stresses: on "Yes" del., those on "Why" and "all" blurred into single ones; single stress upgraded to double on "seeing" and del. on "do". see 3b "nêed" 4 orig. "So proud to call" 6a "fé[igns?]" 13a "God-in-flesh" 6b "fancies, d[eems]" 9b "this...through," [note "warface" for "warfare"] 12b "falls about" 14c "I" [?] mended to "Could".

Marginal "C"s and RB's pencil divisions above them mark the start of the sonnet.

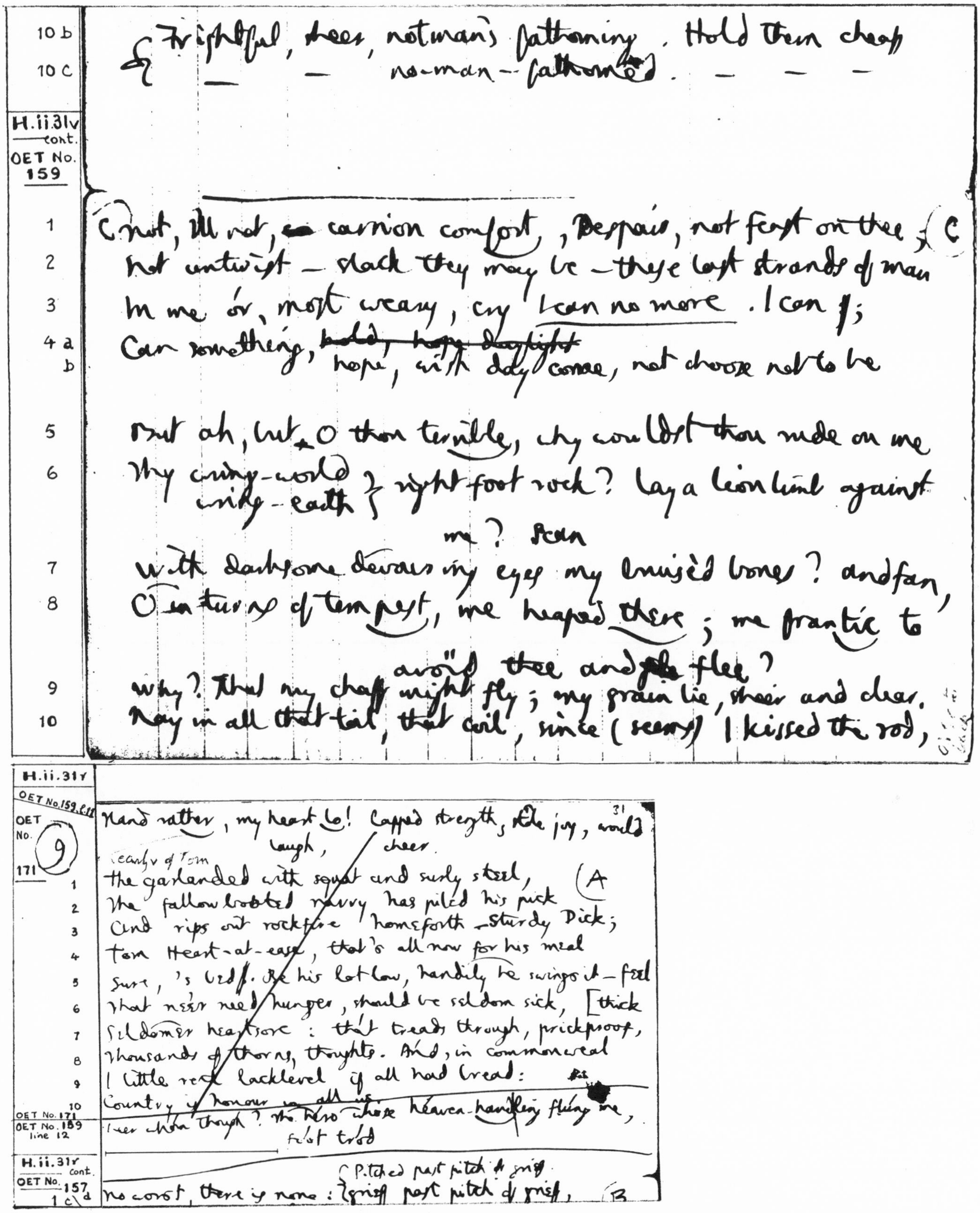

PLATE 459. OET 159. "Not, I'll not, carrion comfort" • 283

Plate 459   OET No. 159: "Not, I'll not, carrion comfort, Despair -- MS. 3: H²

H.ii.31v (lower half, below No. 157, for which see Plate 447a): final autograph (1-10 only). The revised 11 and 12 were squeezed above and below "Tom's Garland" on H.ii.31r (see Plate 492 for full scale reproduction). The final revisions of 13, 14 are missing.

Changes include: 1 "car" blotted   "despair" mended to u.c.   3 "can ✗;   4b "come" m written like a n (?) and mended over original e   5 "but,"   8 "fle"   9 "that" mended to u.c.   Note: 4 has no final stop; 6 "scan" l.c. probably as after other queries in 6 and 7   7 "devouring" slur begun, not finished; 8 "avoid" has diaeresis, not double stress.

RB's "C" marks the beginning of the poem, and at bottom he notes "over to back" (for ℓℓ.11, 12 on 31 recto).

⑤

H.ii. 23r | **OET No. 161**

23

1a	From thee I came, to thee I go,
2a	And all day long like fountain flow
3a	From thy hand out and ⟨sway⟩ move about
4a	Mote-like in thy mighty glow.

2 What I know of thee I bless,
As acknowledging thy stress
On my being and as seeing
Something of thy holiness,

9a	I neglected thee too long,
10a	Weak in will but seeming strong,
11a	Sowed the wind — sir, I winned:
12a	I repent my doing wrong.

13b I repent; I am thy child;
13a { But because I am thy child,
14a Father, be thou reconciled;
15a look on me since I see
16a thou hast on other sinners smiled.
16b that I On other sinners thou hast smiled.

5/ And I have life left with me still / before me still
18 with thy purpose to fulfill;
19 Yet a debt to pay thee yet:
20 Help me, sir, and so fulfill.

Right column (OET No. 161)

1b	Thee, God, I come from, to thee go,
2b	And all day long like fountain flow
3c / 3b	From thy hand out, sway about move about
4b	Mote-like in thy mighty glow.

2c [All day long like some fountain flow]
2d All day long I like fountain flow

9b	From thy presence once I hid,
10b	Doing that thou hadst forbid,
11b	Sowed the wind — sir, I sinned:
12b	I repent of that I did,

3 Once I turned from thee and hid,
9c / 10c Bound on what thou hadst forbid;
11c Sow the wind I would; I winned:
12c I repent of that I did,

4 Bad I am, but yet thy child.
13c / 14b Father, be thou reconciled.
15b Spare thou me since thee
16c / 17b With thy might that thou art mild

H.ii. 23r cont. | **OET No 161 CONT.**

| 21a | 6 But thou bidst, and just thou art, | 21b | But thou bidst, as thou art just |

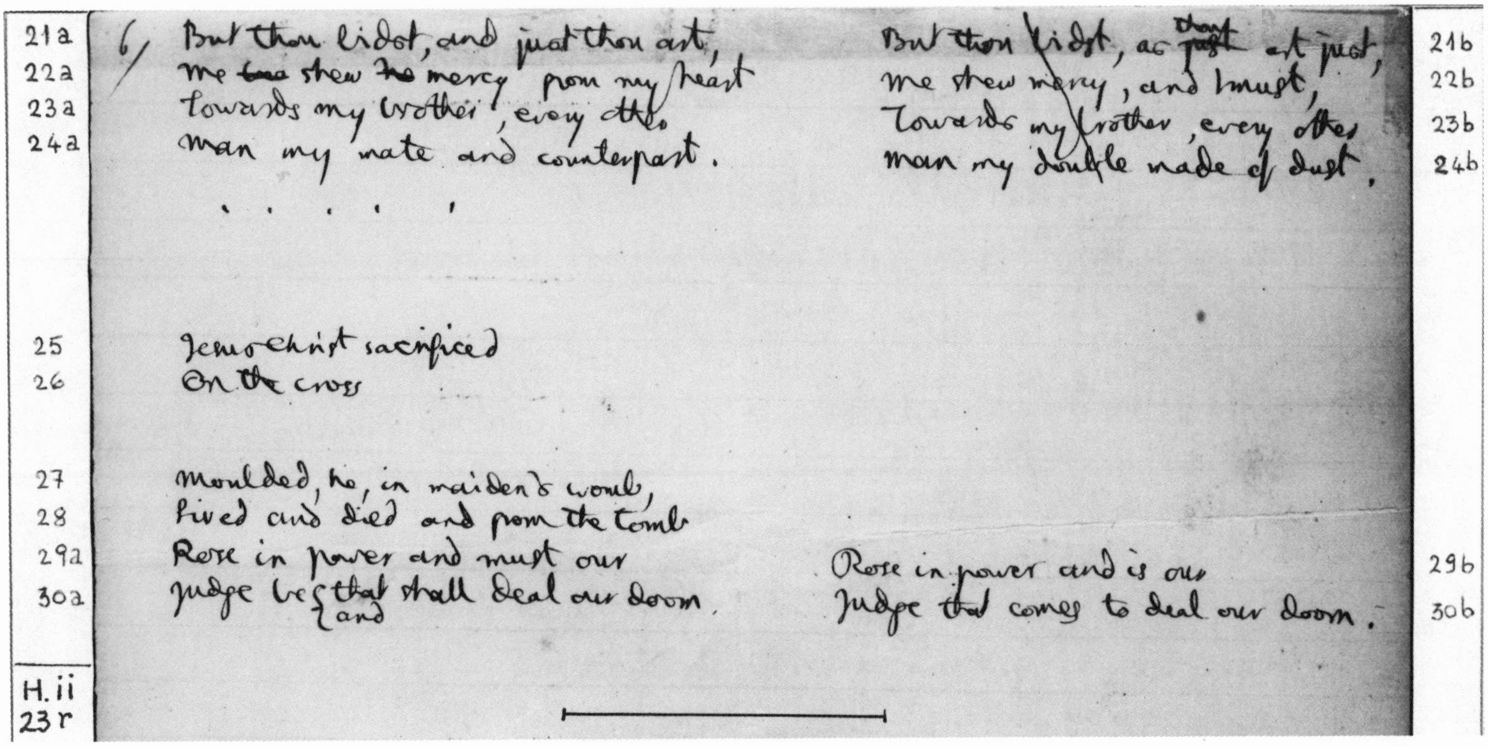

PLATE 461. OET 161. "Thee God, I come from" • 285

21 a	6/ But thou bidst, and just thou art,
22 a	me ~~too~~ shew ~~no~~ mercy from my heart
23 a	Towards my brother, every other
24 a	man my mate and counterpart.

21 b	But thou bidst, as ~~just~~ that art just,
22 b	me shew mercy, and I must,
23 b	Towards my brother, every other
24 b	man my double made of dust.

25	Jesus Christ sacrificed
26	On the cross

27	Moulded, he, in maiden's womb,
28	lived and died and from the tomb
29 a	Rose in power and must our
30 a	Judge be that shall deal our doom.
	{and

29 b	Rose in power and is our
30 b	Judge that comes to deal our doom.

H. ii
23 r

Plates 460 and 461   OET No. 161: "Thee, God, I come from, to thee go" -- Sole MS.

[opposite and above] H.ii.23r--sole autograph (with early draft of No. 158 on the verso). The second column was used for revisions.

GMH's Deletions in ink: *ll*.9a to 12a, 21b to 24b   2d day/day   7 by my   15a An[d]/Smite...as/since   15b since/because [del. in pencil by RB] 17b I   18 And/With   19 And/Yea   22a bea[r?]shew he   21b just/thou

Edited for publication by RB in pencil (1893?). He pencilled numbers beside final versions of sts. 1 to 6; he neatly crossed through in pencil 1a to 4a, 9b to 12b, 13b to 16b, and at first through 2c and 2d, but then he rubbed out the del. line. He del. the undecided alternatives in 3b "out and move" and 15b "because". He enclosed in square brackets 2b and 2c, with an x beside 2b and an arrow leading to 2d.

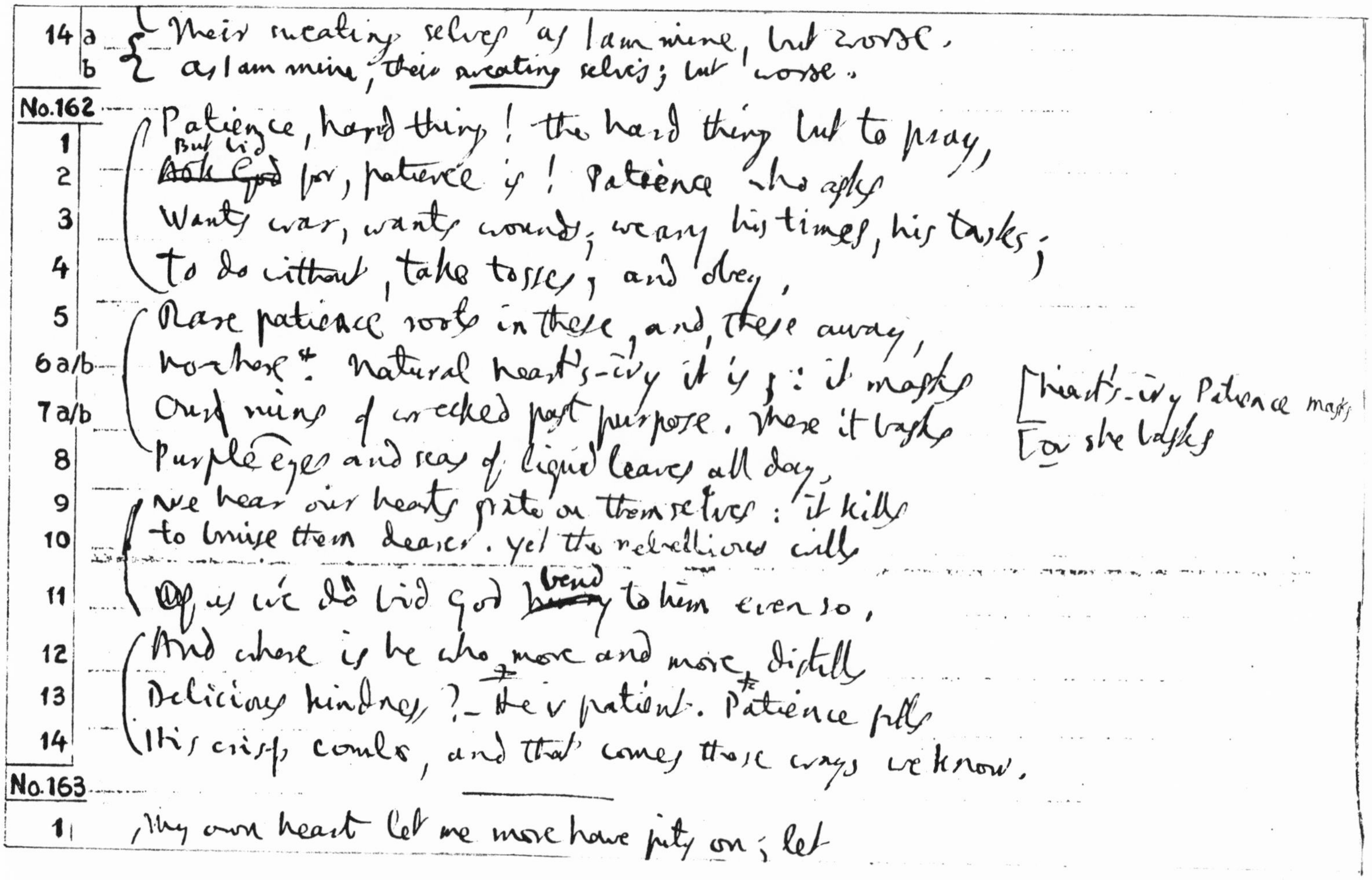

14	a	{ Their sweating selves, as I am mine, but worse.
	b	{ as I am mine, their sweating selves; but worse.
No.162		
1		Patience, hard thing! the hard thing but to pray,
		But bid
2		Ask God for, patience is! Patience who asks
3		Wants war, wants wounds; weary his times, his tasks;
4		To do without, take tosses, and obey.
5		Rare patience roots in these, and these away
6 a/b		Nowhere. Natural heart's-ivy it is; : it masks
7 a/b		Our ruins of wrecked past purpose. There it basks
8		Purple eyes and seas of liquid leaves all day,
9		We hear our hearts grate on themselves: it kills
10		to bruise them dearer. Yet the rebellious wills
11		Of us we do bid God bend to him even so.
12		And where is he who, more and more, distills
13		Delicious kindness? — He is patient. Patience fills
14		His crisp combs, and that comes those ways we know.
No.163		
1		My own heart let me more have pity on; let

(marginal note at 6a/b–7a/b: [heart's-ivy Patience masks / For she basks)

Plate 462   OET No. 162: "Patience, hard thing!" -- MS. H

H.ii.35v--sole autograph, faircopy with a few revisions, following No. 155. The marginal braces mark the quatrains and tercets.

Deletions, etc., include: 6a "No-where" hyphenated, rev. as one word. ..."is ;:"   7a "Our"   11 "W" [We?] mended to "Of"   "hurry/bend". [Daniel Harris reads "bring" but cf. "hurry" in a contemporary MS. L.i.257, ℓ.15 (30 July 1887):

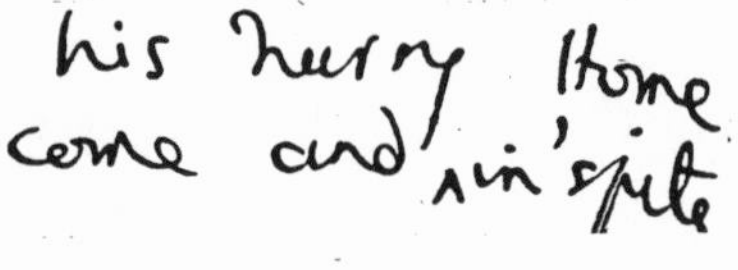

his hurry home
come and in spite

and "hurl" in No. 156, 1b (Plate 446)]   12 "who,"..."more, distills".

Many words have been fumbled and patched, e.g. 2 "Patience"   3 "times"   5 "patience"   8 "liquid" (second i overlaps d; compare the dot over it with the final period in 8 after "day" and with the period in the semicolon in No. 163, 1, included in this plate). In 13 the s of "is" has microscopic loops to distinguish it from the limb of a v.

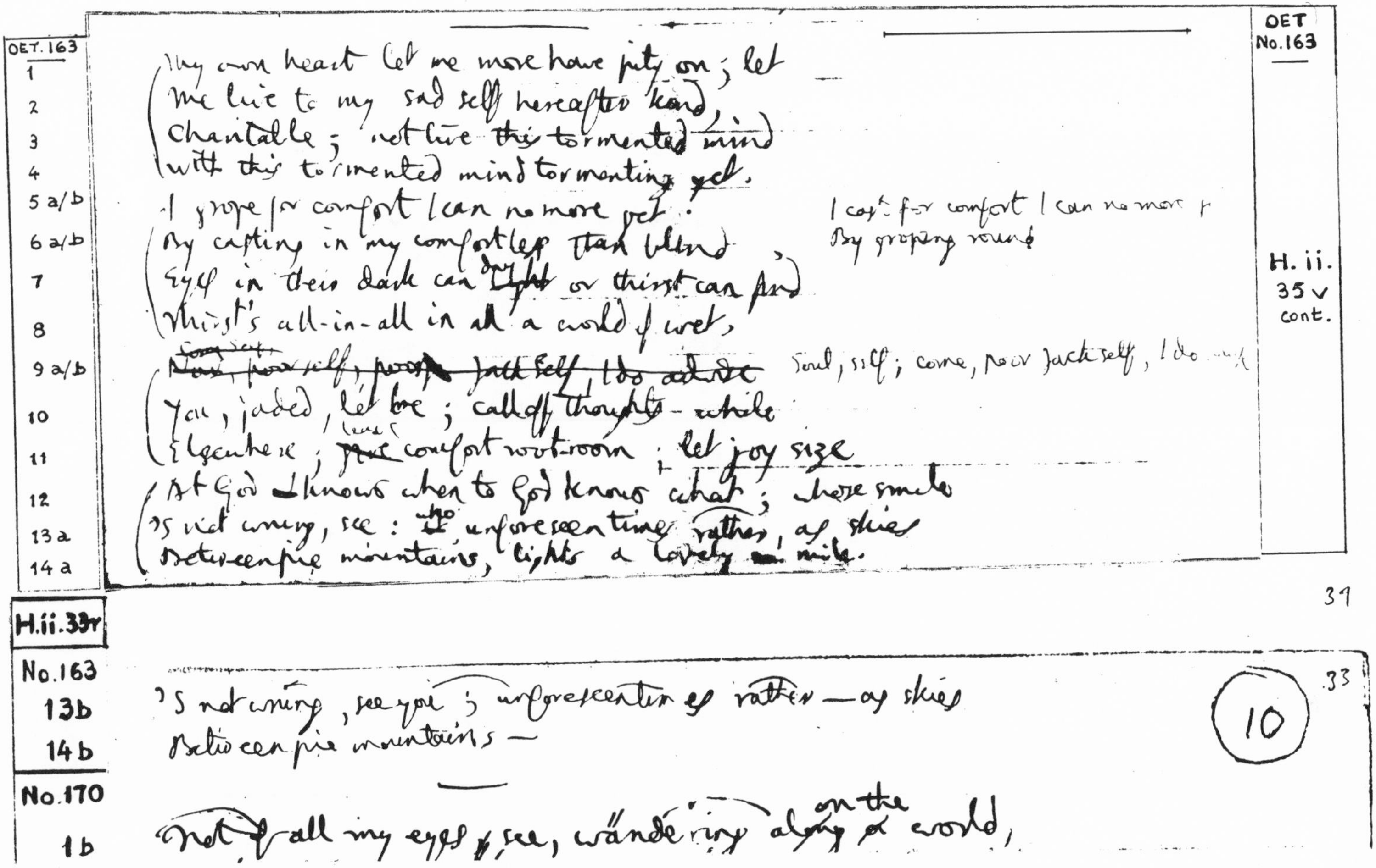

PLATE 463. OET 163. "My own heart"　　•　　287

Plate 463　　　　　OET No. 163: "My own heart let me more have pity on" -- MSS. 1 (H¹) and 2 (H²)

1. (H¹) H.ii.35v--sole complete autograph (below OET No. 162), faircopy, later revised with a different pen. Note the varied dots to the i: a horizontal dash above "live" (3), a period as though ending the previous line above "blind" (6a), a comma above "find" (7--cf. the period after "wet" in 8, which is also a pseudo-comma), and the loop above "advise" (9a).

Deletions, etc., include: 9a "Now, [rev. as "Come" then as "Self,"] poorself, poor Ja[ck] Jack ʃSelf," rev. to "Jackself" in margin ["self" might perhaps be meant as a separate word--more likely as a compound with "poor" in 9a and with "Jack" in 9b; in 9a "Jack Self" must be two words since s is mended to S in 9a.]　　10 "me" mended to "be"; the minute a in "awhile" is barely visible　　12 "At God wh[?] knows when to God o" mended to "knows"　　13 "it/who"　　14a "lovely sm[ile?]

2. (H²) H.ii.33r (which was once part of f.35)--revision of 13 and start of 14 (see Plate 491 for the rest of the MS.). Over "wrung" the beginning of a slur should not be mistaken for a stress.

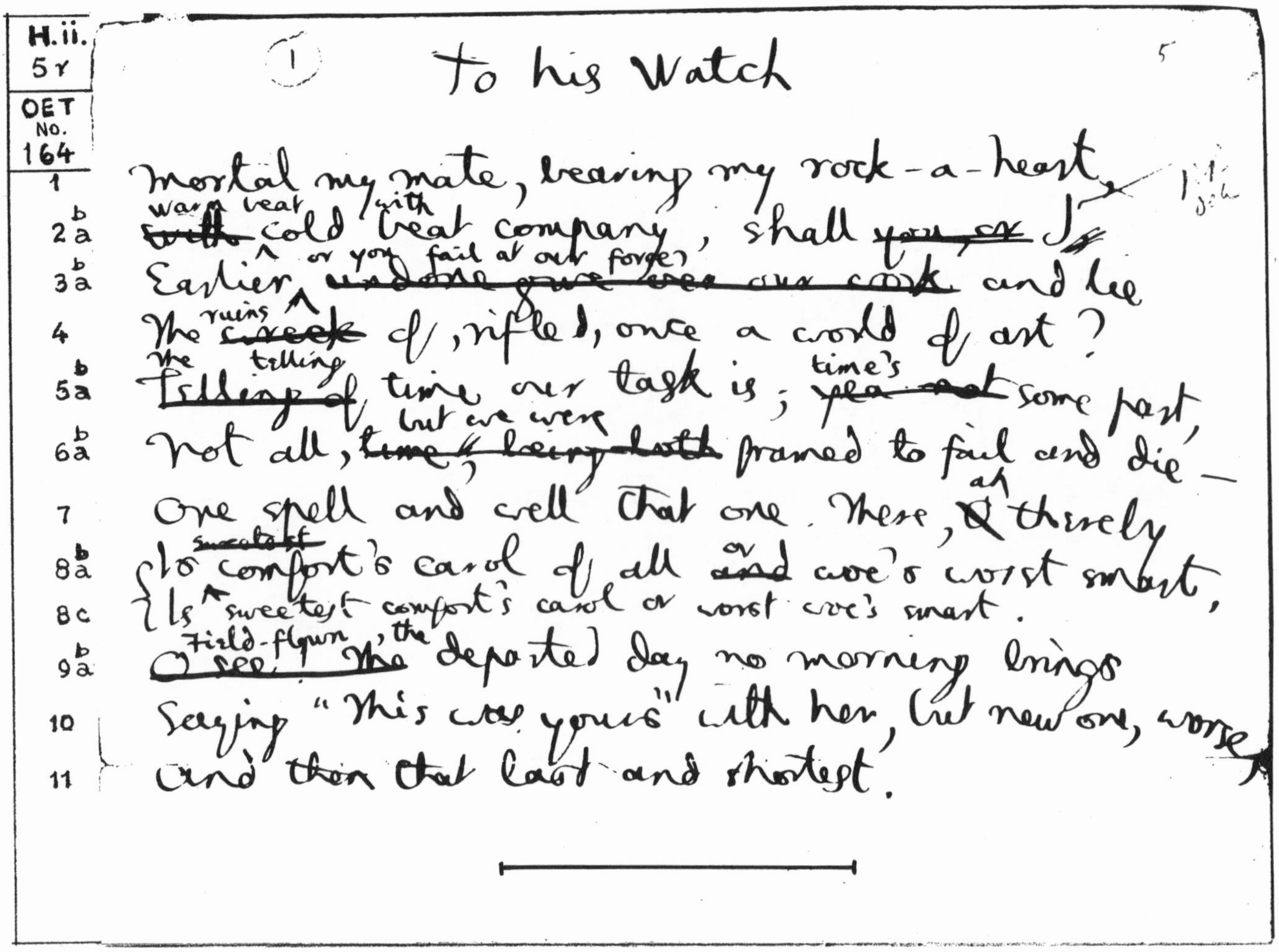

Plate 464 [above]   OET No. 164: To his Watch -- Sole Autograph

H.ii.5r--sole autograph, draft of an unfinished sonnet, with revisions in 6 and 7 while the ink was wet; later revised in other lines, including the addition of 8c, with a different pen and ink.

Obscure readings include: 2a "you, or I,"   3a "undone give o'er our work" 3b "force" or "forge" (see enlargement) 5a "yea not" ("not" deleted twice)   6a "time,"

RB's pencil numbers the poem "1" before the title, and deletes the comma after "heart" (1).

Plate 465 [opposite, left]   OET No. 164: To his Watch -- Enlargement of Lines 1-4.

The OET text of line 3 has an asterisk after "fail at our force" with the footnote "or possibly forge". The ambiguity arises because GMH's interlined revision crosses the tail of the "y" in "company" (2a), which had ended with a slight swerve to the right (level with the bottom of the "e" and of the apostrophe above "o'er" (3a). Two interpretations arise. One is that the tail of the "y" was extended during the revision (or, more likely, after the revision had dried) because he had written "force" and wanted to disentangle that word from "company". The second interpretation, not proposed until 1968, is that the word GMH had interlined was "forge", and that the tail of its "g" unluckily almost exactly coincided with the "y" of "company". Against this it may be argued that if GMH had really intended to write "forge" here, his common figure-of-eight "g" would have prevented any confusion. Why should he deliberately have created difficulty by forming a "g" virtually unique in his autographs?--one made in two distinct stages, separated by a pen lift, a "c" closed off with the tail of a "y"? My manuscript dating files have no parallels among over 1200 dated examples (from his prose and verse) of the lower case "g". Rather different is a single instance where he changed a "c" to a "g": in the Welsh of No. 102c, Plate 268, line x of the prose introduction, he had to turn "cael" into "gael" because in revision he had placed an "i" before it, causing a mutation. In the Introduction to the 4th. edn. of Poems (1970 reprint, lxviii-lxix) I invited scholars to produce examples of an unaltered "g" which would parallel the reputed "g" in "force/forge", a "g" formed in two separate stages: no one has yet been able to point one out. The nearest equivalent I have myself noticed in GMH's MSS. is in the hurried drafts of his last poem (OET No. 179, Plate 522), written when his final fatal illness was already afflicting him. Here I found two "g" forms with "y" tails. In line 11b the word "lagging" has one "g" formed like an open-topped "y", and another "g" like an elongated printed "s": but neither shows a "c" closed off with a separate tail-stroke. See Plate 465 (bot. right) example (v).

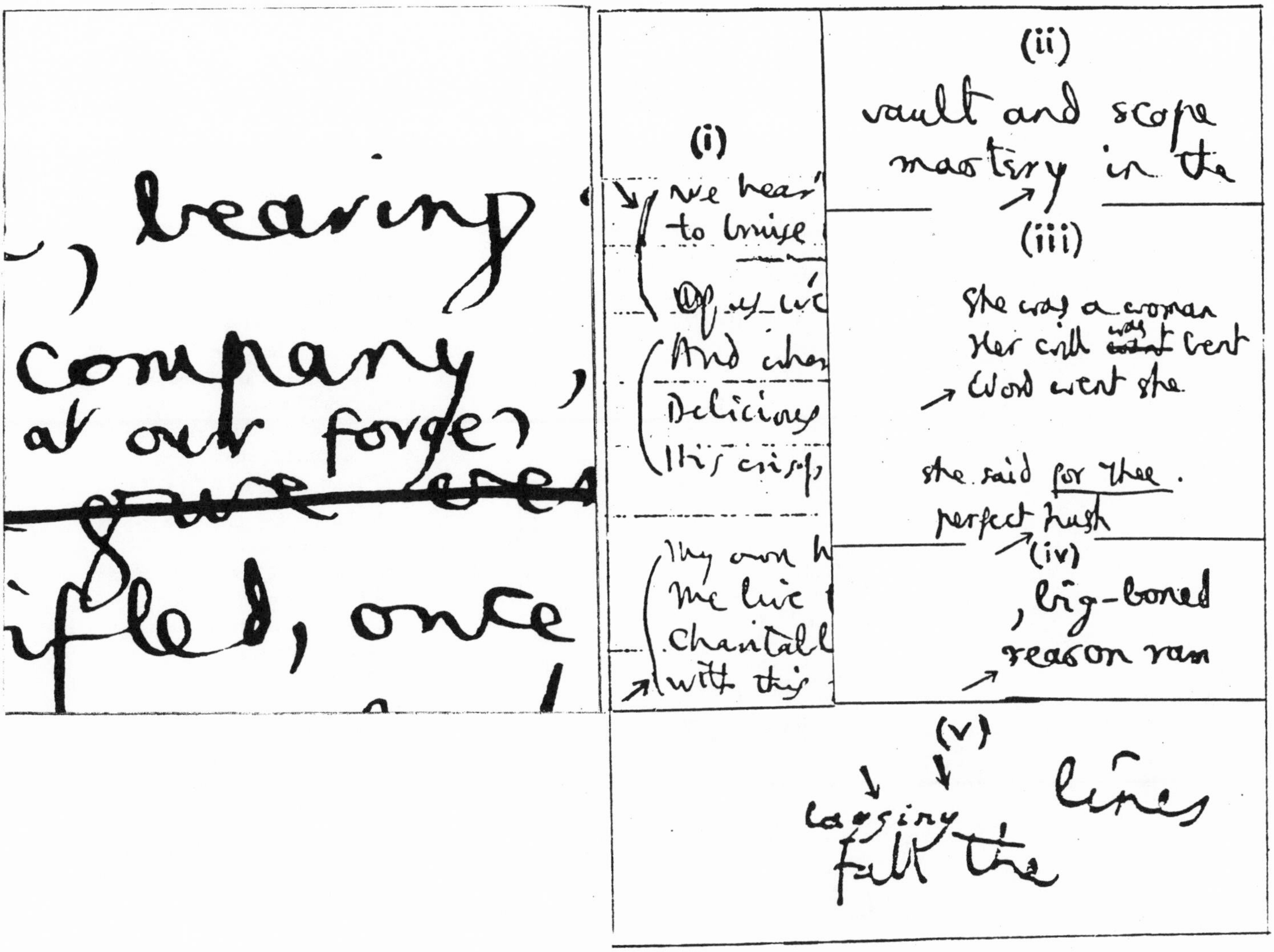

PLATE 465. OET 164. *To his Watch* • 289

Plate 465 [left]: Discussion of the Enlargement.

The sole autograph is reproduced full scale in Plate 464, with a greatly enlarged portion (c. 360%) in Plate 465. To the naked eye the whole "y" tail of "company" (2a) in Plate 464 seems one flowing line. Magnification discloses that its extension, instead of overlapping perfectly as an engraver with a jeweller's loupe in his eye might have drawn it, begins about a quarter of a millimeter to the left of the original line. A poet consumed by the feeling of failure revealed in this poem, hurriedly amending the poetic embodiment of futility, is the last person who would exercise such superfluous care. Readers who are convinced that the disjuncture is proof absolute that the true reading is "forge" may care to try this experiment: print five times in rapid succession the word "company" with a strait-tailed "y", in letters no larger than those in Plate 464, where the word occupies about an inch or 2.4 centimeters. Then add to the length of each tail with a swift curving stroke. Though the unaided eye may approve the extensions as exactly in line, magnification is liable to be disillusioning.

Plate 465 [right]: Examples of GMH's Extensions of Lines elsewhere.

GMH's quill pen can frequently be seen, even without optical aid, to diverge from perfect extensions to letters which he unquestionably tried to amend, and his marginal braces or counterpoint curves are often drawn in two arcs which do not exactly meet. Examples: (i) braces on Plate 462; (ii) the "y" of "mastery" (OET No. 139, ℓ.16, MS. A, Plate 373a); (iii) the "W" of "Word" and the "h" of "hush" (No. 108, ℓℓ.38, 58, Plates 282, 283); (iv) the "r" of "reason" (No. 142, ℓ.3, MS. A, Plate 382).

A third interpretation of the MS. is just conceivable--that GMH first wrote "force" and then mended it to "forge" by the same method as in the Welsh "Cywydd". But the change from failing force, an acceptable description of reduced physical powers (see OET Commentary on this poem, p.464), to forge introduces an image of the poet which many will think unlikely. From his first teaching post onward (1868, L.iii.231) Hopkins had complained of weak health and tiredness. Would a poet pleading bodily and mental debility invite comparison with the Felix Randal he had enviously admired while he was still wielding his sledge hammer (OET No. 142; cf. No. 101, st. 10), or liken the murky chaos of a blacksmith's shop, the "random grim forge", to a "world of art"?

A p. 168
OET No. 165a

Come unto these yellow sands 10/
(from the Tempest)

1 Ocius O flavas has, ocius
O ad arenas
2 Manusque manibus jungite,
3 Post Salve dictum, post oscula, dum neque venti
4 Ferum neque obstrepit
mare.
5 Tum pede sic agiles ~~p~~ terram
pulsabitis et sic
6 Pulsabitis terram pede.
7 Vos, dulces nymphae, spectabitis interea; quin
8 Plausu modos signabitis.

L.i.232
9 Lascivae latrare; ita plaudere! At hoc
juvat: ergo
10 b a nos ~~Et~~ Hecuba et Hecubae nos canes ~~nunc chorus~~
11 Allatrent. ~~hos~~ Gallus sed enim occinit,
occinat: ~~hora~~ aequumst
12 Cantare gallos temperi. ~~aequum erat~~
OET No. 165a

SONGS FROM SHAKSPERE IN LATIN.

No. II.—"COME UNTO THESE YELLOW SANDS."

COME unto these yellow sands
And then take hands:
Courtsied when you have and kissed
(The wild waves whist).
Foot it featly here and there
And, sweet sprites, the burthen bear.
Hark, hark! "*Bow, wow!*"
The watchdogs bark, "*Bow, wow!*"
Hark, hark! I hear
The strain of strutting chanticleer
Cry, cock-a-diddle-dow.

LATINE REDDITUM

Ocius O flavas, has ocius O ad arenas,
Manusque manibus jungite;
Post *Salve* dictum, post oscula; dum neque venti
Ferum neque obstrepit mare.
Tum pede sic agiles terram pulsabitis et sic
Pulsabitis terram pede.
Vos, dulces nymphae, spectabitis interea; quin
Plausu modos signabitis.
Lascivæ latrare; ita plaudere. At hoc juvat: ergo
Et Hecuba et Hecubæ nos canes
Allatrent. Gallus sed enim occinit. Occinat: æquumst
Cantare gallos temperi.

G. H.

<u>Plates 466-472:</u> <u>OET No. 165: [Songs from Shakespeare, in Latin and Greek]</u>

<u>Plate 466</u>: <u>OET No. 165(a): "Come unto these yellow sands"</u>

(i) <u>A.p.168</u> (for ℓℓ.1-8)--autograph faircopy. Omitted from the bottom of the plate is RB's transcription of ℓℓ.9-12, copied from L.i.232 with three changes.

(ii) <u>L.i.232</u> [MS. Letters to Bridges, ii.173] (for ℓℓ.9-12)--autograph, in a letter dated 21 Oct. 1886. <u>Deletions</u>: 10a Et...nunc chorus 11 hos. /...hora 12 aequum erat.

If GMH had amalgamated the two parts into one MS., he would have changed the period ending 8 into a comma, as the sentence is continued in 9.

(iii) <u>Irish Monthly</u>, 15 (Feb. 1887), 92. This differs from the MSS. in various places, owing to editorial and/or authorial changes.

SONGS FROM SHAKSPEARE, IN LATIN.

No. I.

"FULL FATHOM FIVE THY FATHER LIES."

(*The Tempest*, Act I, Scene 2.)

FULL fathom five thy father lies :
  Of his bones are coral made :
Those are pearls that were his eyes :
  Nothing of him that doth fade,
  But doth suffer a sea-change
  Into something rich and strange.
Sea-nymphs hourly ring his knell :
Hark ! now I hear them—ding-dong bell.

Occidit, O juvenis, pater et sub syrtibus his est,
  Ossaque concretum paene coralium habet,
Quique fuere oculi vertunt in iaspidas undae :
  In rem Nereidum et Tethyos omnis abit.
Quidquid enim poterat corrumpi corpore in illo
  Malunt aequoream fata subire vicem.
Exsequias, quod tu miraberis, illi Phorcys
  Delphinis ducunt Oceanusque suis.
Fallor an ipsa vadis haec nenia redditur imis ?
  Glauci mortalem flet, mihi crede, chorus.

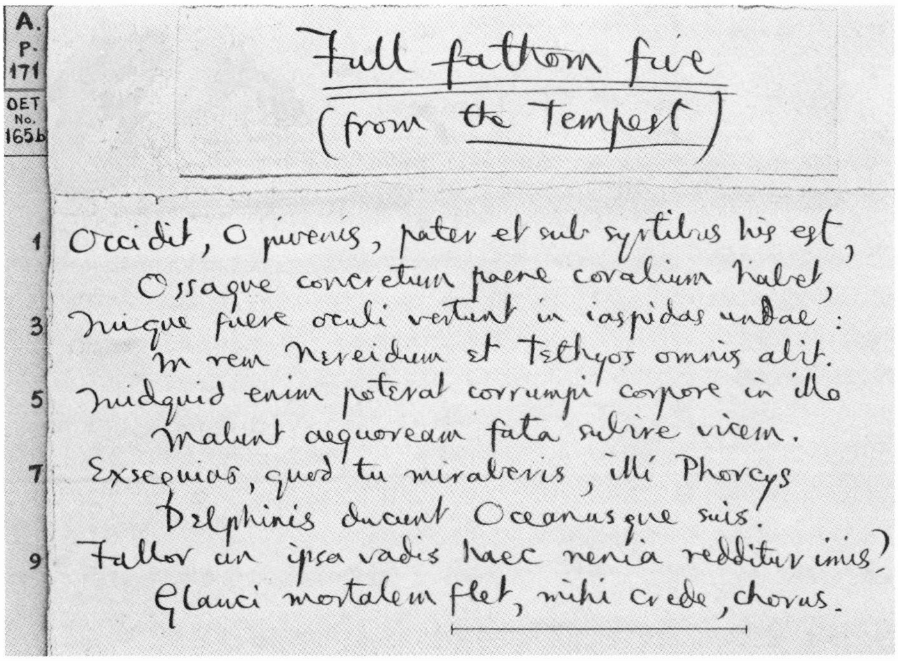

Full fathom five
(from the Tempest)

1 Occidit, O juvenis, pater et sub syrtibus his est,
    Ossaque concretum paene coralium habet,
3 Quique fuere oculi vertunt in iaspidas undae :
    In rem Nereidum et Tethyos omnis alit.
5 Quidquid enim poterat corrumpi corpore in illo
    Malunt aequoream fata subire vicem.
7 Exsequias, quod tu miraberis, illi Phorcys
    Delphinis ducunt Oceanusque suis.
9 Fallor an ipsa vadis haec nenia redditur imis?
    Glauci mortalem flet, mihi crede, chorus.

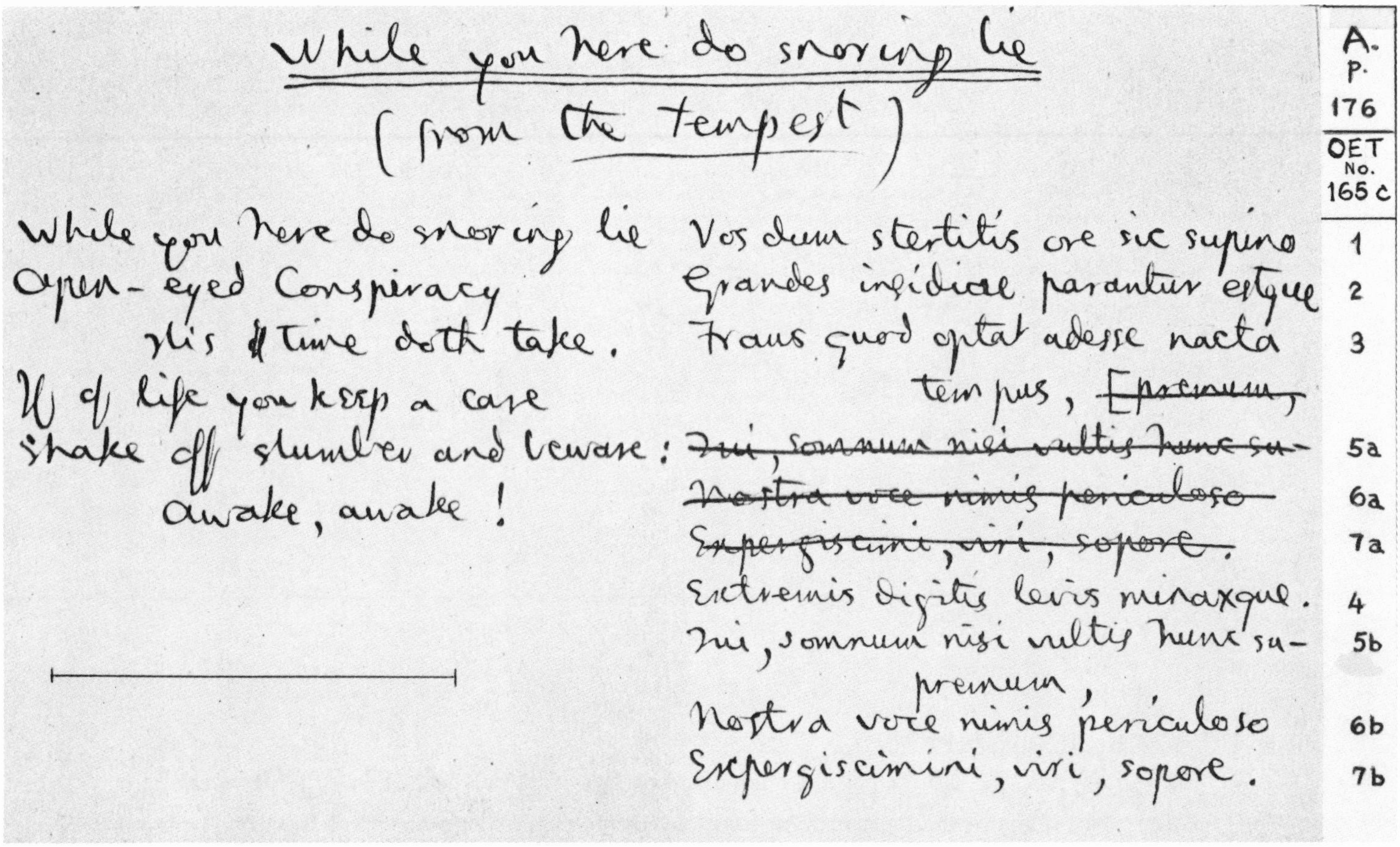

While you here do snoring lie
(from the Tempest)

While you here do snoring lie
Open-eyed Conspiracy
  His & time doth take.
If of life you keep a care
Shake off slumber and beware:
  Awake, awake!

Vos dum stertitis ore sic supino   1
Grandes insidiae parantur estque   2
Fraus quod optat adesse nacta   3
    tempus, ~~Epsum~~
~~Tui, somnum nisi vultis hunc su~~   5a
~~Nostra voce nimis periculoso~~   6a
~~Expergiscimini, viri, sopore.~~   7a
Extremis digitis levis miraxque.   4
Tui, somnum nisi vultis hunc su-   5b
    premum,
Nostra voce nimis periculoso   6b
Expergiscimini, viri, sopore.   7b

Plate 467:   (i) OET No. 165(b): "Full fathom five"
  [top right] A.p.171--autograph faircopy.
  [top left] Irish Monthly, 14 (Nov. 1886), 628--earliest published version, with the English original. Not even GMH's initials were added.
        (ii) OET No. 165(c): "While you here do snoring lie"
  [bottom] A.p.176--autograph faircopy, absent-mindedly made. GMH in the English started to write "doth" before "time" (3), and in the Latin copied 5-7 before realising that 4 had been omitted. Instead of interlining 4 neatly, he scored through 5-7, and rewrote them after copying in 4.

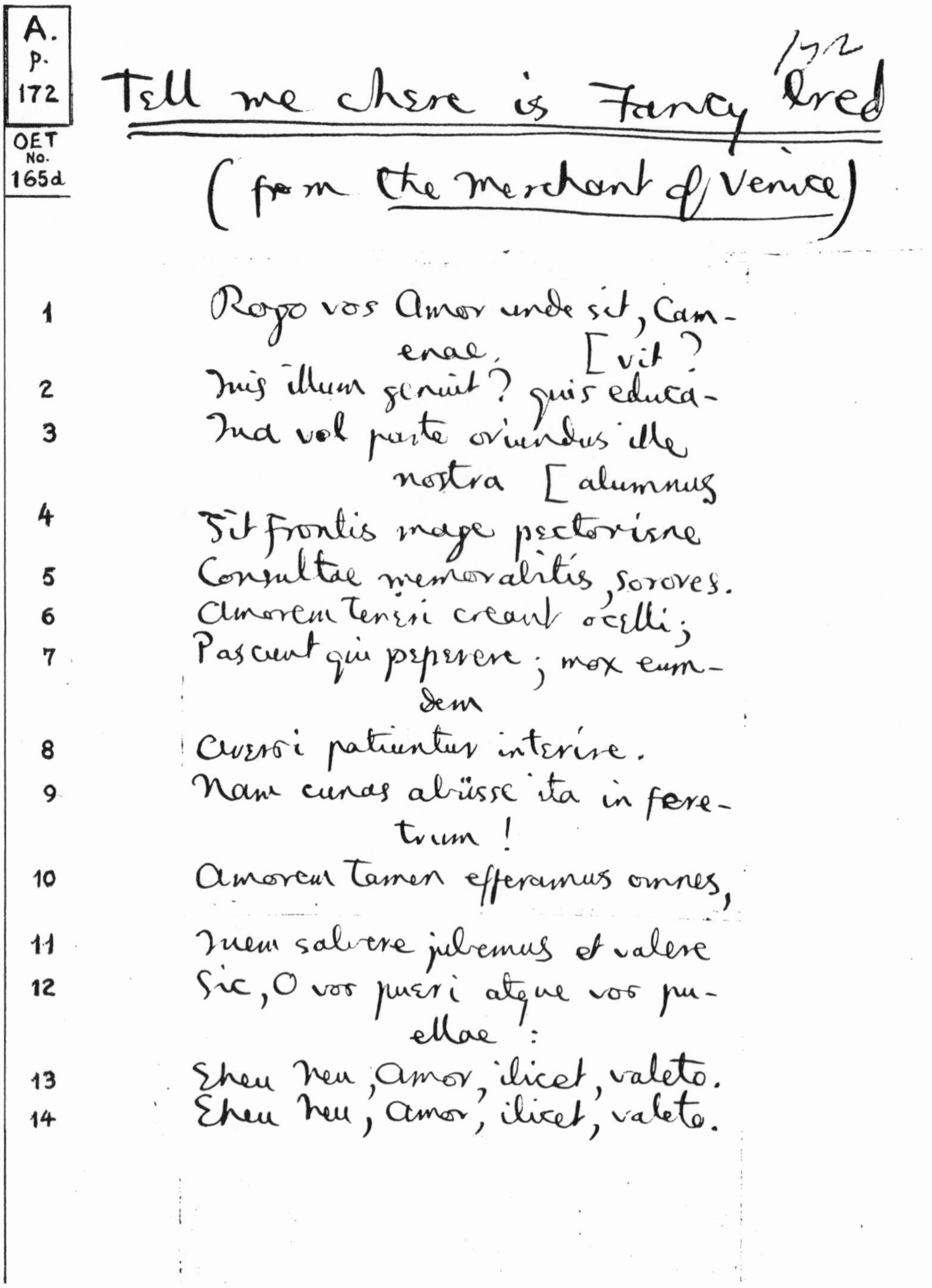

A. **p.** **172** **OET** **No.** **165d**	*Tell me where is Fancy bred* /172 (*from the Merchant of Venice*)

1 Rogo vos Amor unde sit, Cam-
        enae,   [vit ?
2 Quis illum genuit? quis educa-
3 Qua vel parte oriundus ille
                nostra [alumnus
4 Sit frontis mage pectorisne
5 Consultae memoralitis, sorores.
6 Amorem teneri creant ocelli;
7 Pascunt qui peperere; mox eum-
                dem
8 Cueroi patiuntur interire.
9 Nam cunas abiisse ita in fere-
                trum !
10 Amorem tamen efferamus omnes,
11 Quem salvere jubemus et valere
12 Sic, O vos pueri atque vos pu-
                ellae :
13 Eheu heu, Amor, ilicet, valeto.
14 Eheu heu, Amor, ilicet, valeto.

Plate 468:   OET No. 165(d) "Tell me where is Fancy bred" -- Latin

A.p.172--autograph faircopy. RB cut the MS. after 10, probably to omit two deleted lines: GMH seems to have repeated his slip in No. 165(c), as the remnants of the omitted line(s) visible below the end of 10 match the tops and commas of ", ilicet, valeto." (13 and 14).

[opposite]   Plate 469:   (i) OET No. 165(f): 'Orpheus with his lute made trees' -- Latin version

A.p.175--autograph faircopy.

(ii) OET No. 165(h): 'When icicles hang by the wall' -- Latin version

A.pp.177-8--autograph faircopy, with two changes (7 "gelido"   8b "sic"). The last line was deleted and rewritten because the end of 7 was too crowded.

Orpheus with his lute made trees

(from Henry VIII)

	A. p.175
	OET No. 165 f

Orpheus with his lute made trees	Orpheus fertur et arbores canendo	1
And the mountain tops that freeze	Et pigros nive concitasse montes.	2
Bow themselves when he did sing:	Si quid lusserat ille, vitis uvas	3
To his music plants and flowers	Extemplo referebat, herba flores.	4
Ever spring, as sun and showers	Diceres Zephyros eosque Phoebum	5
There had made a lasting spring.	Conspirasse diem in sereniorem	6
	Et ver continuare sempiternum.	7
	tum venti posuere, tum resedit	8
Everything that heard him play,	Omnis fluctus ab obsequente pon-	
Even the billows of the sea,	to. [Sal :	9
Hung their heads and then lay by:	Est hoc imperium artis atque mu-	10
In sweet music is such art	importunior aegriorque nuper	11
Killing care and grief of heart	Cura quae fuerat, loquente plectro	12
Fall asleep or hearing die.	Conticescere vel mori necesse est.	13

When icicles hang by the wall

(from Love's Labour's Lost)

	A. P. 177
	OET No. 165 h
	P. 178

Institit acris hiemps : glacies simul imbrices ad	1
imas	
Promissa passim ut horret haec ! Camillus	2
Pastor, primores quotiens miser afflat ore in ungues,	3
Ut ore, rore, vix fovet rigentes ! [do	4
Grandia ligna foco fert Marcipor uvidis struen-	5
Vestigiis in atrium secutus [mulctris	6
Aut stupet, e ~~gelido~~ tepido quod presserat ~~ipse,~~ ubere	7
~~Haesisse tam liquore posse nulla.~~	8a
ubere ipse, mulctris	7 cont.
Haesisse ~~sic~~ tam liquore posse nulla.	8b

Tell me where is Fancy bred

(Greek: Dorian rhythm, freely syncopated, as in drama)

		A. p. 169 OET No 165 e

στροφή· χο] Τίς Ἔρωτος, τίς ποτ' ἄρ' ἁ πατρὶς ἦν; — 1

ῥυτής α'] Τίς δέ νιν τίκτει, τίς ἔθρεψεν, ἀνδρῶν ἢ θεῶν; — 2

πότερ' αὐτῷ καρδίαν ἢ κεφαλᾶς τί που φίλα εἴπω — 3

μέρος; οὐ γὰρ, οὐκ ἔχω τὰ τάδε ~~θεὶς δὴ τύχοιμ' ἄν~~ — }5
θεὶς δὴ τύχοιμ' ἄν.

ἀντιστροφή· χο] τὸν Ἔρωτ' ἆρ' οὐχ ἑλικοβλεφάροις — 6
ῥυτής β']

ὡς ἐν ὀφθαλμοῖσι τραφέντ' ἀκούεις πρῶτα μέν, — 7

συνέφαβον δ' ἱμέρου καὶ χάριτος τέως νεοθαλοῦς — 8

τέλος ἐκπεσόντα φροῦδον θανάτῳ, φροῦδον ἔρρειν; — 10

ἐπῳδός· κορυφαῖος] φροῦδος Ἔρως, φροῦδος ἡμῖν. — 11

ἡμιχόριον α'] ἀλλ' αἴλινον αἴλινον εἴπωμεν, ἄνδρες· — Ap.170 / 12

ἡμιχόριον β'] αἴλινον γὰρ αἴλινον εἴπωμεν. —

χορός] ἡμῖν — 13

ἆρα φροῦδος, φροῦδος ἆρ' ἡμῖν Ἔρως. — 14

σχῆμα τοῦ εἴδους· στροφὴ καὶ ἀντι-στροφή]

ἐπῳδός]

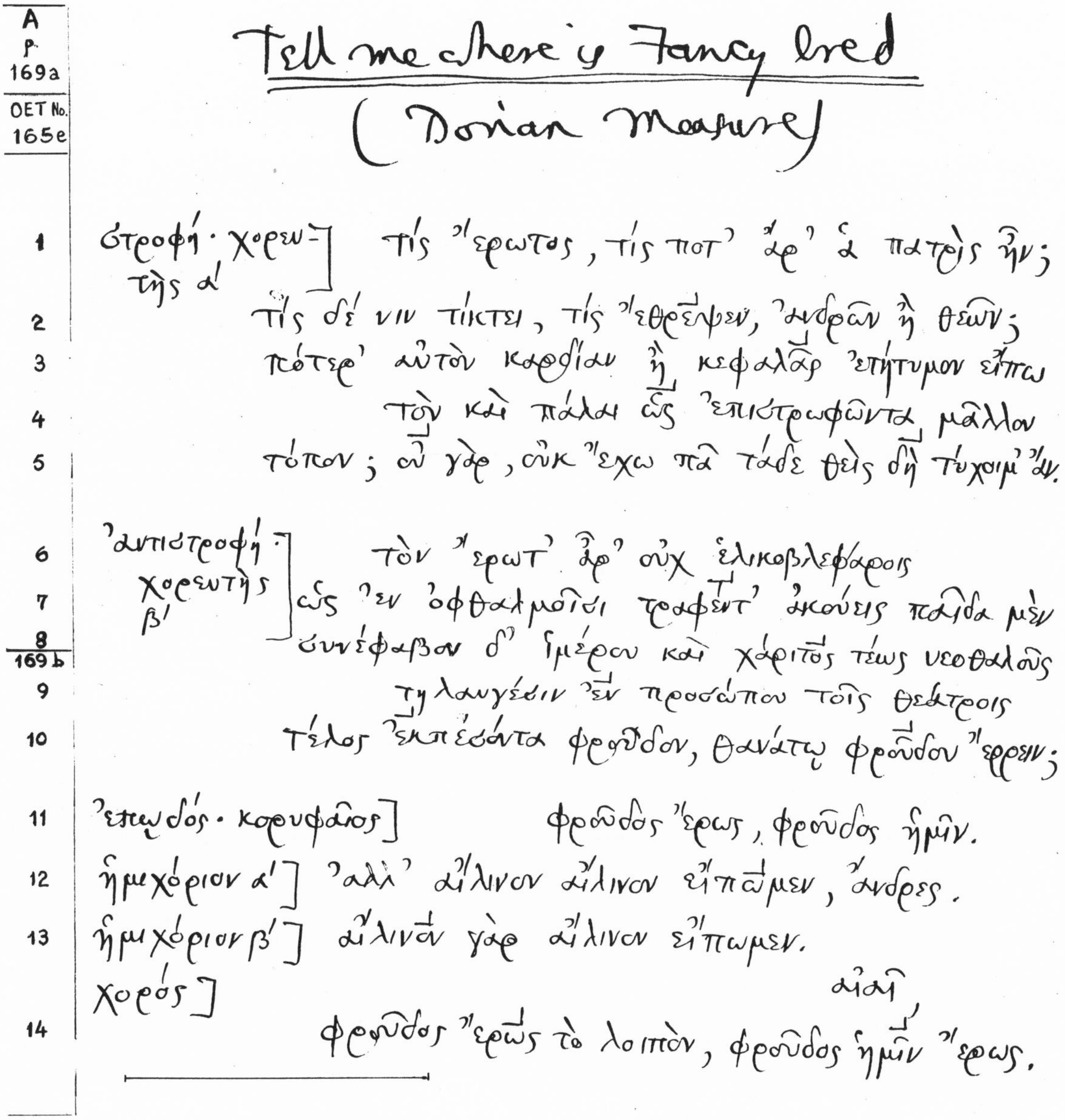

A P. 169a	
OET No. 165e	

Tell me where is Fancy bred

(Dorian Measure)

1 στροφή· χορεῡ-]   τίς ᾽έρωτος, τίς ποτ᾽ ἆρ᾽ ὁ πατρὸς ἦν;
τῆς α'

2   τίς δέ νιν τίκτει, τίς ᾽εθρεψεν, ᾽ανδρῶν ἢ θεῶν;

3   πότερ᾽ αὐτὸν καρδίαν ἢ κεφαλᾶς ᾽ετήτυμον εἴπω

4   τὸν καὶ πάλαι ὡς ᾽επιστρωφῶντα μᾶλλον

5   τόπον; οὐ γάρ, οὐκ ᾽έχω πᾶ τάδε θεὶς δὴ τύχοιμ᾽ ᾽ώ.

6 ᾽αντιστροφή·]   τὸν ᾽έρωτ᾽ ἆρ᾽ οὐχ ἑλικοβλεφάροις
χορευτῆς

7 β'   ὡς ᾽εν ᾽οφθαλμοῖσι τραφέντ᾽ ᾽ακούεις παῖδα μὲν

8 169b   συνέφαβον δ᾽ ἱμέρου καὶ χάριτος τέως νεοθαλοῦς

9   τῃ λαυγέδιν ᾽εν προσώπων τοῖς θεάτροις

10   τέλος ᾽εκπεσόντα φροῦδον, θανάτῳ φροῦδον ᾽έρριν;

11 ᾽επῳδός· κορυφαῖος]   φροῦδος ᾽έρως, φροῦδος ἡμῖν.

12 ἡμιχόριον α']   ᾽αλλ᾽ αἴλινον αἴλινον εἴπωμεν, ᾽ανδρες.

13 ἡμιχόριον β']   αἴλινον γὰρ αἴλινον εἴπωμεν.

14 χορός]   φροῦδος ᾽έρως τὸ λοιπὸν, φροῦδος ἡμῖν ᾽έρως.

Plate 470   OET No. 165(e): 'Tell me where is Fancy bred" -- First Greek Version

A.pp.169,170--autograph faircopy of a shorter version. During pasting up the section carrying 3 to 11 was cut from the rest, and when the revised version of the poem was guarded in between pp.169 and 170 the word for 'semichorus' at the hinge was covered over [here sketched in]. Lines 4 and 9 of the longer version are missing. The metrical scheme suits only this shorter line strophe.

Plate 471   OET No. 165(e): "Tell me where is Fancy bred" -- Second Greek Version

A.pp.169a,169b--autograph faircopy of revised and longer Greek version (on unnumbered pages, guarded in on top of the earlier short Greek version). In 3, καρδίαν was copied from the first translation without the change of case required by the revised syntax, to καρδίας.

A
P.
173

OET
No.
165g

_____

Orpheus with his lute made trees

(Dorian rhythm, syncopated, and with
triplets in resolution)

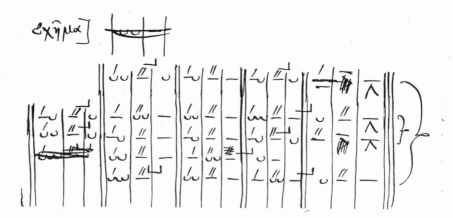

p.174

1 στροφή]   λόγος Ὀρφέως λύραν καὶ δενδρεῖν χορηγεῖν

2 καὶ νιφοκτύπων ὀρέων κορυφαῖσιν θαμά, δαμείσαις πόθῳ,

3 κελαδοῦντι δ' εὐθὺς λυθῆσαι ῥόδοισίν θ' ἄλλοῦ τε

γᾶν καὶ

4 ψακάδος οὐρανίου βλαστήμασι καλλικάρποις

5 ἀντιστροφή] χιόνος κρύος μεσούσας. πόντιον δὲ κῦμα

6 τῶν τ' ἐριβρόμων ἀΐοντ' ἀνέμων πνεύματα γαλάνᾳ

πέσεν.   [παυσίλυπον

7 κιθάρᾳ δὲ ταῖς τε Μούσαις ὡς ἐνεστ' εἰπεῖν τὸ

8 ἀδύνατον· κατεκοίμασ' αὐτίκα πάντα λάθα.

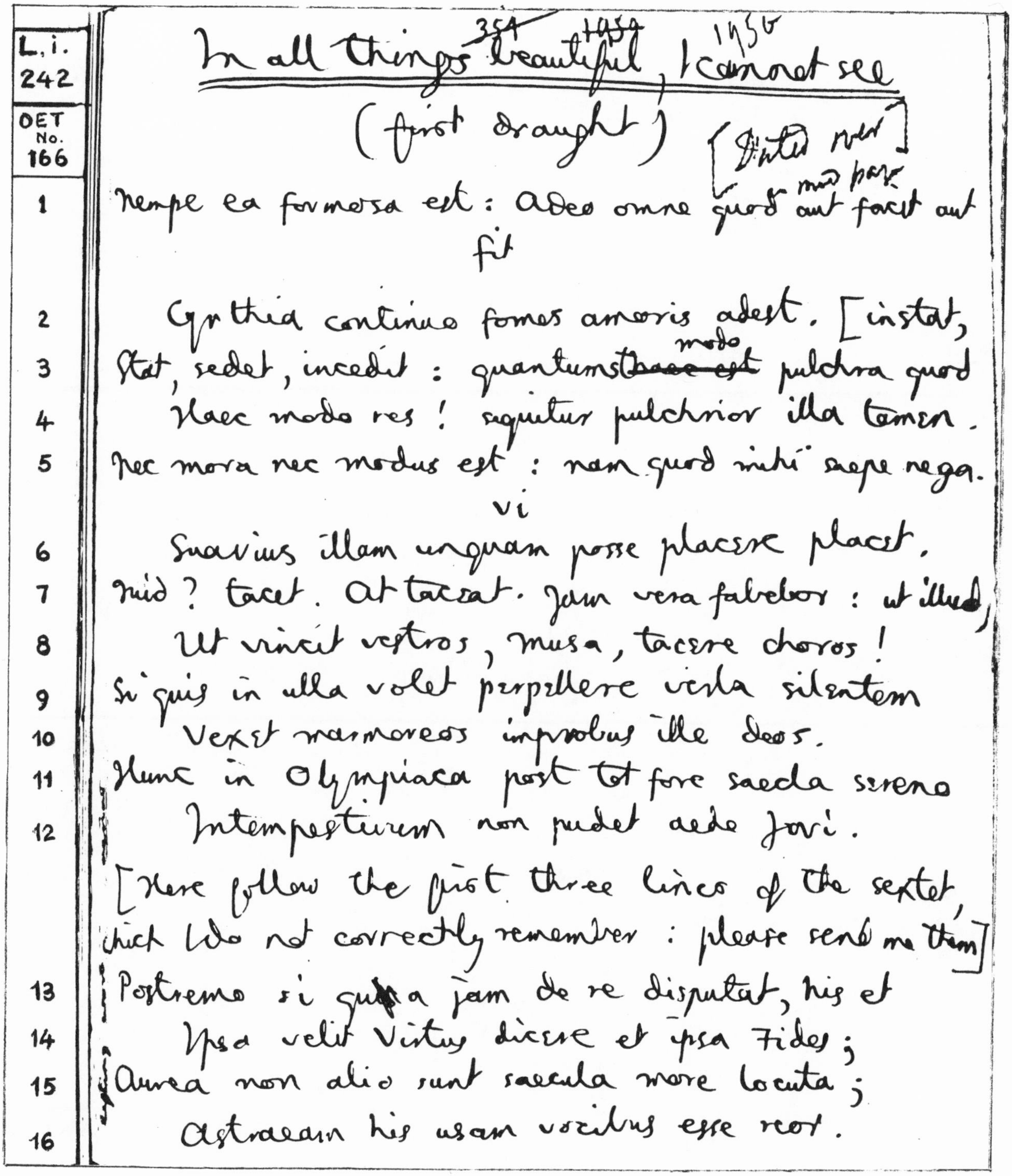

PLATE 473. OET 166. "In all things beautiful" • 297

L, i. **242** **OET** **No.** **166**	**In all things** ~~beautiful~~ **, I cannot see** (first draught) [Dated over] 1 Nempe ea formosa est : Adeo omne quod aut facit aut fit 2 Cynthia continuo fomes amoris adest. [instat, 3 Stat, sedet, incedit : quantumst~~haec est~~ pulchra quod 4 Haec modo res ! sequitur pulchrior illa tamen. 5 Nec mora nec modus est : nam quod mihi saepe negat. vi 6 Suavius illam unquam posse placere placet. 7 quid ? tacet. At taceat. Jam vera fatebor : ut illud, 8 Ut vincit vestros, musa, tacere choros ! 9 Si quis in ulla volet perpellere verba silentem 10 Vexet marmoreos improbus ille deos. 11 Hunc in Olympiaca post tot fore saecla sereno 12 Intempestivum non pudet aede Jovi. [Here follow the first three lines of the sextet, which I do not correctly remember : please send me them] 13 Postremo si qua jam de re disputat, his et 14 Ipsa velit Virtus dicere et ipsa Fides ; 15 Aurea non alio sunt saecula more locuta ; 16 Astraeam his usam vocibus esse reor.

Plate 473   OET No. 166: Robert Bridges: "In all things beautiful, I cannot see" -- Incomplete Latin Version L.i.242 (MS Letters to Bridges, ii.195b). Autograph, sole surviving MS., of all the lines GMH could remember, part of a letter to RB 31 Oct. 1886. RB notes below the title that it is "[Dated over in mid page]": there are three successive paginations at the top. In 1 the capital letter in "Adeo" indicates that the colon before it was originally a period. In 3 "st" was squeezed onto "quantum" when "haec est" was crossed out. In 7 "fabebor" is a slip for "fatebor"; the comma after "illud" was formerly obscured by a scrap of paper adhering to the surface. In 13 "qua" was originally "quis".

H.i.51r — 51

1 Earnest, earthless, equal, attuneable, vaulty, voluminous, . . . stupendous

2a Evening, dealing the dark down, time's o drone, sullen hulk-of-all, hoarse-of-all night,

2b Evening, dealing the drone-dark down, hollow hulk-of-all, home-of-all, hoarse-of-all night,

OET No. 167

Dub.15r — 15

1a Earnest, earthless, equal, attuneable, vaulty, voluminous, .. stupendous

2a b Evening, strained into dark to be, drone-dark tomb-of-all, home-of- all, hoarse-of-all night;

3a Her fond yellow horn light low with the west and the wild hollow hoarlight following the height [us,

4a Waste, and the earliest stars, earlstars, principal lights, overbend

5a Fire-featuring heaven

3b Her fond yellow horn light wound with the west, her wild hollow hoarlight hung to the height [bend us,

4b Waste and her earliest stars, earlstars, stars principal, over-

5b c Fire-featuring heaven. For earth her being now untwinds; has unbound; the dapple is at an end, a-

6a b Stray, aswarm, throughther, in throngs; the o self is on Stray and aswarm self steepèd in self, quite or in her, quite

7a Dismembering, disremembering all.

6c Swarm, swarms, throughther, in throng; now self she has in self steeped in her, quite (or right)

6d

7b Dismembering, disremembering all.

6e Swarm, swarms, all throughther, in throng; self in self steep'd and flush; quite right

7c Dismembering, disremembering all.

2c Evening strains to be time's-well, world's-pit, womb-of-all, home-of-all, hoarse-of-all night

OET No. 167

Plate 474   OET No. 167: Spelt from Sibyl's Leaves -- MS.1: H

[top] H.i.51r--earliest autograph draft, lines 1 and 2 only.

[lower] MS. 2 - Dub.[1] Dublin Note-book, f.15r--autograph draft of 1-7. Deletions include: 2a "into"   3a "horn light" (words then joined--with the imperfect junctures of the link cf. No. 164, ℓ.3)   3b "with/to"   5b "ha[s]" (begun above "unbinds")

PLATE 475. OET 167. *Spelt from Sibyl's Leaves* • 299

DUB
20v

1 Earnest, earthless, equal, attuneable, vaulty, voluminous,... stupendous

2a Evening strains to be time's den, world's delf, womb-of-all, home-of-
-all, hearse-of-all night.

3 Her fond yellowy hornlight wound to the crest, and her wild hollowy
hoarlight hung to the height

4 Waste; her earliest stars, earlstars, stars principal, overbend us,

5a Firefeaturing heaven. And earth her being unbinds; her dapple
is at an end — a-

6a Stray, aswarm, all throughther, in throngs; self in self steepèd
and stillèd; plush; quite

7a Disremembering, dismembering all

6b and plush — fast; quite

5c Firefeaturing heaven. For earth (her being has unpenned;
(unpenned her being; her
dapple is at an end— a-

6c Stray or aswarm, all throughther, in throng; self in self
steepèd and pashèd — flush; quite

7b Disremembering, dismembering all. My heart rounds me right

8a then: Evening is here over us, over us; our night whelms,
whelms: when will it end us?

8b that our evening is over us, our night whelms, whelms: when
will it end us?

9a only the crisp boughs beakèd and dragonish, damask the toolsmooth
b beaked boughs, crispèd and dragonish,

9a bleak light; black,
10 Ever so black on it. O this is our tale too!

c
2b Evening strains to be time's (harbour
a (hush, world's haven
e dock, world's den

2b doom-of-all, womb-of-all, hearse-of-all

OET
No.
167

Plate 475   OET No. 167: Spelt from Sibyl's Leaves -- MS. 3 - Dub.[2]

Dublin Note-book, 20v--autograph draft of 1-10. Deletions include: 2a "womb-of ʄ-all"   After 6b GMH began to draw a brace (cf. one linking 8a, 8b), then struck through 5a to 6b in ink and redrafted them.   6c "self/in"   8a "here ov[er?]"mended to "on"   9a "and/or dragonish,...light,-"   9b "crispèd"

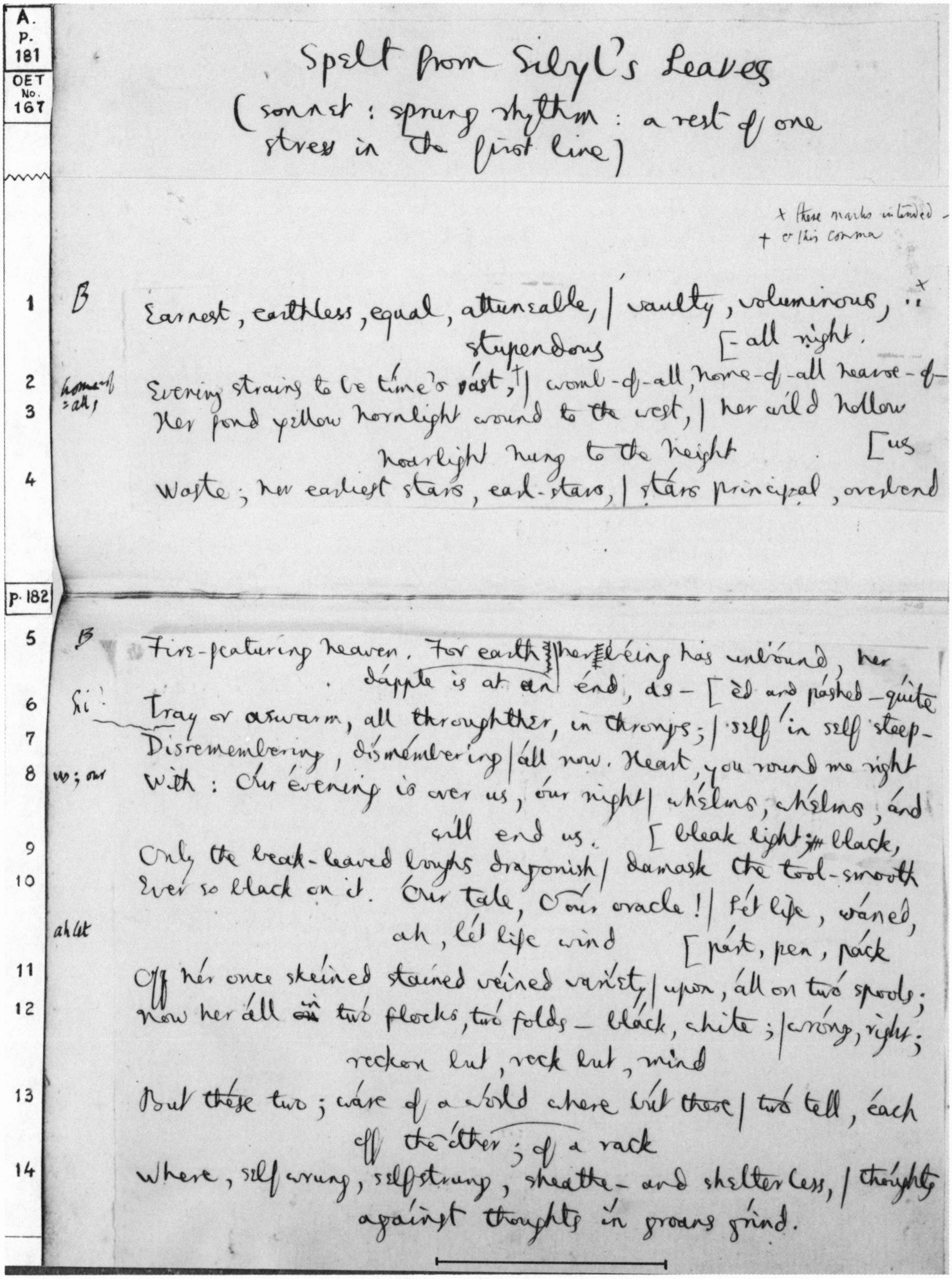

Spelt from Sibyl's Leaves
(sonnet: sprung rhythm: a rest of one
stress in the first line)

x these marks intended —
+ & this comma

1 Earnest, earthless, equal, attuneable, | vaulty, voluminous, ...
   stupendous   [-all night.

2 Evening strains to be time's vást, + | womb-of-all, home-of-all hearse-of-

3 Her fond yellow hornlight wound to the west, | her wild hollow
   hoarlight hung to the height   [us

4 Waste; her earliest stars, earl-stars, | stars principal, overbend

P. 182

5 Fire-featuring heaven. For earth | her being has unbound, her
   dapple is at an end, as — [ed and pashed — quite

6 Sic! Tráy or aswarm, all throughther, in throngs; | self 'in self steep-

7 Disremembering, dísmémbering | áll now. Heart, you round me right

8 With: Our evening is over us, our night | whelms, whelms, and
   will end us.   [bleak light-# black,

9 Only the beak-leaved boughs dragonish | damask the tool-smooth

10 Ever so black on it. Our tale, our oracle! | Lét life, wáned,
   ah, lét life wind   [part, pen, páck

11 Off hér once skéined stained véined variety | upon, áll on twó spools;

12 now her áll in twó flocks, twó folds — black, white; | ríght, ríght;
   reckon but, reck but, mind

13 But these two; ware of a world where but these | two tell, éach
   off thé óther; of a rack

14 Where, self wrung, selfstrung, sheathe- and shelterless, | thoughts
   against thoughts in groans grind.

Plate 476   OET No. 167: Spelt from Sibyl's Leaves -- MS. 4: A

A.pp.181-2--autograph faircopy, separated into three pieces by RB for mounting in album A: in the autograph 1 to 4 had no spaces before and after them. Changes include: 5 caesural divisions del. twice   "at e[nd?"--cf. MS. B] mended to "an end"   9 "light-#;"   12 "on/in"   All stresses are in the same ink as the text. The "dots" over "will" (8) and "mind" (12) could be mistaken for stresses (cf. "quite" in the turnover of line 6).

Above 1 RB has written [1889] "x these marks intended" (i.e. the two dots in 1 indicating the rest referred to in the metrical description) "+ and this comma" (i.e., after "vast" in 2). In the left margin RB has entered variants from B, with a "Sic!" beside "as-/Tray" (5, 6), exclaiming at the capital letter.

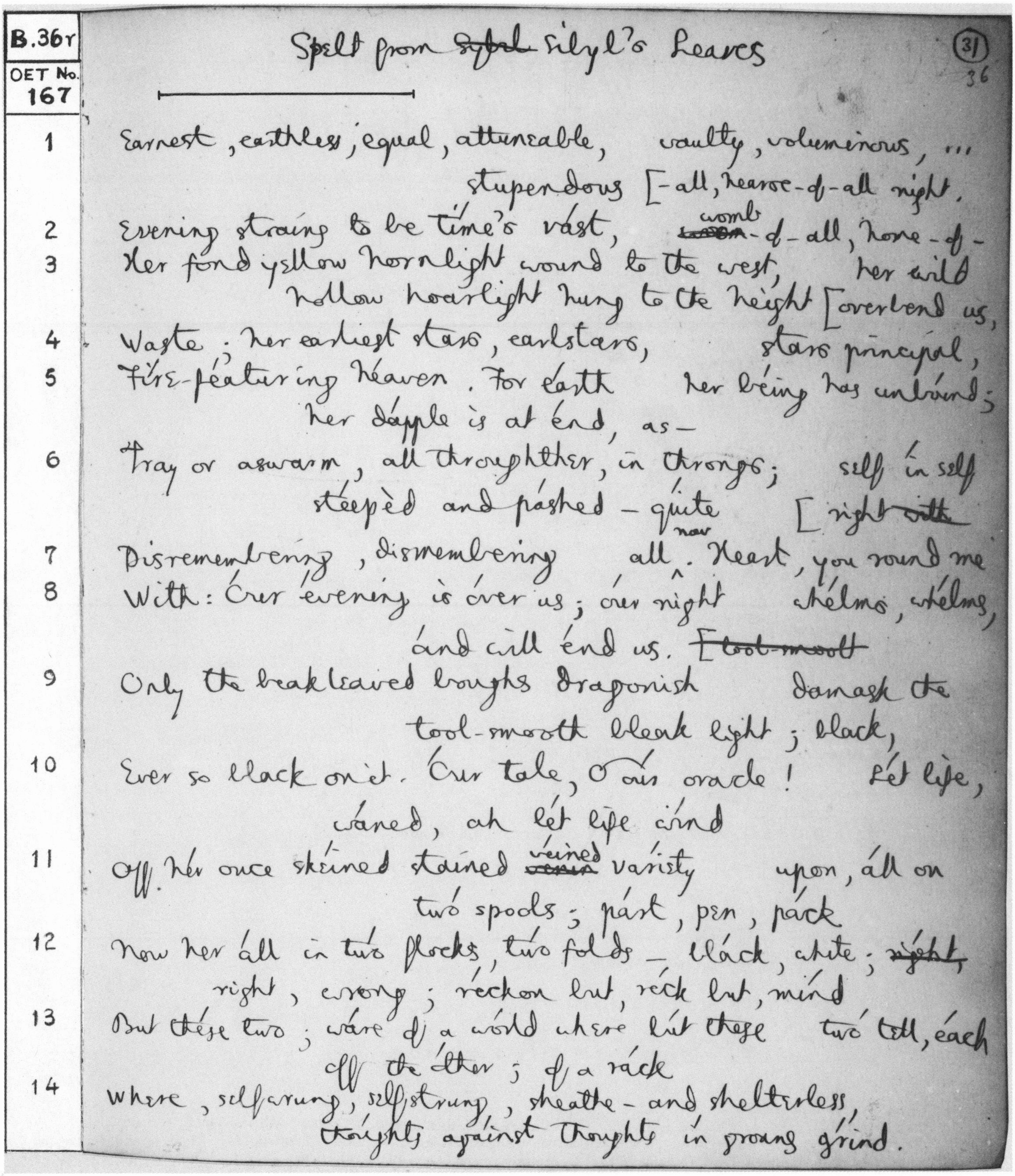

PLATE 477. OET 167. *Spelt from Sibyl's Leaves* • 301

B.36r

OET No. 167

Spelt from ~~Sybyl~~ Sibyl's Leaves

1. Earnest, earthless, equal, attuneable, vaulty, voluminous, ...
           stupendous [-all, hearse-of-all night.
2. Evening strains to be time's vást, ~~womb~~ womb-of-all, home-of-
3. Her fond yellow hornlight wound to the west, her wild
       hollow hoarlight hung to the height [overbend us,
4. Waste; her earliest stars, earlstars, stars principal,
5. Fíre-féaturing héaven. For éarth her béing has unbóund;
       her dápple is at énd, as —
6. Tray or aswarm, all throughther, in throngs; self ín self
       steepèd and páshed — quíte [right~~out~~
7. Dísremembering, dísmembering all. Heart, you round me
8. With: Óur évening is óver us; óur níght ^ whélms, whélms,
       ánd will énd us. ~~tool-smooth~~
9. Only the beakleaved boughs dragonish damask the
       tool-smooth bleak light; black,
10. Ever so black on it. Óur tale, Ó óur oracle! Lét lífe,
        wáned, ah lét lífe wínd
11. Off. Her once skéined stained ~~venin~~ varíety upon, áll on
        twó spools; párt, pen, páck
12. Now her áll in twó flocks, twó folds — black, white; ~~right~~
        right, wrong; réckon but, réck but, mínd
13. But thése two; wáre of a wórld where bút these twó tell, éach
        off the óther; of a rack
14. Where, selfwrung, selfstrung, sheathe- and shelterless,
        thóughts agàinst thoughts in groans grínd.

Plate 477   OET No. 167: Spelt from Sibyl's Leaves -- MS. 5: B

    B.36r--autograph faircopy inscribed in album B. Caesuras are indicated by spaces: in 12 "right" was del. and rewritten (but without its stress), because he had left no space. Other deletions were due to slips: 2 "worm" mended to "woom/womb"   7 "with" (wrong line)   9 "tool-smooth" (no room for the rest of the line)   11 "venin/veined"

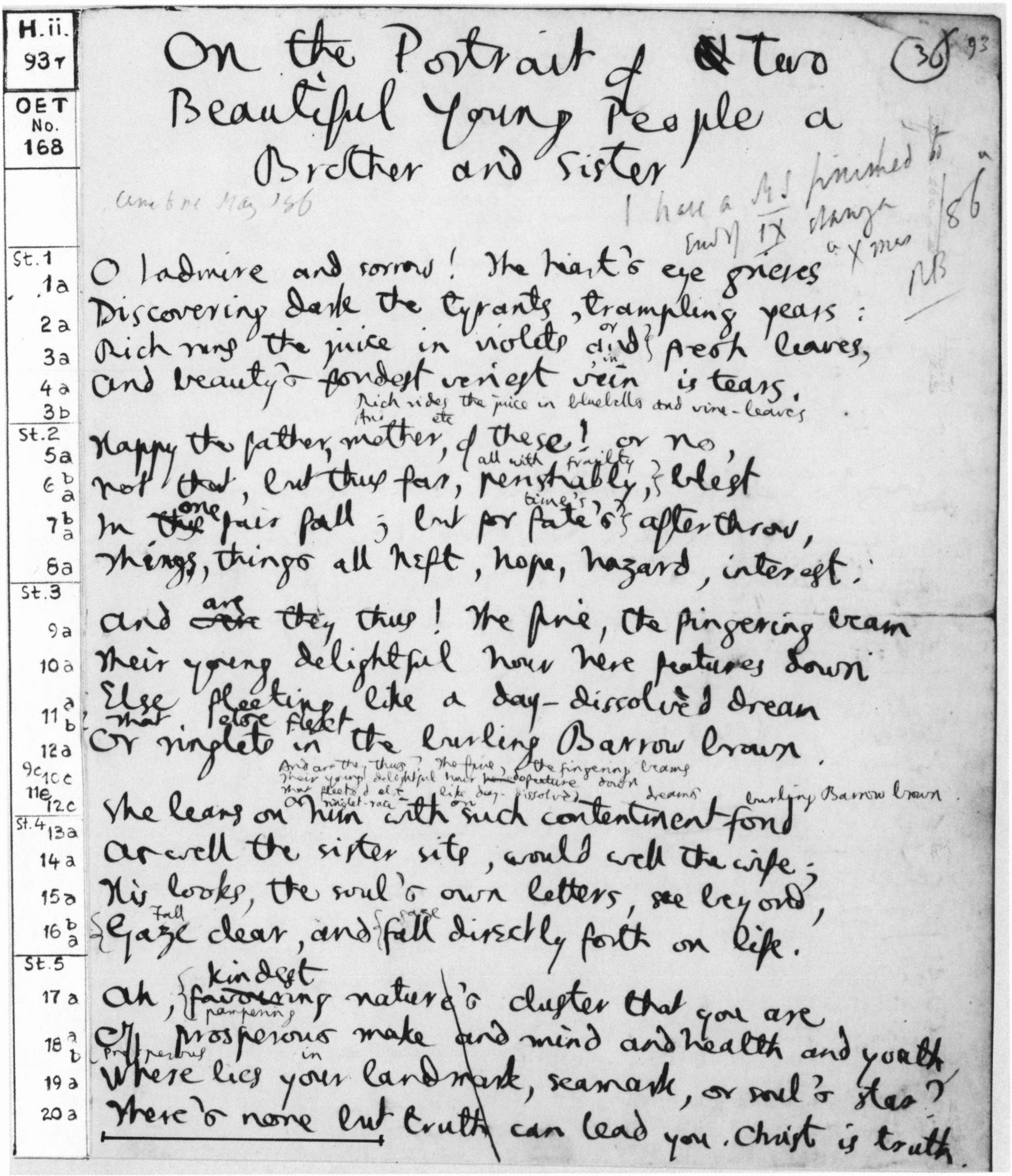

H.ii.
93r

OET
No.
168

St.1
1a
2a
3a
4a
3b
St.2
5a
6 b/a
7 b/a
6a
St.3
9a
10a
11 a/b
12a
9c 10c
11e 12c
St.4 13a
14a
15a
16 b/a
St.5
17a
18 a/b
19a
20a

On the Portrait of Two
Beautiful Young People a
Brother and Sister

Came to me May '86

*I have a MS finished to
end of IX stanza
at Xmas   /86
RB*

O I admire and sorrow! The heart's eye grieves
Discovering dark the tyrants, trampling years:
Rich rung the juice in violets and fresh leaves,
And beauty's fondest veriest vein is tears.
    Rich rides the juice in bluebells and vine-leaves .

Happy the father, mother, of these! or no,
Not that, but thus far, penetrably, blest
In the pair fall; but for fate's after throw,
Things, things all kept, hope, hazard, interest:

And are they thus! the fine, the fingering beam
Their young delightful hour were features down
Else fleeting like a day-dissolved dream
Or ringlets in the curling Barrow brown.
    And are they thus? the fine, the fingering beam
    Their young delightful hour's feature down
    that fleeted else like day-dissolved dreams curling Barrow brown.
    ringlet-race

She leans on him with such contentment fond
As well the sister sits, would well the wife;
His looks, the soul's own letters, see beyond,
Gaze clear, and fall directly forth on life.

Ah, kindest nature's cluster that you are
In prosperous make and mind and health and youth,
Where lies your landmark, seamark, or soul's star?
There's none but truth can lead you. Christ is truth.

Plate 478   OET No. 168: On the Portrait of Two Beautiful Young People -- MS. 1: H^1(1)

   H.ii.93r--autograph, the beginning of the earliest surviving draft (cont. 94r, then 93v, then 94v). Many later revisions were made with a fine steel pen. Because GMH frequently reverted to old readings, the sequence of the drafts may be in doubt. St. 5 was del. (rev. on 94r). Revisions include: 3a "and/or/, in" all bracketed   3b/4 "Rich rides the juice in bluebells and vine-leaves/And etc." 5a exclamation prob. mended, not del.   6b "all with frailty"   7b "this/one" 8a "There," mended to "Things"   9c to 12c: the minute revision of st. 3, later than the version at the top of 94v, is the same as the final text (A--see Plate 485, right); 10c "hour here/do feature"; 12c "Or"--The r is lost in the large h of "him" below it.   16b "Fall clear and gaze"   17a "pampering"   18b "Prosperous in make".

   RB's pencilled note on the left below the title appears on the surface to have no relevance to this poem: "Came to me May '86": GMH did not see the portrait until Dec. 1886, and the MS. A version (sent to RB Jan. 2 1887) and "finished to the end of IX stanza" is, as RB records in the right margin, dated "Xmas/86". May '86 was, however, the date on which GMH visited RB at Yattendon, to meet for the first time his wife Monica whom he had married 8 months earlier. The note would make sense if they discussed heredity. The Bridges' first child was not born till Dec. 1887, just after GMH's second visit, Aug. 1887: see L.i.224-5, 258.

PLATE 479. OET 168. *On the Portrait of Two Beautiful Young People* • 303

H.ii.94r	
St.5/17b	
18 d c	
19 c b	
20 b	
St.6	
21 a	
22 a	
22 b c	
23 a	
23 b	
24 a	
St.8	
29 a	
30 a	
31 a	
31 b	
32 a	
32 b	
29 b	
29 c	
30 b	
30 c	
29 d	
30 d	
31 c	
31 d	
32 c	
OET No. 168	

bright
But ah, ~~your~~ forelock, cluster that you are [youth,
Of favoured in
where ~~prosperous~~ make and mind and health and
that your
where ~~lies~~ ~~this~~ lies ~~you~~ landmark, seamark, or soul's star?
There's none but truth can stead you. Xt is truth.

There's now but good is any good, for you
⎧ Or what should ~~sway~~ with you sway, as this sweet maid.
⎨ Or what swayed ~~by~~ you, as now does this sweet maid.
none as may this sweet maid.
~~And but God good~~
none ^good but God. But that was spoken to
the youth who was found wanting when Christ weighed.

feast of
Your ~~lovely~~ youth and that most earnest air,
call
They do but ~~bid~~ your bones to more carouse;
the
Worst ~~will~~, batten on best: ~~a~~ worms, we ~~say~~, were
there
what cry
Worst will the best: ~~See~~ worms, we ~~say~~, were there
⎧ to pork with havoc so th skyey boughs!
⎨ to have porked with havoc ~~so th~~ you skyey boughs!

eye, ⎫
Youth's festival in you, that most earnest air, ⎬
Your
~~Youth's~~ festival, that in you earnest ~~x~~ ete,
This does but ~~bid~~ on your bones on to carouse.
They does but bid your bones to more carouse.

air; ⎫
The feast of you, that in you earnest eye; ⎬
They may but call your bones to more carouse.
Worst will the best. What worms were here, we cry, ⎫
What worms, we cry, were there ⎬
our
to have havoc-porked so the ~~this~~ thung-heavenward
boughs! there

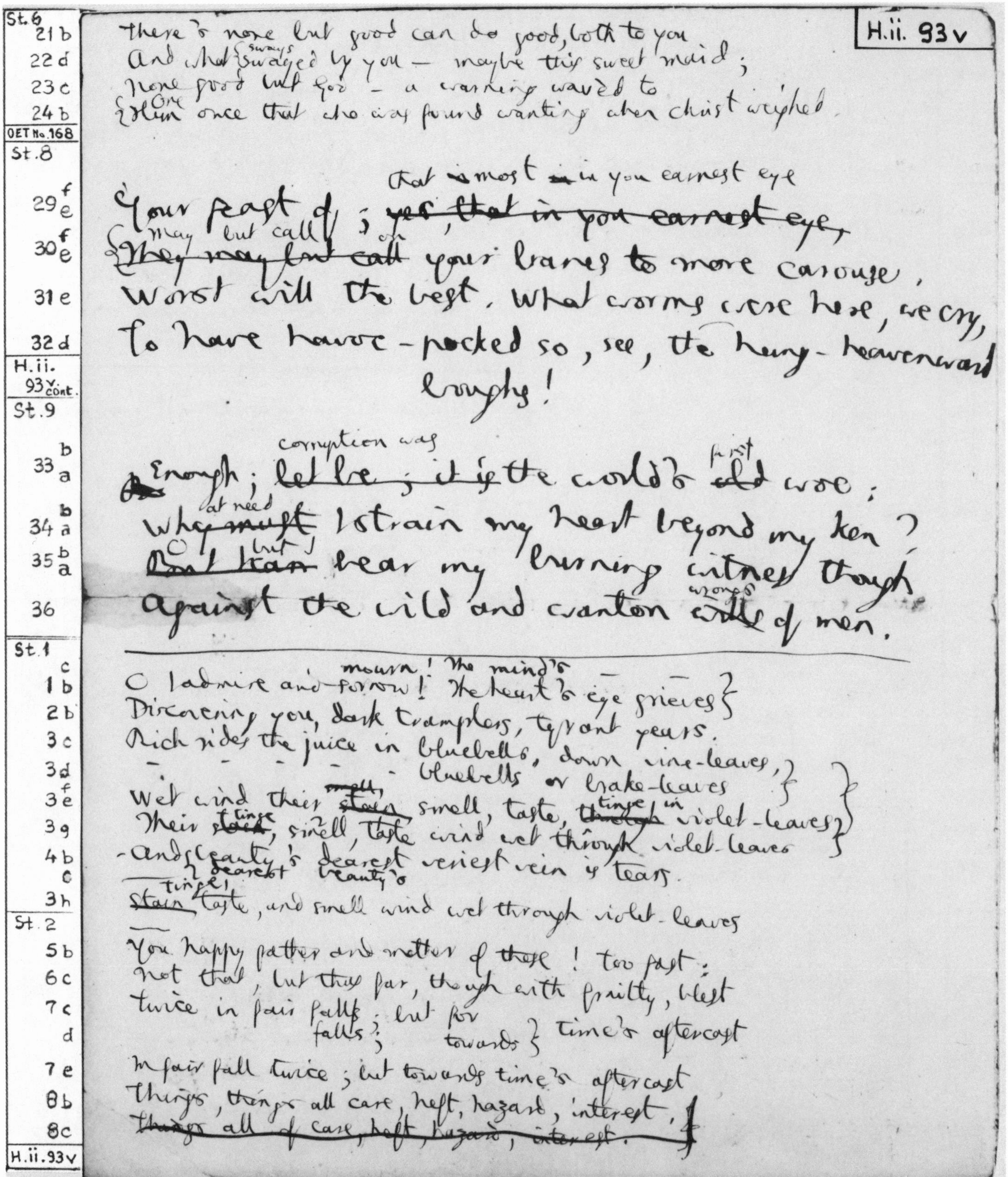

H.ii. 93v

St.6
21 b There's none but good can do good, both to you
22 d And what (sways) swayed by you — maybe this sweet maid;
23 c none good but God — a warning waved to
24 b Him once that she was found wanting when Christ weighed.

OET No.168
St.8
                              that is most in in you earnest eye
29 f Your feast of ; yes, that in you earnest eye,
      May but call ; on
30 f They may but call your braves to more carouse,
31 e Worst will the best, what worms were here, we cry,
32 d To have havoc-pocked so, see, the hung-heavenward
                              boughs!

H.ii. 93v cont.
St.9
                 corruption was
33 b Enough; let be; it is the world's old woe;   first
33 a
      at need
34 b Why must I strain my heart beyond my ken?
34 a
35 b But I bear my burning witness though
35 a
                                        wrongs
36 Against the wild and wanton work of men.

St.1
   c O I admire and mourn! the mind's
1 b O I admire and sorrow! the heart's eye grieves}
2 b Discovering you, dark tramplers, tyrant years.
3 c Rich rides the juice in bluebells, down vine-leaves,}
3 d   bluebells or brake-leaves }}
3 e Wet wind their smell, smell, taste, tinge in violet-leaves}
3 g Their stain, tinge, smell, taste wind wet through violet-leaves}
4 b And beauty's dearest veriest vein is tears.
   c   2 dearest   beauty's
3 h Stain, tinge taste, and smell wind wet through violet-leaves

St.2
5 b You happy father and mother of these! too fast:
6 c not that, but thus far, though with frailty, blest
7 c twice in fair falls; but for
   d   falls;   towards } time's aftercast
7 e In fair fall twice; but towards time's aftercast
8 b things, things all care, heft, hazard, 'interest,}
8 c things all of care, heft hazard, interest.}

H.ii.93v

Plate 480   OET No. 168: On the Portrait of Two Beautiful Young People — MS. 3: H¹ (3)

H.ii.93v--earliest autograph draft, cont. from 94r, then cont. on 94v. The top stanza and bottom half page belong with the revisions made with a fine pen on 93r. Changes include: 29f "in most in in" 33a "B[ut?]" 34a,b "Why must" changed to "What need" 36 "wills/wrongs" 3e "stain,...through" 3f "smell." 3g "stain/tinge, smell, taste" (i.e. Read "taste, smell") 3h "Stain,/Tinge," (u.c. "T") 7c "Falls" 8b,c final brace del. after he had decided against the lower version.

PLATE 481. OET 168. *On the Portrait of Two Beautiful Young People* • 305

St 3	
9 b	
10 b	
11 c	
11 d	
12 b	
st. 4	
13 b	
H.ii.94 v	
OET No. 168	
16 c	
d	
St. 5	
17 c	
18 e	
19 e	
20 c	
St 6	
21 c	
22 e f	
23 d	
24 c	
St.c	
24/1a	
24/2a	
24/3a	
24/3b	
24/4a	
St 7	
25 a b	
26 a	
27 a	
28 a	
26 b c	
OET No. 168	

H.ii.94v

Yea, are they this ? ! Then fine, then fingering beams
Their young delightful hour do feature down
That fleeted else ? like day-dissolved dreams
Fleeting fast else ?
Or ringlet-race on curling Barrow brown.

She leans

And gaze, and ? and fall directly forth on life.
Gaze on, and ?

But ah, bright forelock,
Of favour — make
where lies your landmark, seamark, and hope's star?
there's none

There's none but good can be good, both for you
None good   by you, as may this sweet maid
One once   who hit this sweet maid?

Though he was mild and-lovely ; he very well
to the hand chose lightning-rive striving nor stealth
wrest wrong the least ; ? yet rise he could not ; fell
The least wrest wrong ; ?
Rather; he core that millstone you wear, wealth.

Man lives that list and ? leaning of bare will
list, that ?
Forecasting wisdom dare nor guage nor guess,
His selfless self of self, most strange, most still,
Furled home and fast foredrawn to No and yes.
Wisdom's best forecast ? dare nor guage nor guess
That wisest forecast ?

Plate 481   OET No. 168: On the Portrait of Two Beautiful Young People -- MS. 4: H[1] (4)

H.ii.94v--earliest autograph draft, concl. from 93v. After the revised st. 6 comes a new st. (No. 168c), later omitted from the faircopy in A, but obviously intended to follow ℓ.24 (with a comma after "weighed"). Then at last we meet the first draft of st. 7. Changes include: 9b "this?!" 10b "their ℓ[? mended to]young" 22e (Writing damaged by the crease) "And what swayed with by you, as may this sweet maid;" 24/1 "he yo[?wa]rung"

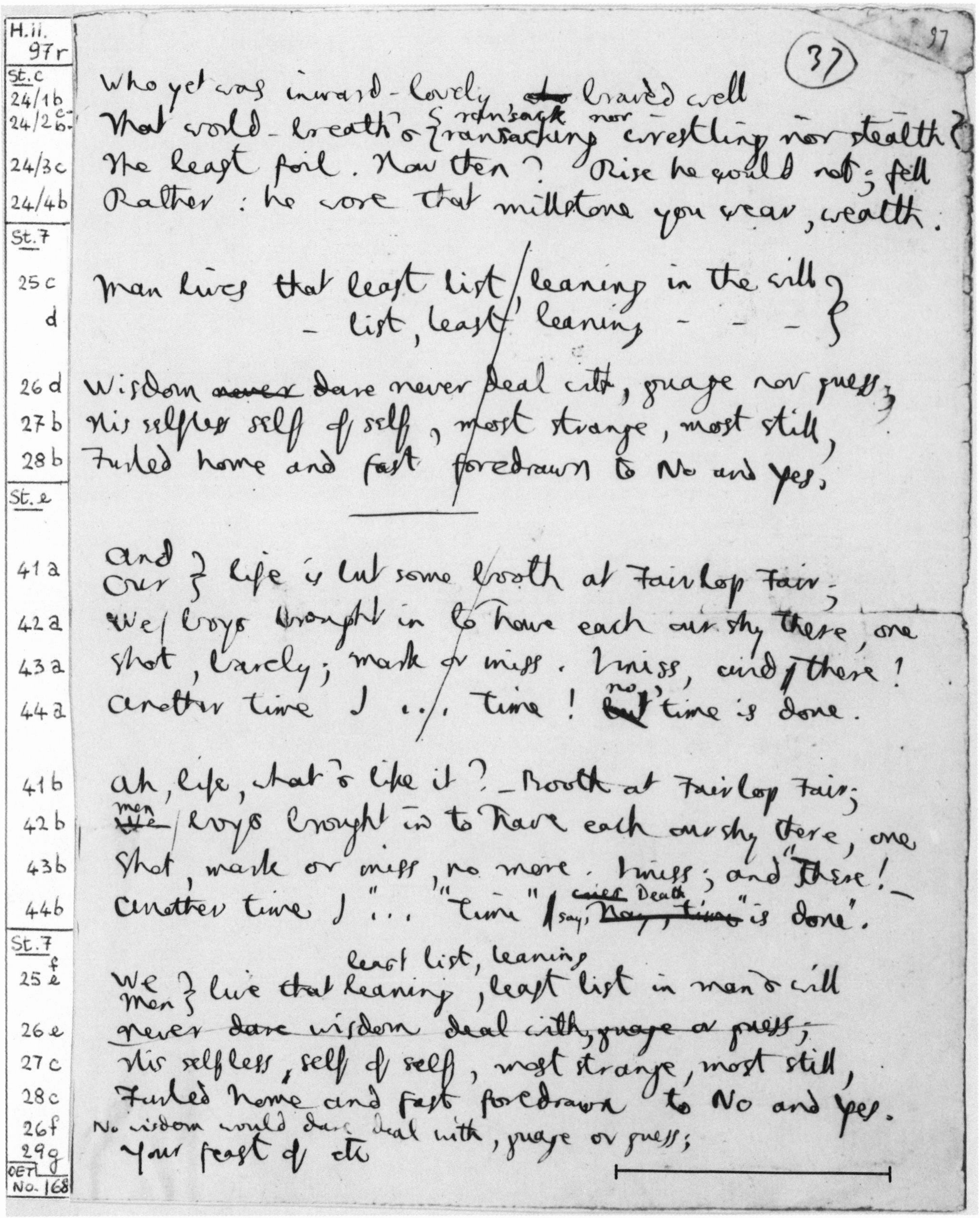

H.ii. 97r   ㊲   97

St.c 24/1b	Who yet was inward-lovely ~~too~~ bravèd well
24/2 e b	That would-breath'd ~~ransack~~ nor ~~ransacking~~ wrestling nor stealth
24/3c	The least foil. Now then? Rise he would not; fell
24/4b	Rather: he wore that millstone you wear, wealth.
St.7	
25 c	Man lives that least list / leaning in the will
d	– list, least leaning – – –
26 d	Wisdom ~~never~~ dare never deal with, guage nor guess;
27 b	His ~~selfless~~ self of self, most strange, most still,
28 b	Furled home and fast foredrawn to No and yes,
St.e	
41 a	And
	Our } life is but some booth at Fairlop ~~Fair~~;
42 a	We/ boys brought in to have each our shy there, one
43 a	Shot, barely; mark or miss. I miss, and there!
44 a	Another time I . . / . time! ~~but~~ no time is done.
41 b	Ah, life, what's like it? – Booth at Fairlop Fair;
42 b	~~Men He~~/ boys brought in to have each our shy there, one
43b	Shot, mark or miss, no more. I miss; and "There!" –
44b	Another time I "... "Time" / says; cries Death, "is done".
St.7	least list, leaning
25 e f	We } live that leaning, least list in man's will
	Men } never dare wisdom deal with, guage or guess;
26 e	His selfless, self of self, most strange, most still,
27 c	Furled home and fast foredrawn to No and yes.
28 c	No wisdom would dare deal with, guage or guess;
26 f	
29 g	Your feast of etc

OET No. 168

Plate 482   OET No. 168: On the Portrait of Two Beautiful Young People -- MS. 5: H[2]

[H[2]] H.ii.97r--autograph draft, on a sheet of cream laid notepaper, opened wide: the verso is blank. The draft probably follows on from H[1], and line numbers are therefore made continuous, though in places the sequence may be in doubt. Deletions, Changes, etc. include: 24/1b "who braved" changed to "bravèd"   26d "never"...final semicolon smudged   42a and b "We/" (virgule)   43a "and, there!"   44a "but/no [first comma on top of t]."   42b "to have" (slur) 43b "t" mended to u.c. "There!" (quotes added later)   44b orig.: [no quotes] Time! Nay, time is done. (rev. to): '"Time" cries/says Death "is done".'   26e del. in same faded brown ink used for 26f and in 43b and 44b for quotes and changes.   27c "selfless,"

PLATE 483. OET 168. *On the Portrait of Two Beautiful Young People* • 307

H.ii. 96r	
OET No. 168	
St. 1	

UNIVERSITY COLLEGE,

Sᵀ STEPHEN'S GREEN,

DUBLIN.

(38) 96

1d O I admire and sorrow! the heart's eye grieves

2c Discovering you, dark tramplers, tyrant years.

3i Rich moisture runs in violets ~~and vein~~ or vine -leaves

4d And beauty's dearest veriest vein is tears.

3j (In bluebells rich juice rides and dawn vine-leaves
     (and etc

St. 2

5c You happy father, mother of these! — too fast:

6d Not ~~that~~, but thus far, though with frailty, blest

7f In two fair pulls; but towards time's aftercast

8d things all care, all heft, hazard, interest.

St. 3

x   X   x   X   x   X

12 d (or ringletrace on Barrow keeling brown)

x : x   x   x   x x

25 g Man lives the list and leaning of a will

26 g/h Wisdom may not ~
        No wisdom may's forecast nor guaye nor guess,

27 d His ~~selfs~~ selfless self of self, most strange, most
                                    still,

28 d all pulled and fast foredrawn to No or Yes.

Plate 483   OET No. 168: On the Portrait of Two Beautiful Young People -- MS. 6: H³ (1)

H.ii.96r--further autograph drafts, on U.C.D. folded notepaper (cont. on the opened inside pages, see Plate 484).

Line numbering follows on from H². 3i "~~and vein~~" (slip from 4)   27d "selfs" mended to "selfless"

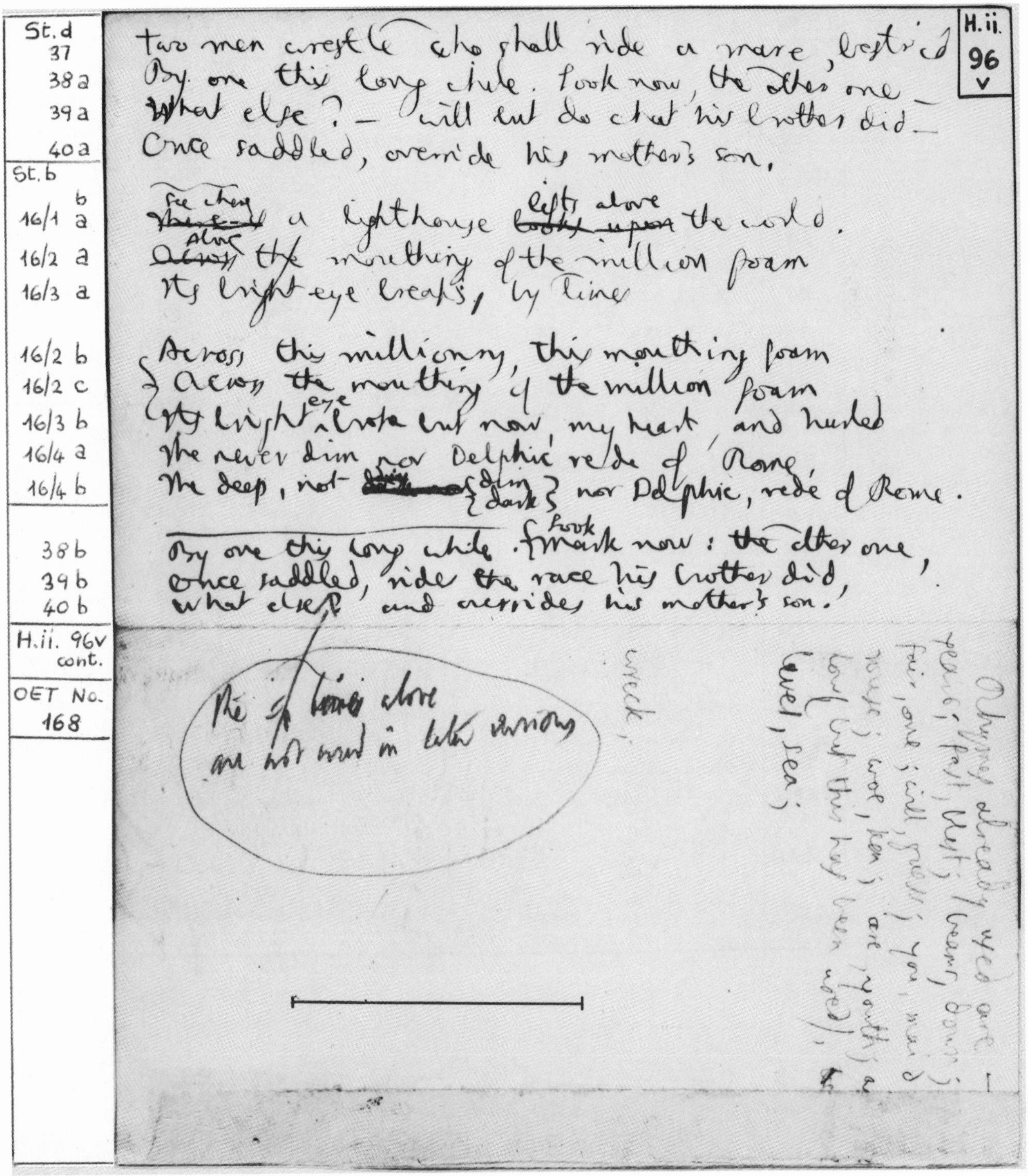

St. d	**H. ii.**
37	**96**
38 a	**v**
39 a	
40 a	
St. b	
16/1 ᵇ/a	
16/2 a	
16/3 a	
16/2 b	
16/2 c	
16/3 b	
16/4 a	
16/4 b	
38 b	
39 b	
40 b	
H. ii. 96v cont.	
OET No. 168	

[facsimile of GMH autograph manuscript draft, with pencil notes at right angles along the margin and an oval-enclosed note reading "The [ ] lines above / are not used in later versions"; marginal words "wreck;"]

Plate 484　　OET No. 168: On the Portrait of Two Beautiful Young People -- MS. 7: H³ (2)

H.ii.96v--begins and ends with sole autograph draft of st. d, not in the faircopy in A: it has been numbered as if meant to follow 36, the last line of No. 168(a), but a bridge would be needed.

Stanza b should really follow st. 5, but ℓℓ.20 and 21-24 must not be separated from each other, so it is here numbered to follow ℓ.16. Obscurities, etc.: 39a "W" in "What" reshaped.　　16/1a "There is/See where"..."looks upon/lifts above"

16/2a "Across/Above"　　16/3a "breaks," (2a and 3a are then deleted)　　16/2b Note coinage "millionry"　　16/4b orig. "not dark nor dim"; rev. to "not dim/dark"　　39b "rides" (s almost a straight line)　　40b "What else? [obscured by head of RB's arrow] and overrides" [RB's note below 40b reads "the lines above are not used in later versions"].

At right angles, GMH's pencil note (partly lost under the hinge and the unfortunate trimming of the sheet) records: "Rhymes already used are--[grieves,] years; fast, blest; beams, down; [fond,? wife;] fair, one; will, guess; you, maid [; eye, ca]rouse; woe, ken; are, youth; w[ell,? stealth;] low, (but this has been used) [where?] be, [more]; lives, sea; [...] wreck, [....]"

PLATE 485. OET 168. *On the Portrait of Two Beautiful Young People* • 309

On the Portrait of
Two Beautiful Young
People

People

a Brother and Sister

St. 1
1 O I admire and sorrow! The heart's eye
2 Discovering you, dark tramplers, tyrant years.
3 A juice rides rich through bluebells,
4 And beauty's dearest veriest vein is tears.

St. 2
5 Happy the father, mother of these! Too
6 fast: I frailty, blest
7 Not that, but thus far, all with
8 In one fair fall; but, for time's after-cast,
   Creatures all heft, hope, hazard, in-

St. 3
9 And are they thus? The fine, the fingering beams
10 Their young delightful hour do feature down
11 That fleeted close like day-dissolvèd dreams
12 Or ringlet-race on swirling Barrow brown.

St. 4
13 She leans on him with such contentment fond
14 As well the sister sits, would well the wife;
15 His looks, the soul's own letters, see beyond,
16 Gaze on, and fall directly forth on life.

St. 5
17 But ah, bright forelock, cluster that you are
18 Of favoured make and mind and health and youth,
19 Where lies your landmark, seamark, or soul's star?
20 There's none but truth can stead you. Christ is truth.

St. 6
21 There's none but good can bé good, both for you
22 And what sways with you, maybe this sweet maid;
23 None good but God — a warning wavèd to
24 One once that was found wanting when God weighed.

St. 7
25 Man lives that list, that leaning in the will
26 No wisdom can forecast by gauge or guess,
27 The selfless self of self, most strange, most still,
28 Fast furled and all foredrawn to No or Yes.

St. 8
29 Your feast of; that most in you earnest eye
30 May but call on your bones to more carouse.
31 Worst will the best. What worm was here, we cry,
32 To have havoc-pocked so, see, the hung-heavenward
   boughs?

St. 9
33 Enough: corruption was the world's first woe.
34 What need I strain my heart beyond my ken?
35 O but I bear my burning witness though
36 Against the wild and wanton work of men.

×   ×   ×   ×

Monasterevan, Co. Kildare. Christmas 1886

Plate 485   OET No. 168: On the Portrait of Two Beautiful Young People -- MS. 8: A (1-4)

A.pp.180a, b, c and d--autograph faircopy of the unfinished poem (nine stanzas), on a four-page sheaf of University College notepaper (here called pp. a to d). Deletions due to slips in transcription: **6** "thus" for "all" (dittography, not a variant); 24 "God" for "Good" (mended from "g"); date "Chist" for "Christmas". Vertical smears affect the end of 18.

Several letters have been touched up, e.g., "A" in "As" (14), "a" in "cast" (7), "hazard" (8), and "f" in "fall" (7): that this is not "Fall" may be confirmed by contrasting the typical capital "F" in "Fast" (28)--after 1875 the cross-bars of his "F" ran off to the left, and the vertical always stopped about the level of the line.

RB's pencil (1918) in 26 indicates that "guage" (a 19th C spelling, described in OED as a "mere blunder") should be transposed as "gauge".

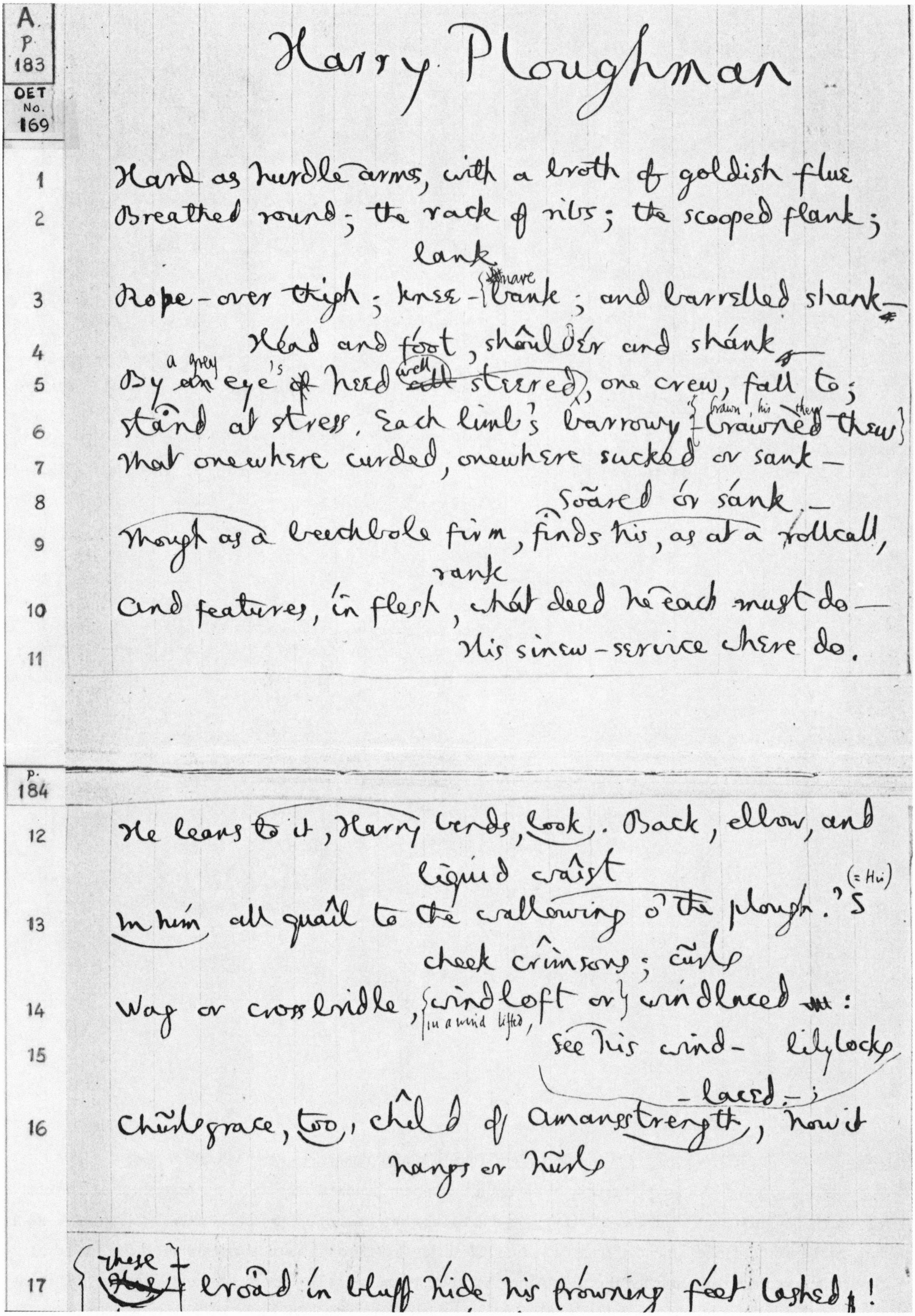

Harry Ploughman

1 Hard as hurdle arms, with a broth of goldish flue
2 Breathed round; the rack of ribs; the scooped flank;
       lank
3 Rope-over thigh; knee-bank; and barrelled shank—
       Head and foot, shoulder and shank
4 By a grey eye's of heed well steered, one crew, fall to;
5 stand at stress. Each limb's barrowy brawn, his thew
6 that onewhere curded, onewhere sucked or sank—
       soared or sank.—
7 Though as a beechbole firm, finds his, as at a rollcall,
8   rank
9 And features, in flesh, what deed he each must do—
10   His sinew-service there do.
11

12 He leans to it, Harry bends, look. Back, elbow, and
       liquid waist
13 In him, all quail to the wallowing o' the plough. 'S
       cheek crimsons; curls
14 Wag or crossbridle, in a wind lifted, windlaced—
15   See his wind- lilylocks
       -laced—;
16 Churlsgrace, too, child of Amansstrength, how it
       hangs or hurls

17 broad in bluff hide his frowning feet lashed!

<u>Plates 486 and 487</u>   OET No. 169: Harry Ploughman -- MS. 1: A

   <u>A.pp.183-84</u>--autograph faircopy, written on two sheets: 1-16 on the first (cut into two for pasting into album A), and 17-19 on the second (no line spaces intended), with "Marks used" (which folded up to fit inside album A).

PLATE 487. OET 169. *Harry Ploughman* • 311

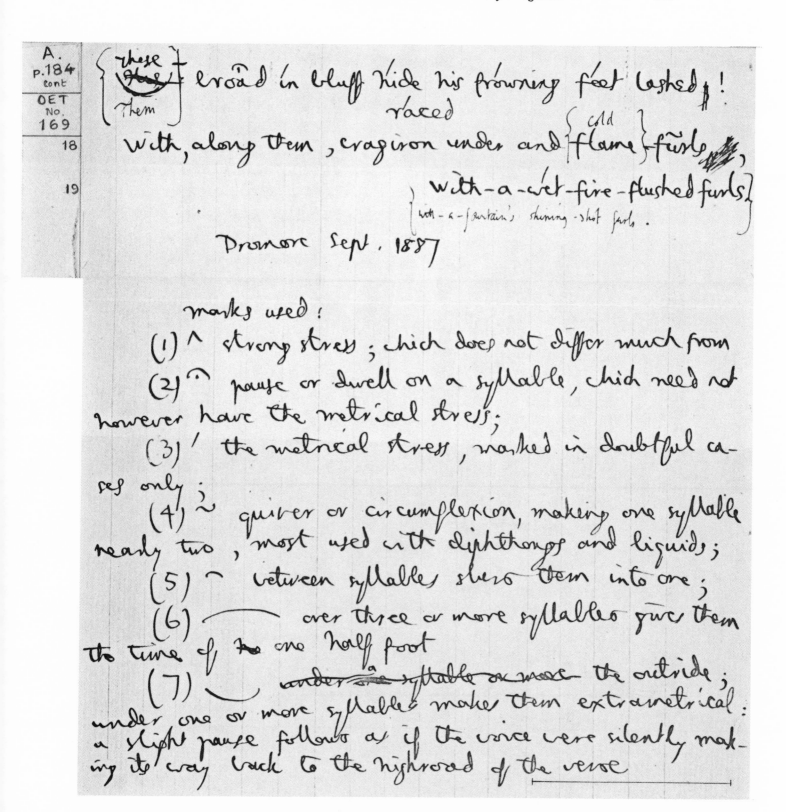

A.
p.184
cont

OET
No.
169

18

19

{ these ~~those~~ }
{ Them }
eroâd in bluff hide his frowning féet lashed ! !
raced
with, along them, cragiron under and { cold { flame } -furls }
} with -a -wet -fire -flushed furls }
{ with - a - fountain's shining -shot furls .

Promore Sept. 1887

marks used:

(1) ^ strong stress; which does not differ much from

(2) ⌢ pause or dwell on a syllable, which need not
however have the metrical stress;

(3) ′ the metrical stress, marked in doubtful cases only;

(4) ˜ quiver or circumflexion, making one syllable
nearly two, most used with diphthongs and liquids;

(5) ⌢ between syllables slurs them into one;

(6) ⌢ over three or more syllables give them
the time of ~~two~~ one half foot

(7) ⌣ ~~under a syllable or more~~ the outride;
under one or more syllables make them extrametrical:
a slight pause follows as if the voice were silently making its way back to the highroad of the verse

---

Changes by GMH: ends of 3 and 4, "⸴" 5 "all/well" 14 "windlaced⸝:" 17 "His⸚"/"These⸚" (short outride under "His" del., longer one drawn under "These") 18 "flame-furls⸝," In "Marks used" [No.] 6 "time of há[lf]" [No.] 7 "under oné/a syllable or more" Note: in ℓ.8 there is a smudge, not comma, between "sank" and the dash; and in 13 there is an elongated dot, not a stress, over "him"--"In him" is extrametrical, being an outride.

RB's fine black ink (1889, after he had seen MS. B) copied into A the revision GMH had made in 5, and the alternatives GMH had added to other lines, inserting brackets to show the start and end of the original alternatives 3 "knave" 5 "a grey [eye]'s"; RB del. "of" and transposed GMH's "well" to follow "steered" 6 "brawn, his thew" 14 "in a wind lifted," 15 after "laced." RB added "--;" but forgot to del. the period; he drew a wavy line to separate "laced" from "Amansstrength" RB also added: 17 "Them" but without the outride implied in B 18 "cold", hyphen left in by mistake 19 "With-a-fountain's shining-shot furls." In 13, after "'S" RB notes (=His)"

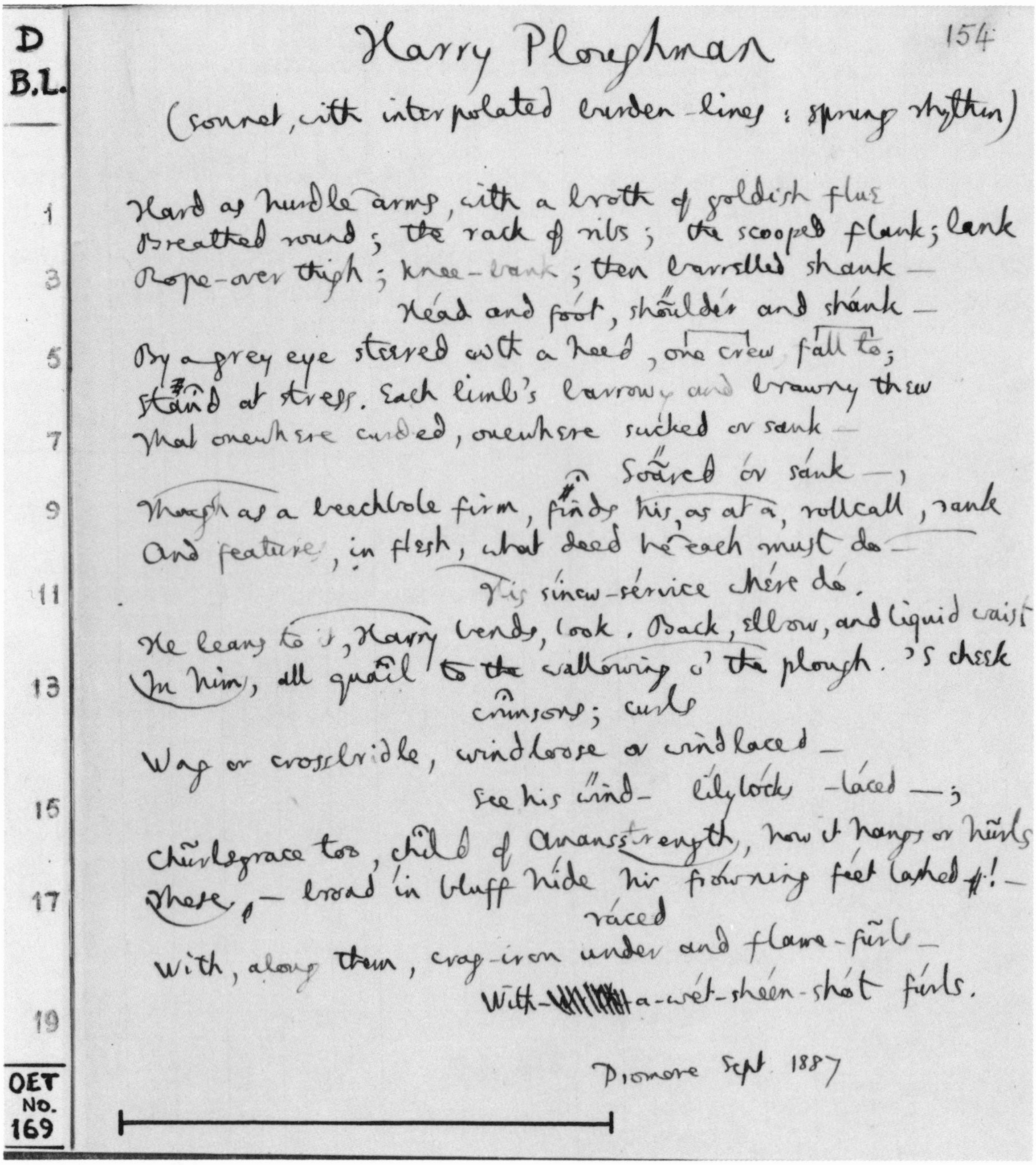

D
B.L.

154

Harry Ploughman

(sonnet, with interpolated burden-lines : sprung rhythm)

1 Hard as hurdle arms, with a broth of goldish flue
2 Breathed round; the rack of ribs; the scooped flank; lank
3 Rope-over thigh; knee-bank; then barrelled shank —
     Head and foot, shoulder and shank —
5 By a grey eye starred with a heed, one crew, fall to;
6 Stand at stress. Each limb's barrowy and brawny thew
7 That onewhere curded, onewhere sucked or sank —
       Soared or sank —,
9 Though as a beechbole firm, finds his, as at a, rollcall, rank
10 And features, in flesh, what deed he each must do —
      His sinew-service there do.

13 He leans to it, Harry bends, look. Back, elbow, and liquid waist
14 In him, all quail to the wallowing o' the plough. 's cheek
      crimsons; curls
15 Wag or crossbridle, windlaced or windlaced —
      See his wind- lilylocks -laced —;
17 Churlsgrace too, child of Amansstrength, how it hangs or hurls
18 There,—broad in bluff hide his frowning feet lashed-+!-—
      raced
19 With, along them, crag-iron under and cold-furl —
      With-~~~~~~ a-wet-sheen-shot furls.

       Dromore Sept. 1887

OET
NO.
169

Plate 488   OET No. 169: Harry Ploughman -- MS. 2: D

D (Brit. Lib. Add. MS. 42711, f.154)--autograph faircopy, sent to Dixon. Changes include: 5 "w" mended in "with" 6 stand (double stress changed to pause)   9 "finds" (same change)   13 the pause mark over "quail" conflicts with the horizontal dash serving as a dot over the "i"   17 "These,--"..."lashed+!--"   19 "With--" was del. and the beginning of the line was moved left by rewriting it. In 10 over "he" the apparent stress is probably only part of the slur; at the end of 10 and start of 11 note the half-slurs which link 'do' and 'His' (as in B).

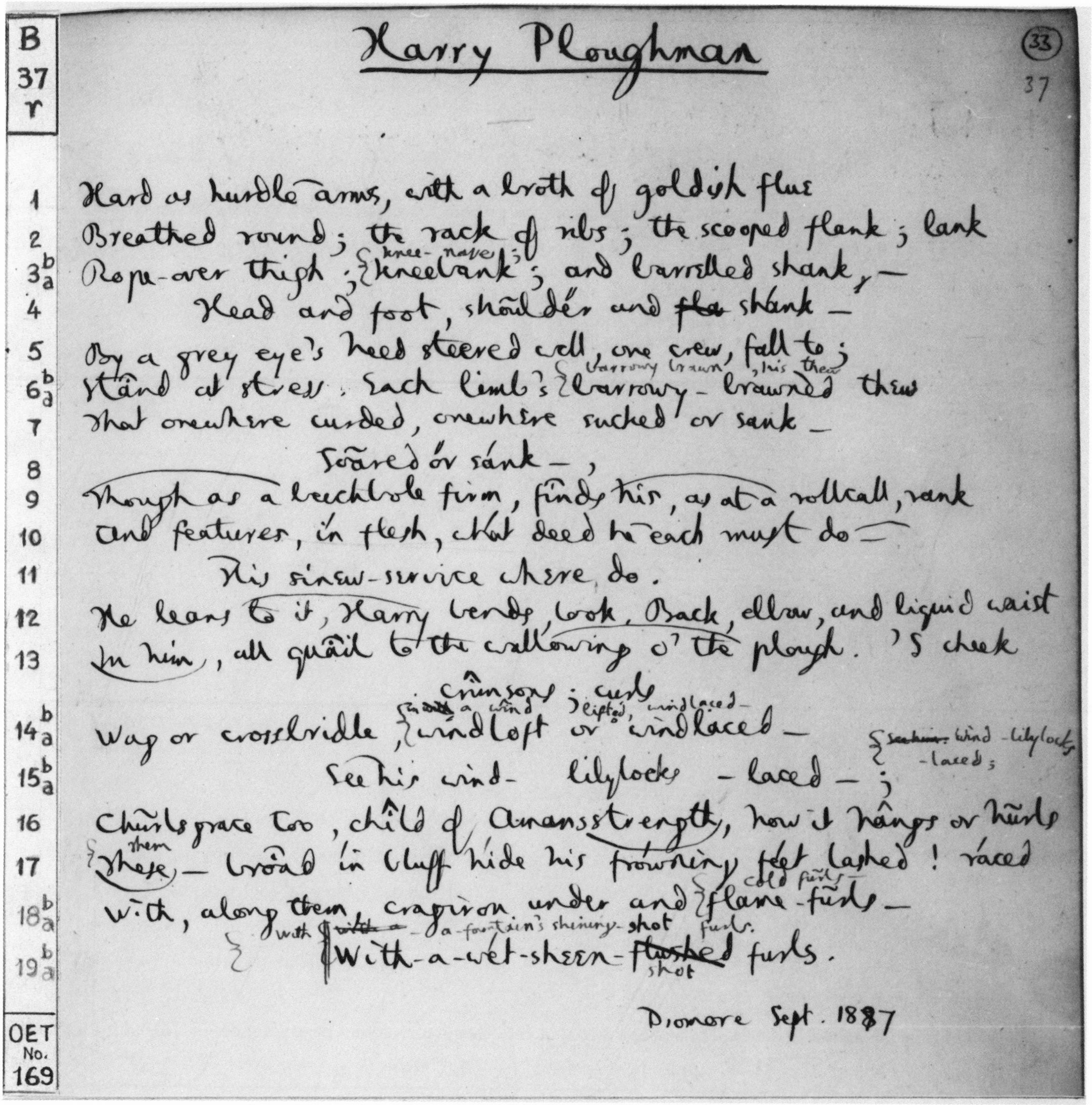

PLATE 489. OET 169. *Harry Ploughman* • 313

Plate 489   OET No. 169: Harry Ploughman -- MS. 3: B

B.37r--autograph faircopy, inscribed in album B, with early changes: 3 "shank,"   4 "fla[nk]"   19 "Flushed/shot" [added above]   Date "187" mended to "1887".

Later alternatives and brackets are in faded brown ink: 3 "knee-nave;"   6 "barrowy brawn, his thew"   14 "in [squeezed in before] with a wind lifted, windlaced--" [the black ball below a vowel marks the heard stress, a white ball the dumb or metrical stress--see L.i.109: 'lifted' seems also to have a stress above the second syllable].   [right margin] 15 "See him ["w" mended to] Wind-lilylocks-laced;" 16 "⌒" added on "hangs"   17 "Them" (presumably also an outride) stress on "hide" 18 "cold furls--"   19 "With a", bracket moved left, "With-a-fountain's shining-shot furls" ("shot" is rewritten below, to preserve the alternative "With-a-wet-sheen-shot furls.")

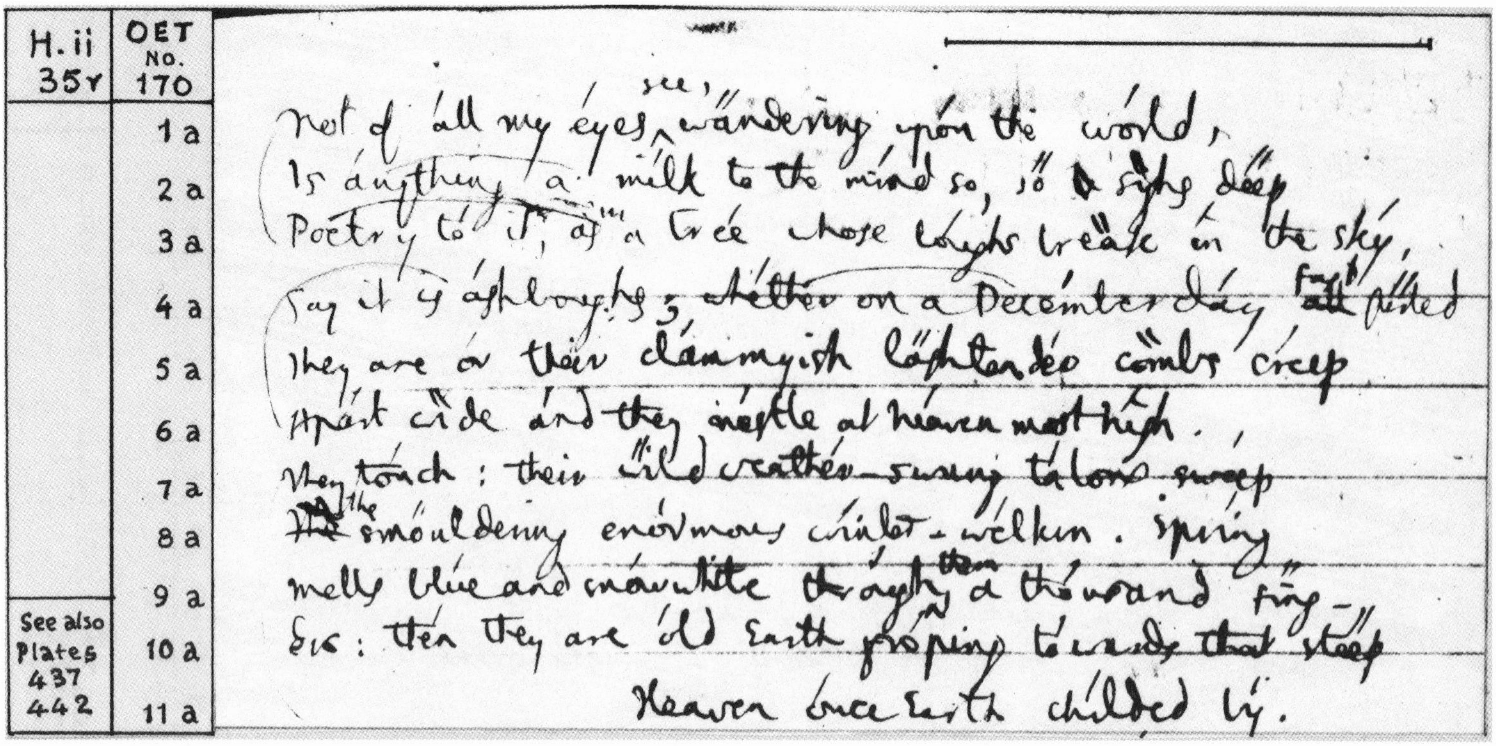

H.ii 35r	OET No. 170	
	1 a	
	2 a	
	3 a	
	4 a	
	5 a	
	6 a	
	7 a	
	8 a	
	9 a	
See also Plates 437 442	10 a	
	11 a	

[Manuscript autograph of the curtal sonnet "Ashboughs", 11 lines in Hopkins's hand]

Plate 490   OET No. 170: "Not of all my eyes see" [Ashboughs] -- MS. 1: H[1]

[above] H.ii.35r--earliest surviving autograph, a faircopy of the curtal sonnet to which RB gave the title "Ashboughs". 2a "so͞b [? confusion with ℓ.3] sighs" (the double grave is not del., but is superimposed on the stroke dotting the "i") 3a Note GMH's doubts as to where the slur should end: after "it" (tail end del.), after "a" (del.), or "as"? [In H₂ the slur covers only "Poetr".]   4a "all/fast"   6a "nistle" [slip? dial.?] mended to "nestle".   7a "wildweather-" probably one word, with a hyphen after it.   8a "The/A The" 9a/10a "fing-/ers" mended to "Ers" (GMH liked every line to begin with u.c.). The marginal braces are in ink.

RB numbered the sheet in pencil "11", and at the foot of H.ii.33r noted that that page (numbered "10", with a revision of this poem) was once part of 11. For prosodic marks see No. 169, Plate 487.

Plate 491   OET No. 170: "Not of all my eyes see" [Ashboughs[-- MS. 2: H[2]

[opposite] H.ii.33r--at the top is a revision of 13, 14 of No. 163, cont. from H.ii.35v (Plate 463): as RB notes in pencil at the foot, "10 and 11 were one sheet" (i.e., 33r and 35r and v). The page is now damaged before 4b. A former vertical pleat in the paper (now pulled open) is marked by breaks in the writing in 1b "wandering", 5b "lashtender", 8b "winter". GMH's pen often ran short of ink (e.g., 3b, 8b, 11b).

The autograph revision of No. 170, 1b to 11b, is followed by an attempt to re-write 7-11 with two extra half-lines or "burden lines" (7ii and 8ii).

Changes: 1b "eyes,"..."along-a/on the"   3b "as as[h?]" mended to "as a tree"   7b,c "hovering/how their"   8b "Spr[ing"--from 35r]   10b "towards that hea[ven]"   11b "that/whom"   7d,e "They touch heaven, tabour" rev. as "They touch, they [comma left undel.] tabour"..."hovering;/hovering", rev. as "hover on it;"   7ii "Their/With"   8c "Eye" is probably an absent-minded slip for its homophone "Ay"   8ii,a,b "More cheer will be/But more cheer is" 9c "and/with"

10c,d "gropes, grasps towards the" rev. as "gropes at for, grasps at"   11c "Heaven that/whom she childs us by." [Above "she" is a del. caret showing where "at" is to be inserted in the line above.]   11d "childs us/them by" rev. as "things by".

PLATE 491. OET 170. [Ashboughs] • 315

H.ii.33r

No.163

13b
14b

'S not ening, see you ; unforeseen as rather — as skies
Between the mountains —

No.170

1b Not of all my eyes see, wandering on the world,
2b Is anything a milk to the mind so, so sighs deep
3b Poetry to it, as a tree whose boughs break in the sky.
4b Say it is ashboughs : whether on a December day and furled
5b Fast or they in clammyish lashtender combs creep
6b Apart wide and new-nestle at heaven most high.
7 c b They touch heaven, talons on it ; how their talons sweep
8b The smouldering enormous winter welkin ! Eye May
9b Melts blue and snowwhite through them, a fringe and fray
10b Of greenery : it is old earth's groping towards that the steep
11b Heaven whom sho childs us ly.

7 e d They touch, they, talons on it, hovering on it ; here, there hurled,
7.ii with talons sweep

8 c The smouldering enormous winter welkin. Eye,
8.ii b a But more cheer when May
with melts blue and snowwhite through their fringe and fray
9 c Of greenery and old earth props at for, prays for the steep
10 d c Heaven whom sho childs us ly.
11 c Heaven with it whom she childs
d this
e things by.

OET No. 170

10 & 11 were one sheet

33

10

H.ii.31r

OET No.159, l.11

OET No. 9

171

And rather, my heart lo! capped strength, idle joy, would
laugh,   cheer.

Entry of Tom

1 Tom garlanded with squat and surly steel,   (A

2 Tom, fallow booted navvy has piled his pick

3 And rips out rockfire homeforth — sturdy Dick;

4 Tom Heart-at-ease, that's all now for his meal

5 Sure, 's bed. Be his lot low, handily he swings it — feel

6 That ne'er need hunger, should be seldom sick, [thick

7 Seldomer heartsore : that treads through, prickproof,

8 Thousands of thorns, thoughts. And, in commonweal

9 A little reck lacklevel if all had bread:

10 Country is honour is all us

OET No. 171

OET No. 159 line 12

reck what though? the Hero whose heaven-handling flung me,
foot trod

H.ii.31r cont.

OET No. 157

1 c\d   no comfort, there is none : { Pitched past pitch of grief.
                                     { grief past pitch of grief,   (B

H.i. 33r

O.E.T. No. 171

1 Tom, garlanded with squat and surly steel

2 Tom; then Tom's fallow oot fellow piles pick

3 By him and rips out rockfire homeforth — sturdy Dick; [for his meal

4a Tom Heart-at-ease, Tom Navvy; who's all

5a Sure, & bed now. Low be it, lustily he his
   { life's lot (feel
   { own

6 That ne'er need hunger, Tom; Tom seldom sick,

7 Seldomer heartsore; that treads through,
   prickproof, thick

8 Thousands of thorns, thoughts) swings though.
   commonweal [bread:

9 Little I' reck no! lacklevel, in, if all had

10 What! country is honour enough in all us—
   lordly head, [thor-ground

11 with heaven's lights high hung round, or, mo-

12 That mammocks, mighty foot. But no way sped

13a Nor mind nor mainstrength; gold go garlanded [sound;

14a with, perilous, O no; nor yet plod safe shod

H.i. 33v

15 Undenizened, beyond bound

16 Of earth's glory, earth's ease, all; noone,
   nowhere, [base

17 In side the world's weal; rare gold, bold steel,

18a Of lath, but ease, share ease

b   Of lath, but ease, share ease

19 This, by Despair, bred Hangdog dull; by Rape,

20 manwolf, worse; and their packs infest the
   age,

Dromore Sept. 1887

13b try : neither garlanded

14b with gold, perilous, nor yet ete

4b   also, he is all for his meal

5b Sure, 's bed now. how be it: he lustily his life's
   (or own]) lot

OET No. 171

PLATE 493. OET 171. *Tom's Garland* • 317

D   153

Tom's Garland :

on the Unemployed

(sonnet, with two codas : the rhythm is not sprung)

1   Tom — garlanded with squat and surly steel
Tom; then Tom's fallowbootfellow piles pick
By him and rips out rockfire homesforth — sturdy Dick;
4   Tom Heart-at-ease, Tom Navvy; that is all for his meal
Sure, 's bed now. Low be it: lustily he his own lot (feel
That need not hunger, Tom; Tom seldom sick,
Seldomer heartsore; that treads through, prickproof, thick
8   Thousands of thorns, thoughts) swings though. Commonweal
Little I' reck ho! lacklevel in, if all had bread:
What! country is honour enough in all us — lordly head,
With heaven's lights high hung round, or, mother-ground
12   That mammocks, mighty foot. But no way sped,
Nor mind nor mainstrength; gold go garlanded
With, perilous, O no; nor yet plod safe shod sound;
            Undenizened, beyond bound
16   Of earth's glory, earth's ease, both; noone, nowhere,
In all the world's weal; comfort, ay, most base
         Of; care, but share the care —
This, by Despair, bred Hangdog dull; by Rage,
20   Manwolf, worse; and their packs infest the age.

                     Sept:
               Dromore, 1887

Plate 492   [opposite]   OET No. 171: Tom's Garland -- MSS. 1 and 3

    (i) [top] MS.1 [H¹] H.ii.31r--earliest autograph version, incomplete, crossed through in ink. Lines 11 and 12 of "[Carrion Comfort]", No. 159, are squeezed in above and below, followed by the sole autograph of "No worst", No. 157--see Plate 447. Changes by GMH: 2 "bot" mended to "booted"   3 "&-Sturdy" treated as a proper noun, "S" confirmed in different ink after the change in punctuation   5 "bed↓." Note stresses: 7 "thát"   8 "Ánd"

    RB's pencil marks it "A", "early v[ersion] of Tom".

    (ii) [opposite, lower left and right] MS.3 [H²] H.i.33r,v--autograph faircopy, on folded grey notepaper embossed "Monasterevan/Ireland"--not visible in the plate. Deletion: 9 "·/in,"   13a "mia" mended to "mind". 16 "noone" seems to be one word as in 14th, 15th C. and other MSS. of this poem.   17 nor/or   18 Half line deleted because he had forgotten to indent it. In the variants at the foot the black balls show the "real or heard stress, the white the dumb or conventional one" (see L.i.109).

Plate 493 [above]   OET No. 171: Tom's Garland -- MS.2: D

    D (Add MS. 42, 711, f.153r, Brit. Lib.)--autograph faircopy sent to Dixon. Deletions: 9 "reck ø[f?]"   12 "no" (italics del.)   18 two dashes.

A.p. 185

OET
No
171

Tom's Garland : upon
the Unemployed (sonnet: // common rhythm,
but with hurried feet: // two codas)

1 Tom — garlanded with squat and surly steel
2 Tom ; then tom's fallow bootfellow piles pick
3 By him and rips out rockfire homeforth — sturdy Dick ;
4 Tom Heart-at-ease, Tom Navvy : he is all for his meal
5 Sure, 's bed now. Low be it : lustily he his low lot (feel
6 That néer need hunger, Tom ; Tom seldom sick, [thick
7 Seldomer heartsore ; that treads through, prickproof,
8 Thousands of thorns, thoughts) swings though. Commonweal
9 Little I reck ho ! lacklevel in, if all had bread :
10 What ! Country is honour enough in all us — lordly head,
11 With heaven's lights high hung round, or, mother-ground
12 That mammocks, mighty foot. But no way sped,
13 Nor mind nor mainstrength ; gold go garlanded
14 With, perilous, O no ; nor yet plod safe shod sound ;

little reck he !

p.186

15   Undenizened, beyond bound
16 Of earth's glory, earth's ease, all ; no one, nowhere,
17 In wide the world's weal ; rare gold, bold steel, bare
18   In both ; # care, but share care—
19 This, by Despair, bred Hangdog dull ; by Rage,
20 Manwolf, worse ; and their packs infest the age,

Dromore Sept. 1887

[Heavy stresses marked double, thus ' and stresses of sense, independent of the natural stress of the verse, thus `]

The key to this obscure poem may be found in the letter at end of this volume

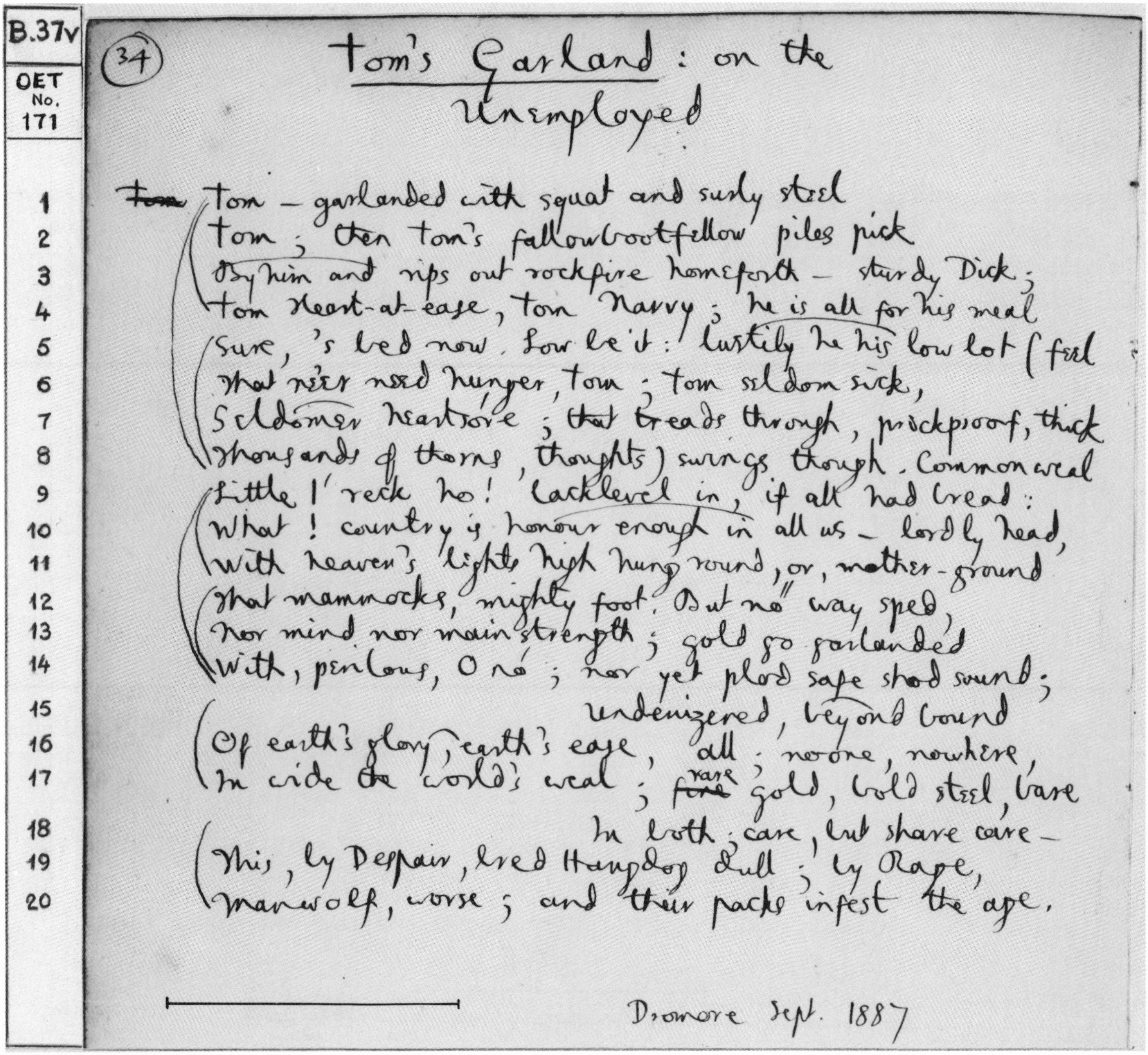

B.37v

OET No. 171

(34)

1
2
3
4
5
6
7
8
9
10
11
12
13
14
15
16
17
18
19
20

Tom's Garland : on the
Unemployed

~~Tom~~ Tom — garlanded with squat and surly steel
Tom; then Tom's fallowbootfellow piles pick
By him and rips out rockfire homeforth — sturdy Dick;
Tom Heart-at-ease, Tom Navvy; he is all for his meal
Sure, 's bed now. Low be it: lustily he his low lot (feel
That need not hunger, Tom; Tom seldom sick,
Seldomer heartsore; that treads through, prickproof, thick
Thousands of thorns, thoughts) swings though. Commonweal
Little I reck ho! Lacklevel in, if all had bread:
What! country is honour enough in all us — lordly head,
With heaven's lights high hung round, or, mother-ground
That mammocks, mighty foot. But no way sped,
Nor mind nor mainstrength; gold go garlanded
With, perilous, O no; nor yet plod safe shod sound;
undenizered, beyond bound
Of earth's glory, earth's ease, all: noone, nowhere,
In cold the world's weal; fine gold, cold steel, bare
In both; care, but share care —
This, by Despair, bred Hangdog dull; by Rage,
Manwolf, worse; and their packs infest the age.

Dromore Sept. 1887

Plate 493a [opposite]   OET No. 171: Tom's Garland -- MS. 4: A

A.pp.185-6--autograph faircopy, cut in two and mounted in album A (the thin severed tail of the "y" in "yet" from 14 seems like a stress on "-den-" in 15.

Deletions: Metrical note "⸝" (twice)   18 "✗care". 14 "no" the single stress (so broad and black) may have been orig. a double stress, as in D. Blots: 12 "mighty" and above "But"   18 above first "care". In the footnote the double acute and double grave are blurred because the strokes were made too close to each other.

RB's marginal note (9), "Little reck he!" was probably a suggested emendation submitted to GMH. He added below the autograph: "The key to this obscure poem may be found in the letter at the end of this volume"--the letter has since been transferred to the volume of MSS. letters from GMH to RB (L.i.272-4).

Plate 493b [above]   OET No. 171: Tom's Garland -- MS. 5: B

B.37v--autograph faircopy inscribed on a page in album B, the last of the autographs so entered (27v-37v). In 1 "Tom" was probably deleted because it was too close to the margin for the braces which identify quatrains, octave, etc. (cf. Plates 516-7 and 523). In 17 "fine" is rev. to "rare".

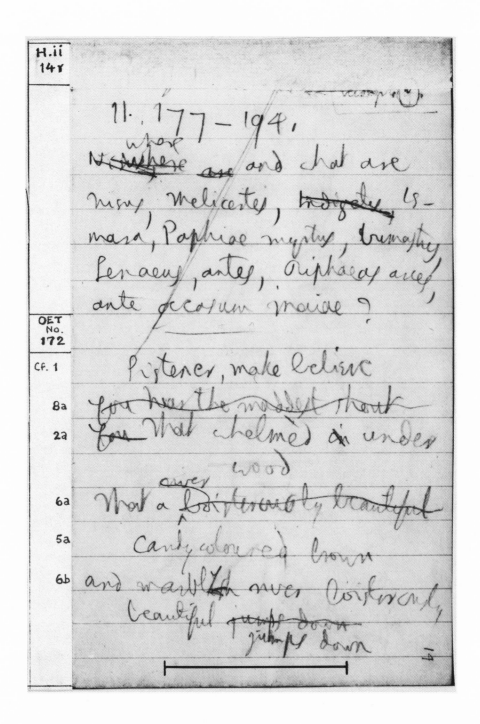

Plate 494   OET No. 172: Epithalamion -- MS. 1: H[1]

H.ii.14r--earliest autograph draft, in pencil, with phrases later used in lines 1, 2, 5, 6, 8. Above it, partly obscured by a hinge, is an examination question on Vergil, Georgics i and ii (prescribed for second year Latin at the Royal University in 1888). 6a "a river boisterously beautiful"   In 6b "marblish" is mended to "marbly". Note: The line numbers and letters have been assigned to each MS. in turn to identify the entries: they begin again with the next draft.

PLATE 495. OET 172. *Epithalamion* • *321*

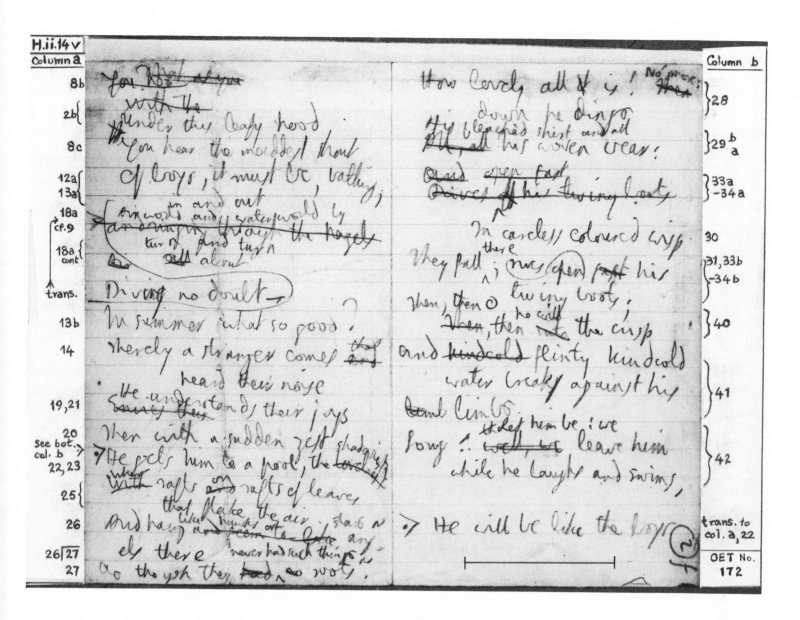

Plate 495   OET No. 172: Epithalamion -- MS.1: H¹ (2)

   H.ii.14v--earliest autograph draft (cont.), in pencil, with phrases later embodied mainly in *ℓℓ*.12-14, 18-34, 40-42. Marginal line numbers, necessarily inexact, facilitate comparison with later versions: the letters after them (8b, 8c, etc.) refer to the sequence in f.14 only.

   Column a continues from *ℓ*.1 on 14r ("make believe"): "That as you/ You he[ar]"   After 2 a marginal arrow is del.

  9 "and ringing through the hazels"   The arrow at 18a marks the insertion point for the ringed phrase below: "Divers" mended to "Diving no doubt--"   18a (cont.) "Air"   "all about"   19 "Envies their"   After 20 the line at the bottom of col. b is to be inserted.   22,23 "loveliest"   25 "With/Where rafts and/on"   26 orig. "And hang and seem to like angels there" rev. to "hang like hawks or stars or angels there"   27 "As though they had no roots." rev. to "they never had such things as roots."

   Column b: 28 "all it is! Then"   29a "All, all his woven wear:"   33a "Rives off" rev. to "And [rives] open fast his twiny boots"   33b "rives open fast" rev. to "open rives his"   40,41 "Then, then into the crisp/And kindcold...water breaks" rev. to "Then, then O then he will the crisp/...water break against his limb [del. because not indented] limbs"

   42 "Long : well, we/th[ere?]" rev. to "Long. Let him be:"

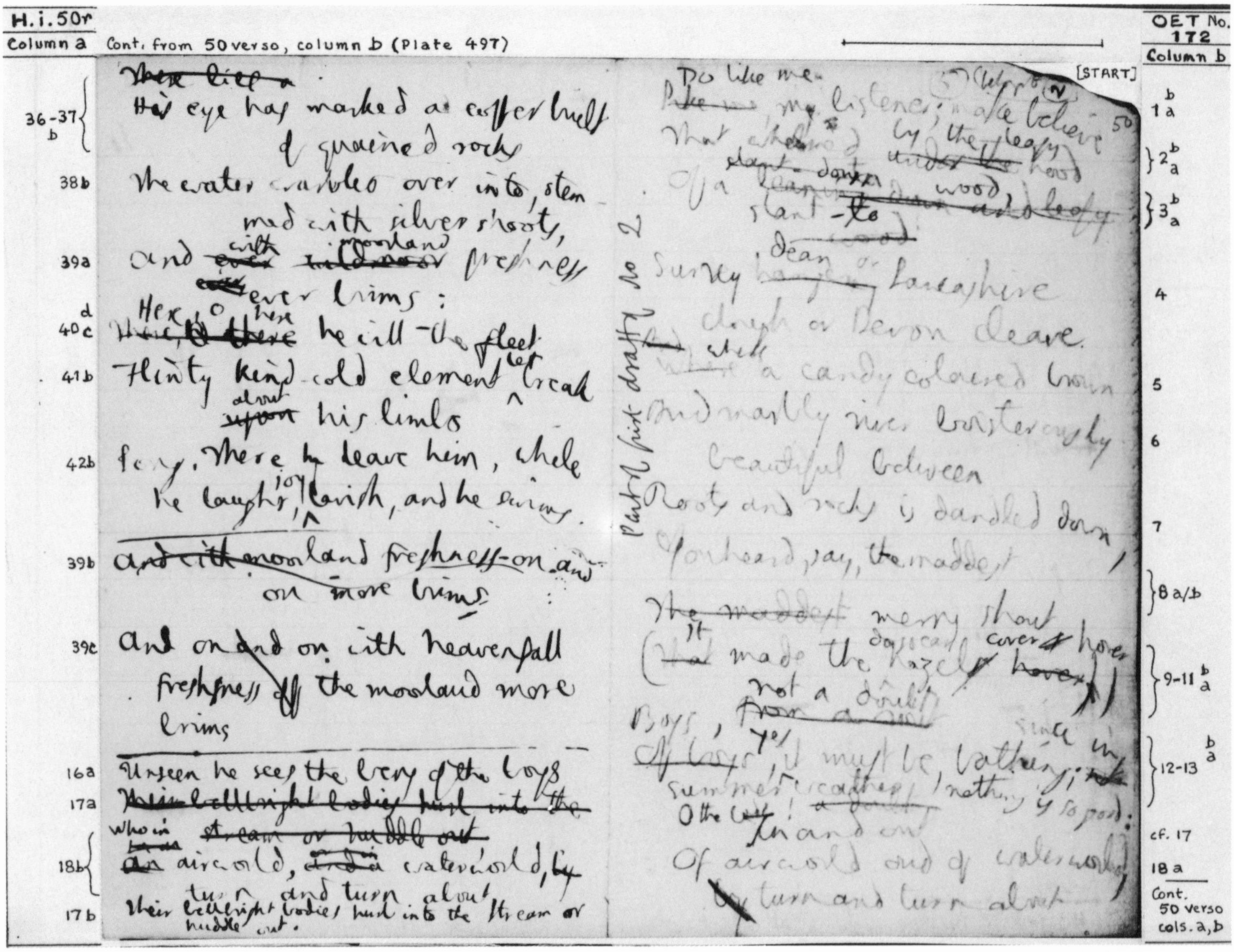

H.i.50r
Column a   Cont. from 50 verso, column b (Plate 497)

OET No.
172
Column b

[handwritten manuscript draft — Gerard Manley Hopkins, *Epithalamion*, column a and column b, with numerous deletions and revisions]

Line markers (column a): 36-37 b, 38b, 39a, 40 c/d, 41b, 42b, 39b, 39c, 16a, 17a, 18b, 17b

Line markers (column b): 1 a/b, 2 a/b, 3 a/b, 4, 5, 6, 7, 8 a/b, 9-11 a/b, 12-13 a/b, cf. 17, 18 a, Cont. 50 verso cols. a, b   [START]

Plate 496   OET No. 172: Epithalamion -- MS. 2: H² (1)

H.i.50r--part of second autograph draft. It begins with column b (in pencil), continues on 50 verso, cols. a and b; then back to 50r, col. a (ink). At the top of right corner b RB notes "5 - belongs to 2", i.e., to the second poem in MS. H.ii album. Vertically down the middle RB notes in red ink: "Part of first draft of No. 2."

Deletions, obscurities include (Column b): 1 "Like me," 2 "whelmèd under the/by the leafy hood" 3 Sequence of drafts uncertain: "Of a leaning down and leafy wood"--(?) "lean-to wood"--"slant-down wood"--"slant-to wood" 4 "Surrey hanger,/dean or" 9-11 "That made the hazels hover" rev. to "(It made the dogsear hazel cover hover) from a rout/Of boys, it must be, bathing; not a doubt" rev. to "Not a doubt/Boys, yes it must be, bathing; since in summer weather nothing is so good: /O the lads!" [not del., but seems so because "in" was mended to "In" on top of "lads"]. 18a "waterworld by turn"

Column a (cont. from f.50 verso, cols. a and b--see Plate 497 next): 36 "There lies a" 39a "ever wildmoor/with moorland freshness ever" 40 "There, th(? O) there" 42 "Long. There he [slip for "we"?] leave him" 39b ink splashes and strokes, not punctuation 17a "Their bellbright bodies hurl into the stream or huddle out," del. 18b "An/In an/Who in airworld, and a/or in waterworld, by" 17b "Their bellbright bodies hurl into the stream or huddle out."

PLATE 497. OET 172. *Epithalamion*   •   323

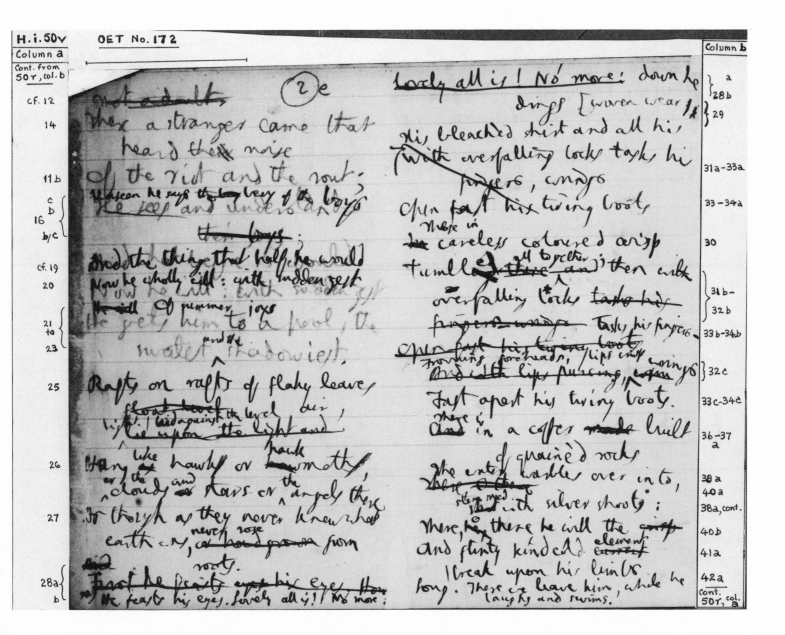

Plate 497   OET No. 172: Epithalamion -- MS. 2 cont.: H² (2)

H.i.50v--second autograph draft, cont.. The large "(2)e" at the top is from RB's pencil. Col. a continues from col. b of 50 recto, and col. b is revised in col. a of 50 recto. Col. a here begins in pencil, revised in ink on top of the pencil; from 25 on the MS. is in ink. A complete transcription of all the successive changes (some necessarily conjectural) would occupy considerable space, and has not been attempted here.

Column a: 12 "Not a doubt." 14 "There a stranger came that heard their noise" 11 "Of the riot and the rout;" 16 orig. "He sees and understands their joys;" mended in ink to "boys"; 16c "Unseen he says [for "sees"--cf. f.50r, bot. col. a, 16a] the bey bevy" 19-23 orig. "And what before he would/Now he will: with sudden zest/He gets him to a pool, the sweetest, shadowiest." rev. to "and the shadowiest." 25 "leaves float level/lie upon the light and/light | [lie mended to] laid against the level air," 26 orig. "[Hung mended to] Hang as hawks or hawmoths, clouds or stars" 27 "As though as [sic] they never knew what earth was, or had grown from roots." 28a "First" rev. to "And first he feasts [eyes] his eyes. How"

Column b: "lovely all is! No more:" [deletion line like italics] 29 "woven weary." [?] 30 "In...wisp" 31b-32c "Tumbling/ed [i.e., "Tumbling" rev. to "Tumbled" rev. to "Tumble"] there and all together; then with overfalling locks [transposition del.] tasks his fingers--wrings/Open fast his twiny boots/And with lips pursing, wrin wrings" rev. to "Frowning foreheads, lips crisp" [rhyme word] 36-7 "And in" rev. to "There is a coffer made built of quainèd rocks/The water warbles over into, shot stemmed with silver shoots:" 40a "There, O there" 40b "There he," rev. "There, O there he will the crisp" [rhyme word not replaced] 41 "kindcold current element | break"

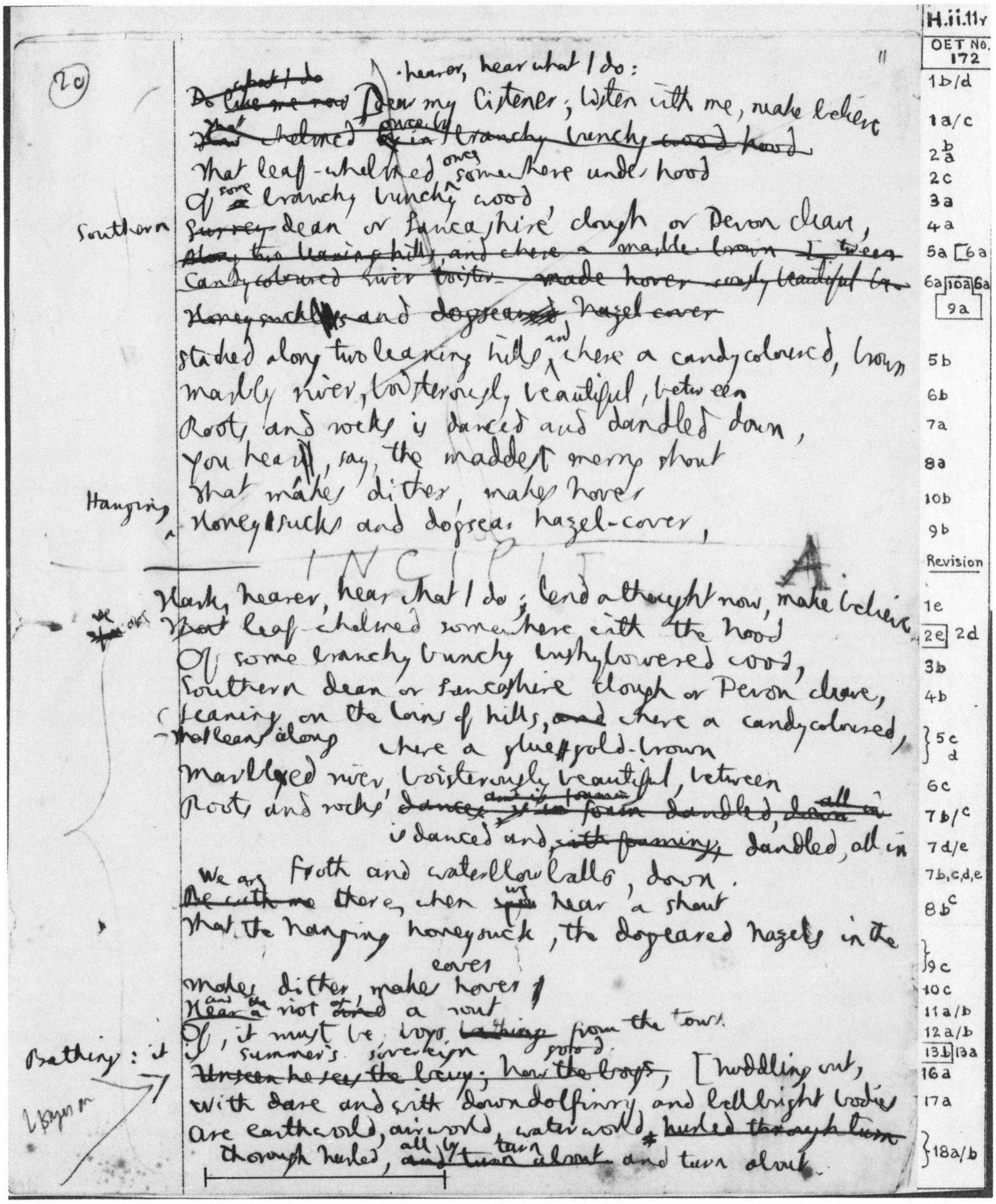

Plates 498-502   OET No. 172: Epithalamion -- MS. 3 (final drafts): H³

H.ii.7r, 9r, 11r, 13r and 13v--third and last autograph drafts, unfinished, left in great confusion, written in ink in a university examination answer book (see Plate 500). The pages are here rearranged more nearly in sequence of line numbers, but GMH reworked passages in irregular order. RB's pencil annotations help: the start of the "final" version is marked "INCIPIT" and "A" (Plate 498); B (Pl. 499) is subdivided into "B alpha", "B beta" (top of page), "B gamma"; "C" is on Plate 501 and we return to Plate 499 for "D" (rev. Pl. 502). RB numbers the pages 2a to 2d.

Plate 498   H.ii.11r--drafts and final version of 1-13, 16-18. The first entry on the page was 2 inches from the top, 10a and 9a: "made hover/Honeysuckless and dogseared hazel cover", all del.; when the poet reached 6 he fitted the line before and after "made hover"--"boister-" on one side and "ously" on the other. Lines 1b to 9b are crossed through in pencil (prob. RB). 1a orig. "Do like me now" rev. 1b "Do what I do, dear my listener;" then "dear" mended to 1c "Dear my listener...believe" then 1d prob. "Dear my hearer, hear what I do:"   2a "How...by in"   2b "That...once by"   5a "Along two leaning hills,"   6a "be-/tween" 5b "hills, where" comma then mended to caret: "hills and where"   8a "heard"   10b "makes"   9b after "Honey" wet ink deletion left no shape for detection under infrared or transmitted light.

Revision. 2e (left margin, torn) "You We are" 2d "leaf-whelmed" (uncertain hyphen, clear in 2c above).   5d "glue\gold", presumably meant to be closed up   6c "Marblyed"   7b stages may have been: "dances, is in foam dandled, down"   7c "dances and is foaming dandled, all in"   7d "is danced and, with foaming, dandled," (stops uncertain)   10c "hover\"   11b "And the riot of a rout"   After 13b GMH's marginal arrow in ink corresponds with the marginal arrow at "B" (Plate 499). RB notes "2 pages on", adding his own large arrow in pencil.

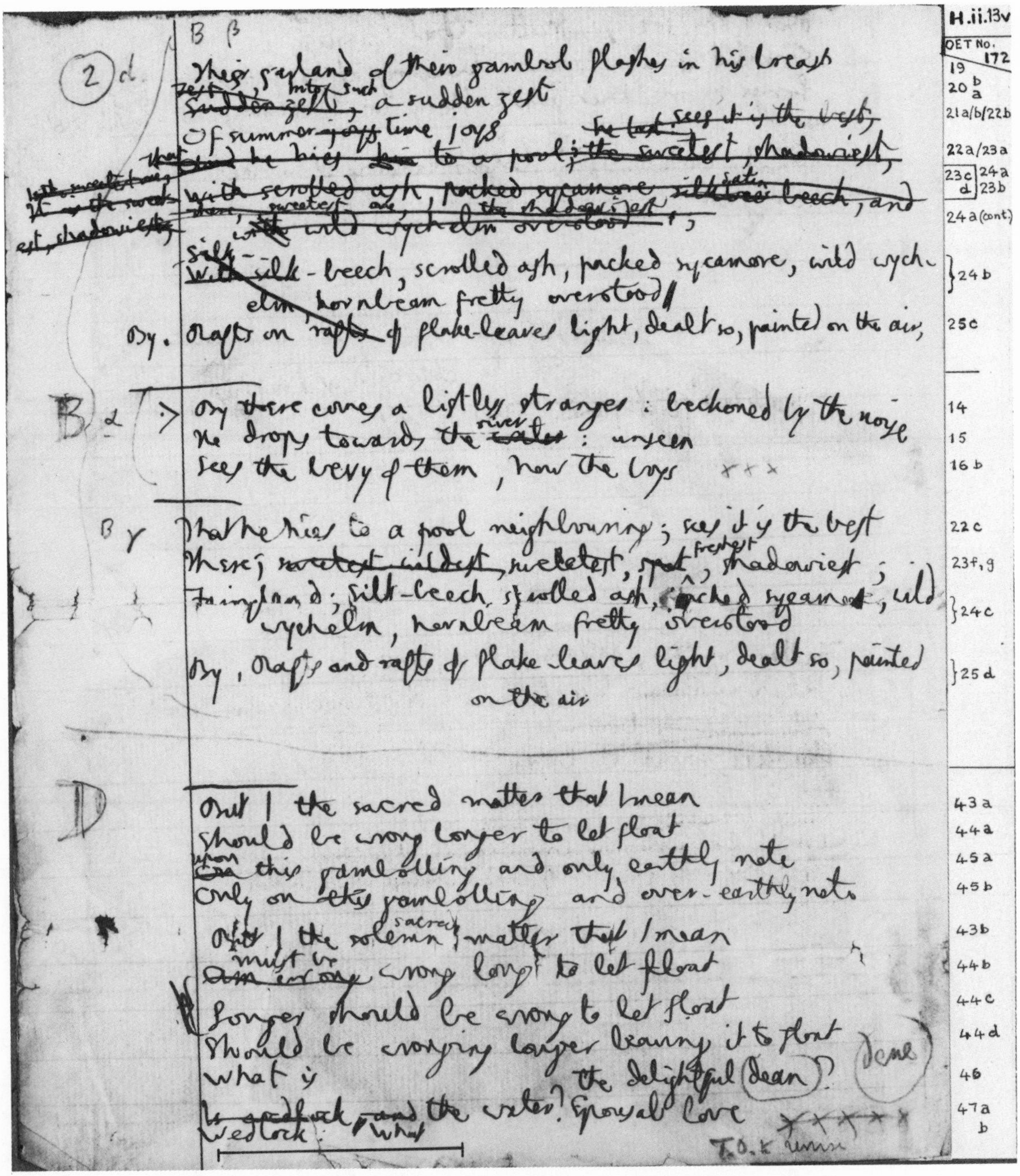

PLATE 499. OET 172. *Epithalamion* • *325*

Plate 499   OET No. 172: Epithalamion -- MS. 3 (cont.): H³ (2)

H.ii.13v (really the recto, with ruled lines)--third autograph draft, cont. (𝓵𝓵.14-16, 19-25, 43-47) RB's pencil brackets the top two-thirds as "B". "D" was rev. on 13r. The page is torn, and badly creased at 24c.

Some changes: 19 "Their" mended to "This garland"   20 three openings: "Sudden zest,"/"Zest,"/"Into such"   21 orig. "Of summer-joys"   22a "[And] That he hies him...pool; the sweetest, [Was the "best" above it meant to fit in here?] shadowiest,"   23c,d (in left margin) "Is the sweetest one,"/"It is the sweet-/est, shadowiest;"   22b/23b "the best/There, sweetest one, the shadowiest"   24a orig. "sycamore, silkbee satin beech, and with wild wychelm overstood;" 24b "...fretty overstood"   25 was drafted on Plate 501

Middle section: 14 Ink arrow in margin corresponds with marginal arrow near bottom of f.11 recto where this passage belongs.   16b Pencilled xxx (RB) and ink line across exam book margin (GMH) indicate a break in continuity (cont. bot. f.11 recto).   23f "sweetest spot,"   24c (bad crease) "Fairyland; silk-beech, scrolled ash, packed sycamore, wild"   25d "flake-leaves" (note curled hyphen, which almost looks like part of "𝓵")

D.   43a "But I"   44b and c marginal bracket del.. "Am wrong/Must be wrong long [tear] to let [𝓵e ? mended to] float"   46 "dean" ringed in pencil by RB, who added the more usual spelling "dene" in the margin.   47 "Is wedlock, and the water?" RB's pencil adds 5 xs to mark incompleteness and "T.O. [Turn Over] to reverse", the real verso, now f.13 recto.

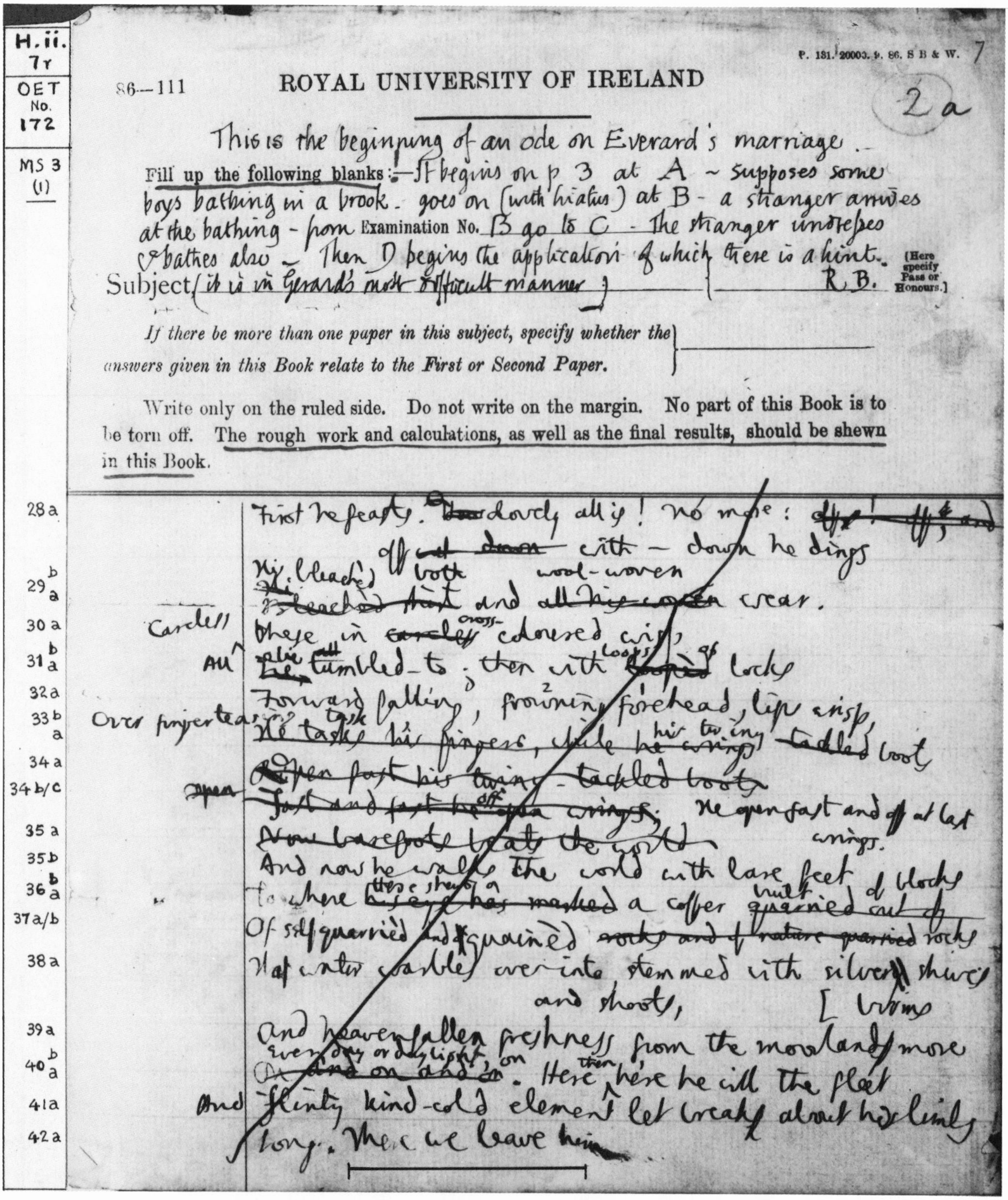

Plate 500   OET No. 172: Epithalamion -- MS. 3 (cont.): H³ (3)

H.ii.7r--third autograph draft (revision of H.i.50 verso) ℓ ℓ.28-42. The old exam answer book (printed 1886) was ruled on rectos only, with wide margins for examiners' marks and comments. The prefatory note is by RB (see Introduction to this vol.).

28a "Q How lovely" mended to "Lovely all is! Nó more: off;\off;; and off wit[h] down"   29a "Bleachèd shirt [dotted i, not stress] and all his woven wear."   29b "His bleachèd both" 30a "These" mended to "Careless these"   31a "Lie all:..looped" 31b "All lie tumbled-to"   33b "twiny/tackled boots"   34a "R[ps?] Open"   34b "open wrings;" 35a "Now barefoot beats the world"   36b "To where these [for there] shews a" 37b "of nature-quarried rocks"   39a "moorlands"

40a "On and on and on"   41a "Flinty" mended to "And flinty"..."breaks" 42a "Long. There we leave him" [ends with a blot]

PLATE 501. OET 172. *Epithalamion* • 327

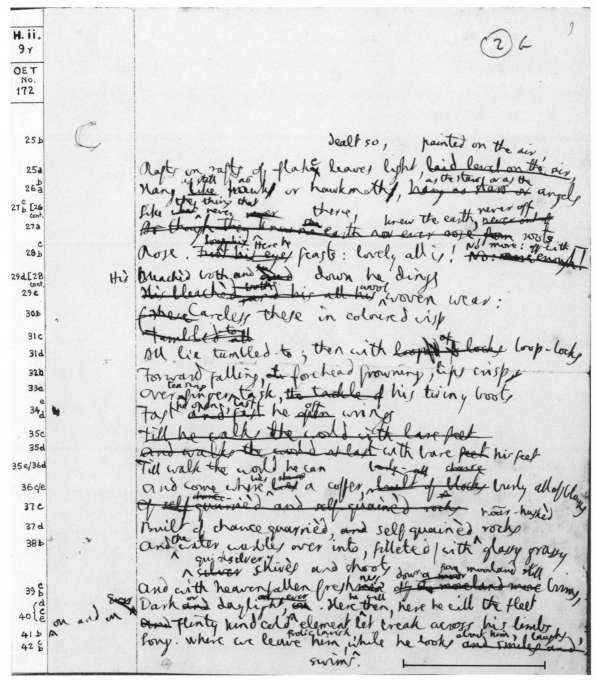

Plate 501   OET No. 172: Epithalamion -- MS. 3 (cont.): H³ (4)

H.ii.9r--autograph redraft and last version of *ll*.25-42.   RB's pencil marks the page "(2)b". His marginal "C" shows where this section fits in with other parts of the poem.

25a "flak*y*/e"   26a "like m [mended to] hawks"   27a orig. "As though they [knew no rev. to] never knew the earth nor ever rose from roots"   27b "Like what never knew"   28b orig. "First his [rev. as "Long his"] eyes feast"   "No: more enough!/Nó more: off with--and/so/down he dings" 29d "Bleachèd" mended to "His bleachèd both and woolwoven" [one word?]   29c "His bleachèd, [and rev. to] both and [his rev. to] all his woven wear"   31c "Tumbled all" rev. as "Tumbled-to"   31d orig. "looped f[alling?] locks" rev. as "loop of locks" then "loop-locks"   32b "falling, etc....crisp," (crease in paper runs across the line)   33c "Over finger-task," rev. as "Over teasing finger-task", then by transposing the caret "finger teasing task" (prob. "fingerteasing" intended as one word, as in 33b, f.7 recto)   "the tackle of"   36c "where lies/shews lies a coffer built of blocks" rev. 36d "coffer, burly-all of chance blocks"   37c "Of [self rev. as] chance-quarrièd and self-quainèd rocks" 37d rev. as "hoar-huskèd rocks"   38b "silver chivès" rev. as "quicksilvery shivès"   39b "heavenfallen freshmen [distracted professor!] off the moreland more"   rev. as "freshness off a moor" then "down from moorland still brims,"   40c "Dark and daylight, on" then (?) "Ever" inserted before it; then "Dark or daylight ever on [or? on ever]", and finally "Dark or daylight, on and on."   41b ["And flinty" mended to] "Flinty kindcold"

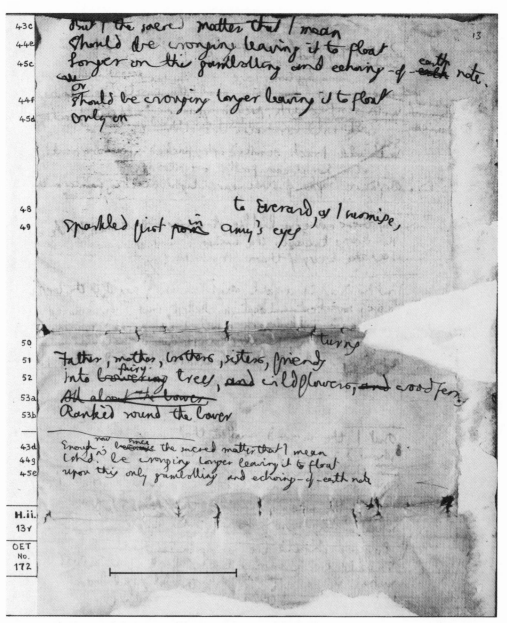

Plate 502   OET No. 172: Epithalamion -- MS. 3 (cont.): H³ (5)

    H.ii.13 recto (really the verso of the examination book page)--end of third autograph draft: redraft and last version of 43-45, and sole versions of 48-53, with spaces left (in vain) for intermediate lines. The page has been badly torn at 50, and repaired, but no lines were probably lost.

    44e "be" was mended--"b" enlarged?   45c "e̱ati̱"

[opposite, top] Plate 503   "Cleaning Dr. Molloy's windows"

    (i)   H.i.49v--pencil sketch by GMH, facing the draft of "Epithalamion" on Plate 496. It is on the back of a draft of No. 176. GMH had begun drawing again (see L.i.227, 232, 240-41, 296).

        Dr. Gerald Molloy had been Rector of the old Catholic University in Dublin, founded by Cardinal Newman. He stayed on in 86 St. Stephen's Green as Professor of Physics after the Jesuits, including GMH, had moved in to run the new University College there. He occupied more of their best rooms than could easily be spared.

[bottom] (ii) OET No. 173: "The sea took pity: it interposed with doom:"

    H.ii.108r--sole autograph in pencil on a scrap of paper. Changes: 1 "and/it"   after "doom," period probably rev. to a colon   2 "daughters,"   3 "winter" mended to "W". RB adds "(45)"--the poem number in album H--and "end".

Cleaning Dr.
Molloy's windows

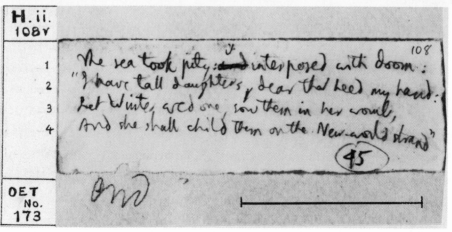

H. ii. 108ᵛ	
	108
1	The sea took pity: ~~and~~ interposed with doom :
2	"I have tall daughters, dear that heed my hand :
3	Let Winter, wed one, sow them in her womb,
4	And she shall child them on the New-world strand"
	45
OET No. 173	

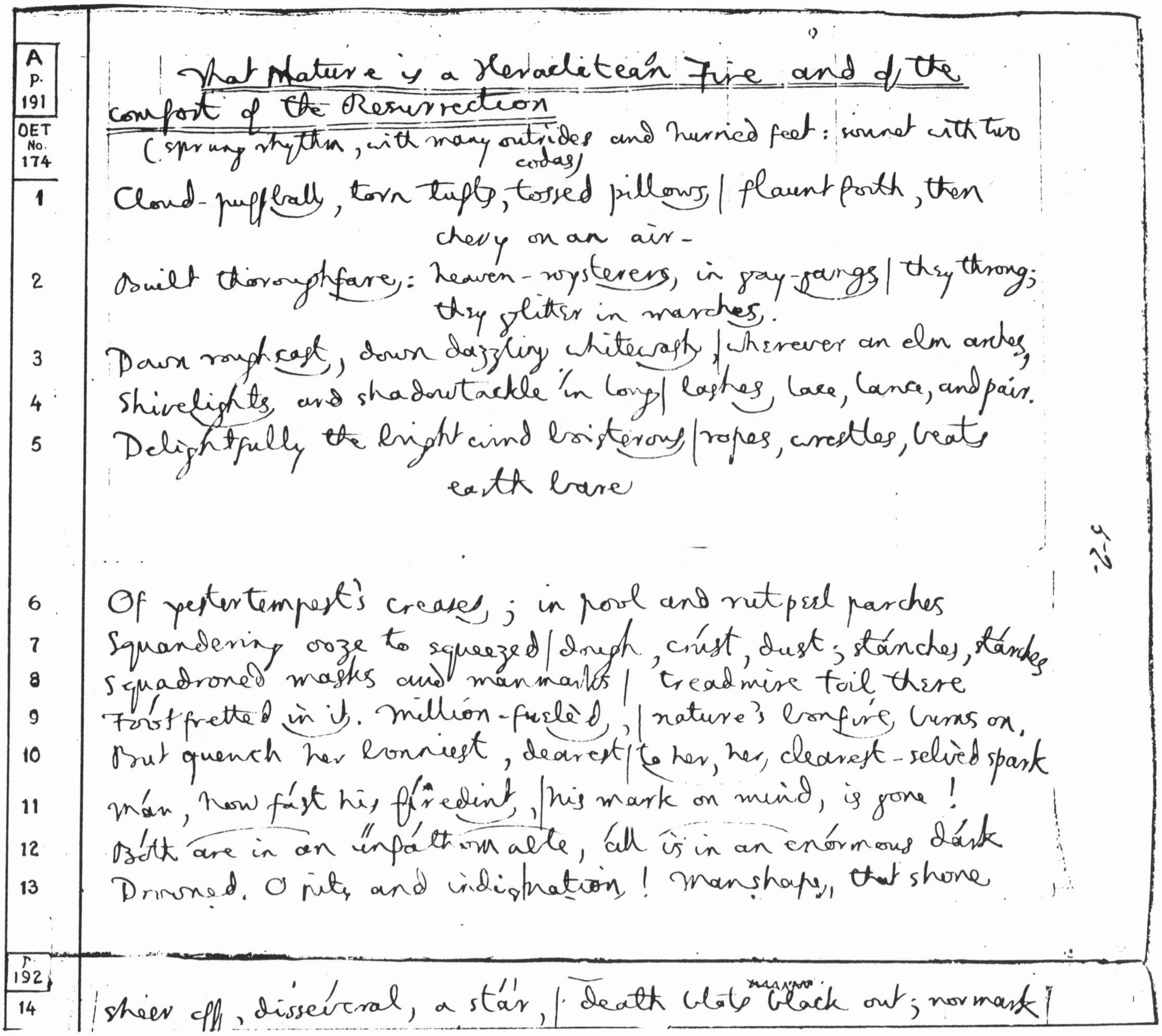

A
p.
191

OET
No.
174

That Nature is a Heraclitean Fire and of the
comfort of the Resurrection
(sprung rhythm, with many outrides and hurried feet: sonnet with two
codas)

1   Cloud-puffball, torn tufts, tossed pillows, | flaunt forth, then
          chevy on an air-
2   built thoroughfare: heaven-roysterers, in gay-gangs | they throng;
          they glitter in marches.
3   Down roughcast, down dazzling whitewash, | wherever an elm arches,
4   Shivelights and shadowtackle in long | lashes, lace, lance, and pair.
5   Delightfully the bright wind boisterous | ropes, wrestles, beats
          earth bare

6   Of yestertempest's creases; | in pool and rutpeel parches
7   Squandering ooze to squeezed | dough, crust, dust; stanches, starches
8   Squadroned masks and manmarks | treadmire toil there
9   Footfretted in it. Million-fuelèd, | nature's bonfire burns on.
10   But quench her bonniest, dearest | to her, her clearest-selvèd spark
11   Man, how fast his firedint, | his mark on mind, is gone !
12   Both are in an unfathomable, | all is in an enormous dark
13   Drowned. O pity and indignation ! Manshape, that shone

p.
192

14 | sheer off, disseveral, a star, | Death blots black out; nor mark |

Plates 504 and 505   OET No. 174: That Nature is a Heraclitean Fire.

MS. A. pp.191-2--sole autograph, a faircopy (with revision in 23, 24), on two sheets of paper, sent to RB. Above it on the first sheet was "To What Serves Mortal Beauty" (No. 158, Plate 453): the looped tail of "g" in its date "Aug." can be seen above the "n" of "Heraclitean". Title: "nature" mended to "N" and "fire" to "F". Outrides, slurs and stresses are in the same ink as the text. Nearly all the outrides are in 1-11; they seem to be displaced by "hurried feet" in 12-20. The autographs had to be cut into three pieces for mounting in album A. Line 5 ended the first sheet--no break was intended. The cut below 13 (to avoid the album hinge) severed the outride under "[indigna]tion" and a deleted outride under "shape", as well as the tails of a "y" and "g": these could now be mistaken for stresses on "[dis]sev[eral]" and "star" in 14.

20 apostrophe in " world's" has been deleted and restored. The last word "diamod." (24b) was corrected to "diamond."
Note: In deciding whether GMH intended adjacent words to form a compound we must compare his penlifts within words in places where no one would suggest that the small gap separated two distinct words: e.g. in "shadowtackle" (4) there are penlifts before the "h" and "d" as well as before the "t". In the title, "Her/acli/tean" breaks into three parts, and "Resur/rection" into two. Note penlifts before a "p" in "ropes" (5), "yestertempest's" (6) as well as in "rutpeel" (6), where there is also a space after the "p"; cf. "fir/edint" (11), "unfathom/able" (12), "in/d/i/gnation" (13). With "mat/ch/wood" (23) cf. "j/oy/less" (17).

In 11 the dot intended for the i in "fire" (to the right of the stress) was mended--it is not an additional prosodic mark.

PLATE 505. OET 174. *That Nature is a Heraclitean Fire* • 331

14	sheer off, disseveral, a star, | Death blots black out; nor mark |
15	Is any of him at all so stark
16	But vastness blurs and time | beats level. Enough! the resurrection,
17	a heart's-clarion! Away grief's gasping, | joyless days, dejection.
18	Across my foundering deck shone
19	A beacon, an eternal beam. | Flesh fade, and mortal trash
20	Fall to the residuary worm; | world's wildfire, leave but ash:
21	In a flash, at a trumpet crash,
22	I am all at once what Christ is |, since he was what I am, and
23	This Jack, joke, poor potsherd, | patch, matchwood, ‿ immortal diamond,
24a	~~Diamond,~~
24b	Is immortal diamond.
	July 26 1888
	Co. Dublin

The last sonnet provisional only

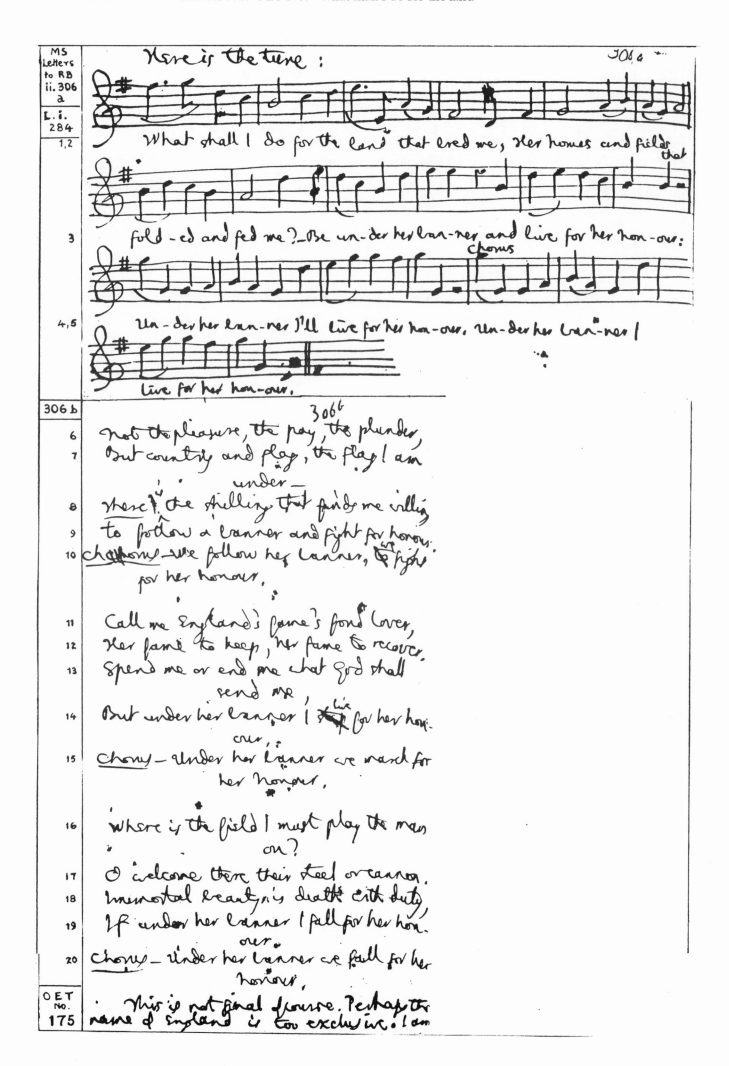

PLATE 507. OET 175. "What shall I do for the land" • 333

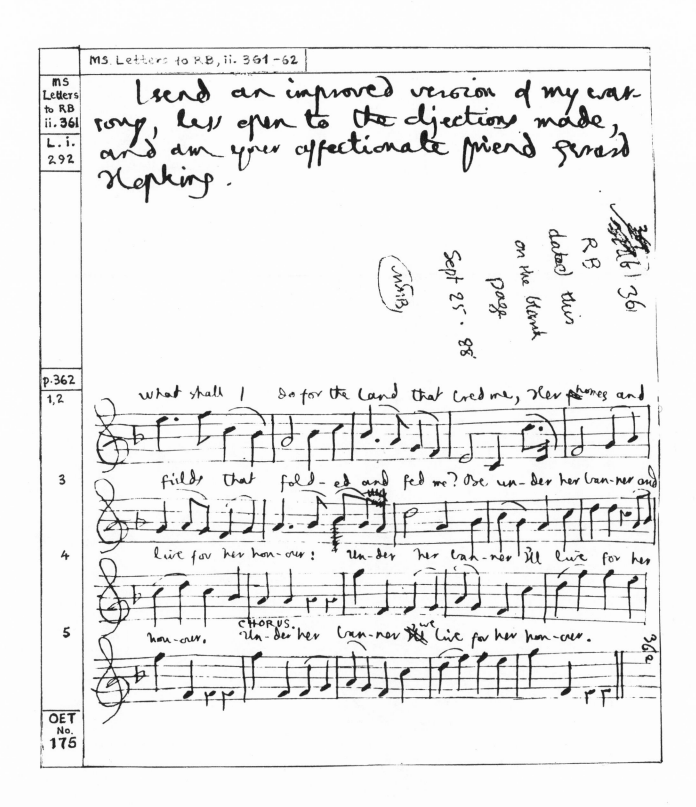

Plates 506,507   OET No. 175: "What shall I do for the land that bred me?"

[opposite, L[1]] MS Letters to Bridges, ii.306a,b--this autograph, part of a letter to RB from GMH, sent 8 Sept. 1888 (the 20th anniversary of GMH's enlistment in the ranks of the Society of Jesus), was mounted in album A, p.188, on a page facing No. 158, "To What Serves Mortal Beauty?" a poem sent to RB in the same letter (see Plate 453). When the Letters of GMH to RB (Oxford Univ. Press, 1935) were being edited by C.C. Abbott, in Feb. 1932 the MS. was cut off with part of the album page itself so that the plate now facing L.i.284 could be made. When it was returned it was restored to the MS. Letters, not album A. Abbott omitted stanzas 2 to 4, reproduced here, in L.i.

[above] Plate 507 -- MS. Letters to RB, ii. pp.361-2--autograph of st. 1, with very minor changes to the words, but with an "improved version" of the melody, in F major instead of G major. Mrs. Monica Bridges notes above the music "RB dated this on the blank page Sept. 25.88 MMB" (the date of the letter to RB containing it, L.i.292).

1 a	Honour is flower from exploit, so we say,
2 b a	And every scar of limb, or dint of shield,
3 a	Std. tongue the time and trumpet of the field
4 a	Stand in the hero came his warrior. day.
5 a	In christ they do; in martyrdom they way.
6 a	But the war was gestet and
6 c	But when the war is in the
6 b	Not the war sword we wield
7 a	seen, nor outwardly the bosom steeled
8 a	Earth hears no hurtle of the fray.
8 b	then from fiercest fray.
4 b	And, on the fighter, forge the heroic day.
7 b	Not seen, the warrior-breast not outward-steeled;
H.i.	
46 v	

9 a	But God that moulds mountain and continent
10 a	With exquisite and increment
9 b	But God, that majory mountain, continent
10 c b	carves, that God else with exquisite increment
11 a	Veins violets and tall trees pines makes more and more
12 a	Crowded career with conquest, while time went
13 b a	Years after years of world without event
14 b	that in Majorca
14 a	For forty years Alphonso watched the door.
9 c	But god that quarries mountains continent
10 d	Carves, god that else with tiniest increment
11 b	Veins violets and tall pines makes more and more,

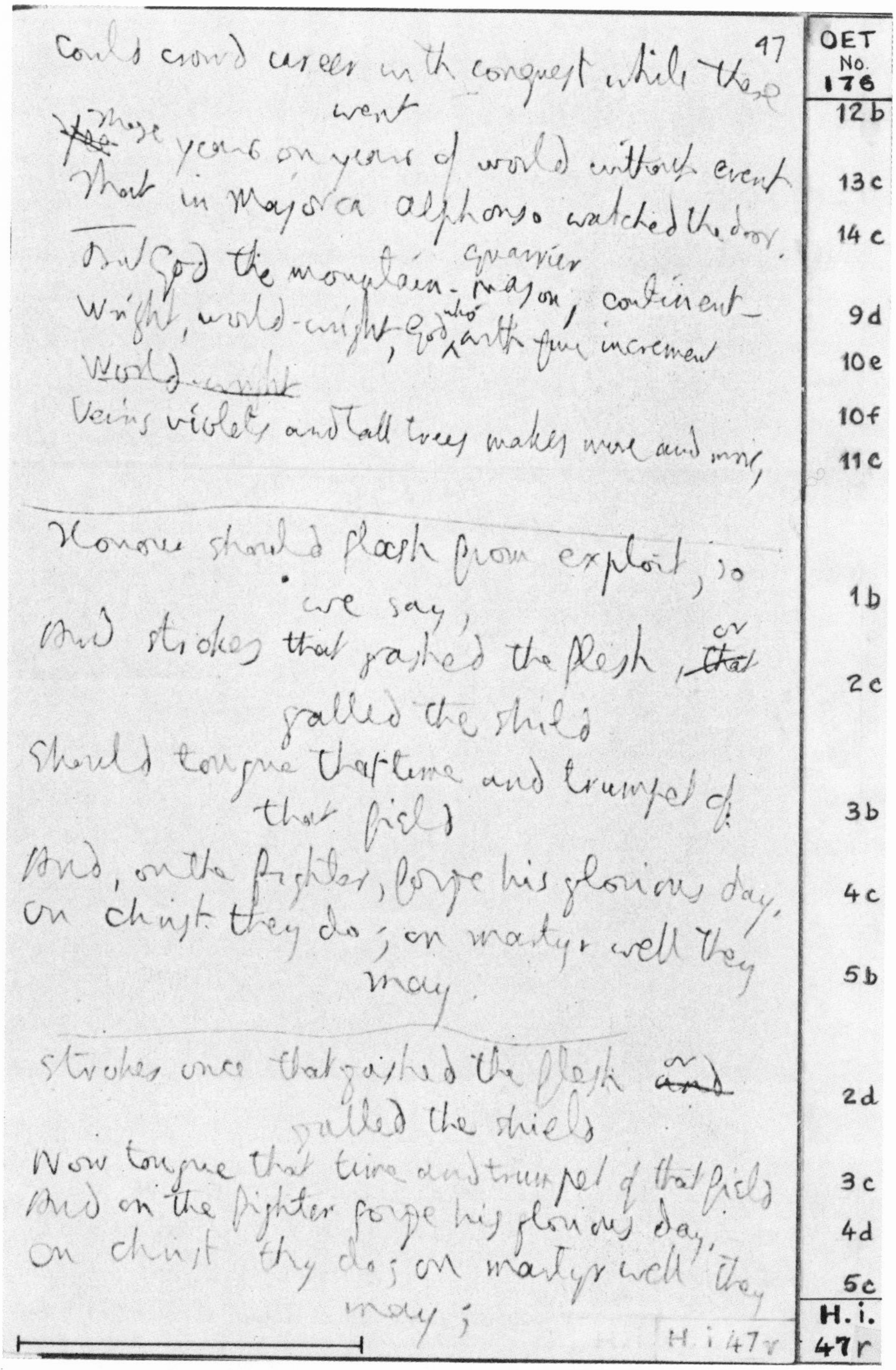

PLATE 509. OET 176. *St. Alphonsus Rodriguez* • *335*

The manuscript facsimile shows handwritten draft text with marginal line references:

	OET No. 176
Could crowd career with conquest while they went	12 b
Those years on years of world without event	13 c
That in Majorca Alphonso watched the door.	14 c
But God the mountain-mason, continent—	9 d
Wright, world-wright, God, with fine increment	10 e
World-wright	10 f
Veins violets and tall trees makes more and more,	11 c
Honour should flash from exploit, so we say;	1 b
And strokes that gashed the flesh, that galled the shield	2 c
Should tongue that time and trumpet of that field	3 b
And, on the fighter, forge his glorious day.	4 c
On Christ they do; on martyr well they may.	5 b
Strokes once that gashed the flesh and galled the shield	2 d
Now tongue that time and trumpet of that field	3 c
And on the fighter forge his glorious day,	4 d
On Christ thy do; on martyr well they may;	5 c
	H. i. 47 r

Plates 508, 509   OET No. 176: In honour of St. Alphonsus Rodriguez -- MS. 1: H¹ (1,2)

[H¹] H.i.46v, 47r and v--autograph rough pencil draft, revised in darker pencil. It occupied the three blank pages of folded notepaper with Dr. Dunne's letter to "Fr. Hospkins" (sic), 28 Sept. 1888 (Plate 510). The draft was completed that same day.

[opposite] 46 verso--a much enlarged reproduction. Deletions, changes include: 1a "grow/flower"   2a orig. "And every scar of limb, or dint of shield," rev. to "The scar that galls the limb, and that dints the shield,"   4a "Ca[rve?]" mended to "And"   "-d" before "day"   6a "But where/say the war was/were secret and we wield"   6b orig. "But say the war were secret," revised to "But when the war's within, the sword we wield"   7a "Unseen/Not seen"   8a,b "the fiercest" revised to "fieriest" or [bracketed below] "from fieriest"   4b commas added   "in/on"   10b "That carves, or" revised to "Carves, that God that"   11a "tall trees/pines"   13a,b "Years after/Those years on"   14b "While/That"   14a [probably the first form of the line] "For forty years Alphonso kept/watched"   9c "quarried" mended to "quarries mountains"   10d "Carved" mended to "Carves"   11b "Veins violets"

[above] 47 recto: 13c "Yea[rs]/Those"   10f "World-wright"   2c "shild" [for "shield"]   5c "Christ thy [they] do;" (note how small the u.c. "C" is here and in 5b).

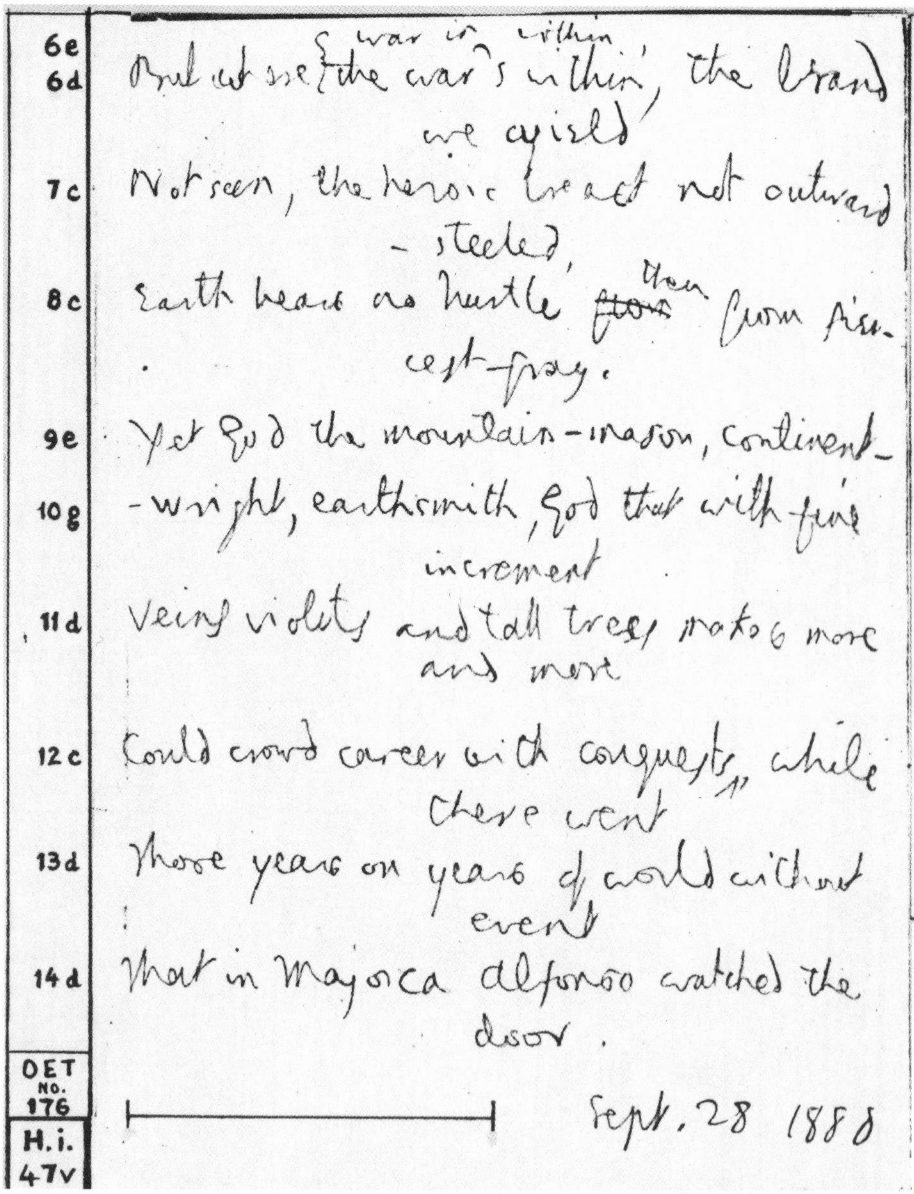

6e
6d
But let me ſee {war is within'}
the war's within', the brand
we wield'

7c
Not seen, the heroic breast not outward
- steeled,

8c
Earth hears no hustle' ~~from~~ then from fier-
cest-fray.

9e
Yet God the mountain-mason, continent-

10g
-wright, earthsmith, God that with-fire
increment

11d
Veins violets and tall trees makes more
and more

12c
Could crowd career with conquests, while
there went

13d
Those years on years of world without
event

14d
That in Majorca Alfonso watched the
door.

Sept. 28 1888

OET
NO.
176

H.i.
47v

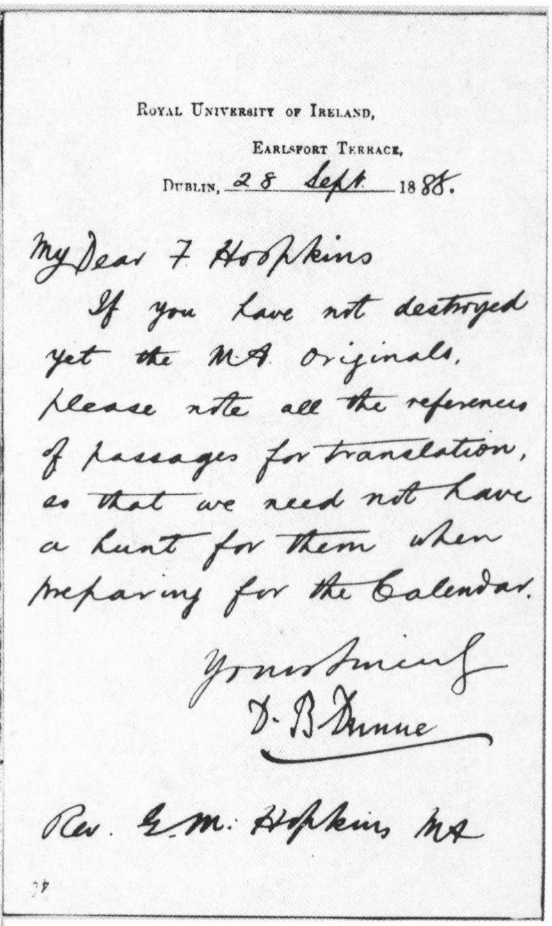

ROYAL UNIVERSITY OF IRELAND,
EARLSFORT TERRACE,
DUBLIN, *28 Sept* 18 88.

My Dear F Hospkins
    If you have not destroyed
yet the MS. originals,
please note all the references
of passages for translation,
so that we need not have
a hunt for them when
preparing for the Calendar.
        Yours sincerely
        D. B Dunne

Rev. G. M. Hopkins MA

Plate 510   OET No. 176: In honour of St. Alphonsus Rodriguez -- MS. 1 (3)

[left] H.i.47 verso--autograph pencil draft, cont. from Plate 509. Note the corrections, some in darker pencil, e.g., in 6d "w" of "where" reshaped   "yield" mended to "wield" (a slip in MSS. L and B also).   8c from/then from fiercest fray"   11d "tres" mended to "trees"   12c orig. "conquest," then "conquests," then comma replaced (?)   Date intends "1888".

[right] H.i.46 recto--letter to GMH from Dr. D.B. Dunne, Catholic Secretary of the Royal University of Ireland. GMH used the three blank pages of its notepaper to make a pencil draft of No. 176--completed the same day as the letter (H[1]).

The Royal University calendars (or catalogues) published in an appendix all the previous year's examination papers, but to save space textual passages set for translation were indicated only by line references. It would appear that GMH on some previous occasion had delayed the editors while he searched for passages he had himself chosen. The suppressed irritation of the letter is softened by the squeezing in of "My" before "Dear", but Hopkins, who was sensitive about his name and easily upset by orders from university officials, may well have felt slighted at being addressed as "Father Hospkins" (cf. the "s" in "Yours [Sincerely]" and see L.i.153, 295; L.iii.173, 176). The name is correctly spelt at the foot.

Dr. D.B. Dunne as a brilliant young student in Rome had taken doctorates in both Theology and Philosophy by the age of 23; returning to Ireland he joined the staff of Newman's Catholic University, where he came to occupy two chairs, largely sinecures, Law and Logic. When the new Royal University replaced it, he became its Catholic Secretary (one of its two registrars, responsible for the University College in Stephen's Green).

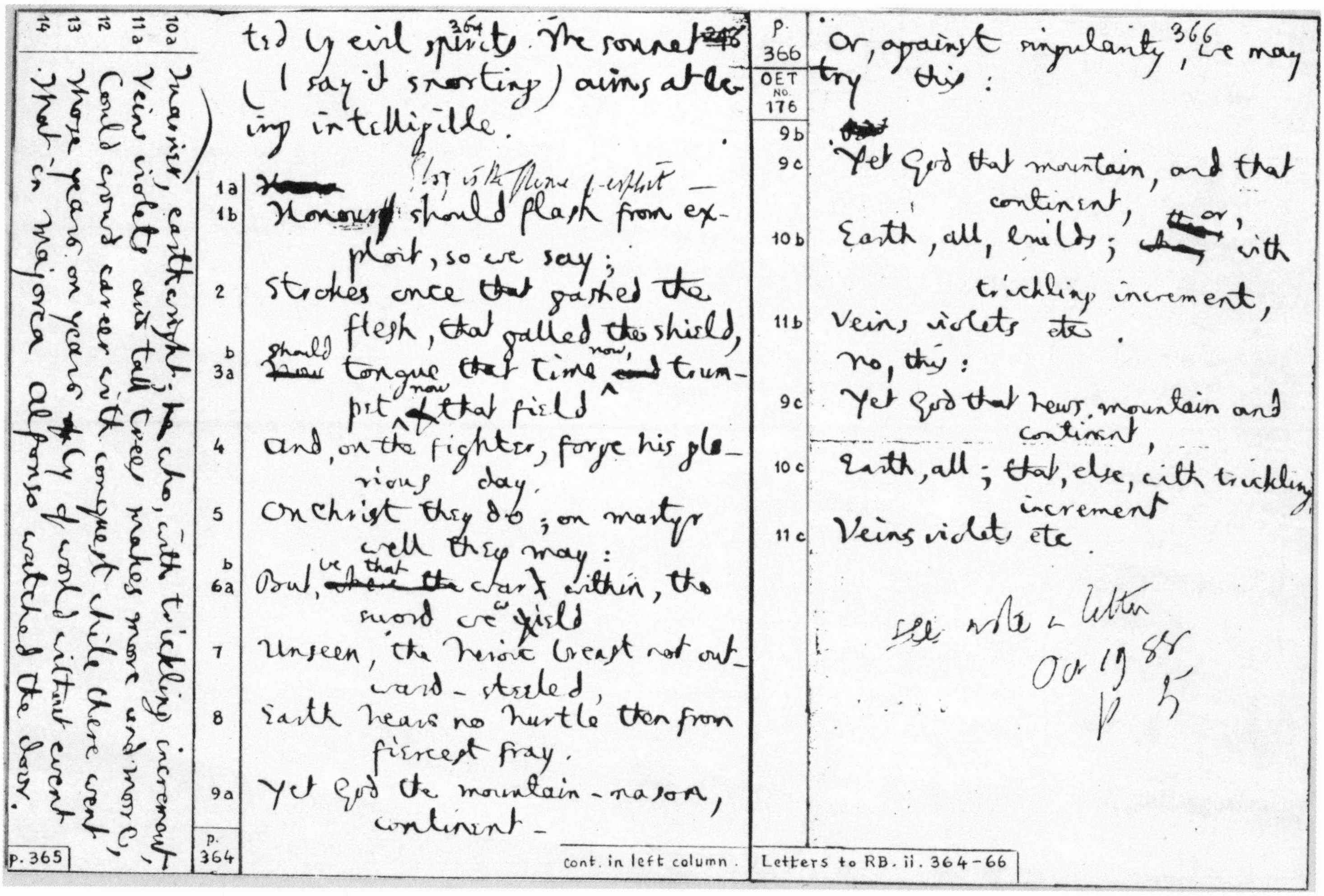

PLATE 511. OET 176. *St. Alphonsus Rodriguez* • *337*

Plate 511   OET No. 176: In honour of St. Alphonso Rodriguez -- MS. 2

[L] L.i.293 (MS. Letters to Bridges, ii.364-66)--autograph revision in ink, part of a letter from GMH to RB, 3 Oct. 1888. Above the poem RB has written in pencil "Glory is the flame of exploit", his recollection of another version of the first line which GMH sent him in a later letter, 19 Oct. 1888 (L.i.297): it should have run "Glory is a flame off exploit, so we say". At the end of p.366 RB adds "see note in letter Oct 19 88 p 5".

Deletions, etc.: 1a Line begun too far to left, so the beginning of "Honour" was blotted out   1b "Honours"   3a "Now" "and" "of"   6a "where the war's" "yield" (i.e. "wield")

Lines 10-14 written at right angles on p.365.   10a "he"   13 "of"   Page 366: 9b "But"   10b "who, then, or,"

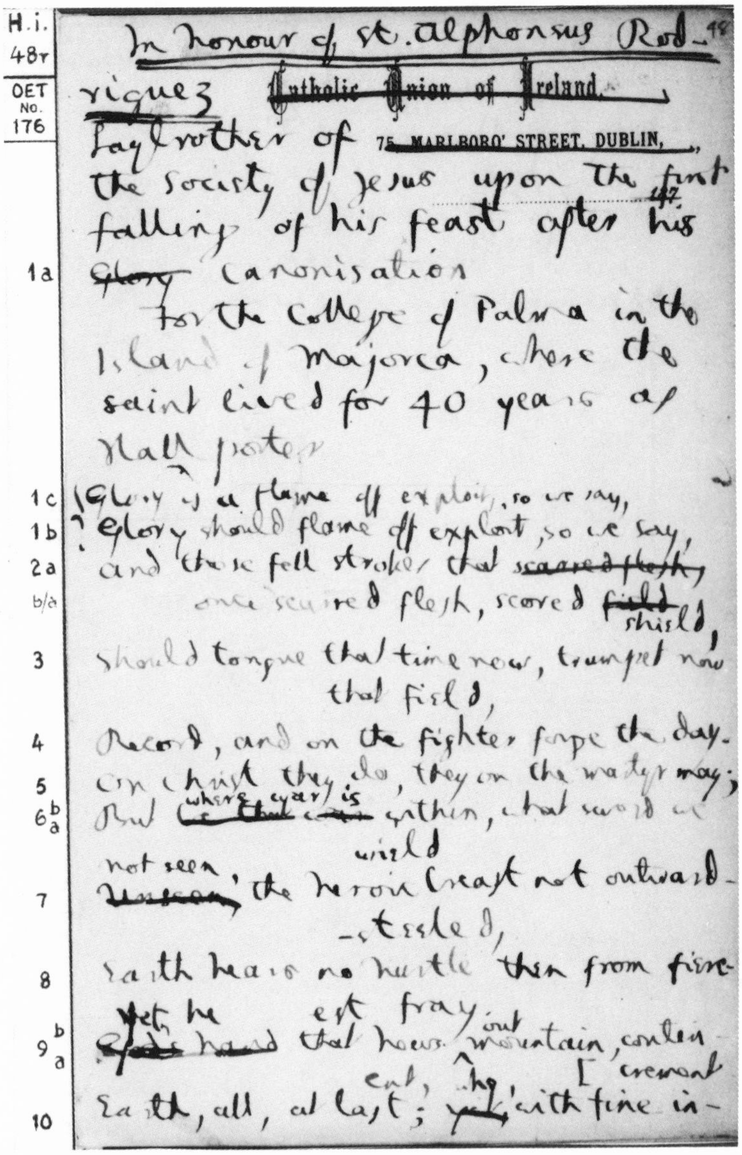

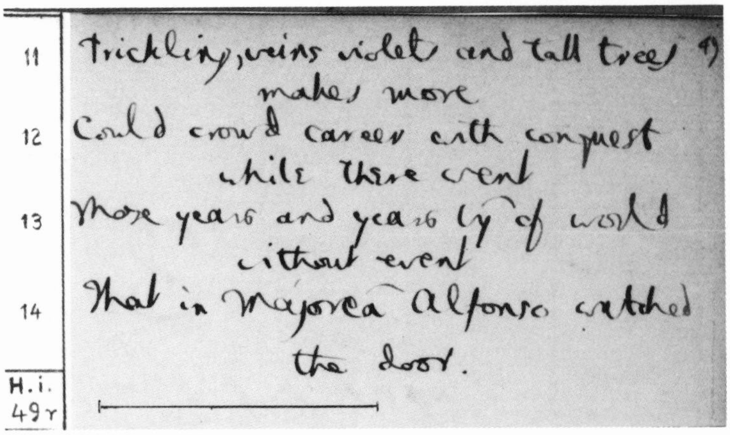

Plate 512   OET No. 176: In honour of St. Alphonsus Rodriguez -- MS. 3: H²

[H²] H.i.48r, 49r--autograph revised draft in weak ink, on a double sheet watermarked 1878, with 48v blank, and a rapid pencil sketch of a man "Cleaning Dr. Molloy's windows" on 49v (see Plate 503). The poem originally began below the printed address and date line, but the first word "Glory" (1a) was deleted when the title was extended.

   Deletions include: 2a "scarred flesh," 2b "field" (absent-minded anticipation of 3) 6a "be that war" 7 "Unseen," 9a "God's hand" 10 "yet,"

   Dr. Catherine Phillips regards this as the final version because it bears the same printed letterhead as GMH's letter to RB on Oct. 19 1888, and is the only MS. to include as an alternative (though not finally adopt) the version of ℓ.1 ("Glory is a flame of exploit") which GMH quoted in the letter as the current reading, adding "I think it must so stand" (L.i.297). This proves that H² was written about the same time as the letter and that GMH then thought the first line quoted was final.

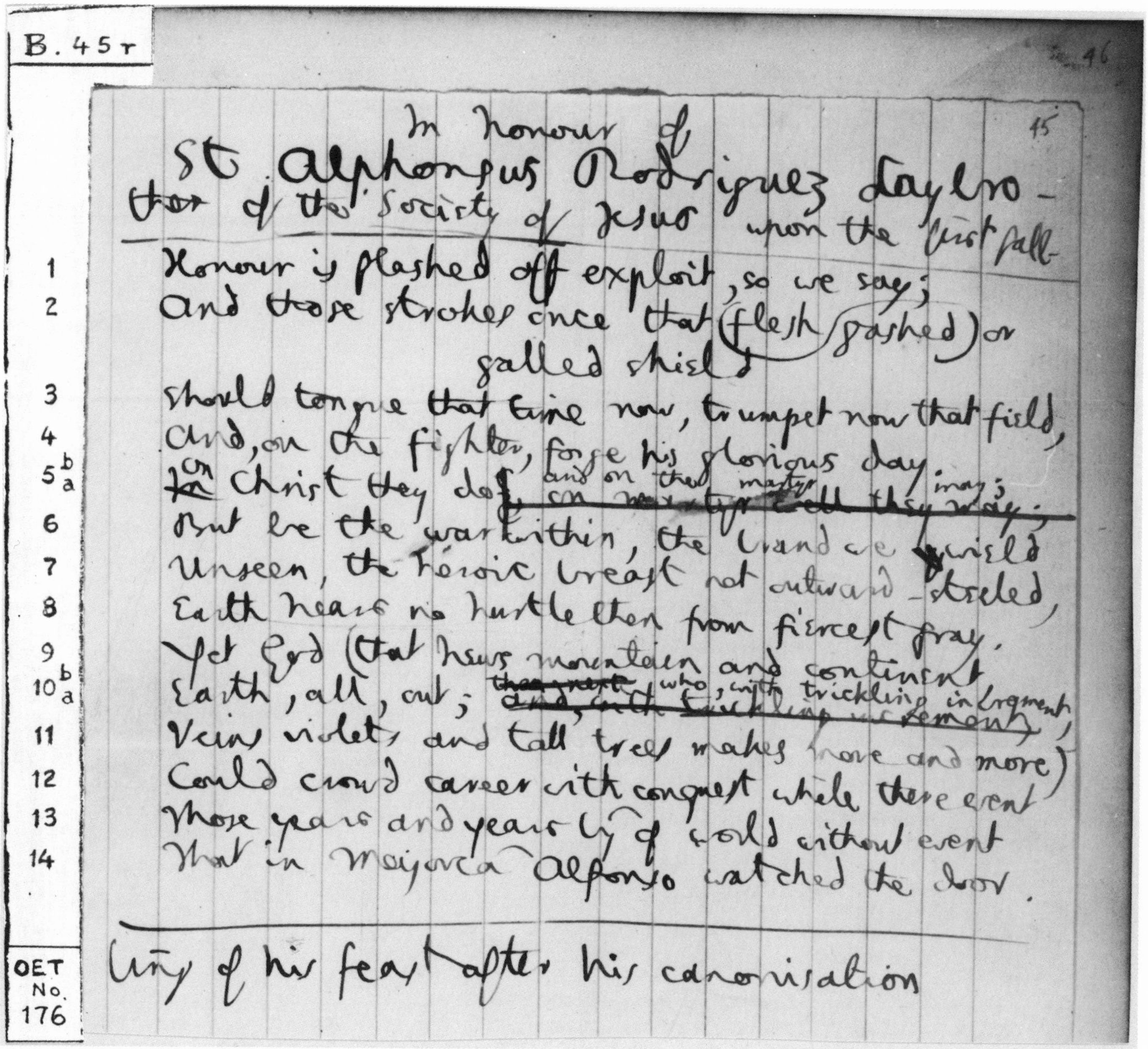

PLATE 513. OET 176. *St. Alphonsus Rodriguez* • *339*

B. 45 r

45

In honour of

St. Alphonsus Rodriguez Laybro —
that of the Society of Jesus upon the first fall

1   Honour is flashed off exploit, so we say;
2   And those strokes once that (flesh (gashed) or
       galled shield
3   Should tongue that time now, trumpet now that field,
4   And, on the fighter, forge his glorious day.
5   On Christ they do, and on the martyr all they may;
6   But be the war within, the brand we wield
7   Unseen, the heroic breast not outward-steeled,
8   Earth hears no hurtle then from fiercest fray.
9   Yet God (that hews mountain and continent
10   Earth, all, out; who, with trickling increment
11   Veins violets and tall trees makes more and more)
12   Could crowd career with conquest while there went
13   Those years and years by of world without event
14   That in Majorca Alfonso watched the door.

Any of his feast after his canonisation

OET No. 176

Plate 513   OET No. 176: In honour of St. Alphonsus Rodriguez -- MS. 4: B

B.45r--autograph draft in faded ink, on ruled paper, probably the final one, pasted onto f.46 of album B. The title was extended after the poem had been copied out, and is continued below it: what appears to be a third "*l*" in "falling" is no doubt an opening parenthesis which was not closed.

Deletions, etc.: Title "Lay" mended (u.c. → *l*.c.?) 2 "flesh" and "gashed" transposed   5 bracket was crossed out when the original smudged version was deleted: ", on martyr well they may"   6 "*y*wield"   10a "and, with trickling increment, [the cross-stroke of the final "t" curls down to form a comma]; "and" revised to "then next"; finally "who, with trickling increment,". This version has been traditionally regarded as the final one, perhaps later than the version sent to Majorca (which has not yet been found in spite of extensive efforts I have made with the generous help of Spanish friends).

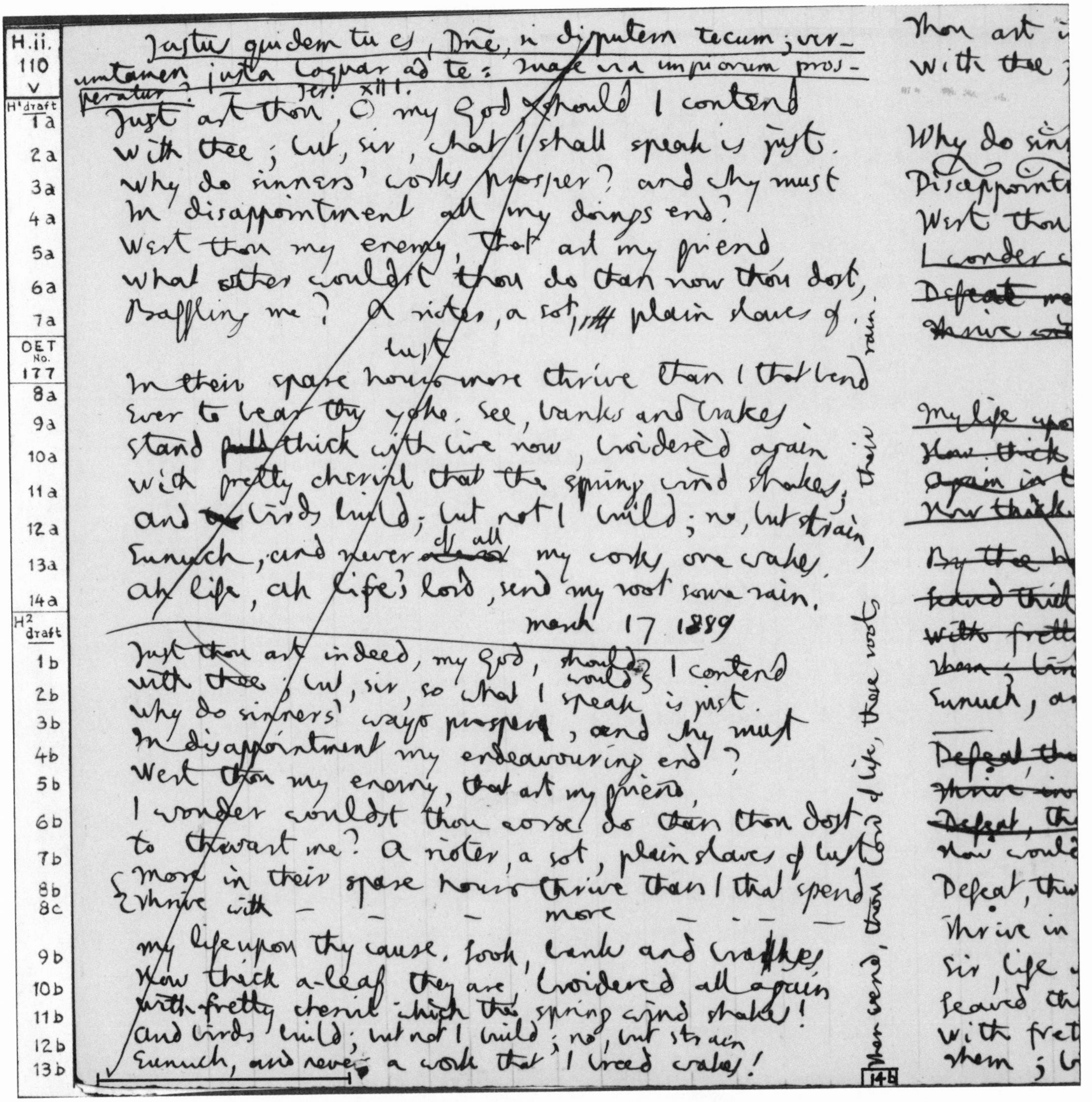

Plate 514   OET No. 177: "Thou art indeed just, Lord" -- MS. 1: H (1)

[above] H.ii.110v--autograph, written in ink on left hand half of a foolscrap page turned sideways, with continuation (111r) on the right. The top part, [H¹] (1a to 14a), the earliest surviving version, was at first intended as a faircopy, ending with a date. It has few changes, though many letters are mended: 7a dash deleted before "plain" and comma moved left.   10a "full"   Note: the epigraph was squeezed in later ("Dn̄e" is an abbreviation for "Domine")   6a "w̄" ["worse"? see 6b] mended to "other"   10a "live" (sic, for "life"; cf. 14a "live's" mended to "life's") 12a "bur̄ birds"   13a "a wor/of all". Whole top half crossed through with a single ink line.

[lower part] [H²]: 1b, 2b pencil line through "thou" and "thee"   3b "prosper$ end" (mended to "and")   9b "banks and branks" (mended to "brakes")   11b "shakes!" (the "s" returns on itself)   14b squeezed in vertically. Whole page crossed through in ink.

Plate 515   OET No. 177: "Thou art indeed just, Lord" -- MS. 1 (cont.): H (2 and 3)

[opposite-top] H.ii.111r--[H³] third autograph draft, alongside 110v. Bad blots on poor paper obscure some ends of words, e.g. 7f "revellers"   10h "again"   12d "build". Deleted words (some crossed out twice) include: 2c "these

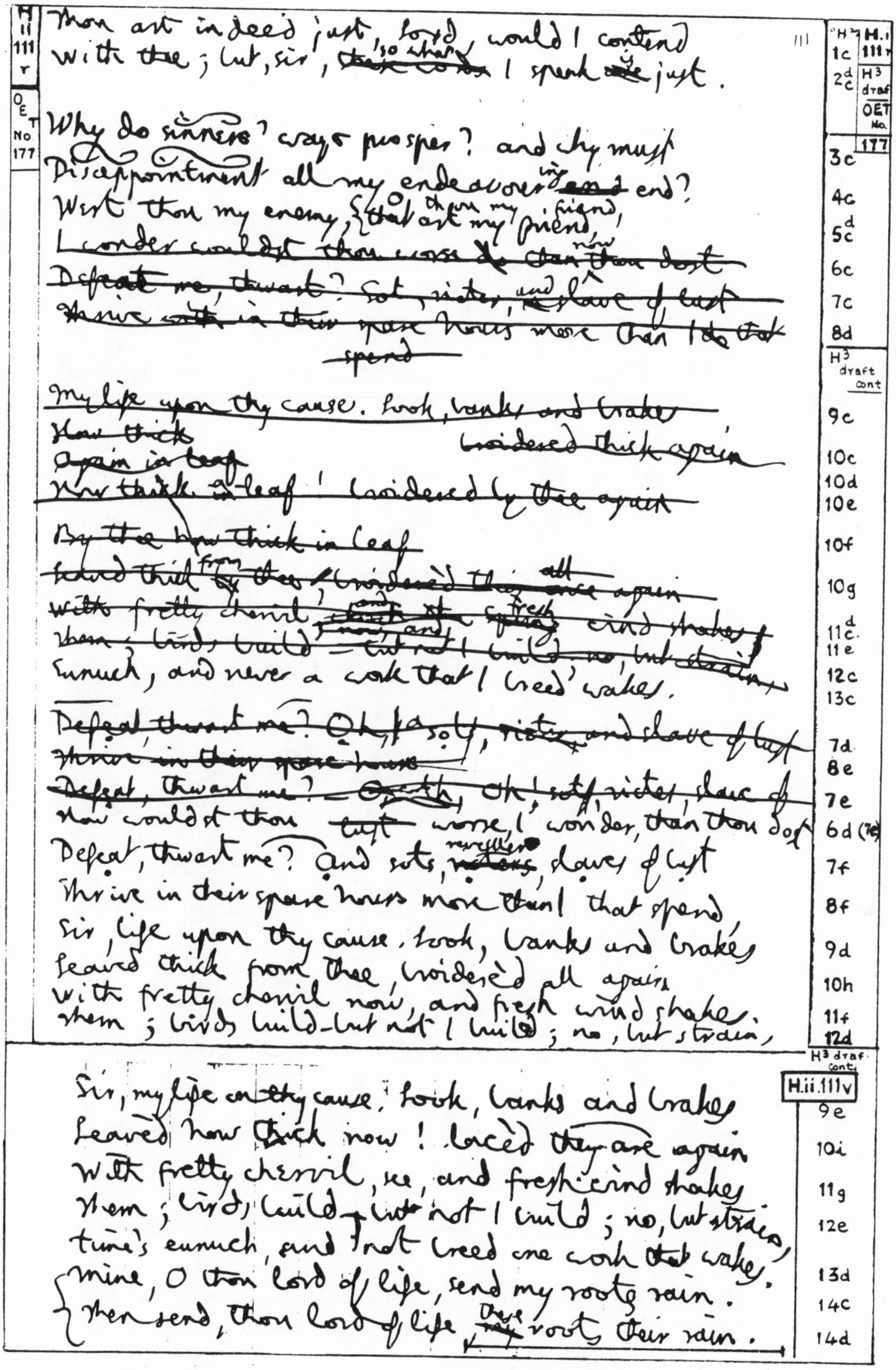

PLATE 515. OET 177. "Thou art indeed just, Lord" • 341

words...are" 4c "end" 6c "wouldst...do" 7c "rioter, slave" 8d "with...do" 10e "in leaf!" (dot over "i" looks like a hyphen before "a") revised to "a-leaf!" 10g originally "Leaved thick by thee, broidered this once again" then "broidered all again" 11c "which the Spring" revised to "and fresh" then ", now, and fresh wind shakes;" 7d originally "Oh! sots" then "Oh, a sot, rioter," 7e originally "O, soth," (sic) then "Oh! sots," 6d "lust" (from end of 7e) 7f "rioters/revellers". Note black balls (explained L.i.109) below stressed syllables: in 7d ("feat" "Oh" "sot"), 7e ("feat"), 7f ("feat" "And" "riot" "slaves" "lust")

[bottom] <u>111v</u>--continuation of H³ on back with blotches showing through from 111r (e.g. below "thick" (10i) and in 12e, 13d 12e semicolon replaced by dash before "but"; "strain," ends the line 14d "my".

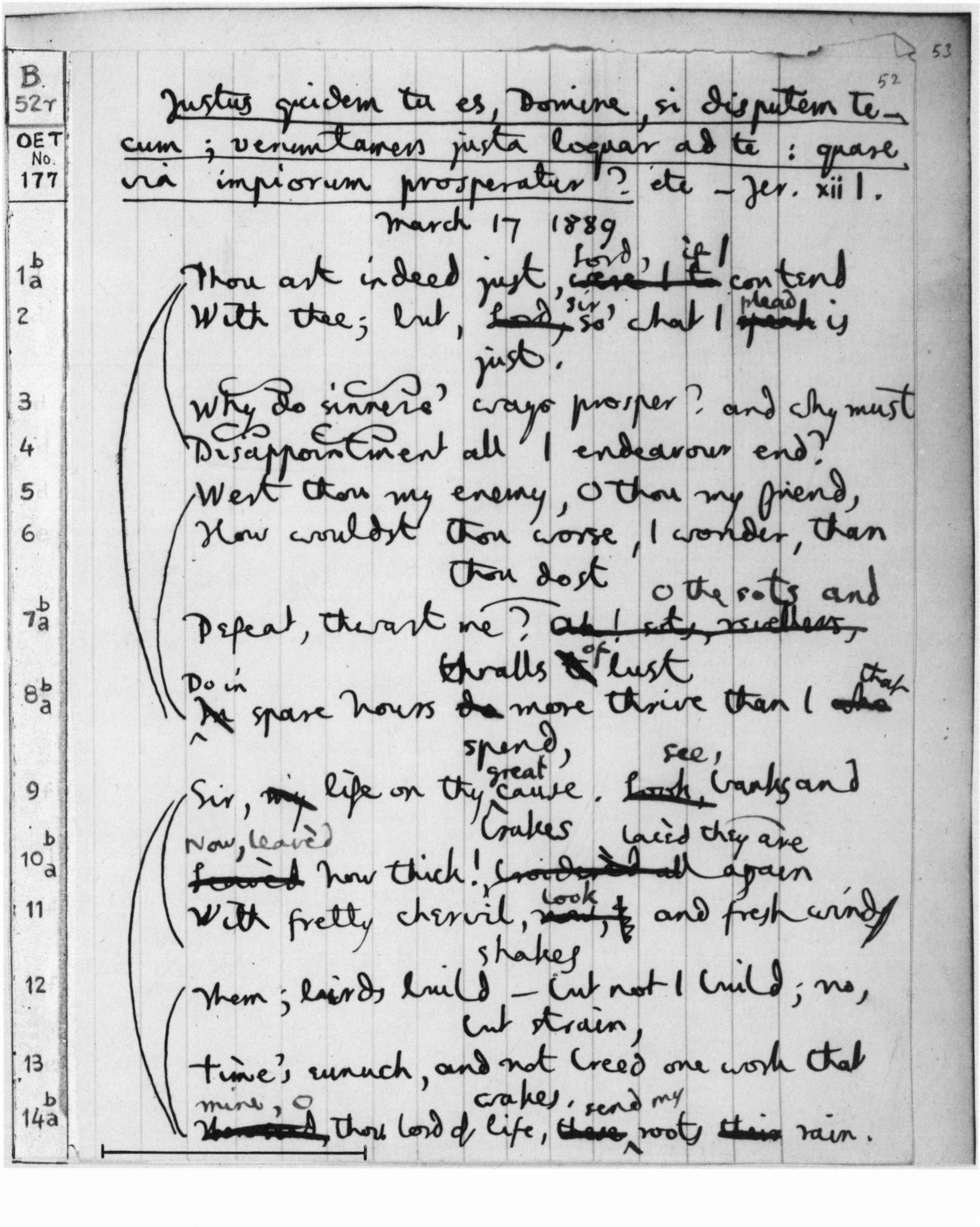

Justus quidem tu es, Domine, si disputem tecum; verumtamen justa loquar ad te : quare
via impiorum prosperatur? etc – Jer. xii 1.

march 17 1889

Thou art indeed just, ~~Lord~~ Lord, if I contend
With thee; but, ~~Lord,~~ sir, so what I plead is
  just.
Why do 'sinners' ways prosper? and why must
Disappointment all I endeavour end?
Wert thou my enemy, O thou my friend,
How wouldst thou worse, I wonder, than thou dost
  Defeat, thwart me? ~~ah! sir,~~ O the sots and
  thralls of lust
Do in spare hours more thrive than I that
  spend,
Sir, life upon thy cause. See, banks and
  brakes laced they are
Now, leavèd how thick! ~~broidered all~~ again
With fretty chervil, look, and fresh winds
  shakes
them; birds build – but not I build; no,
  but strain,
time's eunuch, and not breed one work that
  wakes.
Mine, O thou lord of life, send my roots rain.

Plate 516   <u>OET No. 177</u>: <u>"Thou art indeed just, Lord"</u> -- MS. 2: B

 B.52r, same poor quality ruled paper as H 110v-111v, mounted on album B.f.53. Autograph faircopy, with revisions mostly in faded brown ink.   2 "Lord, sir," [prob. not "Sir"--contr. 9] "speak"   3,4 counterpoint signs as usual indicate reversed (trochaic) rhythm.   7a "sl[aves]" mended to "thralls to lust"   10a orig. "Leavèd how thick, broidered all"; revised in black ink, "laced they are", slur added later (weak brown ink)   11 "With" (dot over "i" looks like accent); "chervil now," revised to "chervil, look,...winds"   12 "bu" mended to "birds"   14a "Then send,...these...their". This plate is reproduced and transcribed by Peter Croft, <u>Autograph Poetry in the English Language</u>, Cassells, 1973, Vol.ii.142: he sometimes quotes the revised reading before the orig. if the caret comes first (e.g. 8). I had the privilege of checking this MS. in Scotland Yard's Document Examination Laboratory with their Infrared Image Converter and a zoom lens which enlarged up to 40x.

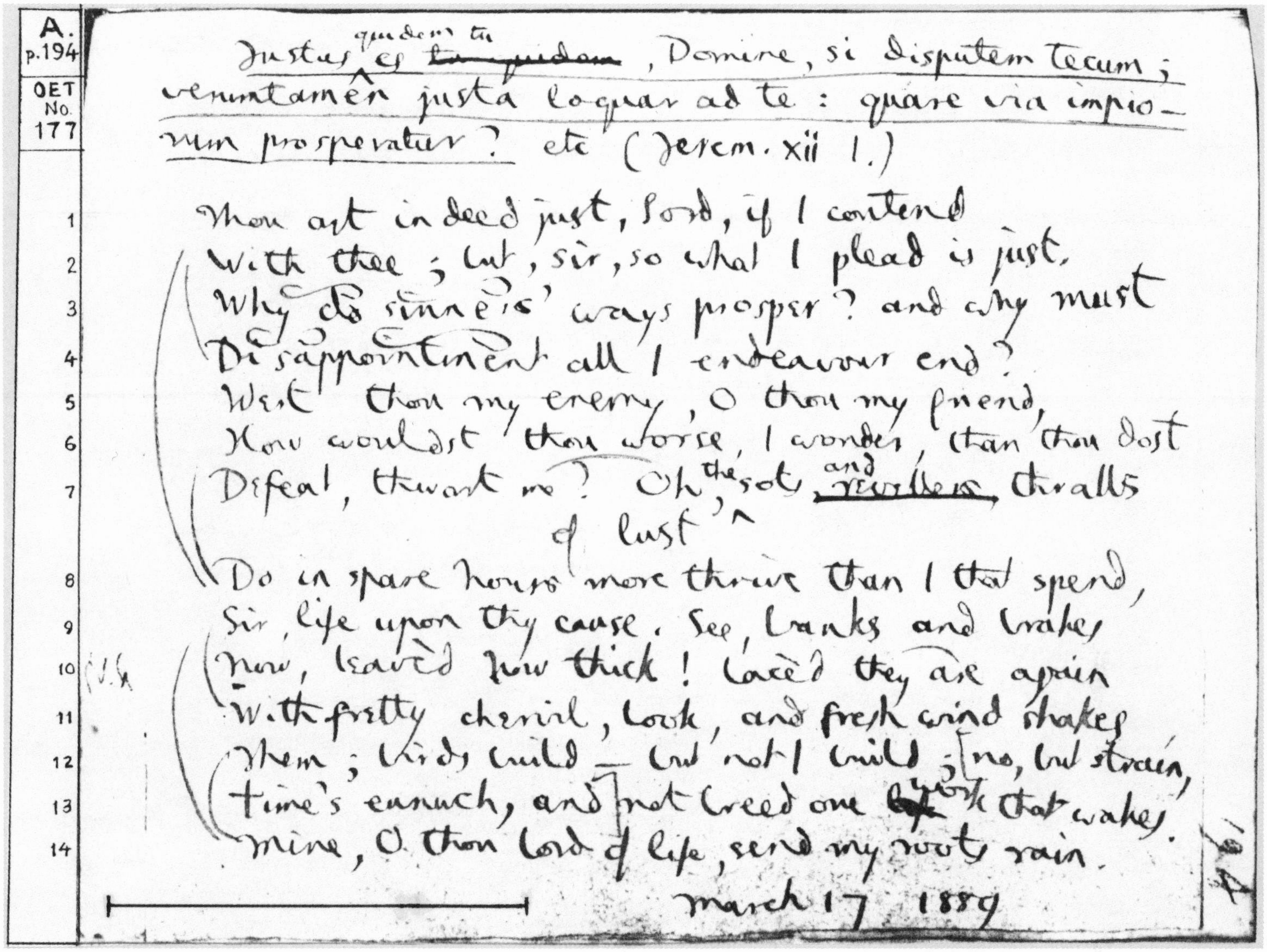

PLATE 517.   OET 177.   "Thou art indeed just, Lord"   •   343

A.
p.194

OET
No.
177

Justus quidem tu es, Domine, si disputem tecum;
verumtamen justa loquar ad te : quare via impiorum prosperatur? etc (Jerem. xii 1.)

1 Thou art indeed just, Lord, if I contend
2 with thee ; but, sir, so what I plead is just,
3 Why do sinners' ways prosper? and why must
4 Disappointment all I endeavour end?
5 Wert thou my enemy, O thou my friend,
6 How wouldst thou worse, I wonder, than thou dost
7 Defeat, thwart me? Oh the sots and thralls of lust
8 Do in spare hours more thrive than I that spend,
9 Sir, life upon thy cause. See, banks and brakes
10 Now, leavèd how thick! lacèd they are again
11 with fretty chervil, look, and fresh wind shakes
12 Them ; birds build — but not I build ; no, but strain,
13 time's eunuch, and not breed one work that wakes.
14 mine, O thou lord of life, send my roots rain.

march 17 1889

Plate 517   OET No. 177: "Thou art indeed just, Lord" -- MS. 3: A

A.p.194--autograph on grey paper, embossed on the other side "Monasterevan/Ireland": final version, embodying the revisions which in B were interlined (except in 9), and like them written in Miss Cassidy's "shocking" weak ink (L.i.303). The correction in the epigraph is due to a slip in copying: so may "life/work" in 13 (see 14)   7 for the revision here, cf. B.

RB in 10 underlines the "N" of "Now" and the "h" of "how", confusingly similar in shape, and draws attention to them in the margin. In 12, 13 he encloses in pencilled square brackets six words for which (probably in 1889, for discussion with GMH) he tentatively suggests on the blank page above "head and brain/Toil impotent", followed by "nor flower [one work that wakes]" (cf. L.i.117-23).

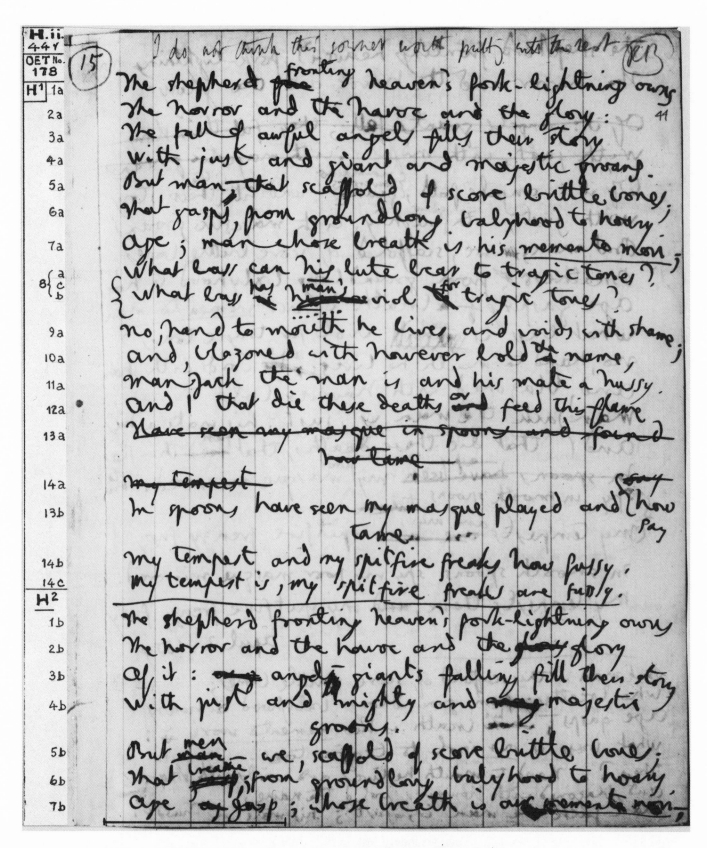

Plate 518   OET No. 178: "The shepherd's brow, fronting forked lightning" -- MS. 1

H.ii.44r--earliest surviving autograph, quite close to a faircopy, but with revisions of 8, 13, 14 [=H¹]; followed by a slight revise of 1-7 [=H²]. These occupy the first page of a folded foolscap sheet; further minor revisions follow on 44v, 45r, with No. 179 on 45v.

Obscurities (Note: When letters still wet were deleted, blobs sometimes washed out the shapes, making recovery uncertain.): [H¹] 1a "fac[ing?]"   5a "man,--that"   8b originally "What bass is his yo[ice?] viol to tragic tones?" revised to "has man's" (the seven dots below "his" probably marked the need for change)   10a "with" (note the long sweeping curve down from the dot over "i") "a/the name" ("the" is not deleted)   12a "and"   13a "how tame"   13b "say"   [H²] 2b "glory [with a poor "r"] glory" 3b probably "a g angels,-giants"--probably meant for "angel-giants", but hyphen looks like a dash   4b "mag" [for "maj"] 5b "man"   6b "gasp;"   7b "a[?] gasp" ["g" like a "j"] "our memento mori--,". Above the poem, RB's pencil reads: "I do not think this sonnet worth putting with the rest RB". He included it in the First edn., but among the "Unfinished Poems and Fragments" (p.87).

PLATE 519. OET 178. "The shepherd's brow" • 345

OET No. 178 **H.ii.44 verso**

H³

1c The shepherd fronting heaven's fork-lightning own; and I
2c The horror and the havoc and the glory my te
3c Of it: angels—giants, fell, they fill their story
4c with just, with might, with majestic groan.
3d Of it: angels fall, giants; and fill their story   The she / The ho
4d with just, with mighty, with majestic groans   Of
5c But man; we, scaffold of score brittle bones;   Of in
6c Breathers, from ground long babyhood to hoary   But in
7c Age gasping breath is our memento mori: Who
8d what ease is our viol for tragic tone?   Age
9b No, hard to mouth he lives, and voids with shame;   What / xe!
10b And, blazoned with however bold the name,   The th
11b man Jack the man is, just; his mate a hussy.   the h
12b And I that die these deaths, that feed this flame,   Of it / Of it
13c my poor masque mirrored: tame   But
13e spy in smooth spoons   who
14d my tempests and my spitfire frenzy fussy.   Age
13f In smooth spoons spy my poor masque mirrored: tame   what / xe!
14e My tempests there, and my spitfire frenzy fussy,   and
april 3 1889   man / and / that

H⁴

5d But man — thy scaffold of score brittle bones;   and
6d who breathes, from ground long babyhood to hoary   that
7d age gasps his breath is his memento mori:
8e what bass is our viol to tragic tone
9c then? — hard to mouth he lives and voids with shame;   my t
10c And, blazoned with however bold the name,
11c Man-Jack the man is, just; his mate a hussy.

Plate 519   OET No. 178: "The shepherd's brow" -- MS. 2

H.ii.44v--autograph, second complete version [H³]; the minor revisions of 5 to the end (begun at the foot), are continued on 45r [H⁴]. Obscurities: [H³] 3c "angels—giants [fell mended to] fall;" 5c "man," rev to ";" 6c "Breathers,," 7c "gasping --a[?]" 8d "is man's/our" 9b "lives, he/and" 10b "And I" [confused with 12b, mended to] blazoned" 13c "spoons have seen/espy"..."how tame" 14d "tempests are and"...fussy,[?]"

[H⁴] 6d after "breathes" a blot from 44r (4b) obscures "; from" (not deleted) 7d "gasps, whose" rev. to "--his"..."mori +:" 11c "Man-Jack" (hyphen).

OET No. 178   H. ii. 45 recto

And I that die these death, that fan this flame,
that ... in smooth spoons 'spy life's masque mirrored: tame
my tempests there and all my fever fussy.

The shepherd's eye fronting forked lightning owns
The horror and the havoc and the glory
Of it. Angels fall, towers, from heaven — a
Of just, giant, majestic groans.
But man — scaffold of score brittle bones;
Who breathes, from ground long babyhood to hoary
Age gasps; whose breath is our memento mori —
What bass is our viol for tragic tones?
He! Hand to mouth he lives, and voids with shame;

The shepherd's brow, fronting forked lightning, owns
the horror and the havoc and the glory
Of it. Angels fall, they are towers, from heaven — a story
Of just, majestical, and giant groans.
But man — we, scaffold of score brittle bones;
Who breathe, from ground long babyhood to hoary
Age gasp; whose breath is our memento mori —
What bass is our viol for tragic tones?
He! Hand to mouth he lives, and voids with shame;
and, blazoned in however bold the name,
man Jack the man is, just; his mate a hussy.
And I that die these death, that feed this flame,
that ... in smooth spoons spy life's masque mirrored: tame
my tempests there, my fire and fever fussy.

                        April 3 1889

H.ii. 45 r

PLATE 521. Notes on Plate 520   •   *347*

[opposite] Plate 520   OET No. 178: "The shepherd's brow" -- MS. 3

H.ii.45r--autograph, continuing [H⁵] the revision of 1-14, then slightly

reworking 1-9 [H⁶] before making a faircopy (the final version) of the whole

sonnet [H⁷].

Obscurities: 1d originally "fork-lightning" ("ed" squeezed in)   3e, 4e,f

"of mended to Of it Of it, angels [mended to].Angels...down from heaven/

their". Then next ": their story/Has just, has giant, has mage" [for "majestic"];

revised as "--a story/Of just, of" etc.   5e "this/we,"   6e "breathes/," 7e

"gasps" "his"   9d "Man!" Grey blots obscure "voids" and [H⁶] 1e "forked".

6f "breathe /," 13h "spy m[y] mended to "life's"..."mirrored:/[?]"

RB's note in the right margin is linked by a pencil line to "groundlong"

underlined; it reads "see first p" (i.e., f.44r, line 6a) where "groundlong" is

clearly a single compound word.

H. ii. **45v**	
OET **No.** **179**	

I have a perfectly finished copy of this.

1a The fine delight that fathers thought, the strong
2b/a Spur, live and lanced like the blowpipe flame,
3b/a Breathes once and, quenchèd faster than it came
4a Yet leaves the mind a mother of immortal song.
5b/a Nine months it, nay years, nine years long
6b/a The widow of an insight lost she lives, with aim
7 Seized and her hand at work now never wrong.
8a/b

9a Delight the sire of muse, my soul wants this;
10a I the rare rapture of an inspiration
11a O in my lagging lines then where you miss
12a The fire, the fall, the courage, the creation
13a Believe my withered world know no such bliss
14a Rebuke no more, but read my explanation.

11c O if then in my lagging lines, you miss
11b O in my lagging lines then you who miss
12b The fire, the fall, the courage, the creation
13c my withered world that breaks into no such bliss
14f Yield, you with certain sighs, our explanation.
13d This withered world of me, that breathe no bliss,
14d Now, yields you, with some sighs, our explanation.

9b But fire the sire of muse, my soul needs this;
10b I want the rare rapture of an inspiration
11e O in my lagging lines then since you who miss
12c The flame, the flag, the carol, the creation,
d will wing, waft, cry, carol and creation,
e the wing, the waft, the carol, the creation,   April 22 1889

PLATE 523. OET 179. *To R.B.* • *349*

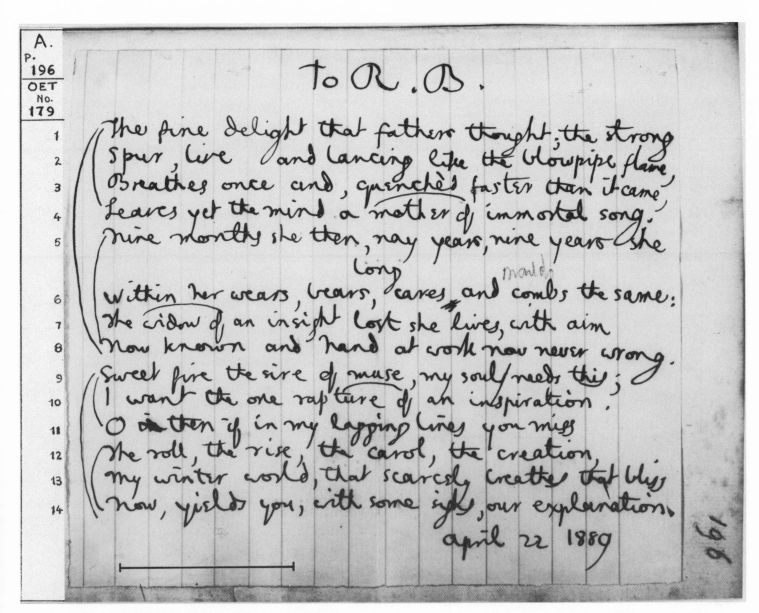

Plate 522   OET No. 179: To R.B. -- MS. 1: H

[opposite page] H.ii.45v--autograph draft, on the back of No. 178. RB notes in pencil at the top: "I have a perfectly finished copy of this" [i.e. A, p.196].

Obscurities: 2b [interlined] "lanced-out like the"   The apparent dash after "out" is only the dot over the "i" of "like" in 2a (cf. 7 "lives, with"; 9a "Delight")   3a "Ma[y]/Can/speak spring and,"   rev. 3b "Breathes once, then" [GMH prolonged the tail of the "e" in "once" through the dash/dot from "spring" (3a)]   The hinge or "guard" covers the ends of 3a "came" (no comma), 13a "bliss:", and the date "1889"--all faintly pencilled in for this plate   6b "wears, bears, cares"   7 "And"   9a "mind needs" 10a "I want"   11a "if"   12a "keenness/courage"   13a "kindles" "bliss:" (note the line curling up to dot the "i")   14a "And"   11b preceded 11c. Note the short horizontal stroke above its "O", marking the end of the first draft: this stroke was later deleted and replaced by a line running the whole width of the page so that 11c could be squeezed in. 11b "laboured" replaced above and below by "lagging".   13b 1st. "My", 2nd "Our", 3rd "My" reinstated. ..."breaks into" ["s" almost a straight line] revised to "that breaks to"..."this" [slip]   14b "But yields" revised to "Yields", apostrophe [slip] deleted..."some"..."this"   11c, 13c, 14c, 14d, 12d, 12e were probably inserted after 9b to 12c and the date.   9b "But/Sweet fire"   10b "the" changed to "that"   11d "laboured lines" [last "e" has no loop] revised to "lagging"   12c "flame, the flow, the courage,/carol,/the creation,"   12d "waft, cry, carol, and"   12e "The wing"

Plate 523   OET No. 179: To R.B. -- MS. 2: A

[above] A.p.196--autograph faircopy, pasted into album A. GMH's changes: 6 "cares,"   9 "souls"   11 "if" (cf. Plate 522, 11a).

RB has pencilled above the difficult word "combs" (6) a possible substitute, taken from No. 151, ℓ.104.

The Irish Monthly.   *Vol. XIV, 1886*

(668)

NURSERY RHYMES.

No. II.—SING A SONG OF SIXPENCE.

SING a song of sixpence,
    A bag full of rye ;
Four-and-twenty blackbirds
    Baked in a pie.

When the pie was opened,
    The birds began to sing ;
And wasn't that a dainty dish
    To lay before the king ?

The king was in his parlour
    Counting out his money ;
The queen was in the pantry
    Eating bread and honey ;

The maid was in the garden
    Spreading out the clothes :
Up jumps a little bird
    And snaps off her nose.

(i)   IDEM LATINE REDDITUM.

Denariorum sex cane canticum,
2 Plenum secalis concine sacculum,
    Dum quatuor crusto latentes
4   Bisque decem merulæ coquuntur.

Quando reclusum crustum erat, alites
6 Cœpere cunctæ carmina fundere.
    Nonne ista laudandi saporis
8   Esca fuit statuenda regi ?

Aes rex in aulâ dinumerat suum,
10 Regina cellâ mel cereremque edit ;
    Pandentis ancillæ per hortum
12   Lintea, nasum avicella raptat.

Nursery Rhymes.   669

(ii) CARMEN SEX DENARIORUM.

Versio Altera.

Sex Denariorum
2   Cane canticum,
Secalis cerealis
4   Plenum sacculum :
Quatuor et viginti
6   Nigræ merulæ
In crusto robusto
8   Sunt conditæ.

Crusto aperto,
10   Cœpere illico
Aves hæ suaves
12   Cantare sedulo :
Nonne fuit ista
14   Esca delicata,
Cœna amœna,
16   Regi præparata ?

Rex in aulâ nummos
18   Computans sedebat ;
Regina in culinâ
20   Cum pane mel edebat.
Famula in horto
22   Lintea pandebat,
Cui nasum abrasum
24   Aviculus carpebat.

O.

(cont. Plate 525

OET [No.180(a) and (b)] published as Appendix C

Plates 524,525   OET No. 180 (publ. as Appendix C): Nursery Rhymes in Latin

Irish Monthly, xiv, 1886: (a) 'Sing a Song of Sixpence', pp.668-9; (b) Three Blind Mice, p.481. I discovered the originals of these witty translations just too late for inclusion in the OET. All three Latin versions are simply signed "O". Hopkins's translation of "Full fathom five" (Plate 467) had no signature when it was printed on p.628; the following year his rendering of "Come unto these yellow sands" was signed "G.H.". In the Irish Monthly articles or poems frequently appeared above single initials, or double or triple ones (e.g. in vol. 18, "S", "W"; F.G., M.R., J.K., etc., etc.,). With single initials the editor probably made no effort to reserve a letter for a particular author. Though Jim Cotter has shown the deep significance of omega for Hopkins, "O" was a modest disguise, a mere zero, used in other numbers of the Irish Monthly by a writer who was clearly not Hopkins: he translated a piece of verse from the Italian, and was the author of a mediocre poem, "The Melancholy Ocean", contributed to The Spectator twelve years earlier (Irish Monthly xiv.384; xviii.502-3). "O" was used by Charles Lever for articles in the Dublin Univ. Magazine up to 1844, and by John Henry Newman (e.g., for four articles on St. Chrysostom in the Rambler, 1859-60). See also Brit. Lib. Cat. sub "O".

Evidence for Hopkins's Authorship. In the OET, pp.512-3, I showed that GMH was thinking about a Latin version of "Three Blind Mice" in Oct. 1884; that there is a strong Jesuit tradition of his authorship (greatly reinforced by the proof on these plates of the accuracy with which the Jesuits have handed down the text, largely orally, for over a century); and I contended that the "linguistic dexterity and witty playing of one sound against another" are in keeping with Hopkins's

PLATE 525. OET 180. Nursery Rhymes in Latin (Appendix C) • *351*

Page 669, cont. from Plate 524   *The Irish Monthly.*

Note.—A distinguished scholar, a Fellow of Magdalen College, Oxford, suspects that this legend, with its tragical conclusion, had a Greek origin. He writes to us as follows :—" Hæc carmina Graeco fonti antiquitus emanasse suspicor; inveni enim versus quosdam valde antiquos, quibus pars certe earundem rerum, nisi fallor, commemorari videtur. Judicet autem qui exemplum corum infra scriptum cum Latinis contulerit.

'Αλλ' ὅτε δὴ πόσιος καὶ ἐδήτυος ἐξ ἔρον ἔντο,
διογενὴς Βασιλεὺς Θαλάμῳ ἐνὶ χρυσὸν ἀριθμῶν
ἵζανεν· ἡ δ'ἀρ ἄνασσα μυχῷ δόμου ὑψηλοῖο
ἀρτον καὶ μέλι ἦσθε καὶ ἤραρε θυμὸν ἐδωδῇ.
εἵματα δ'ἀμφίπολος κήπου περικάλλεος 'εντὸς
λοῦσέν τ' ἐν ποταμῷ κρέμασέν τ'ἐπὶ πείρατι πάντα.
τῇ δ' ἐφάνη μέγα θαῦμ'· ὀρνίθιον οὐράνοθι πρὸ
'εκ νεφέων ποτὶ κῆπον ἐπέσσυτο, τῆς δ'ἀρ' ἔπειτα
ῥῖνας ὀδὰξ ἀπέδρυψε· Διος δ' ἐτελείετο βουλή.

Γ.

<u>The Irish Monthly Vol. xiv 1886</u>

Three Blind Mice.   481

THREE BLIND MICE.

THREE blind mice—see how they run!
  They all run up to the farmer's wife,
She cuts off their tails with a carving knife
Such is the fate of the three blind mice.

LATINE REDDITUM.

Tres oculis capti mures, en quomodo currunt!
Conjugis agricolae curritur usque pedes.
Hæc properat caudas illorum exscindere cultro:
Muribus heu cœcis talia fata tribus!

O.

compositions in English, Latin, Greek and in Welsh his Cywydd. To these arguments we can now add that the versions were published in a Jesuit magazine and in Dublin, and in the very year when GMH began contributing songs from Shakespeare in Latin and Greek to that same periodical.

One peculiarity may also point his way. In his Latin tribute to the Silver Jubilee of Bishop James Brown, OET No. 102(b), ℓ.36, Plates 266-7, he had written "caepimus" for "coepimus", an idiosyncratic spelling based on the analogy of accepted variant pairs (caelum, coelum; caena, coena; caelestis, coelestis; caenum, coenum; etc.). In the last line of 'Three Blind Mice" the anon. "O" uses "coecis" for "caecis" (blind). This form is not given in my large Latin-English Dictionaries by Wm. Smith (London: John Murray, 1857), by John T. White (Lon.: Longman, Green, 1865), nor in the latest <u>Oxford Latin-English Dict.</u> of 1968-82. But the earlier <u>Ox. Lat.-Eng. Dict.</u> by Lewis and Short (1879) in its 1966 impression bluntly heads the word "<u>caecus</u> (not <u>coecus</u>)", proving that the odd spelling does occur. GMH admired and imitated usages "counter, original,...strange", and enjoyed carrying analogies one step further. Another rare form ends the second version of the Song of Sixpence in the <u>Irish Monthly,</u> "Aviculus" for the accepted "Avicula" in the tradition. It would have pleased Hopkins to move further away from the "avicella" of the first version.

Classicists may perhaps feel sufficiently reassured about GMH's probable authorship of these nursery rhymes in Latin as to treat them as OET No. 180(a), i and ii, and (b), although they should in chronology precede the Songs from Shakespeare in Latin and Greek, No. 165.

<u>Deviations in the Orally Transmitted Text from the Originals</u> as published in the <u>Irish Monthly.</u> The editor, Fr. Matthew Russell, SJ (see L.i.230), had no hesitation in "correcting" copy sent him, but there are remarkably few divergences between the two sets of texts, except in punctuation. In (a), 5, 6, <u>ales</u> can be either masc. or fem. (tradition has "alites...cuncti"); in (b) 5 OET prints "Dum quatuor", in 7 "combusto" for "robusto" (still a rollicking line), and in 21 "per hortum". Classicists may enjoy the mock learning of the note on p.669, with the Greek version of "Sing a Song of Sixpence" of which a distinguished Fellow of Magdalen College, Oxford,claimed to be the discoverer.

PRINCIPAL CONTENTS OF MS. A

For the history of MS. A see Introduction, and *OET*, pp. xxxii to xxxv. A full bibliographical study of the album is given by Leo van Noppen in his doctoral dissertation, *Gerard Manley Hopkins: The Wreck of the Deutschland*, State University of Groningen: Krips Repro Meppel, 1980, pp. 42-44. The album contains 316 pages, and is paginated, not foliated. After p.6 odd numbers are always on the left, contrary to convention. The early pages were at first left blank, probably for the insertion of autographs of Hopkins's undergraduate poems, but Hopkins later (1884) dissociated himself from all but two of them. Bridges respected his wish not to dilute his mature Catholic poems with earlier pieces, and, when he had autographs, in two places he added notes directing that they should not be published (pp. 21-22, 67-68). The album now begins with miscellaneous material.

PLATE 526. Sketch of Coventry Patmore • *355*

Plate 526   <u>Sketch of Coventry Patmore</u>

<u>MS.A. p.19</u>: Sketch in blue pencil of Coventry Patmore, "done under difficulties" by GMH, perhaps during the Speechday or "Great Academy" at Stonyhurst College, attended by Patmore. RB adds that "This was when GMH first met C.P." The Rector deputed Hopkins to look after Patmore during his three-day visit, thus starting a friendship and correspondence which lasted the rest of his life. See L.i.184-5; L.iii.205, letter to Baillie, 6 Sept. 1863: "All my pencil sketches are in a book, coloured sketches I have none". This sketch is on paper (with a discarded first attempt on the right), mounted on one of the many blank pages at the beginning of album A.

188   What shall I do for the land that bred me (No. 175)--auto., part of a letter to RB (L.i.284), formerly mounted on this page. Cut off, with most of the page, for facsimile reproduction facing L.i.284 (Plate 506), then restored to MS. Letters to RB, ii.306a,b.

191-2   That Nature is a Heraclitean Fire (No. 174)--auto. (Plates 504, 505).

194   Thou art indeed just, Lord, (No. 177)--auto. (Plate 517).

196   To R.B. (No. 179)--auto. (Plate 523). [pp.198/9 removed]

200-244   *Transcriptions of Poems by RB*

In Oct. 1889, after GMH's death, RB sorted through poems found among his papers or loaned him by the family. The most important he mounted in a new album, MS. H [which I call H.ii], copying into MS. A those new to him. He collated copies with the original MSS in Jan. 1918, while preparing the 1st. Edn.. This he explains pp.208, 210, 212, 214, 215, 217, etc.. He often copied the stress marks (contr. MS. B, where he deliberately omitted them), though sometimes his acutes fell on consonants (e.g., in "Inversnaid", ℓ.1 (A.p.210), they rest on the middle consonants of "horse" and the "w" of "brown"). The text of shorter poems occupies the right-hand page (even numbered), with editorial notes (sometimes in purple pencil or ink) on the left--e.g., he attributes the hyphenation of "horse-back" (Plate 397) to the narrowness of the MS. The text is in fine, careful Italic (ink). These transcriptions are not reproduced, as their originals have survived. In RB's annotations commas may look like periods.

200-08   A Vision of Mermaids [sic] (No. 6);   210 Inversnaid (No. 146);   212 To his Watch (No. 164);   214 Moonrise June 19, 1876 (No. 103) [he copied "Maenefa" as "Manresa", but corrected this 1918];   215-6 Thee, God, I come from (No. 161); 218 Carrion comfort--"(my title RB)" (No. 159). [He notes, ℓ.6, "*lion-limb* doubtful if written as one word. close and not hyphenated."]

220   Yes, why do we all, seeing of a soldier (No. 160)   222 No worst, there is none (No. 157)   224 Not of all my eyes see (No. 170)   "The foll. 5 sonnets were all on one sheet of paper. without date. in writing which was apparently from one pen at one time."   226 To seem the stranger (No. 154)   228 I wake and feel (No. 155) 230 Patience, hard thing! (No. 162)   232 My own heart (No. 163)   Line 14 at first read as "Between fire" with n. "fire is doubtful"   234 The times are nightfall (No. 152)   236 As kingfishers catch fire (No. 115)   238 What things in nature (No. 128d) "Fragment of sonnet (?)"   240 Strike, churl; hurl, cheerless wind (No. 156)   242 O Deus, ego amo te (No. 95). He notes the dittography "lance and lance" for "nails and lance" in other drafts.   244 To him who ever thought (No. 123b). His 1918 collation notes the grammatical oversight in the last line. [246/7 was removed; only the stub is left.]

248   *Later Transcriptions*

[sheet guarded in] Cheery Beggar (No. 136). "Copied Jan. 1918. M.M.B." (RB's wife Monica. RB corrected her "fire" to "fine" in 6, but missed the error in 4, "fineflower". Reproduced Plate 354.   [Remaining copies made by RB in pencil]   250-1 Nondum (No. 78) and 252 Easter (No. 79) were "MSS found by Alfred J. Rahilly in Dublin 2nd hand bk shop 1915 and sent to Father Keating. who lent them to me".

253-4   Remembrance and Expectation (M.H. [= Manley Hopkins], June 14 1868).

254   Mater Jesu mei (No. 91). First 4 only of 72 ℓℓ. transcribed.

255-6   Winter with the Gulf Stream (No. 7). Trans. made from Fr. F.E. Bacon's copy. RB notes that in a letter to him, May 26 1879, GMH said he wrote it at school.

257-9   The Nightingale (No. 76). From "autog. in family".

259-60   Spring and Death (No. 8).

PLATE 527. R.B.'s Contents of MS. A • *359*

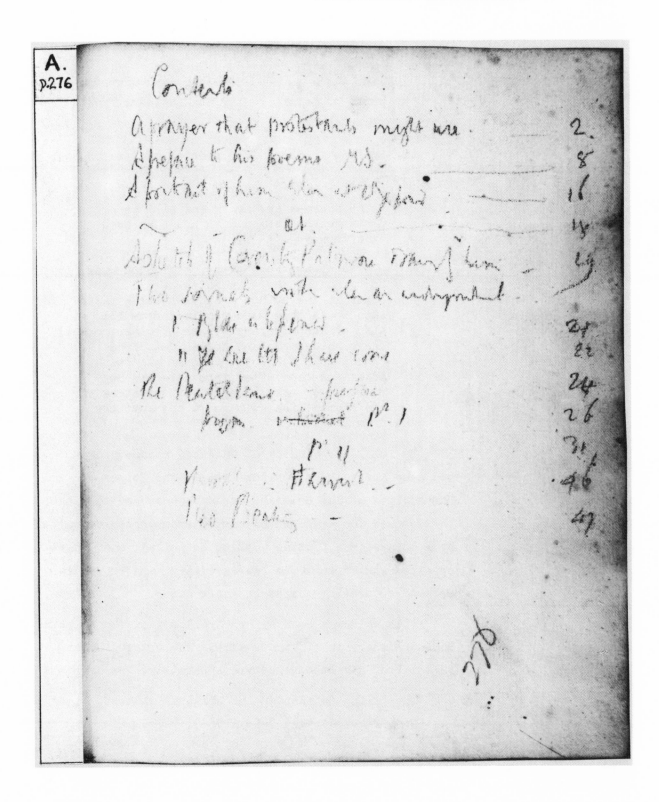

MS. A, p.276--the second pencilled attempt at a Table of Contents by RB (the first, on p.267, headed "Contents of this Bk.", had only one entry, "A prayer written for protestants to use").

A prayer that protestants might use...2   A preface to his poems MS....8   A portrait of him taken at Oxford [1863]...16   ditto aet....18 [1879]   A sketch of Coventry Patmore drawn by him...19   Two sonnets written when an undergraduate: i My love is lessened...21 iiYou[Ye?] see that I have come...22   The Deutschland--preface...24   ...poem [metrical *del.*] Pt. I...26   ...Pt. II...31   Hurrahing in Harvest...46   Pied Beauty...47 [The last entry.]

A.
p.316

The poems of Gerard Manley Hopkins were first published in 1918, edited with notes by Robert Bridges.

The Preface to the Editor's Notes states, on page 94, as follows:

" The sources are four, and will be distinguished as A, B, D and H as here described.

A is my own collection, a MS book made up of autographs - by which word I denote poems in the author's handwriting - pasted into it as they were received from him, and also of contemporary copies of other poems. These autographs and copies date from (18)67 to (18)89, the year of his death. Additions made after that date are not reckoned or used. The first two items of the facsimilies at page 70 are cuttings from A."

By 1967, the binding of MS.A had become broken, and many sheets were working loose. The Keeper of Manuscripts at The British Museum recommended that the best course for a MS of this importance, often consulted by scholars, was for the book to be pulled, each sheet repaired and strengthened as necessary, and the whole rebound on meeting-guards in a new cover.

This work was done by Mr. S A.Scott of The British Museum Bindery in his spare time. The original cover of the book has been preserved separately.

The paging is that of the original sheets. At some date R.B. removed pages 7-13, 198-9, 246-7.

B. March '67

Plate 528   Note on the Rebinding of MS. A.

MS.A. p.316. This typewritten note (initialled by Edward, the first Lord Bridges?) relates details of the professional rebinding of the volume in 1967. The deterioration of the pages and fading of the writing through exposure to light during frequent use has made necessary more stringent restrictions on its consultation.

CONTENTS OF MS. B

<u>MS. B</u> (Bodleian Library, MS. Eng. Poet. d. 149). A brief history of this important volume will be found in the Introduction (see also *OET,* xxxv-xxxix). Handed down in the family, it was purchased from Leo Handley-Derry by the library in 1953 and professionally foliated. Hopkins, writing to his brother Everard, Dec. 23 1885, refers to it as a "black ms book of my own containing nearly all my poems" (*Selected Letters,* ed. Catherine Phillips, 223), but it is now bound in brown cloth. A fine bibliographical description by Leo van Noppen will be found in his Ph.D. thesis: *GMH - The Wreck of the Deutschland* (Groningen: 1980), 44-46.

Hopkins's autograph preface on Rhythm (ff.1-5) may have been written specifically for Coventry Patmore's benefit, because of the latter's interest in metrical law, and have been inserted in album B before it was posted to Patmore in 1884. Bridges wisely transferred it to the safety of MS. A when MS. B was returned to him, but he restored it to its proper place some time after Hopkins's death. The First Edition of the *Poems* printed it on pp.1-6.

Four distinct components should be carefully recognised in B's poetic MSS. The Bridges transcripts (1883) occupy ff.7r to 27r: these were the only poems in the album when on 14 Dec. 1883 Bridges posted it to Hopkins, who had agreed [L.i.189] to "point" [i.e., punctuate it] and "make a few corrections" [rectifying any slips, but also making revisions]. The second component, ff.27v to 35r, consists of autograph poems inscribed in the album by Hopkins before he sent it to Patmore from Dublin a "few days" before 7 March 1884 (L.i.190). We should note that "The Blessed Virgin" (No. 151, f.31v) was then incomplete, ending at line 45, f.32v being left blank for the missing lines. Patmore returned the book in person to Bridges when he visited Bridges in July 1884.

Rereading his own poems in B had been so stimulating that Hopkins in August begged Bridges to make him a gift of the album as an encouragement to further compositions (L.i.195). Bridges swiftly complied, having first copied into the autographs of MS. A in red ink all the revisions he noticed Hopkins having made to the transcripts in B. After taking possession of album B Hopkins completed "The Blessed Virgin", and inscribed another Alexandrine version of "The Handsome Heart". But out of some 30 new poems which he completed in Ireland, or of which he composed substantial portions, he exerted himself to inscribe in album B only 4: "Spelt from Sibyl's Leaves", "To what serves Mortal Beauty?", "Harry Ploughman" and "Tom's Garland". In the five years before his death he filled only ff.35v to 37v. The revulsion Hopkins felt to the very last against copying out his own work (L.i.304) led him to defer over and over again his professed intention to finalise his new poems and enter them in album B. Bridges' scheme to ensure that his editor(s) would have an orderly collection of finished autographs to work from was defeated by the poet's melancholia, scruples and inertia.

The fourth component in MS. B (ff.38r to 53r) consists of poems pasted in, beginning with two printed versions from Bridges' 1918 edition (*OET* Nos. 169, 171), the autographs of four earlier pieces (Nos. 90, 105, 126, 142), but the autographs of only two poems written in Ireland (Nos. 176, 177). There is reason to believe that Bridges and not Hopkins was responsible for this section. In the First Edn. (p.94) Bridges, discussing MS. B, remarks that the "last entry written into this book is of the date 1887", a reference to "Harry Ploughman" and "Tom's Garland" (in the third section of the album). We might infer from this that it was not Hopkins who mounted in B Nos. 176, "St. Alphonsus Rodriguez" (Oct. 1888) and 177, "Thou art indeed just, Lord," (March 1889). Indeed it is likely that the inscribing of "Tom's Garland" on f.37v was the last act Hopkins had the chance to perform in the album: though dated 1887, its double sets of marginal braces suggest that it was not copied into the book till March/April 1889 (see *OET*, p.485), on the verge of his final illness. The six autographs pasted into later folios may have been found loose in album B after his death, and mounted in it by Bridges to make them more secure. All the poet's literary remains were consigned to his parents by the Dublin Jesuits: Bridges was not at liberty to add them to his own collection in MS. A.

ff.1-5 *[Author's Preface on Rhythm]* autograph (*OET*, pp.115-17), formerly in MS. A, pp.8-13, guarded into B professionally on the stub of the first leaf (Plates 221-26).

6r *Bridges' Title Page*   (Plate 220).

ff.7r to 27r *Bridges' Transcripts of Autographs in MS. A, checked by Hopkins*

7r *Pied Beauty* (No. 121) Plate 311   7v *Hurrahing in Harvest* (No. 124) Plate 317   8r *God's Grandeur* (No. 111) Plate 287a   8v *The Starlight Night* (No. 112) Plate 291a, partially rev. by GMH, then crossed through, with "See later" (i.e., 27v)   9r *Spring* (No. 117) Plate 301   9v *The Lantern* (No. 113), Plate 293, title extended by GMH, "out of doors"   10r *Walking by the Sea* (orig. title of No. 118) Plate 303b, crossed through by GMH, with "See later" (i.e., 28r)   10v *The Windhover* (No. 120) transcript of rev. auto. in A.p.96; GMH extended the title ": to Christ our Lord"; Pls. 309, 309a

11r *The Caged Skylark* (No. 122) Pl. 313   11v *In the valley of the Elwy* (No. 119) Pl. 307   12r *Duns Scotus's Oxford* (No. 129) Pl. 333   12v *Henry Purcell* (No. 131) Pl. 341, transcript omits the prose argument   13r *The Candle Indoors* (No. 133) Pl. 345   13v *The Handsome Heart* (No. 134), transcript of a mixed version, *ℓℓ*.1-4 from A¹, rest from A²--see Pl. 349. GMH crossed it through, with "See later" (i.e., 28v)   14r *Andromeda* (No. 138) Pl. 372a   14v *Felix Randal* (No. 142) Pl. 383 15r-20v *The Wreck of the Deutschland* (No. 101) odd numbered plates 231 through 263, and 263b; st.8 is in auto., pasted over RB's transcript.   21r *Binsey Poplars* (No. 130) Pl. 339   21v *Morning, Midday and Evening Sacrifice* (No. 139) Pl. 375   22r *At a wedding* (orig. title of No. 141) Pl. 381   22v,23r *Brothers* (No. 143) transcript of A¹, not A², Pl. 390   23v *Spring and Fall* (No. 144) Pl. 395 24r,v,25r *The Bugler's First Communion* (No. 137) Pls. 367-69   25v,26r,v,27r *The Leaden Echo and the Golden Echo* (No. 148) Pls. 409, 411, 413, 415.

ff.27v to 35r *Autographs added to MS. B by Hopkins before the album was sent to Coventry Patmore*

27v *The Starlight Night* (No. 112) Pl. 291b, replacing transcript on 8v   28r *The Sea and the Skylark* (No. 118) Pl. 303, replacing transcript on 10r   28v *The Handsome Heart* (No. 134b) Pl. 350, rev. autograph in Alexandrines, replacing 13v; crossed through by Hopkins after MS. B was returned to him as a gift, Aug. 1884, with "See later" (i.e., 35v)   29r *Peace* (No. 140) Pl. 377, no auto. previously sent to RB, so no transcript in B   29v *Ribblesdale* (No. 149) Pl. 419; no transcript made by RB because the auto. sent him was described as probably not final.   30r,31r,32r,33r,34r,v *The Loss of the Eurydice* (No. 125) Pls. 319,321,323,325,325b, rev. auto.; Bridges had not been entrusted with the orig. auto., now lost.   30v *The May Magnificat* (No. 126) Pl. 327b; GMH in sending the auto. to RB had written that he saw "little good" in it (L.i.65): see also 47r,v,48r   31v *The Blessed Virgin compared to the Air we Breathe* (No. 151, *ℓℓ*.1-45 only) Pl. 421, auto. made from a transcript of A, sent him by RB but mislaid during GMH's move to Dublin when he had copied only a third of it; not completed till album B was returned to GMH as a gift along with another transcript (32v, Pl. 423)   35r *The Silver Jubilee* (No. 102a) Pl. 265b. This was the last poem in the album when Hopkins sent it to

Patmore. This can be deduced from RB's red ink entries made in MS. A in August 1884 after MS. B had been brought back by Patmore.

35v to 37v *Autographs inscribed in MS. B after Hopkins assumed its Ownership*

31v,32v *The Blessed Virgin...* (see note above)   35v *The Handsome Heart* (No. 134b) Pl. 351, rev. Alexandrine version (cf. 13v and 28v)   36r *Spelt from Sibyl's Leaves* (No. 167) Pl. 477, inscribed more than two years after he had received the album as a gift   36v *To what serves Mortal Beauty?* (No. 158) Pl. 451   37r *Harry Ploughman* (No. 169) Pl. 489, prob. entered c. Oct. 1887   37v *Tom's Garland* (No. 171) Pl. 493b, prob. not copied until c. March, April 1889, on the verge of his final illness (see *OET,* p.485).

38r,38v Printed copies of *Harry Ploughman* and *Tom's Garland* pasted in by Bridges, being pp.65,64 in his 1st. Edn. of the *Poems,* 1918.

40r to 53r *Autographs pasted into MS. B (probably by Bridges)*

40r (guarded in on stub of a leaf) *To Jesus living in Mary* (No. 90), with the orig. Latin by Fr. Condren, 41r (guarded in) Plate 185, *Facs.* i   43r (on 44r) *Penmaen Pool* (No. 105b) Pl.279   45r (on 46r) *St. Alphonsus Rodriguez* (No. 176) Pl. 513   47r,v,48r *The May Magnificat* (No. 126) Pls. 326-27   50r (on 51r) *Felix Randal* (No. 142) Pl. 380, earlier version.   52r (on 53r) *Thou art indeed just, Lord* (No. 177) Pl. 516.

CONTENTS OF MS. H.i.

MS. H.i. Bodleian Library, MS. Eng. Poet. c. 48

This is a modern professionally constructed volume into which the Bodleian guarded all the loose Hopkins MS poems which they purchased from Leo Handley-Derry in 1953, along with MSS. H.ii and B. I have given it the title "H.i" because it now contains some of the MSS sent from Dublin after Hopkins's death and referred to by Bridges and later editors as "H". The contents of the scrapbook in which he mounted "the more important pieces" were later transferred to a volume (now Bodleian MS. Eng. Poet. d. 150) which I have called "H.ii". See *OET,* pp. xxix to xxxi.

MS. H.i also includes *important early autographs* which Hopkins left with his family when he became a Jesuit (ff.1-26v).

1r-9r	The Escorial (No. 1) sole MS, transcript by Manley Hopkins on rectos, notes printed by GMH in disguised hand on versos (Pls. 2-17, *Facs.* i) ff.9v through 18v are blank.
19r,v,20r,v	A Vision of the Mermaids (No. 6) auto., sole MS, with a pen and ink sketch (Pls. 23-25, *Facs.* i).
21r,22r	Barnfloor and Winepress (No. 17) transcript in unknown hand (Pl. 78, *Facs.* i).
23r,v	The Nightingale (No. 76) sole MS., auto. (Pls. 162-63, *Facs.* i).
24r,v	A Complaint (No. 72) auto. (Pl. 160, *Facs.* i).
25r,v	For a picture of St. Dorothea (No. 42a) auto. (Pl. 156, *Facs.* i).
25v	Fair Havens--The Nunnery (an early title of "Heaven-Haven", No. 20a) auto. (Pl. 81, *Facs.* i).
26r,v	Spring and Death (No. 8) auto., sole MS (Pl. 28, *Facs.* i).

Mature Poems in MS. H.i

27r,28r	The Silver Jubilee (No. 102a) auto. used for copying into the presentation album (Pl. 264).
29r	God's Grandeur (No. 111) auto. (Pl. 284).
30r	The Starlight Night (No. 112, MS. 2) auto., footnote revisions (Pl. 288a).
31r,30v	The Starlight Night (No. 112, MS. 5) auto. rev., with alternatives (Pl. 291).
32r,v	Hurrahing in Harvest (No. 124) auto., earliest version (Pl. 314).
33r,v	Tom's Garland (No. 171) auto., rev. (Pl. 492) 34r,v are blank.
35r	Binsey Poplars (No. 130) auto. (Pl. 337).
35v	Printed leaflet on needlework group and language classes, St. Joseph's Convent, Oxford (Pl. 338).

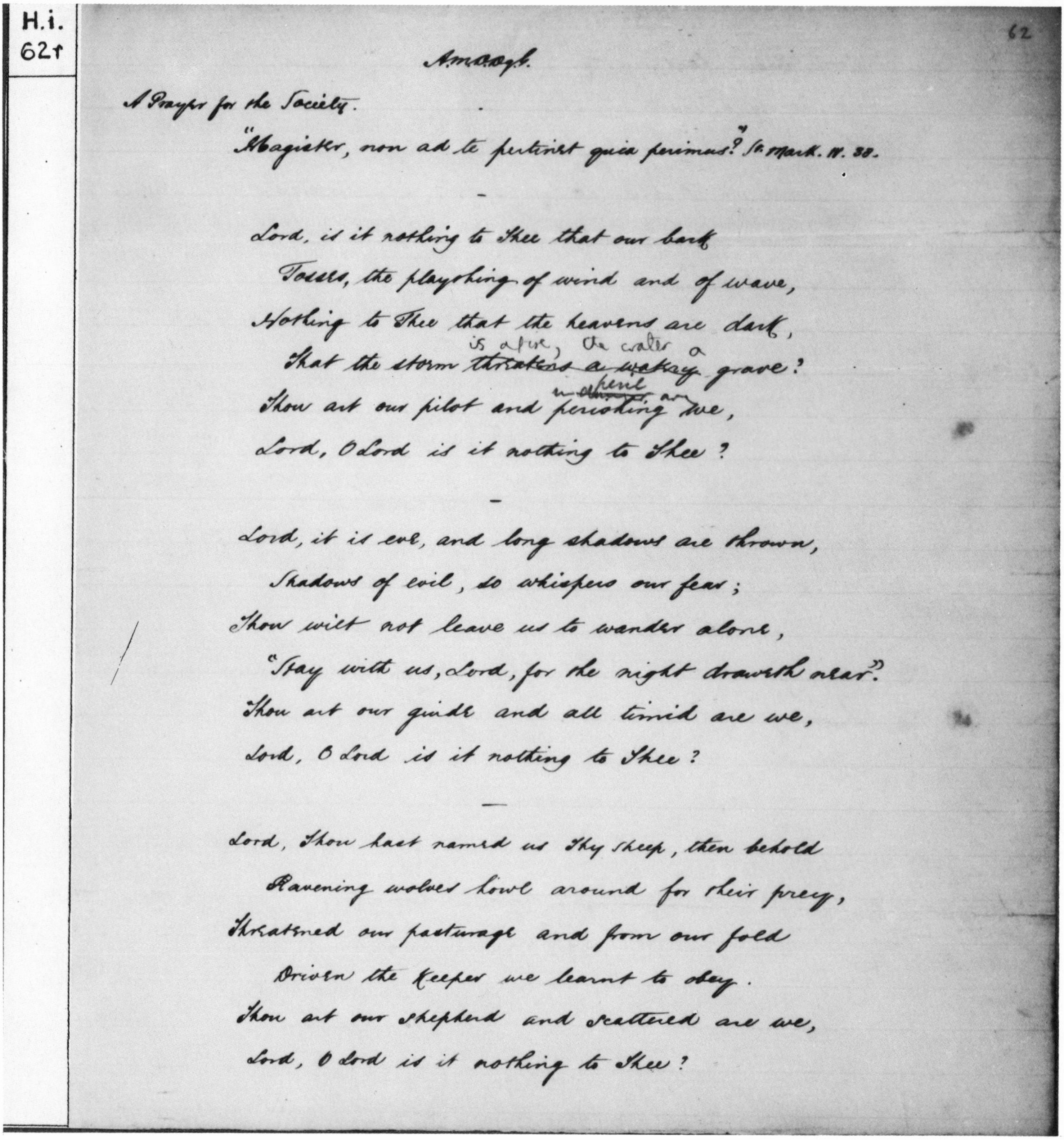

H.i.
62r

62

A.M.D.G.

A Prayer for the Society.

"Magister, non ad te pertinet quia perimus?" *St. Mark. iv. 38.*

Lord, is it nothing to Thee that our bark
    Tosses, the plaything of wind and of wave,
Nothing to Thee that the heavens are dark,
    That the storm threatens a watery grave?
Thou art our pilot and perishing we,
    Lord, O Lord is it nothing to Thee?

Lord, it is eve, and long shadows are thrown,
    Shadows of evil, so whispers our fear;
Thou wilt not leave us to wander alone,
    "Stay with us, Lord, for the night draweth near."
Thou art our guide and all timid are we,
    Lord, O Lord is it nothing to Thee?

Lord, Thou hast named us Thy sheep, then behold
    Ravening wolves howl around for their prey,
Threatened our pasturage and from our fold
    Driven the keeper we learnt to obey.
Thou art our shepherd and scattered are we,
    Lord, O Lord is it nothing to Thee?

Plates 529,530   A Prayer for the Society

MS. H.i.62,r,v--anon. (translation of?) A prayer for the Society of Jesus in time of persecution (e.g., Spain in 1869, L.iii.106; expulsion from Germany, 1872, J.236,424, n.1). The epigraph is from the Vulgate of St. Mark 4:38 (Douay: "Master, doth it not concern thee that we perish?"--alluded to in the opening line of "The Loss of the Eurydice", No. 125). GMH has improved st. 1 (avoiding the cliche of "a watery grave") and the second quatrain of the last extended stanza. From the handwriting I would date it c.1872, but the specimen is too short for precision.

PLATE 530. *A Prayer for the Society* • 367

Lord, Thou hast 'written' us deep in Thy 'hands';

Set us a 'seal on Thy heart' for a sign,

Drawn us to Thee by 'Thy love's triple 'bands';

Save us, O Lord, for at least we are Thine :

Jesus art Thou and Thy namesakes are we,

Jesus, Lord is it nothing to Thee ? —

Voice of Jesus. Does the Sky lower, "Fear not, it is I ";

Is your fold threatened, "Take heart, little flock";

"I am your way", when the darkness is nigh ;

Better than Peter's, My Name is your rock.

Still is there one of my titles unsaid,

Answer me, how would the limbs be without

Pain from the thorns which encircle the head?

"O ye of little faith, why did ye doubt ?"

I am your Head, and my members are ye

How then, how can it be nothing to Me ?

x O ye of little faith, why did ye doubt ?

Still is there one of My titles unsaid :

what the head wears shall the limbs be without ?

Thorns, they are thorns that encircle the head.

L.B.S.

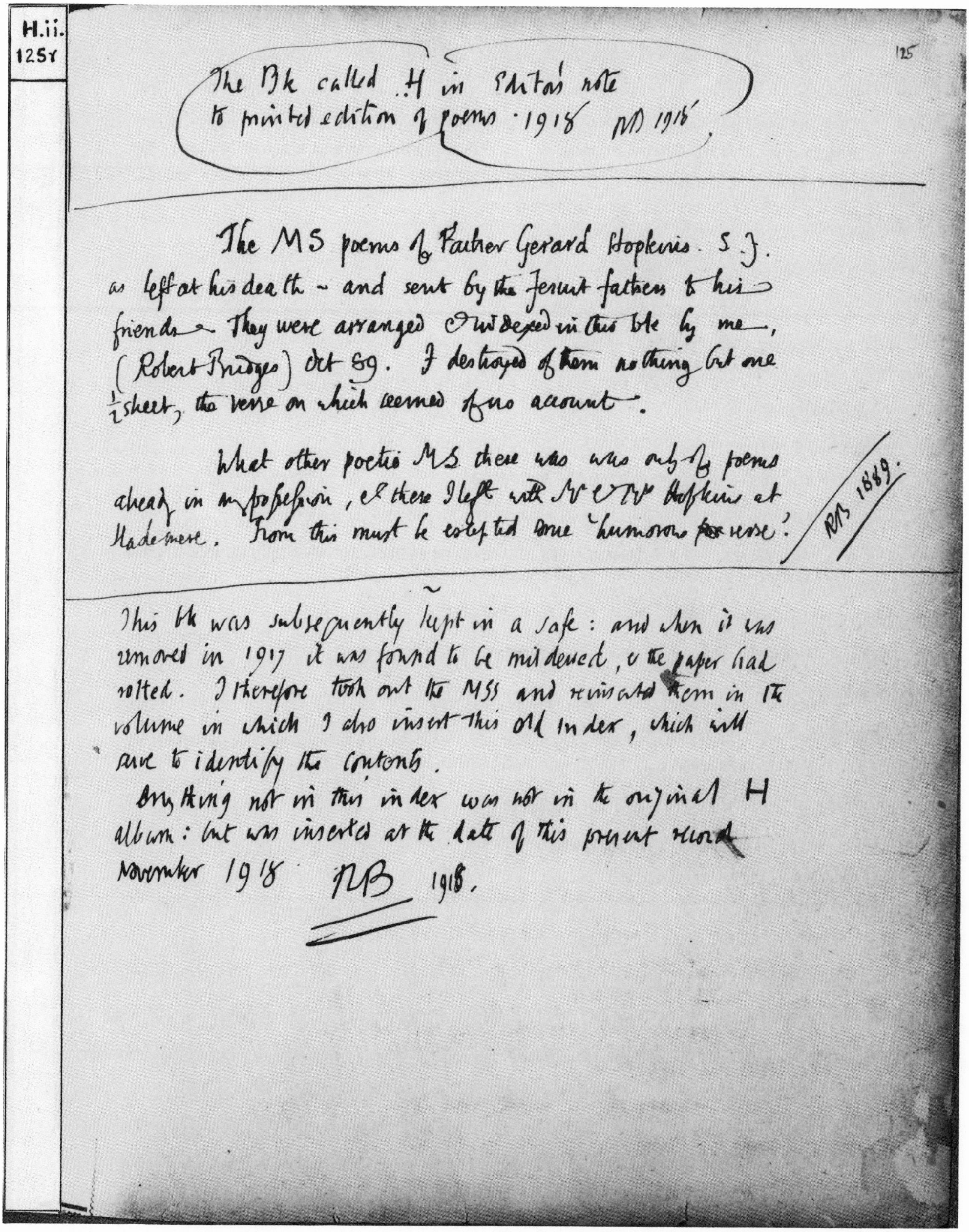

PLATE 531. Bridges's Note on MS.H.ii • *369*

125

The Bk called . H in Editor's note
to printed edition of poems . 1918   RB 1918

The MS poems of Father Gerard Hopkins. S.J.
as left at his death ~ and sent by the Jesuit fathers to his
friends ~ They were arranged & indexed in this bk by me ,
(Robert Bridges) Oct 89 . I destroyed of them nothing but one
½ sheet, the verse on which seemed of no account ~ .

What other poetic MS. there was was only of poems
already in my possession , & these I left with M & Mrs Hopkins at
Haslemere . From this must be excepted some "humorous verse" .

RB 1889 .

This bk was subsequently kept in a safe : and when it was
removed in 1917 it was found to be mildewed, & the paper had
rotted . I therefore took out the MSS and reinserted them in the
volume in which I also insert this old Index , which will
serve to identify the contents .

Anything not in this index was not in the original H
album : but was inserted at the date of this present record
November 1918   RB 1918 .

Plate 532   *Index to MS.H.ii* (Bodleian Lib., MS. Eng. Poet. d.150)

<u>H.ii.125v</u> (cont. 126r): The Table of Contents of the original album H, made by Robert Bridges Oct. 1889 (see Pl. **531**), fastened into the new album with stamp paper. Other poems were added in Nov. 1918 (poems not in the 1889 vol. or mentioned in 1918 are here interspersed in square brackets). The ringed numbers will be found at the top of H.ii.MSS. *OET* Nos., the modern folio references, and plate numbers (some in *Facsimiles* i) are provided below.

1. "To his Watch" (No. 164), 5r, Pls. 464-65.

2. "Epithalamion" (No. 172), 7r, 9r, 13r,v, 14r,v, Pls. 494-95, 498-502.

3. "Inversnaid" (No. 146), 17r,v, 18r, Pl. 397.

4. "Moonrise" (No. 103), 21r, Pl. 269.

5. "Thee, God, I come from," (No. 161), 23r, Pls. 460-61   ; "To what serves Mortal Beauty?" (No. 158), 23v, Pls. 448-49

6. "To him who ever thought with love" (No. 123b) 25r, Pl. 315.

7. "The Cheery Beggar" (No. 136), 27r, Pls. 354-55.

   [Add "The Bugler's First Communion" (No. 137), 27v, Pl.356--earliest draft.]

8. 29v,r, Pls. 438-39. Enlargements: "To what serves Mortal Beauty?" (No. 158), Pl. 450; "Carrion Comfort" (No. 159), Pls. 456-57; "The Soldier" (No. 160), Pl. 458.

   [Add "Tom's Garland" (No. 171), 31r, Pls. 440, 492.]

9. "No worst" (No. 157), 31r,v, Pls. 440, 441, 447, 447a; "Carrion Comfort" (No. 159), 31r,v, Pls. 440, 441, 492, 459.

10. "Not of all my eyes see" (No. 170), 33r, Pls. 444, 491.

11. 35r,v, Pls 442-43: "Not of all my eyes see" (No. 170), Pl. 490; "To seem the stranger" (No. 154), Pl. 445; "I wake and feel" (No. 155), Pl. 446a; "Patience, hard thing" (No. 162), Pl. 462; "My own heart" (No. 163), Pl. 463.

12. "The times are nightfall" (No. 152), 37r, Pl. 425.

13. "As kingfishers" (No. 115), 39r,v; "The dark-out Lucifer" (No. 114), Pls. 294-95.

    [Add "The Handsome Heart" (No. 134), 41r, Pl. 346.]

14. "What being in rank-old nature" (No. 128d), 41v-42v, Pl. 331.

15. "The shepherd's brow" (No. 178), 44r,v,45r, Pls. 518-20; "The fine delight" (No. 179), 45v, Pl. 522.

16. "Strike churl" (No. 156); "I wake and feel" (No. 155), 47r, Pl. 446.

    [Add "The Woodlark" (No. 104), 49r,v, Pls. 270-71a; "Binsey Poplars" (No. 130), 51v, Pls. 334-35.]

17. "The Furl of fresh-leaved dogrose" (No. 127); "Denis,/Whose motionable, alert" (No. 128a), 51r, Pl. 328.

PLATE 532. Index to MS.H.ii   •   371

H.ii.
125v

Index

(Those underlined in red are the finished & unfinished compl. forms which exist only in this book.)

① Beginning of a sonnet " To his watch " p. 1.   [of pencil first draft. & &

② a — f ~ of an ode on Everard's marriage. pp. 2. 3. 4 & a leaf with two leaves

③ "Wet and wildness" a finished lyric ~ p. 5.

④ Moonrise beginning of an unrhymed poem. p. 6.

⑤ "Thee, God, I come from" beginning of hymn p. 7.
     on reverse the rough of the finished sonnet 'To what serves'

⑥ A stanza " The man who ever " p. 8.

⑦ A stanza & a half of " The cheery beggar " (all there is of it) p. 9.

⑧ Draft of sonnets " Mortal beauty ' see ⑤ reverse ⎫
     ' Carrion comfort ' see ⑨   ⎬ p. 11.
     'Soldiers & Tailors' ⎭

⑨ Drafts of sonnets " ✗✗ No worst " and " Carrion comfort " see ⑧ . p. 13

⑩ Second draft of "Not of all my eyes see' p. 14

⑪ First draft of same ~ ~ ~ ~ ~ ~

     draft of sonnet " To seem the stranger ' do ⎫
       " I wake and feel ——— ⎬ p. 15
       " Patience, hard thing —— ⎪
       " My own heart ~~~ ⎭

⑫ Beginning of a sonnet " The times are nightfall ' p. 16.

⑬ Unfinished sonnet " As kingfishers catch fire ' p. 17
     Contains also 3 lines belonging elsewhere .

⑭ 5 or 6 lines beginning 'What things sh^d earlier' p. 18.

⑮ 3 ∧ 4 draft of a sonnet 'The shepherd fronting heaven's' and the first draft of
     'The fine delight' etc ~ ~ between pp. 18 and 19.

⑯ some odd lines, and some of ' I wake and feel '. p. 19.

⑰ some odd lines & verses - Denis etc p. 21.

Plate 533   *Index to MS.H.ii, cont.*

<u>H.ii.126r</u> (cont. from 125v).

18. "Ad Episcopum Salopiensem" [addressed to the Bishop of Shrewsbury--not "Salisbury"] (No. 102b), 53r,54r, poem as originally composed, Pl. 266.

19. Ditto, 56r, 57r, the version after censorship, Pl. 267.

20,21. "O Deus, ego amo te" [formerly attributed to St. Francis Xavier] (No. 95`, 58r,v; 60r,v,61r (also 74v, in item 28 below), Pls. 194-95 (*Facs.* i).

22. "On St. Winefred" (No. 98a), 63r, Pl. 198 (*Facs.* i).

23. "In S. Winefridam" (No. 98b), formerly 68r, Pl. 201 (*Facs.* 1). Removed from album by GMH's nephew, Gerard Hopkins, and presented to Sister Mary Roberta, who later gave it to the College of Notre Dame, Maryland.

24. Greek prose: Dryden's Essay on Satire, trans. into Greek, set at the Royal Univ. of Ireland (prob. as an unprescribed passage for Hons. candidates to translate into English).

25. "Cywydd" (No. 102c), 67r,v, Pl. 268.

26. "Iam si rite" (No. 98c), 68r,v; 69r, Pl. 200 (*Facs.* i).

27. "Ad Rev....Thomam Burke" (No. 116), 71r,v, Pls. 296-97.

28. "O Deus, ego amo te" (No. 95), 74v, Pls. 195, 207 (*Facs.* i).

28 cont.
29,30. "S. Thomae Aquinatis Rhythmus" (No. 100), 73r,v; 74r,v; 76r,78r, Pls. 204-215 (*Facs.* 1).

29 cont.
31,32. "To Jesus living in Mary", beginning "Jesu that dost in Mary dwell" (No. 90), 76v, 80r, 81r, 82v, Pls. 184-85 (*Facs.* i).

33. "Haec te jubent salvere (No. 92), 86r-88v, Pls. 188-89; 33b: "Quique haec membra" (No. 97), 85r, Pl. 199; 33a: "Miror surgentem" (No. 99), 89r,v, Pls. 202-03 (all in *Facs.* i).

34. Latin prose. No longer in H.ii. (Fr. A. Bischoff reported this missing in his survey of GMH's MSS in *Thought,* 26, winter 1951-2, 562.)

35. Latin prose address or citation to a leader of the Royal University in Ireland; draft by GMH with many corrections, beginning "Contigit igitur, dux illustrissime...collegium nostrum regia". 91r,v.

36-38. "On the Portrait of Two Beautiful Young People" (No. 168), 93r-97r, Pls. 478-84.

39. "The Prayer En Ego", del., English translation with corrections by GMH (transcript in A, p.14).

39-40. "Who shaped these walls" (No. 135--RB correctly describes this as a "poem on a work of art"), 99v-100v, Pls. 352-54.

41,42. "Margaret Clitheroe" (No. 108), 102-4, Pls. 282-83.
43. "Hope holds to Christ the mind's own mirror" (No. 109), 106r,v; Pl. 299.

44. "Repeat that, repeat" (No. 132), 107r, Pl. 338.

45. "The sea took pity" (No. 173), 108r, Pl. 503.

46. "Thou art indeed just, Lord," (No. 177), 110v-111v, Pls. 514-15 (RB notes: "added 46 1918)."

47. "O praedestinata bis" (No. 93), 113r, 114r, Pls. 190-91 (RB's pencil note, "MS. added 1819", is a slip for "1918") *Facs.* i.

PLATE 533. Index to MS.H.ii   •   373

H.ii.
126ᵛ

(18) Latin verse address to Bp of Salisbury. as written   p. 22

(19)   same as emended (by authority ?)   p. 23.

(20)(21) Drafts of translatᵒⁿ of Sᵗ Fran Xavier's hymn. pp 24 25   for *final* draft see No (28)

(22) Epigram on Sᵗ Winifred.   p 26

(23)   same in Latin   p. 27.

(24) An exercise in Greek prose p 28

(25) Some Welsh verses (?)   p 29.

(26) pt of Latin elegiac address   p 30

(27) Latin elegiac address to Rev Bourke p 31

(28)* (29)* (30) Drafts of translatᵒⁿ of Rhythm of S Thos Aquinas. between pp 32 – 33

(31)(32) a. & b Translⁿ (& song) of Latin hymn "Jesu that dost in Mary dwell" 34. 35

(33) Latin verses (with 33 a and b) – p 37.   [and see no (29)]

(34) Latin prose   p 39.

(35) Latin prose address – p 41.

(36)(37)(38). Drafts of beginning of the unfinished poem
    "on the Portrait of two beautiful young people". between pp 42 – 43

(39)*
(40) } stanzas of unfinished poem on a work of art { p. 44
                                   { p. 45

(41)(42)   stanzas ———————— on the Murder of Margaret Clitheroe. p 47

(43)
(44) } various stanzas & lines – p 49.
(45)

46 added Feb 1918 Justus es. draft.
47 O praedestinata. MS added 1819..

———————————————————————————

(28)*   Also contains *final* draft of S Francis Xavier. see (20)(21)

(29)*   a. "Jesu that dost in Mary dwell" see (31). (32)

(39)*   on back a prose prayer englished from " En ego "

APPENDIX A

Addenda, Corrigenda to *Facsimiles* Volume I

Plates 534 and 535 reproduce a transcription of *OET* No. 94, "Ad Mariam", made by Hopkins's mother, Kate, from the version printed in the *Stonyhurst Magazine* in 1894, a copy of which is among the Hopkins Family Papers. I am grateful to Leo Handley-Derry for having found the original, which had been mislaid when it was needed to complement Plates 192 and 193 in *Facsimiles* vol. i. Although in this instance her transcription has no authority, an examination of all her transcriptions helps us to evaluate her accuracy when the original she copied has since vanished (see Plate 384).

Plate 536 replaces the top right page reproduced on Plate 37 of *Facsimiles* vol. i, printed in error from a defective negative--though a transcription of the damaged section was provided in the footnote.

Plate 144, ℓ.42 (*Facsimiles* i, p.196). Professor Robert B. Martin, whose biography of Hopkins is expected soon, reads my conjectural "picture of Rosseti's (?)" as "picture of Gosselin". On re-examining my photocopies I agree, and so does Catherine Phillips who was kind enough to look at the original diary on my behalf (C.ii.106). I accept the correction with gratitude for the extra light it throws on Hopkins's battle against temptation.

Gosselin was the fellow Etonian whom Digby Dolben secretly admired. Bridges, in the Memoir prefixed to his 1911 edition of *The Poems of Digby Mackworth Dolben* (Oxford University Press, pp.xxii-iii) tells us that "Manning" (his pseudonym for Gosselin) attracted him "personally as much as any one whom I ever met", though their interests being different he never cultivated his friendship, and that everyone who knew Gosselin either as a boy, in full manhood or in later years "spoke of him only in terms of love and admiration". Gosselin's picture (or carte) must have been sent to Hopkins by Dolben, who after failing to reply to "letters without end" from GMH, had at last written. Plate 142, ℓ.11, 6 Nov. 1865, links the arrival of that letter with Hopkins's celebrated resolution: "On this day by God's grace I resolved to give up all beauty until I had His leave for it: and also Dolben's letter came for wh. Glory to God" (see my discussion in *Facsimiles* i, pp.27-29). Dolben must have been aware that Hopkins was attracted to him as he himself was to Gosselin, and one reason for sending the photograph was surely to show the need for a renunciation in both cases--one-sided friendships which would increase physical tensions. One month later (10 Dec.) Hopkins rejected as unworthy of his spiritual aspirations another temptation: "Looking with evil curiosity at a picture of Gosselin". A rejected temptation is very different from one dwelt upon.

MS. K

OET No. 94

Ad Mariam.

When a sister, born for each strong month-brother,
 Spring's one daughter, the sweet child May,
Lies in the breast of the young year-mother
 With light on her face like the waves at play,
Man from the lips of him speaketh n saith,
At the touch of her wandering wondering breath
Warm on his brow: lo! Where is another
Fairer than this one to lighten our day?

We have suffered the sons of Winter in sorrow
 And been in their ruinous reigns oppressed,
And fain in the springtime surcease would borrow
 From all the pain of the past's unrest;

And May has come, hair-bound in flowers,
 With eyes that smile 'through the tears of the hours,
With joy for today n hope for tomorrow
 And the promise of Summer within her breast.
And we that joy in this month joy-laden,
 The gladdest thing that our eyes have seen,
Oh thou, proud mother n much-proud maiden —
 Maid yet mother as May has been —
To thee we tender the beauties all
 Of the month by men called virginal.
And, where thou dwellest, in deep-groved Arden,
 Salute thee, mother, the maid-month's Queen!

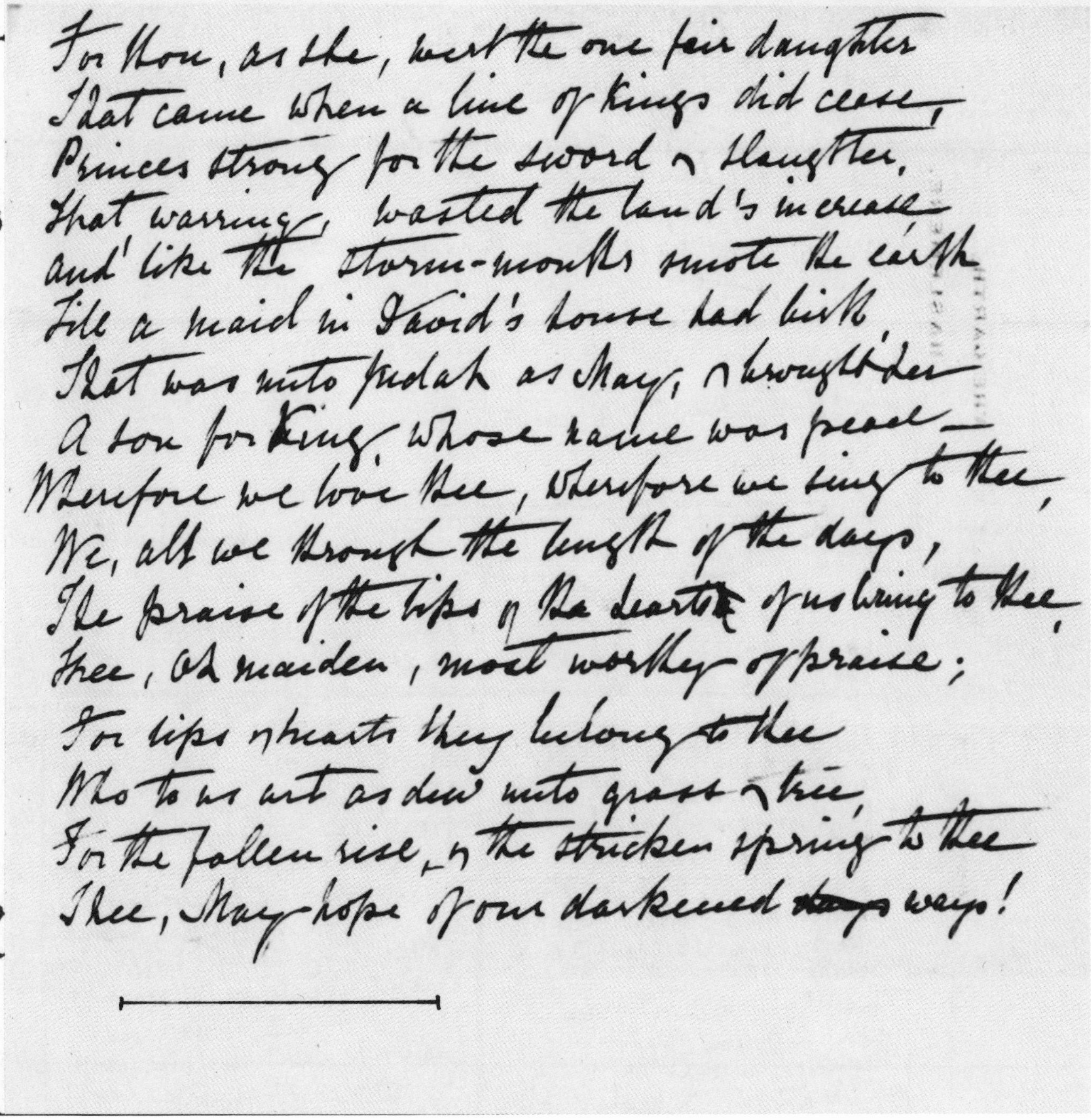

For thou, as she, wert the one fair daughter
That came when a line of kings did cease,
Princes strong for the sword & slaughter,
28   That warring, wasted the land's increase
And like the storm-months smote the earth
Till a maid in David's house had birth
That was unto Judah as May, & brought her
32   A son for king, whose name was peace —
Wherefore we love thee, wherefore we sing to thee,
We, all we through the length of the days,
The praise of the lips of the dearest of us bring to thee,
36   Thee, Oh maiden, most worthy of praise;
For lips & hearts they belong to thee
Who to us art as dew unto grass & tree,
For the fallen rise, & the stricken spring to thee
40   Thee, May-hope of our darkened ways weys!

Plates 534,535   OET No. 94: "Ad Mariam"

MS. K: Transcription made by GMH's mother, Mrs. Kate Hopkins, on printed note-paper headed "The Garth, Haslemere", from the version published in the *Stonyhurst Magazine* (72, 1894, 233-4); this is reproduced Plate 192, *Facsimiles* vol. i (the MS was rediscovered too late to be printed in its correct place). Note such slips as "lighten" for "brighten" (8), "the" for "our" (34).

Other transcriptions by Kate Hopkins will be found in Plates 313b, 374a, 384, 425, 435-36.

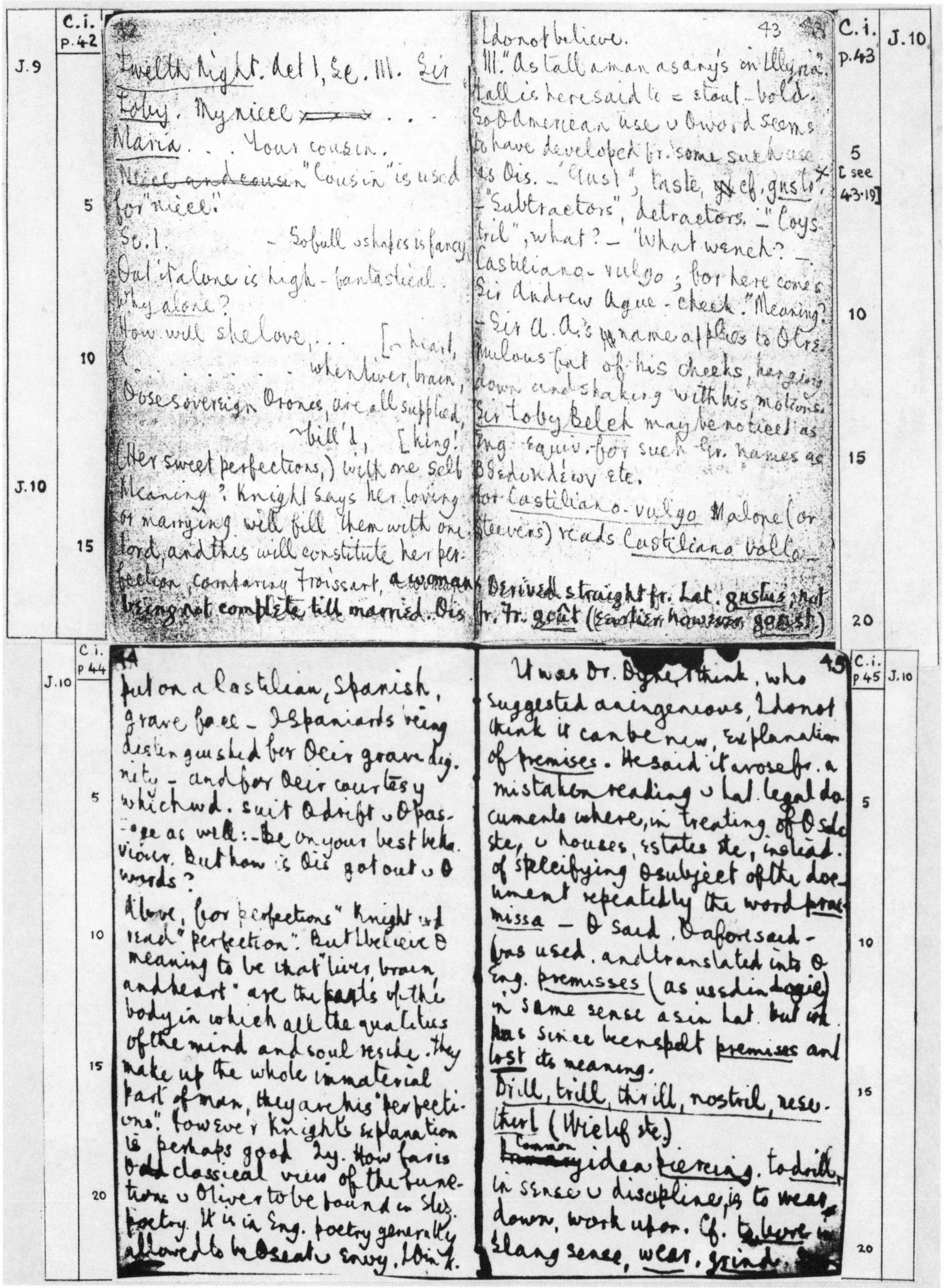

Top left panel (margin: C.i. p.42 / J.9 / J.10)

Twelfth Night. Act I, Sc. III. Sir
Toby. My niece ⸺ . . .
Maria. . . . Your cousin.
"Niece and cousin" "Cousin" is used
for "niece".
Sc. 1. ⸺ So full of shapes is fancy
Out, it alone is high - fantastical.
Why alone?
How will she love, . . . [in heart,
. . . . . . ⸺ whenever, brain,
those sovereign thrones, are all supplied,
⸺ fill'd, [king!
Her sweet perfections,) with one self
Meaning? Knight says her loving
or marrying will fill them with one
lord, and this will constitute her per-
fection, comparing Froissart, a woman
being not complete till married. Dis-

Top right panel (margin: 43 / C.i. p.43 / J.10 / 5 [see 43·19])

I do not believe.
III. "As tall a man as any's in Illyria".
tall is here said to = stout · bold.
So American use o[f] the word seems
to have developed fr. some such use
as this. ⸺ "Gust", taste, × cf. gusto ×
⸺ "Subtractors", detractors. ⸺ "Coys-
tril", what? ⸺ "What wench? ⸺
Castiliana - vulgo; for here comes
Sir Andrew Ague - cheek." Meaning?
⸺ Sir A. A.'s name applies to the
tremulous jut of his cheeks, hanging
down and shaking with his motions.
Sir Toby Belch may be noticed as
Eng. equiv. for such Gr. names as
Βδεόνλέων etc.
For Castiliano-vulgo Malone (or
Steevens) reads Castiliano volto
Derived straight fr. Lat. gustus, not
fr. Fr. goût (earlier however goust)

Bottom left panel (margin: C.i. p.44 / J.10)

put on a Castilian, Spanish,
grave face ⸺ Spaniards being
distinguished for their grave dig-
nity ⸺ and for their courtesy
which wd. suit at drift o[f] pas-
-age as well :⸺ be on your best beha-
viour. But how is this got out o[f] the
words?
Above, (for "perfections" Knight wd.
read "perfection". But I believe the
meaning to be that "liver, brain
and heart" are the parts of the
body in which all the qualities
of the mind and soul reside. they
make up the whole immaterial
part of man, they are his "perfections". However Knight's explanation
is perhaps good. By How far is
the classical view of the func-
tions o[f] liver to be found in Shak-
-peare. It is in Eng. poetry generally
allowed to be seat o[f] envy, I think.

Bottom right panel (margin: 45 / C.i. p.45 / J.10)

It was Dr. Dyce, I think, who
suggested an ingenious, I do not
think it can be new, explanation
of premises. He said it arose fr. a
mistaken reading o[f] Lat. legal documents where, in treating of the es-
tate, o[f] houses, estates etc., instead
of specifying the subject of the document repeatedly the word prae-
missa ⸺ the said, the aforesaid -
was used. and translated into the
Eng. premisses (as used in logic)
in same sense as in Lat. but which
has since been spelt premises and
lost its meaning.
Drill, trill, thrill, nostril, nese-
thirl (Wiclif etc.)
idea herein, to drill
in sense o[f] discipline, is to wear
down, work upon. Cf. to bore in
slang sense, wear, grind.

Plates 36,37: Deletions include: 41.3 "Che[shire]" 42.2 "x x x" 42.4 "Niece and cousin" 43.6 "gu[sto]" 44.19 "old" 45.18 "Primary". In 41.13 "lock. But" orig. "lock, but" 44.6 "be", "Be" superimposed Bot. two lines of 42 and 43 are in ink. 43, ll.19,20 (footnote on gusto) read: "Derived straight from Latin gustus, not from French goût (earlier however goust)." 43, ll.17,18: "For Castiliano-vulgo Malone (or Steevens) reads Castiliano volto--" (cont. top. p.44).

APPENDIX B
Text of the OET Hopkins:
Chief Changes since 1970
Poems Nos. 101 to the End.

The Oxford fourth edition of the *Poems of Gerard Manley Hopkins* (London: 1967), ed. by W.H. Gardner and N.H. MacKenzie, introduced over 400 changes to the text of Gardner's third edition of 1948, as a result of special facilities for comparing the manuscripts generously offered me by their owners: Edward, first Lord Bridges, the Society of Jesus, and the Bodleian Library. Dr. Gardner died in 1969. I was by then already working on the text of my own more specialized edition for the quite distinct Oxford English Texts series. Some corrections that resulted from the renewed study of the manuscripts could be easily incorporated in the more popular fourth edition, and this I did for its paperback reprint of 1970. Others, however, would have involved extensive resetting, especially where I had selected as the *OET* copy-text a manuscript different from the one described as the basis for the fourth edition in notes by RB, WHG, and NHM printed in the paperback. I saved other interesting changes for my own edition, and did not incorporate more than a few until the seventh impression of 1984, when many were released.

In the Oxford English Texts, instead of printing the apparently later of two readings braced together as alternatives by the undecided poet, I have usually given them both. Further, where an earlier version is of special interest or is the only autograph, I have printed it entire, along with the revised version(s)-- see Nos. 105, "Penmaen Pool", 134, "The Handsome Heart" and 176, "St. Alphonsus Rodriguez". The sequence of stanzas has been revised in Nos. 108 "[Margaret Clitheroe]" and 135, formerly called "[On a Piece of Music]". Extra lines have been added to No. 161, "Thee, God, I come from"--as Catherine Phillips did in her Oxford Authors *Hopkins*--and 168, "On the Portrait of Two Beautiful Young People". New fragments have been included: Nos. 110, "Murphy gives sermons", and 128c, "O where is it, the wilderness". The Nursery Rhymes in Latin, published in Appendix C of the *OET,* I would now be willing to number 180 because of new evidence pointing to Hopkins as translator.

The Introduction to the Oxford English Texts edition sets out Hopkins's vacillation in the use of capitals, hyphens, compounds, metrical signs, and punctuation marks, facts that have emerged from my detailed scrutiny of all surviving autographs. Beyond a certain point, a definitive text is defeated by the poet's ambiguities. Nor have I thought it a crime to leave the Oxford University Press single quotes (standard British practice since the first edition of his poems) in place of the double quotes favoured by Victorians.

Prosodic marks have been added to the poems in simplified form wherever the poet's intentions are clear: the many hundreds of changes thus entailed are not recorded below. However my careful scrutiny of his counterpoint signs (see *OET,* liv-lvi) revealed that his identification of the foot in which the rhythm reversed itself was frequently strange and misleading: plain stress marks on the accented syllables have therefore been substituted in the *OET* text. Because sonnet layout provides clues as to when any particular copy of a sonnet was made (see *OET*, lx-lxii), the previously printed format has sometimes been changed to mirror the poet's practice at the time when the sonnet was originally composed rather than when the version adopted as text was copied out.

Among the more interesting revisions are a number in "The Wreck of the Deutschland" where Hopkins's undependability in editing the MS. B transcript induces a greater reliance upon MS. A. The poem about a work of art (No. 135, which I believe was an inspired building, not a "Piece of Music") should be much more intelligible in its radically revised sequence of stanzas. Even though a large percentage of the changes concern accidentals, they may result in improved flow and logic: the reasoning behind these textual revisions may often be found in notes to the *Facsimiles* plates.

In the Fourth Edition the lines were not numbered in the sonnets nor in numerous poems arranged in stanzas: in the rest normally only every tenth line was marked. Among the mature poems left unmarked were those numbered in the *OET* 102a, 103, 105, 126, 137, etc., etc.. To facilitate reference the *OET* numbers every fifth line, consecutive numbering from start to finish being applied to the "Wreck of the Deutschland" (as in the *Oxford Authors*) and "The Leaden Echo and the Golden Echo" (No. 148). In the *Facsimiles* volumes, where there are many versions to be compared, each line is numbered. The running heads and bold lemmas of the *OET* have been designed to make the edition easy to use.

I set out below the changes in the texts of the mature poems, made since the 1970 revised Fourth Edition, that have been incorporated in the *OET* Poetical Works. Occasionally the selection of a different manuscript authority is responsible for a series of small revisions (e.g., "To what serves Mortal Beauty", No. 158). The excellence of Robert Bridges as Hopkins's first editor of the major mature poems saved them from appearing in print with the many corruptions which marred pieces not included in his edition of 1918.

I am deeply grateful to Dr. Catherine Phillips, now of Downing College, Cambridge, for her ready kindness in checking MS readings for me between my research visits. Her Oxford Authors edition of Hopkins edition appeared three months after my *OET* typescript had been submitted, but during the copy-editing stage I was able to adopt some of her corrections that I had overlooked in my revisions: these are indicated in the lists which follow by her initials, "CLP".

OET NO.	TITLE AND TEXTUAL CHANGES

101   *The Wreck of the Deutschland.* Text now frequently follows MS. A, transcribed from the lost autograph, rather than relying upon GMH's somewhat erratic checking of MS. B, which was copied from the transcript in MS. A after the autograph had disappeared. Revisions include: Subtitle--five small changes   st. 2:3 commas after "me" and "tongue"   st. 3:3 and 5 final dashes (concealed in the hinge of A) restored   st. 4:7 "flanks" now "or planks" (footnote)   st. 5:6 "tho ¹" now "though" st. 11:15 "we" now ital.   6 "us," now "us:"   st. 12:7 "did" now ital.   st. 13:2 "haven" now u.c.   st. 14:3 final slur added to show over-rove rhyme   8 "these" now "or there" (footnote)   st. 16:6 now "the to and the fro"   st. 17:2 "not" now "not," 4,5 "sea-romp", "heart-break", "heart-broke" now each one word   st. 20:6 "Christ's lily" comma added   st. 21:2 now "Banned by land"   st. 22:4 "Sacrificed." now comma   st. 24:6 "quails" now comma   st. 26:6 "Way," now period   st. 27:2 now "The jading and the jar"   5 "electrical horror" now hyphenated   st. 28:1 "make" now u.c.   st. 29:7 "Simon Peter" now hyphenated st. 31:5 "Providence" comma added   6,7 final slurs added to indicate over-rove lines   st. 32:6 "being" no comma   8 "Death" comma added   st. 34:6 "dooms-day" now one word   8 "hard-hurled" (paper flaw misread as hyphen) now two words st. 35:4 "King" *l.c.* (in both A and B) now restored   8 "hearts' " now "heart's"   signature "Brân Maenefa" added

102(b)   Ad Episcopum Salopiensem   1-18, rejected by Jesuit censors, now incorporated   36 "coepimus" now caepimus"

103   Moonrise   fuller title "June 19 1876", added in 1978

104   The Woodlark   lacunae, supplied by Fr. Geoffrey Bliss and printed in square brackets, now omitted.   5 "round," no comma 18 del. in MS, now in sq. brackets   final periods omitted in 13, 15, 17, 26   35 no final comma

105   Penmaen Pool   Additional early version (No. 105a). In 105(b), 8 "sculls" now "skulls" (autos.)   5,9 dash added to query

107   Ochenaid Sant Francis Xavier   4 "dan." now "dan;" (stray dot on page taken as the stop instead of the smudged semicolon) 9 "it," apostrophe added 1984

108   [Margaret Clitheroe]   sts. 4 and 5 interchanged to correct historical sequence

109   "Hope holds to Christ"   4,12 alternative lines added

110   "Murphy gives sermons so fierce and hell-fiery"   two-line fragment published, with the hope that more lines may be remembered

111   God's Grandeur   6 "smeared" comma added   9 "And" comma added 1984 (four autos.)

113   The Lantern out of doors   Now no line space after 4   9 "wind" comma added 1984.

114   The dark-out Lucifer   1 (alternative) "hates this," now period

115   As kingfishers catch fire   9 "itself" now "its self"   11 alternative line added

116   Ad Rev. ...Thomam Burke   19 "Godatus"--MS "Gobatus" restored

120   The Windhover   5 "ecstasy" now "ecstacy" (MS)

122   The Caged Skylark   1 "cage" comma added (CLP)   5 "stage" comma del. (CLP)

125   The Loss of the Eurydice   23,67,91 over-rove rhyme shown by final slur

126   The May Magnificat   45 "ecstasy" now "ecstacy" (all autos.)

127   The furl of fresh-leaved dogrose   line space after 4 added 1984   17 longer line moved left

128(a)   Denis   layout altered   alternative added to last line

128(d)   What being in rank-old nature   7 "Or" not in ital. but part of the line

130   <u>Binsey Poplars</u>   12 "country" now u.c.

131   <u>Henry Purcell</u>   6 "love"..."pity" and 12 "seabeach" commas added 1984

133   <u>The Candle Indoors</u>   3 "black," comma omitted (3 autos.) 1984   10 "vault:" semicolon

134   <u>The Handsome Heart</u>   (a) new final pentameter version printed, differing from 4th edn. in 9 lines   134(b) final Alexandrine version added.

135   [On a Piece of Music]   misleading title dropped and sts. radically rearranged; final two longer lines moved left

136   <u>The Cheery Beggar</u>   5 alternative added

137   <u>The Bugler's First Communion</u>   3 rove-over rhyme marked by final slur   30 "Us:" "Us--"   43 "backwheels" comma added

139   <u>Morning, Midday, and Evening Sacrifice</u>   17 "cooling," now no comma

140   <u>Peace</u>   3 "Peace?" dash added 1974

141   <u>At the Wedding March</u>   longer final two lines moved left

143   <u>Brothers</u>   10 "come;" became "come," in 1984   11 "hall;" now "hall."   12 commas del.   13 "him:" now "him."   14 comma del.   19 "lip;" now "lip,"   22 "these," comma removed   26 "Hé" now ital.   37 final dash added   38 "salt;" now "salt!"

146   <u>Inversnaid</u>   subheading "Sept. 28 1881" added

148   <u>The Leaden Echo and the Golden Echo</u>   12 "winding sheets" now one word   22 "ah well where!" now in parentheses (MSS. A and B)   26 "wimpled-water" one word 1984   35 RB's editorial comma after "God" now omitted.   36 "See;" now colon   42 "care-killed" now one word

149   <u>Ribblesdale</u>   3 "To," no comma   10 "man?--" dash del.

150   <u>A Trio of Triolets</u>   (c) 7 exclamation, wrongly printed inside quotes, transposed to outside

151   <u>The Blessed Virgin Compared to the Air</u>   103 "go d of old" now "God" (MS. A)   124 "worldmothering" hyphen in MS. A (as in ℓ1 in A and B), now restored

152   <u>The times are nightfall</u>   undeleted alternatives added in 1,2,4. Line space after 8 closed up.

153   <u>St Winefred's Well</u>   Act II, 5 "my revenge," now no comma   10 "make believe" now one word   Section (c), 17 "recorded)." period removed 1984 (sentence runs on)

154   <u>To seem the stranger</u>   Undel. alternatives printed for 12,13.   Line spaces closed up and marginal braces added from MS for quatrains and tercets.

155   <u>I wake and feel the fell</u>   3 "saw;" now comma   Line spaces closed up, marginal braces printed   12,13,14 undeleted alternatives added.

156   <u>Strike, churl</u>   4 undeleted alternative added

157   <u>No worst</u>   10 undel. alternative added

158   <u>To what serves Mortal Beauty?</u>   Text based on MS. A, not D: 2 "feature, flung prouder form" now "face, prouder flung the form"   3 "See:" now "See,"   9 "needs" now "once"

159   [Carrion Comfort]   now no line space after 4

160   <u>Yes. Why do we all</u> [The Soldier]   6 "It fancies, feigns, deems;" now "It fancies; it deems; dears" with alternative at foot   7 "And fain will find as sterling" now "So feigns it finds as sterling" with three alternatives at foot

161 <u>Thee, God, I come from</u>   17 alternative bracketed in text.   Lines 25-30 added (as also in OSA)

162 <u>Patience, hard thing</u>   2 "for, Patience" now *l.c.*   6 "heart's ivy, Patience" became "heart's-ivy Patience" in 1984   Line spaces closed up, with marginal braces instead.

163 <u>My own heart</u>   6 editorial comma (added by RB 1918) now omitted.   Line spaces replaced by marginal braces.   13 "unforeseen times" now one word.

164 <u>To his Watch</u>   1 "rock-a-heart" now with final comma   2 editorial comma added after "beat"   3 "force" now footnoted "or possibly <u>forge</u>"   8 undeleted alternative added

165 <u>Songs from Shakespeare</u>
   (a) <u>Come unto these yellow sands</u>   1 "flavas, has" now "flavas has,"   "arenas," no comma   2 "jungite;" now ","   3 "oscula;" now comma   8 "signabitis." now comma   9 "latrare:" now semicolon   10 "Et" now "Nos"   11 "Allatrent" now "Adlatrent"   "occinit. Occinat:" now "occinit, occinat:"
   (b) <u>Full fathom five</u>   7 "Phorcys" trans. to end of line, as in MS.
   (e) <u>Tell me where is Fancy bred</u> (Greek)   indenting of lines corrected.
   (f) <u>Orpheus with his lute</u> (Latin)   10 "musae" changed to u.c. 1978
   (g) <u>Orpheus with his lute</u> (Greek)   some Greek metrical marks added.

166 <u>In all things beautiful</u>   7 "Tacet" now *l.c.*   8 "musa" changed to u.c. 1978

167 <u>Spelt from Sibyl's Leaves</u>   5,6 "as-/tray" now "as-/Tray" (as also in OSA)

168 <u>On the Portrait of Two Beautiful Young People</u>   Four extra unassimilated stanzas printed as No. 168 b, c and d.

169 <u>Harry Ploughman</u>   Undeleted alternatives in 3,6,14,15,17,18,19   Space after 11 closed up.

170 <u>[Ashboughs]</u>   a. Line space after 6 closed up   Marginal braces added.   b. 7 square brackets del.   8 "[Eye" square brackets del., text editorially changed to "Ay" (homophone).

171 <u>Tom's Garland</u>   10 "Country" now *l.c.* (MS. B)   16 "no one" now one word (all autographs)

172 <u>Epithalamion</u>   2 "leafwhelmed" now "leaf-whelmed"   5 undeleted alternative reading added.   17 "downdolphinry" changed to "downdolfinry" in 1978   25 "flake leaves" now hyphenated   33 "finger-teasing" now one word.   37 "self-quainèd," comma del.   38 "shives" became "shivès" 1984.   40 "daylight" comma added   new 48,49 added "to Everard, as I surmise,/Sparkled first in Amy's eyes" (perhaps the weakest lines GMH ever wrote).

175 <u>What shall I do for the land that bred me</u>   8 "There" now ital.

176 <u>In honour of St Alphonsus Rodriguez</u>   two additional versions of the whole sonnet added.

177 <u>Thou art indeed just, Lord</u>   Two sets of marginal braces supplied from MS.

179 <u>To RB</u> line spaces between quatrains and tercets closed up, replaced by double sets of marginal braces from MS.

180 (Appendix C) <u>Nursery Rhymes in Latin</u>   Not previously published as by Hopkins

OET Errata

101 <u>The Wreck of the Deutschland</u>   st. 23:8 add final period

117 <u>Spring</u>   12 "lord" add comma   (Slips kindly reported by John Whitehead)

INDEX OF SHORT TITLES AND FIRST LINES

(TITLES ARE SET IN ITALIC, FIRST LINES IN ROMAN. OET POEM NUMBERS, IN PARENTHESES, ARE FOLLOWED BY REFERENCES TO THE PLATES ON WHICH THE POEMS, IN PART OR WHOLE, OCCUR.)